S0-BRA-801

What are the legacies of genocide and mass violence for individuals and the social worlds in which they live, and what are the local processes of recovery? *Genocide and Mass Violence* aims to examine, from a cross-cultural perspective, the effects of mass trauma on multiple levels of a group or society and the recovery processes and sources of resilience. How do particular individuals recall the trauma? How do ongoing reconciliation processes and collective representations of the trauma impact the group? How does the trauma persist in "symptoms"? How are the effects of trauma transmitted across generations in memories, rituals, symptoms, and interpersonal processes? What are local healing resources that aid recovery? To address these issues, this book brings into conversation psychological and medical anthropologists, psychiatrists, psychologists, and historians. The theoretical implications of the chapters are examined in detail using several analytic frameworks.

Devon E. Hinton, M.D, Ph.D., is an anthropologist and psychiatrist, and a Professor of Psychiatry at Harvard Medical School and Massachusetts General Hospital. His work has focused on culturally specific presentations of anxiety disorders, particularly trauma-related disorder, and culturally sensitive treatment of those disorders. He is the first author of more than 100 articles and chapters. He is the coeditor of four volumes, two with Byron Good: *Culture and Panic Disorder* and *Culture and PTSD*. He was a member of the DSM-5 cultural study group, as well as an adviser to the anxiety, OC, posttraumatic, and dissociative disorders work group of DSM-5 (American Psychiatric Association). He is the director of a trauma refugee clinic for Southeast Asian refugees in Lowell, Massachusetts.

Alexander L. Hinton, Ph.D., is Director of the Center for the Study of Genocide and Human Rights, Professor of Anthropology, and UNESCO Chair in Genocide Prevention at Rutgers University. He is the author of the award-winning *Why Did They Kill? Cambodia in the Shadow of Genocide* and nine edited or coedited collections. In recognition of his work on genocide, the American Anthropological Association selected him as the recipient of the 2009 Robert B. Textor and Family Prize for Excellence in Anticipatory Anthropology. He is also the immediate past President of the International Association of Genocide Scholars (2011–13) and was a Member/Visitor at the Institute for Advanced Study at Princeton (2011–13). He has been invited around the globe to lecture on genocide and mass violence.

Genocide and Mass Violence

Memory, Symptom, and Recovery

Edited by

Devon E. Hinton

Harvard University

Alexander L. Hinton

Rutgers University

CAMBRIDGE
UNIVERSITY PRESS

32 Avenue of the Americas, New York, NY 10013-2473, USA

Cambridge University Press is part of the University of Cambridge.

It furthers the University's mission by disseminating knowledge in the pursuit of education, learning, and research at the highest international levels of excellence.

www.cambridge.org
Information on this title: www.cambridge.org/9781107694699

© Cambridge University Press 2015

First published 2015

Printed in the United States of America

A catalog record for this publication is available from the British Library.

Library of Congress Cataloging in Publication data
Hinton, Devon E.
Genocide and mass violence : memory, symptom, and recovery / Devon E. Hinton, Harvard University, Alexander L. Hinton, Rutgers University.
    pages cm
ISBN 978-1-107-06954-1 (hardback) – ISBN 978-1-107-69469-9 (paperback)
1. Genocide – Case studies.   2. Violence – Case studies.   3. Social psychology – Case studies.   I. Hinton, Alexander Laban.   II. Title.
HV6322.7.H54   2015
363.32–dc23   2014020980

ISBN 978-1-107-06954-1 Hardback
ISBN 978-1-107-69469-9 Paperback

Contents

Figures

Tables

Contributors

ORKIDEH BEHROUZAN – King's College London

CONERLY CASEY – Rochester Institute of Technology

VINCENT CRAPANZANO – City University of New York

MARY-JO DELVECCHIO GOOD – Harvard Medical School

NADIA EL-SHAARAWI – Duke University

KOK-THAY ENG – Documentation Center of Cambodia

ERIN FINLEY – The University of Texas Health Science Center

MICHAEL M. J. FISCHER – Massachusetts Institute of Technology

BYRON J. GOOD – Harvard Medical School

DOUG HENRY – University of North Texas

ALEXANDER L. HINTON – Rutgers University

DEVON E. HINTON – Harvard University

CAROL A. KIDRON – University of Haifa

LAURENCE J. KIRMAYER – McGill University

ARTHUR KLEINMAN – Harvard University

BRANDON A. KOHRT – Duke University

HEONIK KWON – Trinity College, University of Cambridge

ROBERT LEMELSON – University of California, Los Angeles

KENNETH E. MILLER – Lesley University

SULANI PERERA – University of Minnesota

ALEXANDRA PILLEN – University College London

CHRISTOPHER C. TAYLOR – University of Alabama at Birmingham

KIMBERLY THEIDON – Harvard University

Foreword: What Does Trauma Do?

Arthur Kleinman

Read the chapters in this book and feel, carry, resist, fight the weight, the heavy yoke of tragedy. Mass violence has been part of the human experience for as long as recorded history and weighs us down to this day. In the American Civil War 750,000 soldiers on both sides lost their lives, and the subsequent decades were dominated by national preoccupation with suffering, loss, and grief (Faust, 2008). Colonialism introduced mass violence to all the continents, with slavery accounting for a huge toll of human misery and death. In the meat grinder of trench warfare during World War I, millions of British, French, and German soldiers were killed and millions more wounded. The Battle of the Somme alone cost the British 450,000 casualties, 50,000 on the first day. That war ended with European societies expressing revulsion against all forms of mass violence, and yet just twenty years later a Second World War killed more than 50 million men and women (most of whom were noncombatants) and displaced hundreds of million more. The war embedded the Holocaust, still the symbol of mass violence as an institutional product of evil. Historians claim that the former Soviet Union may have killed even more people than the Nazis. And this outline of mass violence is only a preliminary to the many and different more recent forms of mass killing described in the chapters that follow.

Whatever the human cost of such immense and continuing destruction it must be staggering. China's Great Leap Forward famine, which killed 30 million rural Chinese, was the unintended consequence of one of the most destructive social policies in human history, but no one knows its toll on families and networks in Chinese villages. The same can be said for the Cultural Revolution (Kleinman et al., 2011). And that is true of much of mass violence. We simply do not know what effect, especially over the long term, it has had on society, on interpersonal bonds, on local moral worlds, and on subjectivity.

So the questions asked of the different forms of twenty-first-century mass violence covered in this book have a lineage. What has changed is the replacement of moral, religious, and legal language with the discourses of psychiatry and the humanities and interpretive social sciences, and with those technical discourses on trauma have arrived the humanitarian interventions that define our age (Abramowitz, 2009; Benton, 2009).

Yet, nothing has stopped the bodies from piling up along with the complex of grieving, revenge, and remembering/forgetting that looms equally enormous in people's lives. So why not regard this record of mass killing and atrocity and the subsequent biological, psychological, and culturewide responses as human tragedy: one face of the human experience that, if anything, is as basic a feature of human conditions under the pressure of modernity as anything else. And just using the term "tragedy," with its reference to the classical world, suggests that mass violence is not just about modernity, either, but resonates down the halls of human history as far back as the earliest civilizations, so that we must think of society and subjectivity as forged out of the catastrophic consequences of violence over the millennia.

Once we see mass violence this way, even recognizing its increasing sedimentation among marginal and poor populations, we are forced to come to terms with its normality (Canguilhem, 2012). There may be pathology among perpetrators and victims, but the phenomenon of mass violence itself is stunning not because it is nonnormative and aberrant, but rather because it is commonplace. Ordinary people participate in atrocity and ordinary people die and are maimed (Browning 1992, 1998). And life goes on. And just so, ordinary people must bear the burden of pain, suffering, remorse, regret, and the powerful sensibility to respond (Kleinman, Das, & Lock, 1997). Because violence leads not only to trauma, but to humanitarian, legal, political, and health responses it is vulnerable to the terrible irony of social suffering: The institutions created to cope with violence and its aftermath are also responsible for contributing to its intensification and bad outcome. Unintended consequences of purposive action, the harmony of illusions, bureaucratic indifference, the iron cage of technical rationality applied to human affairs, biopower – all are theories applied to understand how this happens. But what is the consequence for human experience of these outcomes?

It is for this reason that I purposefully employ the term "tragedy." That term unites moral, religious, existential, and aesthetic practices. Trauma and trauma care are experiences that cross these domains and that need to be seen as simultaneously embodied, felt, and transformed, but first of all tragic. Tragedy does not have to imply passive acceptance and acquiescence. Nor does it mean that our view of human experience is overly romantic and heroic. Rather it evokes the sense that historical processes and political economic/societal transformations have the deepest influence on individual and collective life. That influence, though culturally distinctive, is still a shared condition of our humanity.

The second reality is that these experiences call forth caregiving responses. Not just the health professions, but ordinary people respond to tragedy with care. Beyond individual experience, societal experience of trauma also calls forth social caregiving. Much more emphasis has been put on the causal pathways from mass violence to trauma than on the caregiving responses, be they practically and symbolically helpful or not. The Wenchuan earthquake in China and northern Japan's catastrophic complex of earthquake, tsunami, and nuclear material release drew forth governmental and NGO responses of caregiving, but also individual acts. Both trauma-related suffering and caregiving need to be seen as examples of local biology requiring a biosocial framework to interpret the illness experience and evaluate the outcome response adequately (Lock & Nguyen, 2011). Central here is to see caregiving as a thoroughly moral enterprise that resists the infiltration of market models into everyday life (Sandel, 2011). Trauma, then, may be categorized as an economic burden requiring economic interventions, or as a psychological burden requiring drugs and psychotherapy. But it also can be seen as a nexus linking the moral, the medical, and the political faces of suffering, humanitarian assistance, and technology. And that nexus cannot just be seen as controlling and disciplinary or in other negative terms. For it is also about interventions that help people and that improve social conditions.

Can such an omnibus term bear the weight of so much conceptual and empirical baggage? How is trauma best parsed into subtexts and microthemes? What is useful about the trauma idea for theory, research, and practical implementation projects? What are the limits of trauma as an organizing idea, especially as it is employed to make sense of mass violence? And what are the leading alternative candidates for this role?

All of which leads us to the question of scholarship and empirical research practice. "Trauma," whatever its limits, has fueled an entire field of academic life and professional development. It has built careers, established disciplinary practices, reoriented science and technology, and remade the global humanitarian assistance agenda. It has itself become part of the culture of the academy as much as of everyday global cultural common sense. So, we should ask, What is the upshot for academic pursuits in our time, be they anthropological or psychiatric, humanistic or public health, theoretical or applied? And that is what the chapters that follow offer. They present original and important work on trauma, to be sure. But they also show us where this field is at present and where it is headed; what the possibilities are; and what trauma is good for, academically to think with and practically to do things of use for those in need out in the world.

REFERENCES

Abramowitz, S. A. (2009). Psychosocial Liberia: Managing suffering in post-conflict life. Unpublished doctoral dissertation, Harvard University, Cambridge, MA.

Benton, A. (2009). Yu get to liv positive: HIV, subjectivity and the politics of care in post-conflict Sierra Leone. Unpublished doctoral dissertation, Harvard University, Cambridge, MA.

Browning, C. R. (1992, 1998). *Ordinary Men: Reserve Police Battalion 101 and the Final Solution in Poland.* New York: HarperCollins.

Canguilhem, G. (2012). *Writings on Medicine.* Translated by S. Geroulanos and T. Meyers. New York: Fordham University Press.

Faust, D. G. (2008). *The Republic of Suffering: Death and the American Civil War.* New York: Alfred A. Knopf.

Kleinman, A., Das, V., & Lock, M. (Eds.) (1997). *Social Suffering.* Berkeley: University of California Press.

Kleinman, A., Yan, Y., Jun, J., Lee, S., Zhang, E., Tianshu, P., Fei, W., & Guo, J. (2011). *Deep China: The Moral Life of the Person: What Anthropology and Psychiatry Tell Us about China Today.* Berkeley: University of California Press.

Lock, M. and Nguyen, Vinh-Kim. (2011) *An anthropology of biomedicine.* Malden, MA: Wiley-Blackwell, 2010.

Sandel, M. (2012). *What Money Can't Buy: The Moral Limits of Markets.* New York: Farrar, Straus and Giroux.

Acknowledgments

We would like to thank Susan D. Hinton, M.A., for her help with the editing of the manuscripts in this volume.

Introduction

An Anthropology of the Effects of Genocide and Mass Violence: Memory, Symptom, and Recovery

Devon E. Hinton and Alexander L. Hinton

What are the wounds of mass violence on various experiential levels and how might recovery occur? Despite the emergence of an international human rights movement in the period after the Holocaust and World War II, mass violence has not ended. The late twentieth-century genocides in Bosnia and Rwanda were followed by early twenty-first-century genocides in Sudan and the Democratic Republic of Congo. Civil war remains a central part of many of these conflicts, as illustrated by the atrocities perpetrated in Aceh, Colombia, East Timor, Guatemala, Liberia, Kosovo, Nepal, Peru, Sierra Leone, Somalia, Syria, and Uganda. The United States has recently entered zones of mass violence in a post-9/11 world, and with its allies has waged war in Afghanistan and Iraq while confronting terrorism at home. There is the postconflict legacy of such violence: economies and infrastructures destroyed, families and communities fractured, interpersonal mistrust, grieving, trauma, symptoms, unwanted memories, and many other forms of social suffering.

This volume explores lingering aftermaths of mass violence and the reaction to it. What are the legacies of mass violence for individuals and the social worlds in which they live and how do they seek to recover? Former zones of violence often become sites of humanitarian aid, peace-building efforts, and transitional justice, but scholars and practitioners have paid too little attention to the ways in which individuals and cultural groups react to mass violence through microdynamics of memory, social practice, ritual, coping, understanding, symptoms, and healing. Psychological anthropology should have much to say about these issues given its emphasis on taking into account various levels of human ontology such as social experience, collective representations, and sociopolitical process; brain function and psychology; the phenomenology of lived experience; and the nexus of self, memory, and emotion. But psychological anthropology has only just begun to grapple with the legacies of mass violence

1

(see, e.g., Fassin & Pandolfi, 2010; Kirmayer, Lemelson, & Barad, 2007; Kleinman, Das, & Lock, 1997; Robben & Suárez-Orozco, 2000).

This book aims to fill this gap and to examine the legacy of mass violence in cross-cultural perspective and on multiple levels. How do particular individuals recall mass violence and trauma? How are the effects of such experiences transmitted across the generations in memory, ritual, symptom, and interpersonal processes? How do the legacies of mass violence continue to have effects in the form of "symptoms" and syndromes? How do ongoing justice and reintegration processes, structural inequalities, and collective representations of trauma have an impact on victims? What are local attempts to bring about cure and reintegration? How do these questions vary depending on the subgroups within the population in question, such as women, children, and the poor?

We have organized the book in terms of three key areas of scholarly research, namely, public and private memory, symptom and syndrome, and response and recovery. The section divisions are useful for organizing the volume, but most chapters could have been included in one or both of the other sections. They are closely related domains, and discussion of one usually involves the others. To give one example, memories of a mass genocide often represent a symptom (unwanted recall of the past), and recovery often entails changing the relationship to the memory and the memory's contextual meaning, with these re-memorialization processes involving personal and public processes.[1]

To enrich the volume, we purposefully sought contributors from a variety of disciplines (psychological anthropology, psychiatry, psychology, medical anthropology) and organized sessions at academic events to promote conversation. The authors presented and discussed their research at panels at the meetings of the American Anthropological Association and of the Society of Psychological Anthropology. Then there was a conference – sponsored by a Lemelson grant from the Society of Psychological Anthropology that was awarded to the current book's editors[2] – at the Center for the Study of Genocide, Conflict Resolution, and Human Rights at Rutgers University, Newark. To enhance the experience-near quality of the book and to link it to an alternative mode of representation, four chapters in the volume are linked to documentary films in which given contributors were directly involved.[3] In addition, many of the chapters include case presentations.

We consider the volume to have three main cross-cutting analytic frameworks. One is its division into three parts, namely, "memory, symptom, and recovery," and an analysis of the chapters from that perspective (see this chapter). The second is the analysis of the chapters from the perspective of eight ontological dimensions (see this chapter). As a third analytic framework, at the end of the edited volume is a commentary chapter by Laurence Kirmayer in which he presents an alternative and complementary theoretical framework to examine the effects of trauma and attempted recovery, and that he uses to situate the chapters in respect to trauma studies. His framework posits five realms of experience (body; self/person; interpersonal relationship; communal/political; and spirit world) that may be viewed from four different perspectives, namely, descriptive languages, place of injury or rupture, idioms of distress, and sites of resistance and repair. In Kirmayer's analytic schema, the effects of trauma in each of those five ontological realms, and attempts at recovery in each of these five realms, can be traced by viewing how the impacted realm plays out when viewed from each of these four perspectives.

Thus, in this volume we scrutinize mass violence through three broad frames of analysis: the three-part division of the volume, the eight ontological dimensions, and Kirmayer's schema.[4] In the following we first analyze the chapters from the perspective of the divisions of the volume, and then from the perspective of the eight ontological perspectives. See the end of this volume for Kirmayer's commentary.

The Three Book Sections (Memory, Symptom, and Recovery) and Their Chapters: Key Theoretical Contributions

In the following we perform an analysis of the chapters from the perspective of the book's three-part organizational structure, highlighting key contributions to the literature.

Part I: Private and Public Memory

Part I contains chapters that focus on the memory of mass violence. Here we consider memory broadly to include the ways in which public memory is expressed in contexts such as memorials as well as individual forms of remembering such as nightmares, and we examine how private and public memory impact upon each other. Several of the essays in Part I touch on one of the key "symptoms" of trauma, namely, the unwanted recall of the past in nightmare and during waking. In a sense, Part I is a subsection of the symptom section (Part II), but it considers memory in a broad perspective that embraces public and personal memory. Part I addresses memory in the broad sense, which ranges from personal memory, to humiliation memory, to the generational memory of certain events, to public narrative memory, to hidden transcript memory (e.g., memory that is seemingly played out in an idiom of haunting), to memorial memory that holds and constitutes memory in public space. These and other sorts of memory form a key aspect of the trauma ontology.

In Chapter 1, Heonik Kwon describes different types of representations of the war and how memory is articulated in public spaces in Vietnam. Initially after the war only heroic memory was allowed: There was a proliferation of war memorials such as those featuring a winged tower and incense burner along with a statue of revolutionary heroes and martyrs – heroic memory.[5] But in the early 1990s many members of Vietnamese society advocated for the right to be able to grieve publicly the losses of the war without being labeled as counterrevolutionary. Seemingly addressing this need, there was increasing building and rebuilding of domestic ancestral shrines, family ancestral temples, and community temples for the deceased. At that time, too, the envisioned lifeworld of the spirits of the dead became more prominent in the public imaginary: In the area of the My Lai massacres, mother ghosts were seen tending to the wounds of their children. As Kwon describes, in Vietnam it is believed that a violent and unjust death traps the dead; they are doomed to relive their violent death continually in all its particularity and agony. In this sense, there is a mirror image of a flashback – the repeated reliving of a tragic event as if it were happening again – that is played out in the spirit world. Locals perform rituals to try to help the deceased caught in this jail of memory.

Chapter 1 raises a number of important questions. Is the pained memory of the individual impacted by the public representation of these images of horror? Is this an icon in the spiritual world of the living individual's pained memory? Do rituals that aim to transform the state of trapped spirits aid individual memory, both through the symbolism of the enaction and through the sense of relief at improving the fate of the dead? Is this spirit world a hidden transcript speaking indirectly of personal memory? Kwon's chapter suggests that trauma and its anguish – and perhaps its resolution – can play out in concerns about the spiritual state of the deceased and rituals meant to release them, can play out in concerns about spiritual security and the state of the dead.

Like Kwon in his chapter, Byron J. Good (Chapter 2, this volume) argues for the importance of hauntology, the study of the specters that visit the living in dream and in the waking state. B. Good's research focus is the collective imaginary in Aceh seen through the lens of hauntology, and how various collective specters form part of an individual's subjectivity. Hauntology studies the images that haunt individual consciousnesses in a society and how these may relate to key historical and cultural facts as well as structures of power. Trauma studies typically assess nightmare and only those nightmares that replay the "trauma event" – though in the criteria of the *Diagnostic and Statistical Manual of Mental Disorders-5* (*DSM-5;* American Psychiatric Association, 2013), it is now stated that any disturbing dream whose affect or content resembles the trauma meets PTSD criteria, unlike in *DSM-IV-TR* (D. Hinton & Lewis-Fernandez, 2011). Chapter 2 (and Kwon's [Chapter 1, this volume]) suggests that certain images that form collective images of terror may be the most dreaded type of dream – and more generally the specter may recall a collectively experienced traumatic past.

B. Good's chapter argues for the need to assess the types of dream visitors and collective specter imagery and determine what that imagery indicates about broader social and cultural forces. Trauma sufferers may consider their main problem to be spiritual and therefore cast it in that idiom (on this, see also D. Hinton et al., 2009; D. Hinton, Field, et al., 2013; D. Hinton, Peou, et al., 2013). The traumatized individual may have a sense of great ontological insecurity in respect to the spiritual realm. B. Good's chapter explores this issue in Aceh and how the individual's sense of spiritual insecurity may relate to broader unresolved issues in the social, cultural, and historical realms – be this structural violence or gendered inequality or untold histories of unacknowledged violence. The goal of hauntological analysis is to trace the specters – and the uncanny within a society – and to determine whom they haunt, what state of consciousness they haunt (e.g., sleep in the form of nightmare or the awakening state in sleep paralysis), how they haunt persons in different social classes and genders, and how they haunt classes of psychologically disturbed persons, for example, the person who has "PTSD" in the form of nightmare or the person who has psychosis in the form of hallucination. Such research needs to investigate how such hauntings are cured and protected from and to analyze what those specters mean from a colonial, historical, and cultural perspective (Chapter 10, this volume). Here the question is how the person and the society itself are haunted and the meaning of that haunting as scrutinized through these various analytic frames (see also Crandon-Malamud, 1991).

As B. Good shows, literature, artistic creation, and various performative arts are important sources and sites of production of the imaginary of specters. These are artistic zones where imagery can be created that articulates unspoken fears and quandaries, and this imaginary potentially has an invigorating and healing effect (on how art can serve as a depiction of fear in the abstract and act as a healing and a cure, see also Good & Good, 2008). What does it mean to articulate and experience trauma's effects in a spiritual idiom, particularly in a society with a history of mass deaths, or even genocide, where mass violence events cannot be spoken about openly because of the dangers of speaking about them, because the perpetrators still hold power, because the perpetrators are your neighbors? Hidden transcripts may be spoken in a spiritual idiom.

In Chapter 3, Conerly Casey writes about a society with high rates of PTSD: In one study in postinvasion Kuwait, 70 percent of surveyed children had moderate to severe PTSD. A common complaint is being afflicted by trauma memory during waking and dream. These memories are of mutilated bodies shown on television, bodies dumped in the streets, people disappearing, burning oil wells. Casey suggests that the category of PTSD obscures various key ontological securities that Kuwaitis often treat through substance abuse and other dysfunctional means. She suggests something like a trauma cohort. It is a cohort whose sense of security has been shattered in a profound way owing to the 1990 invasion of their country and the post-9/11 U.S. invasion of Iraq.

The way in which events and external landscapes trigger memory and how trauma recall causes bodily complaints (see Part II for further discussion of how somatic complaints occur in trauma victims) are also foci of the chapter. Memories are triggered by smells and by any image of present-day destruction such as places that have been left in a state of ruin as memorials. Casey describes how reminders of the recent war joined with continuing violence in neighboring Iraq led to multiple types of insecurity: gender-based violence, concerns about poisonous fires, a landscape of destroyed buildings, lack of food, and the constant threat of kidnapping and death. Health complaints were common after the Iraqi invasion of Kuwait. These were of high blood pressure, tension, and somatic complaints such as shortness of breath and gastrointestinal distress. Casey discusses how fear of contamination – from uranium, oil fires, and other sources – led to a hypervigilant surveying of the body that resulted in prominent shortness of breath and other symptoms linked to supposed poisonings, and how fear of contamination led to constant recall of chemical fires and other experienced pollutants. Recall of the time of invasion triggers a sense of extreme insecurity, a sense of extreme betrayal, and fear of permanent body contamination. So there is a further lack of physical health ontological security: the bodily itself has been invaded by a pathogen.

Casey suggests that the burning oil well in Kuwait is a hypersemiotized memory image. It has many symbolic meanings and multiple associations to collective trauma. These webs of significance explain why the burning oil well has deep affective impact. It is a rhizome memory image[6] that is connected to multiple meanings. The "burning oil well" encodes the space-time (chronotope)[7] of the Iraqi invasions and the many traumas and insecurities of that time. It is a space-time evoker that encodes multiple memories: It evokes the idea of violation of space. It evokes ideas of bodily contamination with pollutants that have led or will lead to illness and bodily complaint. The image acts as a self-scape memory that evokes a sense of vulnerability, chaos, contamination, violation, and insecurity (on self-scape in dream, see Hollan 2004). (Analogously, the tattoo of a Holocaust victim [Chapter 5, this volume] conjures the memory of a person being treated as an animal through branding and of other acts of humiliation perpetrated by the Nazis, so that the tattoo acts as a rhizomic trauma image; likewise, among Rwandan trauma victims, the memory of impaled bodies may serve as a rhizomic trauma memory owing to semiotic networks [Chapter 13, this volume; see also Hagengimana & D. Hinton, 2009].)

In Chapter 4, Behrouzan and Fischer address a series of questions. How does the Iranian cultivation of the poetics of depressive affect, which seemingly centers on the memory of Karbala, shape the course of trauma? How too does the layering of memory in dream along with local dream hermeneutics affect the course? How too can trauma's effects be seen from the perspective of the memories of those in an age cohort? The chapter's title echoes that of the edited book *Culture and Depression* (Kleinman & Good, 1985) and recalls the chapter on Iran in that volume, which describes the elaborate cultivation of depressive affect in Iranian culture anchored in the Karbala commemorations and imagery (Good, Good, & Moradi, 1985). In the Behrouzan and Fischer chapter, we see the trajectory of that affect through the lens of trauma and dream. In the Iranian context, is depressive affect a sort of "work of culture" (Obeyesekere, 1990) through which trauma is managed, as exemplified by the well-described Karbala events (a sort of collective mytheme or historeme that is an "affecteme," a collective image evoking a certain set of affects) and the cultivation of a culturally specific bittersweet melancholia? At the heart of Karbala is a trauma image – namely, that of the dying martyr who was the Prophet's grandson – and associated rituals of self-flagellation and repentance honoring that event. The conjured affect is that of sadness, of tragic death, of the betrayal of the Prophet and Islam. Can trauma be funneled into depressive affect to try to reach resolution (see Chapter 11, this volume, for a description of trauma's wounds cast in another religious idiom, an image of Jesus)? May this cultural cultivation of an affective form go awry and lead to true clinical depression and suicide? If the depression is too great, may upsetting dreams overpower? How successful is the attempt by Iranians to treat trauma's depressive dysphoria through dream pondering, psychopharmacology (Prozac™), and new self-help movements that teach skills like emotional acceptance, and how do these treatments influence the course of trauma-related disorder?

Behrouzan and Fischer describe how among Iranians living abroad that trauma perdures in sedimented anxiety and dysphoria. The authors show how this layered sedimentation is most visible in nightmare, where memory fragments – for example, of test exams, siren sounds recalling the bombings in Iran, images of Khomeini – coalesce into nightmare. Nightmares and their imagery bring about palpitations, suffocation, and panic. Sonic memory is particularly prominent in Iranian trauma dreams, and this includes dirges, sirens, bombing sounds, parts of sermons that were mandatory listening, and phrases that were slogans of death against the West and slogans that exhorted the young to give their life in sacrifice for Khomeini. Bombing imagery also seems to be a particularly important aspect of the iconography of dream. Past images enter dreams and , take on new significance by resonating with current events and other distant events and so form new assemblages, new affective configurations. *Nachträglichkeit* (after the fact) – old memories take on new meaning; their meaning is not fixed. Behrouzan and Fischer describe a dream hermeneutics among Iranians that seeks memory and meaning in dream. There is a cultivation of dreams as self-objects, as self-scapes. There is a dream-based trauma subjectivity in which melancholia is cultivated through dream poetics. Dreams become a key place of self-making and affect making. (On dreams among trauma victims, see also D. Hinton et al., 2009; D. Hinton, Field, et al., 2013; D. Hinton, Peou, et al., 2013.)

The authors also argue that the iconography of trauma varies by age cohort. They emphasize the importance of analyzing an age cohort's traumas in cultural-historical context. The traumas of each generation vary, and so too do the manner of socialization and the stock of images that resonate with current trauma. An Iranian generation was made to watch cartoons that represented a depressive dystopia of orphans, dead parents, and children seeking out missing parents, cartoons that were rendered in gray tones and whose soundtrack was lugubrious music. A generation was flooded with images of young men committing a martyr suicide in a state of religious intoxication, rushing out to fight against Iraqi troops. This same generation experienced multiple types of representations of the Karbala. Further layers of that space-time (chronotope) are images and sounds of bombing, the recurrent sirens, and other aspects of the sonic landscape described previously. The chapter details an archaeology of traumas and scrutinizes how these archaeological levels are taken up and remixed in dream as current life events call up past images in the process of *Nachträglichkeit*. The chapter also shows how these processes differ by age cohort.

In Chapter 5, Carol Kidron gives examples of how the sudden reliving of the past traumas may not simply be in the form of visual images. The flashback may be multisensorial and additionally enacted: The person may enact the scenes of the past like eating a potato skin when starving. Her chapter shows that hunger – and related sensorial experiencing such as seeing, cutting, and smelling potatoes – may act as a somatic marker of the past that brings about its reliving. Hunger, food, or even skinniness in oneself or one's children may be sufficient to evoke the chronotope of the Holocaust time – and here hunger may also serve as a metaphor and symbol of emptiness. Such memories show the imprint of the past not in the form of heroic memory, or martyrdom memory, or humiliation memory,[8] but rather in the form of desperation memory (on chronotopes triggered by sensorial experience, see also D. Hinton, A. Hinton, & Eng, Chapter 9, this volume).

Desperation memories are memories that evoke the emotional space experienced when there was constant threat of death during a given period that was a desperation chronotope, a dystopia, a lifeworld of desperation. Kidron's chapter describes how those memories are evoked, and so too other chapters reveal how desperation chronotopes are recalled to mind: Behrouzan and Fischer (Chapter 4, this volume) show how sirens and bombing were repetitive background events of a space-time that if heard now have the power to evoke not just a particular event but an entire period; Casey (Chapter 3, this volume) reveals how the image of burning oil wells plays a similar role; and D. Hinton, A. Hinton, and Eng (Chapter 9, this volume) detail how neck tension and pain were the embodied background of the Pol Pot period (on smell's ability to act as a chronotope marker; see D. Hinton, Chea, Ba, & Pollack, 2004).[9] To put it in Langer's (1991) terms, chronotope memory is "deep memory" as compared to "common memory." It is a memory that recalls the self as it was in a period in the past and reveals a "doubling of self," the self as it is now compared to the self during Auschwitz – deep memory returns the Auschwitz self. In this case it is a flashback-like remembering not of just an event but of an entire time and a certain sense of self – the sense of self as it was experienced when in a particular event, location, and time.[10]

There is also wounded-body memory. Kidron describes the permanent inscription of a trauma event on the surface of the body. A tattoo, the scar from a gunshot wound, or two toes that were frostbitten and now paralyzed: These are permanent memorials of the genocide time. It may be through these body memorials that children most deeply understand a parent's Holocaust ordeals. The child's iconic memory of the Holocaust may be the parent's bodily wound along with the events that the child imagines gave rise to the wound: the memory of a parent's tattoo paired to the mental picture of the parent's arm being branded and the sensorial imagining of the heat of that branding. Or the child's iconic memory may be the parent's bodily wound along with the parent's demonstration of the limitations posed by the wound: the memory of the parent's disabled frostbitten toes paired to the memory of the parent demonstrating that the toes do not move. This is wounded-body memory. There are also world-danger memory and inconsolable-wound memory. Children may hear of some danger that the parent survived, such as a death walk in bare feet, and imagine that to be an imminent danger: The child may place walking shoes beside the bed for fear that the Nazis may come. Here the child's sense of ontological security is greatly threatened as a parent's memory becomes an imagined future. This is world-danger memory. As another evoker of the past, Kidron gives the example of a child's memory of a mother often crying upon awaking from a bad dream that the child presumes to be of the Holocaust. This is inconsolable-wound memory.

A parent may have one or more of these types of memories and may pass them on to his or her child. The child of the trauma survivor may also have a doubling of self: the self as it is now and the self as it was when it experienced a parent reliving the Holocaust. This witnessing of a parent may be a kind of trauma. This memory of the younger self and the affect experienced at that time constitute part of the memory of the parent's trauma. As another form of memory and transmission, each generation hypothesizes their parents to have passed through certain events that are part of collective representation of the trauma in question. This might be called hypothesized trauma, which may well be a sort of memory of some depiction of the event such as a film representing the events of the mass violence.[11] These might be called second-order memories, or genocide-representation memories, that is, memories of depictions of the genocide, which may include novels, autobiography, movies. As another kind of second-order memory, there is a parent's recounting of those events, that is, parental representational memories (see also Hirsch, 1999).[12] The various types of memories discussed above may come to be a core part of the person's sense of self and provide an explanation for his or her own actions and those of family members – a transgenerational frame and sense of self. Kidron's chapter suggests that an important aspect of an anthropology of mass violence is the study of these kinds of memories, how these memories are transmitted across generations, how the memories are recalled to mind, and what effects these memories have.

In Chapter 6, Vincent Crapanzano outlines how among the Harkis, who are the former allies of the French military in Algeria, that trauma experiencing is shaped by the conception of fate and the cultural value of endurance (*sabr*) and accepting destiny (*qda*). He demonstrates how these values influence the particular trajectory of the intergenerational transmission of trauma and memory. Harkis did not usually tell children of their abandonment by the French or the abuses and difficulties they endured in Morocco – the cultural virtue of endurance (*sabr*) makes a virtue of "silence before hardship" and builds self-esteem through enacting it. But this endurance and silence result in rage and a lack of communication. Harki men also highly value the understanding of the role of destiny (*qda*) in determining the life trajectory and the need to accept it, a philosophy that is inculcated through many forms such as a common story form that highlights this aspect of life. Crapanzano suggests that these values lead many Harki men to depression and alcoholism, whereas they serve for others as a resource that aids recovery and provides resilience.

Harki men have high rates of identity loss, suicide, anger, and alcohol abuse, according to Crapanzano. They also have a certain mnemonic community. Harki men often ruminate on their abandonment in Morocco by the French, on the abuse suffered in Morocco after abandonment, and on the difficulties of living in an imprisonment-like state in camps upon arrival in France. The situation of Harki men can be viewed through the optic of historical trauma (Evans-Cambell, 2008; Gone, 2009). In the Harki case, the collective trauma memory centers on being *trahi*, that is, "betrayed." In a contrasting case of historical trauma, that of Native American groups, it is a story of lands taken and forced enrollment in boarding schools far from parents and of loss of culture and language, among other blows. In the Harki case, the master explanatory trauma narrative begins with the Algerian War of Independence and the act of siding with the French. Harki children are twice wounded: They are placed in a position of marginality, characterized by racism and poverty, and they suffer from their parents' emotional instability, such as their father's anger, depression, and sometimes alcoholism.

As described by Crapanzano, a constellation of traumas serves as a communal memory and a self-scape memory for its members. Here the memory of trauma does not just function as an activator of fear. It may be ruminated about and create identity, a perpetually returned to set of events that act as a collective self-identity trauma (see also Antze & Lambek, 1996; Suleiman, 2006; Volkan, 2001). It is a self-scape trauma, in which the person's identity is thoroughly associated with a series of historical events. This tendency to return to the image of the trauma and its effects is strongly influenced by local ideas of destiny and endurance in the case of the Harki – the weight of history is silently and valiantly carried on, a burden that is seemingly passed from one generation to the next.

Part II: Symptom and Syndrome

Part I focused on memory on multiple levels, including as symptom. Part II of this volume explores symptoms, syndromes, and social ruptures experienced in the aftermath of mass violence. These chapters show how various somatic symptoms (e.g., neck soreness or dizziness on standing among Cambodian refugees) and other types of symptoms not in the PTSD criteria (e.g., sleep paralysis) are a central aspect of the response to trauma, and these chapters show that various PTSD and non-PTSD symptoms often form part of local trauma syndromes. As Part II shows, the local trauma ontology can only be understood when these local symptoms and syndromes – and the related ethnopsychology, ethnophysiology, and ethnospirituality – are determined.

In Chapter 7, Robert Lemelson expands on B. Good's (Chapter 2, this volume) analysis from the perspective of individual experiencing of "haunting." Lemelson describes the massacre that occurred in 1965 in Bali and the suppression of that event in public discourse. He shows the haunting of one man by supernatural beings that seemingly begins with those 1965 events. In 1965, Nyoman witnessed a man hacked to death for being a "communist" and nearly suffered the same fate himself because of his affiliation with the Communist Party. His sense of fear was further heightened by nearly dying of pesticide poisoning, having a brother-in-law and many neighbors who were perpetrators, and the fact that former communists like himself continued to be blamed for the chaos of 1965 rather than being considered to be victims of those events. Lemelson discusses the multiple cultural syndromes and idioms of distress that Nyoman experiences. The chapter shows how Nyoman's case can be explicated in terms of a variety of explanatory models, each of which suggests a theory of causation and a type of cure and has certain social implications.

Nyoman's complaints are rooted in local ideas of spiritual and bodily vulnerability. Nyoman thought he was the victim of assaults by small spirits, to which he was more vulnerable because of bodily weakness and soul shock. Nyoman's attempt at cure can be seen in respect to a form of ontological security prominent in Southeast Asia, what might be called "concentric ontological security," in which the individual seeks to have multiple layers of protective powers that prevent assault by dangerous spirits or other negative forces (D. Hinton et al., 2009). In a desperate attempt to create protective layers, Nyoman took to wearing a helmet, protective clothing, a camouflage jacket, and amulets. Following this same cultural logic, one of the traditional healers he first saw seemingly aimed to create further protective layers by giving him an oral medication, a body rub, and a nasal spray. In Nyoman's case, even unwanted thoughts are configured as spirits that invade the brain, passing through the normally protective layers to the very inner recesses of being.

In the next chapter, Nadia El-Shaarawi's analysis recalls Erica James's (2008) *States of Insecurity* in that El-Shaarawi's chapter depicts "insecurity" and its effects but from the refugee's perspective. El-Shaarawi details the experience of Iraqis in Egypt as they confront multiple forms of insecurity: daily-safety insecurity, economic insecurity, and health insecurity. They also suffer from gendered structural violence such as women being stigmatized for being unmarried and childless. This is the current lifescape for Iraqis, a people who already suffered many periods of violence that included the threat of torture and death under Saddam Hussein, the Gulf War, the Iraqi war, and the later post–Iraqi war threats posed by daily bombings, sectarian violence, and kidnappings.

The Iraqis whom El-Shaarawi studied considered trauma and hardship the cause of a multitude of complaints: PTSD symptoms such as insomnia, nightmares, fear, and flashbacks, as well as heart pain, high blood pressure, and sadness. The main complaint was fatigue along with many somatic symptoms for which physicians could find no cause. The complaint of fatigue is a powerful icon of the long journey not yet finished and of being in a transit limbo, and the other various somatic symptoms serve as further embodied testimony of hardship. But the somatic complaints were not unexplained somatization. Rather the Iraqis have an ethnopsychology according to which tiredness and other somatic symptoms are thought to be caused by suffering – it is local conceptualization of psychophysiology that hypothesizes a particular psychosomatic reticulum (Kleinman & Kleinman, 1994).

The chapter calls to mind recent writings that have illustrated how the recovery from trauma is severely hampered by living in contexts of insecurity. This literature suggests that traumatized individuals are hyperreactive not just to loud noises and reminders of trauma but also to worry itself: There is heightened reactivity to worry so that a worry episode rapidly induces severe distress, marked irritability, and multiple somatic symptoms (D. Hinton, Nickerson, & Bryant, 2011). This biological fact amplifies the effects of current life distress and structural violence more generally: It creates vicious circles with a cyclical interaction of impaired coping, worsened trauma symptoms such as irritability and somatic symptoms, and dysfunctional social interactions. Trauma results in heightened reactivity to stress and decreased ability to cope, so that when traumatized individuals confront a stressor they will tend to have more arousal and to adjust poorly. In turn, this arousal and sense of failure heighten reactivity to stress and decrease the ability to cope, and an escalating cycle of worsening may well ensue. In these ways, the biology-driven hyperreactivity to stress causes structural violence to etch symptoms deeply into bodies and minds, and the deepness of the cut is increased exponentially rather than additively as the security situation worsens.

In Chapter 9, Devon Hinton et al. address some questions that emerge from a reading of the other chapters in the volume that describe high rates of somatic symptoms and cultural syndromes among trauma victims (e.g., Casey [Chapter 3]; El-Shaarawi [Chapter 8]; Lemelson [Chapter 7]). How exactly do somatic symptoms and cultural syndromes found among victims of mass violence come to be generated? Are there particular somatic symptoms that tend to be experienced by a certain cultural group under distress, and if so, how are they generated? The chapter shows that somatic symptoms and cultural syndromes form a key part of the Cambodian trauma subjectivity. The chapter illustrates how the dynamic interaction of the biology of trauma, trauma memories, and cultural meanings creates a certain illness reality. This illness reality features hypersemiotized and overdetermined somatic complaints, what might be called rhizomic somatic symptoms, and features cultural syndromes. The chapter aims to be a contribution to trauma sociosomatics,[13] of trauma-somatics, that is, the study of the way in which trauma has reverberating effects through the cultural matrix and social networks to the body.

The chapter shows that traumatized Cambodians have extremely high rates of certain symptoms such as neck soreness when distressed and dizziness on standing, and it explains why. The chapter demonstrates that somatic symptoms should be considered from multiple dimensions (biology, metaphor, ethnophysiology/ethnopsychology/ethnospirituality, trauma associations), and that somatic symptoms should be studied though an ethnography of particular episodes in which the somatic symptoms occur, determining key variables in those episodes such as the particular triggers of the somatic symptoms, the interpretation of the symptoms, and how the symptoms are treated. It is not sufficient simply to state that a group has high rates of "somatic symptoms" or high rates of a particular somatic symptom; rather this form of ethnography should be conducted. The chapter also shows certain cultural syndromes – "*khyâl* attacks," "heart weakness," "the ghost pushes you down" (sleep paralysis) – to be very elevated among Cambodian refugees. The chapter presents a specific model of how syndromes are generated among trauma victims and how those syndromes shape the experiencing of trauma, and it argues for ethnographic-type analysis of episodes of those syndromes.

In Chapter 10, Doug Henry explores a symptom (sleep paralysis) common in Sierra Leone among trauma victims, a symptom that was shown in the previous chapter to be elevated among Cambodian refugees. Sleep paralysis is characterized by being unable to move or speak upon falling asleep or awakening, and often during sleep paralysis a dark shape is seen moving toward the body. This shape, which can take on various forms, acts as a cultural Rorschach. Very high rates of sleep paralysis have been documented among traumatized African American and Cambodian populations in the United States as well as among Nigerians in West Africa (D. Hinton et al., 2005). In Sierra Leone a spiritual distress idiom is seemingly made possible by the biology of trauma. The biology of trauma causes not only sleep paralysis but also hypnagogic hallucinations and hypnopompic hallucinations, that is, hallucinations upon awakening and falling asleep. Religion, group conflict, gendered violence, trauma, biology – these all seem to combine to produce the night visitations that Henry describes.

Henry contextualizes sleep paralysis in Sierra Leone. He shows how it affects the local balance of power and the relationships among groups, how it generates great spiritual insecurity that consists of a sense of imminent attack by dangerous supernatural beings, and how it results in violence and death. During the height of the 1997 conflict in Sierra Leone, the rise of a civil militia with mystical authority was seen locally as upsetting the balance of power between ethnic groups. Large numbers of women began sharing traumatic stories about witches appearing in the night as dark shapes with the intent to rape. Henry suggests that these "sleep paralysis" attacks may have acted as an idiom of distress that expressed the reality of intergroup tensions and the particular vulnerability of women, who were frequently victims of rape and sexual slavery as well as structural violence such as lack of education and low earning potential. Henry's chapter shows how women may articulate their profound sense of insecurity in a spiritual idiom, with the attack in sleep paralysis mirroring the actual fact of frequent victimization of women by "living humans" through rape and other forms of abuse in daily life. But as Henry details, an idiom of distress like sleep paralysis may have a sinister course (on hauntology, see Kwon [Chapter 1] and B. Good [Chapter 2]).

Part III: Response and Recovery

Part III of this volume examines local processes of attempted recovery at the individual and group levels following mass trauma. This includes efforts to reduce symptoms, to provide transitional justice, and to reintegrate perpetrators. Whereas the first two parts of the volume outlined the ravages of war on the psychological, social, and existential levels, this part tries to examine the attempts to recover from trauma and the effects of these attempts at recovery, and how such attempts are affected by local, national, and international forces. It details the trauma ontology in respect to the meaning systems and institutional structures that are used to deal with, make sense of, and respond to the trauma event and its symptoms.

In Chapter 11, Finley explores the varieties of ways in which Iraqi veterans view trauma's effects – through spiritual, psychological, and biological frames – and how the frame that is adopted greatly effects the course of the disorder for an individual: It determines what treatment is sought out for trauma symptoms. Finley shows the production of local "PTSD" subjectivities by examining how the category of PTSD comes to be understood among the military and military clergy as they attempt to label and treat "trauma symptoms." The chapter contrasts the medical view of the effects of trauma as a biopsychological disorder ("PTSD") to a theological view of spiritual wound: Priests configure trauma-related suffering as a confrontation of soteriologies, for which religion is the indicated salve.

Here one might use the term "local PTSD" to depict how PTSD is experienced and understood in a particular sociocultural context. Here one may talk of the production of "local PTSD" that occurs through local diagnostic practices and therapeutic modalities (psychological interventions vs. spiritual counseling), stigmatization, representation in the public media, and the social and economic consequences of the person's being so labeled in a specific context. These local assemblages produce a certain form of "PTSD" (Fassin & Rechtman, 2009; Young, 2007). As part of this assemblage, there is also the local contestation of "PTSD," that is, the various ways in which those in a locality dispute the applicability of that label in that context. These are all parts of the "PTSD assemblage" as currently constellated in the armed forces, and more broadly. In turn, these are all part of the "trauma assemblage" – the broader set of discussions and beliefs about "trauma" and the institutions and practices that are part of the trajectory of trauma.

The category of PTSD is well known among the U.S. military whereas in most other global contexts those who are traumatized are unfamiliar with the category, as Finley points out. Because it is a known category, biolooping occurs: "Traumatized" individuals seek out in themselves symptoms said to be caused by "PTSD," and this self-surveying tends to bring about those very symptoms owing to attentional amplification and other means (on biolooping, see Hacking, 1999; see D. Hinton & B. Good, 2009; Kirmayer & Blake, 2009). But there are multiple views of trauma's and "PTSD's" true effects: those of professionals – such as clergy, psychologists, psychiatrists – and those of the trauma survivor who gleans knowledge from professionals, popular media, and military-provided information, among other sources. These forms of diagnostic practice and treatment mutually influence one another (Giddens 1984, 1987). The "patient" may enact – in a complex process of expectation, mind and bodily surveillance, biological activation – the symptoms and spiritual crises that he or she has heard trauma may cause, and then these enminded and embodied "trauma forms" are treated in certain ways (Young, 2007). Whether "PTSD" is enminded and embodied as a kind of generic distress form – a readily available and well-known distress narrative – or rather as a result of the specific effects of trauma's blow, Iraqi veterans in the United States tend to seek out certain treatments that range from PTSD counseling, Prozac™, finding Jesus, to some combination of these or others, often creating a hybrid treatment ontology.

In the following chapter, Mary-Jo Good describes the results of a study of an Acehnese village that found extremely high rates of trauma, PTSD, and depression. She also documents sources of resilience and recovery. She focuses on women and gives a valuable gendered view of trauma's effects and sources of resilience. The resilience of Acehnese women arises in part from their representation in popular culture as strong and valiant protectors of men and home and children.[14] But this process is neither static nor passive. In postconflict Aceh, women's organizations create billboards extolling the role of women in Acehnese history: Here is a public representation in the form of popular media. As an example of their positive agency, Acehnese women negatively represent government troops as being "Si Pai." In so doing, they show power of word as illocutionary act – an act of naming and potent cursing.

In public representation of Acehnese women as heroines, Acehnese women come to have a sense of agency that counters one of trauma's worst wounds: a self-image of being denigrated, passive, and humiliated (Foa, Ehlers, Clark, Tolin, & Orsillo, 1999). In these images of Acehnese women, we have the opposite of historical trauma – it is "resilience memory" or "resistance memory" rather than "broken-self trauma memory." There is not a sense of centuries of defeat but centuries of successful resistance. Stories about and historical memories of women as valiant and defiant help to counter trauma memory. The chapter suggests that researchers should examine collective trauma-resilience memory (and resistance memory) as well as collective trauma memory, and they should examine such resilience memory on an individual level (but see Kwon [Chapter 1] for an example of how a society's focusing just on "heroic memory" can be damaging if it prevents the expression of pained memory). These public representations seemingly build collective self-esteem, and, in this case, collective self-esteem for women, and they form a narrative of historical resilience to trauma.

In Chapter 13, Christopher Taylor describes *gacaca*, a form of justice that has been used in Rwanda to deal with an extremely large number of persons accused of being perpetrators. *Gacaca* is based on traditional forms of meting out justice in which a judge presides over a public meeting of the accused and witnesses. In Taylor's opinion, *gacaca* is often not successful as a means of justice for many reasons ranging from the accused lying about their actions to a bias against Hutus. But he finds that in many cases *gacaca* seems to help trauma victims to recover, particularly those suffering from *ihahamuka*. *Ihahamuka* (also called *guhahamuka*) is a frequent complaint among those attending the trials, as noted by Taylor and others. *Ihahamuka* is a common syndrome of distress among Rwandan trauma victims that only came into being after the genocide. It features prominent shortness of breath.

Why might *gacaca* help relieve *ihahamuka*? Building on Taylor's analysis of the importance of images of blockage and flow in Rwanda, Hagengimana and D. Hinton (2009) have analyzed how *ihahamuka* illness, with its blockage imagery, involves ontological resonances that reach from the body – as in shortness of breath, configured as the blockage of breath – to multiple other ontological domains that include trauma memory. During the genocide, trauma was perpetrated according to a logic of "blockage as terror." Roadblocks were set up where murder was often committed, and a common form of killing was impaling. According to Rwandan aesthetics, justice in the form of *gacaca* may be configured and experienced as a return of flow – in the exchange of dialogue, in the fact of transgression being dealt with by justice, in the speaking of truth, in the undoing of injustice. *Gacaca* seemingly heals the body through ontological resonances.[15] Through its performance of the flow ideal, *gacaca* may be more effective as a community-based healing ritual for victims – especially those with *ihahamuka* (*guhahamuka*) – than as a method of justice. It is the enacting of the cultural aesthetic of flow, whereas the actual terror of the genocide was conducted according to the logic of blockage. According to Taylor (personal communication, March 6, 2012), "if *ifumbi* was the archetypal illness in Rwandan society before the genocide, its place has been taken by *ihahamuka/guhahamuka*, the new archetypal illnesses of 'blocked flow'" (on *ifumbi*, see Taylor, 1992). *Gacaca* seemingly is one cure for this postgenocide illness.

In Chapter 14 we switch from societal healing that is focused on the "victim" to that focused on the perpetrator. Kimberly Theidon argues that to promote recovery in postconflict societies, one must attend not only to the marginalized voices of victims but also to those of low-level perpetrators. She describes how low-level perpetrators in Colombia lived in fear of being killed by fellow combatants and were also victimized in multiple ways. And how do ex-combatants imagine their futures? Societies and their prospects may be determined by the imaginary of the future, which is itself a key aspect of identity.

Postconflict societies may have various types of individuals in transition who are in the process of self-definition in respect to the past and who are negotiating new life trajectories. Theidon traces how combatants use language and representation to maintain self-esteem and avoid guilt. The combatants often say of murder, "I never killed anyone, just enemies in combat" (cf. M. Good's [Chapter 12] analysis of how trauma survivors in Aceh use language to maintain self-esteem). Combatants may describe the place of combat in spatial metaphors of distance that diminish the sense of culpability. But Theidon also suggests that language may help perpetrators to understand better what they have done: The Spanish term for "consciousness" also means "conscience" in the sense of being aware of the moral dimensions of one's actions.

Theidon highlights the importance of the ethnography of reintegration processes; it can lead to an understanding of how this occurs on the local level. Where can the ex-combatants safely go? Will guilt, resentment, and economic struggle slowly do their damage until further violence occurs? Do others forgive them? Where can they go to start again? What is the new social order, cultural order, and power structure when combatants return to the civil society, and how does this situation affect recovery and reintegration? Theidon describes an ex-combatant's view of reintegration: mental health treatment for the victims so that they can recover from their trauma and spiritual therapy for the victims so that they can forgive; and too the combatants must apologize and repent, necessitating that they receive mental health treatment and spiritual therapy. But Theidon argues that this puts the burden on the victim to "forgive" and leaves out the question of justice. Who decides when forgiveness is necessary rather than justice?

In Chapter 15, Alexandra Pillen examines the *tovile* healing ritual in Sri Lanka and what it reveals about how former perpetrators seek reintegration into society. Whereas in Theidon's chapter it was the ex-combatant who needed to be integrated into cosmology and society, here it is youth who are often locally labeled as the demonic other. Pillen discusses a case of remembering and representation that may be either healing (or as she puts it, a re-humanization, or what might be called a re-cosmologization) or fracturing. Certain Sri Lankan youth are often configured as and conflated with the demonic. Or rather they are often considered as something beyond the demonic owing to their having been among the main perpetrators of violence that is considered "beyond the pale"; they committed violence against family members and performed violence for hire. The *tovile* healing dramas involve the enacting of beings of the Sri Lankan cosmology. Pillen describes how youth intrude into the *tovile* ritual and add their own sequences to the cosmological healing dramas, sequences that are a new representation of the demonic: With effigies, they play out gestures of fatherly love alternating with sexual pranks and other outré behavior.

Pillen suggests that these mini-performances act as a public representation of the horrors of Sri Lankan history, of its multiple periods of brutal violence, as experienced by certain groups of youth. Whether these additions to the *tovile* might bring about "cure" through the integration of a new demon that is a representation of that horror into the Sri Lankan cosmology or whether these actions of youth constitute a sort of intrusion of nightmare-like remembering that retraumatizes and desecrates, these questions are left unanswered, still to be determined in time. Will the *tovile* ritual come to have a new ritual sequence that acts as some sort of taming or purification of this demonic force that helps both youth and the group itself to recover?

Put another way, Pillen presents a case of the uncanny, of hauntology, in which a new "specter" is seemingly created. But here again, just as Henry's chapter warns about the overromanticization of the positivity of the cultural (e.g., spirit beliefs may lead to killing), one wonders whether these additions by youths may lead to more conflict than healing and may act as an assault on traditional cultural resources of healing. The chapter raises certain key questions, among which are the following: What is the representation, sometimes in an abstracted and symbolic form, of a trauma in a culture? When are those representations curative? (Others have written on rituals enacting past traumas; Kidron [Chapter 5, this volume]; see also Argenti, 2007; Berliner, 2005.)

In the following chapter, Kenneth Miller and Sulani Perera give a detailed description of violence – the Tamil massacre at a village – from the perspective of youth. The chapter highlights the particularity of trauma and its horror and how trauma is composed of multiple details that form its memory. The chapter also shows that trauma does not just give rise to "PTSD" in the Sri Lankan context but also to bereavement and associated depressive affect. The authors address several areas of theoretical interest also touched on in other chapters: How do individuals deal with the death of loved ones? What are local ideas about the fate of the deceased? What are cultural means to deal with loss, and how do the living still interact with the dead in dreams or religious rituals? (On these questions, see the Kwon chapter [Chapter 1]; for how this plays out among Cambodian refugees, see D. Hinton, Field, et al., 2013; D. Hinton, Peou, et al., 2013; in Rwanda following the genocide, see Hagengimana & D. Hinton, 2009.)

Miller and Perera explore which forces explain whether someone recovered after the Tamil massacre. They highlight that in this particular Sri Lankan context there was not a tranquil space of recovery from the massacre. Lack of safety and financial insecurity continued as families lived in terror and were dislocated from their homes and rice fields. Miller and Perera highlight how certain factors may influence the course of recovery such as personality traits, maternal support of emotion expression, economic stressors (see also El-Shaarawi [Chapter 8]), and religion. Religion has a complex role in recovery in Sri Lanka, as is documented by Miller and Perera. Certain strands of Buddhism such as compassion or non-attachment may be helpful in recovery for some. In Sri Lanka, *karma* is often invoked to help deal with trauma and is often helpful. But some survivors still suffer inconsolably, for instance, still painfully remember the dead to the point of despair, and they are blamed for not accepting *karma* as a good Buddhist would – by practicing detachment and by recalling the story of the Buddha, who asked the bereaved to find one household that has not known of death. Buddhism helps some to move on and so serves as a successful "work of culture" (Obeyesekere, 1990) but leaves others in a state of unresolved bereavement. As a further complication, some Buddhist rituals of recovery are only available to the relatively wealthy: Making merit for the deceased serves as a way of reducing the pain of bereavement, but in Sri Lanka financial resources are needed to make merit. In the Sri Lankan case, the effects of trauma and recovery may play out in bereavement and local rituals meant to aid the spiritual status of the deceased (for a similar process in Cambodia, see D. Hinton, Field, et al., 2013; D. Hinton, Peou, et al., 2013).

In Chapter 17, Brandon Kohrt examines the use of transition rituals to promote psychosocial well-being of child soldiers in Nepal. Here we see the attempt at social healing with transition ritual. Other chapters in this volume documented forms of social healing: in Taylor's chapter, a local trial form that also acts as communal healing rite; in Theidon's chapter, processes of reconciliation and reintegration of ex-combatants; and in Pillen's chapter, the role of a traditional healing ritual in possibly promoting reintegration. Kohrt's deals with the challenges of integrating the "polluted" and dangerous other back into society (as do chapters by Taylor [Chapter 13], Theidon [Chapter 14], and Pillen [Chapter 15]), and his chapter serves as a cautionary tale against an overromanticization of the local therapeutic interventions for trauma.

Local rituals that aim to heal may instead have negative consequences such as when rituals enact negative representations of women, as Kohrt shows. An uncritical overromanticization of local ritual can lead to a kind of "orientalization" (Said, 1978) in which the exotic other is configured as a continual unmitigated source of some traditional knowledge that is curative (Waters, 2010). Just as Western interventions may have destructive effects when not sensitively applied, so too may local ritual traditions. But many studies have shown that traditional healing rituals and techniques, which are consonant with local metaphors and aesthetic ideals, frequently have important therapeutic elements (D. Hinton & Kirmayer, 2013), and that these traditional healing rituals and local religious traditions give insights into local ideas of the pathological and ideal state of being (Finley [Chapter 11]; Miller and Perera [Chapter 16]; see also Lewis, 2013; Nickerson & D. Hinton, 2011). However, Kohrt's chapter serves as a cautionary tale against a naïve acceptance of local "therapeutic" traditions.

The Ontological Dimensions of the Trauma Survivor

In this section we examine the chapters in the volume using an analytic schema and advocate the use of the model to evaluate and address the survivor of mass violence. We advocate a holistic approach to the study of survivors of mass violence, an anthropology of the effects of mass violence in the broad sense of the term, in which the complex nature of human existence – the human being as a social, cultural, ecological, and biological being – is taken into account (on such an approach, see also Kirmayer et al., 2007). One way to approach the legacies of mass violence holistically is to examine the ontological dimensions that shape the trauma subjectivity and influence trauma experiencing, trauma symptoms, and the trajectory of trauma recovery.

The analytic perspective we provide in this section aims to guard against a distorting decontextualization of the plight of the trauma survivor such as a myopic (or reductive) medicalization or an oversimplistic biologization. It is not sufficient, for example, to address only the symptom dimension: to diagnose someone in a locality that has experienced mass violence as having "PTSD" while ignoring the other dimensions such as social and economic distress that may cause or worsen the symptom dimension (see, e.g., El-Shaarawi [Chapter 8] and Miller and Perera [Chapter 16]; see also Miller & Rasmussen, 2010; Summerfield, 1999). To treat only "PTSD" when other such issues are occurring is to medicalize human suffering and ignore its true origins (Kleinman et al., 1997).

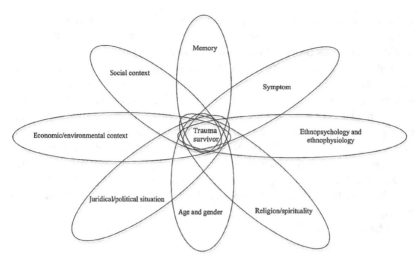

Figure I.1. Multiaxial model of the trauma survivor: Eight ontological dimensions.

The trauma survivor's subjectivity and life situation may be viewed in terms of eight ontological domains: (1) memory, (2) symptom, (3) ethnopsychology and ethnophysiology, (4) gender and age, (5) social situation, (6) economic-environmental context, (7) juridical/political situation, and (8) religion/spirituality (religion here meant in the broad sense that includes spirituality, the local understanding of spiritual realms of being, e.g., what happens to the deceased; we emphasize this by using the term "religion/spirituality"). It should be remembered that each of these ontological aspects is associated with certain practices and institutions. Our multiaxial model of the trauma survivor is illustrated in Introduction Figure I.1. We begin by emphasizing the importance of determining the exact nature of the "trauma" and then we outline the eight ontological dimensions.[16]

The Trauma Events

At the center of this model is the "trauma survivor." The nature of the trauma will affect all the dimensions. A key aspect of the ethnography of the trauma survivor is delineating the exact nature of those events, and their cultural meaning, which includes stigmatization. Acts of violence may be perpetrated in such a way as to inflict symbolic violence (Casey [Chapter 3]; Kidron [Chapter 5]; Taylor [Chapter 13]; for a review, see

D. Hinton & Lewis-Fernández, 2011). Many of the chapters describe particular trauma events and their meanings in situations of mass violence: in Kuwait, bodies dumped in the street with a background of burning of oil wells and destroyed cityscapes (Casey [Chapter 3]); in the Holocaust, having the arm branded, nearly starving to death, and being forced to march barefoot in the snow (Kidron [Chapter 5]); in Bali, witnessing a friend macheted to death (Lemelson [Chapter 7]); in Cambodia, mass killing in which the back of the neck was bludgeoned (D. Hinton, A. Hinton & Eng [Chapter 9]); in Sierra Leone, rape (Henry [Chapter 10]); in Aceh, women being tortured by the pulling of their nails and other means and by their being forced to watch the torturing and killing of their husbands (M. Good [Chapter 12]); and in Sri Lanka, a massacre in a village (Miller and Perera [Chapter 16]). Too often studies ignore the exact nature of the trauma event and its cultural meanings.

Memory Dimension

Here we mean both individual and collective memory. Following mass violence, individuals and cultural groups engage with memory and grapple with the issue of how to represent the past (see all the chapters of Part I; on public memorial, see also Das, Kleinman, Lock, Ramphele, & Reynolds, 2001; A. Hinton & O'Neill, 2009; Suleiman, 2006; Zurbuchen, 2005). An individual may cultivate certain memories or may be haunted by them in waking life or in dream (Behrouzan and Fischer [Chapter 4]), and sometimes the individual and the society itself are haunted by specters that symbolize and evoke past mass violence (B. Good [Chapter 2], Kwon [Chapter 1], Pillen [Chapter 15]). Sometimes a core national narrative is temporarily settled upon; in other situations, alternative visions of the past remain in tension (B. Good [Chapter 2] and Lemelson [Chapter 7]; see also A. Hinton & O'Neill, 2009). Narratives of the past are found in a variety of domains: in ways of describing the events, public memorials, commemorative holidays and events, the literary and visual arts, television, state ritual and rhetorics, public rituals, and even public health initiatives about trauma. Representation of individuals or groups in respect to the time of mass violence may shape the survivor's sense of self: A trauma survivor may be portrayed as a valiant soldier, a passive and weak actor, a liar, untrustworthy, a collaborator, a damaged being, or a participant in a meaningless conflict (see M. Good [Chapter 12], Kohrt [Chapter 17], and Pillen [Chapter 15]). Survivors may find that their own personal memories do not accord with state-level narratives or are explicitly excluded (B. Good [Chapter 2] and Lemelson [Chapter 7]).

Symptom Dimension

There has been much debate as to whether "posttraumatic stress disorder" and its symptoms are present in other cultures or whether it and its symptoms are a culturally specific experiencing only applicable to the West, a sort of Western cultural syndrome or idiom of distress (Summerfield 1999; Watters 2010; Young 1995). See Introduction Table I.1 for the list of the 20 PTSD symptoms in the *DSM-5* (American Psychiatric Association, 2013).[17] Recent work by anthropologists and other scholars clearly shows that many aspects of the PTSD construct do indeed represent a cross-cultural psychobiological fact (for a review, see D. Hinton & Lewis-Fernández, 2011) and that many of the symptoms listed in the PTSD criteria – such as unwanted recall of past trauma events, flashbacks, recurring horrifying nightmares, hypervigilance, startle, anger[18] – capture certain key aspects of the effect of trauma across cultures (on this too, see Casey [Chapter 3]; M. Good [Chapter 12]; and D. Hinton, A. Hinton, & Eng [Chapter 9]).

But each of the "PTSD" symptoms may have a very different meaning and experiential salience in a particular group, as is highlighted in this volume. In a group, "PTSD" symptoms may be considered indicative of a disturbance of psychology or physiology, of a cultural syndrome (see the ethnopsychology/ethnophysiology section later), or of spiritual assault. A symptom such as nightmares may be especially salient in the local trauma ontology owing to an elaborated system of dream interpretation that perceives key meanings in dream such as evidence of spiritual assault (Behrouzan and Fischer [Chapter 4]; see also D. Hinton et al., 2009).

Certain symptoms commonly found in other cultures that result from trauma are not listed in the PTSD criteria, as also illustrated in this volume. Somatic symptoms are a common reaction to trauma in other cultural contexts: weakness in Bali (Lemelson [Chapter 7]), exhaustion among Iraqi refugees (El-Shaarawi [Chapter 8]), neck soreness and orthostatic dizziness among Cambodian refugees (D. Hinton, A. Hinton, & Eng [Chapter 9]), or a general tendency to somaticize (Casey [Chapter 3]; El-Shaawari [Chapter 8]).[19] Trauma-related symptoms such as sleep paralysis seem to be common among some traumatized populations (Henry [Chapter 10], D. Hinton, A. Hinton, & Eng [Chapter 9]; see also D. Hinton, Pich, Chhean, & Pollack, 2005). Complicated bereavement is also often a key issue in situations of mass violence and death: unresolved mourning about those who died during the violence, concerns about how the deceased died, and great distress about not having performed indicated rituals (Kwon [Chapter 1]; see the religion/spirituality section

Table I.1. *Posttraumatic Stress Disorder: DSM-5 Criteria (309.81)*

A. Exposure to actual or threatened death, serious injury, or sexual violation in one (or more) of the following ways:
1. Directly experiencing the traumatic event(s).
2. Witnessing, in person, the event(s) as it occurred to others.
3. Learning that the traumatic event(s) occurred to a close family member or close friend. In cases of actual or threatened death of a family member or friend, the event(s) must have been violent or accidental.
4. Experiencing repeated or extreme exposure to aversive details of the traumatic event(s) (e.g., first responders collecting human remains; police officers repeatedly exposed to details of child abuse).
Note: Criterion A4 does not apply to exposure through electronic media, television, movies, or pictures, unless this exposure is work related.

B. Presence of one (or more) of the following intrusion symptoms associated with the traumatic event(s), beginning after the traumatic event(s) occurred:
1. Recurrent, involuntary, and intrusive distressing memories of the traumatic event(s).
Note: In children older than 6 years, repetitive play may occur in which themes or aspects of the traumatic event(s) are expressed.
2. Recurrent distressing dreams in which the content and/or affect of the dream are related to the event(s).
Note: In children, there may be frightening dreams without recognizable content.
3. Dissociative reactions (e.g., flashbacks) in which the individual feels or acts as if the traumatic event(s) were recurring. (Such reactions may occur on a continuum, with the most extreme expression being a complete loss of awareness of present surroundings.)
Note: In children, trauma-specific reenactment may occur in play.
4. Intense or prolonged psychological distress at exposure to internal or external cues that symbolize or resemble an aspect of the traumatic event(s).
5. Marked physiological reactions to internal or external cues that symbolize or resemble an aspect of the traumatic event(s).

C. Persistent avoidance of stimuli associated with the traumatic event(s), beginning after the traumatic event(s) occurred, as evidenced by avoidance of one or both of the following:
1. Avoidance of or efforts to avoid distressing memories, thoughts, or feelings about or closely associated with the traumatic event(s).
2. Avoidance of or efforts to avoid external reminders (people, places, conversations, activities, objects, situations) that arouse distressing memories, thoughts, or feelings about or closely associated with the traumatic event(s).

D. Negative alterations in cognitions and mood associated with the traumatic event(s), beginning or worsening after the traumatic event(s) occurred, as evidenced by two (or more) of the following:
1. Inability to remember an important aspect of the traumatic event(s) (typically due to dissociative amnesia and not to other factors such as head injury, alcohol, or drugs).

2. Persistent and exaggerated negative beliefs or expectations about oneself, others, or the world (e.g., "I am bad," "No one can be trusted," "The world is completely dangerous," "My whole nervous system is permanently ruined").

3. Persistent, distorted cognitions about the cause or consequence of the traumatic events that lead the individual to blame himself/herself or others.

4. Persistent negative emotional state (e.g., fear, horror, anger, guilt, or shame).

5. Markedly diminished interest or participation in significant activities.

6. Feelings of detachment or estrangement from others.

7. Persistent inability to experience positive emotions (e.g., inability to experience happiness, satisfaction, or loving feelings).

E. Marked alterations in arousal and reactivity associated with the traumatic event(s), beginning or worsening after the traumatic event(s) occurred, as evidenced by two (or more) of the following:

1. Irritable behavior and angry outbursts (with little or no provocation) typically expressed as verbal or physical aggression toward people or objects.

2. Reckless or self-destructive behavior.

3. Hypervigilance.

4. Exaggerated startle response.

5. Problems with concentration.

6. Sleep disturbance (e.g., difficulty falling or staying asleep or restless sleep).

F. Duration of the disturbance (Criteria B, C, D, and E) is more than 1 month.

G. The disturbance causes clinically significant distress or impairment in social, occupational, or other important areas of functioning.

H. The disturbance is not attributable to the direct physiological effects of a substance (e.g., medication, alcohol) or another medical condition.

---

for further discussion of the bereavement issue). Also, local cultural syndromes may form a key part of the local experiencing of trauma (see the next section). Behaviors such as violence and suicidality may be a key aftermath of trauma, and so too psychological disorders such as generalized anxiety disorder or substance abuse (Casey [Chapter 3]).

Ethnopsychological and Ethnophysiological Dimension

Every society has certain ideas about how the trauma event affects a person. There will be certain expected symptoms (e.g., startle) and a certain conceptualization of how these symptoms are produced by psychological and physiological processes and of how these symptoms should be treated. Even if trauma-caused symptoms such as startle and somatic distress are not linked to trauma in that cultural group, these symptoms will be interpreted according to the local ethnopsychology and ethnophysiology. Consequently, the local ethnopsychology/ethnophysiology will have profound effects on the trajectory of trauma in a given context and on how the effects of trauma are experienced and treated. (As described in the "religion/spirituality" section, symptoms may also be understood in a religious/spiritual frame: nightmares interpreted as a spiritual assault or somatic symptoms as indicators of possession according to the local conceptualization of spirituality, or ethnospirituality.)

Often these understandings of trauma and its symptoms in terms of the local conceptualization of psychology and physiology – and the nature of the spiritual domain – are connected to cultural syndromes. These cultural syndromes profoundly affect how trauma-related disorder is experienced and thought to be best treated, how the traumatized person is viewed by others (El-Shaarawi [Chapter 8]; Lemelson [Chapter 7]; D. Hinton, A. Hinton, & Eng [Chapter 9]): Labeling a traumatized person as having *Ngeb* in Bali or "weak heart" in Cambodia will result in a very different trauma ontology than the label of "PTSD." In such societies, the symptoms caused by trauma may be attributed to a variety of local syndromes, and those syndromes will influence how those trauma symptoms are treated and whether the symptoms are stigmatized or thought to be dangerous.

Increasingly as the PTSD construct has become known by laypersons in Western and non-Western cultural contexts, this understanding of the "PTSD" construct shapes the local trauma ontology (see Finley [Chapter 11] on how these issues play out among Iraqi veterans). PTSD itself is not just a trauma-driven biological fact. It may also be experienced as a local idiom of distress, a set of symptoms that are embodied and enminded when experiencing overwhelming distress, depression, and anxiety (on cultural syndromes and PTSD, see D. Hinton, Pich, Marques, Nickerson, & Pollack, 2010; D. Hinton & Lewis-Fernández, 2010; on these "looping" phenomena, see also D. Hinton & B. Good, 2009; Kirmayer & Sartorius, 2007; McNally & Frueh, 2013; Young, 2007).

Age and Gender Dimension

Depending on the person's age and gender, the effects of mass violence may greatly vary. The young may be predisposed to experiencing certain types of traumas and may have a special vulnerability to the effects of trauma, and those of a certain age will form a cohort that will share aspects of socialization, education, and media exposure (Behrouzan and Fischer [Chapter 4]; Casey [Chapter 3]; El-Shaarawi [Chapter 8]; Kohrt

[Chapter 17]; see also Das et al., 2001; Farmer, 1997; Honwana, 2006; Suleiman, 2006; Straker, 1992; Trawick, 2007). Children may be exposed not only to trauma during the mass violence event but also to intergenerational trauma in the postconflict setting. This may include exposure to parental anger and having traumatized parents who have an impaired ability to nurture (Miller and Perera [Chapter 16]). Also, one's gender influences the type of trauma experienced, with women, for example, having high levels of sexual trauma (see the M. Good [Chapter 12] and Henry [Chapter 10]; see also Coulter, 2009), and stigmatization: Female rape victims may be labeled as "polluted beings" (e.g., Kohrt [Chapter 17]). Age and gender may impact exposure to structural violence and ability to recover after mass violence, as when women in certain sociocultural contexts have particularly poor economic prospects after the death of a spouse and are prohibited from remarrying.

Social Dimension

Mass violence and its aftermaths are situated in given social contexts and these may undergo significant transformation during the accompanying upheaval (Lischer, 2005; Lubkemann, 2008; Zraly, Rubin, & Mukamana, 2013). After mass violence, survivors may be displaced, living in camps (El-Shaarawi [Chapter 8]; see also Malkki, 1995). Trauma survivors reside in a certain family and social structure, to which they must adapt after mass violence (Taylor [Chapter 13]; Theidon [Chapter 14]). Trauma may destroy extended families and create a chasm in social networks, and it may force immigration that creates separation. Mass trauma produces social bereavement from death and distance (on bereavement from death and its effects, see Kwon [Chapter 1]). Trauma may shatter a family through the anger of the parent, spouse, or child, or from silences and nonverbal behaviors (Kidron [Chapter 5]; Crapanzano [Chapter 6]; see also Argenti & Schramm, 2010; D. Hinton, Rasmussen, Nou, Pollack, & M. Good, 2009). On a group level, trauma may have its effects through the social structures and social interactions brought about by drug use, violence, and defeatism (Casey [Chapter 3]; Crapanzano [Chapter 6]; see also Evans-Campbell, 2008; Gone, 2009, in press).

Economic-Environmental Dimension

Each person inhabits a certain economic and environmental space that influences the experience of and attempt at recovery from trauma. The person's economic-environmental situation includes safety of self and family members (e.g., the probability of assault), adequacy of housing, and access to adequate water and food. These issues impact on ontological security (El-Shaarawi [Chapter 8], Henry [Chapter 10], Miller and Perera [Chapter. 16]; see also Green, 1999; D. Hinton et al., 2009; James, 2008).[20] If concerns about these life domains are great, then these concerns may intensify the effects of trauma by bringing about an "emergency mode" characterized by repeated activation of the autonomic nervous system. This mode may cause anxiety, irritability, anger, hypervigilance, sleep paralysis, and panic attacks (on such symptoms, see D. Hinton, A. Hinton, & Eng [Chapter 9]; Henry [Chapter 10]; see also Cougle, Feldner, Keough, Hawkins, & Fitch, 2010; Friedman, 2004; D. Hinton et al., 2005: D. Hinton, Nickerson, & Bryant, 2011), and these symptoms may then have reverberating effects on the other ontological levels such as that of the family. Additionally, the impoverished often have limited knowledge of and access to health care, that is, live in a situation of health insecurity, and they may have a heavy load of health care burden – another "stress" and topic of worry, as well as actual biological blow. In these ways, legacies of mass violence are directly affected by economic and security realities structured by relations of power in a society and in broader global contexts.

Juridical and Political Dimension

After a mass violence event, societies confront a range of issues related to redress, one being the new political order (Navaro-Yashin, 2012). Recovery will be facilitated by living in a political order that is perceived to be just. There is the question of what to do with perpetrators, an issue that is directly influenced by whether the perpetrators retain a degree of power in a society (Taylor [Chapter 13]; Theidon [Chapter 14]). Amnesties, such as those given in postconflict Argentina and Chile, are one solution, though one that has been challenged by recent trends in international law. Trials that are linked to symbolic or material compensation (Taylor [Chapter 13]) are an increasingly favored transitional justice mechanism (Fletcher & Weinstein, 2002). Trials are not necessarily benign institutions dispensing universal justice. They are highly politicized and assert a particular, liberal democratic subjectivity. When serving as witnesses or civil parties, victims are directly placed into such a subject position, one that constructs them as a certain sort of being, transmits liberal democratic knowledge, and enables certain sorts of action (A. Hinton, 2010). Trauma victims may also respond with a variety of feelings – hope, upset, vindication, disappointment – during and after a trial, which may become bound up with or reshape public memory (A. Hinton, 2010). In situations in which perpetrators enjoy impunity or face a negligible sentence, victims may experience the ever-present fear that they will be revictimized, a perception that fuels anxiety, anger, and fear. There is a growing recognition that efforts to seek justice must be more finely attuned to local perceptions and realities on the ground (Taylor [Chapter 13]; Theidon [Chapter 14]; see also A. Hinton, 2010; Shaw & Waldorf, 2010).

Religion/Spirituality Dimension

Human suffering may be understood in a variety of registers following mass violence. Religion may be used to comprehend violence and suffering, as survivors seek explanations of why the violence occurred, what the meanings of the symptoms are, and how the resulting suffering should be remedied (Finley [Chapter 11]; Miller and Perera [Chapter 16]). Buddhism, for example, explains trauma and suffering in terms of *karma*; monks may also help people cope with their suffering by listening, reciting scripture, and providing ritual objects and ceremonies thought to alleviate suffering.

Many trauma-related symptoms including somatic symptoms, nightmares, and sleep paralysis may be shaped by and interpreted according to local religious/spirituality ideas such as when trauma symptoms are interpreted as indicating a visitation, attack, or possession by a spirit (on trauma symptoms interpreted in terms of religious/spirituality ideas, see Behrouzan and Fischer [Chapter 4]; Finley [Chapter 11]; Henry [Chapter 10]; and D. Hinton, A. Hinton, & Eng [Chapter 9]; see also D. Hinton et al., 2005; D. Hinton et al., 2009; D. Hinton, Field, et al., 2013; D. Hinton, Peou, et al., 2013).[21] Treatment of trauma-related symptoms may involve local religious traditions: meditation and making merit (Miller and Perera [Chapter 16]), a local possession ritual (Pillen [Chapter 15]; see also Perera, 2001), or purification rites (Kohrt [Chapter 17]; on religion and local recovery, see also Gone, 2013; Hinton & Kirmayer, 2013; Lewis, 2013; Nickerson & Hinton, 2011; Seligman & Brown, 2010).

Religious/spiritual beliefs mediate how a person deals with the death of others, memorializes and commemorates the dead, and imagines what happens to a person after death (Kwon [Chapter 1]; see also Gustafsson, 2009; Hagengimana & D. Hinton, 2010; D. Hinton, Field, et al., 2013; D. Hinton, Peou, et al., 2013; Reis, 2013). What is thought to occur after a person dies a certain kind of death and the indicated rituals to ensure auspicious rebirth often have a profound effect on the meaning of deaths that occurred during mass violence. In many cultural contexts, the manner of death and the lack of death rituals may prevent the deceased from reaching the next spiritual level, may cause the deceased to be a vengeful and dangerous rather protective entity. Bereavement in the context of these beliefs may cause a sense of imminent assault and a lack of spiritual protection (Kwon [Chapter 1]; see also Gustafsson, 2009; D. Hinton et al., 2009; D. Hinton, Field, et al., 2013; D. Hinton, Peou, et al., 2013; Perera, 2001). Consequently, mourning and issues of complicated bereavement, as well as PTSD and other symptoms, may play out in an idiom of spirits – of attack by spirits, of placation of spirits, of making offerings and conducting ceremonies for spirits.

Conclusion: Multiple Levels of Analysis and Intervention

In this Introduction, we have tried to show how the aftermaths of mass violence may be conceptualized through a consideration of multiple types of analysis. We have organized the book in terms of memory, symptom, and recovery and proposed the eight ontological dimensions as a structural phenomenology of the trauma victim. In the sections of this Introduction on the three-part structure of the volume and the eight ontological dimensions, we discussed the chapters and discussed the theoretical contributions of the chapters to the anthropological investigation of situations of genocide and mass violence. In his Commentary at the end of the volume, Kirmayer uses another theoretical framework to examine the chapters, namely, the five realms of experience as seen from four perspectives.

The current volume aims to contribute to the anthropology of mass violence in respect to its effects and how recovery might occur. The chapters in the volume illustrate some of the processes that a recovery-focused anthropology of mass violence must examine. The volume suggests multiple types of possible intervention to alleviate local suffering: articulating and representing "hidden transcripts" of victimization; creating memorials and national narratives that promote reconciliation and resilience; campaigns to address family violence resulting from anger; infrastructure support and direct economic aid; promoting local justice processes; education about trauma's effects (PTSD and locally salient somatic symptoms and syndromes); addressing culturally salient somatic and other types of symptoms (e.g., poor sleep) as well as local cultural syndromes; medication for symptoms like poor sleep and nightmares; and integrating traditional and Western forms of treatment for psychological distress. More generally, recovery will be promoted by a sense of ontological insecurity that ranges from the economic to the spiritual, for example, concerns about the spiritual status of the dead. To use a metaphor, the "pharmacological pill" is not sufficient for recovery: There are the memory pill, the representation pill, the truth pill, the therapy pill, the education pill, the family pill, the economic pill, the justice pill, the traditional therapeutic-ritual pill, and more generally, relating to these and other levels, the ontological security pill.

In the increasingly international contexts in which persons are located, the trauma survivor may receive a treatment or other type of intervention that arrives to that locality through the actions of those in another cultural zone, as is shown in many chapters in this volume (on these issues, see also Biehl & Locke, 2010; Fassin & Pandolfi, 2010). The trauma survivor occupies a certain intervention zone such as a clinic, an area of outreach, a tribunal, a community or group receiving monetary restitution or infrastructure aid, or the radio ambit of an education campaign. Trauma survivors occupy treatment zones, meaning areas where certain treatments are available, and they occupy certain recovery zones, meaning areas where certain resources are available for recovery, with recovery meant in the broad sense of the eight ontological dimensions. One must be careful to differentiate availability from actionability and to determine whether the local population actually makes use of and benefits from the zones and resources.

As there are shifts at the international, national, or local level, what it is thought must be done to redress the effects of mass trauma also morphs. The term "trauma episteme" might be used to refer to ideas about trauma and its effects, and what is needed to recover from it might be called the "trauma recovery episteme,"[22] or to emphasize the institutional settings and various practices, the terms "trauma assemblage" and "trauma recovery assemblage" might be used.[23] This trauma episteme (or trauma assemblage) arises at the international, national, or local level and often forms a hybrid, with particular individuals in a specific place enminding and embodying certain different aspects of these epistemes. Often the salient part of the international trauma recovery episteme is a set of biomedical practices and understandings. Though these biomedical interventions may be beneficial, the effects of the interventions must be examined from the perspective of the various ontological dimensions. One should specify those ontological dimensions of the trauma survivor that are addressed in the intervention, whether the intervention truly has an effect on the dimensions in question,[24] and whether they are key dimensions to address.

The current volume tries to take a broad approach to the effects of and recovery from mass violence. Memory, symptom, and recovery are shaped by local practices and interventions generated at the national and international levels, as are the eight ontological dimensions.[25] Taking a broad cross-cultural approach, chapters in this volume detail various local trauma assemblages in the three sections: Memory, Symptom, and Recovery. The aim of the volume is to contribute to developing an engaged anthropology of mass violence that reveals local forms of suffering and suggests how that suffering might be relieved.

NOTES

1 These rememorialization processes range from public acknowledgment of the trauma events (e.g., the case of Bali; see Chapters 2 and 7, this volume); to changes in public and private representation of the trauma; to changes in group and individual identity and esteem as it relates to the trauma memory; to individual-focused therapeutic processes – local mneumo-therapeutics – that explore how the memory occurs and how to alleviate memory (e.g., current Western models of exposure therapy); to specter therapeutics that aim to banish the demons that relate to past traumas, demons that appear as hauntings in dream and waking (see Chapters 1, 2, and 7, this volume); to types of "compensation" owed to those with "unwanted memory" given the local medical-type diagnostic categories and systems of compensation (e.g., the recall of past traumas as part of "PTSD" in an Iraqi war veteran that warrants disability payments).

2 We would also like to give thanks to the Rutgers University Research Council for providing a supplementary grant.

3 Robert Lemelson's "Afflictions: Culture and Mental Illness in Indonesia" (www.elementalproductions.org), Devon Hinton's (with Siddharth Joshi) "*Khyâl* Attacks among Traumatized Survivors of the Pol Pot Period" (www. khyalattack.com), Kenneth Miller's "Unholy Ground" on Sri Lanka (http:// www.unholygroundfilm.org/), and Brandon Kohrt's (with Robert Koenig) "Returned: Child Soldiers of Nepal's Maoist Army" (www.nepaldocumentary. com).

4 This book does not exclusively explore the effects of mass violence among those traumatized to the point of being diagnosable with a disorder like "PTSD." We explore the subjectivity of those who were traumatized and the subjectivity of those who live in those localities in which mass violence creates collective memory, rituals, and an imaginary that shapes their ontology. For some the mass trauma is more an identity than a biology driven by an actually experienced trauma, and the imagery they draw upon when distressed may well involve events related to the history of violence in the locality or local syndromes and somatic complaints that are said to result from those traumas. When distressed, they may call to mind the aspects of the iconography of mass violence in that locality, a sort of self-identity, and they may embody the idioms of distress and various disorders common in those who were greatly traumatized, such as "PTSD" in localities where it is a diagnosis known by laypersons (Fassin & Rechtman, 2009). In a middle zone are those persons who directly experienced the trauma but not to the point of creating a disorder like PTSD, but who nonetheless enmind and embody the iconography and idioms of distress (e.g., the lay understanding of PTSD) during a distraught state.

5 On types of memory, see Langer, 1991, as well as Kirmayer, 1996b; on memory in general, see Antze & Lambek 1996. On memory and trauma, see also Bal, Crewe, & Spitzer, 1999; Caruth, 1995; Suleiman, 2006; Young, 1995.

6 On "rhizome" in the work of Deleuze and Guattari (1978) and its application to memory, see D. Hinton, Nguyen, & Pollack, 2007.

7 The term "chronotope" is taken from Bakhtin (on "chronotope," see Chapters 5 and 9, this volume). Jane Yager (2009) in her review of Schlögel's *Moscow Dreams* (2008), a book on Moscow during the time of the Stalinist terror, describes Schlögel's use of the term "chronotope" in the following way, which is very close to the usage we intend here: "the Moscow of 1937 as a chronotope, a specific and inextricable bundle of time and space whose defining features are despotic arbitrariness, suddenness, shock, attack out of nowhere, disappearance and the blurring of the line between reality and phantasm." We argue that certain images and somatic symptoms have the power to evoke such space-time, a specific chronotope.

8 On "humiliated" memory, see Langer, 1991; see also Kirmayer, 1996b. As an example of humiliated memory, the person may recall being beaten or having to live without bathing, in tattered clothes, and infested with insects.

9 There is the question of what triggers chronotope memories versus the actual structure of the chronotope memory. For example, certain smells may trigger a chronotrope memory as well as be part of it. Or cutting a potato may act as an evoker of a chronotope memory and be a part of that memory. The chronotope memory might be called webbed memory for its ability to evoke aspects of a time as well as the sense of self.

10 Put another way, certain memories may strongly evoke not only an event but also the sense of self as well as the emotion experienced at that time: humiliation, shame, desperation, rage.

11 To give an example, Alex Haley's book *Roots: the Saga of An American Family* (1976) and its miniseries depicted slavery, including the horrors of the passage in which so many died as well as the horrors of slavery. This movie and miniseries became a collective memory of historical trauma for many African Americans; it shaped the sense of self, as Haley's family became for many an archetypal family. This would be identity by "representation memory," or more specifically, by "past-event-representation memory," that is, identity that is created by imprinting in mind a representation of a past event through such actions as reading a book or viewing a miniseries.

12 And again, these memories have a firstness as well if they include memory of the parent as he or she told the story, the affect and physicality of the parent retelling the event. In this sense, parental representational memories almost always have both qualities, firstness and secondness, have this dual nature.

13 On sociosomatics, see Kleinman and Becker (1988).

14 This source of resilience recalls the representation in African American populations of the "strong black woman," and this representation's supposed importance in promoting self-esteem and resilience (Triffleman & Pole, 2010).

15 For further discussion of how sensations may have multiple ontological resonances, see Chapter 9, this volume (D. Hinton, A. Hinton, & Eng), and see D. Hinton & S. Hinton, 2002; on how "ontological resonance" plays a key role in genocidal and political discourse, see A. Hinton, 2005.

16 These might also be called "ontological spaces." The term "space" or "domain" evokes the fact that each ontological dimension is rooted in certain

institutional spaces and sets of practices and in this way emphasizes the radical emplacement of these ontological dimensions.

17 There were some changes from *DSM-IV-TR* to *DSM-5* but most criteria have remained basically the same (American Psychiatric Association, 2000, 2013).

18 However, certain PTSD criteria, for example, amnesia, may be less applicable to other cultural contexts (for a review, see D. Hinton & Lewis-Fernández, 2011).

19 In many cultural groups, somatic symptoms are a key part of the trauma response (for a review, see D. Hinton & Lewis-Fernández, 2011; see also Jenkins & Valiente, 1995; Kirmayer, 1996).

20 Insecurity may also arise from a feeling of being in a vulnerable spiritual state (e.g., vulnerable to assault by spirits) or of being in a vulnerable bodily state. See the ethnopsychology/ethnophysiology section and the religion/spirituality sections for a discussion of the sources of a feeling of insecurity in those two other domains.

21 Somatic symptoms may be so explained within a culture such as when a distressed Vietnamese trauma survivor attributes somatic symptoms to the embodying of the wounds of the deceased through possession or when a person from Guinea Bissau interprets tinnitus, palpitations, cold extremities, or racing thoughts to possession (Gustafsson, 2009; Igreja et al., 2010; de Jong & Reis, 2010, 2013; Neuner et al., 2012; van Duijl, Nijenhuis, Komproe, Gernaat, & de Jong, 2010).

22 These might also be called the "trauma imaginary" and the "trauma recovery imaginary." On the "pharmaceutical imaginary," see Jenkins, 2011. On the "transitional justice imaginary," see A. Hinton, 2013.

23 On "assemblage," see Biehl & Locke, 2010.

24 Some interventions may even be harmful in respect to the very dimension they claim to address such as "debriefing" therapy that aims to alleviate symptoms after some mass trauma but may in fact worsen them. Or certain psychological therapies such as exposure therapy for trauma victims may have a negative rather than a positive effect if not done sensitively (D. Hinton, 2012).

25 Another type of zone is that of trauma consumerism. The so-called trauma industry consists of local, national, and international groups that try to provide services for the disorders that trauma is said to cause. There are large amounts of money given for international relief for which agencies and individuals compete. The international trauma episteme space and the trauma consumerism zone are in dynamic interaction. Trauma representation – in respect to its causes, effects, means of redress, and those responsible for redress – is a high-stakes game, with major effects on persons in localities of mass violence.

REFERENCES

American Psychiatric Association. (2000, 2013). *Diagnostic and statistical manual of mental disorders*, 4th ed., text revision and 5th ed. Washington, DC: American Psychiatric Association.

Antze, P., & Lambek, M. (1996). *Tense past: Cultural essays in trauma and memory.* New York: Routledge.

Argenti, N. (2007). *The intestines of the state: Youth, violence, and belated histories in the Cameroon grassfields.* Chicago: University of Chicago Press.

Argenti, N., & Schramm, K. (2010). *Remembering violence: Anthropological perspectives on intergenerational transmission.* New York: Berghahn Books.

Bal, M., Crewe, J. V., & Spitzer, L. (1999). *Acts of memory: Cultural recall in the present.* Hanover, NH: Dartmouth College: University Press of New England.

Behrouzan, O., & Fischer, M. J. (2014). *"Behaves like a rooster and cries like a [four eyed] canine": The politics and poetics of depression and psychiatry in Iran.* In D. E. Hinton & A. L. Hinton (Eds.), *Genocide and mass violence: Memory, symptom, and recovery.* Cambridge: Cambridge University Press.

Berger, & Arthur. (1995). *Blind men and elephants: Perspectives on humor.* New Brunswick, NJ: Transaction.

Berliner, D. (2010). Memories of initiation violence: Remembered pain and religious transmission among the Bulongic (Guinea, Conakry). In N. Argenti & K. Schramm (Eds.), *Remembering violence: Anthropological perspectives on intergenerational transmission* (pp. 83–102). New York: Berghahn Books.

Biehl, J., & Locke, P. (2010). Deleuze and the anthropology of becoming. *Current Anthropology, 51,* 317–51.

Caruth, C. (1995). *Trauma: Explorations in memory.* Baltimore: Johns Hopkins University Press.

Cougle, J. R., Feldner, M. T., Keough, M. E., Hawkins, K. A., & Fitch, K. E. (2010). Comorbid panic attacks among individuals with posttraumatic stress disorder: Associations with traumatic event exposure history, symptoms, and impairment. *Journal of Anxiety Disorders, 24,* 183–88.

Coulter, C. (2009). *Bush wives and girl soldiers: Women's lives through war and peace in Sierra Leone.* Ithaca, NY: Cornell University Press.

Crandon-Malamud, L. (1991). *From the fat of our souls: Social change, political process, and medical pluralism in Bolivia.* Berkeley: University of California Press.

Das, V., Kleinman, A., Lock, M., Ramphele, M., & Reynolds, P. (Eds.). (2001). *Remaking a world: Violence, social suffering, and recovery.* Berkeley: University of California Press.

Deleuze, G., & Guattari, F. (1987). *A thousand plateaus: Capitalism and schizophrenia.* Minneapolis: University of Minnesota Press.

de Jong, J., & Clarke, L. (1996). *Mental health of refugees.* Geneva: World Health Organization.

de Jong, J., & Reis, R. (2013). Collective trauma resolution: Dissociation as a way of processing post-war traumatic stress in Guinea Bissau. *Transcultural Psychiatry, 50,* 644–61.

Evans-Campbell, T. (2008). Historical trauma in American Indian/Native Alaska communities: A multilevel framework for exploring impacts on individuals, families, and communities. *Journal of Interpersonal Violence, 23,* 316–38.

Farmer, P. (1997). On suffering and structural violence: A view from below. In A. Kleinman, V. Das & M. Lock (Eds.), *Social suffering* (pp. 261–84). Berkeley: University of California.

Fassin, D., & Pandolfi, M. (2010). *Contemporary states of emergency: The politics of military and humanitarian interventions.* Cambridge, MA: Zone Books.

Fassin, D., & Rechtman, R. (2009). *The empire of trauma: An inquiry into the condition of victimhood.* Princeton, NJ: Princeton University Press.

Fletcher, L., & Weinstein, H. M. (2002). Violence and social repair: Rethinking the contribution of justice to reconciliation. *Human Rights Quarterly,* 24, 573–639.

Foa, E. B., Ehlers, A., Clark, D. M., Tolin, D. F., & Orsillo, S. M. (1999). The Posttraumatic Cognitions Inventory (PTCI): Development and validation. *Psychological Assessment,* 11, 303–14.

Friedman, M. J., & McEwen, B. S. (2004). Posttraumatic stress disorder, allostatic load, and medical illness. In P. P. Schnurr & B. L. Green (Eds.), *Trauma and health: Physical health consequences of exposure to extreme stress.* Washington, DC: American Psychological Association.

Giddens, A. (1984). *The constitution of society: Introduction of the theory of structuration.* Berkeley: University of California Press.

Gone, J. P. (2009). A community-based treatment for Native American historical trauma: Prospects for evidence-based practice. *Journal of Consulting and Clinical Psychology,* 77, 751–61.

(2013). Redressing First Nations historical trauma: Theorizing mechanisms for indigenous culture as mental health treatment. *Transcultural Psychiatry,* 50, 683–706.

(in press). Reconsidering American Indian historical trauma: Lessons from an early Gros Ventre war narrative. *Transcultural Psychiatry.*

Good, B. J., Good, M. J., & Moradi, R. (1985). The interpretation of Iranian depressive illness and dysphoric affect. In A. Kleinman & B. J. Good (Eds.), *Culture and depression: Studies in anthropology and cross-cultural psychiatry of affect and disorder* (pp. 369–428). Berkeley: University of California Press.

Good, M. J., & Good, B. J. (2008). Indonesia Sakit: Indonesian disorders and subjective experience and interpretice politics of contemporary Indonesian artists. In M. J. Good, S. T. Hyde, & B. J. Good (Eds.), *Postcolonial disorders* (pp. 62–108). Berkeley: University of California Press.

Green, L. (1999). *Fear as a way of life: Mayan widows in rural Guatemala.* New York: Columbia University Press.

Gustafsson, M. L. (2009). *War and shadows: The haunting of Vietnam.* Ithaca, NY: Cornell University Press.

Hacking, I. (1999). *The social construction of what?* Cambridge, MA: Harvard University Press.

Hagengimana, A., & Hinton, D. E. (2009). Ihahamuka, a Rwandan syndrome of response to the genocide: Blocked flow, spirit assault, and shortness of breath. In D. E. Hinton & B. J. Good (Eds.), *Culture and panic disorder* (pp. 205–29). Stanford, CA: Stanford University Press.

Hinton, A. L. (2005). *Why did they kill? Cambodia in the shadow of genocide.* Berkeley: University of California Press.

(2013). Transitional justice time: Uncle San, Aunty Yan, and outreach at the Khmer Rouge Tribunal. In D. Mayersen & A. Pohlman (Eds.), *Mass atrocities in Asia: Legacies and prevention* (pp. 82–94). New York: Routledge.

(Ed.) (2010). *Transitional justice: Global mechanisms and local realities after genocide and mass violence*. New Brunswick, NJ: Rutgers University Press.

Hinton, A. L., & O'Neill, K. L. (Eds.) (2009). *Genocide, truth, memory, and representation*. Durham, NC: Duke University Press.

Hinton, D. E. (2012). Multicultural challenges in the delivery of anxiety treatment. *Depression and Anxiety*, 29, 1–3.

Hinton, D. E., Chea, A., Ba, P., & Pollack, M. (2004). Olfactory panic among Cambodian refugees: A contextual approach. *Transcultural Psychiatry*, 41, 155–99.

Hinton, D. E., Field, N. P., Nickerson, A., Bryant, R., & Simon, N. (2013). Dreams of the dead among Cambodian refugees: Frequency, phenomenology, and relationship to complicated grief and PTSD. *Death Studies*, 37, 750–67.

Hinton, D. E., & Good, B. J. (2009). A medical anthropology of panic sensations: Ten analytic perspectives. In D. E. Hinton & B. Good (Eds.), *Culture and panic disorder* (pp. 57–85). Stanford, CA: Stanford University Press.

Hinton, D. E., Hinton, A., Chhean, D., Pich, V., Loeum, J. R., & Pollack, M. H. (2009). Nightmares among Cambodian refugees: The breaching of concentric ontological security. *Culture, Medicine, and Psychiatry*, 33, 219–65.

Hinton, D. E., & Hinton, S. D. (2002). Panic disorder, somatization, and the new cross-cultural psychiatry; or, the seven bodies of a medical anthropology of panic. *Culture, Medicine, and Psychiatry* 26, 155–78.

Hinton, D. E., & Kirmayer, L. J. (2013). Local responses to trauma: Symptom, affect, and healing. *Transcultural Psychiatry*, 50, 607–21.

Hinton, D. E., & Lewis-Fernández, R. (2010). Idioms of distress among trauma survivors: Subtypes and clinical utility. *Culture, Medicine, and Psychiatry*, 34, 209–18.

Hinton, D. E., & Lewis-Fernández, R. (2011). The cross-cultural validity of post-traumatic stress disorder: Implications for DSM-5. *Depression and Anxiety*, 28, 783–801.

Hinton, D. E., Nguyen, L., & Pollack, M. H. (2007). Orthostatic panic as a key Vietnamese reaction to traumatic events: The case of September 11th. *Medical Anthropology Quarterly*, 21, 81–107.

Hinton, D. E., Nickerson, A., & Bryant, R. A. (2011). Worry, worry attacks, and PTSD among Cambodian refugees: A path analysis investigation. *Social Science and Medicine*, 72, 1817–25.

Hinton, D. E., Peou, S., Joshi, S., Nickerson, A., & Simon, N. (2013). Normal grief and complicated bereavement among traumatized Cambodian refugees: Cultural context and the central role of dreams of the deceased. *Culture, Medicine, and Psychiatry*, 37, 427–64.

Hinton, D. E., Pich, V., Chhean, D., & Pollack, M. H. (2005). "The ghost pushes you down": Sleep paralysis-type panic attacks in a Khmer refugee population. *Transcultural Psychiatry*, 42, 46–78.

Hinton, D. E., Pich, V., Marques, L., Nickerson, A., & Pollack, M. H. (2010). Khyâl attacks: A key idiom of distress among traumatized Cambodia refugees. *Culture, Medicine, and Psychiatry*, 34, 244–78.

Hinton, D. E., Rasmussen, A., Nou, L., Pollack, M. H., & Good, M. J. (2009). Anger, PTSD, and the nuclear family: A study of Cambodian refugees. *Social Science and Medicine*, 69, 1387–94.

Hirsch, M. (1999). Projected memory: Holocaust photographs in personal and public fantasy. In M. Bal, J. V. Crewe & L. Spitzer (Eds.), *Acts of memory: Cultural recall in the present* (pp. 3–23). Hanover, NH: Dartmouth College: University Press of New England.

Hollan, D. (2004). Self systems, cultural idioms of distress, and the psycho-biology consequences of childhood suffering. *Transcultural Psychiatry*, 41, 62–79.

Honwana, A. M. (2006). *Child soldiers in Africa*. Philadelphia: University of Pennsylvania Press.

Igreja, V., Dias-Lambranca, B., Hershey, D. A., Racin, L., Richters, A., & Reis, R. (2010). The epidemiology of spirit possession in the aftermath of mass political violence in Mozambique. *Social Science and Medicine*, 71, 592–9.

James, E. (2008). Haunting ghosts: Madness, gender, and *ensekirite* in Haiti in the democratic era. In M. J. Good, S. T. Hyde, & B. J. Good (Eds.), *Postcolonial disorders* (pp. 132–56). Berkeley: University of California Press.

Jenkins, J. H. (2011). *Pharmaceutical self: The global shaping of experience in an age of psychopharmacology*, 1st ed. Santa Fe, NM: School for Advanced Research Press.

Jenkins, J. H., & Valiente, M. (1994). Bodily transactions of the passions: *El calor* (the heat) among Salvadoran women. In T. Csordas (Ed.), *The body as existential ground: Studies in culture, self, and experience* (pp. 163–82). Cambridge: Cambridge University Press.

Kirmayer, L. J., & Blake. (2009). Theoretical perspectives on the cross-cultural study of panic disorder. In D. Hinton & B. Good (Eds.), *Culture and panic disorder* (pp. 31–56). Stanford, CA: Stanford University Press.

Kirmayer, L. J. (1996a). Confusion of the senses: Implications of ethnocultural variations in somatoform and dissociative disorders for PTSD. In A. J. Marsella, M. J. Friedman, E. T. Gerrity & R. M. Scurfield (Eds.), *Ethnocultural aspects of posttraumatic stress disorder: Issues, research, and clinical applications* (pp. 131–64). Washington, DC: American Psychological Association.

(1996b). Tense past: Cultural essays in trauma and memory. In P. Antze & M. Lambek (Eds.), *Tense past: Cultural essays in trauma and memory* (pp. 173–98). New York: Routledge.

Kirmayer, L. J., Lemelson, R., & Barad, M. (Eds.) (2007). *Understanding trauma: Integrating biological, clinical, and cultural perspectives*. New York: Cambridge University Press.

Kirmayer, L. J., & Sartorius, N. (2007). Cultural models and somatic syndromes. *Psychosomatic Medicine*, 69, 832–40.

Kleinman, A., & Becker, A. E. (1998). "Sociosomatics": The contributions of anthropology to psychosomatic medicine. *Psychosomatic Medicine*, 60, 389–93.

Kleinman, A., Das, V., & Lock, M. (Eds.) (1997). *Social suffering*. Berkeley: University of California.

Kleinman, A., & Good, B. J. (Eds.) (1985). *Culture and depression: Studies in anthropology and cross-cultural psychiatry of affect and disorder*. Berkeley: University of California Press.

Kleinman, A., & Kleinman, J. (1994). How bodies remember: Social memory and bodily experience of criticism, resistance, and delegitimation following China's cultural revolution. *New Literary History*, 25, 707–23.

Langer, L. L. (1991). *Holocaust testimonies: The ruins of memory*. New Haven, CT: Yale University Press.

Lewis, S. (2013). Trauma and the making of flexible minds in the Tibetan exile community. *Ethos* 41, 313–36.

Lischer, S. K. (2005). *Dangerous sanctuaries: Refugee camps, civil war, and the dilemmas of humanitarian aid*. Ithaca, NY: Cornell University Press.

Lubkemann, S. C. (2008). *Culture in chaos: An anthropology of the social condition in war*. Chicago: University of Chicago Press.

Malkki, L. H. (1995). *Purity and exile: Violence, memory, and national cosmology among Hutu refugees in Tanzania*. Chicago: University of Chicago Press.

McNally, R. J., & Frueh, B. C. (2013). Why are Iraq and Afghanistan War veterans seeking PTSD disability compensation at unprecedented rates? *Journal of Anxiety Disorders*, 27, 520–6.

Miller, K. E., & Rasmussen, A. (2010). War exposure, daily stressors, and mental health in conflict and post-conflict settings: Bridging the divide between trauma-focused and psychosocial frameworks. *Social Science and Medicine*, 70, 7–16.

Navaro-Yashin, Y. (2012). *The make-believe space: Affective geography in a postwar polity*. Durham, NC: Duke University Press.

Neuner, F., Pfeiffer, A., Schauer-Kaiser, E., Odenwald, M., Elbert, T., & Ertl, V. (2012). Haunted by ghosts: Prevalence, predictors and outcomes of spirit possession experiences among former child soldiers and war-affected civilians in Northern Uganda. *Social Science and Medicine*, 75, 548–54.

Nickerson, A., & Hinton, D. E. (2011). Anger regulation in traumatized Cambodian refugees: The perspectives of Buddhist monks. *Culture, Medicine, and Psychiatry*, 35, 396–416.

Obeyesekere, G. (1990). *The work of culture: Symbolic transformation in psychoanalysis and anthropology*. Chicago: University of Chicago Press.

Perera, S. (2001). Spirit possessions and avenging ghosts: Stories of supernatural activity as narratives of terror and mechanisms of coping and remembering. In V. Das, A. Kleinman, M. Lock, M. Ramphele & P. Reynolds (Eds.), *Remaking a world: Violence, social suffering, and recovery* (pp. 157–200). Berkeley: University of California Press.

Reis, R. (2013). Children enacting idioms of witchcraft and spirit possession in response to trauma: Therapeutically beneficial, and for whom? *Culture, Medicine, and Psychiatry*, 50, 622–43.

Robben, A. C. G. M., & Suárez-Orozco, M. M. (2000). *Cultures under siege: Collective violence and trauma*. Cambridge and New York: Cambridge University Press.

Said, E. W. (1978). *Orientalism*, 1st Vintage Books ed. New York: Vintage.

Seligman, R., & Brown, R. A. (2010). Theory and method at the intersection of anthropology and cultural neuroscience. *Social Cognitive and Affective Neuroscience*, 5, 130–7.

Straker, G. (1992). *Faces in the revolution: The psychological effects of violence on township youth in South Africa*. Athens: Ohio University Press.

Suleiman, S. R. (2006). *Crises of memory and the Second World War*. Cambridge, MA: Harvard University Press.

Summerfield, D. (1999). A critique of seven assumptions behind psychological trauma programmes in war-affected areas. *Social Science and Medicine*, 48, 1449–62.

Taylor, C. C. (1992). *Milk, honey, and money: Changing concepts in Rwandan healing.* Washington, DC: Smithsonian.

Trawick, M. (2007). *Enemy lines: Childhood, warfare, and play in Batticaloa.* Berkeley: University of California Press.

van Duijl, M., Nijenhuis, E., Komproe, I. H., Gernaat, H. B., & de Jong, J. T. (2010). Dissociative symptoms and reported trauma among patients with spirit possession and matched healthy controls in Uganda. *Culture, Medicine, and Psychiatry*, 34, 380–400.

Volkan, V. (2001). Transgenerational transmisssions and chosen traumas: An aspect of large-group identity. *Group Analysis*, 34, 79–97.

Watters, E. (2010). *Crazy like us: The globalization of the American psyche.* New York: Free Press.

Yager, J. (2009). Review of "Moscow Dreams." Times literary supplement, May 29.

Young, A. (2007). Commentary: 9/11: Mental health in the wake of terrorist attacks. *Journal of Nervous and Mental Disease*, 195, 1030–2.

    (1995). *The harmony of illusions: Inventing post-traumatic stress disorder.* Princeton, NJ: Princeton University Press.

Zraly, M., Rubin, S., & Mukamana, D. (2013). Motherhood and resilience among Rwandan genocide-rape survivors. *Ethos*, 41, 411–39.

Zurbuchen, M. S. (2005). *Beginning to remember: The past in the Indonesian present.* Seattle: University of Washington Press.

Part I

Private and Public Memory

1   The Vietnam War Traumas

Heonik Kwon

Books about the Vietnam War abound with stories of painful personal wounds – the wounds that continue to trouble the bodies and souls of those who experienced the brutal and protracted war long after it was over. This is evidently the case in the memoirs written by former U.S. veterans of the Vietnam War in fictional or biographical form. In Philip Caputo's moving autobiographical account, *The Rumour of War*, the war veteran is haunted by the deaths of his fellow soldiers and his Vietnamese acquaintances (Caputo, 1977). He is also troubled by the recurrent memory of an old Vietnamese villager crying out, "Why?" as his thatched house was set on fire by Caputo's unit. Some of these accounts show that the Vietnam War left deep scars not only in individual bodies but also in the collective body – thus the idea of the Vietnam syndrome, which refers to the Vietnam War's enduring, haunting effects on the American collective consciousness and its body politic. According to a commentator, "The Vietnam War was traumatic not only for those who fought in it but also for those who were strongly opposed to it" (Neal, 2005, p. 79).

Traumas caused by the Vietnam War are prominent, moreover, not merely in the popular literary world but also in the scientific literature. According to Allan Young (1995), it was after the Vietnam War that the phenomenon we now call posttraumatic stress disorder (PTSD) came to occupy a firm place in social knowledge and institutional practice, particularly in the United States. He proposes that PTSD is in part a social construct born out of the specific postwar historical context. Furthermore, it is a condition that is identified primarily with the lives of American veterans of the Vietnam War, whose combat experience in a foreign war was presumed to constitute the etiological event for postwar posttraumatic symptoms (p. 113).

The Vietnam War was a turbulent and agonizing experience for many in the United States, but it was surely a much more destructive and violent event for people in Vietnam. Taking this simple fact into account, we may ask the following question: How did the Vietnamese come to terms with the war's destruction after the war was over? Did Vietnam see a similar development after the war – the eruption of an institutional and public interest in traumatic memories?

My answer to these questions is negative. There was no rise of what A. Young calls "psychiatric culture and technology" in Vietnamese society after the devastating war (which in Vietnam is referred to as the "American War"). On the contrary, the political authority of the then-unified Vietnam made enormous administrative and political efforts to shield the society from dwelling on the war-induced personal and communal wounds and sufferings. Since the beginning of the 1990s, by contrast, there has been a sudden eruption of powerful communal interest in these long-held wounds of war across the country, which involved the recognition that the violence of war can cause enduring, traumatic memories. In the following pages, I explore the idea of traumatic memory revealed in this recent development, and, partly in the light of recent discussion about culturally and historically informed understanding of traumatic memories (see D. Hinton & Good, 2009, pp. 2–3, 21–3; Good, Brodwin, Good, & Kleinman, 1992, p. 14), how to situate this idea in proper historical and cultural contexts. The ethnographic details that follow are drawn from my published accounts of the commemoration of war in contemporary Vietnam (Kwon, 2006, 2008).

Postwar Vietnamese society was strongly mobilized to focus its attention on the forward-looking revolutionary vision for a prosperous political community and a collective optimism based on "revolutionary sentiment" and "love of labour." Crucial to this process was the empowerment of a heroic memory of war and related civic morality of commemoration. This process materialized in the form of numerous cemeteries of revolutionary war martyrs and memorials dedicated to their memory, erected in the immediate postwar years at the center of the community's public space throughout the central and southern regions of Vietnam.

The postwar revolutionary optimism is materialized in the public war memorials. Many of these memorials adopt the form known as "bird" to Vietnamese memorial artists, consisting of a pointed neo-Gothic tower and two wings unfolding from the lower level of the tower. A traditional incense burner and an altar are typically placed between the two wings, and in front of the tower on the surface into which is inscribed the classical dictum of the official Vietnamese war commemorative art, "Your ancestral land remembers your merit." In one typical example found in the hamlet Thuy Bo, Quang Nam Province, a sculpture above the inscription shows a family of three including a man in uniform holding the flag of Vietnam. A small boy stands beside the man also holding the flagpole and, behind him, a woman rests her arm on the boy's shoulder while holding a gun with another arm. The self-sacrifice of this revolutionary nuclear family constitutes the radical symbolic transition between the imagery depicted by the two lower wings. The wing on the left paints a historical reality of the wartime village, mixing elements of village history with those of national history, thus showing soldiers in combat gear as well as a legendary local war heroine who is known to have stood against advancing enemy tanks. Moving to the opposite wing, the landscape changes radically, now depicting a peaceful, prosperous view of postwar village life. Children walk to school, women become schoolteachers and mothers, men sit on tractors, and they are surrounded by lush forest and expansive farmland. These installations solidify the memory of heroic death as the threshold through which the violent past of a war trans-forms into the prosperous communal life of the future. The villagers' self-sacrifice for the ancestral land enables this transformation. The nuclear family at the top of the Thuy Bo memorial signifies the transformation of the military command of "All Forward!" into a forward movement in economic development; this motif of regeneration is dominant in Vietnamese war monumental art.

The state-instituted centrality of the heroic memory of war in post-war Vietnamese society also changed the domestic space. The political campaigns focused on substituting the commemoration of heroic war dead for the traditional cult of ancestors, first in the north after the inde-pendence of 1945 and then in the southern and central regions after the unification of the country in 1975. The memorabilia of war martyrs and revolutionary leaders replaced the ancestral tablets in the domestic space; the communal ancestral temples and other religious sites were closed down and these gave way to the people's assembly hall. In the latter, ordinary citizens and their administrative leaders discussed com-munity affairs and production quotas surrounded by the vestiges of the American War in a structurally similar way to how peasants and village notables earlier talked about rents and the ritual calendar in the vil-lage's communal house surrounded by the relics of the village's founding ancestors.

Recent accounts from prominent Vietnamese writers show how this construction of heroic national memory contributed to excluding and stigmatizing the expressions of pain during the postwar era, not only in the public realm, but also in the intimate spheres of communal lives. The stories told by such celebrated writers as Bao Ninh, Duong Thu Huong, and Le Minh Hue commonly take issue, within diverse backgrounds of postwar life, with the inability to express publicly the grief about the destructive past and the losses it incurred in postwar Vietnamese society – without the right to be sad, as one acute observer says (Templer, 1998,

p. 3). They all make a break with the conventional, official narrative of war based on the paradigm of the heroic revolutionary struggle of a unified nation against the intervention by a foreign power. The protagonist in Bao Ninh's *The Sorrow of War*, a survivor of a battle that killed all of his close comrades, finds it impossible to readjust to life after the war is over. He finds it hard "to remember a time when his whole personality and character had been intact, a time before the cruelty and the destruction of war had warped his soul." He is haunted by the memories of the dead and the death he was responsible for, and his own solace is to recover in writing the lost and the killed, known or unknown. Bao Ninh's novel was published in Hanoi in 1991 and was banned immediately after release, although the censorship made his work even more popular in Vietnam and beyond. The works by two other writers mentioned earlier all appeared in the early 1990s and experienced a similar fate to that of *The Sorrow of War*. Their appearance represented the momentous change that engulfed the Vietnamese society at the time.

In the early 1990s, while rumors of these writers were being circulated in towns, Vietnamese rural communities also began forcefully to assert their liberty to express and attend to their war-induced wounds, although in different ways and using different means of expression. Their assertions involved, most prominently, the revival of traditional commemorative rituals and the related change in death commemoration from a conventional postwar practice focused exclusively on the category of heroic sacrifice, to a more inclusive practice that is open to other diverse casualties of war. In the material culture of commemoration, the change was manifested in the form of rebuilding new domestic ancestral shrines, family ancestral temples, and community ancestral halls, all of which mushroomed across Vietnam throughout the 1990s. In many areas, particularly in the central region, this development, referred to as the "commemorative fever" by some observers (Tai, 2001, p. 1), included an equivalent process on the categorically opposite side of ancestor worship in Vietnamese religious tradition, which is the milieu of the spirits of the dead unrelated to the commemorator in ties of kinship. As a result of this development, the structure of contemporary Vietnamese domestic commemorative ritual, in Quang Nam and Quang Ngai Provinces, where I studied the local history of war in the second half of the 1990s, situates the ritual actor between two separate modes of afterlife and milieus of memory. On the one side lies the household ancestral shrine, or the equivalent in the community ancestral temple, which keeps the vestiges of family ancestors and household deities. The other side is oriented toward what Michael Taussig calls "the open space of death," which is the imagined life-world of the tragic, nonancestral, unsettled, and unrelated spirits of the dead (Taussig, 1987, p. 7). The ritual tradition in the central region represents this open space of death in the form of a small external shrine, popularly called *khom* in Quang Ngai and Quang Nam Provinces, which is usually placed at the boundary between the domestic garden and the street. Within this dual concentric spatial organization, the typical ritual action in this region engages with both the interior and exterior milieus of memory through a simple movement of the body. The most habitual act of commemoration consists of kowtowing and offering incense to the house-side ancestors and turning the body to the opposite side to repeat the action toward the street-wandering ghosts. This two-directional act may be accompanied by a single beat of the gong followed by three or four beats of the drum.

This communal development arises in central Vietnam against the enduring wounds of war felt in communal lives as well as against the background of postwar politics of memory, mentioned previously, focused on the heritage of heroic war death. These persisting wounds are forcefully expressed in the stories of apparition of grievous ghosts of war popular in rural Vietnam. In the part of Quang Ngai Province that the international community came to know as My Lai during the Vietnam War, after a tragic mass killing of civilians in March 1968, the residents told me many stories of the spirits of the dead in pain. Some of them vividly recalled the lamentations of ghosts in the villages, cries that they had heard arising from the killing sites. Residents in one particular settlement claimed that they had seen old women ghosts licking and sucking the arms and legs of small child ghosts; they interpreted this scene as an effort by the elderly victims to ease the wounded children's pain. Some people in another settlement graphically described young women ghosts, each walking with a small child in her arms and lamenting the child's lifeless body. The mother ghosts were grieving, the villagers explained, for their dead children. One family living along the dirt road that leads to the seashore claimed that they had seen a group of child ghosts trailing faithfully behind a group of young mother ghosts. According to this family, this happened a night or two before the massacre's anniversary. On this occasion, they could hear the ghosts conversing jovially among themselves.

According to the old village undertaker I often spoke with, the village's "invisible neighbors," as he often referred to these ghosts, could lament their own physical pain or feel pain when their loved ones suffered pain; they might have grievous feelings about their own tragic, unjust death or cry over their children's deaths as if they, themselves, were not yet dead. Their moods and sentiments, and even their forms, fluctuated with the circumstances. The child ghosts appeared dead in their grieving mothers' arms on a moonless night during a rainy season; these same children could be seen playfully running after their mothers on a pleasant evening before the anniversary day. It appeared to me that My Lai's ghosts led lives with their own ups and downs, and that the fluctuations in their lives were intertwined with the rhythms of life among their neighbors.

The My Lai villagers regularly held modest rituals at home and outside their home on behalf of their "invisible neighbors" – offering incense, food, and sometimes votive money notes to the sites of apparitions or elsewhere – and they explained the condition of these invisible neighbors' lives with the concept of "grievous death" or "unjust death" (*chet oan*). The concept entails that the agony of a violent, unjust death and the memory of its terror entrap the soul in negative conditions of afterlife. The human soul in this condition of postmortem incarceration does not remember the terror as we, the living, normally would; rather the soul is believed to relive the violent event, perpetually reexperiencing the agony of violent death. The memory of death for the tragically dead, in other words, is a living memory in its most brutal sense.

The idea that the dead can feel physical pain has a long history in Vietnamese mortuary and religious tradition, and it relates to the notion that the human soul is a duplex entity. It has the spiritual part of *hon*, which may be considered in the light of *spiritus* as opposed to *anima* in the European philosophical tradition, as well as the bodily, material part of *via*. The material soul senses and feels, whereas the spiritual soul thinks and imagines. In a "good" death (which Vietnamese call *chet nha*, meaning "death at home," as opposed to *chet duong*, "death in the street") at home under peaceful circumstances, surrounded by loved ones, after enjoying longevity, the material soul eventually perishes together with the decomposing body. Only the spiritual soul survives a good death (although in a case when the deceased's body is buried in an inappropriate place for entombment, this material soul is reawakened and may feel the discomfort and pain of improper burial). It is believed that the ritually appropriated pure spirit travels across the imaginary threshold between the world of the living (*duong*) and the world of the dead (*am*) eventually to join the pure domain of ancestor worship. The soul of one who experiences a bad death (i.e., violent death away from home, *chet duong*), on the contrary, remains largely intact and keeps its predeath dual formation because of the absence of ritual separation. The material soul is believed to linger near the place of death and the place where its decomposing body is buried. It feels the discomfort of improper burial and awakens the spiritual soul to the embodied memory of the violent death. The material soul's bodily pain and the spiritual soul's painful memory communicate with one another, and this communication between the two kinds of souls can generate the perilous condition, mentioned previously, that the Vietnamese call *chet oan*, or "grievous death." The mass deaths such as those suffered at My Lai, although they took place "at home" and therefore may not be "death in the street," strictly speaking, nevertheless constitute *chet duong* and *chet oan*. In this case, the intensity of violence changed the idea of home, turning it inside out, and resulted in mass graves where people unrelated in kinship were enmeshed together.

Being captivated by the memory of the violent death event, the soul experiencing "grievous death" is unable to depart to the other world until the situation is corrected by the intervention of an external power. This perpetual reexperiencing is conveyed by the idea of "incarceration" (*nguc*) within the mortal historical drama. The grievance of *oan* and the self-imprisonment of *nguc* describe the same phenomenon: Grievance creates the imaginary prison, whereas the prison encapsulates the grievance and augments its intensity.

One man in a village of Quang Nam Province, the village's specialist in death and Taoist rituals, suggested a road accident when he kindly tried to explain the meaning of "grievous death." He said that all accidental deaths on the road are tragic, but only some of them result in the grievous death of *chet oan*. If a man is driving his scooter at a speed that is not permissible, he is doing it in the knowledge that his action could lead to a fatal accident. If he crashes into a tree trunk and dies on the way to the hospital, his death is not necessarily a grievous one, according to the Taoist master. This man did not intend to die, but he helped to create the circumstances of a possible death. Hence, the death that is circumstantially expected circumvents the cultural category of unjust and grievous death. The road accident of a prudent schoolgirl on her bicycle is, on the contrary, clearly a grievous death. She is not responsible, the master explained, for the tiredness of the overworked truck driver who crashed into her bicycle from behind. She neither created the circumstances of the road accident, nor expected any such tragedy on her usual way back from school. Accidental death in these circumstances was not part of the person's self-awareness, and it therefore induces grievous feelings in the spirit of the dead.

The same logic applies to the condition of war. Whereas the soldiers fought the war with a certain awareness of the risk of their activity, the villagers supported their fighting without, in principle, having to risk their lives for doing so. Death of the armed soldiers was anticipated, whereas the unarmed villagers were expected only to till the soil, raise the pigs and children, and protect their families and village. For these two groups, war death takes on different meanings, and the civilian death becomes ritually more complicated to deal with than the soldier's death because of its added meaning of unjustified, grievance-causing death. A large-scale civilian killing in a confined place, such as what happened in My Lai in 1968, is clearly a tragic, unjust event, but its injustice has added meanings relating to a specific cultural understanding of the ethics of war and the morality of memory. This understanding resonates with the legal concept of noncombatant immunity in the theory of justified war, but the "injustice" of death in Vietnamese conception relates further to the morality and ethics of commemoration.

The My Lai villagers mentioned names of certain old villagers as the most grievous victims of the 1968 massacre, and these names belonged to families whose genealogy was decimated by the violence. The decimated family genealogy provoked the strongest sense of injustice and moral indignation in other communities affected by civilian massacres. A grievous death in this context is not only the destruction of innocent lives but also a crisis in the social foundation of commemoration, and the idea of justice implied in the category points to the right to be commemorated and accounted for. According to this culturally specific conception of human rights, the right of the dead to be liberated from the violent history of death is inalienable, and the protection of this right depends on the secular institutions of commemoration.

The concept of "grievous death" signifies a state of imprisonment within the vexing and mortifying memory of experiencing a violent, unjust event, but it also has a progressive connotation that points to concrete measures against captivity. In Vietnamese conception, the liberation from the incarceration of grievous memory is referred to as "disentangling the grievance" (*giai oan*) or "breaking the prison" (*giai nguc*). The work against grievance involves the appropriate intervention of sympathetic others; family- or village-based death commemorations and the provision of ritual offerings to the "invisible neighbors" are two prominent forms of this moral intervention. The commitment to this work of memory, and its demonstration in communal ritual activities, was, as mentioned earlier, one of the most prominent changes in Vietnamese villages in the 1990s.

The work of memory is also a collaborative project. It ought to involve not only acts of outside intervention in the form of death commemoration, but also the fateful inmate's strong will for freedom from history. Apparitions such as those of the mother and child ghosts mentioned earlier are commonly understood as a sign of the growth of self-consciousness and self-determination on the part of the sufferers of grievous historical memory. That the souls of the dead can suffer from the enduring effects of a traumatic historical experience is an established, legitimate idea in Vietnamese moral and cultural tradition. In addition, this idea is firmly present in the eruption of "commemorative fever" and in the related, forceful ritual revival. The idea is bound up with everyday Vietnamese ritual commemorative practices, which paint the world as a place that the living must share with the dead. In this milieu of interaction with the past, the apparitions in My Lai are more than history's ruins or uncanny traces. Rather, these ghosts are vital historical witnesses, testifying to the war's unjust destruction of human life, with broken lives but unbreakable spirits. The sufferings endured by My Lai's ghosts are not the same as those we gloss over as traumatic memory. However, we can imagine that their collective existence is a reflection of the historical trauma the community as a whole suffered.

The political authority of postwar Vietnam sought to come to terms with the destruction of war with a forward-looking spirit and mobilized the heroism of patriotic and revolutionary sacrifice for that purpose. In recent years, the focus of commemoration in the Vietnamese society has shifted from the centrality of heroic memory to the plurality of historical memory. The latter, and its manifestation in recent revival of ancestral and other commemorative rituals, is based on the notion that the spirits of the dead can suffer from traumatic memories and the related awareness that the living have an ethical responsibility to help free them from their confinement in a historical trauma. What we learn from this development is, first, that the constitution of political reality is intimately related to the trauma of war, that is, to the question of whether and how the historical trauma is publicly recognized. To understand this relationship, moreover, it is important to recognize that the trauma of war may have different loci and different ways of being dealt with.

Allan Young (1995) notes, with reference to the reality of PTSD in post–Vietnam War American society, that he intends "not to deny its reality but to explain how it and its traumatic memory have been *made* real" (pp. 5–6, original emphasis). Just as Ian Hacking (1995, p. 16) does in his gripping account of the history of multiple personality disorder partly in relation to modern culture's obsession with repressed memories, A. Young disavows interest in the "reality question" of the object of his investigation. He also makes the plea, however, that his research was far from "trivializing the acts of violence and the terrible losses that stand behind many traumatic memories." His primary interest is instead to show how the reality of the posttrauma was "achieved" and "to describe the mechanisms through which these phenomena penetrate people's life worlds, acquire facticity, and the self-knowledge of patients, clinicians, and researchers" (A. Young, 1995, p. 6). In this light, A. Young highlights the *DSM-III* "revolution" that began in 1974 – the entry of

PTSD into the third edition of the *Diagnostic Statistical Manual*, the psychiatric profession's bible. He also details how this stamp of approval was "inextricably connected with the lives of American veterans of the Vietnam War, with their experiences as combatants and, later, as patients of the Veterans Administration Medical System" (1995, p. 108). If PTSD is partly a "disease of time," as A. Young maintains, how was the rise of this phenomenon related to the experience and memory of the Vietnam War?

A. Young considers the relationship mainly in the institutional settings of veteran care and in terms of the interaction between this institutional establishment and the existing broad psychiatric profession. We may broaden the setting, however. The Vietnam War is commonly referred to as having been a "traumatic" experience for the American society as a whole. According to a commentator, "The Vietnam War was traumatic not only for those who fought in it but also for those who were strongly opposed to it" (Neal, 2005, p. 79). Americans, Marilyn Young observes, indeed remember the Vietnam War mainly as conflicts among Americans: "The Vietnam war, in short, was a civil war, but – and this may puzzle Vietnamese, who are currently discovering the extent to which it was a civil war for them – it was an *American* civil war" (1995, p. 516, original emphasis). The radical division of a nation as to the objective and the conduct of a war that it was compelled to fight had a lot to do with how the memory of this war turned into a "traumatic" memory, and the war's prolific violence against innocent civilians such as the tragedy of My Lai played a major part in provoking and deepening this division. M. Young writes, "More divisive than any conflict Americans have engaged in since the Civil War, the Vietnam War raised questions about the nation's identity. These questions have not been settled. The battle over interpreting the Vietnam War is a battle over interpreting America and it continues to the present day" (1995, p. 516). It is a widely held view among the observers of the post–Vietnam War period that the conflicts within the society as to the war's purpose and related interpretive battles over the nation's identity were intimately tied to the personal alienation that many American veterans of the Vietnam War experienced on their return home. Furthermore, it is argued that this widespread alienation was partly responsible for the way in which their war experience turned to the etiological event for posttraumatic symptoms (Figley & Leventma, 1990). Hence, we may say that the Vietnam War was a traumatic event for many Americans in literal as well as metaphoric senses, in personal as well as collective terms, and that these two separate senses of the term were interconnected in making the event a traumatic memory.

A. Young's book, *The Harmony of Illusions*, includes an ethnographic description of the clinical institutional setting, featuring detailed accounts of the troubling flashbacks and nightmares that torment the veterans diagnosed as PTSD patients. In their accounts, social alienation indeed appears to a major issue. Moreover, A. Young was surprised to discover also that the veterans' troubled memories of the combat experience were not always related to combat. In the case of Brian Murray, whose PTSD diagnosis A. Young (1995, pp. 149–53) introduces, the veteran testifies that he could not readjust to society after he left the service and that he experienced a host of troubles after return home with his family and at his job. He said, "I had a lot of contact with Vietnamese people as a result of my job [as a military police officer], and I thought of them as being a very interesting culture. When I came back to the U.S., everything was silly bullshit. Everybody I came into contact with seemed so childish.... The geography looked the same as before, but the people were all clones" (A. Young, 1995, p. 152). Murray's nightmares return to the place that he had to patrol as a military policeman, a place where captured Vietnamese prisoners and civilians were being interrogated. Murray was later ordered to assist with the interrogations, and this is "where he has his traumatic experience" (1995, p. 150). In a compelling narrative, A. Young introduces stories of these complicated lives, told in the treatment unit where the anguish of the veterans is reenacted in the presence of the treatment staff. The anguish is often of the tortuous mixture of being both a victim and a perpetrator of violence, of the horrors simultaneously experienced and perpetrated by these men.

A. Young says that his history of PTSD is not to prove or disprove the truth of the phenomenon – similar phenomena have long been known since the time of the Great War, as testified by the career of W. H. R Rivers, the eminent British anthropologist who, during the war, worked with shell-shock victims in an Edinburgh hospital – but rather to detail how the phenomenon was made to be publicly truthful in particular historical circumstances, within which he highlights the aftermath of the Vietnam War, and against a particular cultural historical background. This background has been, according to Hacking (1995, p. 5), part of the development in Western medicine to "scientize the soul" since the late nineteenth century. A. Young's ethnography of the development of PTSD is not meant to challenge or trivialize the reality of posttraumatic sufferings; he says emphatically, "The suffering is real; PTSD is real" (1995, p. 10). With the last statement, in my understanding, A. Young means the reality of posttrauma as this is experienced by individual veterans and patients – a reality that should not be confused with the PTSD as a reality and truth in clinical medicine and diagnostic science. It is the latter, and this only, that A. Young makes an object of ethnographical and historical investigation, that is, a contested reality of truth and a historically constituted phenomenon.

I will say the same of the grievous spirits of war dead in Vietnam. My intention in introducing the accounts of grievous war death is not to prove or disprove the reality of the phenomenon that the souls of the dead can suffer from traumas. I have no means to know whether human souls survive the event of death, not to mention whether the agony of reexperiencing violent events of the past can torment these souls of the dead. What I do know is simply that this idea, the trauma of the dead, has helped to form the momentous changes that Vietnamese society has undergone since the Vietnam War. The idea of "grievous death" is a deep-rooted cultural category in Vietnam, and the contemporary manifestation of this idea is a product of history, inseparable from the violent history of a long war and rising against the postwar historical background in which people were not able to engage publicly, under the revolutionary politics of memory, with the multitude of broken human lives and their vital historical traces that did not possess the credentials to qualify as heroic deaths.

The concept of trauma that emerged in postwar Vietnamese society is surely not the same as that which developed in post–Vietnam War American society. It is not possible to assign the trauma suffered by the living and those endured by the dead to the same category. Beyond the plurality of forms and even a categorical incompatibility between the concepts of trauma discussed in this essay, however, it is also inconceivable to think that the traumas of war in Vietnam and those in America are entirely unrelated. I believe it is possible to think of these radically diverging forms of human trauma in relational terms, without diminishing the authenticity of each of these forms. The traumatic memories of the Vietnam-American War among the American survivors of this war and the memories of violent death among the Vietnamese victims of the war – these two different manifestations of trauma have their origin in a common tragedy of human suffering. It is true that they arose from variant historical circumstances and cultural backgrounds. Yet, it is also true that these divergent ways to express what Hacking (1995, p. 4) calls "a wound to the soul" have a shared origin of destruction that created these wounds in the first place. Perhaps it is this question of common historical origin that our concerns about the traumas of war, including those about their plural nature, ultimately point to. For it is in the process of eliciting the common origin that we come to realize the necessity to situate the trauma of war in its proper historical context as well as to recognize the plurality of human culture to express traumatic memories of war.

Acknowledgments

This article draws upon research on comparative Cold War cultural history supported by the British Academy and the Academy of Korean Studies (AkS-2010-DZZ-3104). I thank these institutions for their generous support. I also thank Alexander Hinton, Devon Hinton, Anne Guillou, Ian Hacking, Carol Kidron, Michael Lambek, Allan Young, and Marilyn Young for their comments and interest.

REFERENCES

Bao, N. (1993). *The sorrow of war*. London: Martin Secker & Warburg.

Caputo, P. (1977). *A rumor of war*. London: Macmillan.

Good, M. D., Brodwin, P. E., Good, B. J., & Kleinman, A. (Eds.) (1992). *Pain as human experience: An anthropological perspective*. Berkeley: University of California Press.

Figley, C. R. & Leventman, S. (Eds.) (1990). *Strangers at home: Vietnam veterans since the war*. New York: Routledge.

Hacking, I. (1995). *Rewriting the soul: Multiple personality and the sciences of memory*. Princeton, NJ: Princeton University Press.

Hinton, D. E., & Good, B. J. (2009). Panic disorder in cross-cultural and historical perspective." In D. E. Hinton & B. J. Good (Eds.), *Culture and panic disorder* (pp. 1–28). Stanford, CA: Stanford University Press.

Kwon, H. (2006). *After the massacre: Commemoration and consolation in Ha My and My Lai*. Berkeley: University of California Press.

(2008). *Ghosts of war in Vietnam*. Cambridge: Cambridge University Press.

Neal, A. G. (2005). *National trauma and collective memory: Extraordinary events in the American experience*. New York: M. E. Sharpe.

Templer, R. (1998). *Shadows and wind: A view of modern Vietnam*. London: Abacus, 1998.

Tai, H. H. (Ed.) (2001). *The country of memory: Remaking the past in late socialist Vietnam*. Berkeley: University of California Press.

Taussig, M. (1987). *Shamanism, colonialism, and the wild man: A study in terror and healing*. Chicago: University of Chicago Press.

Young, A. (1995). *The harmony of illusions: Inventing post-traumatic stress disorder*. Princeton, NJ: Princeton University Press.

Young, M. B. (1995). The Vietnam War in American memory. In M. E. Gettleman, J. Franklin, M. B. Young, & H. B. Franklin (Eds.), *Vietnam and America: A documented history* (pp. 515–22). New York: Grove.

2   Haunted by Aceh: Specters of Violence in Post-Suharto Indonesia

Byron J. Good

> to learn to live *with* ghosts. . . . To live otherwise, and better.
> No, not better, but more justly. But *with them*. . . .
> this being-with specters would also be, not only but also,
> a *politics* of memory, of inheritance, and of generations.
>   (Derrida, *Specters of Marx* [1994], pp. xviii–xix)

In November 2005, I returned directly to Washington, D.C., from a short field trip to Aceh, the northernmost province of the island of Sumatra, to participate in a symposium of the annual meetings of the American Anthropological Association, entitled "Uncanny Minds."[1] I had intended to present a paper on the sense of the uncanny produced by the paintings of a Javanese artist friend, Entang Wiharso. However, so unsettling were my experiences in Aceh that immediately upon my return, I wrote a brief account of that trip, entitled "Haunted by Aceh," to present at the symposium. For this volume on mass violence, I begin by reproducing parts of that presentation – something akin to field notes, which provide a vivid sense of the experience of being in Aceh in that eery period, immediately post conflict, when it was far from certain whether the cessation of violence and military repression that followed the signing of the peace accords (August 15, 2005, in Helsinki) would lead to a lasting peace or whether the terrible violence, enacted primarily by members of the Indonesian special forces against the relatively invisible communities in the hills of Aceh, would begin again.

What was it about my experiences in Aceh that made it seem appropriate to discuss in a panel on "the Uncanny"? Why address issues of "haunting" in a book on mass violence? And how do we understand the sudden appearance of ghosts or spiritual forces and the eerie feelings they provoke both during and after conflict? Addressing such questions requires responding to more general issues. What are the sources of the sense of the uncanny? What are the psychological processes at work, and how do the ghosts and apparitions that appear come to have vital power as social actors and social forces? What is the relation between a sense of haunting experienced by ethnographers and the uncanny or haunting experienced by members of the society in which one works? And how do phenomena that are experienced as uncanny relate not only to individual repression and remembering, as Freud suggests, but to "how societies remember," in Paul Connerton's terms (1989), to the political suppression and reemergence of historical memory? These are the larger questions that motivate my attention to the uncanny and to the apparitional in Indonesian society.

I begin with the excerpt of my initial engagement with these questions in 2005. I briefly review recent writing about the uncanny and the spectral in contemporary social life, suggesting some beginning points for what Derrida (1994, p. 10) labels as "hauntology." I then use this vantage to look backward and forward to ghosts of mass violence in Indonesia, ghosts that often remain quiet and out of view, though never fully out of consciousness, but that appear forcefully at particular moments of Indonesian history. And I reflect on the place of ghosts and hauntings in anthropological writing about violence, about conflict and postconflict societies, about how individuals and communities learn to live with ghosts, and about those eerie moments when the ghosts of violence refuse to remain quiet.

2005: Haunted by Aceh

My presentation at the December 1, 2005, panel began as follows.

"Less than a week ago, last Friday, I spent the day in the little town of Sigli, the first major town down the east coast of Aceh from Banda Aceh, the capital of Nanggroe Aceh Darussalam or the Indonesian province of Aceh on the northern tip of Sumatra. I visited Sigli as a member of a team from IOM, the International Organization for Migration, the large, UN-linked intergovernmental organization that has been deeply involved in humanitarian relief in response to the tsunami which devastated much of Aceh one year ago on December 26. Before the tsunami, IOM was contracted by the Indonesian Ministry of Law and Human Rights to assist Acehnese villages and towns suffering violence and dislocation associated with the on-going conflict between GAM, Gerakan Aceh Merdeka, the Free Aceh Movement, and the TNI, the Indonesian national military. Since the signing of a Memorandum of Understanding or peace accord between representatives of GAM and those of the Indonesian government, on August 15 of this year [2005], IOM has been charged with carrying out the 'reintegration' activities of the DDRR process, the process by which the GAM military force, the TNA, is to be 'demilitarized' and 'demobilized,' with former GAM fighters and political prisoners 'reinserted' and 'reintegrated' into their communities within Aceh. I went to Sigli with a small group – one of my graduate students, Jesse Grayman, an Indonesian psychiatrist working part-time for IOM, and an Indonesian general practitioner, also hired by IOM – to initiate a project that would provide a rapid assessment of psychosocial needs in three districts on the east coast of Aceh, communities deeply affected by years of violence.

"We drove the two hours from Banda Aceh through rice paddies, rising into the central hills of Aceh, and then into the coastal area of the district of Pidie, of which Sigli is the capital. We went first to the district health office, where recently trained community mental health nurses were having a monthly meeting with their supervisors, and briefly joined that meeting. We then went to visit members of the AMM, the Aceh Monitoring Mission, the unarmed mission of European and ASEAN nation members charged with monitoring the peace process. Two members of the AMM office there told us about their activities and reported that, quite astonishingly, there has not been a single major eruption of conflict between TNI and TNA (GAM) combatants at any place in Aceh since the signing of the peace accords. AMM members monitor the settlement of returning prisoners – they had carried out interviews with over 120 of them, and told stories about the diversity of this group, particularly the generational differences between the older GAM members still deeply committed to the ideology and the cause of an independent Aceh, and the younger generation mostly intent on resuming their education and moving forward with their lives. Former GAM members are also returning to very different communities, they told us, some to coastal towns and villages where GAM was less strong, some to villages in the mountains, the GAM strongholds, which had suffered far greater violence from the Indonesian Army as well as the GAM fighters.

"The former political prisoners, as well as those soldiers who have begun to return from the hills, find it extremely difficult to pick up their lives; many have no jobs, no income, and many have suffered losses of family members – from the fighting or from the tsunami. The peace agreement stipulates that each of approximately 2000 former political prisoners and 3000 demobilized soldiers or TNA veterans will be paid $600 U.S. over a six month period, will be given two hectares of land, housing, and job counseling. However, to date, the returning political prisoners have received little other than initial cash payments. In spite of this fact, the AMM officials told us, 'incidents' in this region have been limited so far to such events as a fight in a coffee house and complaints about inadequate medical care. The district of Pidie, in particular, is a community that has been very committed to the peace process, we were told. The *bupati* or district officer of Sigli is particularly invested in the process. For example, he opened a public office for GAM in the town, invited GAM to select a representative to interact with the government as well as the public. The GAM leader put into this position is M. Thaib, a former military leader. You should stop and visit him. And by the way, here is his hp (hand phone) number....

"Half an hour later, we sat waiting for a restaurant to open following Friday prayers, and decided to phone the GAM leader. Our Acehnese psychiatrist colleague called; the man answered. Our colleague spoke to him in very honorific terms, asked if we could come by the office. He replied that he would join us at the restaurant. Five minutes later, a car with government license plates drove up and four or five tough-looking men got out of the car. We stood, thinking the GAM leader had arrived with bodyguards. But they walked past us without a glance, sat at a table, chatted and waited about 5 minutes, apparently for the restaurant to open. They then got back into the car and left.

"Ten minutes later, a car with a single occupant drove by a couple of times, apparently visually checking for security, then parked. A single man got out and came over to join us. We sat outside the small restaurant overlooking the *bupati*'s large official residence and the *alun-alun*, the town common, a soccer field now under water from the rains. M. Thaib came alone. After looking uneasy for a few minutes, he was soon chatting fairly openly, telling us about his personal history, about his observations about the demobilization process, and about his concerns for what would happen to the returning soldiers or veterans.

"M. Thaib is a 53-year-old military leader, a graduate of the Indonesian military academy, the TNI's 'West Point' in Magelang in Central Java, in the 1970s. He spent several years in the Indonesian Army in Yogyakarta and Solo, before leaving and joining the GAM guerrilla forces. We talked (mixed Bahasa Indonesia and Bahasa Aceh, our friends translating the Bahasa Aceh) about the problems of the 'veterans' returning to their communities. These are men who have technical skills, Teungku Thaib said. They are very good at making bombs. They know how to use guns. If they do not soon find a means of livelihood, there are other groups in Indonesia who will be quite interested in hiring them. (Apparently, Jama Islamiyah, the Indonesian Islamic group associated with Al Qaeda, regularly approached GAM, seeking collaboration, but GAM has steadfastly refused to cooperate. Now that the command structure is dissolving, of course, there is a far greater opportunity that individuals may be recruited into such organizations.) Or they may turn to criminal activities, he went on. He talked in general about the 'trauma' and 'stress' they experience – words that generate associations of losses from the tsunami, of GAM soldiers whose family members have disappeared, of combat related memories. He talked about the 'lost generation' of young Acehnese who were unable to go to school, unable to grow up normally, owing to the violence. And he was happy to support our research – suggesting that it might be nice to hire some former GAM members for our research team. At the end, we walked to our cars and promised to meet again.

"I left Indonesia planning to write a paper for this panel to be entitled 'Violence, Memory, and the Uncanny in the Paintings of Entang Wiharso.' ... I was going to present such a paper, adding further reflections to the analyses of Entang's work in which Mary-Jo and I have been engaged.[2] But I have found myself instead haunted by Aceh. I have been working in Indonesia for ten years. I have only made two short trips to Aceh, although we expect to work more intensively there over the next several years. But I am haunted by the visual images of the 'utter calamity,' the *hancuran tsunami*, and by the stories that come forth unbidden. I was chatting with a nurse in Aceh's only mental hospital last week, talking about the patients and her role in caring for them. I asked about the tsunami and its effect on her family. 'Yes, I lost 26 members of my family,' she said, still smiling. 'You must miss them,' I said. '*Yah, kami rindu selalu*, we miss them all the time. But we pray, and we have our work, and we go on,' she said still smiling.

"In June we heard explicit ghost stories. 'We often hear people crying at night, calling out,' we were told. 'Then we pray, *berdoa*, and they go away.' 'Do they come in your dreams?' 'I myself often see a woman wearing a *jilbab* [an Islamic head covering]. She is indistinct, comes near, but leaves.' With nearly 200,000 dead, and thousands of homes and whole communities gone, the stories of the sea rising up, the vivid memories of terror and survival while those around perished, and the stories of loss are all unsettling and deeply moving.

"Many Acehnese are haunted by ghosts, and nearly all by memories. I am haunted by stories. But are these hauntings those of Freud's uncanny? Freud's essay on the Uncanny[3] is a kind of reader response theory. What is it about some stories or images that provokes a sense of the uncanny in those of us who are the readers, Freud asks. After describing the uncanny as a special subset of feelings of fear, he tries to identify what is peculiar to those experiences that provoke the sense of the uncanny: 'the uncanny [*unheimlich*] is something which is secretly familiar [*heimlich-heimisch*], which has undergone repression and then returned from it...' '... an uncanny experience occurs either when infantile complexes which have been repressed are once more revived by some impression, or when primitive beliefs which have been surmounted seem once more to be confirmed.' For many Indonesians, stories of haunting ghosts awaken strong recognition and anxiety, in some cases linked to childhood memories of ghosts and spirits and the anxieties they produced. But Freud himself elaborated numerous possible sources of the sense of the uncanny, and the interpretation of the uncanny which Freud develops has been expanded in recent writings in ways that resonate more widely, while holding onto the sense of primitive and irrational anxieties being provoked, even in settings in which danger is real. Nicholas Royle's wide-ranging essays expand the analysis of the uncanny to a variety of experiences that are 'strange, weird and mysterious, with a flickering sense (but not conviction) of something supernatural' (Royle, 2003). He also points to 'a strong evocation of the uncanny as what should have remained hidden but has come to light,' a line Freud took from Schelling (Royle, 2003, p. 3). It is with this sense that I want to return to the uncanny feelings described by Acehnese at this moment as former GAM fighters suddenly appear in the everyday.

"Over the past several years in particular, I was told, there was deep fear in Aceh, a fear tinged with the eerie, with the sense of life being ordinary on the surface but of great danger lurking. 'OTK' – 'orang tidak kenal,' 'unknown persons' – were a constant threat. They would appear at the door of the midwife from a village health center on the day that her paycheck would come, demanding money. One avoided meeting the eyes of strangers on the street – they might be dangerous, OTK. Our friend's brother disappeared for months, then miraculously returned. Who had kidnapped him? OTK.... Many roads were simply in the 'black' zone – no one would travel on them – and even the major roads were largely abandoned at night. In Banda Aceh, the provincial capital, people seldom went out after dark during the height of the violence.

"And then rather suddenly the violence stopped. It stopped in some areas almost immediately following the tsunami. In many of the GAM strongholds – up in the hills, rather than along the coasts – it remained terribly dangerous to travel, particularly at night, up until the 15 August ceasefire. Now the roads are almost entirely open. People are beginning to take the overnight bus from Banda Aceh south along the coast to Medan (in the next province). And GAM officials are suddenly having lunch on the square in front of the bupati's official residence. Some GAM leaders are widely welcomed back. For others, long accustomed to having their way because they carried guns, the welcome is less clear. Yet they too are emerging from the mountains. '... what should have remained hidden but has come to light.' And perhaps it is this that provokes the sense of the uncanny."

I went on briefly, in that 2005 presentation, to reflect on the place of a theory of the uncanny for ethnographic writing on postcolonial subjectivity, before concluding.

"It is in this larger sense, as an effort to explore contemporary forms of subjectivity, to find new ways of linking the psychological and the political, to explore how psychologically powerful memories or anxieties provide motives for political movements, to understand how the social is embedded in everyday psychological experience, that I find discussion of the uncanny to be useful. It of course remains to be seen what will happen with the peace process in Aceh. It is still very new. But there has been enormous suffering, leaving 'poisonous knowledge' (Das, 2000). How the ghosts of those who died in the tsunami will interact with the ghosts of the violence, as perpetrated both by the Indonesian military and the GAM fighters, is yet to be told. At the moment, there is a sense of the uncanny, as that which was hidden, deeply and forcefully repressed, suddenly appears as eerily 'normal' in everyday settings. It is that sense of the moment that I have tried to convey."

Interlude: "Hauntology" or Theorizing the Spectral

The haunting and the powerful feeling of the uncanny that I reported in that talk in 2005 were my response to being present in Aceh and encountering a representative of GAM, an imagined and anxiety-provoking figure who "should have" been hidden but was suddenly sitting before us as a real person, Teungku Thaib, "coming to light." The nature of my reflections was shaped by a commitment to engage the ideas of Freud and the uncanny with members of the panel, but also by a larger project in which we were deeply engaged during the previous months.

In early November, before leaving for Aceh, my colleagues and I had just completed drafting the introduction to *Postcolonial Disorders* (2008), an edited volume on postcolonial subjectivity that we were readying to send to press.[4] The introduction juxtaposed three key terms – subjectivity, the postcolonial, and disorders – to sketch out the shape of a scholarly project "to develop new strategies for investigating and theorizing subjects in postcolonial societies and situations." "Subjectivity," we wrote, "denotes a new attention to hierarchy, violence, and subtle modes of internalized anxieties that link subjection and subjectivity, and an urgent sense of the importance of linking national and global economic and political processes to the most intimate forms of everyday experience. It places the political at the heart of the psychological and the psychological at the heart of the political" (pp. 2–3). Such a project, we argued, would necessarily "pay attention to that which is *not* said overtly, to that which is unspeakable and unspoken, that which appears at the margins of formal speech and everyday presentations of self, manifest in the Imaginary,... and to traumatic memories and hidden transcripts, which may fade from everyday awareness but have explosive power when evoked" (pp. 14–15). My presentation at the 2005 symposium was meant to contribute to this larger scholarly program, and it is in this context, rather than a narrow focus on the haunting ghosts and memories that belong to a tradition of studies of trauma and posttraumatic disorders, that this paper should be read.

A relatively small but critical body of recent writing focuses explicitly on the uncanny, the spectral, and the ghostly in contemporary societies. While I will return in the end to suggest that such work has particular relevance for understanding aspects of remembering and forgetting – and reremembering amid efforts to exorcise memory – in societies that have experienced mass violence, this body of writing has far wider scope, ranging from ethnographic studies to literary criticism, sociology and feminist writing, and postcolonial theorizing. Two theoretical texts, along with associated commentaries, have been particularly important for this work: Freud's psychoanalytic reflections on "the Uncanny" and Derrida's *Specters of Marx* (1994). Freud himself focused rather narrowly on the psychological dimensions of the experience of the Uncanny, on how this "quality of feeling" is produced in texts and storytelling, as well as in everyday lives of adults and children. In his remarkable analysis of the figure of the Sand-Man, incorporated into Offenbach's opera *The Tales of Hoffman*, he argued for the importance of "infantile complexes which have been repressed" being "revived" by some event in everyday life. In the case of the boy Nathaniel, Freud argued, the fear of his childhood boogeyman, the sandman who tears out children's eyes if they do not shut them and go to sleep, was brought back to life in a terrifying way by the menacing figure of Coppelius, the lawyer, associated with the mysterious death of Nathaniel's father. Freud analyzes Nathaniel's fears as rooted in castration anxieties; however, in this strangely unruly text, Freud goes on to enumerate a wide range of psychologically "primitive" feeling complexes that may produce the sense of the Uncanny. Many who have drawn on this text in recent years extend the analysis even further; for some, the uncanny points to historical memories and traumatic anxieties repressed through social and political processes that leave traces in social life and return in disguised forms.

Derrida's "hauntology" (1994, p. 10) focuses explicitly on the social and the linguistic, on the supplement or trace, that which exceeds the formal symbolic structures of meaning, making phantom appearances within language and social life. Haunting is not exclusively psychological, arousing partial awareness of that which belongs to the individual unconscious; nor does it have as referent a single traumatic event in the life of an individual or a society. For Derrida, spirits, ghosts, and phantoms make themselves felt in language as that which stands amid or is excluded by formal dichotomies: "haunting is ... neither present nor absent, neither positive nor negative, neither inside nor outside" (from "To Do Justice to Freud," 1998, p. 88). It is, in Royle's (2003) terms, "the revenant at the origin" (p. 281).[5]

In *Specters of Marx*, Derrida draws on this framework to explore the ghosts of Marx that haunt current social and political analysis. At a time when neoliberalism has become hegemonic, defining everyday reality and sociality in terms of the production of commodities and the "glorification of labor" (Arendt, 1958, p. 4); at a time of growing inequality and "the prospect of a society of laborers without labor" (Arendt, 1958, p. 5); Derrida reminds us that we are haunted by the ghosts of Marx. Not only is the "specter of Communism" still present, though in more apparitional form than in the past, the ghosts (plural) of Marx are still potent when social scientists or intellectuals attempt to understand structures of production and inequalities and that which is too often erased from history. Derrida explores how traces of these erasures reappear as powerful social forces, as ghosts and troubling specters that demand justice for "those *who are not there,* ... those who are no longer or who are not yet *present and living*" (1994, p. xiv). Addressing these specters – and the ghosts of Marx – is part of our responsibility to the generations of the past and the future, those who appear as ghosts demanding justice and those future generations who will be affected by our responses to these ghosts.[6]

How then can these two forms of analysis, the psychological and the political, be drawn together for analyzing subjectivity in societies haunted by ghosts? What does it mean to suggest that such ghosts are specters or phantom remains of colonial or postcolonial violence? And what is the role of the scholar in this matter of ghosts and haunting? While rejecting the "ontological" for the "hauntological," Derrida insists on according ghosts a special status as reality, a reality more often explained away by scholars.[7] "They [scholars] are not always in the most competent position to do what is necessary: speak to the specter," Derrida (1994, p. 11) writes. "There has never been a scholar who really, and as scholar, deals with ghosts. A traditional scholar does not believe in ghosts."

How then do we understand those powerful ghosts or phantoms that haunt the societies in which those of us who are anthropologists work? How do we recognize them, and how do we "speak to the specters," accord them appropriate respect while addressing them at the same time as political and psychological realities? A number of recent ethnographers provide critical insights.

In *Ghostly Matters: Haunting and the Sociological Imagination* (2008), Avery Gordon, who draws explicitly on a feminist reading of Freud as well as on Derrida, takes up Derrida's analytic and moral imperative: "If we want to study social life well, and if in addition we want to contribute, in however small measure, to changing it, we must learn how to identify hauntings and reckon with ghosts, must learn how to make contact with what is without doubt often painful, difficult, and unsettling" (p. 23). While drawing powerfully on Freud and Derrida, she articulates an appropriation of their work that links it with recent ethnographic writing. "Haunting is one way in which abusive systems of power make themselves known and their impacts felt in everyday life, especially when they are supposedly over and done with (slavery, for instance) or when their oppressive nature is denied (as in free labor or national security)" (1997, p. xvi). She distinguishes haunting from "being exploited, traumatized, or oppressed," though they are often copresent.

What's distinctive about haunting is that it is an animated state in which a repressed or unresolved social violence is making itself known, sometimes very directly, sometimes more obliquely. I used the term *haunting* to describe those singular yet repetitive instances when home becomes unfamiliar, when your bearings on the world lose direction, when the over-and-done-with comes alive, when what's been in your blind spot comes into view.

Exploring what exactly the "social violence" linked to haunting is and how it "makes itself known" has been critical for a number of ethnographers. For Michael Taussig's early work, the social violence was that enacted through colonial domination and the imposition of commodity capitalism that displaced Colombian and Bolivian peasants from their land. These are "made known" through dramatic images of the devil and the presence of evil in peasant Christianity ("These peasants represent as vividly unnatural, even as evil, practices that most of us in commodity-based societies have come to accept as natural in the everyday working of our economy, and therefore of the world in general" [Taussig, 1980, p. 3]), as well as through Putumayo healing rituals (Taussig, 1980, 1987, 1992, ch. 1). In Taussig's later work, the silencing of the dirty wars of Peru and Colombia "preserves memory as nightmare" (1992, p. 27), and the "restless souls" of those who died violent deaths "return again and again to haunt the living" (1992, p. 27; cf. Taussig, 2003).

Mary Weismantel (2001) addresses the ghostly figures of the *chola*s and *pishtaco*" in the parts of the Andes in which she has worked for years. The *chola*s, the dark, mixed race women of the market, and the *pishtaco*s, the horrifying white killer, "a creature of the night: a white man with a knife, pale and terrifying," are for Weismantel ultimately the haunting figures of colonial violence. The "signified" to which they refer are not, however, entirely in the past. "For white men, the idea of the *chola* is suggestive, arousing pleasurable fantasies of a woman whose racial and sexual subordination makes her available for almost any use. By the same token, the *pishtaco* frightens Indians, women, and the poor, for it evokes their own vulnerability to the predations of the powerful" (pp. xxi–xxii). "Together, these two figures frame a picture of Andean social life as fraught with racial and sexual anxieties – and alive with transgressive possibilities" (pp. xxi–xxii). Weismantel goes on to demonstrate that the sense of uncanniness associated with the *pishtaco* arises not from the foreignness of all that is white, appearing suddenly in the Andean highlands, but from "the creeping realization, unavoidable yet impossible to acknowledge, that the murderer is not really a stranger at all" (p. 15). The *chola* and *pishtaco* are powerful psychological figures that demarcate racial boundaries, creating "the desperately necessary fiction of territorial autonomy" (pp. 15–16) and a psychologically "defensible space" for Indian communities, while acknowledging more implicitly the economic exchanges between Andean and lowland communities upon which they have become dependent. It is thus not the strangeness of the *pishtaco*, Weismantel argues, referring to Freud, but that which is "deliberately hidden – *estranged* – from conscious awareness" that lends the sense of the uncanny (pp. 11–12).

For Begoña Aretxaga (2008), it was the "mad violence" of the Basque youth involved in the ETA, the Basque separatist movement, that was experienced as uncanny for members of the Basque communities. These young radical nationalists rejected the autonomy granted to the region by the Spanish government and turned sometimes shocking violence on members of the Basque police force, many of whom were intimate members of their own communities. Aretxaga draws on Abraham and Torok (1986), who explore how collective secrets are passed psychologically from generation to generation, to explore the sense of the uncanny. In a fascinating analysis, she hypothesizes that Spain's great collective secret, which "the whole political system endeavors to suppress," "is that the Spanish democracy was the result of a pact with Francoist forces that did not dispose of the former structures but used them in its favor" (2008, p. 49). Even the monarchy, guarantor of democracy, is complicit in this secret. Aretxaga attempts to demonstrate that the ETA violence, however horrifying, thus appears as an unwelcome reminder – or remainder – of that secret.

While these examples could easily be multiplied, taken together they suggest directions for an ethnographic "hauntology," an approach to attending to the presence of ghosts and specters that appear in the

societies in which we work and the sense of the uncanny that they provoke – for anthropologists, as well as for members of the societies in
which we work.

Java 2000: Ghostly Eruptions

April 9, 2000. Purna Budaya theater, Yogyakarta. Performance of *Mayat
Terhormat* (*Honored/Honorable Corpse*), a theatrical monologue by Butet
Kartaredjasa and his Teater Gandrik.[8]

In April 2000, I joined my colleagues from Gadjah Mada University
in Yogyakarta to attend a performance by Butet Kartaredjasa of a new
"monologue" with the ghostly title *Mayat Terhormat,* or "Honored/
Honorable Corpse," in the theater/exhibition hall, Purna Budaya, on
the university campus. We arrived to find the small theater packed with
nearly nine hundred students, faculty members, and leading intellectuals of Yogyakarta. Ticket prices were cheap, and the front area was
reserved for students to sit on the floor on mats, in traditional Javanese
style, while university professors and intellectuals sat in the front rows of
chairs. Butet, playwright and actor and son of one of Java's most famous choreographers, was renowned for his biting caricatures of leading
politicians during the Suharto era. It was now two years since the fall of
the New Order (May 1998). But the ghosts that began to appear months
after Suharto's abdication – the ninjas and the ninja killings, the "dark
forces" President Abdurrahman Wahid blamed for loosing violence and
threatening his Reformasi regime – were still lurking.

The performance begins with lilting folk music performed by Djaduk
Ferianto, Butet's younger brother, and his musical group. Butet strolls/
dances in, dressed in a simple dark blue, loose fitting pants and blouse,
eating from a simple silver plate. He engages the audience in a stand-up
comedy routine, recognizing important persons in the audience, honoring their presence, then with a clever turn in Javanese making them the
objects of hilarious laughter. After some time, Butet, alone on a simple
stage, the band set up on the side, unrolls a screen with a simple painting of the window of a jail. He settles into position on a bench, now
a prisoner, and begins a conversation with the plate, now the face of
a fellow inmate. At the beginning, his conversation alternates between
dark reflections on being a political prisoner and continuation of his
earlier joking. However, the mood turns more somber as he questions
why he, a simple civil person, is imprisoned, and whether his new confi-
dant is really a friend or whether he will report what he is saying to the
aparat, the term used for the military and security apparatus during the
Suharto era. The *aparat*, Butet the prisoner remembers, "forced us into

obedience through terror and fear." He then becomes reflective. "Jail ... graveyard ... what is the difference between the two? Very little.... People don't want to have contact with the graveyard because it reminds them of death. And people don't want to get involved with the prison because it too often leads to death."

And with this turn and a simple change in scenery, Butet becomes Siwi, the keeper of a cemetery, a role he plays for the remainder of the evening. This is a modest graveyard, he says, not a place for heroes or the wealthy, but of ordinary people. These are bodies who do not need air conditioners – they are still warm, recently become corpses, because "they have asked for a raise in their wages." And so we are told where these bodies that appear in Siwi's graveyard are coming from. But why, Siwi asks himself, are so many *mayat*, corpses, being tossed unceremoniously into his simple cemetery. As the stage darkens, and as the bodies pile up, Siwi reflects on the situation, engaging some of the dead – or their ghosts – in conversation. "What did you do while you lived on this earth," he asks a woman/corpse. "I was a laborer." "And why did you die?" "I was accused of leading a demonstration for higher wages." "Surely you are not the one named...." "Don't mention my name. My name has become a ghost (*hantu*) that brings terror to those who proudly killed me to fill their stomachs...." "Your name has become a legend that has shaken the halls of justice.... Can you say the name of those who took out their fury on you?" "Oh no, if I mention their names, surely they will kill me again. I am afraid of being killed a second time."

As the play moves forward, Siwi begins to ask more insistently why so many bodies are being tossed into his small graveyard. So strange.... I hear that there are many killings, a massacre.... On the simple stage, he wanders about in the half dark, and begins to find body parts. He hears the voice of a young man, rushes to find him, pulls him out, finds that he is a student, still alive among the dead. He tries to convince the young man to calm down, assuring him that he is actually alive, not dead despite the fact that it is so dark. The young man speaks with terror about the interrogation and torture he endured in his last days, not sure that he wishes to be alive. The music turns to a Chinese-sounding tune, and Siwi finds his graveyard crowded with the bodies of the Chinese killed in the week after Suharto's death. He hears the cry of a baby and becomes more frantic, rushes madly trying to find the infant, who continues to cry in the dark, exclaiming that even the babies are now being killed without mercy. Madness. Generations ... are being pulled from our era's womb ... and replaced by machines that only know obedience. And so the drama continues.

The monologue ends with the grave keeper reflecting on how he wants to be a simple witness, not a hero; how he wishes only to expiate his feelings of sin for the corpses who have become his friends; and why he has decided finally to testify to what he has seen. Suddenly, massive nets drop from above and capture him. He struggles and rages, becomes weak, finally quiet, and the stage darkens. Butet concluded with a few comments for the current regime, now two years since the fall of Suharto and nearly a year into the presidency of Abdurrahman Wahid, asking why those who know about these matters are still in power while the corpses have not yet been honored.

The fall of the Suharto regime in May 1998 was followed by an outpouring of long-suppressed aesthetic performances and artistic productions, reflecting critically on that which was hidden away during the 33 years of autocratic rule of the New Order.[9] By July 1999, the Festival of Fine Arts in Yogyakarta was filled with paintings by artists young and old commemorating the victims of violence, juxtaposing figures of the *aparat* with hopeful images of the new Reformasi era, and openly portraying the dance of finger pointing, as those in power passed responsibility for the disappearances during the late years of the New Order or the violence against the Chinese in the immediate aftermath of Suharto's abdication from one to another.[10] Intellectuals spoke publicly about the massive human rights violations of Suharto's New Order on countless television talk shows that appeared for the first time, and our friends began to speak openly with us about political repression, the loss of legitimacy of the symbols of Javanese values and *pancasila* that had been usurped to prop up the Suharto regime, and the events of 1965. For the first time we heard stories about how the Vredeburg Museum, the nineteenth-century colonial-era wooden building in the center of Yogyakarta, which served also as the gallery for the Festival of Fine Arts, had been used in 1965–66 as a holding center for leftist prisoners, many of whom were executed or simply left to die of starvation.

By 2000, when Butet performed *Mayat Terhormat*, the mood had turned darker, as artists and intellectuals increasingly recognized that much of the political elite of the New Order was still in power, that the military and the intelligence apparatus continued to operate behind the scenes, and that, as Butet concluded his monologue, ghosts of the victims of the Suharto era had not yet been acknowledged or buried with honor. More than that, the rise of violence throughout Indonesia – the murderous clashes between Christian and Muslim communities in Ambon; the deadly conflict between indigenous Dayak and Madurese communities in West Kalimantan that led to gruesome images of Dayak warriors displaying heads of Madurese they had killed; the vicious military response in East Timor, when Timorese dared to vote for independence from Indonesia – raised more fundamental anxieties about the collapse of social order and hints of nostalgia for the long years of military rule. Accounts of these large-scale conflicts were matched by almost daily reports of *keroyokan*, of sudden mob violence enacting vigilante justice against anyone accused of theft or any petty crime in communities throughout Indonesia (Welsh, 2008).

Among the most haunting were stories of killings of witches and of "ninjas" in rural villages in Banyuangi and around Malang in eastern Java.[11] As early as October 2008, just four months after Suharto relinquished power, eerie stories began circulating about groups of village men going out at night to attack and kill persons accused of being *dukun santet*, witches or sorcerers. But confused stories began to appear at nearly the same time of dark figures, dressed in black – and thus labeled *ninja* – attacking and killing *kyai*, religious leaders belonging to the Nahdlatul Ulama (NU), the large Islamic organization that Abdurrahman Wahid (popularly called Gus Dur) had led before he became president. Village groups that had been mobilized to eliminate *dukun santet* then began to watch for the mysterious ninja figures, which were said to be able to turn into animals and disappear when confronted. Nearly any stranger or individual out of place – including wandering persons with mental illness – was at risk for being identified as a ninja and killed. Stories began to circulate that the so-called ninja figures who were said to be killing *kyai* were hired by military forces who felt threatened by Gus Dur's presidency and sought his political demise. Other stories circulated that the ninjas were actually Communists, finally enacting their revenge on leaders of Nahdlatul Ulama, the Islamic group that had been active in 1965–66 in the civil violence and killings of those identified as members of the PKI, the Communist Party of Indonesia. And thus the ghosts of 1965 began to appear alongside the ghosts of the victims of Suharto's New Order regime.

Throughout the 33 years of Suharto's New Order regime, a fundamental symbolic opposition was drawn between "disorder" and "order," between the massive disorder blamed on the Communists and associated with the last years of the Sukarno era and the order established by Suharto, in 1965, with the support of his circle in the Indonesian Army. This basic dichotomy, which provided the grammar of New Order ideology, could be extended as needed, with the Communists and the threats of the "masses running amok" on the side of disorder, for example, and the "national discipline" associated with Suharto and the military on the side of order.[12] What was hidden by this grammar was precisely the historical fact of the killings of 1965 that put Suharto in power – represented symbolically and narratively as the response of a group of young officers to the G30S, the 30 September movement, the term for the abortive coup in which six Indonesian Army generals were murdered. Led by Suharto, the young officers blamed the Communist Party for the coup and launched a campaign of mass killings, particularly in Java and Bali, that saw between 600,000 and one million persons summarily executed and many more imprisoned or sent into exile. In New Order ideology, the coup and the heroic actions of the army to save the nation mark the gap between the chaos of that period, ironically blamed on the Communists, and the "order" established by the regime. Aside from monuments and a propaganda film shown to all students on Independence Day, which articulate this heroic narrative, however, the events of 1965 were largely unspeakable. At the heart of this political grammar was thus an occulting of traumatic memory. And it was the traces of this occulted memory that made their ghostly appearances in the years following the fall of Suharto.

The argument I have been developing here is that the ghosts that appeared in the simple graveyard in Butet's drama were those loosed by the fall of the Suharto regime. Speaking the unspeakable about the repression and disappearances over the past thirty years was a powerful act and produced a powerful response among audiences such as those students and intellectuals present in the Purna Budaya theater that night in April 2000. I am suggesting, however, that at a deeper level the sense of the uncanny was provoked by the spectral images that represented what remained unspeakable, even in this period of relative freedom of speech: the mass killings of 1965–66. When the first president elected after the downfall of Suharto, Abdurahman Wahid, attempted to eliminate the legal apparatus associated with criminalizing those identified as "communists" and associated with the disorders of 1965, many nationalist and religious leaders responded vehemently, reenacting the basic structure that led to the original killings. The events of 1965, the massive gulag in which those accused of being communist were kept for many years, and the labeling of the family members of those who were killed or imprisoned as "unclean" and dangerous have remained largely unspeakable until today, and it was precisely the trace of this dark secret, present between categories of order and disorder, present and past, that lent a powerful sense of the uncanny to the ghosts that flourished as ninjas and *dukun santet* in 1998 and appeared on Butet's stage in 2000.

In the years of the post-Suharto Reformasi era, many Indonesians were haunted by violence and ghosts of violence hidden from view throughout the era of the New Order. Quite remarkably, the conflict in Aceh, waged by special forces of the Indonesian Army against the GAM militants and the vast network of villages that provided them support, continued on with relatively little attention from most Indonesian activists, in part because

NGOs and human rights groups were not allowed in Aceh. This was a secret "hidden in plain sight" (Cavell, 1988; B. Good, 2012): Evidence of intense military violence against civilians was available but largely suppressed. It took a great act of nature, the earthquake of December 26, 2004, and the terrible Indian Ocean tsunami that killed approximately 160,000 people in Aceh alone, to push these events fully into the open.[13] As national and international humanitarian organizations responded to the calamity, rushing into Aceh, the violence could no longer be hidden. And as Indonesians grieved for Aceh, popular sentiment contributed to the negotiation of the MOU and the cessation of the conflict.

Return to Aceh: Living with Ghosts

The expectation, voiced in the paper "Haunted by Aceh" in 2005, that we would return often to Aceh in the coming years proved correct. From 2005 through 2010, we dedicated much of our time to postconflict mental health work in Aceh. Along with our Ph.D. student Jesse Grayman, Mary-Jo and I directed teams from the International Organization for Migration in conducting a major survey in high-conflict subdistricts – first in three Northeast coast districts, then throughout Aceh – of experiences of violence during the years of the conflict and the "remainders of violence" that manifest as psychological symptoms, memories that appeared unbidden, fear and rage, and nightmares haunted by the ghosts of the violence. We recorded stories, analyzed quantitative data and wrote reports, and became deeply involved in advocating for IOM to develop mobile mental health teams to go into villages most affected by the conflict to provide care for those still suffering the lasting effects of the traumatic violence. Mary-Jo and I continued this work until 2010, serving as consultants to the project and to the teams of young Acehnese doctors and nurses, funded from diverse sources and organized by IOM, who treated more than two thousand persons with trauma-related mental illnesses in 75 villages. We fought to have IOM and the donors support these teams; we worked closely with them, carried out formal evaluations, met with patients to hear stories of violence and recovery, and continued to advocate for this model of care, even as donor funds for Aceh disappeared.[14] We continue to work in Aceh today.

The findings of our initial survey in three high-conflict districts on the Northeast coast of Aceh (PNA1 – Psychosocial Needs Assessment 1)[15] were wrenching: Of our total sample of adults (n = 596), 78 percent had experienced combat; 56 percent of men (and 20 percent of women) reported being beaten; 25 percent of men (and 11 percent of women) reported being tortured; 8 percent of women reported having a spouse killed (cf. M. Good, Chapter 12, this volume). In one district, 68 percent of young men aged 17–29 reported head trauma – being beaten on the head, suffocated, or nearly drowned, usually during interrogation. Although our survey asked whether respondents had ever suffered such events, not who the perpetrators had been, interviews were filled with graphic stories about violence enacted by members of the Indonesian military or the special mobile brigade of the police (Brimob) against members of rural civilian communities considered to be "bases" for support of GAM.

The release of our first report, PNA1, by IOM was fraught with anxiety.[16] The release of the report was scheduled for September 2006, barely one year after the Helsinki peace accords, and the role of the military in the events in Aceh and claims of human rights violations were still extremely sensitive. The study had been funded by the Canadian Foreign Ministry, making the report diplomatically sensitive, and IOM works closely with the central government, given that Indonesia is a member state of this intergovernmental organization. In the end, IOM, along with the Canadian donor, made the decision that the report should not record the graphic stories and that neutral language should be used, not referring to who perpetrated such violence. By allowing the dramatic numbers to speak for themselves, with our agreement, and by keeping the ghosts of the violence off stage, IOM was able to convince a brave minister of health to sign a letter of support for the study, noting that development of mental health services should be an urgent priority for high-conflict areas of Aceh. This in turn allowed IOM to seek donor support to develop mental health outreach teams to address the broad range of mental health problems suffered by men and women in 75 isolated, high-conflict villages.

The surveys (both PNA1 and PNA2) made it abundantly clear that the people of Aceh continued to live with the vivid phantom presence of those who died or disappeared as well as those who perpetrated the violence (Grayman, M. Good, & B. Good, 2009). Those surveyed were asked whether they suffered nightmares and invited to tell about dream experiences.[17] A total of 26 percent (458 persons) of our sample of 1,750 persons provided narrative accounts of dreams. Of these 458 persons, 54 percent (247) reported seeing the spirits of persons who died in the conflict in their dreams. However, many corrected our questions – these were not "nightmares" (*mimpi buruk*, bad dreams); these were often comforting dreams in which they experienced a spouse or a child who visited to chat with them or offer words of comfort and encouragement (128 persons, 52 percent of those reporting being visited by family members who died, reported that these were positive or comforting experiences).

On the other hand, 35 percent (160) of those who told dream stories reexperienced violent conflict, and 22 percent (101) relived violence directed toward them personally. PTSD symptoms were extremely high among those who experienced such genuine nightmares.[18]

It was only when the IOM mental health teams, which we helped organize, began working intensively in villages that the painful memories and troubling ghosts reported in the PNA research could be addressed clinically. Our formal outcome studies suggested that the combined medical and psychosocial treatments offered by these young doctors and nurses were extremely helpful, reducing symptoms for more than 80 percent of those treated, enabling many to sleep without intrusive dreams, and allowing many who were seriously disabled to return to work, often in their fields, gardens, and small businesses (B. Good & M. Good, 2010b).

Our qualitative and ethnographic observations provided equally impressive findings. At the beginning of the program, we often met individuals in early stages of treatment who were completely overwhelmed by the memories of violence they had experienced or witnessed. Some told vivid stories in the present tense, describing events as though they had happened in the past week – when eventually the stories would reveal that the events had happened several years earlier, or in some cases more than fifteen years before. They described sudden episodes of intrusive memories that evoked profound fears; they told of being awakened after a few hours of sleep with a vivid dream of the conflict, producing terror and anxiety that prevented them from sleeping again. At the end of the project, many of these same individuals talked quietly about these traumatic events in the past tense, as something they did not want to talk about in depth but as belonging to their past. They also described the intrusive memories and sleep problems as rare or gone entirely.

Despite the recovery of individuals and communities, the people of Aceh continue to live with the ghosts of the violence. The formal Memorandum of Understanding signed in Helsinki called for a truth and reconciliation process. Although some human rights activists continue to urge that such a process go forward, neither the Indonesian government, particularly the military, nor former GAM members, many of whom are now actively involved in the political process, show an inclination to awaken the ghosts of the past. "It would be easy to resolve these things," a former GAM leader who organized a cooperative movement for combatants, told us. "If someone wrongs you and comes and says 'I did this and that and I am sorry,' we can forgive and move on. However, when that person comes and sits with you and refuses to acknowledge what

happened, it never goes away." For the Indonesian military and nationalist forces within the government, such acknowledgment is unlikely.

Derrida (1994, pp. 45–8) describes Marx's analysis of capital and
the monetary system as being "the figure of appearance or simulacrum,
more exactly of the ghost." "Marx does not like ghosts any more than his
adversaries do," he goes on. "He does not want to believe in them. But
he thinks of nothing else." Marx attempts to distinguish the spectral from
"actual reality," Derrida writes, opposing them "like life to death, like
vain appearances of the simulacrum to real presence." But he can only
do so by attempting to conjure them away, to exorcise the ghosts. But
exorcism requires its own use of magic. "Effective exorcism pretends to
declare the death only in order to put to death.... It is in fact [*en effet*] a
matter of a performative that seeks to reassure but first of all to reassure
itself by assuring itself, for nothing is less sure, than what one would like
to see dead is indeed dead."

When representatives of the Indonesian military took the stand for
hearings of the Commission for Reception, Truth and Reconciliation in
East Timor in 2005, they blatantly declared their innocence. Theirs was
exorcism in the sense described by Derrida, a performative act seeking to assure themselves that that which they wished to be dead – the
vicious human rights violations of the military in East Timor – is indeed
dead. But such exorcism, however magically performed, could not put
the ghosts of Timor to rest. And so it is with Aceh. The ghosts of the
past are still vital actors in local and national politics. No exorcisms, no
declarations that the dead are really dead, can erase the spectral presence
of the past. And so the people of Aceh continue to live with the ghosts of
this conflict, as do people throughout Indonesia with the ghosts of the
Suharto era and of 1965.

Concluding Thoughts

I have not in this essay neatly distinguished between the sense of haunting that I experienced when meeting former combatants or hearing stories of state terror and the experiences of those haunted by memories
of that violence or engaged in the process of "beginning to remember"
(Zurbuchen, 2005). The essay has a disjointed quality – juxtaposing
experiences in Aceh with those in Yogyakarta, vivid memories of stories
of torture and violence, dramatic performances, and reports of dreams of
ghosts of victims of the violence, taking place at quite different moments
in recent Indonesian history and evoking memories of more distant
events. The stories represent a kind of free association of memories
linked by "emotions in the field" (Davies & Spencer, 2010), disjointed

memories of being affected by the violent and traumatic, long hidden, moving mysteriously into the open.

My broad argument here has been that attention to the spectral, and to that which we as ethnographers as well as members of the societies in which we work experience as uncanny or haunting, is critical for understanding how societies deal with mass violence. Remembering and forgetting, and rerememering amid efforts to exorcise memory, are continuous processes for individuals as well as societies. Ultimately, Derrida reminds us, the ghosts of mass violence cannot be effaced. "To learn to live *with* ghosts," and to live "more justly" – this is the task at hand. Engaging this learning requires, as he said, "a *politics* of memory, of inheritance, and of generations." One task of scholars and activists alike is to participate in this process of learning and thus in the politics of memory.

NOTES

1 The panel was organized by Sarah Pinto and Michael Oldani. See Pinto, 2005.
2 See M. Good and B. Good, 2008.
3 I refer here the 2003 Penguin edition of *The Uncanny* (Freud, 2003 [1919]), translated by David McLintock.
4 The following paragraph is drawn from the Introduction to that volume (B. Good, M. Good, Hyde, & Pinto, 2008).
5 "If deconstruction is inseparable from a logic of spectrality, it is because the trace or difference is ghostly: all language, every manifestation of meaning, is the phantom effect of a trace which is neither present nor absent, but which is the condition of possibility of the opposition of presence and absence. The trace cannot become present, or absent, in its essence: it is the revenant at the origin." (Royle, 2003, p. 281)
6 See Fischer, 2007, 2008, for related reflections.
7 See, for example, Lewis (1999) for a discussion of Derrida's juxtaposition of hauntology to ontology.
8 I use for this analysis a text of the monologue *Mayat Terhormat*, in Indonesian, available on the Internet at http://sastradrama.wordpress.com/2010/10/11/ mayat-terhormat-monolog/. Translations are partly mine, partly those of John MacDougal, whom I thank for providing a complete translation of this remarkable monologue.
9 See, for example, Halim, 1999.
10 For a full description and analysis of the 1999 Festival of Fine Arts and several of the key critical artists in Yogyakarta, see M. Good & B. Good, 2008.
11 The fullest analysis is found in James Siegel's *Naming the Witch* (2006), a Derridean analysis of the killings in Banyuangi. For excellent analyses of this phenomenon, see also Cribb, 2000; Retsikas, 2006; Welsh, 2008; Beatty; 2009; Herriman, 2010. Cribb (2000) links the killings explicitly to the so-called Petrus death squads of the late Suharto era (cf. Siegel, 1998).

Welsh demonstrates that *keroyokan,* or mob, vigilante justice has a far longer trajectory and has been found throughout Indonesia, although rates increased in the years immediately following the fall of Suharto.

12 For a fuller analysis, see B. Good, 2010 (see also B. Good & M. Good, 2001; B. Good, Subandi, & M. Good, 2007; B. Good & M. Good, 2010).

13 See, for example, Drexler, 2008, for a description of this period.

14 The technical reports for this work were published as two reports of the psychosocial needs assessments by IOM (B. Good, M. Good, Grayman, & Lakoma, 2006; M. Good, B. Good, Grayman, & Lakoma, 2007), and as a final project evaluation report of the intervention program (B. Good & M. Good, 2010). Anthropological reports on our Aceh work are published as M. Good, B. Good, & Grayman, 2010; Grayman, M. Good, & B. Good, 2009; M. Good & B. Good, 2013; and M. Good, this volume, Chapter 12.

15 The survey was conducted – and reported – in two parts. The Psychosocial Needs Assessment Part 1 (PNA1) was conducted in three districts (B. Good, M. Good, Grayman, & Lakoma, 2006; results were summarized in an Indonesian mental health journal, B. Good, M. Good, Grayman & Lakoma, 2007). The Psychosocial Needs Assessment Part 2 (PNA2) reported on an extension of the project to an additional 11 districts throughout Aceh and reports on findings from all 14 districts (M. Good, B. Good, Grayman, & Lakoma, 2007). Here we mention only a few brief highlights.

16 For the full story of this release, see M. Good, B. Good, & Grayman, 2010.

17 See Grayman, M. Good, & B. Good (2009) for a full report on both the quantitative and qualitative data on dreams and conflict-related nightmares among those who responded to the IOM survey.

18 Acehnese have a complex theory of dreams and the meaning of the appearance of diverse spirits and ghosts in dreams. See Grayman, M. Good, & B. Good (2009) for a more detailed account. The presence of ghostly spiritual forces in dreams has been explored in a special issue of *Culture, Medicine, and Psychiatry,* edited by D. Hinton (2009). D. Hinton provides detailed analyses of this phenomenon among survivors of the killing fields of Cambodia (D. Hinton, 2009; D. Hinton, Field, Nickerson, Bryant, & Simon, 2013; D. Hinton, Peou, Joshi, Nickerson, & Simon, 2013; D. Hinton, A. Hinton, Pich, Loeum, & Pollack, 2009; D. Hinton, Pich, Chhean, & Pollack, 2005).

REFERENCES

Abraham, N., & Torok, M. (1986). *The wolf man's magic word: A cryptonymy.* Minneapolis: University of Minnesota Press.

Arendt, H. (1958). *The human condition.* Chicago: University of Chicago Press.

Aretxaga, B. (2008). Madness and the politically real: Reflections on violence in postdictatorial Spain. In M. J. Good, S. Hyde, S. Pinto, & B. J. Good (Eds.), *Postcolonial disorders* (pp. 43–61). Berkeley: University of California Press.

Beatty, A. (2009). *A shadow falls in the heart of Java.* London: Faber & Faber.

Cavell, S. (1988). The uncanniness of the ordinary. In *In quest of the ordinary: Lines of skepticism and romanticism* (pp. 153–80). Chicago: University of Chicago Press.

Connerton, P. (1989). *How societies remember*. Cambridge: Cambridge University Press.

Cribb, R. (2000). From *petrus* to ninja: Death squads in Indonesia. In B. B. Campbell & A. D. Brenner (Eds.), *Death squads in global perspective: Murder with deniability* (pp. 181–202). New York: St. Martin's Press.

Das, V. (2000). The act of witnessing: Violence, poisonous knowledge, and subjectivity. In V. Das, A. Kleinman, M. Ramphele, & P. Reynolds (Eds.), *Violence and subjectivity* (pp. 205–25). Berkeley: University of California Press.

Davies, J. & Spencer, D. (2010). *Emotions in the field: The psychology and anthropology of fieldwork experience*. Stanford, CA: Stanford University Press.

Derrida, J. (1994). *Specters of Marx: The state of the debt, the work of mourning, and the new international*. New York: Routledge.

(1998). "To do justice to Freud": The history of madness in the age of psychoanalysis. In J. Derrida, *Resistances of psychoanalysis* (pp. 70–118). Stanford, CA: Stanford University Press.

Drexler, E. F. (2008). *Aceh, Indonesia: Securing the insecure state*. Philadelphia: University of Pennsylvania Press.

Fischer, M. (2007). Epilogue: To live with what would otherwise be unendurable: Return(s) to subjectivities. In J. Biehl, B. J. Good, & A. Kleinman (Eds.), *Subjectivity: Ethnographic investigations* (pp. 423–46). Berkeley: University of California Press.

(2008). To live with what would otherwise be unendurable. II. Caught in the borderlands of Palestine/Israel. In M. J. Good, S. Hyde, S. Pinto, & B. J. Good (Eds), *Postcolonial disorders* (pp. 260–75). Berkeley: University of California Press.

Freud, S. (2003) [1919]. *The uncanny*. New York: Penguin.

Good, B. J. (2012). Theorizing the "subject" of medical and psychiatric anthropology. *Journal of the Royal Anthropological Institute*, 18, 515–35.

Good, B. J., & Good, M. J. (2001). "Why do the masses so easily run amuk?" Madness and violence in Indonesian politics. *Latitudes*, 5, 10–19.

(2010a). *Amuk* in Java: Madness and violence in Indonesian politics. In B. J. Good, M. Fischer, S. S. Willen, & M. J. Good (Eds.), *A reader in medical anthropology: Theoretical trajectories, emergent realities* (pp. 473–80). Chichester, UK: Wiley-Blackwell.

(2010b). Final evaluation report: IOM DHPAP extension program. Unpublished manuscript.xf

Good, B. J., Good, M. J., Grayman, J. H., & Lakoma, M. (2006). *Psychosocial needs assessment of communities affected by the conflict in the districts of Pidie, Bireuen, and Aceh Utara (PNA1)*. Geneva: International Organization for Migration.

(2007). Violence, trauma, and mental health consequences in post-conflict Aceh: Report of an empirical investigation. *Ataraxis: The Indonesian Journal of Mental Health*, 1, 33–40.

Good, B. J., Good, M. J., Hyde, S., & Pinto, S. (2008). Postcolonial disorders: Reflections on subjectivity in the contemporary world. In M. J. Good, S. Hyde, S. Pinto, & B. J. Good (Eds.), *Postcolonial disorders* (pp. 1–40). Berkeley: University of California Press.

Good, B. J., Subandi, M. A., & Good, M. J. (2007). The subject of mental illness: Psychosis, mad violence and subjectivity in Indonesia. In J. Biehl, B. J. Good, & A. Kleinman (Eds.), *Subjectivity: Ethnographic investigations* (pp. 243–72). Berkeley: University of California Press.

Good, M. J. (2015). Acehnese women's tales of traumatic experience, resilience, and recovery. In D. E. Hinton & A. L. Hinton (Eds.), *Genocide and mass violence: Memory, symptom, and recovery*. Cambridge: Cambridge University Press.

Good, M. J. & Good, B. J. (2008). *Indonesia sakit*: Indonesian disorders and the subjective experience and interpretive politics of contemporary Indonesian artists. In M. J. Good, S. Hyde, S. Pinto, & B. J. Good (Eds.), *Postcolonial disorders* (pp. 62–108). Berkeley: University of California Press.

Good, M. J., & Good, B. J. (2013). Perspectives on the politics of peace in Aceh, Indonesia. In F. Aulino, M. Goheen, & S. Tambiah (Eds.), *Radical egalitarianism: Local realities, global relations* (pp. 191–208). New York: Fordham University Press.

Good, M. J., Good, B. J., & Grayman, J. H. (2010). Complex engagements: Responding to violence in post-conflict Aceh. In D. Fassin & M. Pandolfi (Eds.), *Contemporary states of emergency: The politics of military and humanitarian interventions* (pp. 241–66). Cambridge, MA: MIT Press.

Good, M. J., Good, B. J., Grayman, J. H., & Lakoma, M. (2007). *A psychosocial needs assessment of communities in 14 conflict-affected districts in Aceh (PNA2)*. Geneva: International Organization for Migration.

Good, M. J., Hyde, S., Pinto, S., & Good, B. J. (Eds.). (2008). *Postcolonial disorders*. Berkeley: University of California Press.

Gordon, A. F. (2008). *Ghostly matters: Haunting and the sociological imagination*. Minneapolis: University of Minnesota Press.

Grayman, J. H., Good, M. J., & Good, B. J. (2009). Conflict nightmares and trauma in Aceh. *Culture, Medicine and Psychiatry*, 33, 290–312.

Halim, H. D. (1999). Arts networks and the struggle for democratisation. In A. Budiman, B. Hatley, & D. Kingsbury (Eds.), *Reformasi* (pp. 287–98). Clayton, Australia: Monash Asia Institute.

Herriman, N. (2010). The great rumor mill: Gossip, mass media, and the ninja fear. *Journal of Asian Studies*, 69, 723–48.

Hinton, D. E. (2009). Introduction to the special section: Nightmares of trauma victims – cross-cultural perspectives. *Culture, Medicine and Psychiatry*, 33, 216–18.

Hinton, D. E., Field, N. P., Nickerson, A., Bryant, R. A., & Simon, N. (2013). Dreams of the dead among Cambodian refugees: Frequency, phenomenology, and relationship to complicated grief and posttraumatic stress disorder. *Death Studies*, 37, 750–67.

Hinton, D. E., Hinton, A. L., Pich, V., Loeum, J. R., & Pollack, M. H. (2009). Nightmares among Cambodian refugees: The breaching of concentric ontological security. *Transcultural Psychiatry*, 33, 219–65.

Hinton, D. E., Peou, S., Joshi, S., Nickerson, A., & Simon, N. (2013). Normal grief and complicated bereavement among traumatized Cambodian refugees: Cultural context and the central role of dreams of the deceased. *Culture, Medicine, and Psychiatry*, 37, 427–64.

Hinton, D. E., Pich, V., Chhean, D., & Pollack, M. H. (2005). "The ghost pushes you down": Sleep paralysis–type panic attacks in a Khmer refugee population. *Transcultural Psychiatry, 42*, 46–77.

Lewis, T. (1999). The politics of "hauntology" in Derrida's *Specters of Marx*. In M. Sprinker (Ed.), *Ghostly demarcations: A symposium on Jacques Derrida's specters of Marx* (pp. 134–67). London: Verso.

Pinto, S. (2005). Uncanny minds: Emerging politics of the uncanny. Unpublished manuscript.

Retsikas, K. (2006). The semiotics of violence: Ninja, sorcerers, and state terror in post-Soeharto Indonesia. *Bijdragen, tot de Taal-, Land- en Volkenkunde, 162*, 56–94.

Royle, N. (2003). *The uncanny.* New York: Routledge.

Siegel, J. T. (1998). *A new criminal type in Jakarta: Counter-revolution today.* Durham, NC: Duke University Press.

(2001). Suharto, witches. *Indonesia, 71*, 27–78.

(2006). *Naming the witch.* Stanford, CA: Stanford University Press.

Taussig, M. T. (1980). *The devil and commodity fetishism in South America.* Chapel Hill, NC: University of North Carolina Press.

(1987). *Shamanism, colonialism, and the wild man: A study in terror and healing.* Chicago: University of Chicago Press.

(1992). *The nervous system.* New York: Routledge.

(2003). *Law in a lawless land.* New York: Free Press.

Weismantel, M. (2001). *Cholas and pishtacos: Stories of race and sex in the Andes.* Chicago: University of Chicago Press.

Welsh, B. (2008). Local and ordinary: "*Keroyokan*" mobbing in Indonesia. *Journal of East Asian Studies, 8*, 473–504.

Zurbuchen, M. (2005). *Beginning to remember: The past in the Indonesian present.* Singapore: Singapore University Press.

3 Remembering and Ill Health in Postinvasion Kuwait: Topographies, Collaborations, Mediations

Conerly Casey

Awakened by the pummeling blasts of nearby explosions, Dalia was unable to fall back asleep. Trembling, she crawled under her bed to hide, then ran to find her mother in the living room of their family's home. Dalia knew immediately from her mother's whispers and worried expression that Iraqi soldiers had invaded Kuwait. Dalia's family, unlike many others who fled to neighboring or to European countries after the August 2, 1990, Iraqi invasion, remained in Kuwait during the seven-month occupation, covering their windows with blankets and sticky tape, little protection from the shattering glass of mortar explosions and gunfire. They talked their way past heavily armed Iraqi soldiers to search for food and water and, later, lived in sooty darkness, breathing in the residues of burning oil fires and other war contaminants.

The 1990 Iraqi invasion and occupation of Kuwait led to highly mediated, emotionally charged ideas, images, and sounds of war, affective mediations of violence that continue to circulate. Less accessible to media audiences is the Harvard School of Public Health (HSPH, 2005) finding that Kuwaitis, aged fifty years or older, who had remained in Kuwait for all or part of the occupation, were at 20–30 percent greater risk of mortality than those who fled the country. John Evans (2008; HSPH, 2005), director of the Harvard School of Public Health assessment of postinvasion health, suggested that smoke from more than seven hundred oil fires burning from January to November of 1991 contributed to these higher mortality rates, though not in ways sufficient to cause the observed increases. After screening for "other contaminants – such as volatile organic compounds, polycyclic aromatic hydrocarbons and metals from the oil lakes and marine oil spills; and depleted uranium," the HSPH (2005) team concluded that "exposures to these compounds were unlikely to lead to appreciable risks to public health." The HSPH team, collaborating with Professor Jaafar Behbehani (Kuwait University Faculty of Medicine) and his colleagues at Kuwait's Al-Riggae Specialized Centre (Hammadi, 1994), suggested instead that a combination of oil smoke and PTSD would explain the higher prevalence of mortality in the fourteen years since independence (HSPH, 2005). Oil smoke, PTSD, and depression became dominant lenses through which researchers and Kuwaiti government and private health care providers understood, structured, and treated war traumas (Abdel-Khalek, 1996, 1997; Abdullatif, 1995; Al-Naser, al-Khulaifi, & Martino, 2000; Dockery, 2009; Evans, 2008; Hadi & Llabre, 1998; Hammadi, 1994; Llabre & Hadi, 1997; Nader, Pynoos, Fairbanks, al-Ajeel, al-Asfour, 1993).

My interest in remembering and ill health among Kuwaitis had a different valence. In 2006, I moved to Kuwait to teach in the anthropology and psychology programs at the American University of Kuwait, and I was eager to learn about Kuwaiti young adults and families. Within months, I became alarmed at the numbers of students and their age mates employed in government and private businesses who spoke of having tumors, gastrointestinal and reproductive problems, tension and severe headaches – a constellation of symptoms that may result from exposure to toxins. I reviewed the research on war contamination in Kuwait, but none of the literature addressed chronic, low-level, incremental exposures to the combination of known war pollutants (and other sources of pollution) in children and young adults. Over the three years I spent with young Kuwaitis, the dearth of information about chronic, low-level exposures to war pollutants impressed on me the need to find other modes of understanding. I began to trace their memories of war in topographical, collaborative, and mediated remembering – in ill health and distress, bombed and bullet-ridden homes left standing, talk of families and neighborhoods blown apart by war, or in images of Failaka, a former resort, left abandoned to war artillery and to war tours. Embodied memories of occupation, and memories evoked by structures such as the Liberation Tower and War Museum, or reenacted in liberation parades, appeared to converge with discussions of war in *diwaniyas* and families. These diverse memory streams further converged with media, and media emphasis on present pasts – what Huyssen (2002, p. 61) refers to as the "traumatic side of memory culture," the evermore, ubiquitous discourses of trauma, recovering memories, mass violence, memorials, commemorations, and apologies.

Using a combination of methods – person-centered, semistructured and informal interviews; participant observations; a review of print, broadcast, and Internet media; popular art, poetry, music, and literature, I sought to understand Kuwaiti remembering of the 1990 invasion and occupation, in affective sensorial attunements to danger, self-reports of ill health, and the changing dynamics of self, self–other, and self–society referencing. My research suggests that remembering the 1990 Iraqi invasion and occupation of Kuwait *became* increasingly traumatic for young adults in their teenage years, after the start of the 2003 U.S. war in Iraq, with dramatic changes in their self-perceived health during this period. Most significantly, Kuwaiti young adults perceived their health declines in relation to embodied affects of Internet social media conversations with youths of neighboring countries who blamed Kuwaitis for both the 1990 Iraqi invasion and the 2003 U.S. war in Iraq.

Topographies, collaborative stories, and media images and story lines, all stretch out and collapse temporal and spatial sources of danger, channeling and repeating affective information (Casey, 2009, 2010). Topographical, collaborative, and mediated referents to the affective sensorial of violence, and to sources of danger with the 2003 U.S. war in Iraq, reverberated with the 1990 Iraqi invasion of Kuwait. Referents of these two wars brought about amplifying waves of conflicted moral appraisal, ambivalence about identity and security, and affective responses to parental emotion, with visceral responses to war as the time and space of family closeness and Kuwaiti national cohesion, yet also of abandonment and betrayal, domestic violence, and substance abuse. Young Kuwaitis spoke of heightened concerns emerging from these *two wars* about the environment – natural/contaminated, built/blown apart, social/fractured, and political. These structuring narratives of war differ from PTSD diagnostics in which a "primary trauma" results in symptoms of posttraumatic stress.

Experiences of the 1990 invasion and the 2003 U.S. war in Iraq, as they intertwined through narrative and embodied processes, both constructed – and further amplified the magnitude of – felt memories; the invasion and war in Iraq also led to dissonant and harmonic resonances with personal and familial experiences. These resonances condensed pre- and postinvasion regional wars, and Kuwaiti societal problems and ill health, into narrations of the 1990 invasion. In this chapter, I focus on postinvasion remembering and ill health in terms of affective sensorial memory processes and the topographical, collaborative, and mediated narrative structuring of trauma. But these forms of remembering and narrating are dynamically related to forgetting, to social silencing, *and* to the materialities of pre- and postinvasion life, those bound by nation and time, such as dead bodies and destroyed infrastructures, and those, boundless, such as Internet media reports or blowing sand, contaminated by war chemicals.

Remembering and ill health in postinvasion Kuwait, heavily structured by an oil fire and PTSD framework, has primarily been documented in research conducted for the State of Kuwait, and under the auspices of the United Nations Compensation Commission, charged with evaluating Iraq's liability for harm to Kuwaitis. PTSD and Iraqi liability construct and underpin support for burgeoning psychological services in Kuwait, which have had mixed reviews. Dr. Naif Al-Mutawa (2009) describes an "invisible plague visited on the most vulnerable people, made double victims of their psychological problems by a largely unregulated gaggle of pseudo-professionals who offered psychological advice under a dozen different self-descriptions."[1] The dominant framing of war remembrances as PTSD, supported by an unprecedented number of psychological services, obscures and hides alternative rememberings of the invasion and occupation as they articulate with pre- and postconflict life in Kuwait.

Remembering War

In the aftermath of the 1990 Iraqi invasion and occupation, the diagnostic criteria for PTSD in *DSM-IV* – exposure to a traumatic event and symptoms from each of three groups: intrusive recollections of the trauma event, avoidance of reminders of the event and emotional numbing, and hyperarousal – framed nearly all studies of Kuwaiti children and adults. These studies established correlations between the Iraqi invasion and PTSD and depression, with higher prevalence rates for children than for adults (Abdel-Khalek, 1996, 1997; Abdullatif, 1995; Al-Naser et al., 2000; Hadi & Llabre, 1997, 1998; Nader et al., 1993). Implicit in the PTSD diagnosis was the notion that the Iraqi invasion and occupation were the traumatic events that resulted in symptoms of PTSD.

Shortly after the August 1990 invasion, Nader et al. (1993) found that many children who remained in Kuwait during the occupation had multiple war-related exposures, with 70 percent of his respondents reporting moderate to severe posttraumatic stress reactions. Witnessing death or injury and viewing explicit graphic images of mutilation on television had a measurable influence on the severity of children's trauma (Nader et al., 1993; Hadi & Llabre, 1998). In March of 1991, in the wake of the liberation of Kuwait City, Garbarino (1994) interviewed 45 children between five and thirteen years of age, and found that 62 percent had direct experience with a traumatic event such as seeing a body "dumped" in their neighborhood or a person killed. Garbarino found more than 50 percent of the children had what appeared to be psychological effects of trauma, most prominently repetitive dreams related to a traumatic experience or generalized fear of Iraqis. Children who had a martyr or POW in the family (Abdullatif, 1995) and boys (Llabre & Hadi, 1997) reported higher levels of depression, with social support a protective buffer for girls. Several years after the occupation, Al-Naser et al. (2000) reported a prevalence of PTSD of 28.4 percent in a sample of Kuwaiti citizens, with a higher prevalence of 45.6 percent in a subsample of teenage students, who the authors suggest have increased sensitivity to traumatic stress.

In 2006, Kuwaiti young adults, regardless of whether they had experienced prior symptoms of PTSD or depression, reported heightened sensitivity to traumatic stress in their teenage years, and significant health problems, with an appreciable increase in sensitivity and ill health after the 2003 U.S. war in Iraq. The PTSD diagnosis, as Kirmayer, Lemelson, and Barad (2007, p. 7) remind us, is distinguished from other psychiatric disorders by "the attribution of causality and the role that memory plays in its symptomatology." Young's (1995) compelling study of a U.S. Veterans Administration psychiatric unit specializing in PTSD convincingly illustrates how the structure of PTSD narratives exists *prior* to their content, selecting and organizing the content. My interest here is to question how PTSD narrations of war experience select and organize the content of Kuwaiti sensorial memories, changing the identifications, meanings, and interpretations of trauma that circulate in Kuwait. What do PTSD narratives reveal *and* hide about Kuwaiti experiences of trauma prior to, during, and after the invasion and occupation? How might PTSD narratives direct attention away from alternative expressions of trauma (Young, 1995); the moral appraisals that shape the selection, use, and interpretation of remembrances of violence (Cole, 2003; Kirmayer, 1996; Lambek & Antze, 1996); collaborative and relational remembering (Capps & Ochs, 1995; Wertsch, 2008; Wikan, 2000); the various forms of mediation that situate and inscribe violence (Casey, 2009); and the amplifications of violence in resonant events and interactions (Casey, 2009, 2010; Hagengimana & D. Hinton, 2009; A. Hinton, 2004; D. Hinton & S. Hinton, 2002)?[2] Remembering and forgetting converge and resonate, in harmonics and dissonance of affective sensorial experience, condensing and abridging, or widening and deepening, specific memories, while reforming affective bodily inscriptions of memory in social and political relations.[3]

A majority of the young Kuwaitis I interviewed described the 2003 U.S. war in Iraq as a pivotal period in their self-assessments of ill health, in that heavily mediated moral appraisals of the war and war sensoria – especially loud noises, and images of smoke, weapons, and death – all brought about affective bodily remembrances of the 1990 Iraqi invasion and occupation. But the timing of the 2003 U.S. war was also critical to youths' participation in family and *diwaniya* appraisals of these two wars, and in real-virtual exchanges about both wars with Kuwaiti and regional youths. Compression of the Iraqi invasion and the U.S. war in Iraq ignited and amplified affective bodily inscriptions of victim and perpetrator identities. Young Kuwaiti adults remembered Muslim solidarities and betrayals; anxieties about parental capacities to protect them from harm; the sounds, smells, and landscapes of war; and Kuwaiti martyrs still missing. These ongoing insults to the body politic of Kuwait heightened tensions about the potential overspill of violence into Kuwait from neighboring Iraq and Iran.

The importance of family reputation and the weighty stigma of admitting psychological distress further compressed social worlds and resulted in affective bodily inscriptions of "tension" and "anxiety" in young adults who resorted to "double" or "hidden" lives – those in which control of one's body and *nafs* (desires and emotion of self) amplifies disjuncture within the self. These double "public" and "hidden" selves articulated further with polarizing real-virtual rhetoric and bodily experiences of whom to hold accountable for war and suffering. Youths from neighboring countries, in social media and blogs, blamed Kuwaitis for the 1990 Iraqi invasion and held them complicit in the 2003 U.S. war in Iraq. Young Kuwaitis with whom I spoke felt victimized by these depictions, but they also acknowledged strong ambivalence about whom to blame – Saddam Hussein, the Emir and Kuwaiti government officials, or parents who may have fled, leaving them in harm's way. "Ultraliberal" and "ultrareligious" identifications in Kuwait, pre- and postconflict intergroup blame, and generational framings of whom to hold accountable for the war and its aftermath reconfigured the nexus of identity, morality, and security.

While I interviewed a few child witnesses of the 1990 Iraqi invasion who had direct experiences of violence, particularly young men actively resisting occupation, Dalia, and the majority of others, did not witness violent events or any interactions they considered traumatic. Dalia never experienced childhood symptoms of PTSD or depression; her parents did not express concern about her behavior; nor did she seek treatment for health or mental health problems until her teenage years. In her self-assessment, Dalia felt moderate to severe affective bodily distress after the 2003 U.S. war in Iraq, and she reported a combination of tension, headaches, low mood, gastrointestinal problems, tumors, and discord with family, friends, and regional youths, amplified in real-virtual mediations of the 2003 U.S. war in Iraq. The resonant sensorial affective features and moral appraisals of the 1990 Iraqi invasion and the 2003 Iraqi war, highlighted in her experiences of these *two* wars, further amplified Dalia's fear of past and future dangers from Iraq and Iran.

Dalia

At the time of the invasion, 8-year-old Dalia lived with her mother and father, both about 50 years of age; with two elder sisters, one aged 20 and another 23 years of age; and with two brothers, ages 3 and 16. Dalia's maternal grandmother had lived with the family but died just before the invasion of heart disease complications Dalia associated with "aging." Her paternal grandfather also died prior to the invasion: "We think it was good for them – that they didn't have to go through the invasion."

The family lived in Surra, a neighborhood of Kuwait City that Dalia remembered as "quiet" and "like a family." There were some non-Kuwaitis living in the neighborhood who "disappeared," but Dalia did not know what happened to them. Prior to the invasion, Dalia often visited other children from the neighborhood. She and her cousins played with Barbie dolls inside their family homes and fearlessly rode bicycles on neighborhood streets. Dalia's family, similar to other Kuwaitis, lived close by their relatives, whom they visited during the week, and then on weekends they drove to a seaside chalet at the border with Saudi Arabia, where her extended family gathered to talk, eat, and swim.

The morning of the invasion Dalia recalled her mother telling her, "It's ok – not to worry, but it made me realize the problem. If it was ok, she would not say that. It was just my thinking." In the process of remembering, Dalia said, "I started to feel afraid like it might be the Palestinian war with Israelis, fighting in the streets. I saw it on television. After the invasion, I thought Chemical Ali was living in Surra. Iraqis were living in the neighborhood." Iraqis on Dalia's streets, family discussions of dangers, and mediated Israeli and Iraqi violence, past and present, infused her body and neighborhood with lethal harm.

Throughout our interview Dalia made frequent references to "loud noises," "waking up with noises," "feeling very afraid with each blast," "running, very afraid, with no electricity," and "Iraqis shooting at the house and the windows." Each time, her speech became pressed, and the volume changed, growing louder with descriptions of war sensorial and moral appraisals of war, at times softer, almost inaudible, in narrating her own thoughts and actions. News flashes of the 2003 U.S. artillery and bombings in Iraq became points of similarity and multiplicity in her feelings of both wars.

Dalia's family slept in an interior hallway to get away from the windows that might shatter from Iraqi gunfire or mortar blasts. Dalia's mother took turns sleeping beside the youngest children, who clung to her in fear. At times the family survived on milk, corn flakes, and beans. It was difficult for her father to go out for resources since Kuwaiti men were prime targets for Iraqi attacks, so Dalia's older brother felt compelled to find assistance for the family. Dalia said, "My older brother was not excited to kill but excited to do something. My mother and sisters said not to go out. It's not easy to kill someone." Gendered displays of emotion were also evident in Dalia's description of her father being "afraid for his family." She said, "It's very scary to see your father crying. My grandmother was not in Kuwait. I saw him crying when he heard they were coming into Kuwait. When you see your father cry, it is like it destroys the house."

Iraqi soldiers occupying Dalia's neighborhood did not kill anyone, but she remembers family discussions of dangers and particularly fears of rape and remembers feeling very afraid at an Iraqi checkpoint where gun-wielding soldiers examined her parents' identification cards. She also recalled an Iraqi soldier yelling at her cousin in a supermarket where she had gone with her aunt and cousin to find food. Scared by this, Dalia's aunt left them at the supermarket. "My aunt left us. I couldn't believe it. She has a very weak heart." Iraqi soldiers kidnapped three of Dalia's cousins, causing her family members great worry, but all were released without physical harm.

Dalia said that after the invasion, "All Kuwaitis have high blood pressure." Dalia's mother was diagnosed with high blood pressure and had to take medication for the first time. Dalia's 3-year-old brother developed "tension" and "fear" at 4–5 years of age and became disruptive at his kindergarten, so that her mother took him to see a general practitioner, who prescribed an unknown medication. Dalia said he remained "close to her mother" and continued to have "tension" and to be "very afraid" well into his teenage years.

Dalia, though fearful during the occupation, reported feeling far more distressed by the televised 2003 U.S. war in Iraq. Dalia, then living with her father, mother, and younger brother because her older siblings had married, watched televised news reports of the U.S. attack, and she started to worry – "we are close"; "war can get into our country"; "everybody is against us." In 2003, these narratives circulated among Kuwaiti young adults in social media and blogs, and in response to Kuwaiti air siren drills.

Dalia said her father was "ok" with the war; "Kuwaitis after the invasion don't like Iraqis and they're ok with the war." But, Dalia "did not like this way of thinking," and she began to turn to religion for help with the growing conflicts inside her. Dalia veiled and prayed more frequently. She felt she could not express herself, whether at home or outside the home, and she became increasingly quiet, with alternating bursts of anger. Dalia developed "tension," "headaches," and "problems with her colon," and she went to a general practitioner who prescribed medication, but she did not feel better. Dalia then thought it might be a problem with her ovaries. She went to another doctor, who found a tumor, which he diagnosed as benign.

Dalia described herself as increasingly "emotional." She was living in the family home where she had experienced the 1990 Iraqi invasion and occupation. In 2003, Dalia became increasingly tense owing to televised depictions of tanks destroying other tanks and of bombing. She stopped watching television and turned to the Internet for information, but responding again to age mates in neighboring countries Dalia found "everyone against us" or "against the invasion" and U.S. occupation of Iraq. Dalia began having trouble with sleep, waking throughout the night, feeling depressed, crying easily at "anything that has sensitivity or emotion." Dalia felt she used to be stronger. She wanted to "catch her emotions" but felt very angry, sometimes "saying angry things" to an older sister she very much admired. Dalia e-mailed "professionals" to "get their advice" but she never made an appointment to see anyone; nor did she consult her mother, citing stigma against "depression" as the main reason. Eventually, Dalia stopped watching news of Iraq but began fervently watching news of Iran, worrying that "Americans and Iranians would start fighting."

Children and Idioms of Distress

Children adopt certain feelings, ideas, and ways of acting and remembering through direct interaction, and by indirectly "attending to how persons around them are representing and constructing their world through language" (Capps & Ochs, 1995, p. 10). The acceptability of certain Kuwaiti cultural idioms of distress – such as having "tension" and "fear," and in particular narrative and somatic forms such as high blood pressure – along with stigmatization of anxiety and depression, both channel and constrain what is possible to say and feel in Kuwaiti contexts (Kirmayer, 1996; Lambek & Antze, 1996). In Dalia's case, fear and dissonance between her own feelings about the U.S. war in Iraq and those of others produced an excess of feelings as she empathized with the emotions of others, yet a contraction of her own feelings that constructed, amplified, and channeled her war memories (Casey, 2009; White, 2005). Dalia's "tension" grew with affective bodily responses to moral appraisals of the 2003 U.S. war in Iraq, with conflicts in family discussions, and in her Internet exchanges about the 1990 and 2003 wars with age mates in Kuwait and the region. The feeling of dissonance between her moral appraisals and those of others, a sense of being silenced by the potential for social discord, and embodied sensorial remembrances of war, all seemingly conjoined and caused Dalia to search for guidance from professionals, religious and psychological, who had sites on the Internet. Most distressing to Dalia were Internet blogs of teenagers from neighboring countries who depicted Kuwaitis as "elitist" and "selfish" and having themselves to blame for the Iraqi invasion of Kuwait, responses that continually reemerged in ongoing news reporting of the U.S. war in Iraq and Iraqi deaths.

A majority of the other young adults with whom I spoke similarly reported heightened "tension" and somatic symptoms in their teenage years just after the 2003 U.S. war in Iraq. These included an array of symptoms: tensions, headaches and body aches, sleeplessness, respiratory problems, gastrointestinal and reproductive problems, tumors, and cognitive and speech impairments. The similarity of these symptoms to those of U.S. troops with "GulfWar syndrome," a syndrome often attributed by sufferers to contaminants such as the smoke of oil fires, may result from exposures to toxins, trajectories of catastrophic cognitions and fearful surveying of the body for symptoms of poisoning, or a combination of both (Bloom, Miller, Winkler, & Warner, 1994; Harley, Foulkes, Hilborne, Hudson, & Anthony, 1999; D. Hinton & Good, 2009). Young adults also paid close attention to their bodies as teenagers during the 2003 U.S. war in Iraq, either increasing religious observances such as prayer and conservative styles of dress *or* indulging in heavy drug and alcohol consumption. These patterns of attention to the body in modulating war experiences also occurred after the 1990 Iraqi invasion.

The 1990 Iraqi invasion of Kuwait and the 2003 U.S. war in Iraq were events that marked time for Kuwaitis in terms of before and after war. These temporal references to war – the before and after of war – became framing devices in popular cultural forms such as paintings, stories, music, and poetry, as well as in Kuwaiti news reports of government and medical health research. Several young adults spoke of friends who had taken overdoses of heroin, methamphetamines, and/or benzodiazepines in response to "tensions" and stress after the 2003 U.S. invasion of Iraq. Young Kuwaitis spoke of fears that the war in Iraq would spill over into Kuwait, tensions with family and friends over the morality of the war, and conflicted feelings about Muslim and Iraqi identities, since many Kuwaitis have married Iraqis and their extended families live on both sides of the border.

Stigmas, Gag Orders, and Forgetting

In Kuwait, acknowledging psychological distress has, until the last few years, been highly stigmatized with consequences for family reputation, marriage, and extended family relations. Prior to the recent burgeoning of psychological and hypnosis clinics, affective bodily inscriptions of war tended to be rendered as the somatic distress of physical illnesses and concerns about war contaminants or other "outside assaults." Kuwaiti young adults made numerous topographical referents to the invasion – bombed homes riddled with bullet holes, burned abandoned cars, torture houses, dead bodies in the streets, the War Museum, the Liberation Tower – that evoke, become, and write memory into Kuwaiti landscapes. In dynamic relation, difficulty breathing, headaches, body aches, and weakness brought about concern of contamination and danger in postinvasion topographies and environments.

The lack of information about child and teenage health effects of oil fires, and chronic, low-level exposures to depleted uranium, pesticides, and other war contaminants is notable (Cecchine, Golomb, Hilborne, Spektor, & Anthony, 2000). Each winter, young Kuwaitis go camping in the desert or to farms that border Iraq, where they play football in the sand. Though U.S. government funded reports, the International Atomic Energy Agency (2003), and the Kuwaiti government deny causal relationships between depleted uranium and health consequences for Kuwaitis, the U.S. government placed gag orders on many U.S. government funded organizations (Harley et al., 1999) and transported 6,700 tons of sand contaminated with depleted uranium to the American Ecology Corporation's Idaho's Grand View low-level radiation waste facility in the Owyhee Desert of Idaho (Williams, 2008). Iraqi forces were not the only ones potentially culpable and thus financially liable for war contaminations (Bloom et al., 1994). Iraqi and coalition forces set hundreds of oil fires, whose plumes of black oily soot endangered humans and environments not only locally but globally (Hilder, 1994). Child witnesses of these war fires described intense darkness, "not being able to tell night or day," "having trouble breathing," and black soot on their fingers and mucus. A 23-year-old woman said, "I heard cannons. It was always dark. My family and I felt isolated because it was unsafe for us to leave the house. Life was depressing and frightening and everyone felt anxious and tense. I still can't look at anything related to the war or POWs without feeling extremely very sad." A 29-year-old woman recalled, "There was black smoke everywhere, especially a few months into the occupation. It looked like nighttime all day long. The sea was very contaminated. I saw dirty and dead wildlife on the streets and ocean coasts, mostly birds."[4]

Identities and Betrayals

Beyond anxieties about their health, young Kuwaitis offered moral appraisals of the 1990 Iraqi occupation of Kuwait that resonate with the 2003 U.S. war in Iraq, highlighting Muslim identities and betrayal. One woman remarked, "We always looked up to Saddam protecting us from Iran and then he invades us." Young Kuwaitis also focused on differences in the levels of violence between neighborhoods. Kuwaiti children living in neighborhoods occupied by the Iraqi Republican Guard Ba'athist troops witnessed far more physical violence than those occupied by regular Iraqi troops. They described the Ba'athist troops as violent, "bad Muslims," who had chosen to harm them, while those under regular army troops remembered troops as "children," "forced to do wrong," who "cried," "begged for food," and asked "to play football" with the children of their families. These dissimilar remembrances of intra-Muslim violence and agency in violent acts were strongly gendered, with young boys frequently the ones parents asked to go out for bread or water because their fathers, mothers, and sisters were presumed to be at greater risk for physical and sexual assault in Ba'athist occupied neighborhoods. Narratives by young men living in these neighborhoods tended to depict heroic action outside the home with affective bodily experiences such as humiliation and anger that evoked cautioning responses from their mothers and sisters. Young women, by contrast, spoke of comforting their mothers and siblings, feeling sad and anxious. Dalia's 16-year-old brother's excitement to "do something," while her mother and sisters attempted to contain his emotions, exemplifies this dynamic. Kuwaiti family collaborative remembering generally involved strong moral action input from adults and boys, who were more likely to have had personal experiences with violence and with heroism. Collaborative remembering conjoined with these social and cultural mediations of violent experiences tended to ground memories in identity affiliations and betrayals, by drawing attention to particular topographical and media referents to violence, and to differing social perceptions of the legitimacy of the 2003 U.S. invasion of Iraq.

"Part of the way violence is carried into the future," as Nordstrom (2004, p. 226) suggests, "is through creating hegemony of enduring violence across the length and breadth of the commonplace world, past and present. The normal, the innocuous, and the inescapable are infused with associations of lethal harm." Child witnesses of the Iraqi invasion vividly recalled the dangers of Iraqi checkpoints on main roads and the destruction of community centers, religious sites, public parks, schoolyards, and marketplaces, places where war was brought home. Many of these cityscapes have never been repaired, but rather are inscribed as communal memory, in some places with plaques attesting to particular incidents of violence. Males, more often than females, recalled intimidation, humiliation, loss of control, and powerlessness at Iraqi soldier checkpoints in response to sexually aggressive or inappropriate advances toward their mothers.

Young men, out of the home more often than their sisters during the 1990 invasion and occupation, vividly described seeing maimed and murdered bodies in communal areas close to their homes: A 24-year-old described "torture houses" and "piles of dead bodies, and a tortured man, still alive, led from the torture house to an ambulance." He recalled children playing football with the head of a murdered Iraqi after the U.S.-led liberation of Kuwait. A 22-year-old remembered "men being executed in front of my own eyes." He said, "I felt helpless, not only because I was a child, but my family could not control anything … no one could protect me." He said, "My older brother took a soldier's decapitated head and kicked it to me. I was scared and still remember how I felt when I saw it." Another 22-year-old described "seeing a dead man hanging from a light post" and "walking by workout facilities and cafes with dead bodies." A 23-year-old spoke of "children making poisonous drinks as a game to kill Iraqi soldiers," to regain a sense of control and to take revenge. During the occupation, places associated with safety such as the home were recast as lethal and inhumane or as refuges for Iraqi soldiers. Some Kuwaiti neighborhoods were unchanged in terms of family composition, while in others, neighbors moved away, their houses destroyed or vandalized beyond repair. A 23-year-old male described Ba'athist soldiers breaking into his family's home: "Iraqi soldiers broke down our door. My brother spilled water on the soldier, and he got angry; he yelled at my brother." Living in an area occupied by non-Ba'athists, a 24-year-old male said: "Soldiers cried; they didn't want to be there. They were forced. They needed food. The soldiers played with children, and joked." Neighborhood differences with regard to treatment by Ba'athist and non-Ba'athist Iraqi troops led to contrasting Kuwaiti sentiments and narrations of experience that were emplaced or tied to particular topographies. As neighborhoods themselves were destroyed or divided by their experiences of occupation, so too were familial, social, and national narrations of it. Empathy or indifference to the plight of Iraqis under U.S. occupation tended to mirror these social divisions.

Most children remembered the occupation as a time of both their worst and best memories with their families. Though stress and family conflicts may have resulted in domestic violence and substance abuse, young Kuwaitis also felt closer to their families. A 23-year-old female said: "It was perfect. No one had to be there. Everyone was there because they wanted to be there. We were never so close." Others described the "fun" of sleeping in the same room with their extended family members. This social channeling of remembrances – the ways in which children collectively remember and forget trauma and remember and forget "fun" or increased care and cohesion – is a powerful aspect of group identification and recovery that impacts the likelihood of future resilience and future risk of violence (Casey, 2009; White, 2005).

The issue of identities – familial, ethnic, religious, and national – became a central feature in remembrances of 'trust' during the occupation. Kuwaitis recalled their families obtaining fake identification, using other languages and dialects, and the increase in Iraqi prejudice toward Kuwaitis, with Kuwaiti intolerance of Palestinians and Bidoon (in Arabic, "without"), meaning persons without state citizenship. Kuwaitis accused Palestinians and Bidoon of collaborating with the Iraqi army during the occupation, and in the summer of 1991, Kuwaiti officials started to detain Palestinian children and teens, pressuring them to confess that their fathers and older brothers were Iraqi collaborators (Marzoued, 1994). Government officials arrested many Palestinian fathers and brothers on the basis of these confessions. Constructions of identity and feelings of betrayal emerged through a majority of interviews. A young man asked, "Why should there be trust? We trusted Palestinians. We gave them jobs. They made money. They were our brothers and look how they stabbed us in the back." A young woman recalled, "They wrote Kuwait is for Palestinians" on city walls. Another said, "I know it is wrong to hate people because of their race, but I hate Palestinians because my mother and father told me to. A Palestinian almost killed my father." A young woman of Palestinian family background and Kuwaiti citizenship described increased isolation and harassment, as Palestinians were fired from jobs. Roughly 200,000 Palestinians fled Kuwait during the Iraqi occupation, losing their homes and businesses, then in the aftermath of the war, the Kuwaiti government expelled an additional 200,000 Palestinians and more than 100,000 Bidoon (Gabra, 1991; Marzoued, 1994; Rosen, 2012).[5]

Affective Inscriptions of National Memory

Immediately after their invasion of Kuwait, Iraqi soldiers attempted to destroy Kuwaiti national identity and memories, changing the names of streets, neighborhoods, and buildings; looting and torching the National Museum; cutting phone lines; collecting all radios and fax machines; and placing signs around Kuwait claiming Kuwait as their own (Wheeler, 2000). Iraqi forces destroyed the satellite earth station at Umm al-'Aysh and crushed public utilities and infrastructure. Reestablishing communication technologies became a symbolic national endeavor and led to a proliferation of new media. By the late 1990s, Kuwaiti Internet savvy teenagers and young adults were communicating more across gender lines and with diverse Muslim populations than they had prior to the invasion (Wheeler, 2000). They had greater exposure to Kuwaiti radio and television shows that addressed the aftermath of the Iraqi invasion as well as to satellite TV from neighboring countries. Many child witnesses spoke of being obsessed with the Internet and televised communications of the 2003 U.S. war in Iraq; others seemed disengaged and asserted that "Iraqis deserved what they are getting"; or yet others, similar to Dalia, found media depictions of the U.S. war to be "emotionally overwhelming" for them. By 2006, Wheeler found Kuwaiti teenagers and young adults, particularly women and Islamists, to be among the most frequent Internet users, further impacting the politics of gender and religion in Kuwait.

Kuwaiti memories and moral assessments of the 1990 Iraqi invasion and occupation of Kuwait, and the 2003 U.S. invasion and occupation of Iraq, took on additional emotive resonance with questions at local and regional levels about the colonial formation of Iraq and Kuwait. Ideas about citizenship and the ownership of oil resources, regional support for the Iraqi invasion of Kuwait, and violence toward Muslims around the globe, all became points of contention in face-to-face and social media conversations. Structuring narratives of the U.S. assistance with the liberation of Kuwait, prominent in Liberation Day celebrations and in the War Museum, represented, for many young people, an appreciation of U.S. recognition and support of Kuwait. But, within changing regional and global contexts, this support entailed societal fracturing, increased sectarianism, and ambivalence, if not hostility, from some of Kuwait's neighbors.

Remembering, Amplified

While the majority of the child witnesses I interviewed had never been diagnosed with PTSD or depression, most described periods of low mood, isolation, emptiness, and emotional disconnectedness, feelings that grew unbearable in their teenage years after the 2003 U.S. war in Iraq. Young Kuwaitis felt they lacked a sense of loyalty or trust, recounting instead fear, betrayal, dependency on friends and immediate family, anger and frustration, and either increased reliance on religion, as in Dalia's case, or on alcohol and street drugs. But attributing dependence on either religion or alcohol and street drugs to the trauma of invasion has hindered efforts to understand social, political, and environmental causes of stress and ill health and their resounding effects on Kuwaiti youths.[6]

Child witnesses of the 1990 Iraqi invasion experience sensitivity to explosive sounds such as the backfiring of cars or the explosions at building demolition sites or in films. They react to sights and smells of destruction and pollution, particularly to bombed or bullet ridden buildings, to oil fire residues and oil slicks, and to intrusive images of tortured and mutilated bodies. Such sights, sounds, and smells, whether in the Kuwaiti environment or via contemporary media, resonate with topographies, collaborative remembering, and mediations of the 2003 U.S. war in Iraq. These sensory experiences may result from a confluence of veridical recall, obsessional worry, and vivid ruminations of "worst case scenarios" from the 1990 Iraqi invasion, but they may also be constructions and amplifications of memories – experiences of two wars that converge and resonate in narrative, performative, and incorporating memory practices, evoking, repeating, and channeling affective information *as trauma*.

Remembrances of the 2003 U.S. war in Iraq and the 1990 Iraqi occupation became increasingly traumatic in the form of sensorial experiencing, in real-virtual topographies of contamination and destruction, and in collaborative remembering and mediations of war violence. Nostalgia about preinvasion social cohesiveness and safety gave way to traumatic aftereffects – affective bodily incorporations of felt familial, Kuwaiti national, regional, and global betrayals, as well as insults to the Muslim body, the body as family, body politic, and national terrain. Bombed out buildings and burned cars, the stuff of everyday life, left like abandoned bodies, provide few alternative standpoints of encounter, few sensorial and narrative possibilities with which to encode the devastation of resonant wars.

In postwar Kuwait, rememberings and forgettings of violence as they converged and resonated amplified the magnitude of affective power in the emotional anchoring (and unmooring) of sensorial experiences, and in channeling and repeating some memories and not others. Harmonic and dissonant reverberations of war memories within households and across neighborhoods, and Kuwaiti cultural idioms of distress, further widened and deepened, condensed, and abridged particular memories. The "tensions" and "double lives" that emerged as young Kuwaitis dealt with these memory processes gave way to health problems, and to self-other, self-society dialectics that fractured and silenced public remembrances of war, often confining them to psychological and religious sites of interaction.[7] Affective sensorial inscriptions of memory (bodily, topographical, collaborative, and mediated), structured and anchored in PTSD narratives or in religious practices, obscure and hide the destructive presence of social and political tensions in Kuwait and persistent, as well as more recent, forms of violence in Kuwait and in the region.

Acknowledgments

I would like to thank the Kuwaiti young adults who have allowed me into their lives, and my former students, colleagues, and friends in Kuwait who have helped me to learn about Kuwait and the region. My thanks also extend to Alexander Hinton and Devon Hinton for organizing the conference from which this volume originates and for their editorial comments. A Paul and Francena Miller Research Fellowship funded the writing of this chapter, and I am grateful to the Millers for their support of this research through their sponsorship of faculty research at the Rochester Institute of Technology.

NOTES

1 Dr. Naif Al-Mutawa (2009) wrote this in an obituary for his colleague, Dr. Jaabar Behbehani, who expressed concern about the growing, unregulated psychological services industry in Kuwait.
2 See A. Hinton's (2004) analysis of the "ontological resonances" with Khmer Rouge violence that shape meaning and experience in today's Cambodia. See D. Hinton and S. Hinton (2002, p. 17) for an integrative perspective on somatic sensations in panic, an ontological resonances analysis of somatic sensations (see also Hagengimana & D. Hinton, 2009, for an ontological analysis of sensations among Rwandan genocide survivors): The analysis takes into account "the full spectrum of panic attack sensations (the sensation body), the biological generation of panic sensations (the biological body), sensation as invoking an ethnophysiology (the ethnophysiological body), sensation as metaphor (the metaphoric body), sensation as invoking the landscape (the landscape body), sensation as invoking catastrophic cognitions (the catastrophic cognitions body), and sensation as invoking memory (the memory-associational body)." The tensions described by young Kuwaitis were persistent, closely tied to the affective-sensorial of war, and to social relations, conflict, and betrayal, and did not manifest as panic, but did have somatic symptoms as primary complaints. The literature on "embodied memory" (Stoller, 1995), the "ontological resonances" of violence (A. Hinton, 2004), and the multidimensional and ontological analysis of sensations (D. Hinton & S. Hinton, 2002; see also Hagengimana & D. Hinton, 2009), fits well with the research described in this chapter.
3 An excellent example of this is Stoller's (1995) analysis of Songhay Hauka, who, possessed by European colonial spirits, "embody colonial memories," triggering sensorial, affective remembrances that resonate with and impact past and present power relations in Niger.
4 Despite strong anecdotal evidence of post-1990 elevations in the prevalence rates of cancer, respiratory illnesses, gastrointestinal and reproductive disorders, and 1,573 postinvasion deaths attributed to a variety of causes – unknown (344), circulatory (686), neoplasms (183), endocrine (95), and respiratory (67) (Dockery, 2009) – Kuwaitis have not been tested for chronic, low-level exposures to war and other pollutants.

5 The numbers of Palestinians and Bidoon who fled during the Iraqi invasion and were denied return or who were expelled by the Kuwaiti government vary somewhat by study. Marzoued (1994) estimates the number of persons exiled at 250,000 Palestinians and 100,000 Bidoon. Rosen (2012) reports 200,000 Palestinians fled during the occupation and were denied return, and then later, from March to September of 1991, the Kuwaiti government expelled an additional 200,000. Shafeeq Gabra (1991) similarly estimates the number of Palestinians who fled during the Iraqi occupation to be 200,000. He describes the complexities of Palestinian–Kuwaiti relations after the invasion, damaged by the PLO's actions at the beginning of the crisis, while enhanced by Palestinian involvement with Kuwaiti resistance and mutual caretaking in mixed neighborhoods.

6 See Demerdash et al. (1981) for a study of preinvasion alcohol and drug dependence among mental health patients, and Bilal and Angelo-Kharrar (1988) and Bilal (1989) for alcohol casualties and alcoholism in preinvasion Kuwait. Radovanovic, Pitcher, al-Nakib, and Shihab-Eidden (2000) performed 28,548 tests on 3,781 samples from Kuwaitis and found cannabinoids positive in 40 percent of the tested samples, opiates in 24 percent, ethanol in 10 percent, and amphetamines in 5 percent. Radovanovic et al. found a significant increase in the proportion of positive results for ethanol, amphetamines, and benzodiazepines from 1992 to 1997, but there have been no similar studies to help us evaluate the prevalence of pre- and postconflict substance use, nor the social contexts in which people use substances. Please see Conrad (2011) for news reports about the prevalence of domestic violence in Kuwait.

7 The 1990 Iraqi invasion dealt a heavy blow to the arts communities within Kuwait, resulting in a period between 1990 and 2003 with few public arts events and expressive cultural opportunities for public discussion of war. While the Kuwait National Memorial Museum exhibited a dramatization of the Iraqi invasion prior to 2003, the 2003 opening of the Modern Art Museum, and the opening from 2005 to 2006 of a number of smaller galleries, such as the Sultan Gallery, JAMM Consultancy, Contemporary Art Platform, MinRASY projects, and Dar al-Athar Al-Islamiyya, substantially reinvigorated public arts and debate about the 1990 and 2003 wars and their aftermaths. In the past few years, child witnesses of war (Al-Qadiri & Al-Garaballi, 2012) and the plight of Palestinians and Bidoon exiled during the 1990 war have emerged as subjects of art exhibitions, literature, and social political protest. The May 2012 Modern Art Museum installation called *UNPLIFIED*, for instance, elicited a rethinking of Ghasson Kanafani's novel *Men in the Sun and Other Palestinian Stories* (1963), contrasting the life of a Palestinian refugee in Lebanon who paid to be smuggled into Kuwait in a water tanker with those of Palestinians who, after the Iraqi invasion, were banished. In 2012, Mai Al-Nakib, a professor of literature at Kuwait University, gave a talk entitled "The People Are Missing" to suggest that the expulsions of Palestinians call for political cinema that "reinvents missing people." Al-Nakib has also published *The Hidden Light of Objects* (2014), a fictionalized account of a young Kuwaiti girl, named Amerika, who honored the U.S. role in the liberation of Kuwait but who, after the 2003 U.S. war in Iraq, becomes ill at ease with this name as new restraints under an increasingly conservative public come into play. Conservative identity politics,

religion, and changing gender dynamics have emerged as central themes in postwar and "Arab Spring" Kuwaiti expressive cultures, highlighted by the recent censorship of a May 2012 exhibition of paintings by Shurooq Amin called *It's a Man's World* and her 2013 series of paintings *Popcornographic*.

REFERENCES

Abdel-Khalek, A. M. (1996). Factorial structure of the Arabic children's depression inventory among Kuwaiti subjects. *Psychological Reports*, 78, 963–7.

(1997). A survey of fears associated with Iraqi aggression among Kuwaiti children and adolescents: A factorial study 5.7 years after the Gulf War. *Psychological Reports*, 81, 247–55.

Abdullatif, H. I. (1995). Prevalence of depression among middle-school Kuwaiti students following the Iraqi Invasion. *Psychological Reports*, 77, 643–9.

Al-Khaled, A. (2007, March 8). Domestic violence common in Kuwait. *Kuwait Times*, p. 1.

Al-Mutawa, N. (2009). The last wow. Retrieved January 12, 2014, from http://www.al-mutawa.com/1270cp.html

Al-Nakib, M. (2014). *The hidden light of objects.* New York: Bloomsbury Publishing.

Al-Naser, F., al-Khulaifi, I. M., & Martino, C. (2000). Assessment of posttraumatic stress disorder four and one-half years after the Iraqi invasion. *International Journal of Emergency Mental Health*, 2, 153–6.

Al-Qadiri, F., & Al-Garaballi, K. (2012). *Children of war: Kuwait.* Retrieved September 2, 2013, from http://gulfartguide.com/g/wpcontent/uploads/2012/08/ Children-of-War-Bidoun-interview-FaQ-KhaGh.pdf

Antze, P., & Lambek, M. (1996). *Tense past: Cultural essays in trauma and memory.* New York: Routledge.

Bilal, A. M. (1989). Prospective study of alcoholism treatment in Kuwait: A 5-year follow-up report. *Drug and Alcohol Dependence*, 23, 83–6.

Bilal, A. M., & Angelo-Khattar, M. (1988). Correlates of alcohol-related casualty in Kuwait. *Acta Psychiatrica Scandinavica*, 78, 417–20.

Bloom, S., Miller, J., Winkler, P., & Warner, J. (1994). *Hidden casualties: Environmental, health and political consequences of the Persian Gulf War.* Berkeley: North Atlantic Books.

Capps, L., & Ochs, E. (1995). *Constructing panic: The discourse of agoraphobia.* Cambridge, MA: Harvard University Press.

Casey, C. (2009). Mediated hostility: Media, "affective citizenship," and genocide in northern Nigeria. In A. L. Hinton & K. O'Neill (Eds.), *Genocide, truth and representation: Anthropological approaches*, (pp. 247–78). Durham, NC: Duke University Press.

(2010). Remembering genocide: Hypocrisy and the violence of local/global 'justice' in northern Nigeria. In A. L. Hinton (Ed.), *Transitional justice: Global mechanisms and local realities after genocide and mass violence*, (pp. 119–36). Rutgers, NJ: Rutgers University Press.

Cecchine, G., Golomb, B., Hilborne, L., Spektor, D., & Anthony, C. R. (2000). *A review of the scientific literature as it pertains to Gulf War illnesses.* Volume 8. *Pesticides.* Santa Monica, CA: RAND.

Cole, J. (2003). Narratives and moral projects: Generational memories of the Malagasy 1947 rebellion. *Ethos*, 31, 95–126.

Conrad, L. (2011, July 5). One in three women in Kuwait is a domestic violence victim. *Kuwait Times*, p. 1.

Demerdash, A. M., Mizaal, H., Farouki, S. E., & El-Mossalem, H. (1981). Some behavioural and psychosocial aspects of alcohol and drug dependence in Kuwait Psychiatric Hospital. *Acta Psychiatrica Scandinavica*, 63, 173–84.

Dockery, D. (2009). *Kuwait Longitudinal Health Study: Environment and health in Kuwait*. RAC-GWVI Meeting Minutes, 30–48, June 29–30, 2009.

Evans, J. (2008). *The Kuwait oil fires*. Retrieved December 21, 2011, from www.sra-ne.org/seminars/kuwait.ppt.

Figley, C. R., Chapman, P. Ashkanani, H., Al-Naser, F., & Donnelly, E. (2010). Well-being in a deeply religious society in the shadows of war: Results of a household survey of Kuwaitis. *American Journal of Orthopsychiatry*, 80, 593–600.

Gabra, S. (1991). The PLO in Kuwait. *Middle East International*. Retrieved November 10, 2013, from https://www.greenleft.org.au/node/1457.

Garbarino, J. (1994). The experience of children in Kuwait: Occupation, war and liberation. In S. Bloom, J. Miller, J. Warner, & P. Winkler (Eds.) *Hidden casualties: Environmental, health and political consequences of the Persian Gulf War*, (pp. 203–5). ARC/Arms Control Research Center, San Francisco, CA: North Atlantic Books.

Hadi, F. A., & Liabre, M. M. (1997). Social support and psychological distress in Kuwaiti boys and girls exposed to the Gulf crisis. *Journal of Clinical Child Psychology*, 3, 247–55.

(1998). The Gulf crisis experience of Kuwaiti children: Psychological and cognitive factors. *Journal of Traumatic Stress*, 11, 45–56.

Hagengimana, A., & Hinton, D. E. (2009). Ihahamuka, a Rwandan syndrome of response to the genocide: Blocked flow, spirit assault, and shortness of breath. In D. E. Hinton & B. J. Good (Eds.), *Culture and panic disorder* (pp. 205–29). Stanford, CA: Stanford University Press.

Hammadi, A., Staehr, A., Behbehani, J., & Staehr, M. (1994). *The traumatic events and mental health consequences resulting from the Iraqi invasion and occupation of Kuwait*. Kuwait: Al-Riggae Specialised Centre.

Harley, N., Foulkes, E., Hilborne, L., Hudson, A., & Anthony, C. R. (1999). *A review of the scientific literature as it pertains to Gulf War illnesses.* Vol. 7. *Depleted uranium*. Santa Monica, CA: RAND.

Harvard School of Public Health. (2005). *Harvard scientists report public health impact of 1990 Iraq invasion of Kuwait: Higher rates of mortality evident among Kuwaiti civilians who remained in Kuwait during occupation*. Retrieved December 11, 2010, from http://www.hsph.harvard.edu/news/press-releases/archives/2005-releases/press06292005.html

Hilder, L. (1994). The gag order: Did the U.S. government hide facts about the fires? In S. Bloom, J. Miller, J. Warner & P. Winkler (Eds.) *Hidden casualties: Environmental, health and political consequences of the Persian Gulf War* (pp. 95–102). ARC/Arms Control Research Center, San Francisco: North Atlantic Books.

Hinton, A. L. (2004). *Why did they kill? Cambodia in the shadow of genocide.* Berkeley and Los Angeles: University of California Press.

Hinton, D. E., & Good, B. J. (Eds.) (2009). *Culture and panic disorder.* Palo Alto, CA: Stanford University Press.

Hinton, D. E. & Hinton, S. D. (2002). Panic disorder, somatization, and the new cross-cultural psychiatry: The seven bodies of a new anthropology of panic. *Culture, Medicine & Psychiatry,* 26, 155–78.

Huyssen, A. (2001). Present pasts: Media, politics, amnesia. In A. Appadurai (Ed.), *Globalization,* (pp. 57–77). Durham, NC, and London: Duke University Press.

International Atomic Energy Agency. (2003). *Radiological conditions in areas of Kuwait with residues of depleted uranium: Report by an international group of experts.* Retrieved December 22, 2011, from http://wwwpub.iaea.org/MTCD/publications/PDF/Pub1164_web.pdf

Kanafani, G. (1998 [1963]). *Men in the sun and other Palestinian stories.* Washington, DC: Three Continents.

Kirmayer, L. (1996). Landscapes of memory: Trauma, narrative and dissociation. In P. Antze & M. Lambek (Eds.), *Tense past: Cultural essays in memory and trauma* (pp. 173–98). London: Routledge.

Kirmayer, L., Lemelson, R., & Barad, M. (Eds.). (2007). *Understanding trauma: Integrating biological, clinical, and cultural perspectives.* New York: Cambridge University Press.

Llabre, M., & Hadi, F. A. (1997). Social support and psychological distress in Kuwaiti boys and girls exposed to the Gulf crisis. *Journal of Clinical Child Psychology,* 26, 247–55.

Marzoued, M. (1994). Palestinian youth in Kuwait. In S. Bloom, J. Miller, J. Warner, & P. Winkler (Eds.), *Hidden casualties: Environmental, health and political consequences of the Persian Gulf War* (pp. 206–7). ARC/Arms Control Research Center, San Francisco: North Atlantic Books.

Mattingly, C., & Garro, L. (Eds.) (2000). *Narrative and the cultural construction of illness and healing.* Berkeley: University of California Press.

Nader, K. O., Pynoos, R. S., Fairbanks, L. A., al-Ajeel, M., & al-Asfour, A. (1993). A preliminary study of PTSD and grief among the children of Kuwait following the Gulf crisis. *British Journal of Clinical Psychology,* 32, 407–16.

Nordstrom, C. (2004). *Shadows of war: Violence, power, and international profiteering in the twenty-first century.* Berkeley: University of California Press.

Radovanovic, Z., Pitcher, C. W., al-Nakib, T., & Shihab-Eideen, A. (2000). On substance abuse in Kuwait (1992–1997): Evidence from toxicological screening of patients. *Journal of Substance Abuse,* 12, 363–71.

Rosen, S. (2012). Kuwait expels thousands of Palestinians. *Middle East Quarterly,* 75–83.

Stoller, P. (1995). *Embodying colonial memories: Spirit possession, power, and the Hauka in West Africa.* New York and London: Routledge.

Wertsch, J. V. (2008). The narrative organization of collective memory. *Ethos,* 36, 120–35.

Wheeler, D. (2000). New media, globalization and Kuwaiti national identity. *The Middle East Journal,* 54, 432–44.

(2006). *The Internet in the Middle East: Global expectations and local imaginations in Kuwait*. Albany: State University of New York Press.

White, G. (2005). Emotive institutions. In C. Casey & R. Edgerton (Eds.), *Companion to psychological anthropology: Modernity and psychocultural change* (pp. 241–54). Malden, MA, and London: Blackwell.

Wikan, U. (2000). With life in one's lap: The story of an eye/I (or two). In C. Mattingly & L. Garro (Eds.), *Narrative and the cultural construction of illness and healing* (pp. 221–36). Berkeley: University of California Press.

Williams, T. D. (2008). *The depleted uranium threat*. Centre for Research on Globalization. Retrieved December 18, 2011, from http://www.globalresearch.ca/index.php?context=va&aid=9847.

Young, A. (1995). *The harmony of illusions: Inventing post-traumatic stress disorder*. Princeton, NJ: Princeton University Press.

"Behaves Like a Rooster and Cries Like a
[Four Eyed] Canine": The Politics and
Poetics of Depression and Psychiatry in Iran

Orkideh Behrouzan and Michael M. J. Fischer

We are the *daheh shasti* (the [13]60s, the sixties [1980s])
generation.[1] We are now scattered around the world. We wear
colorful clothes but our insides are all black, dark, and depressed
... we want to extract this bitterness from life and show it to
you the way Gholam Hossein Sa'edi[2] did. We are the
most screwed up generation.

We are the *Khāmushi* generation, born and raised under those
periods of khāmushi [lights turned off, silenced, asphyxiated].
We have had no voice. We want to have a voice.

–Radio Khāmushi podcast, Tehran, spring 2009

I. Introduction: The Topological Twist and the Traumatic Self

In January 2009, the Ministry of Health of the Islamic Republic of Iran
issued a statement that there was too much sadness in the country and
that new programs in engineering happiness should be introduced. Of
the three differently culturally marked generations born since the 1979
Islamic revolution, a central one, "the 1360s (1980s) generation," calls
itself the "khamushi or silenced generation" or "the 'lights out' generation," stemming from its experiences of the bombings of Iran's cities
during the Iran-Iraq War (1980–8) huddled in darkened basements and
bomb shelters. Now in their thirties, many are successful professionals.
Many have left Iran, but still suffer the psychological effects, manifested
in nightmares and other symptoms of generational and transgenerational
emotional repressions. Many other well-educated adults are unemployed
in Iran (Behrouzan, 2010a). The 2009 underground podcast serial Radio
Khamushi is one of the media that voice this generational experience.[3]
Blogs are another of the media used as affective spaces in which shared
traumas can be retrospectively recognized and shared, shattering the suffering in isolation and fear of public articulation.

The phenomenological description of melancholia we use in our title
is from a much older discursive time, from the famous Persian physician

105

Ali ibn al-Majusi (d. 982–4), whose medical textbook was studied in Europe as the *Liber Regalis* or *Regalis Dispositio*[4] and is technically about one particular kind of melancholia but illustrates a poetic power that both articulates the disjunction between public face and private feeling, repeated in the epigram from Radio Khamushi, and draws upon a rich nexus of continuing symbols that every Iranian knows.[5]

The more explicit discourses of "psychiatric selves" that have arisen in the past twenty years are influenced in part by European and American neurology, psychiatry, and self-help discourses (Behrouzan, 2014). We discern successive powerful moments and layers – neurology, Freud, Jung, Tavistock, psychopharmacology, child psychiatry – of Persianized imports from Europe and the United States over the course of the past seventy years. These inflect and alloy with the powerful affective mix of Persian politics. Changing forms of the unsayable periodically redirect, reformulate, and reshape the circulation of affects.

We begin with five types of contemporary nightmare: blocked processing of sedimented anxieties; allegorical affective insults to the body politic causing individuals to feel isolated; the emotional labor and fatigue of stuckness; failures of self-help therapies; and technomusic remixes of wartime songs that recall confused feelings of nostalgia, dysphoria, and anger. Along the way we acknowledge psychosocial analytic readings of Persian cinematic dreamwork, and the history of Iranian psychiatry and self-help movements. In section III we turn to intra- and intergenerational communication across four generations: those born before the revolution with memories of their youthful parts in it; those born between 1965 and 1970 who came of age during the Iran-Iraq War; those born after Khomeini's 1981 call for more babies to fuel the armies of sacred defense; and those born in the late 1980s and 1990s who are coming of age through today's Green Wave (*mouj-e sabz*) struggles over the affective structure of the state in the aftermath of the tenth presidential elections in June 2009.

Thirty years after the establishment of the Islamic Republic of Iran (IRI), in January 2009, and after a decade of allowing small girls to wear more colorful attire to school, with suicide and addiction rates rising, the Ministries of Internal Affairs, Education, and Health announced a need for an initiative to engineer happiness. It is a remarkable admission of the effects of thirty years of unrelenting efforts to suppress public displays of happiness in the name of stoicism or steady patience (*sabr*) to achieve the goals of an Islamic society, which increasingly has deteriorated from notions of social justice (*adalat*) and competence to mere commitment (*ta'ahod*) to a hierarchical structure. Without denying the existence of laughter and joy, psychiatrists worry about the deadening of affect among many youth who consult them with obsessive adoption of Islamicist self-discipline and complaints of not knowing how to relate to the opposite sex.[6]

In the past twenty years there has been an explosion of interest in psychiatric and psychological discourses on self-help talk shows on radio and television that attract calls from all strata of society, rural as well as urban. The directness of the language used for interpersonal, sexual, infidelity, mental illness, psychic distress, and traumatic relations is of a kind unimaginable twenty years ago, when such subjects would have been indirectly expressed through poetry and philosophical melancholia (Behrouzan, 2010b, 2014).

Any serious anthropological exploration of trauma, posttraumatic stress disorder (PTSD), depression, as well as the rise of new psychiatric discourses of the self in Iran and its diasporas, requires at least three rings of engagement: (i) explanation or causal social analysis, (ii) explication or interpretive cultural hermeneutics, and (iii) psychodynamics or individual and social life histories.

II.   Five Kinds of Nightmare

His voice, his tone, the long alarm siren that followed his words, will never leave me. Nothing makes me feel worse than hearing this thing again; it gives me palpitations. And thanks to the Internet, after all these years, I hear it again because some of my friends find it nostalgic and feel they should e-mail and share it with me (interview with 29-year-old Sara, London, September 15, 2009/OB):

shenavandegan-e aziz,	dear audience,
shenavandegan-e aziz	dear audience,
Alamati ke ham aknun mishenavid	the siren you hear now is a red siren of warning
...	...
Va ma'na va mafhoum-e an in ast ke	And what it means is
Mahalleh eghamat e khod ra tark kardeh	leave wherever you are
va be nazdiktarin panahgah...	and go to the nearest shelter

[siren sounds]
– "The Announcement of the Red Siren" during the nights of Iraqi air attacks on Tehran

Five kinds of nightmares: (i) anxieties that continue to haunt, (ii) allegorical insults to the body politic, (iii) the emotionally exhausting labor of being stuck, (iv) projections and transferences through an emerging culture of therapy, and (v) disorienting "remixes" of contemporary sound tracks with sounds of war, traditional religious chants, and older-generation pop music.

Psychic traumas by definition refuse to be located in time and place and are never grasped and experienced fully at the moment of their occurrences. They actualize in their belatedness, their *Nachträglichkeit*, their recognition only "after the fact." This temporality is both a mechanism of survival (repression) and of "working through" rather than encrypting, monumentalizing, or becoming trapped within trauma. This temporality is also the connection to history, to the interaction between social causalities and individual resilience. Herein also lies the importance of the unsaid, what cannot be said, like the massacres of 1988, questioning the continuation of the war beyond 1982, lifting and repressing of sexual mores, or intergenerational shifts of sensibility. The burden of the unspoken and the unspeakable does not dissipate when one leaves Iran. It is not simply that the psychic demands of constructing new anchorages in new environments inhibit reflecting upon the past. More important are the painful scars that cannot easily be reflected upon at all.

Here ethnographic and linguistic details become signifiers. Generational slang, or memories of children's television programs (dark in the early 1980s, more colorful with the late 1980s with shows like *Kolāh Ghermezi* [Red Hat]), create a difference in affective memory for people in their thirties from those in their twenties. These different bodily inscriptions produce frequent situations of nontranslatability across generational fractions. One of these affective marks perhaps is the comment one young Iranian biomedical engineer on the MIT campus made on the anniversary of the Universal Declaration of Human Rights, declining to attend a talk on Iran: "Human rights? Leave these things alone; they make you sad.... I don't want to think about these things" (December 26, 2008: 00:34:20/OB).

i.   *Anxieties That Haunt*

My imagination was obviously open. Very freaky. I was receiving a lot of information that I did not have the capacity to process.

Still today the repetitive dreams are: I am in massive cinemas and auditoriums, not in themselves necessarily negative, but if something flies over my head – airplanes, balloons, and such – it always crashes. ("Neda," artist in her early forties)

Neda grew up immersed in daily news reports and weekly television footage of the eight-year-long "Imposed War" between Iraq and Iran and remembers the 1979 revolution indirectly as a young child: "I remember someone had gone to the city and seen a strike downtown, and came back home and said that he had seen a cut off head, and you hear stuff like that." At the time she had nightmares of a "huge worm that had eaten up my mother; and my dad and I are marching in the street and mourning." She remembers her grandmother cleaning up vomit so that the local *komiteh* ("committee" policing fundamentalist "religious" codes) could not see the evidence of a party her brother had given during which another boy had thrown up, and overhearing in the background that the boy had died. "Vomit and illness and all these associations were really horrible.... My imagination was obviously open. Very freaky. I was receiving a lot of information that I did not have the capacity to process. And I was feeling very unprotected ... this paranoia thing. We used to have Sri Lankan maids," who, she fantasized, were planning to kidnap her at night. There were stories about servant uprisings, recalled also by Goli Taraghi in her collection of short stories, *Khāterehā-ye Parākandeh* (Scattered Memories). Taraghi recalls her own "fragmented memories" that their previously loyal maids and their chef, Hassan Agha, confronted her parents demanding their rights immediately after the revolution, arguing "otherwise, why did we have a revolution at all?"

Neda remembers the headline story in the press at the time of a boy named Mehdi who was kidnapped and found dead in a well. (The name Mehdi is symbolically overdetermined: It is a common name, but also refers to the Mahdi, the eschatological savior, the *saoshyant*, the Twelfth Imam, who occulted himself in a well until the end of time, when he will return.)[7] Neda suffered many death nightmares including one that her brother, who was at the time studying in London, had died of an overdose of heroin, even though, she claims, she has no idea where at that point in her life she would have learned the term "heroin overdose." He would die a few years later, but not of an overdose, and not in London. Neda reflects that "death was a major thing, always a major thing," and still today, while death is not there directly, "there is always this somberness in my art, it is gritty, very real" (interview with Neda, LA, February 2009/OB). Neda's story is not unique for her generation.

Death is always present for this generation – children during the revolution and during the Iran-Iraq War – but this artist's anxiety structures are layered also with the anxieties of exile and with still older parental anxieties that children pick up along with the anxieties of the stress of the present: "My mom was sent to England at age six. She too had these abandonment issues, but for different reasons." Raised in an affluent family forced to flee to England with almost nothing after the revolution (her mother had presciently sold some lands just before the revolution), Neda was sent to boarding school. This she experienced as a second exile from the family, even if it was only for weekdays, and responded with self-invented superstitious rituals to keep her parents alive while she was away from them: wearing the same clothing every day, eating exactly the same amount each day in between phone calls from her mother. One day her mother failed to call, and she panicked thinking the mother dead. Although she was a good student in Iran, language problems interfered. As many immigrant teenagers report, "When you are twelve or thirteen, you are too embarrassed to raise your hand and ask ... it was a cultural barrier unless someone had picked up on it and fixed it." Although she had to repeat some of her O levels, she did go on to university. Around that time, her brother, having suffered a nervous breakdown in America and diagnosed with schizophrenia, committed suicide. She claims that because the brother was using so many medications, she herself avoids medication even when suffering bouts of depression. Her mother "is the opposite: she is from the generation that says, oh let's take a Valium to go to sleep, she takes everything." The topic is unbroachable between them. It forms, she says, part of the political and social conscience behind her artwork, which focuses on women and makeup, women and identity, women outside motherhood.

In 1992, Neda returned to Iran for the first time, to visit her parents, who had returned to a quiet and isolated life because they could not afford to stay abroad. "There are still moments when these feelings mix up. When I got to Iran, I was petrified at the airport, everyone had guns in their hands, faces were different, nothing like the Iran I had in [my] mind, and I was so scared. So I go to the window and show my pass-port. The officer, the scary officer, without looking at me, asks, 'name? [esm!]' ... and he doesn't even ask me how to spell it! So there was an immediate sense of connection, a spiritual connection with this man I have nothing in common with, and who scares me; but he knows how to spell my name!" Sedimented anxieties reappear not only across gen-erations but in an exile's fears upon return to a strange and uncannily intimate land.

ii.   *Insults to the Body Politic*

In my dream, a bus full of passengers falls off the mountain road into the abyss. Everyone is scared. Some are so despairing they are willing to die.
    Sarzamin-e Royāyi (Dreamland), blog of female Tehran University professor[8]

In the blog's comments section, a number of people say that the bus symbolizes Iran in the same way as the apartment building in the film *Ejareh Neshinha* ("The Tenants," directed by Dariush Mehrjui, 1986) symbolizes Iran, an enclosed space of marginalization, strife, and repression. More importantly, they see it as a repetition of the 1995 bus transporting members of the Writers Association to Armenia that was sent tumbling into a ravine in a failed mass assassination. The Writers Association (Kanoon-e Nevisandegan-e Iran) has been under constant attack since the 1979 revolution. Serial murders of members were organized by the Ministry of Intelligence during the 1990s. In 1995 when the writers' bus went off the road, the writers survived, the plot was exposed, and the incident became inscribed in the public memory as iconic of the state treatment by the Islamic Republic of Iran of intellectual free thought.[9]

A variant of the bus dream is much more disturbing:

I had a dream I was on a bus and they tell us another bus should come and stick to ours for support. The other bus comes next to us, and we go side-by-side, very fast. Then, slowly, the two buses merge. They mesh into each other. Suddenly they are full of cadavers. Piles of cadavers. We have cadavers on our laps. Everyone is wearing olive green, like soldiers, like the bassejis. And suddenly there is a boy on my lap, ten to twelve years of age, very thin, I feel his bones, alive, and moving, and I realize, oh my God, there is one person who is alive and I can save him, and instead I am so scared and disgusted that, you know, I just push him away. I keep pushing him away. And I wake up trembling. I love kids. Why did I push him away? Death: I often dream of masses, faceless, death. Occasionally individuals dead, mostly masses and faceless death. Also, I felt stuck on the bus, with the boy, for how long? I feel stuck all the time. Yet the bus is going so fast. Too fast. The speed is unbelievable. We cannot stop this thing. The emotional power of stuckness. (December 26, 2008/MF/OB)

The dreamer, a 31-year-old female who left Iran at the age of 24, is a doctor and now lives in the United States. One could speculate that at a surface level many young Iranian professionals who entered the United States in the aftermath of the 9/11 attacks suffered such anxieties because of their immigration status. Given only single entry visas, they were unable to leave the United States without risking their return to their jobs and schools. The émigré feels at home neither here nor there, and the concept of home becomes fluid, liminal, ungrounded. Moreover, like many others she suggests that for participants in youth culture and those from secularized families who were born since the revolution there was already in Iran a sense of internal exile.[10] "I felt like an outsider when I lived in Iran; we were the 'other' all the time, the '*degar-andishan*', the secular ones, the bad ones." Moreover, she insists almost obsessively, since this is well known, "There is an abundance of literary work and poems on the concept [of estrangement, of internal exile], from the classical poetry of Hafez's '*man az diar e habibam na az belad e gharib*' – whose lifelong struggle with censorship and religious authority made him the ultimate '*rend*' [rogue, carouser] – to that of recent poets such as Ahmad Shamlou and Akhavan Sales."

It is to the contemporary context of the dream that one of us (OB) draws attention, the emotional stuckness, of the diasporic but unsettled, neither émigré nor immigrant, status, rather than to the bus or the war surface content. It is the acceleration, the speed, that stikes the other of us (MF), an image of being stuck in a slowed time warp, while both Iran and the diaspora worlds speed on, leaving the dreamer hanging in between.[11] This is the most figural of three dreams reported by this dreamer (see next section) and seems the most disturbed and disturbing, working, like Ibrahim Hatamikia's *Ruband-e Germez* (*The Red Ribbon*) on a figural emotional level rather than a cognitive, linguistic one. In *The Red Ribbon*, three individuals, differently deranged by the war, have to learn to interact despite their disabilities and miscommunications. In the bus dream, natural emotion (love for children) is disturbed, becomes fearsome, and is abjected; the divisions between the dead and living dead are blurred; one is stuck in a world moving too fast, too fast to gain any sense of grounding. If modernity is grounded in the thrill of speed, here (post)modernity speeds out of control, leaving the dreamer caught, stuck, disempowered.

iii.   *Exhausting Labor of Being Stuck*

They both smile, but behind them, instead of the flowers and trees, I see airplanes raining down bombs on the house. Everything is sepia and dark and dusty. I take my eye from the camera and look over it, and all is the garden again. (31-year-old female doctor, 2006)

The same dreamer sees President George W. Bush and his wife. The year was 2006, when talk of a probable United States attack on Iran's nuclear facilities was in the headlines. "They are in our house in Tehran. My parents are going out of their way to be hospitable. We are in the Vanak house where I grew up. It is summer. We are sitting by the swimming pool in the beautiful garden. I am pissed off that my parents are so kind to the Bushes. As if they don't know why they are here. Then they suggest we go on a boat in the pool (we don't have a boat). The couple go on a boat and ask me to take a photo for them. I take the camera and look through the lens. Shocking! They both smile, but behind them, instead of the flowers and trees, I see airplanes raining down bombs on the house. Everything is sepia and dark and dusty. I take my eye from the camera and look over it, and all is the garden again. I look through the lens again. I see airplanes. They keep smiling. I am terrified, but no one else can see what I see. This was one of the most horrifying nightmares I ever had" (July 6/OB). The dream recirculates the filmic device of Mohsen

Makhmalbaf's *Arusi Khuban* (*Marriage of the Blessed*, 1988), in which a disillusioned war photographer sees the contrast between the egalitarian promises of the 1979 revolution and the corruption of the postrevolutionary period with new elites living well, while poverty increases. Each click of the camera shifts time between past and present. The fear of an American attack on Iran was pervasive in 2006 under President Bush's belligerent stance, merging in the dream uneasily with both the imagery of Iraqi bombs falling on Tehran and the good feeling and diasporic relations between the Iranian middle classes and the United States with the ironic wish/denial that the United States intervene in Iran.

Another dream from a young male Iranian circulated online in blogs barely transposes everyday anxieties of being stuck between worlds, trapped by single entry student visa to the United States, unable to predict whether if one travels home or even on a research trip to London or Paris the visa will be renewed. Just after the election of President Barack Obama in which Iranian Americans expressed an unprecedented excitement and participation, this dream was posted and circulated through linked blogs: "We were talking, he and I. He was very nice. He asked me why I am sad. I said, 'President Obama! Do you remember when your grandmother was ill and you flew to Hawaii?' He said yes. I then said, 'You know, we all have grandmothers who are getting old, who we love so much, but we cannot see them before they die.' He looked at me and extended his hand to me and pointed to my passport. I gave it to him. He opened it and wrote something in it, then handed it back to me, and smiled and said, 'You are all set' (last phrase in English)." (November2008/OB)

A 28-year-old engineer in Cambridge, Massachusetts, says he has recurrent dreams about his grandmother's house in Ardebil, a small city in the province of Azerbaijan, where he lived until age 9, when his family moved to Tehran. Ardebil remained intact during the war. For him, the grandmother's house is the only safe home in his dreams. "I dream a lot that I am back in Iran, and cannot get a visa back to the US, and I am stuck, in our Tehran house.... I dream that I am back in my grandma's house, which I love and where I long to be. But once there, I feel awkward. I want to get out. But sometimes, I feel happy. I feel it is mine again, and that makes me happy" (March 2009/OB)

He has another recurrent dream, a common anxiety about exams and schooling, exacerbated by the fear that failure in the high-pressure, highly competitive, exams could result in being sent to the war front. It is about failing the national university entrance exam (*konkur*), "that sick and pathological competition that fucked up our minds and souls.... In my dream, I am a PhD student, but I still have to take the *konkur* [national exams for university admission], I don't know why. And I fail. The anxiety takes my breath away. It is horrible. Sometimes, the place where I am taking the exams, is bombed." The anxieties of the past merge into the anxieties of a present when he too, like many of his generation, asserts "that war never ended. It never will"(March 2009/OB). These themes – war, exam anxiety, home – are repeated by many others in strikingly similar accounts. More importantly, it is the way the dreamers link their dreams to historical and generational traumas that makes them function as dreamwork, either repetitively producing anxiety or occasionally allowing some "working through" into acceptance if not quite resolution.

iv.   Projections and Transferences

Exiles (*avareh*), says the psychiatrist-writer Gholam Hossein Sa'edi, are different from migrants (*muhajir*).... *Avareh* feel themselves paralyzed or suspended in an unreal limbo or purgatory (*barzakh*) unable to move forward into a new life, unable to return to their roots. (Fischer and Abedi, 1990, pp. 253–5)

It seems sudden and new, a fad of the last fifteen years, in both Tehran and California: the passion for therapy and self-help and for television and radio talk shows about one's psychological and relationship problems, about addiction, domestic abuse, and depression. In the 1980s, although depression was recognized among Iranian exiles in California (Good, Good, & Moradi, 1985), therapeutic discourse was also found to be restricted in Persian and somewhat easier in English (Lotfalian, 1996). In Persian complicated taboos inhibited, and lexemes for taboo subjects were not available; both were easier to negotiate in English as a foreign, second, nonfamilial, nonintimate language. Acting out psychological distress frequently took the forms of divorce, spousal murder, self-immolation (often covered with political overtones), and even a dramatic hostage taking. This last, near the Berkeley campus, was deciphered by Lotfalian (1996) as an infiltration of deforming and demeaning media stereotypes processed through the disturbed discourse of an individual in extreme distress.

With the growing popularity of therapy and self-help culture in both Iran and its diasporic community in southern California (where more than twenty-eight Iranian TV channels that also had audiences inside Iran were based), dreams have entered the popular discourse of Iranians in ways different from traditions of religious visions and interpretation, more attuned to displacements of complicated manifestations of traumatic or exilic pasts, as well as more obvious stress and anxiety. Talk shows and celebrity psychologists took hold in the 1990s with public talk of family dysfunction and other psychosocial mental health problems. That films and television soap operas paved the way, and that most Persian language self-help books are translations of American ones, can obscure the history of psychiatry, psychology, and self-help movements in Iran.

One of the more important of the self-help movements in Iran is Parvaresh-e Nirooha-ye Ensani (Training in the Skills of Being Human, PANA) founded by Belgian-educated Ebrahim Khajeh-Nouri and continuing in Tehran today.[12] Its vocabulary has been taken over by the celebrity psychologist Ebrāhim Holākoui in Los Angeles, whose talks can draw audiences of a thousand or more and who is but one of a generation of immigrants who have found new professional careers as psychological counselors. The discourse, the vocabulary, of PANA includes *mehr-talabi* (hunger for compassion, for acceptance) and *pishraft-sanji* (evaluating one's progress). In the decades after the revolution Ebrāhim Khajeh-Nouri's legacy was continued by his students, who created a training curriculum for group leaders or teachers (*ostad*). Two hour sessions in Tehran occur in private houses, rotating among members of a circle. Attendees are mainly women, but there are also sessions for men, for children, and for couples. The first hour is a discussion of concepts: the art of forgiveness, of telling people why you were upset by something they did, emphasizing the "I feel" rather than "you are a bad person" or "you did this to me." In the second hour, participants share their experiences of the past week and how they had practiced the concepts, for instance, forgiving their husbands. This is called *pishraft-sanji* (evaluating progress by reviewing the actions of the week in accord with the PANA concepts). Participants share success stories. There are tea and sweets. The socializing creates good friendships and support networks.

PANA in a way is the opposite tactic to that of psychoanalysis: It avoids the hurt, and rather than digging deep, it teaches letting go, making situations look good, not struggling with repressed emotions. This is the strategy adopted also by Farhang Holākoui and other self-help gurus, both Iranian and American. Holākoui acknowledges his own dilemmas. He was a Baha'i, and so while he loves Iran and wants to contribute and ideally go back to Iran, he cannot. His two California born sons, he says, speak Persian to him and are "totally Irani although they have never been to Iran." But then: "My kids love LA and don't want to go anywhere else." Still, he insists to make the point, "all their friends are Persian, all fifty of their friends," deploying one of his frequent numerical emphatics, a gestural rhetoric not meant to be taken quite literally. Presumably the Iran to which his sons cathect is his Iran, not the actually existing Iran today. A couple of his closest friends were executed in Iran, one on the day Holakoui's younger son was born and after whom the son then was named. He admits, "It has been very hard to cope." Outwardly a very successful man, he changes the subject when PANA in Iran is mentioned, (interviews, LA, February 2009/OB). Perhaps it is not just a desire to project a singular genius without predecessors, but more symptomatically a denial that his picture of Iran is often dated, dependent on people in Iran who call his radio show and present their personal cases detached from social context. There is a tendency to create an image of Iran, through these cases, as a disturbed and maladjusted society, not unlike the rhetoric of Los Angeles Persian language television in the 1980s, described by Hamid Naficy (1993). Indeed women-marriage-and-family therapists at another well-known therapeutic establishment, the Personal Growth Center, with three satellite locations in southern California often talk about the way in which Los Angeles culture of the first generation migrants who arrived at the time of the revolution is often frozen in the Iran of the 1970s, constituting a unique subculture that exists nowhere else.[13] The center's founder left Iran at age 13 with her mother after the revolution and was forced by her mother, a former television anchor in Tehran, to read the Persian poetry of Hafez and Sa'edi every night (and be tested). As rebellion, she jokes, she told her mother, "OK, I'll read Hafez for you, but Iraj Mirza for myself." Iraj Mirza, a Qajar prince, was a late nineteenth-century poet whose satirical poetry and prose are full of sexual references, mocking religious dogmatism and traditional Iranian values. Another of the therapists is a well-known pop song lyricist, and while she observes that lyrics (*taraneh*, using colloquial Persian) are given less status than formal poetry, one wonders whether the *taraneh* do not provide as much entry into therapy as the poetry on which Iranians claim to model their – philosophical and saturnine – emotional dynamics. Pop music from Los Angeles, as well as now rap, rock, and hip hop from Tehran, has become the coin of a transnational Persian youth culture; the former speaks of love; the latter of rebellion and demands for telling things as they are.

While there is faddish cultlike behavior around some of the self-help movement, there are also pragmatism and cynicism among a public long accustomed to not accepting matters at face value. A former Tehran University medical student, now married in Los Angeles to an engineer, gushes about Holākoui, "He saved my life. When I got here, I was homesick and all … I would have gone crazy if it were not for Dr. Holākoui and his programs" (M, LA, February 4, 2009/OB). Holakoui's charisma is palpable. A handsome man in his sixties with salt and pepper hair and gray eyes, he is a consummate verbal performer. His voice is strikingly beautiful. His choice of words is both sophisticated and fun. He peppers his speech with jokes and anecdotes drawn from his radio shows. He has numbers and statistics for everything, even if most are made up: "Twenty percent of people in Iran are depressed but only half of them seek help." He has, says a local Westwood, Los Angeles, bookseller who carries his books, both *hafezeh* and *lafezeh* (the gift of memory and a silver tongue, respectively). He is very smart, but "you know, at the end of the day, he is an *akhund* [preacher]; he was a Baha'i missionary-*akhund* before they kicked him out" (interview, LA, February 2009/ OB). There is something important about all these terms – *hafezeh, lafezeh, akhund, Baha'i*. Baha'ism not only is a modern reform movement that began in Iran in the mid-nineteenth century; it promotes an ecumenism that sees similarities in all the world religions' moral codes and says becoming Baha'i does not entail rejecting one's previous religion, only understanding it in more universalistic terms. An *akhund* is a preacher. In Iran, the role of *akhund* is both admired for its skill in orchestrating emotional moods and its rhetorical powers, and at the same time (as in Plato's rejection of sophists) cynically viewed as a business (*dokan-e mazhab*, shop of religion) and purveyor of empty moralisms. So too, of course, are many California-style self-help gurus. Still, self-help has been a powerful movement from the Norman Vincent Peale (also a religious figure, a Protestant preacher) power of positive thinking, enrolled by the advertising industry, to various therapeutic protocols (the twelve step programs in Alcoholics Anonymous and its Narcotics Anonymous offshoot in Iran [Erami, 2009]), and more recently the evolution of executive and life coaching (Ozkan, 2007).

A 2009 Holakoui event at UCLA attracted a sold-out crowd of more than a thousand. He made a majestic entry – late, of course, and after the hall was packed. People ran toward him, from one end of the hall to the other, to greet him. He barely deigned to return greetings. He walked like a king visiting one of his provinces. This event, organized by UCLA students, is unlike other of his talks: There are a lot of young people here. There is a lot of makeup, hairdos, designer suits and dresses. Young people walk in pairs, with their friends, checking out others, throwing seductive looks at the other girls or guys across the room. To do this they promenade the hall, even crossing paths. Girls almost catwalk, in very high heels, looking away when you look at them. Parents introduce their children to one another in hopes of striking marriage interest. Beginning an hour and a half late, the talk goes on and on, with an intermission only at almost 10:30 p.m.

Holākoui is but one of a generation of immigrants who have found new professional careers as psychological counselors. There is an "elective affinity," Max Weber might have said, between their pragmatic need to earn a living in a new society where previous professional qualifications may be hard to reestablish and their own psychological need to be recognized as cultural translators, both for their own self-esteem and for recognition as father figures for the insecurities and feelings of loss and meaninglessness of fellow migrants. There is simultaneously widespread skepticism toward the Iranian therapy offerings in Los Angeles. The bookseller, a former leftist who now owns a bookstore on Westwood Avenue in Los Angeles, acknowledges both sides, the con-man actor and the taboo-freeing healer: "You know, in this city, no one has identity, all the *motrebha-ye khaiboon Cyrus*" ["buskers of Cyrus Street," an idiom from early twentieth-century Tehran] are now here. And they look for a cultural identity. They are lost. They are fake, full of *pedar soukhteh baazi* [charlatanry]." He names television personalities and political pundits. He goes on: "They go to this or that college and pay and get a one year certificate on *moshāvereh* [counseling] and then they practice as *ravanshenas* [psychologists]."

And yet, Holākoui with his great skills of *hafezeh* and *lafezeh* is "like a *nishtar* [scapel] for the infectious cysts of this society; he releases the pus, so he is doing something" (B interview, LA, February 2, 2009/ OB). A physicist and another therapist concur: Holākoui is not practicing therapy, but he has broken a taboo and popularized the concept of therapy and created a discourse. That itself is a contribution (F&AN, LA, February 4, 2009/OB). He breaks taboos of silence about sexuality, interpersonal relations, marriage and divorce, alienation, addiction, and so on, and allows people to live more freely. He represents the loss that people feel but do not want to forget. He is a father figure, with all the comfort and failure to think for oneself that father figures impose.

v.   Technoremix

New CDs of Kuwaitipour now with gray hair, with headphones on his head like a pop star ... remixed with like "oops oops" ... [and] with keyboards. It has become a hip thing, the Ashura night ... black make-up, black nail polish, very hip (D&OB interview, LA, February 2009)

"I dreamt I was dead: people were wearing white, people were lost and wandering." "I dreamt I was running in a Metro tunnel and the train was chasing me like a missile." "I dreamt it was the day of resurrection." "I dreamt about the man in the chocolate cloak [i.e., President Khātami: *mardi baa abaye chocolati*)." "I dreamt about the Imams and the Prophet."

"I had a dream that we were all in high school, and suddenly a group of people broke in with guns." "I dreamt of my twenty-first birthday when the *komiteh* [morals police] arrested me and my boyfriend; they treated me like a whore. Instead of wanting a bribe, the *komiteh* guy wanted me: it was horrible." "I dreamt Bush attacked Iran; the sounds were those of the Iran-Iraq War." "I dream a lot about air attacks."

There is an abundance of dreams reported by Iranians aged 25–35, filled with war images. There seems to be a rich reservoir of images and sounds recorded in the minds of the then-children whose experience of the war ranged from immediate destruction and bombing, to subtler resonances of the war in children's programs on TV, extracurricular school activities, radio shows, soap operas, slogans wishing death to the Imperialist West they had to practice at school, mobility of exiled peers to and from schools in different cities, anthems and dirges (*nouhehs*), sermons (*khotbeh*) to be reported on for school, and a wide range of visual and auditory input carrying Karbala paradigm concepts and war-related meanings.

"The war never ended," says a 32-year-old female Ph.D. student. "It stayed with us. In our dreams, In our collective memories that would make sense to no one except ourselves. It never ended if you ask me. We internalized it. And yet we were the lucky ones, children of Tehran. Tehran remained intact except for the periods of city bombings. But no Iraqi set foot in Tehran. We only got to see the destroyed buildings, the dust and rubble left after each attack, the hasty phone calls after the all clear siren, to see which relative's house was damaged, to see who was dead and who was alive. At that age, you only know that when the red siren goes off, you have to run to the basements, to the shelter. That's all you know. There were nights where the entire family was sleeping in the basement; in one room. It was so much fun. My grandma would bring lots of snacks and candies and nuts. We would play. It felt as if we had a tree house like in the movies. Lots of imagination was at work I suppose, you see, I was only eight" (OB, 2008/MF).

Fear is intermixed with childhood memories of warmth and pleasure. A young male Ph.D. student recalls, "At the age of 7, I knew the meaning of death. I knew that after that siren goes off – oh, the bloody siren, it still makes me want to puke – but we knew that after that moment, we might die. The house might not exist after a few moments. But still, we were living our lives. People would have weddings and birthday parties disrupted by the sirens. Then they would go back upstairs and continue dancing. It was not like what you see on news footage. We had a life. We too, have childhood memories filled with Cinderella and spaceships you know. But I think we are older souls than our peers in the West. We were too close to death at a very young age, without even knowing. They took away our school playground, and in its place they built a [bomb] shelter. There was construction as long as I remember elementary school, and we had nowhere to play. I detested them for doing that" (R, Cambridge, March 2009/OB).

"We all share a fucked up history," D says. She is commenting on a Persian blog with a post about the children's program series from the 1980s called *Chāgh o Lāghar* (The Fat Man and the Thin Man). It was the story of two SAVAK detectives[14] who consistently failed to block revolutionary activities in the 1970s. There was particularly a 10-year-old boy they could not defeat. The actors wore puppet masks and it aired during the first ten days of February, the annual celebrations of the victory of the 1979 revolution. The blog post shows a photo of the two detectives and directs readers to three YouTube videos of the program. The post itself reads, "It has been a long time that I have buried them in my unconscious. The stupid detective pair we knew from Channel 2 (when the country only had two channels, with only two hours of children's programs per day, always interrupted by the call to prayer and the prayers that followed). This was the special program for *daheye fajr* [the ten days of the month of Fajr (February)]. Today I found three videos of them on YouTube. When I shared it with others on Friendfeed, I received very interesting comments back. Half said they used to be scared of the detectives. Someone said he always wondered why they had human hands (in white gloves) but doll heads. I never had a good feeling about them. The truth is that the feel of most of the cartoons we used to watch was very gray, very gloomy, filled with misery and misfortune. All we knew was orphans who had either lost their mother or father and spent their lives searching for them. Indeed almost all cartoons were about finding a mother who was often in fact dead. And at the end of the day, they never found anything. All the cartoons we watched were filled with ideology: that this world is nothing but misery, and you children are no exception, lest you think there can ever be a happy life awaiting you. This is who we are: the envious generation. We envied, and we envy, and envy, and envy."[15]

Of the 35 comments on this post, most talked about fear and how gray and somber everything was. Some recalled other cartoons: *Hāch* (the bee looking for its lost mother), *Hana* (the farm girl who had to work hard for her living), and *Nell*, the saddest of all with sad music and gloomy colors that turned Paris into a dull village. Nell looks for her mother, who is said to have gone to the city called "Paradise." OB remembers when she was about seven, she got excited when she recognized the pun and that "paradise" meant heaven in English. At the end of each episode, Nell's grandfather would arrive in a carriage to pick her up. His face was invisible; he had long gray hair and a beard. The music made you want to cry. Then there was the show *Ali Koochooloo* (whose father was away at war so he was the man of the house; the images dark and dull); *Pesar-e*

Shojā' and *Ramkal,* both stories about orphans. One brighter comment said, "I used to love the detective pair: I loved their old Jian [the Persian name of the Citroen 2VC or deux cheveaux][16] which was colorful and could fly; I was a boy fascinated with cars back then."

The blog stimulated other memories, and D talked about the slogans students had to shout in the morning. From 7:00 to 7:30 a.m., they would line up in queues, listen to the Qur'an, shout slogans, do exercises, and then march to class. Amid the slogans of "death to" (death to Amrika, to Israel, to Englis [England], to 'anti-*velayat-e faqih*' [the opponents of the doctrine of the guardianship by the theologian], to the imperialist [hardly knowing what the word meant]), "the creepiest slogans," she recalled, "were the ones that came after morning prayers: '*khodāyā!* [oh God! protect the revolution of the twelve imams, protect Imam Khomeini until the reappearance of the Mahdi'] and '*khodāyā! az omre man bekah o bar omre rahbar afza* [oh God! cut off years from my life and give them to extend the years of life of the leader!]. "How on earth would you make a 7-year-old pray to live a shorter life so that the 1,000,000-year-old Khomeini should live longer? One can only laugh. No wonder we are all fucked up" (D, LA, February 2009/OB).

YouTube and blogs provide ever-present availability for reviving sounds and images, increasingly remixed with new accompaniments or contexts. One of the most famous voices of the war was that of the singer Kuwaitipour, who sang the *nouheh* (lament), *chang-e del ahang atash mizanad-naleye eshgh ast o atash mizanad* (my heart's melodica is playing the song of fire; it is the song of love and it burns all). The beautiful poetry in the form of a long *qasideh,* mystical in content (*erfani*), performed in the singing style of religious *nouheh* (laments), worked many youths into a state of willingness to charge across minefields (as "cannon fodder" to explode the mines for infantry following behind, so as not to waste expensive tanks). On the nights of each of the *amaliyāt* (military actions, attacks), there were rituals, they sang together and they reached this *hal* [state of ecstasy] and they just went, these teenagers. This is when they are said to have been given keys to heaven in the event they should become martyrs. Many young Iranians abroad have access to Kuwaitipour on YouTube and listen to it nostalgically. For slightly older Iranians the recirculation of the sound of Kuwaitipour's *nouheh* evokes painful nostalgia. They blame Kuwaitipour for contributing to the deaths of thousands of teenage boys on the battlefield. Still, the beauty of the poetry and the sound of the *nouheh* remain deeply moving. "Of course I know it [Kuwaitipour's *nouheh* renditions]; I listen to it on YouTube," a 20-year-old tells a surprised 30-year-old, who thinks of the younger man as being too young to remember.

There are also video clips of interviews on the battlefront with teenagers. "And they talk; they are thirteen, fourteen, and they are talking about, you know, how nothing matters but what the Imam says, and if he wants me to be here, I should be here. It's just crazy. And these whole interviews are in the form of *nouhehs*; they just turn into *nouhehs*.[17] I don't know how to put it, but there is a lot being done with this music, and also the music in the cities that we grew up with in school, on TV, everywhere, now it is being recycled and remixed. There are new CDs of Kuwaitipour now with gray hair, with headphones on his head like a pop star, and they are remixed with like 'oops oops' because these are very rhythmic. Except back then there were only drums, and now they are remixed with keyboards. And they are sold on the streets.

"So if you go to Tehran on an Ashura night (memorializing the death of Imam Hussain) which is now turned into the Husain party – you know about the whole Hussain party thing – so it has become a hip thing, the Ashura night. Young people go. There are certain spots, Meidan Mohseni, Andishah, and certain other neighborhoods. Young people go there; they wear black. Black is the color of Ashura, traditional *dasteh*, groups of young men chanting dirges about Husain and beating their chests or swinging *zangir* (chains) onto their backs, wearing black shirts. Here young people also dress in black, but they have black makeup, black nail polish, very hip [MF: almost Gothic]. Almost Gothic. But it is also like a meat market, so people exchange phone numbers and everything, and then many really luxury cars are just basically racing in [the neighborhood called] Shahrak-e Gharb and other places. And the loud music is this, except it is techno now" (OB, December 26, 2008/MF). These dreams and figurations in their variants, displacements, and repetitions circulate like jagged-edged and turbulent shards across the generations of children born after the revolution and across the gaps between parents and children.

III.   Intergenerational Transfer

saroomad zemestoon	The winter is over
shekofteh baharoon	The spring has blossomed
gol e sorkh e khorshid baz oomad	the red flower of sun is back
o shab shodeh gorizoon	and the dark night is running away
kooha laleh zaran	The mountains are covered with tulips
laleh ha bidaran	The tulips are wide awake
to kooha daran gol, gol, gol,	In the mountains flowers, flowers, flowers
aftab o mikaran	and "the Sun," they are planting

(Leftist song refunctioned by
Mir-Hussein Mousavi campaign
May–June 2009)[18]

In the contested June 2009 tenth presidential elections and its after-math, something dramatic happened. Youth and their parents joined in the mass demonstrations of June and July 2009 against the manipulation of the tenth presidential elections.[19] It was a moment of reconciliation (*āshtī*) between generations who had been unable to speak.[20]

In the streets, parents and children refunctioned slogans and songs from 1979. A leftist song used by Mir Hossein Mousavi's campaign for president at first outraged leftists and secularists around the world, who accused him of hijacking a song for which many had been executed dur-ing his prime ministership in the 1980s. A month later, when Mousavi proved a courageous leader who stood by the protesters after Khāmenei declared Ahmadinejād the winner a few hours after the election polling stations closed, many leftists willingly joined his cause, happily allowing their anthem to become one of the main symbols of the "Green Wave" reform movement.

For a long time, the songs and anthems and sermons of the war-time were the stuff of memories and dreams. They belonged in "school textbooks, dull and boring; where were fed lies about our history," says one of our informants, a 26-year-old graphic designer whose active involvement in election campaigns forced her to flee to Europe after the June 2009 coup. "Those concepts like martyr, brother, sister, solidar-ity, sacrifice, they all belonged to our fathers and their idealistic dreams of changing the world when we were not even born. The word martyr always reminded me of obligatory school anthems, of pictures of com-manders and baseejis after whom streets were named. They were differ-ent. They were the past. They didn't use the Internet. They didn't blog. They were another generation. And now, suddenly, I am using the word, choking, calling for my sisters and brothers who are dying on the street, who are 'martyrs.' And I am so willing to use this word now, with pride. Because now you see, we have dreams too. Dreams to fight for. [Our fathers] always accused us of being carefree, of being indifferent, of only obsessing with MTV and Hollywood. Now you see, we have dreams to fight for. We want our votes back. We want our country back. And for that, we are happy to die" (R, London, September 2009/OB). Yet, "those memories were always in the background" a 27-year-old female student in physics tells me. "No matter how much we hated the official narra-tive of the revolution and so forth, I think part of us always envied our parents' generation for having had those ideals. Maybe we had waited for this moment all our lives."

In the light of what happened in summer 2009, it is strikingly interesting how not only inside Iran, but also among the diaspora, the same Khāmushi generation is slowly finding an anchor around a com-mon voice. They insist that they are a united voice "but with different demands and hopes." A 30-year-old female graduate student puts it this way: "We are all green, but green has different shades. This is our chance to educate and practice precisely this – that we are different shades of green; but we are all green." "Whatever happens, we have come a long way and achieved a lot," a young architect tells me in London, sitting among fifteen peers who have gathered to plan a protest against Ahmadinejād's trip to the UN in September 2009. Another friend interrupts him. "You know, what really strikes me is that the concept of 'each citizen is one medium' has come true." For the Green Wave, the slogans and songs, at least, have taken on renewed emotional charges as the Islamic Republic sheds its republican pretentions for a more coercively Islamic state that openly advocates ideological commitment (*ta'ahod*) over expertise (*takhasos*), being a "servant of God" over being a citizen, and that targets youth culture as not merely frivolous (*bidard*, without pain) but an addictive disease (Westoxification, *gharbzadegi*), rails against cultural invasion through the media (*tahajom-e farhangi*) and a moral crisis (*bouhran-e akhlaq*), and makes statistically charted "deviance" studies (of rates of addiction, suicide, runaway girls, depression) that are stamped "secret" as matters of national security. Even the Ministry of Education as early as 2000 worriedly reacted to surveys about the extent of depression and suicide attempts among the youth by urging elementary school girls to begin wearing brightly colored clothes, and by organizing festivals of laughter and joy (*jashn-e khande va shadi*) to counter the melancholia discipline of puritan state ideology. Surveys of the youth are stamped "secret" and "national security" matters, and Khosravi argues (2007) that these surveys are in fact the documentation of the result of their own unceasing emphasis on the dangers of cultural invasion (*tahajom-e farhang*) from the West and emphasis on the youth as vulnerable targets of Western seduction who need constant correction (*eslah*) and guidance (*ershad*) through such agencies as the Ministry of Islamic Guidance.

The third generation (*nasl-e sevvom*) of the Islamic revolution in Iran, born after 1981, is fractured into parts: the exiles, the emigrants (born abroad), the *baseeji* or *hezbullāhis* (paramilitary supporters of the Islamic Republic), and the chafing middle-class youth. All but those born abroad are deeply, if differentially, marked by the Iran-Iraq War. The *khāmushi* generation or the "sixties" (1360 [1980s]) generation, in one of its fractions also calls itself "the unfortunate generation," "the burnt generation [*nasl-e soukhteh*], the envious "generation." The third generation has no memories from before the revolution and today constitutes some three-quarters of the population. Born after Khomeini's call for producing children to empower the army of Islam, they are the guinea pigs of the Islamic Republic of Iran's cultural revolution and casualties of Iran's poorly planned social revolution. After the Iran-Iraq War, Iran reversed its natalist policies and the rate of population growth dropped from a wartime high above 4 percent to 1.5 percent. The population explosion of the 1990s has created a crisis in education and employment, produced high levels of crime and drug use, polarized the polity, and resulted in a brain drain with annual emigration applications exceeding 150,000, the majority with university education, and 38,000 working as illegals in Japan in the late 1990s (Sassen, 1998, p. 66). The social crisis, with its mental health burdens (depression, drug use), is recognized by the Iranian government as a moral crisis (*bouhran-e akhlaq*).

In understanding the laments of the different generations and their contrastive fractions, historical references and the delayed public circulation of memoirs and memories become catacoustically powerful. For many Iranians now in their forties, the experiences chronicled in Marjane Satrapi's comic book and film *Persepolis* read like their own diaries, but these experiences are quite different for a younger generation who were university students in the euphoric days of hope in the late 1990s under President Khātami, when from the office of the president there were calls for strengthening civil society, public sphere debate, dialogue of civilizations, and in general taking spirit of change away from repressiveness and for whom the crushing of liberal hopes in the elections of President Ahmadinejād occurred as disillusionment and despair.

For men born in the 1960s, the war was experienced on the front or in political prisons. Memoirs of war veterans and political prisoners and accounts of the large-scale massacres of 1982 and 1988 of leftist or secular reformers have begun to recirculate after twenty years of silence, especially in the aftermath and as a reaction to the June 2009 elections.[21] Women of this generation either stayed and lived a *Persepolis 2* life in Iran (Satrapi, 2009) or left Iran in the 1980s.

All of these gendered and fractional experiences, echoes of war, oppression, fear, anxiety, and displacement, manifest in dream and dreamlike life-worlds years later, including in therapy groups in California.

M. dreams he is taking his visiting mom and sister to a city that feels like somewhere in the central part of the United States, a place he has never been. There is a temple. Very calm. Pilgrims come and go. Then Ahmadinejad and family arrive! M. starts to talk with him. Friendly. Giving him a chance. He has vivid images of his face, of the lines around his eyes. He even says Ahmadinjead was funny and personable. Then Ahmadinejad says something like "for managing the country, it doesn't really matter if a few people get killed." M. explodes. Starts swearing and calling him names. Really bad. He can't stop. Ahamdinejad looks at him as if he doesn't hear him. Smiles even. Ignores. The scenes shift to New York City, in front of the United Nations, where Ahmadinejad is being filmed and photographed. In the background, M. is standing, with fists up in the air, swearing and yelling, but no one hears him. He is invisible to them. He wakes up shaking. Too much anger. Even when he recalls the dream, he is infuriated

(July 2009, i.e., just after the contested presidential election and the crushing of protests in the streets of Tehran and cities all over Iran)

IV.   Conclusions

Everyone is on Fluxetin (Prozac). (Psychiatry resident, Tehran, 2009/OB)

"Human rights? leave these things alone; they make you sad … I don't want to think about these things." (MIT graduate student, summer 2009)

Work on the self has been a psychocultural thematic of Iranian reform movements over the last century and a half, but perhaps never in as intense and differentiated ways as in the aftermath of the 1977–9 revolution, the eight-year-long Iran-Iraq War (1980–8), the second wave of postrevolution emigration abroad, and the interweaving of satellite television and the Internet into the fabric of Iranian and Persian culture. It is perhaps no surprise that so many of the second and third generations, particularly in the diaspora, but also their age mates in Iran, should be turning to psychology as both therapy and profession.

Persian nightmares often occur as (i) metadreams (I dream I was dreaming [*khab didam ke khab mididam*]) that express a sense of unreality about the real or bewilderment in reading the signs of the real (*khabe gong didam*);[22] (ii) catastrophic disruptions of ordinary life plans, sustaining feelings of being unsettled whether in the turmoil of postwar Iran or that of exile and migration into the diaspora; and as (iii) remixes of traditional religious imagery, 1980s Iran-Iraq War sounds and imagery, and allusions to the violence of the 1990s culture wars.

Dreams occur as repetitions, displacements, and prefigurations. In Persian, nightmares (Arabic, *kabus*; Persian *khāb-e bad, khab-e narahat, khoftak or khoftu, faranjak, bakhtak,* and many other colloquial variants) are described as causing feelings of suffocation, strangulation, weight on one's chest, paralysis, fright attacks, anxious dreaming, and sadness-increasing dreams (*ghamasa, khab-e narrahat va gham afza*).[23] Both "sadness" (*gham*) and "dream" (*khab*) are loaded terms, the first with emotional roots both in the philosophies of melancholia and stoicism and in the Shi'ite passion plays of Karbala in which the heroes are abandoned and made to feel as strangers (*garib*), hidden or occulted (*gheib*), amid the corruptions of the world and injustices of the hegemonic; the second (*khab*) with emotional roots in the moral discourses of purity amid a corrupt world, the visions of prophets and poets that cannot be conveyed to ordinary people because of the emotional layeredness of the imagery, the philosophical training required to counter emotional chaos, the deafness and unwillingness of people to know, or the psychological defenses of scarring and need for survival.

Catastrophe disrupts life expectations, creating layered psychologies and personas, multiple consciousness, feelings of alienation and fracturing, disseminating anxiety, guilt, and feelings of helplessness about the inability to put the genie-jinn back whence it was contained. Much of this inability is not personal, but social. Dreams come as repetitions, displacements, and prefigurations of the social fracturing. They come as remixes of cultural bits and bytes: childhood political chants in school, ephemeral pop songs, and wartime radio emergency warnings that inscribe generational differences into the depths of the autonomous reflexes of the body. Their inscriptions are also to be found in a wide array of cultural detailing: in blogs, in YouTube videos, in television psychology talk shows, in videos of interviews with teenage soldiers in the war formatted as religious *nouheh* (mourning chants), as music compact discs with recycled and remixed old *nouheh* and *sorood*s (martial anthems), in the Goth-like recycling of the black dress for Ashura with black makeup and nail polish, and technomusiclike syncopation to old wartime *soroods*,[24] and dreams with their sounds of sirens, battlefield images, signs of the undead, of being chased by trains and other noisy machines, of explosions.

The sexuality of nightmares is a theme that is highly dramatized in the techniques of interrogation and torture used by the Iranian state. Anyone paying the least attention cannot fail to be impressed that reports by victims of interrogation techniques in Iranian prisons always focus on making one confess to sexual deviances, crimes, or indiscretions, and torture escalates to involve various forms of rape. Rape is devastating and bears the profoundest stigma to women and to men alike. It is intended to break people. Iranians often like to claim melancholy as a distinctive tap root of philosophical Persian culture, but Europe too in the Baroque period saw melancholy as a sign of gravitas and realism The intertwined mandrake-like roots of melancholia in the Islamic and European worlds go back to the humoral theory (in Persian, called *junani* [Greek] medicine) of balancing the four humors, and of melancholia as the overabundance of the black (*melas*) bile (*kholes*), hence "melancholia." Hippocrates in the fifth–fourth century B.C. diagnosed a symptomatology of melancholia. Ishaq (Isaac) ibn Imran (d. 908) wrote of the mood disorder *malikhuliya*, and Ali ibn Abbas al-Majusi (d. 982) wrote of a personality disorder in which the "victim behaves like a rooster and cries like a dog, the patient wanders among the tombs at night, his eyes are dark, his mouth is dry, the patient hardly ever recovers and the disease is hereditary" (see Youssef,

Youssef, & Dening, 1996). Ibn Sina (Avicenna) in the eleventh century identified phobias and paranoias associated with the melancholic mood disorder.

The "Karbala paradigm" and Persian passion plays have been analyzed as, in many ways, parallel to the Lutheran Baroque theater as analyzed by Benjamin; and more generally Persian cultural politics over the course of the twentieth century turned upon the struggle between public rituals that emphasize melancholy and those that emphasize happiness, optimism, and future orientation (Fischer, 1973, 1980). The rituals of Muharram, memorializing the death of Imam Hossein on the battlefield of Karbala, also include rhythmic chanting, chest beating, marching, drums, and high theatrical and gender-charged emotion.[25] High-ranking clerics would routinely dismiss this display of emotion and the preaching that went with it (*rouzeh-khani*, sermons that always begin and end with stories of Karbala and weeping) and emphasize instead the philosophical realism and sadness of living in this corrupt world. Reza Shah Pahlavi in the 1930s and 1940s pursued an explicit national goal to rid Iran of excessive sadness rituals, replacing them with civic rituals of joyousness, emphasizing the optimism and happiness in the ancient Zoroastrian heritage of Iran.[26] After the Islamic revolution a counterideology attempted to repress music and color, expanding the Karbala paradigm as an all-encompassing stoicism for a regime feeling itself embattled and claiming to fight for justice in a corrupt world. Khomeini used his own public unsmiling visage as an emblem of gravitas and anti–Western consumer capitalism (Fischer 1983). Culturally, the Iran-Iraq War provided new venues and forms for reinforcing the Karbala theme, from rituals to put soldiers into a *hal*, an ecstasy of willingness to sacrifice themselves running through minefields or facing the fire of Iraqi mortars; to "sacred defense films" showing footage from the front to citizens at home framed in Karbala terms, focusing little on the Iraqi enemies, but rather on the struggles over the self, to conquer fear, to become strong, to regard death as incidental to one's spiritual trajectory (Sorabi, 1995; Varzi, 2006).

But clinicians have noticed since the 1980s, despite the effervescence of many aspects of Iranian life, that all too many young people, especially among the religiously committed, present signs of dysphoria (Sanati/MF2007). "Everyone is on Prozac," say doctors in Iran (Behrouzan, 2010b). One says, "In my psychiatric rotation, I had at least two to three successful suicide admissions per night. I cannot say there is an epidemic of clinical depression, but there is an epidemic of dysphoria, of social hopelessness" (B, Tehran, 2008/OB). A

33-year-old doctor turned filmmaker who is on antidepressants says his generation's depression is not existential, but "I have very simple reasons to be depressed: my best friends have left the country one after another; there is no public space we can meet new friends or girls, and of course there is our intergenerational struggles with our parents and their values – isn't that enough to drive you crazy?" (AA, 2008/OB). The stresses of long years of pressured study for the *konkur* [27] and living double lives radically different in private and in public take their toll. Calculated use of drugs is often a "rational" strategy in a setting where there is "no solution: I can't change the society, I can't change my parents, I can't change this government, and if I don't want to leave my country, I have to make a decision how to cope with all of this, that's what the pill does for me."[28]

NOTES

1 The date 1360s in the Iranian Shamsi calendar corresponds to the 1980s in the Common Era calendar.

2 Gholam Hossein Sa'edi (1936–85) was a renowned writer, trained as a psychiatrist in Tabriz (where he wrote his dissertation "Social Causes of Psychoneuroses in Azerbaijan") and Tehran, where he did his residency at Ruzbeh Hospital. His monograph on the zar cult among pearl divers in the Persian Gulf (*Ahl-e Hava*, "People of the Air") is a classic study of ritual and mental health; his screenplay for the celebrated film *Gav* ("The Cow") is a study of grief gone awry in a village after the death of a cow, used as an allegory for conditions of repression in Iran. But the reference here is also to his exile, when he first wrote a sarcastic play, *Othello in Wonderland,* in which Islamic censorship in a step-by-step fashion turns Shakespeare into a religious passion play, and then eventually fell into depression and drank himself to death.

3 They podcasted six programs between January and May 2009: http://stillness-radio.blogspot.com/. Each podcast opens with a replay of the sirens of city bombings in the 1980s.

4 *The Complete Book of the Medical Arts* (*Kitab Kamil as-Sina'a at-Tibbiyya,* also known as *The Royal Book* (*Kitab al-Maliki*) and known in Europe as *Liber Regalis* or *Regalis Dispositio.*

5 "Its victim behaves like a rooster and cries like a dog, the patient wanders among the tombs at night, his eyes are dark, his mouth is dry, the patient hardly ever recovers and the disease is hereditary." Technically this is a description of clinical lycanthropy (delusion of becoming a dog or wolf or other animal). The dog is a contested symbol in Iran. In Zoroastrianism the four-eyed dog is used in funerary rituals to see into the next world, to discern whether the body is in fact dead, and to ward off the demons of impurity. Zoroastrians take care of dogs, while in many Islamic communities the dog is ill-treated. In the Shi'ite compendia of ritual rules put out by anyone claiming to be an ayatuallah, the

dog is *najes* (unclean), as are Jews and Zoroastrians. But in the Qur'an (18:9–26) the good dog guards the seven sleepers in the cave (a fragmentary transformation of the Seven Sleepers of Ephesus). The dog was made a powerful modern symbol of urban repression and abandonment by the writer Sadegh Hedayat in his famous short story "Sag-e Velgard" ("Abandoned Dog"). The duality of al-Majusi's rooster-dog image resonates well with the contemporary feelings that there are "colorful clothes but our insides are all black" (and inversely memories of learning to dress in black or drab colors for school, but lie to teachers about how one lives at home, and what one really believes) and the constant, wearying friction between public/private, *zahir/batin*, "having no voice, we want a voice." But, as we will argue, over the past decades there has been a dramatic change from philosophical, poetic, or parable indirection of expression to psychiatric and self-help psychological address of the wounds of revolution, war, and emigration.

6 MF interview with Dr. Muhammad Sanati, 2007.

7 The imagery of the Twelfth Imam withdrawn into a well and into metaphysical occultation draws on the ancient Iranian motif of the Saoshyant, the Zoroastrian eschatological savior who is withdrawn into a sacred lake. The press circulated the story of the boy. Whether true or not, it is always already infiltrated with traditional religious imagery in a revolution that traded on such imagery. The Islamic Republic of Iran still employs such imagery in weekly sermons (*khutbeh*) and political discourse, particularly that of Ayatullah Mesba-Yazdi, of the imminent return of the Mahdi from his well of occultation, and of his follower and enabler President Ahmadinejad.

8 Blog URL is available on authors' files.

9 It also repeats the public memory of the death of Samad Behrangi, the author of the children's story for adults from the late Pahlavi period before the revolution, *Mahi Siah Kuchilu* (*The Little Black Fish*, 1968). The story is of a fish who leaves the security of his local stream to explore the world down to the sea. It was read as an allegory of breaking out of the parochialism and ideology of Iran. An Azeri, Behrangi preferred writing in Turkish but translated his work into Persian because state law forbids publishing in Azeri. An educational reformer, Behrangi taught for eleven years in rural schools in Azerbaijan, introducing village children to books and the idea of libraries. He often crossed out words in textbooks that referred to objects and concepts from abroad that were unavailable to the children's experience, or were archaic, replacing them with ones that were more appropriate. Behrangi is said to have died in a swimming accident in the Aras River between Azerbaijan and Armenia. A famous poem of the time mocks the official story: Why would you voluntarily swim, Samad, in the freezing river? It was widely believed the accident was arranged by the secret police. He, too, like his fish, dies for his curiosity and openness to the world. He too, like the 1990s writers' bus, is on the way to Armenia, or betwixt and between Armenia and Iran. The Aras River flows from Erzerum in Turkey along the borders of Turkey, Armenia, Iran, and Azerbaijan. It became the border between the Persian and Russian Empires by the Treaties of Gulistan and Turkmenchay. A number of Iranian communists escaped to the Soviet Union during the Cold War across the Aras.

10 See, for instance, Shahram Khosravi's 2007 ethnography of youth culture in the Shahr-e Garb neighborhood of middle-class Tehran, and also for an earlier generation Taghi Modarressi's essay on émigrés, "Writing with an Accent" (*Chanteh*, 1992), quoted in Rahimi (2012).

11 See also the discussion of the term *avareh*, this emotional purgatory of being able to go neither back nor forward among exiles in the 1980s in Fischer and Abedi (1990).

12 See http://maktabpanah.com; http://www.farhangsara.com/fnamdaran_iran_khajehnori.htm.

13 See the M.A. thesis by Talieh Rohani, which differentiates (i) generations of migrants and of children of migrants, (ii) double migrants (first to Europe or Canada, then to California) versus direct migrants, and (iii) local media contexts in San Francisco versus Los Angeles or Washington, D.C. She focuses on the difference between the young Iranian-Swedish migrants to California in San Francisco (who have a playful, open, and somewhat cavalier attitude toward authenticity) who staff Bebin-TV, on the one hand, and the LA based culture, on the other hand (more concerned with purity of Persian culture, nostalgia for modernist Iran, and concern with material wealth). A third underexplored contrast is with the Washington, D.C., community, on which, however, see also Nahal Naficy's 2007 dissertation.

14 The secret police under Muhammad Reza Shah Pahlavi was called Sazeman-e Ettela'at va Amniyat-e Keshvar (Intelligence and Security Organization of the Country, or SAVAK). After the 1979 revolution, it was called Sazman-e Ettela'at va Amniat-e Melli-e Iran (Information and Security Organization of the People of Iran, or SAVAMI).

15 See http://zebelkhan.wordpress.com/2008/12/07/chagholagharism/.

16 Manufactured in Iran in a joint venture between Citroën and Iran National until 1979, when it was continued by a nationalized Iran National without Citroën. Designed as a low-cost, reliable, simple to maintain, and off-road car, the *deux chevaux vapeur* or "two steam horses" (the horsepower taxable rating) was produced in France from 1949 to 1990. The prototype, TPV (Toute Petite Voiture, "Very Small Car"), with a Bauhaus inspired body, was built before World War II and was hidden from the Nazis during the wartime occupation. It was originally designed for farmers to drive goods to market on unpaved roads or even across plowed fields, and to encourage the French to adopt cars. Redesigned after the war, it became phenomenally popular as well as the butt of many jokes.

17 Morteza Avini, the filmmaker of the Sacred Defense war films, sent back weekly clips of the battlefront to be shown on television during the Iran-Iraq War. He carefully edited and framed them in the mystical terms of self-sacrifice for God. See Naficy, 2007; Sorabi, 1995; Varzi, 2006; Zeyadabadinejad, 2009; see also for more recent films Danesh, 2007, on how war and spiritual films are inflected under the presidencies of Khatami and Ahmadinejad.

18 The references are to the genealogy of leftist struggles from the *nezhat-e jangali* (forest movement) led by Mirza Kouchak Khan (1914–21) to the 1971 Mujaheddin attack on a police station in the Caspian village, Siakhal,

that signaled the beginning of a small guerrilla activity against the rule of Muhammad Reza Shah Pahlavi. The verses continue:

> In the mountains
> his heart is alive and awake
> he carries in his hands
> flowers and wheat and a gun
> in his heart
> *jaan, jaan, jaan,* [life, soul; full of life, zest for life]
> he carries a forest of stars
> his lips are the smile of light
> his heart is all flames of love
> his voice is a spring in the mountains and
> his memory is like the *ghazal* of the farthest forests.

19 This was followed by violent repression of objection, including forced confessions in front of television cameras of intellectuals and reform leaders (many originally revolutionaries thirty years ago), all under the self-fulfilling allegation that a "velvet revolution" was developing against the regime. Initially meant as a reference to U.S.-supported democratic movements in Ukraine, Serbia, and Georgia, it gradually expanded to orders that all academics should cease any interactions with scholars abroad, that degrees earned abroad would not be recognized, and that intellectuals and reform leaders could be punished for introducing into Iran books by Max Weber, Jurgen Habermas, and Talcott Parsons.

20 *Qahr-ashti*: *Qahr* is the state of a fight when neither side is talking to the other and often requires a third party to help them reconcile (*ashti*). In this case, it is not so much that they did not talk at all, but that the shared experiential referent points were missing. Parents often expressed displeasure at how much time the younger generation spent on the Internet, seeing it as frivolous. After the Internet and cell phones proved their worth in getting images and information about the June–February 2009 demonstrations out of the country around government efforts at censoshp, the parental generation embraced the skills of their children. Inversely revolutionary songs that seemed inappropriate nostalgia for aspirations long denied by the revolution, these songs of hope and defiance gained salience for the younger generation in ways they could never have known previously.

21 For example, former People's Mujahedin member Iraj Mesdaghi's four volume *Memoirs of Prison 1981–1991* (published in Stockholm, 2004), and his collection of prison songs about the massacres of 1988, *Bar Sagehi-e Tabieda-ye Kanaf* (2007).

22 *Khab gong-e didam* (glossed as "mute dreams" in the title of *Mute Dreams, Blind Owls and Dispersed Knowledges* [Fischer 2004]) refers to (a) that moment of bewilderment when waking from a dream and attempting to decipher the images of the dream and separate the present feeling of the dream from the waking sense of presentness; or to (b) prophetic vision images or divine language that the prophet feels cannot really be translated to ordinary people, who hear but do not listen, who look but cannot see. The filmmaker Mohsen

Makhmalbaf uses the phrase as the title of his early collection of stories and essays on film, and indirectly it also underlies Abbas Kiarostami's philosophy that he does not care whether you fall asleep during his films as long as days or weeks later the film is still resonating and its puzzles are being worked out by the viewer. In a famous poem, Farrokh Farroghzad opens with a wish for deliverance, *khab didam ke khab mididam* ("I dreamt that I was dreaming"), but in her poem there is less reflexivity than a form of the type 3 dream. A better, simple example of a metastructure, is in Makhmalbaf's film *Arusi Khuban* (1989), about a shell-shocked war photographer, whom camera shutter clicks toggle between seeing the promise of social justice of the early days of the revolution and the 1980s decay of the ideals and practices of the revolution into legitimation for injustice, inegalitarian practices, and ouright corruption. *Arusi Khuban* (a marriage made in heaven) refers to the photographer's marriage to the daughter of a wealthy high-living merchant, for whom the photographer's revolutionary purity is a badge of respect and protection in the corruption of the early postwar period, and whose hypocrisy exacerbates the derangement of shell shock and posttraumatic stress disorder.

23 *Khoft* is a colloquial form of *khab* (dream), and *-u* and *-tak* are diminutives; *bakhtak* has an even stronger connotation than the etymologies of *kaabus* and nightmare; *faranjak* (perhaps from *faranji*, foreigner, Frenchman). The diminutive may refer to the ephemerality of these acute, severe, and recurring frights, which nowadays we try (not very successfully) to track in rapid eye movement versus non-REM sleep).

24 Particularly in Shahrak-e Gharb (see later discussion), Meidan-e Mohseni, Andishah, and certain other neighborhoods, such fun making on a central day of the annual ritual cycle commemorating the death of Imam Hussain at the Battle of Karbala, is, of course, rebellious. But its status as real parody as opposed to just finding an occasion to have fun is ambiguous. Above all, it is an intensification of the fine line of acknowledging religion and objecting to its being turned into a policing mechanism by those in power to maintain power, and to attempts, as Khosrovi puts it, to criminalize youth culture.

25 It was often remarked in the 1970s that when the authorities wished to prevent Ashura *dastehs* from using knives on flagellation chains or for cutting their foreheads, if they prevented women spectators from lining the street, the men would not engage in these ecstatic, but also macho, bloodletting rites.

26 See Fischer 1973 and 2004 for analyses of the dialectic between happiness and sadness in the ways Zoroastrian and Muslim sensibilities are deployed. The former provides an account of the 1930s under Reza Shah. The latter provides an account of how Muslims and Zoroastrians use the stories of the Shahnameh differently, and how mystical Muslims and fundamentalist ones read those stories.

27 The path to higher education starts with an intense competition held once a year, with more than ten applicants for each seat available, and the competition to be admitted into the best schools much more intense. Many spend a year or two in near-isolation preparing. Male candidates work under the

additional pressure of having to serve in the military if they are not admitted to university. Exam preparation has become a marker of class divisions as well with expensive private tutorial businesses promising to prepare students for the exams.

28 On the calculated use of antidepressants and other mood drugs to remain "high-functioning" in the United States, see Kramer (1993) and Greenslit (2007); for use more generally to be "dependent-normal" see Dumit, (2012). Valium, of course, was widely prescribed for suburban housewife anomie in Canada and the United States in the 1950s and 1960s.

REFERENCES

Behrouzan, O. (2014). Writing Prozāk Diaries in Tehran: Generational Anomie and Psychiatric Subjectivities. *Culture, Medicine and Psychiatry* (under review).

(2010a). An epidemic of meanings: The significance of history, gender and language in HIV/AIDS epidemics. In J. Klot & V. K. Nguyen (Eds.), *The fourth wave: Violence, gender, culture and HIV in the 21st century* (pp. 319–45) New York: SSRC, and Paris: UNESCO.

Behrouzan, O. (2010b). Prozàk diaries: Postrupture subjectivities and psychiatric futures. Unpublished doctoral dissertation, Massachusetts Institute of Technology.

Danesh, M. (2007). The rule of the game: 25th international Fajr film festival (February 21, 2007). *Iranian Film Quarterly.* Retrieved from http://www. filminternational.com/archives/articles. asp?id=18

Dumit, Joseph. (2012). *Drugs for life.* Durham, NC: Duke University Press.

Erami, N. (2009). The carpet bazaar in Qum. Unpublished doctoral dissertation, Columbia University.

Fischer, M. M. J. (2009). Iran and the boomeranging cartoon wars: Can public spheres at risk ally with public spheres yet to be achieved? *Cultural Politics,* 5, 27–62.

(2004). *Mute dreams, blind owls, and dispersed knowledges: Persian poesis in the transnational circuitry.* Durham, NC: Duke University Press.

(1993). Five frames for understanding the Iranian revolution. In K. Kenneth (Ed.), *Critical moments in religious history* (pp. 173–97) Macon, GA: Mercer Press.

(1989). Legal postulates in flux: Justice, wit and hierarchy in Iran. In D. Dwyer (Ed.), *Law and politics in the Middle East* (pp. 115–42) New York: J. F. Bergin.

(1987). Repetitions in the revolution. In M. Kramer (Ed.), *Shi'ism, resistance, revolution* (pp.117–32) Boulder, CO: Westwood Press.

(1983). Imam Khomeini: Four ways of understanding. In J. Esposito (Ed.), *Voices of Islamic resurgence* (pp. 150–74). New York: Oxford University Press.

(1980). *Iran: From religious dispute to revolution.* Cambridge, MA: Harvard University Press.

(1973). Zoroastrian Iran: Between myth and praxis. Unpublished doctoral dissertation, University of Chicago.

Fischer, M. M. J., & Abedi, M. (1990). *Debating Muslims: Cultural dialogues between tradition and postmodernity.* Madison: University of Wisconsin Press.

Good, M. J. D., & Good, B. (1988). Ritual, the state and the transformation of emotional discourse in Iranian society. *Culture, Medicine, and Psychiatry,* 12, 43–63.

Good, B., Good, M. J. D., & Moradi, R. (1985). The interpretation of Iranian depressive illness and dysphoric affect. In A. Kleinman & B. Good (Eds.), *Culture and depression* (pp. 369–428). Berkeley: University of California Press.

Greenslit, Nathan. (2007). Pharmaceutical relationships: Intersections of illness, fantasy, and capital in the age of direct-to-consumer marketing. Unpublished doctoral dissertation, MIT.

Khosravi, Shahram. (2007). *Young and defiant in Tehran.* Philadelphia: University of Pennsylvania Press.

Kramer, Peter D. (1993). *Listening to Prozac.* New York: Viking Press.

Lotfalian, M. (1996). Working through psychological understandings of the diasporic condition. *Ethos,* 24, 36–70.

Mesdaghi, Iraj. (2004). *Na zistan na marg* ("Neither life nor death"): Prison memoirs in four volumes: The descent of sunrise; The sorrow of the phoenix; Restless rasberries; Till the dawn of grapes. 1850 pp. Stockholm (in Farsi).

(2007). *Bar Sagehi-e Tabieda-ye Kanaf.* Stockholm (in Farsi).

Naficy, H. (1993). *The making of exile cultures: Iranian television in Los Angeles.* Minneapolis: University of Minnesota Press.

Naficy, H. (2007). Cinema and national identity: A social history of Iranian cinema in the 20th century. Unpublished manuscript.

(2011–13). *A social history of Iranian cinema,* 4 volumes. Durham, NC: Duke University Press.

Naficy, N. (2007). Persian miniature writing: An ethnography of Iranian organizations in Washington, D.C. Unpublished doctoral dissertation, Rice University.

Ozkan, E. (2007). Executive coaching: Crafting a versatile self in corporate America. Unpublished doctoral dissertation, Massachusetts Institute of Technology.

Rahimi, Nasrin (2012). Translating Taghi Modarressi's writing with an accent. In B. Aghaei & M. Ghanoonparvar (Eds.), *Iranian languages and culture: Essays in honor of Gernot Ludwig Windfuhr,* Costa Mesa, CA: Mazda.

Rohani, T. (2009). Nostalgia without memory: Iranian-Americans, cultural programming and Internet television. Unpublished master's thesis, Massachusetts Institute of Technology.

Sa'edi, G. H. (1345 [1966]). *Ahl-i hava.* Tehran: Chupkhaneh Daneshgah.

(1350 [1971–2]). *Gav: A story for a film.* Tehran: Aghah.

Sassen, Saskia. (1998). *Globalization and its discontents.* New York: New Press.

Satrapi, Marianne. (2007). *The complete Persopolis.* New York: Pantheon.

Sorabi, N. (1995). Weapons of propaganda, weapons of war: Iranian war-time rhetoric 1980–1988. Unpublished bachelor's thesis, Massachusetts Institute of Technology.

Taraghi, G. (1994). *Khaterhai parakandeh (scattered memories).* Tehran: Bagh-e Ayeneh Publishers.

Varzi, R. (2006). *Warring souls: Youth, media and martyrdom in post-revolutionary Iran*. Durham, NC: Duke University Press.

Youssef, H. A., Youssef, F. A., & Dening, T. R. (1996). Evidence for the existence of schizophrenia in medieval Islamic society. *History of Psychiatry, 7*, 55–62.

Zeydabadinejad, S. (2009). *The politics of Iranian cinema: Films and society in the islamic republic*. London: Routledge.

5   Embodying the Distant Past: Holocaust Descendant Narratives of the Lived Presence of the Genocidal Past

Carol A. Kidron

In accordance with diverse scholarly epistemologies, surviving traces of mass violence and human suffering are carried over beyond the individual psychic experience of the direct victims of violence. The legacy of genocide is thought to live on inevitably in the intimate social milieu of familial relations and consequently in the everyday lived experience of descendant generations. Foundational paradigms in psychology and Holocaust and genocide studies have explored descendant legacies and their subjective experience of the traces of difficult ancestral pasts. Highlighting the experience of distress and at times disorder, these paradigms have asserted that trauma descendants share a legacy of PTSD-related psychosocial scars (Danieli, 1998; Rousseau & Drapeau, 1998) and childhood memories of a familial "conspiracy of silence" (Bar-On, 1992). Familial genocide history of parental suffering is considered to be shrouded in oppressive silence. The legacy of genocide descendants is thereby portrayed as one of potential suffering in the face of the silent and haunting presence of psychosocial distress and disorder. They are also portrayed as searching for narrative voice and historical knowledge regarding foundational events that have shaped their lives. Talk therapy and public forms of verbal articulation and testimony are put forth by mental health practitioners and genocide scholars alike as not only psychically healing but also sociopolitically redemptive.

The anthropology of genocide (A. Hinton, 2002) and the relatively new field of anthropology of memory have explored descendants' resistant passage from oppressive silence to liberation through voice. Research has examined this shift toward voice within collective monumental forms of testimonial commemoration, or local ritual performative forms of religious or artistic representation (Kwon, this volume; Argenti, 2007). Social historians and family studies scholars have also documented and interpreted the preceding processes of narrativization, however, within the more private domestic practice of intergenerational transmission of pivotal parental tales of survival (Hollander-Goldfein, 2002). It may be claimed, however, that the scholarly focus on voice has overshadowed the phenomenon of silent, tacit, and visceral multisensorial forms of mnemonic representation. Consequently, we know little regarding the taken-for-granted processes in which these corporeal representations may have been intergenerationally transmitted from genocide survivors to their descendants (Kidron, 2009). Aiming to explore this tacit and sensorial legacy of descendant memory, this chapter will present an ethnography of Holocaust descendant embodiment of the Holocaust past.

Intergenerational Transmission of Genocidal Legacies

According to psychological research, trauma victims may suffer from a multitude of emotional and behavioral symptoms diagnosed as posttraumatic stress disorder (PTSD) (*DSM IV*; American Psychiatric Association, 1994). In studies of Holocaust victims (Barocas & Barocas, 1973) and Vietnam War veterans (Rosenheck & Fontana, 1998), the disorder was found to impair survivor/veteran parenting, whereby the effects of PTSD may potentially be transmitted to their children. Although nonclinical findings have failed to show evidence of psychopathology (Sagi-Schwartz et al., 2003), both clinical and nonclinical studies have found that descendants of Holocaust victims and Vietnam War veterans may suffer from maladaptive behavioral patterns and a damaged sense of self (Dansby & Marinelli, 1999; Zilberfein, 1995).[1] According to the logic of the PTSD paradigm, if left untreated, the long-term psychosocial effects of survivor and/or shell shock trauma could be transmitted from generation to generation. Therapeutic treatment entails working through the effects of one's family's distant past and resultant reintegration of painful legacies (Bar-On, 1992; Danieli, 1998). Talk therapy in particular would allow the descendant to integrate the past narratively and to heal and "historically redeem" the destructive legacy (Herman, 1992; Leys, 2000).

The preceding research on Holocaust survivors and Vietnam War veterans has served as a prototypical model for more recent psychological studies on unexplored collective traumatic events such as the Cambodian genocide (Kinzie, Frederickson, Ben, Fleck, & Karls, 1984), Armenian genocide (Altounian, 1999), First Nations forced migration and cultural trauma (Brave-Heart, 1998), as well as African American slavery (Cross, 1998). Research has focused both on first- (see D. Hinton, A. Hinton, & Eng, this volume) and second-generation traumatization (Dansby & Marinelli, 1999; Rousseau & Drapeau, 1998; Sack, McSharry, Clarke, & Kinney, 1994). Consistent with foundational paradigms, these studies conclude that survivors continue to suffer from PTSD-related emotional scars and somatized bodily distress (see D. Hinton et al., this volume; see

Becker, Beyene, & Ken, 2000; Stevens, 2001). Descendants have been found to exhibit increased symptomology causally related to their parents' premigratory traumatic experience (Rousseau, Drapeau, & Rahimi, 2003).

Critical psychology and medical anthropology have deconstructed posttraumatic stress disorder, charting its cultural constitution as an idiom of illness (Breslau, 2004; Kirmayer, Kienzler, Afana, & Pedersen, 2009; Young, 1995). Culture-specific idioms of distress have been found to shape trauma survivors' phenomenological experience of suffering and enable or disable the articulation of difficult pasts (see D. Hinton et al. and Lemelson, this volume; see Kleinman, 1980). In some cases, culture-specific idioms of wellness and illness and related meaning worlds provide a "protective layer" toward resilience. This transcultural approach to traumatic distress has sensitized scholars and health practitioners alike to the great diversity of psychic experience and the role of culture in the subjective and collective experience of trauma sufferers (see, e.g., the chapters of B. Good and M. Good, this volume). These studies have most certainly contributed to culture-sensitive health care. Nevertheless, with the exception of my earlier work on a support group for children of Holocaust survivors (Kidron, 2003), no parallel attempt has been made to assess critically the transmitted PTSD construct or the descendant's subjective phenomenological experience of wellness or illness (Kidron, 2009). One might ask, has first-generation genocidal suffering constituted trauma-related maladaptive descendant lifeworlds, or alternatively, are their lifeworlds characterized by unique emotive, embodied, and intersubjective experiences overshadowed by trauma theory?

The Politics of Voice and Testimony

Culture studies (Alexander, 2004), collective memory studies (Levy & Sznaider, 2002), and human rights discourse and practice (Fassin, 2009) also call for the voicing of individual silenced narratives of victimization and subjugation (see Theidon, this volume; see too Munyas, 2008). From this perspective, the narrativization of survivor and descendant legacies facilitates the civic and moral act of public testimony (Fassin, 2009; McKinney, 2007). As genocide scholars have asserted, pathos-filled and cathartic testimonies at "truth tribunals" not only document the violent past and contribute to the collective stock of memory, but ideally facilitate restitution, reconciliation, and coexistence.

In the same interventionist spirit, scholars of ethnicity and immigrant studies who have worked with traumatized populations have called upon descendants to work through and publicly testify to their genocide past.

These community-based scholars believe that promoting knowledge and intergenerational dialog surrounding the difficult past will help close the generation gap and ultimately empower the socioeconomically challenged and marginalized ethnic minority (Ledgerwood, Ebihara, & Mortland, 1994). Once again, despite the earlier scholarly work on the politics of memory and community activism, questions remain. Beyond verbal accounts of their legacies and public commemorations of violent histories, are there other channels of "remembrance" interwoven in the social milieu of everyday life (Halbwachs, 1980)? As critically posed by other pioneering critical scholars, when globally exporting Eurocentric models of traumatic suffering and resistant testimonial voice to victims around the world, to what degree have interventionist discourse and practice taken culture-specific conceptions of suffering and healing or culturally particular memory work into account (Fassin, 2009; McKinney, 2007)? Pertinent to the present study, these culture-specific conceptions of suffering might marginalize or obviate the need for vocal and public forms of working through and testimony while sustaining the embodied tacit lived experience of the familial past.

The holistic and emic perspectives of anthropology could potentially pave the way for a more grounded and culturally sensitive exploration of the descendant's phenomenological experience of transmitted PTSD, allowing descendants to articulate their "lived experience" of suffering and voice. There have, however, been few attempts to apply this approach to genocide descendant experience. Recent scholarship has presented a culture-sensitive portrayal of the impact of trauma on suffering selves and the ways survivors and descendants have resisted victimhood and subjugation (Argenti, 2007; Berliner, 2005), examining alternative creative forms of representation and commemoration. Again, however, the anthropological gaze has focused thus far on the passage from silence and repression to resistant voice and public performance. It is proposed that the lived experience of the silent or silenced past may, however, not always be politically motivated, performed as acts of resistance. It is asserted once again that we have yet to understand how everyday taken-for-granted mnemonic practices are sustained and transmitted to create the lived presence of the past interwoven in the social milieu of everyday life.

Aiming to explore the lived experience of the Holocaust past, a broad ethnographic study of Israeli Holocaust descendants was undertaken between 2000 and 2005. The study entailed 55 in-depth interviews with children of Holocaust survivors and participant observation at survivor and descendant sites of memory. In-depth interviews were conducted using a semistructured and thematic format. Descendant interviewees were asked open-ended questions about themselves and their families, allowing them to narrate and present the self as they saw fit. The assumption in such an ethnographic stance (Fontana & Frey, 2000, p. 652) is that the interviewees will reveal the cultural and discursive forms that enable them to speak their identities. In accordance with the concept of "narrative truth," the issue at hand is not whether they present phenomenologically "true" identities (Lieblich, Tuval-Mashiach, & Zilber, 1998), but rather the way in which they narratively construct and selectively represent selfhood.

Descendant narratives depict the survivor home as embedding the nonpathological presence of the Holocaust past within silent embodied practices, within person-object interaction and person-person interaction. These silent traces were seen to form an experiential matrix of Holocaust presence that functions to sustain familial "lived memory" of the past and to transmit tacit knowledge of the past within the everyday private social milieu (Kidron, 2009).

In the present chapter, I would like to focus on descendant embodied memory of the parental traumatic past. Illustrative vignettes of descendant accounts of recollections of parental and descendant embodied memory are presented. An analysis of these vignettes will allow us to isolate the emotive and intersubjective processes through which intergenerational transmission of embodied memory may in fact have taken place. Before turning to descendant accounts, their experience must be socially and historically contextualized.

Contextualizing Descendant Accounts

The Holocaust is perceived as Israel's national founding event, legitimating sovereignty in the Jewish historical homeland after 2,000 years in the Diaspora (Friedlander, 1992). The causal link between Holocaust suffering and national sovereignty gave birth to a grand narrative of "Holocaust and Redemption." Grafted onto the Jewish traditional narrative of exile and messianic redemption, the modern secular narrative positioned the Holocaust as the climax of centuries of anti-Semitism. National redemption and revival, however, were to be dependent on the physical prowess and fighting spirit of the Israeli. Referred to as the "New Hebrew," the Israeli was culturally constituted as the antithesis of the passive Diaspora Jew, epitomized by Holocaust victims. Survivors were disdainfully labeled "sheep to the slaughter" for having passively accepted their fate (Liebman & Don-Yehiya, 1983).

This hegemonic narrative and the embedded critique of survivors shaped the contours of public and private Holocaust commemoration during the first decades of statehood. Commemorative ceremonies, museum exhibits, and school curricula focused primarily on the small minority of valiant partisan fighters, engendering another grand narrative of "Holocaust and Heroism," whereas personal tales of noncombatant survivor suffering were derided or merely relegated to the private domain. Survivors and their children avoided painful verbal references to the Holocaust past, leading to a "conspiracy of silence" (Bar-On et al., 1998). Subsequent to the trial of Adolf Eichmann and Israel's near-defeats in the 1967 and 1973 wars (which destabilized the myth of the New Hebrew), a shift occurred in hegemonic narratives and public opinion, leading to renewed public interest in the accounts of noncombatant survivors. Subsequently, thousands of survivors broke their silence, with their public testimony taking center stage in the growing number of public commemorative practices. It is within this context that children of survivors "came out of the closet" on both the private and public fronts. Referred to as "second-generation Holocaust survivors," descendants began to ask parents about their Holocaust past and to attend public events at which they might explore their unique legacy (Berger, 1997). Nevertheless, as Shapira (1996/7) notes, the previous absence of survivor testimony and descendant memory work in the Israeli public domain should not imply that the domestic and communal domains were not rife with the silent presence of the Holocaust in everyday life.

Embodied Memories of the Holocaust Past

How may we understand the concept of embodied memory? Even if one may assume that our bodies can embed or embody sensual visceral memories of past events, can memory be transmitted to other bodies, transmitted intergenerationally in the intimate family domain? Finally can this memory become a form of knowledge and a transmitted legacy, and how does it impact the self (or body-self) and family relations of those who share an intercorporeal memory?

Embodiment has been understood by pioneers of body studies – such as Csordas and Merleau-Ponty – as a prereflexive and prerational process. According to Csordas (1990, 1994, p. 10), embodiment marks the lived experience of the subject of and in the body as one's primary ontological experience of "being in the world." The (practicing) body and consciousness are thought to be inseparable (Merleau-Ponty, 1962). Yet memory and the process of remembering are clearly reflexive – as we must reflect in order to recall events that have occurred in the past. How then are the terms "embodiment" and "memory" juxtaposed in the term "embodied memory"? "Embodied memory" refers to a prereflexive or areflexive experience of memory, namely, the imprints of the past on the sensuous body, the imprints of pain, pleasure, the smell or taste of home cooking, someone's touch (Young, 2002). Although the bodily mnemonic response may be prereflexive, it is clear that once activated it can usher us back into the past, as in the case of Yonit's sensuous memory evoked as she describes her mother's embodied memory:

One day I walked into the kitchen and found my mother sitting at the kitchen table – peeling potato peels. Within seconds she began to finger the peels, put them up to her nose, smell them, and before I could do anything – she began eating them. Shocked, I asked her, Mom, what are you doing, you're eating potato peels!!! She had this glazed look in her eyes and even though she was looking right at me it took her a moment to actually see me, and then she said "This is what there is to eat." She looked back down at the peels, suddenly shook her head, started cleaning up the table, throwing out the peels and continued cooking. It was really scary to see her that way, to see how easy it was for her to … go back there, to the point of eating a potato peel.

Although one might diagnose Yonit's mother's practice as a pathological reexperiencing of her traumatic past or the experience of a dissociative state, from her daughter's point of view, the sensuous commensal and motoric hand movements entailed in the reenactment of past acts of peeling, touching, and smelling the potato actually transport the survivor back to the Holocaust founding event. Her body and more specifically perhaps her taste buds remember the event – although she may have not "reflected" upon it. The body as vehicle of memory ushers the survivor to the temporal location "there," a fact verified by the mother's claim "there is," rather than "there was," "nothing else to eat." Strangely recalling the trapped souls depicted by Kwon (present volume), she seems destined to move between present life- and deathworlds.

The literature provides little material on the embodiment of personal visceral memory within the family. Though the fields of illness and disability studies have explored the body's experience and memory of physical pain and discomfort (Crossley, 1999; Frank, 1993), this literature is framed with assumptions regarding a rather reductionist dichotomy of the victimhood or empowerment of the illness experience. For example, Katherine Young (2002) describes somatic therapy, in which the therapist reads and interprets a patient's bodily gestures and postures as inherited "ways of being in the world" that materialize in the body. Bodily memories of interpersonal or intercorporeal parent-child distressing relations imprinted on the body allow therapist and patient to engage with the past and work through "family-body" relations. Again, the focus is on the absence of wellness and treatment where the body is therapeutically assisted to remember the past.

However, as our ultimate concern is with the question of the private familial intercorporeal transmission of genocidal memory, what of the body as a vehicle of commemoration of one's own past, as in Yonit's mother's case, as a receptacle in which to store, remember, reenact, and even perform one's past? Argenti (2007) and Berliner (2005) document the fascinating process of ritual reenactment of past trauma. The ethnographies, however, deal with public ritual events rather than what Halbwachs (1980) has termed lived memory, the weaving of the past in the everyday mundane private social milieu, where one might assume taken-for-granted familial transmission may take place. In search of an understanding of lived memory – or the everyday mundane sensuous experience of the past – Seremetakis (1994) describes the lingering taste of and longing for oranges that only grew in her hometown in Greece, and Stoller (1997) too has provided pioneering work on the nostalgic memory of smell in Malta. Yet this of course takes us far afield from our concern with the corporeal commemoration and transmission of difficult pasts.

We also cannot avoid noting that these studies relate to the embodiment of one's own personal memories, and they also do not move us any closer to an understanding of the possibility of intercorporeal transmission or what might be considered an intersubjective sharing of personal memory. In the preceding case Yonit in no way develops a taste for potato peels, and peeling them will not transport her back to the Holocaust past.

Let us turn again to the literature on the body as vehicle of an experience other than one's own or the possibility of sharing memory with or of others. Empson's (2007) work on rebirth in Mongolia, on reincarnation, shows the body to act as a receptacle that allows the living to record the memory of deceased relatives, enabling the dead and the living to share in the experience of sustained relations. Lambek's (1996) study of possession in Mayotte and Malagasy also depicts possession by spirits as a channel of communication and conduit for social relations with ancestors. Both may be understand as well as a form of commemoration through which one sustains the presence of the past in the present. Although these cases do explore the transmission and sharing of memory in family relations, both possession and reincarnation are ritualized and mystified as alternative states of consciousness. We therefore still do not know how everyday mundane intimate family intercorporeality actually occurs and how the transmission of embodied memory may be part and parcel of family relations.

Ricki gives us a first glimpse of attempted intercorporeality and perhaps the transmission of embodied memory:

I used to sit with my father and stare at his number ... long and hard ... (long pause, tears well up in her eyes). I would try to imagine what it was like to be ... branded. What it felt like when they burned it into his flesh. Did it hurt? Was he scared? I would stare until (her voice breaks) ... I could (she can't speak, long pause) ... until I could ... (she composes herself with difficulty) ... feel it on my arm. (During her description, Ricki's hand moves to touch her arm, as if the body re-senses – her vicarious branding.)

In this moving text, Ricki utilizes the tattoo as Bell's (1997) "portable place," as medium of chronotopic travel capable of taking her to her father's Holocaust past. Despite temporal/spatial barriers, if she stares at it long enough, she may accomplish the empathic feat of vicariously "being together in concerted time" with her father during his "branding." She does not seek factual knowledge of why or when or who did this to her father but rather whether "it hurt" or "it scare[d] him." Ricki longs for what Young (2002) describes as a shared experiential world via the "memory of the flesh." Yet how could Ricki possibly feel the branding of her own arm? One might refer to this vicarious experience as a "phantom of desire." Just as an amputee may feel a missing leg, Ricki might "break apart objective reality to create an alternative" phantom experience. But before borrowing the analogy, one must consider that Ricki has never been branded, so how then could she imagine the experience? Psychological discourse might diagnose Ricki as suffering from heteropathic identification, the pathological ability to take on the memory of others. Young (2002), however, asserts that "patterns of love, yearning and desire" (p. 45) can create a sense of embodiment even if that past has not been personally experienced.

Although recalling moments of potential intercorporeality, children of survivors are not always willing to experience embodied pain vicariously. Ilana tells of her discovery of her father's Holocaust wounds as follows:

When I was little, I noticed a strange mark on his shoulder I had never seen before. It looked like shriveled skin, kind of rubbery looking. I remember hesitatingly putting out my finger to touch it, but I was ... too disgusted to touch it. I asked him what it was. He said he was shot in the *lager* [concentration camp] and the bullet went right through his shoulder. I looked at the other side of his shoulder and found the other mark. Then I looked at his face ... really scared. He never actually told me anything about the war. It was strange, he looked kind of proud of his scar, not like other times when I knew he was thinking of the camp and looked miserable ... he then looked down at his bare feet and pointed to his toes and said I also almost lost those two toes in the death march, I can't move them ... see. He curled his toes you know ... showing me they didn't move. I was speechless. This was … too much … all at once. This time I didn't even think of touching them. I just asked, what do you mean you almost lost them? He explained they got frostbite from the cold. When that happens, they can fall off, or like me, if you're lucky, you just can't move them anymore.

The scars and altered toes transport both father and child to the concentration camp and the death march. In the beginning of the recollected parent-child interaction, the relations are sensual, as the daughter examines the texture of the scar and hesitatingly considers touching it. Yet despite what Csordas (1990) terms her "somatic attention" to her father's embodied scars, the descendant ultimately responds with disgust, unable to share fully the intense intimacy and candor triggered by the otherwise "dormant embodied bearers" (Parkin, 1999, p. 308) of her father's past. In contrast to Ricki's accounts, it is the descendant child and not the parent who severs the potential for intercorporeality and the stream of narrative knowledge it embeds.

One might assert, however, that Ricki's and Ilana's experiences are only a rare attempt at empathy and vicarious experience or failed intercorporeality. These descendants could not experience or sense the imprint of their own vicarious tattoo or scars in everyday life. We may ask then whether there are embodied traces of the Holocaust past embedded within the everyday taken-for-granted lives of children of survivors. Dina recounts the following recollections:

When I was little, finishing the food on your plate was a big deal. If we didn't eat, my mother would say "Do you know what we would have done for this food." The fridge, the kitchen cabinets … there was always more than we could eat. My father would say over and over, "Eat, eat, so you won't be hungry." The way he said hungry, you knew it wasn't just regular hunger but starvation he was remembering. Well look at me now (she points to her obese figure). They definitely succeeded. The last thing you would think was that I was ever hungry. I'm just a walking symbol of abundance – or I guess of their survival. When my kids started to put on weight I got scared and thought, okay that's enough. Maybe I have to literally carry the Holocaust with me everywhere but they don't. Well … at least not this way.

Dina depicts one of the more stereotypical markers of survivor parenting, namely, their fear of hunger and obsessive concern over their children's nourishment (Epstein, 1979). Recalling the survivor who transmitted the Holocaust past to her descendant children every morning as she fed them their oatmeal with her surviving soup spoon from Auschwitz (Kidron, 2009), here too commensal practices constitute the embodiment of the past in the everyday social milieu. According to the descendant, her present obesity may be traced back to these most mundane yet no less formative family meals, which for her parents were experienced as continued acts of survival. Her eating disorder takes on commemorative dimensions as Dina cynically describes herself as a living symbol who "literally carr[ies] the Holocaust with her everywhere." Perpetually embodying the genocide past, she resists transmitting "this" form of corporeal memory to her children. Recalling Serpente's reading of Hirsch's post memory in the Chilean and Argentinian second-generation case (Serpente, 2011), descendants may be committed to the remembering the past but do not wish to be consumed by it.

Emma too provides an account of the presence of the past in her nightly practice of preparing for bed:

E: The one aspect of daily life that I can link to the Holocaust was that every night, at a very young age, maybe 6 or 7, I would prepare my shoes, placing them next to my bed, so that if the Nazis came I would have shoes ready. I would also fold my clothes in a way that would be easy to put on.

C: Do you know where you got this habit?

E: I remember placing the shoes in the center of the floor in front of my bed so that if I had to get up and I had to wear the shoes in a hurry I would be able to. Why were shoes so important? My mother apparently told me how she walked in the snow. I remember her saying how cold it was, how she almost froze. Now I know it was the Death March. Then it didn't matter what it was, just that it was something terrible. Then I just desperately wanted to have shoes handy … so that I wouldn't have to walk barefoot in the snow, so I would prepare it in such a way, so that if the Nazis came.… I specifically took the Nazi as the enemy, because it was so terrible. Now it wasn't that my mother sat down and told me what had happened to her. I think I just picked up on all sorts of things that floated in the home.

Emma experiences the presence of the Shoah not in structured parent-child storytelling, but rather in the silent mundane practices or "micro-moments and micro-acts" of daily life (Bakhtin, 1981). In Emma's case, the habitual practice of preparing for bed and laying out one's clothes for the following day becomes shaped by association with the experientially distant conditions of the Holocaust deathworld. Echoing Helen Epstein's (1979, p. 10) account of her perpetual fear of murderers who might at any time attack her home, for the seven-year-old Emma, shoes were not merely another piece of attire recklessly worn in the morning, but an essential tool of survival, which if prepared in advance, would allow her to walk in the freezing snow.

When I ask Emma to trace the source of her practice, she repeats again the habitual motions of placing the shoes in the front and center of her bed, as if both the cause and effect of her mundane past were stored and remembered in the motions of the kinetic body. Like people attempting to recall where they misplaced something, the repetition of Emma's childhood bodily motions appears to take her back to microacts in which "the material and the mental interact" (Turnbull, 2002). However, despite her repetition of the "motions," when attempting to trace the actual source of her practice, Emma insists she does not recall being directly taught to prepare her shoes for a potential death march; nor did she ever "sit down" with her mother to be told a full narrative about her traumatic march in the snow. As Merleau-Ponty asserted, practice too is prereflective so that consciousness is primarily a pragmatic matter of "I can do" a certain practice, rather than an intellectual "I know" why I do it (Merleau-Ponty, 1962). Her insistence that her practice is a product of her own inferential efforts to "put things together" preserves Emma's cited depiction of the survivor home as a place of silence and her own Holocaust related childhood knowledge of the formative event as tacit and partial.

But if Emma is ignorant of the source of her practice – or the actual parental memory that generated her own – what kind of transmitted legacy is this? If the body is to be a vehicle of commemoration, how can there be commemoration without knowledge? Can we consider this kind of embodied memory, or embodiment, to be an alternative form of knowing?

Eve's description of the presence of the past in the home points us perhaps in the right direction. She recalls placing her head under her pillow at night so as not to hear her mother's almost nightly cries and getting up to wake her father so that he would stop her from crying. After hearing the story, I asked Eve whether she remembered understanding at the time why her mother was crying. Eve responded:

I didn't know why she was crying; I knew she was having a bad dream, that it must have been something very frightening or painful and that it was about the Holocaust. I think my father may have told me it was because of the Holocaust. I didn't know what she was dreaming about the Holocaust or really what the Holocaust was, but ... *I knew it was about what I didn't know.*

I understood at that point that a new alternative category of knowing Holocaust emerged in Eve's tale, a knowing without words, narrative, history; a knowing through the body that wakes up at night, night after night; through the habitual taken-for-granted practice of covering one's head with a pillow and waking up one's father. So if this is embodied knowledge, what does this second hybridic synthetic concept mean and how can we make sense of it?

Returning to Ricki and Emma, if the child interacts empathically with the parent and shares participation in everyday taken-for-granted Holocaust life-deathworld signification, the survivor "may be made present and known" to the child (Buber in Josselson, 1995, p. 31). Over time, "mutual coordinated interaction" (Gergen 1994, p. 269) engenders a "local ontology of relationship" in which shared meaning emerges. Meaning and knowledge need not be exclusively conditional upon words as such, for they only "generate meaning by virtue of their place within the realm of human interaction." In Eve's case one might say that through her repeated mundane "mutual coordinated interactional" practices of placing her head under her pillow and at times waking her father to wake her screaming mother, Eve empathically came to know the meaning of her mother's nightly attacks. Their wordless relationship could still engender an empathic and communal form of knowledge of the past without having experienced or even having been told the historical narrative of the founding event. She could in fact "know" why her mother screamed without historical Holocaust knowledge.

McHugh's (1968) definition of personal knowledge extends descendant empathic knowledge of the past to actual "personal knowledge." McHugh asserts that one has personal knowledge of another's most "private experience" without experiencing the event, for when "defining a situation" we only need to know what is felt by the other and not actually experience the feeling. When taking the place of the other, we need only know what he/she "makes of his place." Feelings, according to Mchugh, "are not private property ... they are performances ... public and observable" (McHugh, 1968, p. 134). Having observed their parents' performance of feelings and what they "make of their place," the descendants define the situation toward "personal knowledge" of the survivor experience.

If descendants have what Mchugh would define as personal knowledge of the parental past how may we explain the commonplace descendant disavowal of knowledge? Polanyi (1958) proposes that personal knowledge entails tacit knowledge that can either not be "adequately spoken" or has as yet to be articulated: "We know many more things than we can tell, knowing them only in practice as instrumental particulars and not as objects. The knowledge of such particulars is therefore ineffable" (p. 87) until we reflexively narrate our experience.

Discussion

It may be concluded that contrary to the literature on the absence of presence of the Holocaust past and the absence of descendant knowledge of the past in the survivor home, ethnographic accounts of Holocaust descendants depict an alternative genocidal legacy and transmission process. The survivor home is seen to embed the presence of the Holocaust past within silent embodied practices, person-object interaction, and person-person interaction. It has been proposed that these silent traces form an experiential matrix of Holocaust presence that functions to sustain familial "lived memory" of the past and to transmit tacit knowledge of the past intergenerationally within the everyday private social milieu.

As there appear to be multiple ways in which the genocidal past is sustained in everyday life, findings suggest that we might reconfigure the more narrow usage of the terms "commemoration," "family memory," "intergenerational transmission," and "traumatic knowledge of the genocidal memory." In contrast to the "dead" or "duty memory" (Nora, 1989) of monumental sites of commemoration briefly visited only to be forgotten in our daily lives, survivor-descendant intercorporeality, visceral transmission, and the resultant descendant practicing body act as tacit monuments to the distant past in ways that may sustain the lived copresence tightly interwoven in everyday family life. Echoing Henry's (this volume) analysis of the body as site in which meanings are managed, the body as receptacle of mnemonic menacing may thus silently yet perpetually commemorate the genocidal past. Contrary to Pillen's analysis of the legacy of emptiness and nothingness (this volume), having vicariously felt what the survivor "makes of his place" in the aftermath of mass violence, it is asserted that descendants may be said to have accessed and re-presented nonnarrative embodied knowledge of the difficult past.

Findings regarding the descendant's embodied presence of the past also problematize the construct of transmitted trauma as pathology, maladaptive behavior, or even distress. If the traces of the Holocaust past on and in the body of the survivor and vicariously in the visceral experience of the descendant commemorate that past in everyday life, then we might reconsider the viability of certain taken-for-granted therapeutic concepts, practices, and trajectories of healing. For example, the processing and integration of memory related to social suffering and ultimate closure and recovery may be less applicable in sociopolitical contexts such as Israel where personal and collective memory are valorized.

Regarding the question of illness and distress, although as Mary-Jo Good (this volume) warns, there is no doubt that Yonit's mother's posttraumatic responses should not be psychosocially deconstructed and normalized, the question remains whether Yonit, Emma, and Ricki's legacy should be classified as maladaptive or even distressful. As stated previously, the phenomenological experiences of these descendants are inconsistent with the pathologizing construct; beyond the scope of the present study, descendants interviewed recounted their self-attributed sense of wellness (Kidron, 2009). Rather than considering the possibility of repression, denial, or false consciousness, I would propose that we reconsider our own therapeutic gaze. Our culture-specific "comfort zone" may be misreading intense human emotion, empathy, or anxiety over the pain of loved ones as markers of trauma-related distress. Echoing Young's (1995) important distinction between the horrendous "reality" of human suffering and the necessity of expert care, on the one hand, and the construction of disorders, on the other, the harm entailed in the reproduction of victimhood should remain a constant concern for practitioners and scholars alike.

Moreover, if embodied memories of traumatic pasts and their intergenerational transmission are in fact experienced as silent yet normative family specific traces of the past interwoven in the mundane lifeworld of the family, we might want to call into question expert intervention in "silent" survivor populations. This is particularly so where silence does not signify distancing but rather alternative forms of silent articulation. Therapeutic discourse has been most influential in casting a hermeneutics of suspicion surrounding silence in family dynamics, promoting the redemptive power of talk therapy and working through (Kidron, 2009). The moral missionaries of humanitarian psychiatry and disaster relief herald the same call for public articulation of silent memories be it in talk therapy or for more politicized purposes of national truth commissions. These agendas most certainly aim to ameliorate the emotional well-being of survivors and their families and/or politically empower and liberate the silenced and subjugated. Nevertheless, a culture sensitive examination at a microlevel of specific local/communal or religious/ethnic conceptualizations of the subtle meanings of silence, the role of memory in everyday life, of commemoration and mourning, and the represence of traces of the past, and finally wellness and illness, is called for prior to the collective enlistment of patients, witnesses, and trauma-related testimony.

This exploration of the microsetting of the survivor home also calls upon us to consider how mass violence engenders deathworlds that resonate decades later in normative and "normalized" survival practices, embodied experience, and uniquely empathic intergenerational relations. In keeping with the call by contributors in this volume for a rethinking of the anthropology of suffering and a renewed analysis of trauma as culturally dependent (see, e.g., Casey, D. Hinton et al., Pillen, Taylor, this volume), an analysis of the cultural logic and practice of genocidal deathworlds and their legacies might move us closer to an understanding of the way violent pasts leave their trace in the present. Beyond explorations of the inner workings of the traumatized individual psyche haunted by a recurring past, we might examine how individuals, families, and communities have persevered by attuning their bodies, emotions, practices, and relations to the ever more frequent reality of social suffering and its intergenerational legacies.

NOTES

1 In contrast to clinical studies, the majority of nonclinical studies have found no significant differences between the second generation and control groups. Having found no evidence of psychopathology or severe emotional problems, recent studies have tested for alternative attachment behavior and representations (Bar-On et al., 1998; Sagi-Shwartz et. al., 2003). Once again, evidence of maladaptive behavior has not been found. These findings have brought about a shift in terminology in clinical studies from the transmission of trauma (or secondary traumatization) to the "intergenerational effects of trauma."

REFERENCES

Alexander, J. C. (2004). Toward a theory of cultural trauma. In J. C. Alexander, R. Eyerman, B. Geisen, & P. Sztompka (Eds.), *Cultural trauma and collective identity* (pp. 1–30). Berkeley: University of California Press.

Altounian, J. (1999). Putting into words, putting to rest and putting aside the ancestors: How an analsyand who was heir to the Armenian genocide of 1915 worked through mourning. *International Journal of Psycho-Analysis*, 80, 439–48.

American Psychiatric Association (1994). *Diagnostic and statistical manual of mental disorders: DSM IV*, 4th ed. Washington, DC: American Psychiatric Association.

Argenti, N. (2007). *The intestines of the state:Youth, violence, and belated histories in the Cameroon grassfields.* Chicago: University of Chicago Press.

Bakhtin, M. M. (1981). *The dialogic imagination.* Austin: University of Texas Press.

Barocas, H. A., & C. Barocas. (1973). Manifestations of concentration camp effects on the second generation. *American Journal of Psychiatry*, 130, 820–1.

Bar-On, D. (1992). Israeli and German students encounter the Holocaust through a group process: "Working through" and "partial relevance." *International Journal of Group Tensions*, 22, 81–118.

Bar-On, D., Eland, J., Klebe, R. J., Krellm, R., Moore, Y., Sagi, A., Soriano, E., Suedfeld, P., van der Belder, P. G., & van Ijzendoorn, M. H. (1998). Multigenerational perspectives on coping with the Holocaust experience: An attachment perspective for understanding the developmental sequelae of trauma across generations. *International Journal of Behavioral Development*, 22, 315–38.

Becker, G., Beyene, Y., & Ken, P. (2000). Memory, trauma and embodied distress: The management of disruption in the stories of Cambodians in exile. *Ethos*, 28, 320–45.

Bell, M. M. (1997). The ghosts of place. *Theory and Society*, 26, 813–36.

Berger, A. L. (1997). *Children of Job: American second-generation witnesses to the Holocaust.* Albany: State University of New York Press.

Berliner, D. (2005). An "Impossible" transmission: Youth religious memories in Guinea-Conakry. *American Ethnologist*, 32, 576–92.

Brave-Heart, M. Y. H., & DeBruyn, L. M. (1998). The American Indian Holocaust: Healing historical unresolved grief. *American Indian and Alaska Native Mental Health Research*, 8, 56–78.

Breslau, J. (2004). Cultures of trauma: Anthropological views of post-traumatic stress disorder in international health. *Culture, Medicine and Psychiatry*, 28, 113–26.

Casey, C. (2015). Remembering and ill health in post-invasion Kuwait: Topographies, collaborations, mediations. In D. E. Hinton & A. L. Hinton (Eds.), *Genocide and mass violence: Memory, symptom, and recovery*. Cambridge: Cambridge University Press.

Cross, W. E. (1998). Black psychological functioning and the legacy of slavery. In Y. Danieli (Ed.), *International handbook of multigenerational legacies of trauma* (pp. 387–400). New York: Plenum Press.

Crossley, M. L. (1999). Stories of illness and trauma survivors: Liberation or repression? *Social Science & Medicine*, 48, 1685–95.

Csordas, T. J. (1990). Embodiment as a paradigm for anthropology. *Ethos*, 18, 5–47.

(1994). Introduction: The body as representation and being-in-the-world. In T. J. Csordas (Ed.), *Embodiment and experience* (pp. 1–24). Cambridge: Cambridge University Press.

Danieli, Y. (1998). Introduction: History and conceptual foundations. In Y. Danieli (Ed.), *International handbook of multigenerational legacies of trauma* (pp. 1–17). New York: Plenum Press.

Dansby, V. S., & Marinelli, R. P. (1999). Adolescent children of Vietnam combat veteran fathers: A population at risk. *Journal of Adolescence*, 22, 329–40.

Empson, R. (2007). Enlivened memories: Recalling absence and loss in Mongolia. In J. Carsten (Ed.), *Ghosts of memory: Essays on relatedness and remembering* (pp. 58–82). Malden, MA: Blackwell.

Epstein, H. (1979). *Children of the Holocaust: Conversations with sons and daughters of survivors*. New York: Putnam.

Fassin, D. J. (2009). The humanitarian politics of testimony: Subjectification through trauma in the Israeli-Palestinian conflict. *Cultural Anthropology*, 23, 531–58.

Fontana, A., & Frey, J. H. (2000). The interview: From structured questions to negotiated text. In N. K. Denzin & Y. Lincoln (Eds.), *Handbook of qualitative research* (pp. 645–72). Thousand Oaks, CA: Sage.

Frank, A. W. (1993). The rhetoric of self-change: Illness experience as narrative. *The Sociological Quarterly*, 34, 39–52.

Friedlander, S. (1992). *Probing the limits of representation*. Cambridge, MA: Harvard University Press.

Gergen, K. J. (1994). *Realities and relationship: Surroundings in social construction*. Cambridge, MA: Harvard University Press.

Good, M. J. (2015). Acehnese women's tales of traumatic experience, resilience, and recovery. In D. E. Hinton & A. L. Hinton (Eds.), *Genocide and mass violence: Memory, symptom, and recovery*. Cambridge: Cambridge University Press.

Halbwachs, M. (1980). *The collective memory*. New York: Harper Colophon Books.

Henry, D. (2015). Attack of the grotesque: Suffering, sleep paralysis, and distress during the Sierra Leone War. In D. E. Hinton & A. L. Hinton (Eds.), *Genocide and mass violence: memory, symptom, and recovery*. Cambridge: Cambridge University Press.

Herman, J. L. (1992). *Trauma and recovery*. New York: Basic Books.

Hinton, A. L. (2002). *Annihilating difference: The anthropology of genocide*. Berkeley: University of California Press.

Hinton, D. E., & Hinton, A. L. (2015). An anthropology of the effects of genocide and mass violence: Memory, symptom, and recovery. In D. E. Hinton & A. L. Hinton (Eds.), *Genocide and mass violence: Memory, symptom, and recovery*. Cambridge: Cambridge University Press.

Hinton, D. E., & Hinton, A. L., & Eng, K. T. (2015). Key idioms of distress and PTSD among rural Cambodians: The results of a needs assessment survey. In D. E. Hinton & A. L. Hinton (Eds.), *Genocide and mass violence: Memory, symptom, and recovery*. Cambridge: Cambridge University Press.

Hollander-Goldfein, B. (2002). "Family dynamics as the mediator of trauma." *Living the legacy*. Chicago, July 2, 2000. Association of the Descendants of Shoah Annual Conference.

Josselson, R. (1995). Imagining the real: Empathy, narrative, and the dialogic self. In R. Josselson and A. Lieblich (Eds.), *The narrative study of lives* (Vol. 3) (pp. 27–44). Newbury Park, CA: Sage.

Kidron, C. A. (2003). Surviving the distant past: A case study of the cultural construction of trauma descendant identity. *Ethos*, 31, 1–32.

(2009). Toward an ethnography of silence: The lived presence of the past in the everyday lives of Holocaust trauma descendants in Israel. *Current Anthropology*, 50, 5–27.

Kinzie, J. D., Frederickson, R. H., Ben, R., Fleck, J., & Karls, W. (1984). Posttraumatic stress disorder among survivors of Cambodian concentration camps. *American Journal of Psychiatry*, 141, 645–50.

Kirmayer, L. J., Kienzler, H., Afana, A., & Pedersen, D. (2009). Trauma and disasters in social and cultural context. In D. Bhugra & C. Morgan (Eds.), *Principles of social psychiatry*, 2nd ed. New York: Wiley-Blackwell.

Kleinman, A. (1980). *Patients and healers in the context of culture*. Berkeley: University of California Press.

Kwon, H. (2015). The Vietnam War traumas. In D. E. Hinton & A. L. Hinton (Eds.), *Genocide and mass violence: Memory, symptom, and recovery*. Cambridge: Cambridge University Press.

Lambek, M. (1996). The past imperfect: Remembering as a moral practice. In P. Antze & M. Lambek (Eds.), *Tense past: Cultural essays in trauma and memory* (pp. 235–54). New York: Routledge.

Ledgerwood, J., Ebihara, M. M., & Mortland, C. (1994). Introduction. In M. M. Ebihara, C. A. Mortland, & J. Ledgerwood (Eds.), *Cambodian culture since 1975: Homeland and exile* (pp. 1–26). Ithaca, NY: Cornell University Press.

Lemelson, R. (2015). "The spirits enter me to force me to be a communist": Political embodiment, idioms of distress, spirit possession, and thought disorder in Bali. In D. E. Hinton & A. L. Hinton (Eds.), *Genocide and mass violence: Memory, symptom, and recovery*. Cambridge: Cambridge University Press.

Levy, D., & Sznaider, N. (2002). Memory unbound: The Holocaust formation of cosmopolitan memory. *European Journal of Social Theory*, 5, 87–105.

Leys, R. (2000). *Trauma: A geneology*. Chicago: University of Chicago Press.

Lieblich, A., Tuval-Mashiach, R., & Zilber, T. (1998). *Narrative research: Reading, analysis, and interpretation*. Thousand Oaks, London, and New Delhi: Sage.

Liebman, C. S., & Don-Yehiya, E. (1983). *Civil religion in Israel: Traditional Judaism and political culture in the Jewish state*. Berkeley: University of California Press.

McHugh, P. (1968). *Defining the situation: The organization of meaning in social interaction*. Indianapolis: Bobbs-Merril.

Mckinney, K. (2007). Breaking the "conspiracy of silence": Testimony, traumatic memory and psychotherapy with survivors of political violence. *Ethos*, 35, 265–99.

Merleau-Ponty, M. (1962). *The phenomenology of perception*. London: Routledge & Kegan Paul.

Munyas, B. (2008). Cambodian youth: Transmitting (his)tories of genocide to second and third generations in Cambodia. *Journal of Genocide Studies*, 10, 413–39.

Nora, P. (1989). Between memory and history. *Representations*, 26, 7–25.

Parkin, D. (1999). Mementoes as transitional objects in human displacement. *Journal of Material Culture*, 4, 303–20.

Pillen, A. (2015). Atrocity and non-sense: The ethnographic study of dehumanization. In D. E. Hinton & A. L. Hinton (Eds.), *Genocide and mass violence: Memory, symptom, and recovery*. Cambridge: Cambridge University Press.

Polanyi, M. (1958). *Personal knowledge: Towards a post-critical philosophy*. London: Routledge & Kegan Paul.

Rosenheck, R., & Fontana, A. (1998). Transgenerational effects of abusive violence on the children of Vietnam combat veterans. *Journal of Traumatic Stress*, 11, 731–42.

Rousseau, C., & Drapeau, A. (1998). The impact of culture on the transmission of trauma: Refugees' stories and silence embodied in their children's lives. In Y. Danieli (Ed.), *International handbook of multigenerational legacies of trauma* (pp. 465–85). New York: Plenum Press.

Rousseau, C., Drapeau, A., & Rahimi, S. (2003). The complexity of trauma response: A four-year follow-up of adolescent Cambodian refugees. *Child Abuse and Neglect*, 27, 1277–90.

Sack, W. H., McSharry, S., Clarke, G. N., & Kinney, R. (1994). The Khmer adolescent project: Epidemiologic findings in two generations of Cambodian refugees. *Journal of Nervous and Mental Disease*, 182, 387–95.

Sagi-Schwartz, A., Van Ijzendoorn, M. H., Grossmann, K. E., Joels, T., Grossmann, K., Scharf, M., Koren-Karie, N., & Alkalay, S. (2003). Attachment and traumatic stress in female Holocaust child survivors and their daughters. *American Journal of Psychiatry*, 160, 1086–92.

Seremetakis, C. N. (1994). The memory of the senses, Part I. Marks of the transitory. In C. N. Seremetakis (Ed.), *The senses still: Perception and memory as material culture in modernity* (pp. 1–18). Boulder, San Francisco, and Oxford: Westview.

Serpente, A. (2011). The traces of post-memory in second generation Chilean and Argentinean identities. In F. Tessa & V. Druliolle (Eds.), *The memory of state terrorism in the Southern Cone: Argentina, Chile, Uruguay* (pp. 133–56). New York: Palgrave Macmillan.

Shapira, A. (1996–7). The Holocaust: Private and public memory. *Zmanim*, 57, 4–13.

Stevens, C. A. (2001). Perspectives on the meaning of symptoms among Cambodian refugees. *Journal of Sociology*, 37, 81–98.

Stoller, P. (1997). *Sensuous scholarship*. Philadelphia: University of Pennsylvania Press.

Theidon, K. (2015). Pasts imperfect: Talking about justice with former combatants in Colombia. In D. E. Hinton & A. L. Hinton (Eds.), *Genocide and mass violence: Memory, symptom, and recovery*. Cambridge: Cambridge University Press.

Turnbull, D. (2002). Performance and narrative, bodies and movement in the construction of places and objects, spaces and knowledges: The case of the Maltese megaliths. *Theory, Culture and Society*, 19, 125–43.

Young, A. (1995). *Harmony of illusions: Inventing post traumatic stress disorder.* Princeton, NJ: Princeton University Press.

Young, K. G. (2002). The memory of the flesh: The family body in somatic psychology. *Body and Society*, 8, 25–47.

Zilberfein, F. (1995). Children of Holocaust survivors: Separation obstacles, attachments and anxiety. In J. Lemberger (Ed.), *A global perspective on working with Holocaust survivors and the second generation* (pp. 413–22). Jerusalem: JDC-Brookdale Institute & Amcha.

6 Half Disciplined Chaos: Thoughts on Destiny, Contingency, Story, and Trauma

Vincent Crapanzano

The career of this stubborn adventurer signally illustrates the idea that since all human affairs are subject to organic disorder; since they are created in, and sustained by, a sort of half disciplined chaos; hence, he who in great things seeks success, must never wait for smooth water; which never was, and never will be; but with what straggling method he can dash with all his derangements at his object, leaving the rest to Fortune.

– Herman Melville (Israel Potter, 1985, p. 555)

"Half Disciplined Chaos" is divided into two parts. The first is a theoretical alert, if I may use that expression, for calling attention to a domain of human experience – the contingent – that has not received the attention it deserves in psychiatric anthropology, in anthropology generally. The second is concerned with how the articulation of contingency figures in the response to drastic misfortune, a wound, which we all too readily describe as trauma and embed in *our* psychological understanding. I will discuss the role notions of destiny, fate, and chance play in the lives of the Harkis – those Algerians, Berbers and Arabs alike, around 250,000, who sided with the French during the Algerian War of Independence (1954 to 1962). Tens of thousands were brutally slaughtered at the war's end by an angered Algerian population. Those who managed to escape to France, despite the opposition of the Gaullist government, were incarcerated, some for sixteen years, in camps and forestry hamlets.

I am particularly interested in the passage of the wound from generation to generation. I suggest that the Harkis' sense of destiny mediates their experience of the war and its aftermath in a way that is quite different from that of their children. Raised in France, the children have lost their parents' sense of destiny and the solace it offers them. They live in the "modern" world of luck and chance, in which the unexpected, as Anthony Giddens (1990, pp. 29–31) observes, "is thought to come from risk rather than the

This paper was given as the Rappaport Lecture at the joint meeting of the Society for Psychological Anthropology and the Society for the Anthropology of Religion in 2009.

intervention of fate or the divine." They assume their parents' wounds, which, at a remove, often displace their conflicted relationship with them and their ambivalence toward France. As such, the wound becomes a trauma for them. They, like their parents, are trapped in what I have called a frozen, repetitive discourse, which stops time and narrative elaboration, marking, as it were, an ill-fitting destiny (Crapanzano, 2009).

Part One

Contingency and a constellation of associated concepts – destiny, providence, fate, fortune, chance, and luck – are the center of my theoretical concern. Ancillary concepts such as necessity, predestination, determinism, causation, and freedom, and what I call (Crapanzano, 2004, pp. 188–90) the "wholly unexpected" will have, for lack of space, to remain in the background. Their range of meaning varies from one linguistic community to another. The German *Schicksal* refers, for example, to both fate and destiny and does not have the "heroic ring" that "destiny" has at times (Newton, 1985, p. 521). *Geschick* appears to be more closely related to the movement of history and may even be subject to manipulation. The French *destin, providence, sort, fortune, hasard,* and *chance,* though closer to their English counterparts, have different semantic weight. *Hasard,* for example, is often used for peril in a way in which the English "luck" and 'chance" are not.

The ancient Greek *moira,* usually translated as "fate" or "destiny," refers to an impersonal force, associated with justice and the necessity to which both humans and the gods are subject. It can also mean an individual's lot or share. It was personified as three old women – Clotho, Lachesis, and Atropos – who were depicted as spinning. When their thread breaks, death follows. The Moirai contrast with the *daimôn,* a divine power that is attached to a person whose whole life it determines (Vernant & Vidal Naquet, 1990).[1] Oedipus (Sophocles 1991, sect. 1. 816) asks, "Would it not be correct to conclude that my misfortunes are the work of a cruel *daimôn?*" Greek tragedy can be conceived as a working out (but never a resolution) of the relationship between the individual and the impersonal force of destiny. Insofar as the fate of the tragic hero rests on a fault (*harmatia*), human responsibility, recognized or not, figures ambiguously in the tragic plot. It is not fully moralized.

Differences are even greater in non-Indo-European languages. There has been considerable debate among Muslim theologians over the difference between the Arabic *qada* and *qadar*. *Qada* usually refers to divine decree perduring for all eternity, and *qadar* to divine decrees operating existentially in time, setting limits to each and everything. It reflects a distinction often made between cosmic and local destinies (Gardet, 2009).

The Quran and the Hadith refer, on the one hand, to Allah's will and, on the other, to the responsibility humans have for their acts.[2] Despite Allah's unassailable will, efforts are frequently made to influence it through intermediaries – saints, or *waliyyin* – or by making a vow, sometimes modeled on prevailing contractual arrangements (Sather, 1997, pp. 287–90).

According to Meyer Fortes (1983), the notion of fate is well developed in many West African societies. For the Tellensi, fate, which is determined prenatally, is closely integrated with their "insistent" lineage and kinship structure. Fate is reflected in the gap between social organization and the contingencies of biographical existence. For Dahomeans, who have a more flexible notion of fate, the divine trickster Legba offers escape from inexorable destiny if appropriately propitiated. Fortes notwithstanding, I suggest that the constellation of terms associated with contingency can rarely (if ever) be *immediately* reduced to refractions of social organization in either simple or complex societies.

This is clearly evidenced in Weber's (1946) discussion of the quest for meaningful existence. At one point, he figured the dichotomy between irrationality and suffering and a meaningful existence in terms of "the incongruity between destiny and merit " (*das Inkongruenz zwischen Schicksal und Verdienst*) (p. 275; see Shafir 1985, p. 519). Merit – living a legitimate, meaningful life – can only be defined in terms of destiny, Weber argued. He understood destiny, not as an impersonal force, but broadly as an irrational and inescapable dimension of life.[3] Death was, of course, central to Weber's understanding of destiny, as it appears to be, in its unpredictability, in most, if not all, articulations of destiny. In rendering suffering meaningful, the theodicies of the so-called higher religions attempt to reconcile destiny and merit through a rationalized ethic. The bureaucrat, *per contra*, can only achieve a formal reconciliation, as Weber saw it, through a continual adjustment of his inner convictions to whatever has been destined without raising significant existential questions or creating genuine moral value (Shafir, 1985, pp. 521–2). Indeed, at least in Gershon Shafir's (1985, p. 527) reading, Weber held that "when the merits which have hitherto infused fate with ethical content disappear, the irrationality of the world, expressed in pervasive suffering returns to its dominant position as fate."

My point is that the configuration of contingency is deeply rooted in language, religious belief, ethnopsychologies, and assumptions about freedom, risk, responsibility, blame, determinism, and causation. Their translation demands critical reflection, for translation assumes an ordering of both the conceptual and rhetorical usage. The messiness, the contradictions in everyday, unreflected (and even reflected) conceptual understanding and application – Melville's "half disciplined chaos" – are sacrificed to an analytically justified ordering that often bears a striking resemblance to systemic theology. I am not advocating the abandonment of orderly description and analysis, but I am suggesting that such descriptions and analyses have to reckon with "half disciplined chaos" that cannot simply be "writ away" through contextualization, if only because it figures in the constitution of that contextualization.

Contingency can be taken, at least heuristically, as a universal category of experience, however it is explained in its particularity, as an event or conjuncture of events the occurrence of which could not have been, or were not, foreseen: an accident, a casualty, an unexpected juncture. Insofar as its occurrence is dependent on an uncertain event or events, it arouses suspense and anxiety and inspires prediction, prophecy, and, in contemporary parlance, calculations of probability and risk management. If it is desired, it is couched in hope, and realistic or magical attempts to bring it about are undertaken when possible. If it is dreaded, it prompts apotropaic practices, which may be realistic or unrealistic precautions and preparations for its advent. My focus in this chapter is on contingent events that have already occurred and not on future ones. The recognition of the inevitability of future contingencies, most notably death, does, however, affect the response taken to those that have already occurred.

Evans-Pritchard (1950) comes to mind whenever an anthropologist thinks of contingency, particularly negative contingencies, which he refers to in *Witchcraft, Oracles, and Magic among the Azande* as "misfortunes." He argues, quite famously, that witchcraft answers the question why a misfortune occurs and not necessarily how it occurs. His classic example is the granary that collapses, injuring the Azande who have taken shelter from the sun under it. The Azande know that the granary collapsed because of the termites that had been eating its supports. What they ask – and try to determine – is why these two events occurred at the same time. It is witchcraft, which appears to be ubiquitous among the Azande.

Unlike the how of the event, which can be explained – to use Evans-Pritchard's not altogether satisfactory terms – by a sequence of causally related "natural happenings," the why of the event demands narrative explanation: that is, a story. The philosopher Robert Solomon (2003, p. 443) refers to the "narrative necessity" of such (fatalistic) stories, which he likens loosely to the logic of a novel or the plot of a movie or play. Unlike causal or scientific explanations, such stories, he suggests, somewhat ethnocentrically, are teleological.

I believe a case can be made that all stories are triggered by a contingent event or set of events the why of which is frequently masked by a series of causal events that lead up to it. I say "frequently masked" since there are stories whose aim is to call attention to the impossibility of ever answering the ultimate why. They turn impossibility into a rhetorical figure, playing on mystery, the harrowing acknowledgment of the unexplainable – the unknown – the comic, and, as among the existentialists, the absurdity of existence. The contingent figures dramatically in Christian and Muslim preaching, but also, implicitly at least, in ordinary stories like the accounts of everyday life I heard in Morocco. These stories stressed repetitive contingencies and recursive convergences of seemingly unrelated events and characters – unexpectedly meeting someone, for example, several times in a day – rather than the dénouement so characteristic (shaggy dog stories aside) of Western narratives. Reminiscent of the overlapping strands in an arabesque, the structure of these stories highlights the contingency of existence – a destiny that can be neither mastered nor explained away but always produces wonderment, fascination, at times humorous pleasure, at times terror.

Most stories, however, are bound by genre and conventions that formulate the "appropriate" why and hinder, if not preclude, recognition of the artifice of their formulations and the impossibility of ever arriving at a final why. (Lest I be accused of ethnocentrism, I hasten to add that there are cultures that are not particularly concerned with origins, teleological progressions, and the ultimate why and have, in consequence, different narrative structures.) But for those stories that are organized around the why, the artifice of the full stops to why regressions is often bolstered by religious beliefs and practices; that is, it is, at least implicitly, sacral.

When the full stops fail to convince us of their finality, thereby calling attention to the limits of our culturally condoned understanding, we look to forces that impinge upon us for solace, release from epistemological anguish, and the reaffirmation of the meaningfulness of our lifeworld. We turn for explanation to (the will of) gods, spirits, and witches or to abstract forces that are seemingly possessed of a certain constancy, such as destiny, fate, and karma, or to more capricious ones such as luck and chance, though these impinging forces are often backed by myths, theologies, and cosmologies that do not necessarily figure directly in the explanation of a particular event. Their invocations, like *destino*, so frequently made in Latin cultures, are iconic condensations. They may require the eventual elicitation of a background narrative, theoretical justification, or simply active – ritual – remediation that may enact conventional narratives, however fragmented, or affirm theoretical understanding.

The domain in which why stories operate varies from the vaguely articulated to the cosmic, the divine, the sociopolitical, as in Marxist narratives, and the psychological. Heraclitus (Kahn 1979, fragment 104) famously observed that "character for man is destiny" (*êthos anthrôpôi daimôn*), and though he surely meant by "character" (*êthos*) and "destiny" (*daimôn*) something far removed from our own under-standing, his aphorism does call attention to the way in which what *we* call the psychological – the psyche – often serves as a locus for many of the why narratives.[4] Take, for example, both professional and popular psychoanalytic paradigms. They provide motivational answers to the why of some contingent events. Like destiny, necessity, and chance, they refer to forces over which the individual has little if any control: I am thinking specifically of unconscious motivations, drives, and desires that are inte-riorized and individualized equivalents of the exterior forces of destiny, necessity, and chance and reflect modernity's rampant individualism (see Chalier, 2002, p. 12). Needless to say – and here again I call attention to the messiness of experiential reality – these psychoanalytic accounts figure among many other prevailing ones, ranging from God's will to her-edity, character, blood, and nowadays DNA, which are often invoked to explain the same event by the same individual.

Whatever else they do, the narratives, theoretical understanding, and ritual enactments situate a contingent event in a larger frame that gives it a significance that transcends its particularity. Solomon (2003) stresses the sense of necessity that contingent – in his terms "fated" – events have. I am not convinced of the inevitability of this sense of necessity. Would it be the same in societies like the Azande where there are procedures for determining the why of misfortune and possible remediation? In societies where prophylactic prayers and other apotropaic measures are thought efficacious? Among people like the Breton peasants who in the 1980s were caught between supernatural and scientific explanations (Badone 1989, pp. 285–6, 320–4)? Or, as exemplified in this Dinka hymn, where there seems to be no claim to understand but only to question?

> I have been left in misery indeed,
> Divinity, help me!
> Will you refuse [to help] the ants of this country?
>
> When we have the clan-divinity Deng
> Our home is called "Lies and Confusion."
> What is all this for, O Divinity?
> Alas, I am your child. (Lienhardt, 1987, p. 45)[5]

Whether the fated – the contingent – is related to necessity or seen as a limitation – an "unpenetrated cause" in Emerson's (1983, pp. 952, 958) words – there is, at least in complex societies, a tendency to under-stand the why in transcending teleological terms the purpose of which remains a mystery. Such understanding assumes an external force that is usually, if only implicitly, personified, insofar as it is endowed with intention, inclination, or predisposition. We speak of God's will, the hand of destiny, the voice of necessity, Lady Luck, or the writtenness of the universe, as though they were somehow intended. Frequently, but not inevitably, they are seen as a punishment for a moral fault.

There is probably no society that explains every contingent event in terms of a single power, though when pushed for an explanation, they may refer to such a power. Rather – and here again the messiness appears – there seems to be ever-shifting reference to different causes of contingency – that cannot be fully correlated with the significance of the event. In Morocco, among the urban and rural poor, I found that though every event was at some level the result of God's will (*qudret Allah*), and his will was invoked for both significant and trivial events, these same events were also explained in terms of destiny (*qda*) or as written, *mektub*. They were evoked when someone died, for Muslims believe that the time of death, *adjal*, is ordained at, or even before, birth.[6] But most trivial or relatively insignificant events were ascribed, if not to the foibles of character or to an indefinite sense of luck (*zhar*), then to amoral demons, *jnun*, who were quick to take offense and could cause all manner of misfortune (though final responsibility lay, paradoxically, with the offender); or, often with humor, *shitani*, or little devils, who were responsible for sexual and other peccadilloes; and more nefarious forces such as sorcery (*shur*), the cold (*l-berd*), the evil eye (*l-'ain*), and impersonal envy (*l-hsed*). The unfortunate often went to a *fqih*, or teacher; a seer; or a popular religious brotherhood (*tariqa*) of exorcists to discover the cause of their misfortune and were provided with a narrative and a remedy. If they were not satisfied with the explanation or the remedy did not work, they shopped around for another story or remedy and often constructed out of these stories explanations and remedies of their own.

Belief in fate does not necessarily correlate with fatalism.[7] (Indeed, in English, we sometimes speak of "actively assuming our fate" or "taking destiny into our own hands.") Confounded, fate and fatalism have supported stereotypes of Arabs, Hindus, and other "exotic" peoples. The response to fated events, particularly misfortunes, demands discipline (*askesis*) however that discipline is practiced. We speak – my ethnocentrism here should be evident – of fortitude, courage, endurance, patience, stoicism, perseverance, realism, and resignation.

To cite an example that is relevant to my discussion of the Harkis is the Arabic *sabr*, which is usually translated as "patience," "endurance," and "forbearance" but can also mean "resignation," "submission," and even "renunciation" (Wensinck, 2009). It has been associated with the Stoic *ataraxia* – a disengaged tranquility of mind – and "tenacity" in a holy war (*jihad*). As silence in suffering the blows of fate, *sabr* is a preeminent value among the Harkis and relates, I believe, less to an abstract sense of destiny than to a more situated sense of being caught up in the sweep of history that defies human understanding.

Part Two

Though the term *Harki* is now used for any Algerian who fought with the French in one capacity or another, strictly speaking, Harkis are those Algerians who served as auxiliary troops (*supplétifs*) with the French army.[8] They worked for a pittance, usually without contracts on a monthly basis with few benefits. For the most part they did menial jobs, like KP, but as they knew the local terrain and population, they also served as scouts, went out on night mission, and participated in interrogations in which some of them, fewer than was popularly assumed, were ordered to use torture. Although most Harkis proved to be trustworthy, as some were discovered to be working secretly for the liberation forces, they were treated with caution. Some of them sided with the French because they believed that Algeria would be better off under them, but most of them, poor, illiterate peasants, did so to survive in a war-torn country. Many had suffered at the hands of the FLN, the militant and often brutal Front de Libération Nationale, which led Algeria to independence. Its military wing would requisition all their food, and sometimes as an initiation, a volunteer would be made to kill someone, even a relative, in his village to prove his loyalty. Despite warnings of likely bloodshed, de Gaulle ordered the demobilization of the Harkis after the signing of the Treaty of Evian on March 18, 1962. The general had little sympathy for the million *pieds noirs*, the European settlers in Algeria, who were fleeing to France, and even less for the Algerians who had sided with France. In the ensuing months as many as 150,000, but probably no more than 80,000, Harkis were tortured, mutilated, and killed by the Algerian population at large. I myself heard stories of Harkis whose throats were cut in front of their wives and children and of children taken from school to see the torture and beheading of a Harki. Despite the Gaullist government's opposition, and thanks to increasing pressure in the French press, almost 50,000 Harkis managed to escape to France by the end of September 1962. By 1967 another 60,000 had arrived (Jordi & Hamoumou, 1999, p. 49).

Once in France most Harkis were incarcerated in camps and forestry hamlets, forced to live in miserable conditions, subjected to abusive discipline and constant humiliation, and offered, if any, the lowliest of jobs. Those who could not find work outside the camps remained, some for more than sixteen years, until the last of the hamlets was closed in 1978. (Some Harkis still live in or around former camps and hamlets.) They suffered the pathologies associated with abjection: identity loss, depression, bouts of violence, suicide, and, among the men, alcoholism. Women found themselves in a double purdah: forced to remain in their homes – a tent or barrack – by their husbands and afraid to walk out into a strange and alien world. (Most of the women had never left their villages until their flight to France; some I talked to had never even seen a European until then.) Children not only suffered discrimination at school but lived under their father's silent and often violent regime. They did not understand why they were treated as they were; nor did their fathers tell them what they had gone through. But, despite their parents' silence, they came to know, if only by indirection, the Harkis' story and experienced, at a remove, their parents' confusion, anger, humiliation, and ambivalence toward France.

Condemned as traitors by the Algerians, abandoned by the French, anxious not to be identified with Algerian immigrant workers, who reject them in any case, the Harkis and their children have found themselves treated as half-citizens (though they have the rights of any French citizen), mistrusted, marginalized, and often subject to virulent racism. The Harkis themselves did not speak up; they did not protest. For the most part they lost themselves in anger, shame, and despair.

Unlike most of their parents, many Harki children, particularly those in what has been called the *génération charnière*, the hinge generation, now in their fifties, have taken an activist stance, forming political associations, lobbying for the recognition of the sacrifices their parents made for France, demanding compensation for the losses their parents sustained, and demanding an apology, which they know they and their parents will never receive (Crapanzano, 2012) They have, in fact, received some compensation, but, until recently, it has been doled out, after long delays, in often shamelessly small amounts. Official recognition was slow in coming. It was only in 2001 that the French president, Jacques Chirac, declared September 25 a day of national homage to the Harkis (Langelier, 2009, pp. 231–4). No apology for their treatment has been made to date. Many if not most Harki children and grandchildren have, however, entered one segment or another of French society, some with very considerable success and others, like so many North African immigrant workers and their children, condemned, so it seems, to a life of endless unemployment. Though most Harkis do not deny their identity, many, perhaps the majority, only make it known when they are eligible for government compensation. There is, in fact, no way of knowing how many descendants of the Harkis there are, since the French census does not discriminate origins.[9]

The Harki novelist Zahia Rahmani (2003, p. 9) refers to the old Harkis, lost in silent rumination, as *soldatmorts*. They dwell obsessively on their having been betrayed and abandoned by the French. It was the leitmotif in all my conversations with them and the mark of their identity and membership in a community defined by memory, which is dispersed across an alien and unwelcoming country.[10] Often when I asked them about their wartime experiences, they would cut off or punctuate their replies with *trahi* and *abandonné*. (Even when they spoke Arabic, they usually used the French words.) The words seemed to condense their whole history, giving expression to the emotional bolus that had over-whelmed them. Often they would turn helplessly to their children, if they happened to be present, to explain what they themselves could not express, but, given their refusal – their inability – to describe their expe-riences to them, the children could say little more. If their wives were present, they would echo whiningly their husband's anger, despair, and shame, reminding me of a Greek chorus that provided the passion pro-voked by the tragic events. They were, in fact, more willing than the men to describe their feelings during the war, but they tended to speak in generalities about their fears, their worries about their husbands and par-ticularly their children, if they were old enough to fight; how difficult it was to get enough to eat; and the humiliations they were made to suffer by neighbors who were in sympathy with the FLN.

It can be argued that the Harkis' accusing the French of having aban-doned and betrayed them resonates with their own betrayal of their people, as the Algerians insist, but I think it would be a mistake to push this par-allel too far. I found little evidence of guilt among them if only because they do not consider joining the French a betrayal. Rather, they view it as a necessity. They had no choice, as they see it, despite their reluctant rec-ognition that other Algerians in similar circumstances did not act as they did.[11] It is for them simply a fact. If they do justify themselves defensively, it is through facts, incontestable in their eyes and for which there is more than sufficient evidence. They insist with trenchant, stubborn realism that were they faced with the same situation, they would do as they had done but they would not allow themselves to be duped by the French. What haunts them, I believe, is their having been duped and the *fact* of that dupery is so insistent that it refocuses and rearticulates their past in such a manner as to preclude repression and doubt. What is traumatic for them is the clarity of the past, which is never past for them.

The old Harkis situate their story – the misfortunes they suffered – within the grand sweep of a transcending history they do not understand and know they can never understand. We may call it destiny, but it seems more historically situated than destiny. They may call it *qda*, but figure it more concretely in terms of the writtenness of the world and attrib-ute it to God's inscrutable will. Many of the old Harkis, who have not turned to alcohol or fallen into paralyzing depression, find solace in such a view, a patient wisdom, which I observed among those who gathered each afternoon to pray in a small mosque in a village where I did some of my research. I knew then that I would never understand the meaning of destiny, as they did, and experience what comfort it gave them. But that was of little consequence. What I also knew is that the Harki children and their progeny had lost that sense of destiny. Though most of the Harki children were only nominally Muslim, I would not want to relate their loss of a sense of destiny to their commitment to Islam.

In focusing on the role of destiny in old Harkis' response to the wounds they suffered, I do not want to underplay the role of faith in the way they responded to their suffering. The Harkis did not, however, discuss the way their religion eased their suffering and gave meaning to what had happened to them, but some of their children did suggest that their fathers (and to a lesser extent their mothers) were able to find comfort in their faith. They did not speak of the afterlife, though several of the old Harkis did refer to paradise, but I cannot say how their beliefs in paradise (and hell) affected their response to what befell them.[12]

The children can, of course, take no responsibility for what they inherited from the cradle on. They are doubly wounded. They have suffered in the camps and bear the frustrations of a marginalized people, as they attempt to integrate in an unwelcoming society. And they have suffered the effects of their father's wounds – an emotional transfer – without knowing what they were and unable to express the anger they feel toward their fathers.[13] (It should be remembered that traditionally among North African Arabs and Berbers the relationship between fathers and sons was distant and formalized. Fathers had absolute authority and demanded total obedience from their children.) The children cannot resurrect their father's experiences in their particularity because they never knew them in their particularity. They cannot even repress them in their particularity, though no doubt they repress some of their effects: a silence, an absence, a negation, a negativity that has paradoxically to cover over, I surmise, their anger and other feelings generated by that silence and the complex of behavior associated with it. Most of them – the sons more than the daughters – were unable to talk about the effect of their father's temper, his drinking (if he happened to be a drunk), or his depressions on them. They are tortured by an unknown they can never know. They strive to know, or they deny any interest, or they simply act for their cause. What they all have – the seekers, the deniers, and the activists – is a generalized story, one that contains, to be effective, fragments of particular stories but is in its generality, removed from the particular, from that which can be possessed and transmitted in its particularity. Their story can never,

I believe, satisfy their desire, their curiosity, indeed "their wish to forget." It can only be a frozen – lifeless – discourse that loses what little vitality it has on each repetition. It is the effect of what I (Crapanzano, 2009) have called "the dead but alive, the alive but dead father," who exhibits in silence and rage the effects of his wounds. His silence is perhaps the last remnant of his masculinity. *Sabr* demands silence before hardship.

Although most Harki children do not talk about their relations with their father, they readily discuss their own children. Several told me that they had to balance the preservation of their and their parents' mistreatment with trying to lead a "normal life." When I asked some of them if they had ever wondered whether their father had been a torturer, many were shocked by the very idea. Their rage was focused on the French in terms of both their parents' abandonment and their own internment. Though they blame the French – rarely the Algerians – for what happened to them, like their fathers, they stress their loyalty to France. Caught in a paradox, they often burst into anger or suffered a sudden, transitory emotional collapse that seemed incommensurate with its provocation. In my experience, both anger and collapse were provoked by what they saw as a breach of promise or an arbitrary assertion of authority by the French. One man was so angered by receiving a notice for jury duty for March 19 – the anniversary of the day the Treaty of Evian was signed – that he occupied the Prefecture of Marseilles for eight hours!

Azzedine, a particularly sensitive Harki son, an activist, in his forties, often refers to the pain the Harkis and their children feel. He bears that pain – "the pain of the fathers," he calls it – with rare intensity. He and his parents left Algeria when he was too young to remember it, but he recalls with extraordinary vividness the miserable conditions of camp life, the fights he had seen there, the suicides, and the look of those men who had returned from psychiatric asylums to which they had been sent by the camp authorities. "They were the living dead. Their eyes were lifeless. They had lost their souls," he told me.

Azzedine remembers crying, the anger he felt, as he lay in bed at night, thinking about how the camp authorities had humiliated his father. He does not describe, however, his father nor talk about his relations with his parents. They are an absent but insistent presence – an elliptical reference point. Assuming their pain and the pain of the Harkis generally, he focuses on himself in what I take to be defensive egoism – a refusal to acknowledge any resentment, anger, or disappointment he feels toward his father. They are just below the surface and emerge in tone rather than in substance.

Although Azzedine and his wife, Malika, live a few miles from the camp where he and his parents had been interned, they do so, not out of fear of moving to an unfamiliar area, but because of their jobs. Azzedine works with troubled youth, mostly the children of immigrant workers, at a nearby school. He relates his commitment to them to his own camp experiences and the difficulties he had in adjusting to school. "The teachers I had – well, they weren't real teachers, just soldiers who had been ordered to discipline us. They didn't teach us anything. I revolted; I refused to follow instructions." Azzedine was sent for several years to a brutal reform school, where he was continually beaten. "It was like boot camp. I hated it, but they broke me. When I was sent back to my parents I studied hard and got a diploma in physical education. That was not so easy since we [the Harkis] were always discriminated against. I got used to that, but not really – never."

Malika, the daughter of a Harki, is a secretary. She is the realist: independent, practical, and efficient. Though she respects Azzedine, she does not indulge his preoccupation with the suffering Harkis.

Azzedine and Malika are especially proud of their house, a comfortable *pavillon* in a middle-class, mostly European neighborhood. Their neighbors are friendly, if distant. Azzedine takes an active part in raising his children. He is opposed to the veil, believes strongly in women's rights, and is only nominally a Muslim. He and his wife visit their parents, who live in a nearby village, several times a week. They feel a strong obligation to help them in any way they can.

Azzedine often talked about preserving memory and the passage of "trauma" – his word – from generation to generation. He does not want his children to suffer his pain, but he does want them to know the Harki story. "It's their heritage. They must know France. But you must choose the right moment to tell them, when they are old enough to understand and are not just traumatized." The Harkis have a special perspective on society, he tells me. "We are always in and out at the same time. We see things the ordinary French don't." When I asked him if he would want his children to lose this perspective, he hesitated, finally said no, and quickly added, "It would be impossible. We will always be outsiders."

When Azzedine described his life in the camps and school, I was not always sure whether he was talking about his own mistreatment, his parents', or that of the Harkis generally. Their separate experiences evoked the same humiliation, bodily assault, and loss of dignity, honor, masculinity, and autonomy. Conjoined, they created an emotional bolus that was so drawn in on itself that it precluded referential differentiation.[14] They were all subsumed in the Harki story, which, as he told it, oscillated between the personal and the impersonal – the "*je*" and the "*on*," the "I" and the "they."

Did the impersonal deflect the pain of the personal? Perhaps, but I think such an explanation blinds us to the responsibility the Harki story demands. The Harkis feel a continual responsibility to pass on their collective story, which overrides any desire they may have to tell their own story. Azzedine relates this responsibility to the respect he has for his father and the need to honor what he and his mother had endured. He is particularly saddened by his father's deep depression. When I suggested how burdensome this must be, he nodded but said nothing. He seemed incapable of acknowledging any anger or resentment he might feel toward his father for having made a decision that disrupted and stigmatized his family. His denial was absolute – cold for someone as warm as he was. When I asked him whether I could meet his father, he said that would be impossible because his father would not talk to me. "He never even talked to me. He's too old." This often meant, in my experience, that the father was a drunkard. I felt the pain of contorted feelings Azzedine's expression revealed: that of separation, shame, not knowing, and an unacknowledgeable resentment that was folded into the depths of his psyche. I had seen similar expressions on many of the Harki children. I also felt, in Azzedine's case, that he might have been jealous if his father had talked to me. His father's silence was *his* possession, around which he spun his own identity. He did not want to share it. He was, however, especially helpful in introducing me to other old Harkis who were willing to talk to me. Indeed, he encouraged them. They were witnesses.

Though many, if not most, Harki children have passed into one segment or another of French society, no longer acknowledging but not denying their Harki identity, children, both male and female, of the "hinge generation," particularly activists such as Azzedine, cling to the Harki story. It provides them with a fixed – a stigmatized – identity and membership in a community of memory. It also shields them from the force of chance – the roll of the dice – that is not tempered by a sense of transcending and unquestionable destiny. The Moirai have surrendered to the *tuchè* of modernity, and with that surrender the loss of solace they may once have given.[15] But, can a frozen story, repeated over and over again, ever be more than a fated destiny – a story that has lost its *destin*-ation?

NOTES

1 *Daimôn* is derived from *daio*, which, like *meiromai*, means to allot, divide, or share (Balaudé, 2002, p. 22).
2 See Watt (1948, chapter 2) for a discussion of the two opposing trends.
3 We might say that his particular use of *Schicksal* reflects the disenchantment of destiny that arises with modernity.

4 Other editions refer to the fragment as B119.

5 The Dinka often refer to themselves as ants in the eyes of divinity.

6 See Sura 63, verse 11 of the Quran: "God will not defer [the death of] any person when his time [*adjal*] comes; God is well informed of what ye do."

7 Solomon (2003, p. 435) defines fatalism as "the idea that what happens (or has happened) in some sense *has* to (or *had* to) happen."

8 For details and extensive bibliography, see Crapanzano, 2011.

9 The estimates I have heard range from 700,000 to 1,500,000.

10 See Cappelletto (2003) for the notion of a mnemonic community.

11 Today they sometimes say, neither apologetically nor defensively, that they were never opposed to Algerian independence but to the FLN.

12 See Shoeb, Weinstein, & Halpern (2007, pp. 455–6) for the adequacy of PTSD as a diagnostic category among Iraqi refugees.

13 Rahmani (2003, p. 9) is one of the few Harki children to express the conflict between feeling compelled to bear the stigma imposed on them by their father's act and the desire to be rid of it. She writes with passion about her father's suicide, the guilt she bears in consequence of his fatal decision, the impossibility of forgiving him, and the recognition that his "error" is her heritage, her flesh.

14 It becomes a ruthless indexical because it cannot be referentially contained. It indexes itself and, as such, indexes its context. Figuratively speaking, it cannot be exorcised, although it may fade away with time.

15 I am referring here not only to Tuchè the Greek goddess of luck and chance (Latin, Fortuna), to chance and luck themselves, but also to Lacan's (1973, pp. 52–63) use of *tuchè* as the sudden – traumatizing – intrusion of the real (*réel*) into the symbolic.

REFERENCES

Badone, E. (1989). *The appointed hour: Death, worldview, and social change in Brittany.* Berkeley: University of California Press.

Balaudé, J. F. (2002). La "part" de l'homme: Entre démon et nécessité. In C. Chalier (Ed.), *Le Destin* (pp. 1–33). Paris: Autrement.

Benyoucef, M. (2005). *Le nom du père.* Nointel, FR: L'Embaccadère.

Cappelletto, F. (2003). Long-term memory of extreme events: From autobiography to history. *Journal of the Royal Anthropological Institute, 9,* 241–60.

Chalier, C. (2002). *Le destin.* Paris: Autrement.

Crapanzano, V. (2004). *Imaginative horizons: An essay in literary-philosophical anthropology.* Chicago: University of Chicago Press.

(2009). The dead but living father, the living but dead father. In L. Kalinich & S. Taylor (Eds.), *The dead father: A psychoanalytic inquiry* (pp. 163–74). New York: Routledge.

(2011). *The Harkis: The wound that never heals.* Chicago: University of Chicago Press.

(2012). *The contortions of forgiveness: Betrayal, abandonment, and narrative among the Harkis.* In J. Skinner (Ed.), *The interview: An ethnographic approach* (pp. 195–210). London: Bloomsbury.

Emerson, R. W. (1983). *Emerson: Essays and lectures.* New York: Library of America.

Evans-Pritchard, E. E. (1950). *Witchcraft, oracles, and magic among the Azande.* Oxford, UK: Clarendon.

Fortes, M. (1983). *Oedipus and Job in West African religion.* Cambridge: Cambridge University Press.

Gardet, L. (2009). Kada; Wa 'l-kader. In *Encyclopaedia of Islam*, 2nd ed. Leiden, NL: Brill.

Gerth, H. & Mills, C. W. (Eds.) (1946). *From Max Weber.* New York: Oxford University Press.

Giddens, A. (1990). *The consequences of modernity.* Stanford, CA: Stanford University Press

Jordi, J. J., & Hamoumou, M. (1999). *Les Harkis: Une mémoire enfoulé.* Paris: Autrement.

Kahn, C. (1979). *The art and thought of Heraclitus.* Cambridge: Cambridge University Press.

Lacan, J. (1973). *Les quatre concepts fondamentaux de la psychanalyse.* Paris: Seuil.

Langelier, E. (2009). *La situation juridique des Harkis (1962–2007).* Poitiers, FR: University of Poitiers.

Lienhardt, G. (1987). *Divinity and experience: The religion of the Dinka.* Oxford, UK: Clarendon.

Melville, H. (1985). *Pierre, Israel Potter, the Piazza Tales, The Confidence-Man, Billy Budd, uncollected prose.* New York: American Library.

Newton, R. P. (1985). "Destiny" in Hesse's *Demian. The German Quarterly*, 58, 519–39.

Rahmani, Z. (2003). *Moze.* Paris: Sabine Wespieser.

Sather, C. (1997). *The Bajau Laut: Adaptation, history, and fate in a maritime fishing society of south-eastern Sabah.* Kuala Lumpur, Malaisia: Oxford University Press.

Shafir, G. (1985). The incongruity between destiny and merit: Max Weber on meaningful existence and modernity. *British Journal of Sociology*, 36, 516–30.

Shoeb, M., Weinstein, H. M., & Halpern, J. (2007). Living in religious time and space. *Journal of Refugee Studies*, 20, 441–61.

Solomon, R. C. (2003). On fate and fatalism. *Philosophy East and West*, 53, 435–54.

Sophocles (1991). Oedipus Rex. In D. Grene & R. Lattimore (Eds.), *The complete Greek tragedies*, Vol. 1. Chicago: University of Chicago Press.

Vernant, J. P. & Naquet, P. V. (1990). *Myth and tragedy in ancient Greece.* New York: Zone Books.

Watt, M. (1948). *Free will and predestination in early Islam.* London: Luzac.

Wensinck, A. (2009). Sabr. *Encyclopaedia of Islam*, 2nd ed. Leiden, NL: Brill.

Part II

Symptom and Syndrome

7 "The Spirits Enter Me to Force Me to Be a Communist": Political Embodiment, Idioms of Distress, Spirit Possession, and Thought Disorder in Bali

Robert Lemelson

Introduction

The question of how to frame extraordinary experiences that resemble the symptoms of schizophrenia or related mental illness, yet have other polyvalent cultural meanings that may make such psychiatric evaluations irrelevant or orthogonal to the lived experience and subjectivity of the person concerned, is one of interest to social scientists and clinicians attempting to interpret the relations among culture, psychiatric illness, and phenomenology. This chapter explores this issue through an in-depth case study of an older man in rural Bali who has struggled for much of his adult life with the intrusion of what he terms "shadows" or apparitions (in Indonesian [Ind.], *bayangan*).

"Nyoman" is a 53-year-old Balinese Hindu rice farmer. He was born and has lived his entire life in a small rural village located at the center of the southern Balinese rice bowl – a densely settled part of Bali about thirty kilometers north of the capital city Denpasar, and one of the most agriculturally productive areas of Indonesia. This village is situated on a major road linking a number of tourist destinations and has witnessed the massive changes Bali has gone through in the past generation as it has been transformed into Indonesia's premier vacation spot. Geographically and figuratively, village life bridges vast changes brought on by electrification, nationalization, the impact of mass media, and globalization, on the one hand; and rural time, which is marked by a complex ritual calendar, adherence to village customary law (Ind., *adat*), and the daily and cyclical routines of wet rice irrigation, on the other. Nyoman still lives in his patrilocal natal family compound with his wife and two adult children and their families, as well as other extended kin. He has worked all his life in the fields, farming several hectares of rice land and occasionally taking additional construction jobs. His wife works in the market selling religious offerings.

Nyoman is small and thin, with a deeply etched and sun-darkened face. His expression is usually alert, although at times he seems apprehensive, preoccupied, or wary. He occasionally appears a bit disheveled, but there is nothing unusual about his hygiene given his occupation. In fact, much about Nyoman's presentation is culturally appropriate. When he is feeling well he is active in neighborhood activities, particularly the *seka gong*, or local village gamelan orchestra. He feels comfortable having familiar guests in his home and understands the normal social graces and expectations that Balinese culture requires, politely offering a rug to sit on, snacks, and tea. When in conversation he makes suitable eye contact, and while a bit shy or guarded when first getting to know someone, he can be quite affable, engaging, and thoughtful.

He speaks candidly and openly about his relationship with his spirit beings and seems most interested and attentive discussing the efforts he has made to care for them or make them leave him. His speech only becomes a bit pressured when he struggles to describe their world and how he participates in it. He says he has been living in two worlds (Ind., *dua dunia*), the world of his family and community and the world of the spirits, for the past 35 years.[1]

Life History

The third of five children born to a Balinese rice farmer, Nyoman does not remember any serious illnesses in childhood; nor does he know of any history of psychiatric illness in his family.[2] However, he was born in the thirtieth week of the Balinese calendar (in Balinese [Bal.], Wuku Wayang). This is considered an inauspicious time to be born, and a potential portent of numerous social and emotional problems.

He was not able to finish high school because of financial problems and went to work in the rice fields. Nyoman traces his illness back to 1965, when, at the age of 21, he witnessed the massacre of several fellow villagers during the aftermath of the "September 30" attempted coup. This coup destabilized the country and catalyzed an intense period of nationwide violence and mass killing, carried out by both local and military perpetrators. This terror affected Nyoman when military and paramilitary (Ind. *tameng*) forces purportedly belonging to the Indonesian Nationalist Party (PNI) went to his village looking for suspected members of the Indonesian Communist Party (PKI) and other left-wing organizations. Several villagers participated in the hunt. Nyoman remembers the accused villagers, including several of his family members, being marched off to the cemetery (Ind. *kuburan*). He remembers trailing the procession with some of the other villagers at a safe distance when suddenly he felt an overwhelming sense of terror. Even though he had not been singled out for execution he felt that he could be hurt or killed because he himself was affiliated with the PKI. He quietly left the group and climbed a tree near the *kuburan*. From the branches of the tree he witnessed the accused being systematically macheted to death. Several days later, in a ruse, his father was summoned out into the street by a nephew; PNI forces were waiting and he was brutally slain in front of Nyoman. For decades after that time he never spoke about these incidents with anyone, including those members of his village who had also witnessed the massacre. This was understandable, since the perpetrators were still living in the region; several of the squad members were local village officials and even teachers.

Nyoman's long-standing problems with social withdrawal and fear appear to have begun after this terrifying experience, which he believes weakened his life force (Bal. *bayu*). He says that his ongoing problems with feeling his heart beating rapidly began at this time. He also felt an "inner pressure" (Ind. *tekanan batin*) weighing down his body. For months after the massacre he had difficulty eating and became very thin and withdrawn. His eyes felt as if they were deeply sunk in his head. He remembers being jumpy and easily startled, and experiencing periods when he felt his mind go blank. He had difficulty falling asleep, and nightmares revolving around themes of being chased and people being butchered frequently interrupted his sleep. Though Nyoman said he does not feel frightened or anxious (Ind. *cemas*, Bal. *nyeh*) when guests arrive in his family compound, he became very afraid in social gatherings and avoided public places and events. He withdrew from the common social activities of his *banjar* and stopped participating in community work projects. He often had "quiet" or "closed" (Bal. *nyebeng*) social presentation. These problems continued to disturb Nyoman in the years following the violence, but he never sought treatment or medical care.

Then, in 1972 he accidentally ate some eels he had caught in an irrigated rice field that had been sprayed earlier that day with endrin, a potent organochloride insecticide. He became very ill, experiencing continual vomiting and severe stomach pains for several days. He became confused and felt constantly dizzy. These symptoms lasted for six months. During that time he withdrew socially even more, rarely leaving the house except to work in the rice fields.

Nyoman married a member of his clan (Bal. *dadia*) in a cross-cousin arranged marriage in 1980. Before their marriage, Nyoman's wife had heard that he had some type of mental problem and tended to isolate himself socially; she had not wanted to marry him because of the stigma associated with such a person. In 1980 she was forced to visit his compound with her family to make arrangements for the marriage. She ran away but was soon found, and her family convinced her to accept the union. In the first year and a half she ran away several times in an attempt to return to her natal family, but after this initial period of protest she ultimately stayed with Nyoman for good.

Nyoman's wife gave birth to a son the following year. In 1984, when their first child was three, she gave birth to their second child. She had a difficult labor and delivery, and the infant died soon after. Nyoman had to bury the child himself, as his wife had been rehospitalized. Nyoman described this as his most difficult time. He cried continuously for several weeks. He had trouble sleeping and became very fearful of other people, continually plagued by thoughts that they were carrying knives and axes and plotting to kill him. When he had to appear at public events or places, he would always bow his head to avoid looking at people. When caught in a crowd, he felt very weak and thought that his chest was tightening. He felt that his eyes absorbed the images of the people around him and that those images entered his brain.

At that time he also began seeing small, black figures, which he believed to be spirits known as the *wong samar*, literally the "indistinct people." Nyoman first saw the *wong samar* after cutting the grass in the rice field. He said the creatures were wandering over the grass and hiding in stagnant water. At first they made noises that he could not understand, but gradually, the noises solidified into language. He felt the figures were competing with one another to enter his head and take possession of his body. When entering his head they would ask him, "Why don't you take care of yourself? Will you take care of us?" He would hear other figures vying with each other over who was going to enter his body. Some were *wong samar*; others were related Balinese spirits, such as the Buta Kala (spirits of the underworld distinct from the *wong samar*). He thought that there was something in his mind attracting those spirits to enter his body.

After the *wong samar* entered him he would feel his body become heavy. He believed that the *wong samar* entered his nerves (Ind. *saraf*) and absorbed his life force (Bal. *bayu*) so that he felt weak. He would feel continuously confused, nervous, and restless because he could not stop these recurring visions. Yet at times he seemed to seek out a relationship with the spirits by going to their suspected dwelling places. When these spirits possessed him he would go to remote places to be alone. He avoided social contact by hiding in rice fields or in the deeply cut canyons that crisscross the Balinese landscape, knowing that the spirits could be found in these quiet locations.

He would sometimes leave his home for days at a time. When he returned he explained to his family that he had been taken into the *wong samar* world and that he had been forced to marry a beautiful spirit woman. Whereas the spirits he classified as *wong samar* were small and black, the woman he said he married looked like a normal human, except she floated an inch off the ground and her upper lip was flattened. It is a common Balinese belief that *wong samar* sometimes take these human forms in order to mix with human society and find victims who are weak, such as the very young, the very old, and people who are ill.

Although Nyoman had been experiencing significant distress and symptoms since the 1965 massacre, he only sought treatment after this exacerbation of his condition following the death of his child, particularly his increasing inclination to withdraw socially. When he ultimately refused to leave his room to go to work, family members took him to a *balian* in a distant *banjar*, who lived isolated in a mountainous region northeast of Nyoman's village. *Balians* are traditional healers whose activities include healing of illness, specialization in religious ceremonies, sorcery, counsel of bereaved family members through the channeling of deceased relatives' spirits, and advice and charms for attracting or keeping lovers (Connor, Asch, & Asch, 1986). *Balians* view madness as having various causes, such as inherited factors, congenital influences, ancestral or divine curses, bewitchment, and sorcery through introduction of small *bebai*, or creatures, into the victim's body (Lemelson, 1999).

According to the *balian*, who is a *balian usadha* – one who reads and interprets sacred ethnomedical texts inscribed on palm fronds – Nyoman's illness was caused by witchcraft, the result of ill wishes of unspecified village members (Bal. *pepasangan*). The healer also noted that Nyoman's nerves were weak (Ind. *lemah syaraf*). Nyoman spent one month living at the healer's compound. The healer prescribed herbs to be administered as a body rub, as a nasal injection, and as an herbal drink. He and his wife and family also gave advice and psychosocial support to Nyoman. The *balian* believed that Nyoman had a variant of *bebainan*. *Bebainan* is a common explanatory model for sorcery-induced illness that is specific to Bali (Suryani, 1984). People undergoing *bebainan* experience a sudden sense of blankness, loss of desire or will, and confusion. These are often accompanied by dysphoric somatic conditions, such as stomachache or headache. Victims often cry uncontrollably, shout or scream, become mute or incessantly talk angrily to themselves, and occasionally become violent.

Because of Nyoman's worsening condition, and the belief that in addition to sorcery Nyoman's illness was caused by his weak nerves, the healer took Nyoman to the Dutch-built state mental hospital in Bangli, 30 kilometers northeast of Denpasar, saying that he would recover more quickly there. After this stay, when Nyoman was prescribed medication that ameliorated his symptoms, he was discharged and then soon after, briefly rehospitalized.

After these hospitalizations, he returned to work. He reported that he took his medication for only a brief period after discharge and then stopped taking it regularly because it was prohibitively expensive and locally unavailable. For several years he would occasionally go to the general hospital to receive medication, or buy medicine at the local pharmacy or *puskesmas*, a small community health center usually staffed by nurses and a general practitioner, with other specialties rotating on a weekly or monthly basis. He also continued to consult numerous traditional healers over the years. Periodically, he was able to engage in community activities, but he often struggled in his social relations. He continued to have difficulty sleeping and experienced both visual and auditory hallucinations.

Nyoman's experiences with spirit beings have gradually waned over time, and he describes long periods when he would not see or hear them at all. However, during the national election campaigns in 2002–3, when Indonesia elected its first-ever democratically elected president, the spirits returned. This time they were asking Nyoman to rejoin the Communist Party. In response, Nyoman would wear a camouflage jacket and military helmet and would sleep in his family temple courtyard. He believed these actions prevented the spirits from entering his body and forcing him to rejoin the PKI.

While Nyoman's symptoms are largely in remission, his attitude toward these spirits, however disturbing they may be to him at times, is one of acceptance that they will be with him in the future. Nyoman's wife, who feels that he will never recover from his condition, seems quite dissatisfied with the marriage and Nyoman's behavior. She said he is always quiet and does not often engage in casual conversation. When he does talk he gets stuck on the subject of his spirit beings and their involvement in his life, a subject she finds repetitive and boring. He states he really loves his wife, while his wife once said in a joking manner (in his presence) that she loves him, but only a little. Nyoman feels that he has a good relationship with his sons and that he communicates well with them.

Balinese Context and Interpretation

Nyoman's sense of living in two worlds speaks to some of the fundamental and commonly cited binary distinctions in Balinese culture: the *buana alit* (lit. "little world") and *buana agung* (lit. "great world"), the Niskala (lit. "the unseen world") and Sekala (lit. "the visible world"). Others have referred to Sekala and Niskala as "natural" and "supernatural" domains, and *buana alit* and *buana agung* are usually glossed as "microcosm" and "macrocosm" (Eisman, 1990). These worlds interpenetrate and influence each other, and balance must be maintained between these domains or illness is perceived to result.

Numerous spirits and ghosts, with various names and different attributes (*wong samar, roh jahat, tonya, memedi*), are believed to inhabit rivers, graveyards, ravines, and banyan trees (Howe, 1984). This type of complex spirit taxonomy is common throughout Southeast Asia (Ebihara, 1968; Keyes, 1977). Illness is often seen as a punishment for offenses against the many spirits that inhabit the village and surrounding countryside. These spirits are believed to cause illness or emotional or interpersonal problems when they have not been sufficiently propitiated with offerings or are upset by buildings placed improperly or by a ceremony done incorrectly or not at all (Lemelson, 2003). Yet given the complexity of the Balinese ritual calendar, this is almost inevitable. Therefore, while having complex relationships with spiritual beings, including seeing and hearing them, would be prima facie evidence of a "bizarre delusion" as diagnosed by most psychiatrists in Western countries, there is a strong cultural context for the "normalization" of Nyoman's seeming visual hallucinations around the *wong samar*.

The *wong samar* are a potent class of spirit beings that have linkages to Balinese history, mythology, and culture stretching back at least seven hundred years. During the migration and wars in the Majapahit era, a semimythical leader from Java, I. Macaling, led an army of high-class spiritual beings called *wong samar* to conquer Nusa Penida, an island off the coast of southern Bali. The *wong samar* were involved in a variety of spiritual battles but finally were defeated. It was believed that the *wong samar* lived on in the spirit world after the battle, and that people could avoid illness and death by treating them with proper respect, subservience, and offerings. This clearly provides a cultural framework for understanding why Nyoman's primary experiential relationship with the *wong samar* is framed in terms of caring for them, propitiating them, and allowing them to possess him.

While it may seem bizarre that Nyoman became married to a spirit, in Bali it is believed that people can take *wong samar* as wives. They are reputed to be affectionate yet fickle spouses, who desire to make their husbands happy but if neglected become angry and cause misfortune and illness. Indeed, most of Nyoman's beliefs about the *wong samar* (e.g., they have flattened upper lips, they float an inch above the ground, they live in canyons or remote rice fields) and other spirit beings are widely shared and accepted as fact by many Balinese.

It is also understood that those involved in the spirit world, such as Nyoman, will have a different presentation due to these relationships. In Bali, spirits are seen to have a relation to certain states of mind and emotional feelings. This is seen in naming practices for states of dysphoria or anxiety. Anyone overwhelmed by emotional distress or displaying violent feelings or actions can be said to be possessed by demonic spirits (Bal. *kasurupan kala*) (Hobart, 1997).

Members of Nyoman's community have varying perspectives on what has been troubling him over the years. It is significant that Nyoman was specifically not referred to as crazy/mad (Ind. *gila*, Bal. *buduh*) (Connor, 1982) by family members, neighbors, or other community members of his *banjar*. Although madness in Bali is deeply intertwined with magicoreligious elements, there is a clear distinction between those who are *buduh* and those who channel spirits for healing and spiritual power (Ind. *sakti*, Bal. *kesakten*) (Geertz, 1994). Regarding the latter, traditional Balinese categorizations differentiate among spiritual possession, spirit channeling, and psychic distress caused by angry spirits (Ruddick, 1986). Often these categorizations include symptoms that Westerners would see as both "physical" and "psychological." In general, definitions of what constitutes madness involve extremes of behavior, such as running away or refusing to be restrained (Bal. *nglumbar*), having unintelligible or nonsensical speech (Bal. *ngemigmig*), and leaving the village and wandering the roads in a disordered state (Connor, 1982). Nyoman did not engage in the disordered actions that typified "insane" behavior, characterized by *ngamuk* (Ind. *mengamuk*), that is, by being loud, violent, or disruptive (Browne, 2001).

One fellow villager said that Nyoman was not crazy, but rather his problems were caused by his particularly intense and ever-present involvement with the spirit world. On the other hand, it is significant that Nyoman's wife perceived him to be mentally troubled at the time of their arranged marriage in 1980, which took place years before his auditory and visual hallucinations began. Given his two hospitalizations in Bangli and Denpasar, his family was well aware that biomedical practitioners perceived Nyoman as being mentally ill. In describing his condition, his wife used the modern Indonesian term *penyakit jiwa*, literally "psyche/ soul illness," the biomedical terminology for mental illness.

Several other villagers classified him as *buduh kadewan-dewan*, literally "madness from the gods," or what Connor (1982) refers to as "blessed madness." Connor notes that people with this label often experience it on the "margins of settled society" and often wander far from their villages to remote locales. The illness is usually precipitated by an event such as the death of close kin or marital problems.

Thus, opinions about the cause and type of illness varied across family members, village members, psychiatric treatment providers, and healers. Nyoman's "madness" seems to be a matter of debate or ambivalence among his family, neighbors, healers, and physicians. In addition, the ways in which Balinese categorize "mental illnesses" are also highly contested and subject to historical change, as in, for example, Nyoman's wife's usage of the modern biomedical term *penyakit jiwa*.

Perhaps what is clearer is the problematic aspect of Nyoman's social withdrawal. Social participation in a sociocentric society like Bali is expected on a relatively continual basis. In Bali, individuals are fully integrated into extended families, clans, work or interest groups, irrigation societies, and hamlet associations, as well as being identified by caste (Jensen & Suryani, 1993), and the sense that one is being observed and judged by one's "consociates" is particularly intense. In "face-to-face societies," where behavior is intricately observed by everyone around and privacy is minimized in personal and social life, people feel even greater pressure to participate socially and manage the social presentation of social behavior through "emotion work" (Hollan & Wellenkamp, 1994). If one does not participate, a number of negative personality descriptors, such as "arrogant" (*sombong*), can be applied, with highly stigmatizing results. The fear of witchcraft and poisoning increases the emphasis on polite and frequent social interactions.

Bali is also famed as one of the most ritually regulated societies in the world, with a high degree of religiosity as manifested by the daily offerings, the incredibly complex ritual calendar, and the extensive temple systems. Given the centrality of religious ritual performance, complexity, and action in everyday life; the ever-present expectations for sociality and social engagement; and the responsibilities of hamlet members, Nyoman's social avoidance, fear, and disengagement become all the more debilitating. Inability to participate in this life would be seen as a major role failure and would subject one to gossip. These pressures compounded Nyoman's isolation and oddity.

Psychiatric Interpretations

When Nyoman was initially hospitalized at the state mental hospital he was diagnosed on the basis of the *PPDGJ* (*Pedoman Penggolongan dan Diagnosis Gangguan Jiwa*), the Indonesian diagnostic manual, which is based on the *ICD* and the *DSM*. The initial diagnosis was Paranoid Acute Problem (298.30). A subsequent diagnosis, which was made at the one-year evaluation, was Schizophrenia Paranoid type (295.3). Nyoman was provisionally diagnosed with schizophrenia on the basis of the following

DSM-IV-TR criteria: delusions resembling thought insertion, auditory and visual hallucinations, and delusions of a persecutory nature. His social functioning is also significantly impaired, and both his active symptoms and his overall illness have persisted for decades. Nyoman was given chlorpromazine, 50 mg three times a day; trifluoperazine, 5 mg three times a day; and a multivitamin. In response to the medication, the voices of the *wong samar* gradually decreased in frequency and prominence, until after about one week they had become "hazy and unclear." He was hospitalized for three weeks and then discharged.

After Nyoman was discharged, he stayed at home for one week. It is unclear whether he continued taking the medication while at home. His symptoms resumed and his family took him to the Wangaya Government Hospital in Denpasar, which had a small inpatient psychiatric unit. According to the initial intake notes he appeared dazed or expressionless (Ind. *melamun*, Bal. *bengong*) with a vacant or forgetful demeanor. He often appeared confused or panicky (*bingung*) and had disturbed thinking (Ind. *pikiran terganggu*, Bal. *kenahe sing luwung*). He reported that he often felt breathless (*sesak napas*) and dizzy (Ind. *pusing*, Bal. *pengeng*). Nyoman was hospitalized at Wangaya for one week. He was given trifluoperazine, 5 mg three times a day, and an unspecified dosage of trihexyphenidyl to reduce the dystonia and akesthesia brought on by the trifluoperazine. Nyoman thought the medication from the Bangli state mental hospital was more powerful than that of the Wangaya Hospital, as it reduced his symptoms more.

Whereas many hallucinations/delusions of schizophrenics in Western industrialized countries involve very negative images and commands, for Nyoman the spirits' main command is that he needs to take care of them and then they will not disturb him. They also encourage him to take care of himself, instructing him to take his medicine when he is ill and advising him how to use the herbs, amulets, and special articles of clothing that he received from traditional healers. At times it appears that he even welcomes the intrusion of these spirits into his mind and body. He gives his body over to the spirit beings and says to them, "It's up to you that you enter my body ... do it ... serve yourselves ... go ahead ... I do not care." He said he is not scared of the *wong samar* because he already has good relations with them.

Nyoman clearly has a passive reception of a somatic sensation imposed from an outside agency. For example, if he sees the shadow of a vehicle passing by, he feels that the vehicle's shadow can crush his shadow. Afterward he feels sore and uneasy. He always feels that his mind "pulls" (Ind. *menarik*) or "absorbs" (Ind. *menyedot*) things into it. If he sees a chicken or a lizard, he feels it is pulled into his mind and can stay there a long time. He may grow scared because the image does not disappear. This seems to indicate a type of "thought insertion," in that Nyoman always feels that objects are being pulled into his mind, and then he cannot "stop them from appearing" in his thoughts.

Nyoman also at times has a sense of control over the form and content of his hallucinations. For example, he has formed a relation with the *barong*, a good and protective spiritual figure represented by a dragon-like mask. The *barong* often has a particular temple devoted to it within the central village temple. The spirit of the *barong* can possess people for short periods, both in temple festivals and in theatrical performances such as the Calonarang. Nyoman feels that he is able to pull the *barong* into his mind when he goes to the temple on auspicious days, such as *wage* or *kliwon* on the Balinese calendar. The *barong* also enters his body whenever he takes part in community work activity dedicated to temple maintenance or other religious duties. As the *barong* enters him, he feels his body get lighter and his pains disappear. When particular *wong samar* spirit beings are disturbing him, he feels he can call on the *barong* to act as a protective spirit and make them leave his body. He believes the *barong* offers him a form of protective medicine.

Given the preceding information, could Nyoman's experience be seen as an extended form of positive spirit possession? There is a culturally normative context for possession states to be associated with spiritual beings associated with strong spiritual power (Bal. *kesaktian*) such as the *barong* or the *wong samar*. However, Nyoman's case differs from Connor's examples in that many of her case studies used this experience to become healers. The disorder would disappear after purification and consecration ceremonies, neither of which Nyoman underwent. Furthermore, Nyoman's relationship with these spirits extends far beyond what is culturally typical. While his relationship is not culturally bizarre (e.g., like the notion that the CIA has implanted transmitters in one's head), the degree to which he has withdrawn from society due to his involvement with the *wong samar* is particularly stigmatizing and disabling in the Balinese cultural context.

The story regarding Nyoman's hallucinations, delusions, and negative symptoms is even more complex. He has what appears on the surface to be auditory and visual hallucinations. He occasionally sees, but more often hears, the many types of spirits and voices, from different places, that interact with him and with his other spirits in different ways. They have voices like people. He also has visceral or somatic hallucinations related to his visual and auditory ones. The latter can be linked to his more primary hallucination regarding his participation in the spirit world. While the spirits are in his body he believes that they absorb his *bayu,* causing him to become weak. When he feels them entering his body, he believes they lodge in his nerves and make his body feel heavy and cause his skin to become thicker.

A diagnosis of paranoid schizophrenia appears to be warranted given that Nyoman has delusions and hallucinations with a relative preservation of cognitive functioning and affect, and that these delusions and hallucinations are organized around a coherent magicoreligious theme. His hallucinations share the characteristics of a psychogenically based disorder rather than an organic one. They are fleeting and transient, shadowy and misty, and occur in shades of gray. Making such a diagnosis remains problematic, however, as some of its associated characteristic features are absent in this situation. Although Nyoman appeared shy and at times anxious, both while being observed in the village and in the interview context, this demeanor did not seem to be coterminous with affective flattening or avolition, which are prominent negative symptoms of some forms of schizophrenia. His speech production was normal, grammatical, and semantically appropriate and could not be classified as alogia. While his range of activities was restricted when he was actively "delusional," he had a range of volitional activities adequate for his roles in his *banjar.*

Nyoman's other negative symptoms (his social isolation and loss of interest in the social world) seem clearly attributable to his involvement with the world of spirits and, as such, should not be considered outright symptoms of schizophrenia. As previously discussed, there is a rich and complex cultural context for this involvement. Nonetheless, Nyoman's relationships with the self-same spirits extend far beyond what is culturally normative in terms of his social withdrawal. They would not be, in the *DSM* nomenclature, "culturally sanctioned," for example, taking place in a normative culture context, such as a magicoreligious ritual or symbolic healing performance.

It is significant that many of Nyoman's symptoms began after he was poisoned with pesticides. Ingestion exposure to an organochlorine such as endrin is known to have a neurotoxic effect, causing sensory disturbances, headaches, dizziness, mental confusion, and psychosis (Donkin & Williams, 2003). This could account for the late onset of some of his psychotic symptoms. However, he would not fit the criteria for substance-induced psychotic disorder, because while some of the features of his larger clinical picture (e.g., confusion, social withdrawal) began or were exacerbated after the pesticide exposure, his delusions and hallucinations only began after the death of his second child, almost a decade later.

In addition, even Nyoman's poisoning with endrin can be questioned as an actual cause. In 1965 there was gossip that spread among the members of the local *subak* (the irrigation society that controls water flow for rice fields in the watershed) that *subak* members who were also members of the BTI (the Barisan Tani Indonesia), a group affiliated with the PKI, were spreading excess endrin in the irrigation channels to poison those *subak* members who were not affiliated with the PKI. Endrin was also – as Baygon is today – famous as a cheap and effective method of committing suicide (Santikarma, personal communication). It seems significant that Pak Nyoman only became sick upon hearing that he had potentially been poisoned. It is possible that he was not actually poisoned but had an acute fear or panic response, given the multiple meanings and triggers that endrin represented.

Nyoman also has the cardinal features of chronic posttraumatic stress disorder (PTSD) with psychotic features. He witnessed an event in which some of his fellow villagers and family members were brutally macheted to death, which frightened and horrified him, and he nearly died of pesticide poisoning, a severe trauma in itself. From the time of witnessing the murder he has had persistent symptoms of increased arousal and associated physiological reactivity, as indicated by tachycardia, difficulty concentrating, confusion, and dizziness, and he has had nightmares and other persistent sleep disturbances. In terms of avoidance and numbing criteria, given that several of the perpetrators of the 1965 massacre were members of Nyoman's *banjar*, his reluctance to frequent public places, engage in village activities, and socialize may be attributable to a sensible or healthy response to the highly fraught political and social history of his immediate surroundings.

A diagnosis of PTSD with psychotic features would encompass some additional aspects of Nyoman's illness experience and his subsequent relationships with spirits. By comparison, among Cambodian refugees who experienced the numerous traumas associated with the Khmer Rouge regime, a prominent cultural pathoplastic shaping of PTSD symptomatology is visitations by ghosts and other spirit beings (D. Hinton, A. Hinton, D. Chhean, Loeum, & Pollack, 2009; Sack, Clarke, & Seely, 1995). It is conceivable that there is some connection among Nyoman's initial traumas in 1965; the reactivation of loss, fear, and sadness as a result of losing his child in 1984; and his subsequent experience of the spirit beings. In the Balinese case, however, most people (and they numbered in the hundreds of thousands) who witnessed horrific events in 1965 did not develop such close relationships with *wong samar*.

In addition, there is clearly a dissociative possession component to Pak Nyoman's clinical picture. For example, his relation with the *barong* spirit is similar to the interactions that persons with Dissociative Identity Disorder have with a protective alter, as opposed to his relation to the more distressing forms of spirits that he believes attempt to inhabit his body.

1965 and *Ngeb*: Implications of the Social Suppression of Political Violence

Nyoman himself described his illness as '*ngeb*,' which has two distinct, but related, meanings and presentations in Balinese culture. *Ngeb* is an illness caused by witnessing something horrific, frightening, or bizarre, such as the devastating cholera epidemic that swept through Bali in the 1920s. Seeing spirits, such as the *wong samar*, causes another variant of *ngeb*. As a result of these frightening or horrific experiences, sufferers put themselves in a self-imposed exile characterized by "muteness" (*membisu*) and lack of participation in the social world. Nyoman's *ngeb* began with the witnessing of the massacre in 1965. After the death of his infant, his initial *ngeb* was compounded by visual and auditory hallucinations of the *wong samar* world.

Nyoman believed that his *ngeb* began through his witnessing of the massacre and the shock/startle (Ind. *terkejut*, Bal. *makesiab*) that, as a result, weakened his *bayu*, or life force (Wikan, 1989). This fits well with the notion that illness may be precipitated by accidents, shocks, or fainting fits resulting from emotional disturbance. Throughout insular and mainland Southeast Asia, *bayu* is seen as present in all matter, both living and dead (Keyes, 1977; Laderman, 1991). However, it is a force that is sensitive to disturbance and can be depleted through startle, fear, or other disturbance of balance. *Bayu* needs to be strong or large (Bal. *gede*) to maintain health. Nyoman felt that his continually weakened *bayu* accounted for the predilection of his spirit beings to visit him. *Bayu* can be affected by emotional states such as sadness, and there is a cluster of familiar symptoms – such as weakness, heaviness, and feeling empty – that indicates that *bayu* is weak or gone. This is often seen as the result of black magic. When asked whether he believed that someone was practicing sorcery that caused his problems, however, Nyoman responded in Indonesian in a way that suggested either ambivalence or difficulty expressing himself in that language, '*Tidak mungkin tapi kemungkinan ada* ("Definitely not, but the possibility exists").

Whether or not *ngeb* is an illness is certainly contested among the Balinese. Many actively contrast *ngeb* with illness, as in '*Tiang ngeb kewala ten gelem* ("I'm *ngeb*; I'm not ill"). While psychiatrists may refer to *ngeb* as mental illness, *ngeb* is also quite resonant with the Balinese practice of *puik* (Mead & Bateson, 1942; Geertz, 1973), intentional silence and social avoidance, or a kind of social commentary, *koh ngomong* (literally, "fed up with speaking") (Santikarma, 1995). Given the preceding, the illness category of *ngeb* does not correspond with or translate neatly into a *DSM* diagnosis.

Nyoman's *ngeb* should also be considered in historical context. The killings he witnessed were part of a military bloodbath that swept across Bali and other areas of Indonesia in response to a purported communist-backed coup attempt in September 1965 (Robinson, 1998). Between 80,000 and 100,000 Balinese, or approximately 5–8 percent of the population, were killed between December 1965 and March 1966 (Cribb, 2004). The events of 1965 had reverberations for decades (Dwyer, 2004; Dwyer & Santikarma, 2004), as the New Order regime of former president Suharto (1966–98) led a campaign to frame these events officially in a certain way and to stigmatize, ostracize, and blacklist those who were perceived as supporting the communists. This included not only former PKI members, but also their extended families. A "clean environment" policy (Ind. *lingkungan bersih*) legally banned family members of the PKI from the civil service and the media and from participation in civil society organizations, such as NGOs. Family members also had limited access to other civil rights, such as the "good behavior letter" (Ind. *surat kelakuan baik*) necessary to obtain a passport, a university scholarship, or permission to move from one district to another. Until Suharto's fall in 1998, any public discussion of the events of 1965 that was at variance with the official government version was forbidden, and those who engaged in it were jailed or "disappeared."

Individuals who have *ngeb* arising from 1965 can thus be seen as mute witnesses against the domination (Ind. *kekuasaan*) and control that the Suharto regime imposed on Indonesia after its ascendancy in 1965 (Santikarma, 2003). It is significant that Nyoman has several friends who are similarly characterized as *ngeb* and similarly avoid social gatherings. His closest neighbor has symptoms very similar to his own, is also classified as *ngeb*, and also witnessed the events of 1965.

In this context it is extremely significant that, while it seems obvious to outsiders that Nyoman is a victim and survivor of a politically based massacre, bordering on genocide, he is viewed by members of his community as being a perpetrator or instigator of the events of 1965, because he was a sympathizer with the Communist Party. Only in 2004 could his brother say that Nyoman himself had been forgiven by villagers for causing the "disorder" of the events of 1965.

The events of 1965 not only penetrated deeply into his intrapsychic life, but also affected his social support network. At the time of the 1965 violence, Pak Nyoman was the only male in the house responsible for defending the family home (Bal. *nindihan natah*) when it was attacked by the *tameng*. His younger brother was away at school in Singaraja and another brother was living in Sumbawa. Pak Nyoman took this all very hard because he also saw his older sister forced to marry one of the most vicious of the paramilitaries after 1965. This man is now his brother-in-law. Family members clearly linked this relationship to the continuing *tekanan* or weight of his fears.

Another neighbor also believed that a good part of the reason why Pak Nyoman was so troubled was that it was his second cousin (*mindon*) who encouraged the *tameng* to attack Nyoman's home because the cousin wanted to take the land. She stated that the people you are really afraid of are your family members (the ones who know you well enough to inform on you) rather than strangers or the state. Both violence over land reform (Robinson, 1998) and anger and resentment toward close relatives over their role as informants (Dwyer & Santikarma, 2004) are common themes related to the events of the September 30 movement (*G-30-S: Gerakan tiga puluh September*) in Bali.

Nyoman only sought out psychiatric treatment when his suffering became intolerable after the death of his son in 1984. Why did he not seek psychiatric or other forms of help after his witnessing of the 1965 massacre, given the severity of his distress and symptoms? This could be partially explained by the Balinese cultural emphasis on emotional regulation and deemphasis on the expression of negative emotional experiences and states (Jennaway, 2002; Wikan, 1990). However, perhaps more important is the dangerous political nature of these experiences, as discussed earlier.

When in 1997 Nyoman first disclosed to R. B. L. the nature of his experiences and trauma, particularly the events of 1965, R. B. L. felt honored that he would confide such information to him. Toward the end of the fourth interview, Nyoman received a visit from a neighbor of approximately his same age whom he had known for many years, and Nyoman invited him to be part of the interview. They began to discuss the events of 1965, and for the first time Nyoman disclosed what he had experienced during that period to a member of his village. R. B. L. felt this was a courageous step for Nyoman. In follow-up interviews in 2003–9, the family and village members were much more open about the events of 1965 and had lively discussions concerning the memories and meanings of those horrific times.

Nyoman later told R. B. L. that his experience of the *wong samar* world had lessened significantly after his original disclosure to him. As part of the research project, R. B. L and members of his field team had encouraged Nyoman to return to a recently opened *puskesmas* near his village and receive antipsychotic medication, which he gladly did. When R. B. L. returned for an interview several weeks later, Nyoman was not at home. His wife said it was the first time he had engaged in community work for temple maintenance in many years. Whether this was a result of the medication, the disclosure of his trauma and its potentially cathartic effects, the natural course of his disorder, or part, all, or none of the above, is difficult to say.

In the years following the fall of the New Order regime, the political climate in Indonesia surrounding discussion and debate of the events of 1965 has changed considerably. The press regularly covers debates over the events of this history and their meaning, and there is a fledgling and contested movement to redress the human rights violations and genocide through the formation of a National Truth and Reconciliation Commission (Komisi Kebenaran dan Rekonsiliasi Nasional) (Dwyer, 2004; Dwyer & Santikarma, 2004). It is not surprising that it is in this context that many of Nyoman's symptoms receded, only to be reactivated under the pressures and memories that political campaigns evoke.

Conclusion

Nyoman presents a complex clinical picture, with a complex etiology and personal history, set in one of the most culturally "dense" societies in the world. His illness and his adaptations to it exist on multiple levels.

In one sense, his complex relation with the spirits can be seen as a compensatory mechanism to cope with the overwhelming grief and sadness at the loss of his child. His relations with the spirit world provide a culturally acceptable and understandable mode for managing his socially avoidant and anxious states. This grief response is overlaid on a personal history of severe trauma. Of course, it seems clear that the biological diathesis model (e.g., a vulnerability to psychotic states, suggested by the diagnosis of schizophrenia) is relevant here, as many other Balinese suffered similarly in 1965 without a similar progression into delusion, social isolation, and spirit possession.

By focusing only on Nyoman's clinical symptoms, or on a psychodynamic, defense model of his symptomatology, however, we lose extremely important aspects of the social and historical context in which these symptoms are embedded. A unidimensional diagnostic formulation is wholly inadequate in this case. This is a man whose symptoms and suffering have a complex etiology, stemming from being poisoned with a toxic agent, suffering great personal loss and tragedy, and witnessing horrific acts of political violence. His disability is compounded by the complex interaction of Balinese notions of hierarchy, which help to create anxiety about authority and social presentations and emotion management. These are further compounded by a national political culture that, until the fall of Suharto, made expressing distress and remembering 1965 politically and socially dangerous, if not fatal, behavior. Nyoman's social avoidance and isolation, as defined by *ngeb*, have their origins in witnessing a trauma that, until recently, had a schematized and politically monolithic construction in Indonesia's historical memory, and a fear-inducing and stigmatizing enactment on a daily level in village life.

Suppression of these social memories took place at all levels of Indonesian society and was supported by notions regarding the negative effects on mental health, economic development, and Indonesia's national status of discussing these traumatic events. This is compounded by a cosmological context that leads to further suppression of social memory. *Ngeb* has been viewed (Santikarma, 2003) as a means of political protest that can take two forms. One is the muteness that acts as a form of a resistance against political authority, in which the memorializing and even recall of a specific traumatic event, caused by state terror, have been suppressed. The other meaning of *ngeb* is a fear of memorializing or resisting cosmological authority, which it is believed causes the community to risk natural disasters, such as epidemics or volcanic eruptions.

Nyoman's case clearly fits, if not wholly, into this historical frame. However, his complex psychiatric and individual history cannot be simply subsumed by relating it only to this historical model and context. Given the multiple models of illness causation; the differing and, at times, changeable definitions of madness; and the many forms of healing available, it is a complex task to relate these to Nyoman's personal experience. He drew on these models and was shaped by them and by his historical context, and this multilayered interaction helped create a complex illness picture that does not provide an exact fit with a neat historical determinism or the categorical strictures of the *DSM*.

NOTES

1 Portions of this paper first appeared in Lemelson, Kirmayer, & Barad (2007) and Lemelson & Suryani (2006).

2 The author first met Nyoman at his home in 1996 as part of a wider World Health Organization study on the course and outcome of acute psychosis in the developing world. During 1996–7 and 2003–9, R. B. L. conducted at least ten home visit interviews with Nyoman, his wife and extended family, and members of his hamlet (*banjar*). While Nyoman's first language is Balinese, he is also fluent in Indonesian. The interviews were conducted in both Indonesian and Balinese. R. B. L. is fluent in Indonesian, and a field assistant, who was present at three of the interviews, helped translate from Balinese to Indonesian as needed. This history is based on the original case notes, which included an inpatient observation, evaluation, and interview in 1984; the subsequent home interviews in 1984 and 1985; and the follow-up interviews in 1996–7 and 2003–9.

REFERENCES

Browne, K. (2001). (Ng)amuk revisited: Emotional expression and mental illness in Central Java, Indonesia. *Transcultural Psychiatry*, 38, 147–65.

Connor, L. (1982). The unbounded self: Balinese therapy in theory and practice. In A. Marsella (Ed.), *Cultural conceptions of mental health and therapy* (pp. 251–67). Dordrecht: Reidel.

Connor, L., Asch, P., & Asch, T. (1986). *Jero Tapakan: Balinese healer*. Cambridge, MA: Cambridge University Press.

Cribb, R. (2004). The Indonesian genocide of 1965–66. In S. Totten (Ed.), *Teaching about genocide: Issues, approaches, and resources* (pp. 133–42). Fayetteville: University of Arkansas Press.

Donkin, S., & Williams, P. L. (2003). Neurotoxicity: Toxic responses of the nervous system. In P. L. Williams, R. C. James, & S. M. Roberts (Eds.), *Principles of toxicology* (pp. 146–56). New York: John Wiley & Sons.

Dwyer, L. (2004). "Pathetic souls" and restless remains: Ritual politics of reconciliation in Bali, Indonesia. Paper prepared for the seminar Truth, Justice and Redress in Post-Conflict Societies, Harvard University Weatherhead Center for International Affairs, November 1–3.

Dwyer, L., & Santikarma, D. (2004). When the world turned to chaos: 1965 and its aftermath. In R. Gellately (Ed.), *The specter of genocide: Mass murder in historical perspective* (pp. 289–306). Cambridge: Cambridge University Press.

Ebihara, M. (1968). *Svay: A Khmer village*. New York: Department of Anthropology, Columbia University.

Eisman, F. (1990). *Bali: Sekala and niskala*. Berkeley, CA: Periplus Editions.

Geertz, C. (1973). *The interpretation of cultures*. New York: Basic Books.

Geertz, H. (1994). *Images of power: Balinese painting made for Gregory Bateson and Margaret Mead*. Honolulu: University of Hawaii Press.

Hinton, D. E., Hinton, A., Chhean, D., Pich, V., Loeum, J. R., & Pollack, M. H. (2009). Nightmares among Cambodian refugees: The breaching of concentric ontological security. *Culture, Medicine, and Psychiatry*, 33, 219–65.

Hobart, A. (1997). *The people of Bali*. London: Blackwell.

Hollan, D., & Wellenkamp, J. (1994). *Contentment and suffering: Culture and experience in Toraja*. New York: Columbia University Press.

Howe, L. (1984). Gods, peoples, witches and spirits: The Balinese system of person definition. *Bijdragen vor den Taal-, Land-, en Volkenkunde*, 140, 193–222.

Jennaway, M. (2002). *Sisters and lovers: Women and desire in Bali*. New York: Rohan and Littlefield.

Jensen, G., & Suryani, L. K. (1993). *The Balinese people: A reinvestigation of character*. Oxford: Oxford University Press.

Keyes, C. (1977). *The golden peninsula: Culture and adaptation in mainland Southeast Asia*. New York: Macmillan.

Laderman, C. (1991). *Taming the wind of desire: Psychology, medicine and aesthetics in Malay shamanistic performance*. Berkeley: University of California Press.

Lemelson, R. (1999). Re-checking the color of chickens: Indigenous, ethnographic and clinical perspectives on obsessive-compulsive disorder and Tourette's syndrome in Bali. Unpublished doctoral dissertation, University of California, Los Angeles.

(2003). Obsessive-compulsive disorder in Bali: The cultural shaping of a neuropsychiatric disorder. *Transcultural Psychiatry*, 3, 377–408.

Lemelson, R., Kirmayer, L. J., & Barad, M. (2007). Trauma in context: Integrating biological, clinical and cultural perspectives. In L. Kirmayer, R. Lemelson, & M. Barad, (Eds.), *Understanding trauma: Integrating cultural, psychological and biological perspectives*. Cambridge: Cambridge University Press.

Lemelson, R., & Suryani L. K. (2006). Cultural formulation of psychiatric diagnoses: The spirits, *penyakit ngeb* and the social suppression of memory: A complex clinical case from Bali. *Culture, Medicine and Psychiatry*, 30, 389–413.

Mead, M., & Bateson, G. (1942). *Balinese character*. New York: New York Academy of Sciences.

Robinson, G. (1998). *The dark side of paradise: Political violence in Bali*. Ithaca, NY: Cornell University Press.

Ruddick, A. (1986). *Charmed lives: Illness, healing, power and gender in a Balinese village*. Providence, RI: Department of Anthropology, Brown University.

Sack, H., Clarke, G. N., & Seely, J. (1995). Posttraumatic stress disorder across two generations of Cambodian refugees. *Journal of the American Academy of Child and Adolescent Psychiatry*, 34, 1160–6.

Santikarma, D. (1995). *Koh ngomong, the Balinese tactic and the spirit of resistance*. Fourth International Bali Studies Conference, Sydney University.

(2003). Dari stres ke trauma: Politik ingatan dan kekerasan di Bali. *Kompas*, July 30.

Suryani, L. K. (1984). Culture and mental disorder: The case of bebainan in Bali. *Culture, Medicine and Psychiatry*, 1, 95–113.

Wikan, U. (1989). Illness from fright or soul loss: A North Balinese culture-bound syndrome? *Culture, Medicine and Psychiatry*, 13, 25–50.

(1990). *Managing turbulent hearts: A Balinese formula for living*. Chicago: University of Chicago Press.

8 "Everything Here Is Temporary": Psychological Distress and Suffering among Iraqi Refugees in Egypt

Nadia El-Shaarawi

Psychological problems ... begin from Iraq and continue where they (refugees) live now or where they settled in Egypt. It is concern about the war itself, second about the life, and the shortage of life facilities. Also about the unclear future; the future is an important thing to the person, to the human being. If the future is not clear, some problems will begin. (Laith, NGO physician, Cairo, 2007)

Living in Egypt has an effect on my health. Of course. Every day I wake up, I feel that I am older by ten years.... Every day, ten years. Because of the sadness and because I am scared. Maybe one day the Egyptian government will say that we cannot accept Iraqis and will make us go back. I cannot go back. I will kill myself before I go back. The media is saying that things are better in Iraq, but they are lying. Our families there, they tell us it is as bad.... So I am afraid of going back to Iraq, and I am afraid of staying here in Egypt. So I have no choices. We came here as a station. It is a temporary place. I can't be excited for anything. I can't be excited for tomorrow. If I want to buy anything I say no, maybe the money can help in another place. The future is unknown and we cannot decide anything. We are waiting for an unknown future. So we are very sad here. I can't stay more in Egypt. I hate myself. (May, Iraqi refugee woman, Cairo, 2008)

I had asked May, an Iraqi woman living in Cairo, about her health in exile and she tied together her experiences in Iraq, her life in Egypt, and her desire to move elsewhere into a single narrative of suffering and anxiety. We were sitting together in the office of a local nongovernmental organization (NGO) that provides legal assistance to refugees in Egypt. May had gone to the office with her siblings, with whom she lived in Egypt, to seek resettlement to another country. That afternoon, as on many other days, the office was full of Iraqis seeking the same thing, and in a quiet moment, we sat together and May explained her desire to leave Egypt. I had initially gone to Egypt in 2007 to understand the health and psychosocial needs of the Iraqi refugees who had fled there in the aftermath of the 2003 invasion and subsequent violence and instability in their country. Yet I soon came to see, as illustrated by the statements of May and Laith, that health and psychosocial well-being were inextricably linked not only to experiences in Iraq, but to the uncertainty and insecurity of life in Egypt and to existential anxiety about the future.

195

The refugees with whom I spoke linked this insecurity directly to their suffering and psychological distress, including feelings of depression and anxiety, trauma and somatic complaints.

May's Story

When I met May, she was forty years old, highly educated, unmarried, and living with her siblings and their families in a flat in a Cairo suburb. Her family had initially struggled to take her to the NGO's downtown office, as she rarely left the house except to go to work. I remarked on the fact that she had found employment in Egypt, where refugees are not granted work permits and many cannot find any employment at all. In addition to working in the informal sector under conditions she found unacceptable, May was caring for a disabled family member. Despite her family's open concern about her psychological condition, May had not sought any professional treatment or care.

May spoke to me about her experiences in Baghdad both before and immediately after the 2003 invasion. As a Shi'a woman, she had felt oppressed under the regime of Saddam Hussein, and had initially hoped that she and her family would find freedom in the new Iraq. These hopes were soon disappointed when a bomb was dropped on their house, destroying nearly the entire building. May and her family members were all able to escape to a nearby shelter, but lived in fear and desperate conditions for several weeks without heat, electricity, or running water as they waited for the situation to stabilize so that they could rebuild their home. Despite their hope for the future, May and her family were afraid of the American forces and the growing violence and instability in the country. One summer night while the family was sleeping on their roof for relief from the heat, a bomb exploded near the house, creating a terrible blast. Her mother had developed severe anxiety during the first Gulf War and was startled by the explosion. In fright, she went down into the house to pray. She never returned, and when May went to check on her, she saw that her mother had died while praying. Her mother's death profoundly affected her, making it difficult for her to continue with her work and studies.

May recounted how she was only able to continue her studies because of the support and encouragement of her best friend, Noora. However, in 2006, May and Noora were walking down the street in the middle of the day when armed men burst out of cars and abducted Noora, leaving May unharmed. During the period 2005–7, threats of violence and kidnapping at the hands of militias or gangs were widespread (Al-Mohammad, 2012). May recognized that the kidnappers were from a Shi'a militia and thought that her friend might have been targeted because she was Sunni. May thought that because she was Shi'a, she might be able to intervene, but when she tried to inquire about Noora, the militia threatened May's life too. Her family was terrified and urged her to flee the country. May fled to Egypt in 2006 and later learned that Noora's body had been found a few days later.

As a single Shi'a Iraqi woman, May faced considerable difficulties living as a refugee in Egypt. She reported overwhelming sadness and difficulty adjusting to life in Egypt. In Iraq, May's unmarried status was seen as an unfortunate side effect of a society in which many young men had been killed by war and was shared by other women her age. However, in Egypt, a society where marriage is expected and childlessness is considered a great misfortune, May felt ostracized. She was repeatedly asked to explain her marital status and felt that people assumed she was "not a good woman" because she was unmarried. As a Shi'a Muslim, she experienced additional isolation from the predominantly Sunni Muslim Egyptian society, as neighbors and strangers alike openly questioned her about her faith, sometimes derisively. She reported feeling like an outsider in Egyptian society.

When I asked May about her psychological state, she told me that she had developed a nervous condition at the beginning of the war, which had become progressively worse with the death of her mother, with her friend's kidnapping, and throughout her time in exile in Cairo. She explained her suffering in terms of fear, anxiety, trauma, and what she termed psychological tiredness. The idea of being psychologically tired (*ta'aban*), which emerged repeatedly in interviews, refers to a deep and overwhelming fatigue that is experienced by the sufferer as bodily exhaustion but attributed to psychological, emotional, or social causes, especially stressful, difficult, or overwhelming life circumstances. May framed her anxiety in terms of insecurity and uncertainty about the future:

I cannot find peace in my mind and I am constantly afraid for the lives of my loved ones or anxious about the dark future ahead. I cannot sleep at night because my mind is too full of thought and sadness. I know that we have changed place and that it is safer here but it is still very uncertain. Everything here is temporary. The lack of security I feel in my job only makes things worse. In the past all my friends used to tell me that I had a great sense of humor and now they say that they miss me and they are sad without me. But the truth is I no longer have a sense of humor. I never even smile anymore.

May's description of how her suffering in Iraq and in Egypt affected her life and self illustrates one of the key issues that I address in this paper, namely, the implications of an insecure and uncertain life in exile for suffering and psychological distress. In this chapter, I consider the experiences of Iraqi refugees, particularly in terms of the implications of the uncertainty and insecurity of life in Egypt for psychosocial well-being and recovery from traumatic experience. In this context, I explore how the experience of suffering is intimately tied up with the conditions of life in exile, particularly when the place of exile is not understood as a refuge, but instead as a liminal, temporary stage, a stage that may in fact contribute to a refugee's suffering. Much literature has described the mental health of refugees who have fled violence and arrived in their final postmigration setting (Beiser, 1999; D. Hinton, Nickerson, & Bryant, 2011; Ingleby, 2005; Jenkins, 1991; Kinzie, 2007; Kirmayer et al., 2011). However, these findings may not apply to refugees who see themselves in a temporary place and who feel that recovery cannot occur in that space. Moreover, there may be important implications for health and psychosocial well-being when what is originally conceived of as temporary exile, a liminal, in-between stage, becomes long-term displacement with no end in sight.

Few researchers have considered the effects of ongoing, uncertain efforts to seek stability and rebuild lives on the mental health and well-being of refugees (though scholars recently have focused on the effects of daily stressors on mental health and severity of PTSD; for a review, see D. Hinton et al., 2011). For example, there are significantly fewer studies of the mental health of asylum seekers who are in the process of seeking legal status and do not yet have refugee status than of recognized refugees (Gross, 2004; Haas, 2012; James, 2009; Silove, Sinnerbrink, Field, Manicavasagar, & Steel, 1997). One study of Iraqis in the asylum system in the Netherlands found that those who had been in the system for two years or more had significantly higher levels of psychopathology, especially depressive and anxiety disorders, than newly arrived Iraqi asylum seekers (Laban, Komproe, Gernaat, & Jong, 2008). This study is in contrast to research with resettled refugees, which has shown stable or decreasing levels of psychopathology over time (Beiser & Hou, 2001; Boehnlein et al., 2004; Steel et al., 2006; Westermeyer, Neider, & Vang, 1984) and suggests that lengthy asylum processes in which refugees' current and future status is uncertain may be associated with psychosocial problems. Similarly, Steel and colleagues (2011) have found that refugees living with restrictive, insecure legal statuses showed an increase in psychopathology while mental health concerns decreased for refugees who had permanent resettlement status. With the increased fortification of borders (Gibney, 2004), generally decreasing numbers of refugees applying for asylum (Hatton, 2009), and most refugees living in countries of the global South, it is worth considering the effects of uncertainty on refugees in countries of first asylum. To this effect, this chapter considers Iraqi refugees' emic understandings of uncertainty, suffering, and psychological distress to elucidate the meaning and experience of living in an uncertain status and its effects on health and well-being.

When we met, May was coping with the realization that her stay in Egypt, which she had thought would be temporary, was growing progressively longer. Her anxiety seemed to stem primarily from a feeling of being without place – she argued that she could not go back to Iraq, could not stay any longer in Egypt, and did not have the freedom to go anywhere else. Although she missed home, May was afraid to return to Iraq because of ongoing violence and her belief that she was still threatened. Yet resettlement, which she and many other Iraqis desired, is available to only a small number of refugees who meet specific criteria. The United Nations High Commissioner for Refugees (UNHCR) estimates that less than 1 percent of refugees are resettled[1] (UNHCR, 2013). Resettlement is legally understood not as a right, but as a measure afforded when individual refugees are in need of more protection than is available in the country of first asylum. Unable to return to Iraq, unable to travel elsewhere, and unable to integrate into Egyptian society, May and others spoke of their suffering and anxiety about the future. In this chapter, I discuss Iraqi refugees' self-reported psychological distress and the ways in which this suffering is related to an existential sense of anxiety evoked by the insecurity of an uncertain life in exile.

Methods

This paper is based on ongoing fieldwork in Egypt. I conducted ethnographic interviews with 70 Iraqi refugees in refugees' homes and in an NGO that provides legal and psychosocial services to refugees in Cairo.[2] Additional data were collected through interviews with health care providers who serve Iraqi refugees in various capacities and participant observation within the NGO and in the community. The NGO in which I was a participant observer in December 2007 and January 2008 was originally an informal organization that sought to assist Iraqi refugees in Egypt, particularly those who might qualify for resettlement. The office assisted refugees with taking testimonies, preparing cases, and acting as advocates. In addition, the office was a place where Iraqi refugees showed up throughout the day seeking assistance of many kinds. When I returned in the summer of 2009, the NGO had become more formalized but still provided many of the same services. In addition to legal services, the office had developed a psychosocial department, which provided psychosocial assistance including counseling, referral, and group support to clients. While the office had previously specifically served Iraqi refugees, by 2009 it had broadened its scope to assist refugees of all nationalities, although Iraqis continued to make up more than 80 percent of the clientele.

A "Temporary Place": Life in Egypt for Iraqi Refugees

To understand May's desire to leave Egypt and seek her future elsewhere, it is important to situate her experiences within the broader context of conditions for Iraqi refugees in Egypt and to understand why Egypt is seen as a "temporary place" by many Iraqis. Despite the length of their stay in the country, Egypt is understood as temporary by Iraqi refugees for a number of reasons that emerged in the interviews. The political realities of Egypt, where Iraqi refugees are implicitly treated as temporary visitors (Sadek, 2010, 2011), combined with Iraqis' own desires, construct a dynamic whereby settlement or integration in Egypt is only possible for a few. In the following I discuss some of the factors that influence Iraqis' understanding of their stay in Egypt as temporary and consider the implications of these conditions for self-reported well-being.

Current estimates of the numbers of Iraqi refugees remaining in Egypt vary; a statistical survey published in 2008 estimated a population of seventeen thousand (Fargues, El-Masry, Sadek, & Shaban, 2008) but numbers have declined significantly since then. Most of the Iraqi refugees with whom I spoke had fled to Egypt before or during 2007, at the height of sectarian violence and political instability in their country (Fargues et al., 2008). Iraqis traveled to Egypt with the expectation that their stay would be temporary and that they would either be able to return home or be resettled to another country. Many traveled to Egypt via Syria or Jordan, the countries that have hosted the largest numbers of Iraqi refugees (Devi, 2007). When asked why they went to Egypt instead of fleeing to another country, most mentioned that life in Egypt was more affordable than in other countries in the region. However, a variety of other reasons were mentioned as well, including the distance of Egypt from Iraq. The proximity of Syria and Jordan to Iraq made some participants uncomfortable as they noted that militias operated in those countries, and they did not want to be around other Iraqis after what they had suffered in their country. In addition, some mentioned that Egyptians were more sympathetic to Iraqis and frequently remarked on the millions of Egyptians who traveled to Iraq to work in the 1980s, from which they attributed a certain preexisting relationship between Iraqis and Egyptians.[3] Participants also mentioned a familiarity with Egyptian society from songs and films, as Egypt has historically been a major producer of entertainment for the region.

In Egypt, Iraqi refugees live mostly in urban areas such as Cairo, Sixth of October City, and Alexandria. Despite living among the general population, integration into Egyptian society is not possible for most Iraqi refugees. Egypt struggles in many ways to provide for its own population, and it likewise struggles to provide for refugees (Coker, 2004). Egypt is a signatory to the 1951 Convention on the Rights of Refugees yet has entered reservations that restrict refugees' ability to work, attend public schools, and access public health care. As a result, many Iraqi refugees in Egypt are unable to generate income and must rely on savings or remittances from family living elsewhere. Iraqis living in Egypt face some unique challenges as a self-settled urban refugee population. Despite decades of conflict, Iraqis have enjoyed a higher average standard of living than is common in Egypt, and many Iraqis in Egypt, many of whom are well-educated middle-class professionals, have found it difficult to adjust to living as refugees. While a small number of refugees who have managed to start or continue businesses are well off, many Iraqis have watched their savings dwindle and are left with almost no possibility of earning a living in Egypt. Egyptians, however, sometimes conflate Iraqi refugees with other wealthy visitors or migrants from the Persian Gulf, and some refugees reported stress caused by the incongruity between locals' perceptions of their ability to pay for goods and services and their actual, sometimes dire, financial situation. Participants also spoke about barriers to education and the importance of their own and their children's education to their success in life.

Family separation was another important cause of suffering mentioned by participants. After the influx of large numbers of Iraqis fleeing to Egypt in 2006–7, the Egyptian government restricted visas, making it extremely difficult for Iraqis to enter the country. As a result, family members who either did not join their family on the initial trip or who have left Egypt for any reason find it challenging and sometimes impossible to rejoin their families in Egypt. Resettlement is another cause of family separation. Adult children, siblings, and other relations are often processed for resettlement separately from other family members, a circumstance that can lead to their resettlement to another country at a significantly different time than their family and cause separation that may span months or more than a year. In addition, the circumstances of recent forced migration from Iraq and the existing Iraqi diaspora mean that participants had close relatives in many different countries and this separation was often discussed with a profound sense of sadness. Personal and family security was also mentioned as a cause of feelings of anxiety related to security and safety in Egypt, security of family members and loved ones in Iraq, and imagined future security concerns. This existential insecurity and uncertainty about the future was mentioned by participants as a reason for their inability to integrate into Egyptian society and was identified as a major cause of suffering and psychological distress.

Hala Nufsia: Psychological Distress and Suffering

Psychological distress, such as that expressed by May, was a recurring theme in the interviews. Participants spoke about their personal psychological suffering and the psychological well-being of their families. When asked about health, many participants discussed psychological suffering, while others presented somatic complaints. Many of the research participants had directly experienced events such as kidnapping, torture, detention, an explosion, or a direct threat to their lives. Others had close friends or family members who had been killed or who were victims of threats or violence. In addition, many interviewees spoke of the generalized conditions of violence, fear, and uncertainty that they had experienced in Iraq before they fled to Egypt. All of the participants had directly experienced one or more events that would qualify as traumatic events in the sense of the *DSM-IV* definition of posttraumatic stress disorder (American Psychiatric Association, 2000). Although psychological suffering was a pervasive theme in the interviews, not all participants reported psychological distress, and not all participants attributed their suffering to these traumatic events, but instead focused on conditions of life in exile. May, however, discussed her distress in terms of trauma:

I feel that I suffer the extreme effects of trauma. I can only remember sad things, not anything happy or even mundane such as a telephone number or a person's name. If you tell me to go and get something for you I will forget what it is and if you tell me words I will not remember them. I find that often I am staring into space, only thinking of the bad things that have happened to me and the people I love. I know that I am not really mentally well because on one occasion I went to the doctor and I was wearing two different shoes. I cannot be bothered to look after myself. These days I find that I am often thinking that I just want to die.

May articulated her suffering in terms of a lack of "mental wellness" and related this to the suffering that she has experienced. The symptoms and other manifestations of psychological distress mentioned by participants included insomnia, isolation, nightmares, loss of appetite, anxiety, fear, flashbacks, lack of enjoyment of life, loss of trust, suicidal ideation, sadness, and feelings of loss. Other, more somatic, complaints were also associated with psychological suffering, including heart pain, skin problems, weight gain or loss, high blood pressure, and fatigue.

Others similarly articulated their ongoing distress in terms of psychological problems caused by events in Iraq, such as a man named Basim, who spoke of how his previous experiences in Iraq left him struggling with anxiety in Egypt:

I have also acquired psychological problems as a result of these incidents in Iraq. I get distracted easily and it is rare that I laugh. I am always checking to make sure that the windows are closed and the flat is secure because I am constantly worried that we will be attacked in some way. I have to do everything myself and I do not trust anyone.

Another man, Salman, who had been detained and tortured in Iraq for an extended period before being released and fleeing to Egypt, continued to suffer from the lingering effects of his ordeal. He describes these effects in terms of "anxiety" and being "psychologically tired":

Anxiety is the most difficult disease that I have. Although I used to be social in nature, I am not anymore. I have lost my appetite entirely. I have very much trouble sleeping. For example, I sleep at 5 a.m. and wake up at 10 a.m. I have such bad nightmares. When I try to fall asleep, I just cannot. I feel psychologically very tired.

Tiredness *(ta'aban)* was the most commonly expressed psychological ailment. Participants attributed this deep sense of fatigue to both experiences suffered in Iraq and the challenges of life in exile in Egypt. This expression of existential fatigue seemed in many ways to be a result of the cumulative experiences of surviving political violence, living in exile, and dealing with the uncertainty of the future.

Not all of the experiences of violence that continued to affect the health of Iraqi refugees in Egypt were related to the 2003 war and subsequent sectarian violence, even though this violence was the reason for flight from Iraq. Instead, participants referred to stressors in Egypt as well as events from various points in the legacy of war, violence, and repression that make up Iraq's recent political history. For example, one man, Bilal, recounted the long-term physical effects of torture at the hands of Saddam Hussein's security forces as his primary health concern. Arrested and detained in the early 1990s, Bilal was physically and psychologically tortured for a month. More than fifteen years later, when asked about his health, he stated:

I am still suffering permanent effects of this mistreatment. My kidneys have never worked normally after the torture and started producing stones soon after my release. I regularly experience serious pain in my kidneys. As I found out after I married my wife, I also acquired temporary impotence. I still have nightmares about the torture and suffer from flashbacks to the episodes of my mistreatment.

The long-term effects of this violence were such that they remain Bilal's primary health concern to this day. Salman, who had been kidnapped, tortured, and detained for an extended period after the 2003 invasion of Iraq, recounted similar psychological and physical effects. He explained that in Cairo

I really do not eat and I sleep only a few hours a night, because I do feel strongly that I am slowly dying. Until now, the ghost of torture is in front of my eyes, they knocked out all of my teeth and I have high blood pressure, diabetes and a heart disability.

In addition to discussing suffering in terms of psychological distress, some refugees, such as Salman, experienced somatic complaints after violent or traumatic experiences. The significance of these complaints is that while refugees sometimes conceptualized their somatic ailments as originating in psychological suffering, at other times they recounted seeking medical attention but having their concerns dismissed as "psychological." These somatic complaints included heart pain, back pain, stomach pain, loss of breath, loss of speech, nocturnal enuresis, thyroid conditions, skin conditions, and allergies. Salman informed me that he had physical pain in his heart and that he became out of breath with little exertion. He had repeatedly visited doctors in Egypt; yet none could find any problem with his heart. He was told that his pain was psychological, an explanation he was reluctant to accept. This theme of somatic complaints was recurrently mentioned by participants, who occasionally rebelled against physicians' inability to diagnose their disease and other times accepted doctors' advice that their illnesses were psychological in nature.

The suffering experienced by Iraqi refugees in Egypt was often described in terms of the quality of one's *hala nufsia*. *Hala nufsia* is a term that was used repeatedly in the interviews and that I also heard frequently in observations of the community. It can best be understood as an expression of a person's well-being or suffering, expressed through somatic ailments, behavioral problems, or emotional afflictions, which are understood to be psychological or existential in origin. Importantly, *hala nufsia* is not necessarily associated with mental illness requiring the care of a psychiatrist, which might invoke social stigma, but is often dealt with in the family through coping methods such as religion, family support, and learning to bear one's suffering. *Hala nufsia* was invoked by Iraqis when speaking of themselves, as a way of expressing their *ta'aban* or other somatic complaints. It was also used by Iraqis when referring to each other as a way of expressing care and understanding for one another's suffering. (Many cultures have an ethnopsychology, or ethnopsychophysiology, according to which worry and suffering are thought to cause somatic symptoms, and those somatic symptoms are so read by others in that cultural context; see, e.g., D. Hinton, Pich, Marques, Nickerson, & Pollack, 2010; D. Hinton, S. Hinton, Um, Chea, & Sak, 2002).

Psychological Distress and the Uncertainty of Life in Exile

Understanding the effects of life in exile on health and well-being is crucial to understanding and supporting recovery from violence for refugees. To this effect, I sought to understand whether Iraqi refugees perceived that their health and psychosocial well-being had improved in Egypt, specifically, whether or not they were able to recover in their place of asylum. The responses were ambivalent, with key social and economic factors in exile contributing to refugees' accounts of their well-being, and in some cases, entirely superseding or supplanting complaints related to the war in Iraq. In many cases, however, the narratives were additive, with conditions in exile an additional insult that compounded those experienced in Iraq. Uncertainty and insecurity repeatedly emerged as a cause of suffering and anxiety for Iraqi refugees.

Refugees' narratives indicated ambivalence about whether recovery was occurring in Egypt or health and well-being were in fact worsening. While some refugees, especially those who had experienced severe or repeated violence or threats in Iraq, affirmed that their health had improved in Egypt, more participants had an almost opposite response. For example, Omar attributed the worsening of his and his family's health to the uncertainty of their situation in Cairo. Speaking of his family's illnesses, he said:

Most of the problems happened in Iraq from the anxiety, thoughtfulness and depression. Sure they have got worse in Egypt. I don't sleep well here. We are in the bottom. When I look at my children at home, and my wife, I don't know what to do for them. I don't know what to do for myself also.

Refugees cited safety concerns, worry for the future, anxiety about friends and family in Iraq, and worry about their lives in Egypt as reasons for continued distress and ill health. While some participants felt that the threats to their lives that they had experienced in Iraq continued in Egypt, others felt safe from the violence of war in Egypt. For example, Ahmed, whose wartime experiences included neighborhood bombings, the occupation of his house by the American forces, and death threats by militias, argued: "We feel safe here and we feel comfortable psychologically. Because when we were in Iraq, and we hear the shots or the airstrikes we become stressed and feel tension, feel terrified." Despite expressing distress about his situation in Egypt, Ahmed insisted that his security had improved greatly and that his *hala nufsia* was improved. In general, refugees who felt continued threats in Cairo reported that this perception caused them worry and distress, while those who felt that they had escaped from the violence in Iraq did not report the same kind of safety concerns.

In interviews, the theme of uncertainty was repeatedly mentioned by participants and linked to the quality of their *hala nufsia*. Refugees mentioned feeling in limbo in Egypt – they were unable to return to Iraq, unable to live in Egypt, and unable to go elsewhere. As a result, their future, and that of their children, was uncertain, and this status was identified as a major cause of anxiety and suffering. For example, Ahmed, the elderly man who spoke to me of his comfort in Egypt compared to Iraq, later spoke of his family's uncertain situation in Egypt and their anxiety about the future. Ahmed's wife, Ghada, had a severe allergy, which they said had developed in Iraq as a result of shock or trauma and manifested in fainting attacks, swelling, hives, and yellow skin. They articulated how conditions of life in Cairo had exacerbated the allergy. In describing the origin of the allergy, Ahmed said: "The doctor said that this allergy came because of being nervous suddenly. He said she had a sudden strong reaction and it did not leave her.... When she feels the difficult situation of living in Cairo, she has allergy." Ghada related the continuation of her allergy to the circumstances of life in Cairo: "Whenever I look at my children, who are not working and not studying, I become depressed and I have the allergy." Like Ghada, other parents related uncertainty to concern about their children's future. The relationships among uncertainty, past trauma, health, and well-being are particularly apparent in this statement by a father, Mohamed, who spoke about his children's suffering and the ways in which his uncertain future, to him, was akin to a form of death:

My daughter speaks while she is sleeping, but sometimes she cries alone.... My older son just sits alone and starts to drift away. It is as though he is not present at all. But his pronunciation and his speaking have been affected. Now he is not speaking clearly or correctly. Sometimes he wakes up suddenly (shocked) in the middle of the night. But generally, they don't speak for long times. All of us are like this. We sleep a few hours per day, because we are thoughtful all the time. How can we solve this? It reached the point where we are reaching the point of death. It has passed life threatening. We don't think it is easy to overcome. We have an unknown future, my family and I. We don't know what to do. We don't know what will happen tomorrow.

Mohamed's despair about his family's life is evident in his suggestion that their situation has "passed life threatening." For Mohamed, the uncertainty of life in Cairo was more than simply a threat to his health, but a threat to life itself. May expressed a similar sentiment when discussing the uncertainty of her life in Egypt. She argued that living in Egypt affected her health, but that she was powerless to change it as she could not go anywhere else. She spoke about her fear of returning to Iraq, her fear of living in Egypt, and her anxiety about the future as the sum of her suffering. The theme of uncertainty was strongly related to an expression of loss of control over one's life, as expressed by May when she repeatedly said, "I have no choices." Far from neutrally describing circumstances in exile, Mohamed and May both perceive the uncertainty of their lives in Egypt as a threat to security, well-being, and life itself. Refugees argued that their inability to make a life for themselves or their family in Egypt, and their inability to know what the future could hold, caused them suffering and negatively affected their health and well-being.

Conclusion

The effects of displacement as a result of violence include physical, mental, and social disruptions (Henry, 2006). Indeed, the power of violence and persecution lies in their ability to break apart interconnections and communities, leaving survivors struggling to recreate meaning in a changed world (Das, Kleinman, Lock, Ramphele, & Reynolds, 2001). Anthropologists have studied how people displaced by violence seek to make meaning in this context and reorder their lives (Becker, Beyene, & Ken, 2000a, 2000b; Coker, 2004; D. Hinton et al., 2010; Jenkins, 1996; Nordstrom, 1998; Ong, 2003). In this chapter, I have drawn on Iraqi refugees' expressions of suffering and explored the ways in which this suffering is tied up in experiences of uncertainty and insecurity in Egypt.

Iraqi refugees, such as May, fled to Egypt seeking temporary respite from a country rendered unsafe by war, political instability, and sectarian violence. Years after the beginning of the 2003 war, much of Iraq remains unstable and unsafe for return (UNHCR, 2010). As a result, Iraqi refugees' temporary exile in Egypt has stretched into years of uncertainty and a feeling that life is on hold or in limbo. Restrictive resettlement programs mean that the majority of Iraqi refugees are unable to leave Egypt, and the extended nature of their stay in this "temporary place" has implications for psychosocial well-being. While May and others expressed their suffering in terms of trauma, anxiety, and depression, they also drew on emic concepts of *ta'aban* (tiredness) and *hala nufsia* (a local conceptualization of well-being) to express the suffering associated with exile and uncertainty. These emic idioms recognize the cumulative effects of violence, exile, and an uncertain future on the health and well-being of Iraqi refugees in Egypt.

I argue that it is not only the suffering and trauma of past persecution that affect refugees and that should be attended to by policy makers and practitioners, but also the suffering associated with life in limbo – which, for Iraqi refugees in Egypt, includes the feeling of uncertainty about one's legal, economic, educational, personal, or familial security, in combination with traumatic experiences in wartime. The legal definition of a refugee focuses exclusively on past persecution before flight from the country of origin; however, the meaning and experience of past persecution are colored by conditions in the place of asylum. The importance of these conditions is particularly apparent in the case of Iraqis in Egypt, whose weaving together of narratives of war, political instability and repression, conditions in exile, and hopes for the future formed an intricate web of meaning that influenced their psychosocial well-being and that subverted categories of premigration, migration, and postmigration stages (Desjarlais, Eisenberg, Good, & Kleinman, 1996). This continuum of experience and meaning and its effects on well-being have implications for recovery from mass violence, particularly in the context of lives made insecure not by the threat of imminent violence but by the anxiety-provoking effects of a life in limbo.

NOTES

1 The UNHCR estimate is for all refugees. Resettlement numbers for Iraqis are somewhat higher because of programs such as the "Direct Access" program in the United States, which was established after it became increasingly clear that Iraqis who supported the U.S. mission in Iraq were under threat because of their association with the Americans. By 2013, more than eighty thousand Iraqis had been resettled to the United States under this program (United States Citizenship and Immigration Services [USCIS], 2013).

2 A combination of purposive and convenience sampling was used for this study. The exploratory nature of this study, combined with the difficulty of accessing the population of interest, justified this approach. The sample, mostly drawn from Iraqi clients of the NGO, may be biased toward those Iraqis in Egypt who were seeking assistance, and this group may be different from those Iraqis who do not. Unfortunately, the somewhat hidden nature of the general Iraqi refugee population in Egypt made a random sample impossible. However, some participants were not clients of the organization and were not seeking legal services. Service providers, who served as key informants, were sampled purposively in order to gain information about services available to refugees and providers' perceptions of the health situation of Iraqi refugees. This study is unable to provide data that can be generalized to the general population of Iraqi refugees in Egypt. Rather than estimating parameters, this study provides opportunities to generate information about issues of concern and suggest

directions for more in-depth research. This project was reviewed by the Case Western Reserve University IRB.

3 This relationship was sometimes problematic. While some Iraqi respondents stated that Egyptians understood them better because of the time that Egyptians had spent working in Iraq, others felt that this led Egyptians to have incorrect expectations for Iraqi refugees. For example, Iraqis reported that Egyptians often assumed they were wealthy, possibly on the basis of Egyptians' experiences of the standard of living that they had witnessed in Iraq.

REFERENCES

Al-Mohammad, H. (2012). A kidnapping in Basra: The struggles and precariousness of life in postinvasion Iraq. *Cultural Anthropology*, 27, 597–614.

American Psychiatric Association. (2000). *Diagnostic and statistical manual of mental disorders*, 4th ed., text rev. Washington, DC: American Psychiatric Association.

Becker, G., Beyene, Y., & Ken, P. (2000a). Memory, trauma, and embodied distress: The management of disruption in the stories of Cambodians in exile. *Ethos*, 28, 320–45.

(2000b). Health, welfare reform, and narratives of uncertainty among Cambodian refugees. *Culture, Medicine, and Psychiatry*, 24, 139–63.

Beiser, M. (1999). *Strangers at the gate: The "boat people's" first ten years in Canada.* Toronto: University of Toronto Press.

Beiser, M., & Hou, F. (2001). Language acquisition, unemployment and depressive disorder among Southeast Asian refugees: A 10-year study. *Social Science & Medicine*, 53, 1321–34.

Boehnlein, J. K., Kinzie, J. D., Sekiya, U., Riley, C., Pou, K., & Rosborough, B. (2004). A ten-year treatment outcome study of traumatized Cambodian refugees. *Journal of Nervous and Mental Disease*, 192, 658–63.

Coker, E. M. (2004). "Traveling pains": Embodied metaphors of suffering among Southern Sudanese refugees in Cairo. *Culture, Medicine and Psychiatry*, 28, 15–39.

Das, V., Kleinman, A., Lock, M., Ramphele, M., & Reynolds, P. (2001). *Remaking a world: Violence, social suffering, and recovery*, 1st ed. Berkeley: University of California Press.

Desjarlais, R., Eisenberg, L., Good, B., & Kleinman, A. (1996). *World mental health: Problems and priorities in low-income countries.* New York: Oxford University Press.

Devi, S. (2007). Meeting the health needs of Iraqi refugees in Jordan. *Lancet*, 370, 1815–16.

Fargues, P., El-Masry, S., Sadek, S., & Shaban, A. (2008). *Iraqis in Egypt: A statistical survey in 2008.* Cairo: Center for Migration and Refugee Studies, The American University in Cairo. Retrieved from http://www.aucegypt. edu/GAPP/cmrs/Documents/Iraqis%20in%20Egypt%20Provisional%20 Copy.pdf

Gibney, M. J. (2004). *The ethics and politics of asylum: Liberal democracy and the response to refugees.* Cambridge: Cambridge University Press.

Gross, C. S. (2004). Struggling with imaginaries of trauma and trust: The refugee experience in Switzerland. *Culture, Medicine and Psychiatry*, 28, 151–67.

Haas, B. M. (2012). Suffering and the struggle for recognition: Lived experiences of the U.S. political asylum process. Unpublished doctoral dissertation, University of California, San Diego.

Hatton, T. J. (2009). The rise and fall of asylum: What happened and why? *The Economic Journal*, 119, F183–F213.

Henry, D. (2006). Violence and the body: Somatic expressions of trauma and vulnerability during war. *Medical Anthropology Quarterly*, 20, 379–98.

Hinton, D., Hinton, S., Um, K., Chea, A., & Sak, S. (2002). The Khmer "weak heart" syndrome: Fear of death from palpitations. *Transcultural Psychiatry*, 39, 323–44.

Hinton, D. E., Nickerson, A., & Bryant, R. A. (2011). Worry, worry attacks, and PTSD among Cambodian refugees: A path analysis investigation. *Social Science & Medicine*, 72, 1817–25.

Hinton, D. E, Pich, V., Marques, L., Nickerson, A., & Pollack, M. H. (2010). Khyâl attacks: A key idiom of distress among traumatized Cambodian refugees. *Culture, Medicine and Psychiatry*, 34, 244–78.

Ingleby, D. (2005). *Forced migration and mental health: Rethinking the care of refugees and displaced persons*. New York: Springer.

James, E. C. (2009). Neomodern insecurity in Haiti and the politics of asylum. *Culture, Medicine and Psychiatry*, 33, 153–9.

Jenkins, J. H. (1991). The state construction of affect: Political ethos and mental health among Salvadoran refugees. *Culture, Medicine and Psychiatry*, 15, 139–65.

(1996). The impress of extremity: Women's experience of trauma and political violence. In C. Brettell & C. Sargent (Eds.), *Gender and health, an international perspective* (pp. 278–91). New York: Prentice Hall.

Kinzie, J. D. (2007). PTSD among traumatized refugees. In L. J. Kirmayer, R. Lemelson, & M. Barad (Eds.), *Understanding trauma: Integrating biological, clinical, and cultural perspectives* (pp. 194–206). New York: Cambridge University Press

Kirmayer, L. J., Narasiah, L., Munoz, M., Rashid, M., Ryder, A. G., Guzder, J., Hassan, G., et al. (2011). Common mental health problems in immigrants and refugees: General approach in primary care. *Canadian Medical Association Journal*, 183, E959–E967.

Laban, C. J., Komproe, I. H., Gernaat, H. B., & de Jong, J. T. V. (2008). The impact of a long asylum procedure on quality of life, disability and physical health in Iraqi asylum seekers in the Netherlands. *Social Psychiatry and Psychiatric Epidemiology*, 43, 507–15.

Nordstrom, C. (1998). Terror warfare and the medicine of peace. *Medical Anthropology Quarterly*, 12, 103–21.

Ong, A. (2003). *Buddha is hiding: Refugees, citizenship, the New America*. Berkeley: University of California Press.

Sadek, S. (2010). Iraqi "temporary guests" in neighbouring countries. In E. Laipsan & A. Pandya (Eds.), *On the move: Migration challenges in the Indian Ocean littoral*. Washington, DC: Henry L. Stimson Center.

(2011). Safe haven or limbo? Iraqi refugees in Egypt. *International Journal of Contemporary Iraqi Studies*, 5, 185–97.

Silove, D., Sinnerbrink, I., Field, A., Manicavasagar, V., & Steel, Z. (1997). Anxiety, depression and PTSD in asylum-seekers: Associations with pre-migration trauma and post-migration stressors. *British Journal of Psychiatry*, 170, 351–7.

Steel, Z., Momartin, S., Silove, D., Coello, M., Aroche, J., & Tay, K. W. (2011). Two year psychosocial and mental health outcomes for refugees subjected to restrictive or supportive immigration policies. *Social Science & Medicine*, 72, 1149–56.

Steel, Z., Silove, D., Brooks, R., Momartin, S., Alzuhairi, B., & Susljik, I. (2006). Impact of immigration detention and temporary protection on the mental health of refugees. *British Journal of Psychiatry*, 188, 58–64.

UNHCR. (2010). *Note on the continued applicability of the April 2009 UNHCR Eligibility Guidelines for Assessing the International Protection Needs of Iraqi Asylum-Seekers.* Geneva: UNHCR.

(2013). *UNHCR global resettlement statistical report 2012.* Geneva: UNHCR, Resettlement Service.

United States Citizenship and Immigration Services (USCIS). (2013). *Iraqi refugee processing fact sheet.* Washington, DC: USCIS.

Westermeyer, J., Neider, J., & Vang, T. F. (1984). Acculturation and mental health: A study of Hmong refugees at 1.5 and 3.5 years postmigration. *Social Science & Medicine*, 18, 87–93.

9 Key Idioms of Distress and PTSD among Rural Cambodians: The Results of a Needs Assessment Survey

Devon E. Hinton, Alexander L. Hinton, and Kok-Thay Eng

Introduction

This chapter describes key idioms of distress among Cambodian refugees and their manner of generation, and it reports on the results of a needs assessment survey of rural Cambodians that was undertaken by the Documentation Center of Cambodia (DC-CAM) as part of their Victims of Torture (VoT) project.[1] The VoT project was conceived by the director of DC-Cam (Youk Chang) and implemented by a VoT project team leader (Kok-Thay Eng). The purpose of this project was to document experiences under the Khmer Rouge, to identify rural villagers who had significant distress, and to provide services to those suffering from PTSD. Members of DC-CAM went to rural villages in Kampot, Takeo, and Kandal Provinces and asked local officials (e.g., the commune or village chief) and villagers to identify individuals who had psychological problems owing to the Pol Pot period. After being interviewed, all participants were given basic mental health information, including instruction about the use of relaxation and breathing techniques to reduce stress, and those individuals who were found to have significant mental health concerns were provided with psychological services, including referral and modest funds to visit the closest mental health clinic and to pay for any prescribed medications.

To date, what little formal knowledge we have about mental health in Cambodia has been derived from a handful of instruments, such as the Harvard Trauma Questionnaire[2] and the Hopkins Checklist.[3] During a pilot version of the Victims of Torture project, DC-Cam team members noted that the instruments were not culturally sensitive in that they did not assess many symptoms of concern among those surveyed such as dizziness. After discussing these issues, the DC-CAM staff asked to include the Cambodian Symptom and Syndrome Inventory (C-SSI), an instrument devised by the first author based on work with Cambodian

Table 9.1. *The Cambodian Symptom and Syndrome Inventory (SSI): The somatic symptoms and cultural syndromes subscales*

Somatic symptoms	Syndromes
1. Dizziness	1. *Khyâl* attacks
2. Standing up and feeling dizzy	2. Standing up and feeling poorly to the point you feared fainting, *khyâl* overload, or heart attack
3. Blurry vision	
4. Tinnitus	3. Neck soreness to the point you feared the neck vessels would burst
5. Headache	
6. Neck soreness	4. "Heart weakness"
7. Palpitations	5. *Khyâl* hitting up from the stomach, making you fear you might die of asphyxia
8. Shortness of breath	
9. Cold hands and feet	6. "Thinking too much"
10. Sore arms and legs	7. "Ghost pushing you down" (sleep paralysis)
11. Weakness	
12. Poor appetite	

Note: This is more accurately called the abbreviated C-SSI because there is a longer version.

Americans in a Massachusetts clinic, as an addendum to the existing assessment survey in order to seek a more culturally sensitive means of assessing psychological distress in Cambodia. The C-SSI is an addendum of symptoms and syndromes (see Table 9.1) that are a key aspect of the presentation of trauma-type distress among Cambodian refugees but are not among the seventeen symptoms listed in the PTSD criteria of the *Diagnostic and Statistical Manual of Mental Disorders-IV-TR (DSM-IV-TR;* American Psychiatric Association, 2000*)* or among the updated list of twenty symptoms in the PTSD criteria of the *DSM-5* (American Psychiatric Association, 2013).

Historical Background

On April 17, 1975, after a brutal civil war in which hundreds of thousands of Cambodians died and many more were injured, displaced, or impoverished by the fighting, the Khmer Rouge took power. Over the next three and a half years (April 17, 1975, to January 6, 1979), the Khmer Rouge under the leadership of Pol Pot implemented a series of radical socioeconomic reforms in an attempt to enable Cambodia, renamed Democratic Kampuchea (DK), to make a "super great leap forward" into socialism (Becker, 1998; Chandler, 1999; A. Hinton, 2005).

Economic activity was dramatically reshaped as production was collectivized. Money, markets, and courts disappeared. Freedom of speech, travel, religion, and communication were severely curtailed.

In their effort to create a pure society of revolutionaries who would be loyal primarily to the state, the Khmer Rouge rusticated the cities, banned Buddhism, and splintered families: Family members were often separated for long periods, sent to work in other areas, where they labored long days though provided only starvation rations. Spies crept about at night searching for signs of subversion. Meanwhile, the Khmer Rouge established a security apparatus that targeted suspect groups – former soldiers, police, civil service personnel, professionals, the educated, the urbanites – for reeducation, imprisonment, torture, and often murder. By the time the Khmer Rouge were overthrown in January 1979 by a Vietnamese invasion, almost a quarter of Cambodia's eight million inhabitants had died of disease, starvation, overwork, and execution.

The suffering of Cambodians did not stop there. For more than a dozen years (1979–93), hundreds of thousands of refugees lived in difficult circumstances in camps along the Thai-Cambodian border. Some of these camps were highly militarized and subject to forced recruitment and shelling as a new civil war, enmeshed in Cold War politics, broke out among the new Vietnamese-backed Peoples Republic of Kampuchea government; the Khmer Rouge, who, after being routed by the Vietnamese troops, had been backed up, rearmed, and supplied by an odd coalition of Thailand, Cambodia, the United States, and other allies; and some smaller resistance groups (Shawcross, 1984; Terry, 2002). Even after a peace deal was brokered and the refugees were repatriated as part of a UN-sponsored election held in 1993, the new Royal Government of Cambodia continued to battle the Khmer Rouge, who had pulled out of the elections, until 1999, when the movement finally collapsed after Pol Pot's death and a series of defections. Besides dealing with this prolonged conflict, Cambodian villagers have had to deal with extreme economic difficulties: In certain years, floods or droughts resulted in diminished or nonexistent rice harvests, with the threat of starvation.[4]

Owing to these traumas and hardships, in Cambodia there are high rates of PTSD, with one study showing a 14.2 percent rate among those at least three years old at the time of the Pol Pot period (Sonis et al., 2009). But assessing PTSD symptoms is not sufficient to profile the effects of trauma in a cultural context. It is true that cross-cultural research indicates that many of the *DSM-IV* (and *DSM-5*) items such as nightmares, startle, and vivid unwanted recall of trauma events are a core part of the universal response to trauma (D. Hinton & Lewis-Fernández,

2011).[5] But many key symptoms and syndromes that are a central part of the trauma response in a particular cultural context are not assessed in the PTSD criteria. The Cambodian Symptom and Syndrome Inventory (SSI) is designed to survey such symptoms and cultural syndromes in the Cambodian context. In the following we review the items of the SSI before turning to the results of the needs assessment survey conducted in Cambodia.

Cambodian Symptom and Syndrome Inventory (C-SSI)

The C-SSI consists of two main parts, as is shown in Table 9.1, namely, culturally emphasized somatic complaints and key cultural syndromes that are common among traumatized Cambodians (for studies using the C-SSI among Cambodian refugees in the United States, see D. Hinton, Kredlow, Bui, Pollack, & Hofmann, 2012; D. Hinton, Kredlow, Pich, Bui, & Hofmann, 2013).

Somatic Complaints Assessed in the C-SSI

The Cambodian C-SSI assesses the 12 somatic symptoms listed in Table 9.1. To understand why these symptoms are common among traumatized Cambodians, each of these culturally salient somatic symptoms can be thought of as potentially generated in four different ways:

- By the biology of trauma that – for example, through trauma-caused arousal and reactivity – leads to somatic symptoms by activation of the autonomic nervous system and other biological means;
- By the local conceptualization of the disorder indicated by the symptoms such as a cultural syndrome (cultural syndrome here meant in the broad sense that includes local ideas about disturbances in the mental, bodily, and spiritual realms[6]), with that conceptualization producing catastrophic cognitions about somatic symptoms that in turn result in attentional amplification (e.g., seeking the body and mind for symptoms associated with the syndrome) and a fear response (e.g., a surge of autonomic arousal), both processes that increase somatic symptoms;
- By metaphoric resonances that increase the emotional salience of certain somatic symptoms such as through calling to mind current distress issues that are evoked by the somatic-type distress metaphors related to those somatic symptoms; and
- By trauma associations that lead to certain somatic symptoms activating trauma networks that are encoded by those somatic symptoms.

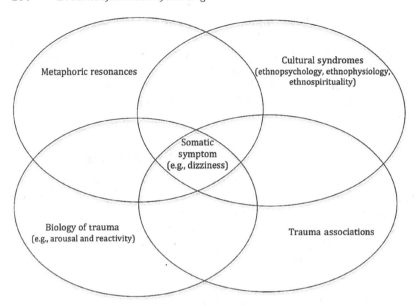

Figure 9.1. Four symptom dimensions of a somatic sensation.

We refer to the elucidation of these dimensions as a four-dimension symptom analysis. In Figure 9.1 we depict these four symptom dimensions using a Venn diagram, and in Figure 9.2 we show how these four symptom dimensions produce somatic symptoms among trauma victims in particular episodes. In the following sections we do a four-dimension analysis (Figure 9.1) of the SSI somatic symptoms, which reveals why those somatic symptoms would give rise to and result from the processes shown in Figure 9.2 – for example, the somatic symptoms are easily triggered owing to biology of trauma, the somatic symptoms give rise to prominent catastrophic cognitions, the somatic symptoms have extensive trauma associations and metaphoric resonances – and thereby cause the SSI somatic symptoms to be prominent in the Cambodian trauma ontology.[7]

The Biology of Trauma   Cambodians experienced extreme trauma during the Pol Pot period, and trauma can result in changes in the nervous system and psychological states that produce constant anxiety. The resulting chronic anxiety can generate all the somatic symptoms of the C-SSI by biological means (D. Hinton & Good, 2009a): palpitations and shortness of breath (from the sympathetic nervous system), dizziness (from anxiety effects on the balance system and the vagal system), neck soreness (from muscle tension), and cold extremities (from vasoconstriction).

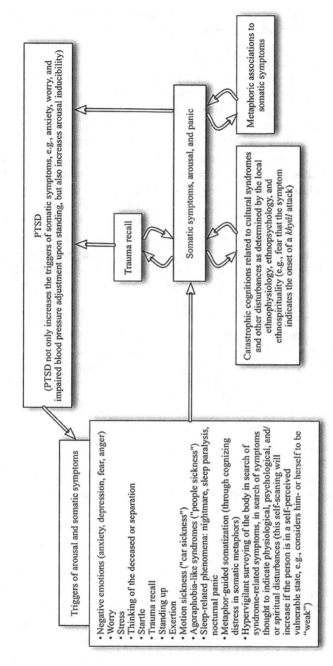

Figure 9.2. The multiplex model of the generation of somatic symptoms among trauma victims.

PTSD
(PTSD not only increases the triggers of somatic symptoms, e.g., anxiety, worry, and impaired blood pressure adjustment upon standing, but also increases arousal inducibility)

Metaphoric associations to somatic symptoms

Trauma recall

Somatic symptoms, arousal, and panic

Catastrophic cognitions related to cultural syndromes and other disturbances as determined by the local ethnophysiology, ethnopsychology, and ethnospirituality (e.g., fear that the symptom indicates the onset of a *khyâl* attack)

Triggers of arousal and somatic symptoms

- Negative emotions (anxiety, depression, fear, anger)
- Worry
- Stress
- Thinking of the deceased or separation
- Startle
- Trauma recall
- Standing up
- Exertion
- Motion sickness ("car sickness")
- Agoraphobia-like syndromes ("people sickness")
- Sleep-related phenomena: nightmare, sleep paralysis, nocturnal panic
- Metaphor-guided somatization (through cognizing distress in somatic metaphors)
- Hypervigilant surveying of the body in search of syndrome-related symptoms, in search of symptoms thought to indicate physiological, psychological, and/ or spiritual disturbances (this self-scanning will increase if the person is in a self-perceived vulnerable state, e.g., considers him- or herself to be "weak")

Trauma not only results in a highly activated state of the nervous system but also increases reactivity – that is, the tendency for arousal and anxiety to be rapidly induced by any of multiple causes, ranging from sounds (noise-induced "startle") to emotions. For example, with worry about a problem like the acting out behavior of a child or not having money to buy food, an easily activated nervous system may cause a trauma victim rapidly to become very anxious and to experience multiple somatic symptoms such as palpitations, dizziness, and neck soreness. Trauma victims also exhibit such reactivity with a variety of emotions other than worry, such as stress, anxiety, anger, and even pained, nostalgic recall of the dead, and, as indicated previously, this reactivity extends to certain stimuli: the classic examples of noise-caused startle and of hyperreactivity to trauma reminders, two types of reactivities that are *DSM-IV* and *DSM-5* PTSD symptoms (D. Hinton, Nickerson, & Bryant, 2011). By bringing about this combination of arousal and arousability, that is, by bringing about a combination of a state and a predisposition to a state, the psychobiology of trauma may cause traumatized Cambodians to have extreme emotional states and multiple symptoms such as the somatic symptoms in the Cambodian SSI.

Cross-cultural differences in biology also seemingly cause certain of the C-SSI symptoms to have the salience they have among psychologically distressed Cambodians (D. Hinton & Good, 2009a; D. Hinton et al., 2010). Some Asian populations, such as Cambodian refugees, appear to be particularly predisposed to both motion sickness and orthostatic dizziness (dizziness on standing), and these two vulnerabilities worsen during anxiety states and after trauma (D. Hinton & Good, 2009b; D. Hinton et al., 2010). Arousal, more generally, may be greater in certain populations as a result of biologically driven differences in rates of certain anxiety-related symptoms: Cambodian and African American populations seem to be particularly predisposed to sleep paralysis after trauma (see later discussion), which leads to further arousal and somatic symptoms.

Cultural Syndromes (Ethnopsychology, Ethnophysiology, and Ethnospirituality) Concerns about a disturbance in mental, bodily, and spiritual integrity and the occurrence of a related syndrome may lead Cambodians to be hypervigilant in regard to the somatic symptoms listed in the C-SSI. The symptoms are thought to indicate an ethnophysiological or other type of disturbance, and these concerns are particularly great when the person is in a self-perceived vulnerable state. Hypervigilance toward somatic symptoms increases these very somatic symptoms by attentional amplification – even a slight symptom such as incipient dizziness may be perceived. And the fear experienced upon noticing one of the dreaded symptoms, or even anticipating that it will occur in a certain situation, such as upon standing up, may induce a given symptom by activating the physiology of fear. Then a vicious cycle of worsening may occur and lead to panic because fear itself may worsen the symptom, and then the worsened symptom causes yet more fear, and so forth. Through this combination of attentional amplification and the physiology of fear, cultural syndromes lead to the worsening of symptoms associated with those syndromes.

Cambodians fear that the C-SSI somatic symptoms indicate several different types of mental, bodily, and spiritual disturbance, which are discussed in the section below on C-SSI cultural syndromes. Here we give the example of the culture syndrome "*khyâl* attack." All the C-SSI symptoms are considered by Cambodians as possibly indicating the onset of a "*khyâl* attack," or "wind attack" (D. Hinton, Pich, Marques, Nickerson, & Pollack, 2010). In a *khyâl* attack, blood and a wind-like substance called *khyâl* are thought to surge upward in the body to cause various somatic symptoms and potentially various bodily catastrophes: Neck soreness may be attributed to a surge of *khyâl* and blood into the neck and give rise to fears of rupture of the neck vessels, and dizziness may be attributed to a surge of *khyâl* into the head that may cause syncope. In this way, a panic attack focusing on a somatic symptom may occur, such as a neck-focused panic attack in which rupture of the neck vessels is the predominant fear (D. Hinton, Um, & Ba, 2001b). Figure 9.3 shows the Cambodian conceptualization of the pathophysiology of a *khyâl* attack, and Table 9.2 lists each somatic symptom of a *khyâl* attack and describes how the symptom is thought to be generated by disordered physiology and what catastrophic event it is feared that each symptom indicates.

Metaphoric Dimensions   Many of the C-SSI somatic symptoms have important metaphoric resonances in the Cambodian language that increase their emotional salience. This is true of dizziness and neck soreness. In the Cambodian language, distress is often described through tropes of spinning: A Cambodian may say, "My son shakes me" (*koun kreulôk khyom*), meaning "my son is upsetting me," or a Cambodian may say, "My brain is spinning" (*wul khueu khabaal*), meaning "I am overwhelmed." Neck soreness is also related to several tropes such as the following: A Cambodian may say of a problem, "It has arrived at my neck" (*dâl gâ*), meaning "I can't take it anymore," or a Cambodian may say, "I'm carrying a heavy load on my shoulder" (*reek thnguen*), meaning "I'm overburdened with responsibility."[8]

If a language has extensive somatic metaphors to express distress, there may occur both "metaphor-guided somatization" and "metaphor-

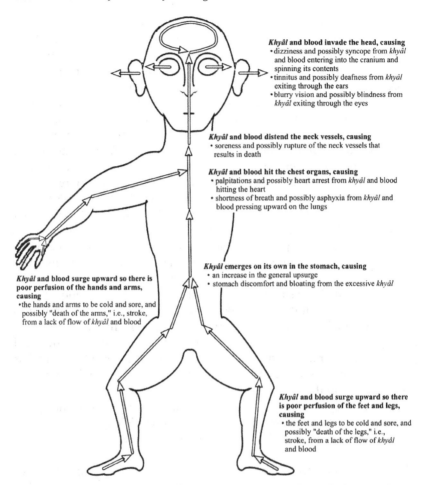

Khyâl and blood invade the head, causing
• dizziness and possibly syncope from khyâl and blood entering into the cranium and spinning its contents
• tinnitus and possibly deafness from khyâl exiting through the ears
• blurry vision and possibly blindness from khyâl exiting through the eyes

Khyâl and blood distend the neck vessels, causing
• soreness and possibly rupture of the neck vessels that results in death

Khyâl and blood hit the chest organs, causing
• palpitations and possibly heart arrest from khyâl and blood hitting the heart
• shortness of breath and possibly asphyxia from khyâl and blood pressing upward on the lungs

Khyâl and blood surge upward so there is poor perfusion of the hands and arms, causing
• the hands and arms to be cold and sore, and possibly "death of the arms," i.e., stroke, from a lack of flow of khyâl and blood

Khyâl emerges on its own in the stomach, causing
• an increase in the general upsurge
• stomach discomfort and bloating from the excessive khyâl

Khyâl and blood surge upward so there is poor perfusion of the feet and legs, causing
• the feet and legs to be cold and sore, and possibly "death of the legs," i.e., stroke, from a lack of flow of khyâl and blood

Figure 9.3. A *khyâl* attack: Ethnophysiology, symptoms, and associated disasters.

network activation by a somatic sensation." Metaphor-guided somatization may occur if a Cambodian thinks about a current problem in terms of the somatic metaphors described previously: If a mother uses the trope "My son shakes me" to cognize her son's disrespectful behavior, doing so may cause dizziness, or likewise if a Cambodian considers current problems and thinks, "I'm carrying a heavy load at the shoulder" (*reek thnguen*), this thought may bring about neck soreness. Metaphor-network activation by a somatic sensation may occur if a Cambodian experiences dizziness or neck soreness for some reason: If autonomic

Table 9.2. *The interpretation of somatic symptoms in terms of a* khyâl *attack: Correlated physiological state and feared consequence*

Symptom	Correlated physiological state	Feared consequence
Dizziness	A surge of *khyâl* and blood into the cranium.	Syncope, "*khyâl* attack," and "*khyâl* overload" (*khyâl koeu*).
Tinnitus	A pressure-like escape of *khyâl* from the ears, with tinnitus called "*khyâl* exits from the ears," or *khyâl ceuny taam treujieu.*	Deafness, syncope, *khyâl* attack, and *khyâl* overload.
Blurry vision	A pressure-like escape of *khyâl* from the eyes.	Blindness, syncope, *khyâl* attack, and *khyâl* overload.
Headache	A rush of *khyâl* and blood into the head and its vessels.	Syncope, *khyâl* attack, and *khyâl* overload.
Neck soreness	A surge of *khyâl* and blood into the neck vessels.	Bursting of the neck vessels, *khyâl* attack, and *khyâl* overload.
Nausea	Excessive *khyâl* in the stomach and abdomen, which may rise upward in the body.	*Khyâl* rising upward from the abdomen into the body to cause asphyxia, cardiac arrest, and various cerebral catastrophes, to cause a *khyâl* attack and *khyâl* overload.
Palpitations	*Khyâl* presses on the heart and causes palpitations, having risen upward from the stomach or limbs. The limbs have blocked vessels, and so the heart must work harder to pump blood and *khyâl* through the body, which also results in heart strain and palpitations.	Cardiac arrest and all disasters associated with a weakened heart, such as poor circulation in the limbs resulting in coagulation in the limbs, which causes an upward surge of *khyâl* and blood in the body, to cause a *khyâl* attack and *khyâl* overload.
Shortness of breath	*Khyâl* surges upward from the limbs or stomach to press on the lungs, which inhibits breathing.	Asphyxia, *khyâl* attack, and *khyâl* overload.
Soreness in the legs or arms	Blockage of the flow of *khyâl* and blood at the joints, with sore joints being called "plugged vessels" (*cok sosai*) or "blocked *khyâl*" (*sla khyâl*).	"Death" of the limbs from a lack of outward flow along the limbs, a surge of *khyâl* and blood upward in the body to cause the various disasters listed above: asphyxia, heart arrest, neck-vessel rupture, and syncope.

(*continued*)

Table 9.2. (*cont.*)

Symptom	Correlated physiological state	Feared consequence
Cold hands or feet	Blockage of the flow of *khyâl* and blood in the limbs.	"Death" of the limbs from a lack of outward flow along the limbs, a surge of *khyâl* and blood upward in the body to cause the various disasters listed above: asphyxia, heart arrest, neck-vessel rupture, and syncope.
Poor appetite	A direct effect of excessive bodily *khyâl*.	Poor food intake may result in weakness, which in turn causes various physiological consequences: dizziness on standing, palpitations upon exposure to stimuli, and a predisposition to *khyâl* attacks.
Out of energy	Serious depletion of the bodily energy supplies, a direct effect of excessive bodily *khyâl*.	The body is depleted, potentially causing a weakened heart, which may result in heart arrest and in *khyâl* attacks because the weakened heart does not adequately pump to circulate the *khyâl* and blood, thus causing plugs in the limbs, with those plugs resulting in an upward surge of *khyâl* and blood into the trunk.

arousal produced by anxiety causes one of these two symptoms, the somatic symptom may evoke all the life issues encoded in mind by the associated somatic trope, such as dizziness's calling to mind emotional tropes (e.g., "My brain is spinning," *wul khueu khabaal*), which then evoke the idea of being overwhelmed with problems and thoughts of current problems such as conflicts with children or financial concerns.

Trauma Associations to Somatic Sensations   The C-SSI somatic symptoms are also prominent because of their association with trauma events. Below we first discuss how somatic symptoms are linked to trauma events among Cambodian refugees, then delineate how the linking of somatic symptoms to trauma events increases somatic symptoms and how somatic symptoms may serve as chronotope encoders, as evokers of a spacetime that includes somatic symptoms and a certain sense of self.

Many Cambodians experienced traumas in the Pol Pot period that are now linked to somatic symptoms. This linking sometimes occurred when fear during the trauma event evoked somatic symptoms through the biology of the fear response[9] or sometimes when the nature of trauma itself resulted in certain strong somatic sensations. Let us consider how the nature of the traumas in the Pol Pot period specifically caused neck soreness as well as dizziness.

Neck and shoulder soreness were induced by the most common form of slave labor during the Pol Pot period: being forced to carry heavy loads of dirt placed in two baskets while starving, with each basket being hung at opposite ends of a pole balanced on the shoulder. Many Cambodians were hit in the neck and head as punishment, and some were hit in the back of the neck with a club in intended execution (this being be far the most common method of execution), but survived, awakening in a burial pit. Neck soreness also occurred during the malaria bouts that almost every Cambodian suffered during the Khmer Rouge period. In respect to dizziness, it was induced during slave labor while starving, and this labor not uncommonly caused collapse and even syncope. And as indicated above, Cambodians were often hit in the head by the Khmer Rouge as a punishment, which also caused dizziness. Moreover, almost all Cambodians had severe malaria that brought about extreme dizziness and other symptoms (D. Hinton, Hsia, Park, Rasmussen, & Pollack, 2009). Yet still, Cambodians often experienced traumas that evoked a mix of nausea, dizziness, and fear: They witnessed executions that sometimes involved evisceration and extraction of the liver and gallbladder (later to be consumed by the Khmer Rouge; A. Hinton, 2005), and they often saw corpses marked by the manner of killing (e.g., bludgeoning to the head) and in various states of decay, sometimes surrounded by flies and infested by maggots.

This linking of trauma events to somatic sensations may increase those somatic symptoms – and their emotional salience – by two processes. For one, if a Cambodian experiences a symptom such as dizziness for any reason, the symptom may bring to mind the trauma event that featured that somatic symptom, such as being threatened with death and feeling dizzy or doing slave labor and feeling dizzy, what might be called "somatic-symptom activation of the trauma network."[10] And, second, thinking about a trauma event ("I remember being threatened with death" or "I remember doing slave labor while starving") may worsen and even bring about the somatic symptom experienced during the trauma event (e.g., dizziness) by a somatic flashback and by the physiology of fear (D. Hinton et al., 2008), what might be called "trauma-recall induction of a somatic symptom."

Dizziness and neck soreness were so prominent throughout the Pol Pot period, as a result of traumas and the nature of life and work, that those two sensations may now act as chronotope markers, that is, evokers of the space-time of the Pol Pot period (on the notion of "chronotope," see the Introduction, this volume). Dizziness evokes starvation and overwork, and neck soreness evokes the main forced labor, with these two somatic symptoms forming part of the experiential background of the Pol Pot period. Therefore, currently having these somatic sensations may bring to mind the entire period, and the sense of the self as it was at that time, such as the self as powerless victim, and emotions experienced at that time, such as rage, sadness, and fear (Langer, 1991; see the Introduction, this volume, for further discussion). Hunger sensations and gastrointestinal distress more generally also seemingly play such a role among Cambodian genocide survivors (see Chapter 5, this volume, for how this plays out among Holocaust survivors, e.g., in respect to hunger), acting as a chronotope marker – and evoker.

Cultural Syndromes Assessed in the C-SSI

The C-SSI also assesses for cultural syndromes that are a prominent aspect of the Cambodian response to trauma. Figure 9.4 illustrates how cultural syndromes are produced among trauma survivors and how the syndromes interact with PTSD to create a certain illness reality. The seven cultural syndromes are listed in Table 9.1 (on these syndromes, see D. Hinton, S. Hinton, Um, Chea, & Sak, 2002; D. Hinton, Um, & Ba, 2001a; D. Hinton et al., 2001b).[11] Of note, the concept of PTSD is usually not known by laypersons in Cambodia and so they use it infrequently to explain their symptoms.

As described previously (see Figure 9.3 and Table 9.2), Cambodians greatly fear *khyâl* attacks. Most Cambodians consider *khyâl* to be a potentially pathogenic element (D. Hinton et al., 2010). In a healthy state, *khyâl* flows throughout the body alongside blood and exits the body by passing through the hands and feet, by exiting through the skin pores located all over the body, by the action of burping, or by downward movement through the gastrointestinal tract. Sometimes the normal flow of *khyâl* suddenly becomes disturbed, and it surges along with blood upward in the body toward the head, causing the symptoms and disasters described in Figure 9.3 and Table 9.2. Such an event is referred to as a "*khyâl* attack," or *kaeut khyâl*. (In the *DSM-5*, *khyâl* attacks are one of the nine cultural concepts of distress [American Psychiatric Association, 2013]. For a detailed description of *khyâl* attacks, including film footage of their traditional treatment, viz., "coining," see www.khyalattack.com.)

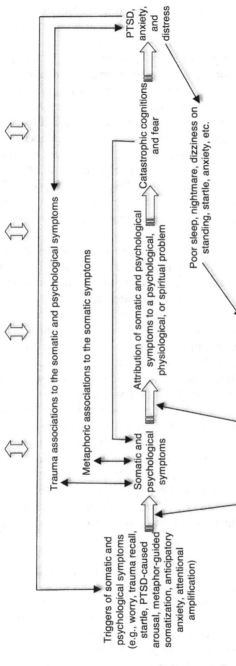

The following text appears within the figure:

- The role of the syndrome as a culturally sanctioned manner of expressing negative affect, distress, or despair
- Interpersonal and personal effects of having a bout of the syndrome: how it changes relationships, how others act towards the person during episodes, stigma associated with the condition, economic effects of having the condition
  - The effects of received treatment resulting from self-labeling as having the condition

PTSD, anxiety, and distress

Catastrophic cognitions and fear

Poor sleep, nightmare, dizziness on standing, startle, anxiety, etc.

Trauma associations to the somatic and psychological symptoms

Metaphoric associations to the somatic symptoms

Attribution of somatic and psychological symptoms to a psychological, physiological, or spiritual problem

Somatic and psychological symptoms

Triggers of somatic and psychological symptoms (e.g., worry, trauma recall, startle, PTSD-caused arousal, metaphor-guided somatization, anticipatory anxiety, attentional amplification)

Hypervigilant surveying of the body and mind for syndrome-related symptoms owing to a self-perceived vulnerability: owing to being "weak" from not sleeping well, to having endured an event (e.g., a trauma or a fright) said to cause the syndrome, to having noticed some of the syndrome symptoms in the recent past, or to having had episodes of the syndrome in the past

Figure 9.4. The multiplex model of the "cultural syndrome" – PTSD interaction among patients who have PTSD.

225

It is believed that an attack may be triggered in many ways: by worry, by any kind of anxiety or fright such as that brought about by a nightmare or a loud noise, by going into a crowded room, by exhaustion. A particularly severe *khyâl* attack may be triggered by standing up and is called "wind overload" (*khyâl koeu*). Cambodians have elaborate ways of treating these *khyâl* attacks (for a description, see D. Hinton et al., 2010). The SSI (Table 9.1) assesses not only how those surveyed were bothered by *khyâl* attacks in the last month but also how much they were concerned about physiological disasters thought to occur during a *khyâl* attack: *khyâl* hitting up from the stomach to the point of causing death by asphyxia; neck soreness to the point of the neck vessel bursting; or dizziness and other symptoms upon standing up to the point of fainting and *khyâl* overload. We assess these items to determine whether the person has the catastrophic cognitions about physiological disturbances thought to occur in a *khyâl* attack.

Many Cambodians who self-diagnose themselves as having "heart weakness" fear that it may cause heart arrest and that it may produce strong reactivity to stimuli such as sounds and smells and predispose to certain negative emotional states such as being easily frightened, frequently becoming angry, and being unable to stop worrying (D. Hinton et al., 2002). Heart weakness is also thought to cause palpitations and shortness of breath (breathing is considered to be driven by a piston-like action of the heart) and dizziness upon standing up, and a weak heart is thought to pump blood and *khyâl* poorly, thereby predisposing to cold extremities and *khyâl* attacks. Heart weakness is considered to have a number of causes that include poor sleep, poor appetite, and excessive worry. If Cambodians note in themselves any of the processes that can weaken the body (e.g., worry, poor appetite, or poor sleep) or any symptoms that indicate bodily weakness (e.g., startle, smell sensitivity, palpitations, or frequent *khyâl* attacks), they may fear having heart weakness and imminent heart arrest. This fear often leads to a constant hypervigilant surveying of the body and emotions for any symptoms of heart weakness, and if any such symptom is found, it will likely be interpreted as a harbinger of heart arrest or a *khyâl* attack.

The C-SSI also assesses the cultural syndrome called "thinking a lot" (*kut caraeun*). This complaint describes a mental state characterized by the following: (1) One thinks of upsetting topics such as current problems like being unable to pay the rent and acting-out children, past trauma events like those that occurred during the Pol Pot period, and separation from loved ones due to their death or to living far from them; (2) one has a hard time not thinking about these topics; and (3) one thinks about them to the point that it may damage mind and body since the excessive thinking may deplete one's mind and body, predispose one to heart weakness and *khyâl* attack, and overheat the brain to the point that there are permanent memory loss, a state of forgetfulness, or even insanity. "Thinking a lot" episodes, worry episodes (which are often labeled as "thinking a lot"), and standing up are considered to be three of the most common causes of *khyâl* attacks.

Because of its prevalence in the Cambodian population and its strong association with PTSD and trauma, we also assessed one sleep-related complaint, namely, sleep paralysis (D. Hinton, Pich, Chhean, & Pollack, 2005). Sleep paralysis in the Cambodian context is given a culturally specific meaning and is referred to as "the ghost pushes you down" (*khmaoch sangot*). In sleep paralysis, the person is unable to move or speak either upon falling asleep or awakening from sleep. During sleep paralysis, Cambodians almost always see a shape, usually a black shadow, that presses down on the body, and Cambodians often experience chest tightness and shortness of breath as the shape approaches and seemingly pushes down on the body. Cambodians refer to this event as "a ghost pushes you down." Cambodians often consider this to be a dangerous assault by a malevolent being such as the ghost of a person they saw killed during the Pol Pot period or of someone who died in the house in which they are now living.

The Needs Assessment Survey

As described previously, as part of the Victims of Torture project DC-CAM staff traveled to three provinces in Cambodia to interview villagers who were identified by the community as continuing to have psychological distress due to events of the Khmer Rouge period. At the onset of the interviews, team members explained the goals of the survey to participants, including providing of services to those identified as having distress, and asked whether they wished to participate. Those who agreed to participate were interviewed about their experiences during the Khmer Rouge regime and assessed for psychological distress. The needs assessment included the 17-item trauma-event section of the Harvard Trauma Questionnaire (to assess the severity of Pol Pot traumas), the PTSD Checklist (to assess PTSD severity), the Self-Perceived Health-3 (SF-3; to assess self-perceived health functioning), and the C-SSI (to assess culturally specific complaints and syndromes).

Measures

Harvard Trauma Questionnaire: Trauma Event Section The Harvard Trauma Questionnaire was developed initially for evaluating Southeast

Asian populations and has been extensively used for evaluating trauma victims (Mollica, Mcinness, Poole, & Tor, 1998). It contains a section that evaluates whether the person has experienced any of 17 trauma events such as imprisonment, torture, or lack of food and water.

PTSD Checklist (PCL)   The PCL assesses how much each of the 17 *DSM–IV* PTSD criteria has bothered someone in the last month, each assessed on a 1–5 Likert-type scale: 1 (*not at all*), 2 (*a little bit*), 3 (*moderately*), 4 (*quite a bit*), and 5 (*extremely*). The Cambodian version of the PCL has excellent test-retest (at one week) and interrater reliability (r = .91 and .95, respectively) (D. Hinton, Rasmussen, Nou, Pollack, & Good, 2009). In the current study, we used a score of 34 as the cutoff for probable PTSD, which is a conservative cutoff score (McDonald & Calhoun, 2010).

Cambodian Symptom and Syndrome Inventory (SSI)   In order to profile the response to trauma in a culturally sensitive way, we created a scale that assesses symptoms and syndromes that are particularly salient in the Cambodian population. The C-SSI items, which are listed in Table 9.1, can be divided into two types: 12 somatic symptoms and 7 cultural syndromes. Each item is assessed on a 0–4 Likert-type scale, asking those interviewed how much they were bothered by certain somatic symptoms or syndromes in the last four weeks: 0 (*not at all*), 1 (*a little bit*), 2 (*moderately*), 3 (*quite a bit*), and 4 (*extremely*). The current survey is the abbreviated version of the C-SSI; there is a longer version that assesses additional symptoms and syndromes (D. Hinton et al., 2013).

Self-Perceived Health: Three-Item Assessment   It is important to assess self-perceived impairment in health (D. Hinton, Sinclair, Chung, & Pollack, 2007). One source of self-perceived impairment in health is an actual poor physical health condition such as diabetes or hypertension, whereas another is psychological disorder. Psychological illnesses such as PTSD and panic disorder lead to multiple somatic complaints, to low energy, and to decreased ability to engage in exertion. These psychological disorders may decrease the ability to engage in exertion because they decrease the sense of energy, cause dizziness and other symptoms (e.g., from autonomic arousal) that then limit exertion, and cause catastrophizing so that any symptoms induced by exertion may be perceived to indicate a serious problem of health and lead to stopping of exertion and possibly panic.

Brief measures of self-perceived physical health have been extensively used. For this survey, 3 items of the SF-36 were used. The SF-36 has been shown to be a reliable instrument as used in Cambodian populations (D.

Hinton et al., 2007). The SF-3 consists of three items, one of which assesses self-perceived general health and two that assess self-perceived impairment in physical functioning. The three items are (1) How good is your health? (2) Does your health limit you in your ability to do activities such as moving a table or carrying groceries? and (3) Does your health limit your ability to do activities such as climbing several flights of stairs? Item one, self-perceived health, is rated on a 1–4 Likert-type scale (1 = *excellent* to 4 = *poor*), and self-perceived function on a 1–3 Likert-type scale (1 = *no, not limited at all* to 3 = *yes, limited a lot*).

Results

Sixty-three percent of the participants were women, and the average age in the entire sample was 60.3 (SD = 10.1). Among the 17 trauma items in the Harvard Trauma Questionnaire, the average number of experienced trauma items was 8.2 (SD = 1.6) of the assessed items. All participants had PTSD as determined by a PCL ≥ 34. The mean total PCL score was 57.2 (SD = 13.5) and the mean item score on the 1–5 Likert-type scale was 3.4 (SD = 0.8). The C-SSI score was extremely elevated as well, with an item average on the 0–4 Likert-type scale of 2.0 (SD = 0.9). The two scores were highly correlated (r = .61). To examine the relationship of the PCL score to the SSI further, we divided the PCL scores into three levels of severity, namely, mild PTSD (2.0–2.8), moderate PTSD (2.9–3.8), and severe PTSD (3.8–5), and then examined the severity of the C-SSI score and individual C-SSI items at each level of PTSD severity. In the mild PTSD group (n = 24), the average C-SSI score was 1.6 (SD = 0.7); in the moderate PTSD group (n = 18), the average C-SSI score was 1.9 (SD = 0.8); in the severe PTSD group (n = 24), the average C-SSI score was 2.6 (SD = 0.6), which was statistically different, $F(2, 63)$ = 8.1, p < .001.

As indicated in Table 9.3, all the C-SSI items were much more severe at each level of PTSD severity. Certain items were highly elevated. Dizziness was extremely elevated in the severe PTSD group, much more so than symptoms like palpitations and shortness of breath, and dizziness differentiated well among the three groups of PTSD severity. Other items that were extremely elevated in the severe PTSD group were blurry vision, weakness, heart weakness, "thinking a lot," and standing up and feeling dizzy. As we hypothesized, patients who had PTSD had great fear of having the various syndromes and associated ethnophysiological disasters, such as fear of dying from neck-vessel rupture and fear of having a "weak heart."

The trauma event total was more highly correlated with the C-SSI than the PCL (r = .61 vs. r = .41), with more variance in the trauma

Table 9.3. *Degree of being bothered by various Cambodian SSI items (somatic symptoms and cultural syndromes) in the last month: A comparison of those rural Cambodians with mild, moderate, and severe PTSD*

Item (degree of being bothered by the symptom or syndrome in the last month)	Mild PTSD M (SD)	Moderate PTSD M (SD)	Severe PTSD M (SD)	F value
1. Dizziness	1.0 (0.9)	2.3 (1.6)	3.7 (0.9)	26.1*
2. Standing up and feeling dizzy	2.3 (1.2)	2.9 (1.7)	3.4 (0.9)	3.8*
3. Blurry vision	2.3 (1.8)	2.7 (1.9)	3.6 (0.7)	6.4*
4. Tinnitus	2.0 (1.8)	2.3 (1.5)	2.8 (1.4)	4.1*
5. Headache	1.3 (1.2)	1.5 (1.4)	2.6 (1.9)	4.4*
6. Neck soreness	1.6 (1.5)	2.3 (1.7)	3.1 (1.5)	6.1*
7. Palpitations	0.5 (0.9)	1.0 (1.6)	1.8 (1.4)	3.9*
8. Shortness of breath	0.6 (0.9)	0.9 (0.8)	1.7 (1.4)	4.2*
9. Cold hands and feet	0.5 (1.0)	1.7 (1.9)	1.9 (1.5)	6.2*
10. Sore arms and legs	2.1 (1.9)	2.7 (1.6)	3.5 (0.7)	10.6*
11. Weakness	2.7 (1.2)	3.0 (1.7)	3.8 (1.4)	5.8*
12. Poor appetite	1.6 (1.2)	2.3 (1.6)	3.5 (1.0)	12.1*
13. *Khyâl* attack	1.5 (1.5)	2.1 (1.1)	2.8 (1.4)	5.2*
14. *Khyâl* hitting up from your stomach, making you fear you might die of asphyxia	0.8 (1.6)	1.3 (1.8)	1.9 (1.7)	3.3*
15. "Weak heart"	1.3 (1.5)	1.7 (1.0)	3.0 (1.5)	7.8*
16. Standing up and feeling poorly to the point you feared fainting, *khyâl* overload, or heart attack	1.0 (1.6)	1.8 (1.4)	2.6 (1.9)	4.9*
17. Neck soreness to the point you feared the neck vessels would burst	1.4 (1.8)	1.7 (1.9)	2.2 (1.8)	3.9*
18. "Thinking too much"	2.8 (1.2)	3.4 (0.4)	3.7 (0.4)	18.9*
19. Sleep paralysis	1.0 (1.3)	1.2 (1.2)	2.1 (1.4)	5.1*

* Indicates a statistically significant difference among the three groups.

SSI = Symptom and Syndrome Inventory. The SSI is rated on a 0–4 Likert-type scale. The severity of PTSD is rated on the PCL, a 1–5 Likert-type scale: mild PTSD, PCL score of 2.0–2.8; moderate PTSD, PCL score of 2.9–3.8; and severe PTSD, PCL score of 3.8–5.0.

event total explained by the C-SSI (16 percent vs. 36 percent). One item that was highly correlated to both scales was imprisonment ($r = .52$ and $r = .46$, respectively).

On the first item of the SF-3 that assessed self-perceived health, the mean score was 3.4 ($SD = 0.51$) on the 4-point scale (viz., "4" denotes poor health), indicating that most villagers considered themselves to have poor health. On the second and third items of the SF-3 that assessed the degree that health limited activities, the mean score was 2.3 ($SD = 0.7$) on the 3-point scales (viz., "3" denotes "limited a lot"), indicating poor functioning. To see which was a better indicator of self-perceived health functioning, we then examined the correlations of self-perceived health functioning (the mean of the three items) to the PCL and C-SSI score. The C-SSI was more highly related to the total score than the PCL score ($r = .38$ vs. $r = .31$).

Discussion

In the Introduction we described the items of the C-SSI and how they are generated, and then we described a needs assessment using the C-SSI of rural Cambodians locally identified as being distressed as a result of the Pol Pot period. Those assessed were found to have experienced many trauma events, and all were found to have PTSD, and many had extremely severe PTSD. Having PTSD symptoms was highly associated with being bothered by culturally salient somatic symptoms and by concerns about having several culturally specific syndromes: Scores on the Cambodian C-SSI were elevated and the scores and all the items increased significantly across each of the three levels of PTSD severity. All the C-SSI somatic symptoms and syndromes were progressively more severe at each level of PTSD severity, and all significantly differentiated among the three levels of PTSD severity (Table 9.3). Self-perceived health was very poor. Indicating that the C-SSI captures a core aspect of the response to trauma, the C-SSI was a better indicator of the severity of past trauma events and of self-perceived health than the PCL.

Some of the C-SSI somatic symptoms and syndromes were extremely elevated in those surveyed. Dizziness was a particularly severe complaint and the best differentiator among the three levels of PTSD. The four-dimension analysis described in the Introduction reveals why dizziness is such a prominent complaint in the Cambodian context (see Figure 9.1): It is associated with the biology of trauma and anxiety, especially among Asian populations (e.g., Cambodians have high rates of orthostatic dizziness and motion sickness); it is a key indicator of ethnophysiological disturbance (e.g., of *khyâl* rushing into the head during a *khyâl* attack such as during *khyâl* overload upon standing) and of syndromes (e.g., of "weakness" and of *khyâl* attack); it has extensive metaphoric resonances in the Cambodian language (e.g., spinning images in expressions used to convey distress); and it is associated with multiple trauma events (e.g., slave labor when starving, head blows, and malaria episodes). Other authors have noted the prominence of dizziness among Cambodians and Asian populations more generally (D. Hinton & Good, 2009a; Kleinman & Kleinman, 1994). Kleinman and Kleinman (1994) found dizziness to be one of the three paradigmatic distress complaints in China; the two others were exhaustion and pain; and a recent survey of a student population in the United States found dizziness complaints to be particularly elevated in the panic attacks of Asian populations as compared to white and African American students (Barrera, Wilson, & Norton, 2010).

Weakness was also a very severe complaint in the current survey and has been found to be so among other Asian groups. As indicated, "exhaustion" is another of the three paradigmatic distress complaints in China according to Kleinman and Kleinman (1994). Like many Asian groups, Cambodians are very concerned about bodily energy and consider it to be a key symptom to attend to – hence the common use of multiple traditional medicines and other means to increase bodily energy in these groups (D. Hinton et al., 2002, 2007). As indicated previously, weakness is feared by Cambodians because it leads to heart weakness and predisposes to *khyâl* attacks. Another prominent complaint in the survey, namely, poor appetite, is also feared because it leads to weakness and weakness-associated dangers, and poor appetite is itself a symptom of a *khyâl* attack. Sore arms and legs were also a very common complaint, and, as discussed, Cambodians often attribute these symptoms to the blocked flow of *khyâl*, so that sore arms and legs create fears of having the *khyâl* disasters shown in Figure 9.3 and Table 9.2. Another very elevated symptom was blurry vision, a symptom that others have found to be a common complaint among Cambodian populations (Caspi, Poole, Mollica, & Frankel, 1998), one thought to indicate a *khyâl* attack.

Among the syndromes, the complaint of "thinking a lot" was extremely elevated, and differentiated particularly well among the three groups. The complaint's commonness is not surprising given the multiple financial and other problems of these rural villagers and the fact they are beset with many disturbing trauma memories. We have shown elsewhere how worry leads to great worsening of PTSD among traumatized groups (D. Hinton et al., 2011), and worry is a key aspect of "thinking a lot." Other very good differentiators of the three levels of PTSD severity were heart weakness and *khyâl* attacks.

This chapter reveals that PTSD symptoms are just the "tip of the iceberg." When PTSD is present, so too are multiple other somatic symptoms and syndromes. It should be emphasized that though Cambodian villagers are not familiar with such biomedical concepts as "PTSD," they are keenly aware of and concerned about both culturally emphasized trauma-related somatic complaints such as dizziness or neck soreness and culturally emphasized trauma-related syndromes, including *khyâl* attacks, weak heart, or "thinking a lot." But in some of the cultural syndromes PTSD symptoms are key symptoms; for example, "weak heart" has startle and irritability as key symptoms. More generally, PTSD and somatic symptoms and cultural syndromes are in dynamic interaction (Figure 9.2 and 9.4).

The current chapter suggests that researchers and clinicians use symptom and syndrome inventories (locally specific SSIs) designed for the cultural group with which they work in addition to a measure of "PTSD." In this way, a more adequate depiction of the local response to trauma can be attained and the symptoms and syndromes of concern in that locality can be addressed, increasing empathy and efficacy and resulting in a more experience-near understanding (on the clinical utility of evaluating idioms of distress, see D. Hinton & Lewis-Fernández, 2010). But for these treatment goals to be attained, the researcher and clinician must determine how the symptoms and syndromes are generated and their local meaning.

The current chapter suggests that the biology of trauma generates a certain potential "symptom pool" (Shorter, 1992), of which PTSD symptoms represent one part (see Figure 9.5). Certain of the symptoms produced by the biology of trauma will be more salient in a particular culture for several reasons. Because of their extremely disruptive and dysphoria-inducing effects, certain PTSD symptoms, such as poor sleep, nightmares, unwanted recall of trauma, and anger, will almost always be prominent in a traumatized group. In addition, these PTSD symptoms and others in the trauma-produced symptom pool – such as somatic symptoms, sleep paralysis, orthostatic dizziness, and worry episodes marked by arousal – will be interpreted in terms of a group's ethnopsychology/ethnopsychology/ethnospirituality and related cultural syndromes, causing certain symptoms to be amplified by attentional mechanisms and by fear responses; and depending on the disturbance the particular symptom is attributed to, the person will have certain ideas about the cause, severity, and indicated manner of redress of the symptom. And as discussed in the Introduction, somatic symptoms that are part of the symptom pool may have metaphoric resonances and trauma associations that then increase those somatic symptoms, and their affective valence, in a group.

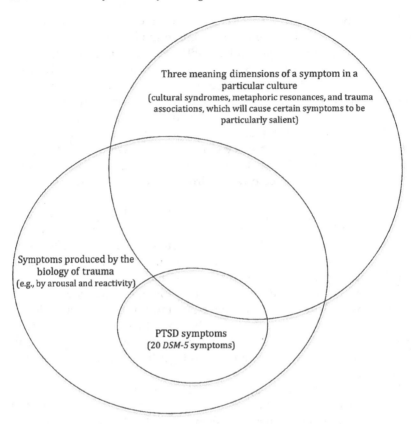

Figure 9.5. The interaction of the biologically generated symptom pool, PTSD symptoms, and culturally specific meaning dimensions.

For these reasons, as indicated in this chapter's Introduction, a four-dimension analysis (Figure 9.1) needs to be conducted of each somatic symptom that is found to be prominent in a cultural context. There should also be an episode analysis (Figure 9.2) that includes the determination of frequent causes of the somatic symptom: The episode may be triggered by worry, anger, a noise, stress, or encountering a trauma reminder. Among traumatized groups, these triggers may rapidly induce symptoms owing to trauma-caused arousal and arousability, part of the biology of trauma. Once somatic and psychological symptoms are generated by some trigger, they will be interpreted according to the three semiotic dimensions (Figure 9.6). Only through a four-dimension analysis (Figure 9.1) conjoined with episode analysis (Figure 9.2) can the

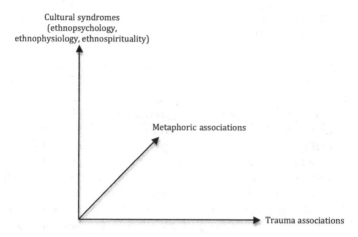

Figure 9.6. The three-dimension analysis of the meaning of somatic and psychological symptoms.

meaning and manner of generation of somatic symptoms become clear, and effective treatments be designed.[12]

As with somatic symptoms, syndromes that are prominent in a locality need to be adequately researched. As highlighted in Figure 9.4, not only does this entail examining the four dimensions of somatic symptoms and conducting episode analysis, it also includes determining the syndrome's role as a sanctioned way of expressing distress, the syndrome's personal and interpersonal effects (e.g., how it affects relationships), and how the attempts at cure influence the trajectory of the syndrome.[13] Cultural syndromes – and key somatic symptoms – should be examined in these ways to scrutinize trauma's effects on the local level, as those effects reverberate across social relationships, existential state, and economic status. "PTSD" in the United States also functions as a syndrome in the way outlined in Figure 9.4. This is because it is a concept known by lay-persons, so that it represents a sanctioned way of experiencing distress (Fassin & Rechtman, 2009). In an extreme case, a cultural syndrome like "PTSD" as understood by a layperson in the United States or "weak heart" in Cambodia may be enminded and embodied purely as a result of its role as a sanctioned form to express distress, for example, when in an intolerable social situation, such as living with an abusive spouse; for its role, when facing a bleak social and financial future, in accessing financial resources and other resources; and for its role in creating a certain self-narrative and self-image, for example, in the case of "PTSD" in the United States, that of wounded hero (McNally & Frueh, 2013).

This chapter has tried to show the importance when evaluating trauma-related disorder of assessing not only PTSD but also locally salient somatic symptoms and syndromes. Not assessing such symptoms and syndromes results in "category truncation," a truncated view of trauma-related disorder in the locality (D. Hinton, Peou, Joshi, Nickerson, & Simon, 2013). The chapter has shown the importance of the C-SSI somatic symptoms and syndromes in the local trauma ontology by illustrating how they are generated by multiple processes, form an illness reality, and constitute key cogs of the generation of distress, and by showing how those culturally salient complaints are related to PTSD, trauma, and self-perceived health. The chapter has argued that it is not sufficient to state that a certain somatic symptom or syndrome is present in a cultural context; how it is generated must be examined through an investigation of the biology of trauma and semiotic dimensions and through the ethnography of particular episodes of somatic symptoms or syndromes. As indicated earlier, analysis should also include a consideration of how the complaint functions as a sanctioned idiom of distress (e.g., a last resort or "ethnobehavioral pathway" for an abused wife: Carr & Vitaliano, 1985), what are its personal and interpersonal effects, and how it is treated. By knowing how the complaint is generated, including how it is worsened by and worsens "PTSD" (see Figures 9.2 and 9.4), effective treatments can be designed for trauma-related disorder and more emphatic understanding attained, an experience-near understanding of the local trauma ontology. The current chapter aims to be a contribution to trauma sociosomatics,[14] the way in which trauma has reverberating effects through the cultural matrix and social networks to the body.

NOTES

1 For more details, see www.dccam.org.
2 The Harvard Trauma Questionnaire (HTQ; Mollica et al., 1992) combines an assessment of the 16 *DSM-III-R* criteria with an addendum of symptoms such as guilt that pertain to all traumatized refugees.
3 The Hopkins Symptom Checklist (Mollica, Wyshak, Marneffe, Khuon, & Lavelle, 1987) contains scales to assess anxiety and depression.
4 For a discussion of the Cambodian genocide, see A. Hinton, (2005); see also A. Hinton (2010) and A. Hinton and O'Neill (2009). In Cambodia, at the time of the writing of this current volume, an international hybrid tribunal is under way to bring the lead Khmer Rouge perpetrators to justice.
5 But as discussed in the Introduction to the current volume, other *DSM-IV* PTSD items such as amnesia or numbing seem to be much less salient aspects of the trauma response in non-Western cultures (for a review, see D. Hinton & Lewis-Fernández, 2011). Of note, in the *DSM-5* (American Psychiatric Association, 2013), the numbing item has been replaced by inability to

experience pleasure, a more easily translated concept, but the amnesia item has been retained.

6 In many cultural contexts, somatic symptoms may be linked to spiritual fears such as when bodily lightness is attributed to soul loss (Rubel, O'Nell, & Collado-Ardón, 1984; Weller, Baer, Garcia de Alba Garcia, & Salcedo Rocha, 2008), a common fear among Cambodians or certain Latino groups, or when symptoms such as tinnitus are interpreted as a sign of possession, common in certain African groups (de Jong & Reis, 2010, 2013; Reis, 2013).

7 On the multidimensional analysis of somatic symptoms, see also Barsky (1992), Good (1977), D. Hinton and Good (2009a), Jenkins and Valiente (1994), Kirmayer (1996), Kirmayer and Sartorius (2007), Kleinman and Kleinman (1994). For a detailed description of these four processes in respect to "tinnitus" in the Cambodian context, see D. Hinton et al. (2008).

8 For a discussion of the metaphors associated with dizziness, neck soreness, and tinnitus in the Cambodian context see D. Hinton and Good (2009b); for how these processes relate to American expressions such as "back pain," see D. Hinton and Lewis-Fernández (2010).

9 Local biologies (Lock, 1993) influence the fear response and these processes. There is some evidence fear is more likely to cause dizziness among Cambodian refugees, and this may relate to biological causes, such as suggested by evidence of a greater predisposition to motion sickness among Asian populations, which is a marker of greater conditionability to dizziness (D. Hinton & Good, 2009a). If true, this would mean that trauma events are more likely to be encoded by dizziness among Cambodian refugees.

10 Worse yet, the activation of the memory network increases the somatic symptom through somatic flashback and arousal, and then the increased somatic symptom activates yet more the memory network, and so on, creating an escalating vicious circle.

11 The survey assesses not only cultural syndromes but also specific catastrophic cognitions related to cultural syndromes. For example, we asked not only about *khyâl* attacks but also about fear of "neck vessel" rupture. If a somatic symptom strongly activates one of the three meaning dimensions (the four symptom dimensions include three meaning dimensions and a biological-causation dimension), such as ethnophysiology concerns, we consider it to be a syndrome: "sore neck syndrome." That is, we consider a cultural syndrome to be present when there is any linking of symptoms to a cultural conceptualization of disorder in the psychological, physiological, or spiritual realms, with some cultural syndromes being more elaborated.

12 The model of the generation of somatic symptoms and cultural syndromes among trauma survivors shows how somatic symptoms and cultural syndromes worsen PTSD, and so has clear treatment implications. For example, the model indicates that particular causes of distress episodes such as worry must be addressed; that episode-associated catastrophic cognitions should be addressed; and that episode-associated trauma associations should be elicited and explored. For a detailed discussion of how the model of the generation of somatic symptoms and cultural syndromes outlined in this chapter informs treatment, see D. Hinton, Rivera, et al. (2012).

13 These analytical dimensions should also be applied to somatic sensations.

14 On sociosomatics, see Kleinman and Becker (1998).

REFERENCES

American Psychiatric Association (2000, 2013). *Diagnostic and statistical manual of mental disorders*, 4th ed., text revision and 5th ed. Washington, DC: American Psychiatric Association.

Barrera, T. L., Wilson, K. P., & Norton, P. J. (2010). The experience of panic symptoms across racial groups in a student sample. *Journal of Anxiety Disorders*, 24, 873–8.

Barsky, A. J. (1992). Amplification, somatization, and the somatoform disorders. *Psychosomatics*, 33, 28–34.

Becker, E. (1998). *When the war was over: Cambodia and the Khmer Rouge revolution*. New York: Public Affairs.

Carr, J. E., & Vitaliano, P. P. (1985). The theoretical implications of converging research on depression and the culture-bound syndromes. In A. Kleinman & B. J. Good (Eds.), *Culture and depression: Studies in anthropology and cross-cultural psychiatry of affect and disorder* (pp. 244–67). Berkeley: University of California Press.

Caspi, Y., Poole, C., Mollica, R. F., & Frankel, M. (1998). Relationship of child loss to psychiatric and functional impairment in resettled Cambodian refugees. *Journal of Nervous and Mental Disease*, 186, 484–91.

Chandler, D. P. (1999). *Voices from S-21: Terror and history in Pol Pot's secret prison*. Berkeley: University of California Press.

de Jong, J., & Reis, R. (2010). *Kiyang-yang*, a West-African postwar idiom of distress. *Culture, Medicine, and Psychiatry*, 34, 301–21.

(2013). Collective trauma resolution: Dissociation as a way of processing post-war traumatic stress in Guinea Bissau. *Transcultural Psychiatry*, 50, 644–61.

Fassin, D., & Rechtman, R. (2009). *The empire of trauma: An inquiry into the condition of victimhood*. Princeton, NJ: Princeton University Press.

Good, B. J. (1977). The heart of what's the matter: The semantics of illness in Iran. *Culture, Medicine, and Psychiatry*, 1, 25–58.

Hinton, A. L. (2005). *Why did they kill? Cambodia in the shadow of genocide*. Berkeley: University of California Press.

(Ed.). (2010). *Transitional justice: Global mechanisms and local realities after genocide and mass violence*. New Brunswick, NJ: Rutgers University Press.

Hinton, A. L., & O'Neill, K. L. (Eds.) (2009). *Genocide truth, memory, and representation*. Durham, NC: Duke University Press.

Hinton, D. E., & Good, B. J. (2009a). A medical anthropology of panic sensations: Ten analytic perspectives. In D. E. Hinton & B. J. Good (Eds.), *Culture and panic disorder* (pp. 57–81). Stanford, CA: Stanford University Press.

(Eds.) (2009b). *Culture and panic disorder*. Palo Alto, CA: Stanford University Press.

Hinton, D. E. & Hinton, A. L. (2015). An anthropology of the effects of genocide and mass violence: Memory, symptom, and recovery. In D. E. Hinton & A. L. Hinton (Eds.), *Genocide and mass violence: Memory, symptom, and recovery*. Cambridge: Cambridge University Press.

Hinton, D. E. & Hinton, A. L., Eng, K. T. (2015). Key idioms of distress and PTSD among rural Cambodians: The results of a needs assessment survey. In D. E. Hinton & A. L. Hinton (Eds.), *Genocide and mass violence: Memory, symptom, and recovery.* Cambridge: Cambridge University Press.

Hinton, D. E., Hinton, S. D., Loeum, J. R., & Pollack, M. H. (2008). The "multiplex model" of somatic symptoms: Application to tinnitus among traumatized Cambodian refugees. *Transcultural Psychiatry,* 45, 287–317.

Hinton, D. E., Hinton, S., Um, K., Chea, A., & Sak, S. (2002). The Khmer "weak heart" syndrome: Fear of death from palpitations. *Transcultural Psychiatry,* 39, 323–44.

Hinton, D. E., Hofmann, S. G., Orr, S. P., Pitman, R. K., Pollack, M. H., & Pole, N. (2010). A psychobiocultural model of orthostatic panic among Cambodian refugees: Flashbacks, catastrophic cognitions, and reduced orthostatic blood-pressure response. *Psychological Trauma: Theory, Research, Practice, and Policy,* 2, 63–70.

Hinton, D. E., Hsia, C., Park, L., Rasmussen, A., & Pollack, M. H. (2009). Cultural anthropology and anxiety diagnoses. In D. McKay, J. S. Abramowitz, S. Taylor, & G. J. Asmundson (Eds.), *Current perspectives on the anxiety disorders: Implications for DSM-V and beyond* (pp. 245–74). New York: Springer Press.

Hinton, D. E., Kredlow, M. A., Bui, E., Pollack, M. H., & Hofmann, S. G. (2012). Treatment change of somatic symptoms and cultural syndromes among Cambodian refugees with PTSD. *Depression and Anxiety,* 29, 148–55.

Hinton, D. E., Kredlow, M. A., Pich, V., Bui, E., & Hofmann, S. G. (2013). The relationship of PTSD to key somatic complaints and cultural syndromes among Cambodian refugees attending a psychiatric clinic: The Cambodian Somatic Symptom and Syndrome Inventory (SSI). *Transcultural Psychiatry,* 50, 347–70.

Hinton, D. E., & Lewis-Fernández, R. (2010). Idioms of distress among trauma survivors: Subtypes and clinical utility. *Culture, Medicine, and Psychiatry,* 34, 209–18.

(2011). The cross-cultural validity of posttraumatic stress disorder: Implications for DSM-5. *Depression and Anxiety,* 28, 783–801.

Hinton, D. E., Nickerson, A., & Bryant, R. A. (2011). Worry, worry attacks, and PTSD among Cambodian refugees: A path analysis investigation. *Social Science and Medicine,* 72, 1817–25.

Hinton, D. E., Peou, S., Joshi, S., Nickerson, A., & Simon, N. (2013). Normal grief and complicated bereavement among traumatized Cambodian refugees: Cultural context and the central role of dreams of the deceased. *Culture, Medicine, and Psychiatry,* 37, 427–64.

Hinton, D. E., Pich, V., Chhean, D., & Pollack, M. H. (2005). "The ghost pushes you down": Sleep paralysis-type panic attacks in a Khmer refugee population. *Transcultural Psychiatry,* 42, 46–78.

Hinton, D. E., Pich, V., Marques, L., Nickerson, A., & Pollack, M. H. (2010). Khyâl attacks: A key idiom of distress among traumatized Cambodia refugees. *Culture, Medicine, and Psychiatry,* 34, 244–78.

Hinton, D. E., Rasmussen, A., Nou, L., Pollack, M. H., & Good, M. J. (2009). Anger, PTSD, and the nuclear family: A study of Cambodian refugees. *Social Science and Medicine*, 69, 1387–94.

Hinton, D. E., Rivera, E., Hofmann, S. G., Barlow, D. H., & Otto, M. W. (2012). Adapting CBT for traumatized refugees and ethnic minority patients: Examples from culturally adapted CBT (CA-CBT). *Transcultural Psychiatry*, 49, 340–65.

Hinton, D. E., Sinclair, J., Chung, R. C., & Pollack, M. H. (2007). The SF-36 among Cambodian and Vietnamese refugees: An examination of psychometric properties. *Journal of Psychopathology and Behavioral Assessment*, 29, 38–45.

Hinton, D. E., Um, K., & Ba, P. (2001a). *Kyol goeu* ("wind overload"). Part I. A cultural syndrome of orthostatic panic among Khmer refugees. *Transcultural Psychiatry*, 38, 403–32.

(2001b). A unique panic-disorder presentation among Khmer refugees: The sore-neck syndrome. *Culture, Medicine, and Psychiatry*, 25, 297–316.

Jenkins, J. H., & Valiente, M. (1994). Bodily transactions of the passions: *El calor* (the heat) among Salvadoran women. In T. Csordas (Ed.), *The body as existential ground: Studies in culture, self, and experience* (pp. 163–82). Cambridge: Cambridge University Press.

Kidron, C. A. (2015). Embodying the distant past: Holocaust descendant narratives of the lived presence of the genocidal past. In D. E. Hinton & A. L. Hinton (Eds.), *Genocide and mass violence: Memory, symptom, and recovery*. Cambridge: Cambridge University Press.

Kirmayer, L. J. (1996). Confusion of the senses: Implications of ethnocultural variations in somatoform and dissociative disorders for PTSD. In A. J. Marsella, M. J. Friedman, E. T. Gerrity, & R. M. Scurfield (Eds.), *Ethnocultural aspects of posttraumatic stress disorder: Issues, research, and clinical applications* (pp. 131–64). Washington, DC: American Psychological Association.

Kirmayer, L. J., & Sartorius, N. (2007). Cultural models and somatic syndromes. *Psychosomatic Medicine*, 69, 832–40.

Kleinman, A., & Becker, A. E. (1998). "Sociosomatics": The contributions of anthropology to psychosomatic medicine. *Psychosomatic Medicine*, 60, 389–93.

Kleinman, A. & Kleinman, J. (1994). How bodies remember: Social memory and bodily experience of criticism, resistance, and delegitimation following China's Cultural Revolution. *New Literary History*, 25, 707–23.

Langer, L. L. (1991). *Holocaust testimonies: The ruins of memory*. New Haven, CT: Yale University Press.

Lock, M. M. (1993). Encounters with aging mythologies of menopause in Japan and North America. Retrieved from http://hdl.handle.net/2027/heb.04079

McDonald, S. D., & Calhoun, P. S. (2010). The diagnostic accuracy of the PTSD Checklist: A critical review. *Clinical Psychology Review*, 30, 976–87.

McNally, R. J., & Frueh, B. C. (2013). Why are Iraq and Afghanistan War veterans seeking PTSD disability compensation at unprecedented rates? *Journal of Anxiety Disorders*, 27, 520–6.

Mollica, R. F., Caspi-Yavin, Y., Bollini, P., Truong, T., Tor, S., & Lavelle, J. (1992). The Harvard Trauma Questionnaire: Validating a cross-cultural instrument for measuring torture, trauma, and posttraumatic stress disorder in Indochinese refugees. *Journal of Nervous and Mental Disease*, 180, 111–16.

Mollica, R. F., Mcinness, K., Poole, C., & Tor, S. (1998). Dose-effect relationships of trauma to symptoms of depression and post-traumatic stress disorder among Cambodian survivors of mass violence. *British Journal of Psychiatry*, 173, 482–8.

Mollica, R. F., Wyshak, G., Marneffe, D., Khuon, F., & Lavelle, J. (1987). Indochinese version of the Hopkins Symptom Checklist-25: A screening instrument for the psychiatric care of refugees. *American Journal of Psychiatry* 144, 497–500.

Reis, R. (2013). Children enacting idioms of witchcraft and spirit possession in response to trauma: Therapeutically beneficial, and for whom? *Culture, Medicine, and Psychiatry*, 50, 622–43.

Rubel, A. J., O'Nell, C. W., & Collado-Ardón, R. (1984). *Susto: A folk illness*. Berkeley: University of California Press.

Shawcross, W. (1984). *The quality of mercy: Cambodia, Holocaust, and modern conscience*. London: Andre Deutsch.

Shorter, E. (1992). *From paralysis to fatigue: A history of psychosomatic illness in the modern era*. Toronto: Maxwell Macmillan Canada.

Sonis, J., Gibson, J. L., de Jong, J. T., Field, N. P., Hean, S., & Komproe, I. (2009). Probable posttraumatic stress disorder and disability in Cambodia: Associations with perceived justice, desire for revenge, and attitudes toward the Khmer Rouge trials. *JAMA*, 302, 527–36.

Terry, F. (2002). *Condemned to repeat? The paradox of humanitarian action*. Ithaca, NY and London: Cornell University Press.

Weller, S. C., Baer, R. D., Garcia de Alba Garcia, J., & Salcedo Rocha, A. L. (2008). Susto and nervios: Expressions for stress and depression. *Culture, Medicine, and Psychiatry*, 32, 406–20.

10   Attack of the Grotesque: Suffering, Sleep Paralysis, and Distress during the Sierra Leone War

Doug Henry

Beware the *njombo-bla*, they just want to part your legs like THIS (CLAP)!

Song sung by schoolgirls,
Kenema, Sierra Leone, 1997

Mariama was a displaced woman in her early thirties from Kailahun, Sierra Leone. I met her in the town of Kenema in eastern Sierra Leone in 1997, at a point during the eleven-year war when the whole world seemed to turn upside down. A military coup had displaced the president, and the rebels were invited to become part of a power sharing government. A civil militia who had become local heroes by aggressively taking back villages from rebels was suddenly outlawed, and was being asked to disband voluntarily. Drunk or stoned soldiers from the army would ply the streets to make a living by extortion or theft. Whereas most violence had before taken place along roadsides in the forest, or in small villages, now towns were the center of unrest. Kenema was experiencing gun battles between the militia and the army; dead bodies on the streets had become a fact of daily life.

Despite the tense milieu of our first meeting, Mariama on the surface seemed remarkably self-assured. A widow since just before the war started, she had lost her husband to cancer in 1989. She had become displaced when rebels attacked her town and burned down both her house and the school where she worked. She had made her way to the safety of Kenema and had here begged for a job with the Kenema Diocesan Development Office, funded through the Catholic Archbishops, and Catholic Relief Services. They were one of the better run local NGOs operating in the area; their workers were actually paid a livable wage, and (the war permitting) on time. Her life was on the surface somewhat enviable; unlike many displaced people who crowded into IDP camps, she was able to contribute to the household income of her uncle's family and so shared a room with three others in a house in town.[1] What made her unusual was that Mariama was one of the few women in town who had survived, and would talk about, attempted nighttime rape by a witch spirit.

I had been doing doctoral fieldwork among refugees in the Southeast of the country. Over the course of thirteen months between 1997 and 1998, I lived in two displaced persons camps on either side of the Sierra Leone–Guinea border, conducting a larger study about the reconstruction and reinvention of health systems in the context of sociopolitical violence. In addition to participant observation, I conducted 220 structured, semistructured, and informal interviews with displaced persons, soldiers, rebels, militia fighters, camp managers, and aid workers. Because of the nature of doing fieldwork in an active war zone, my methodology had to be somewhat flexible and adapt to the exigencies of what could be an unstable social and political situation; fieldwork became more the ethnography of an unfolding process rather than that of a particular place.

When I first arrived, women in and around the IDP camp began experiencing terrifying collective nighttime incidents that came to be known as the *njombo-bla*, or "*njombo-bla* attacks." In Mende,[2] the local language, *njombo-bla* literally means "splitting the pubic hairs." In the Mende experience, this was considered an attack by a witch spirit capable of changing form and forcing sexual intercourse on its victims. Women who experienced this reported that a "dark mist" could appear in the middle of the night that seemed to put them into an immobilized swoon. It could undress you, and when you could not move, force sex on you, sometimes very violently.

The experience was profoundly terrifying. Once you found your voice, you could scream, at which time, coherent with West African cosmology, the witch spirit would change form, often turning into a dog and running away into the night. Though these events were experienced individually, the terror then quickly became collective, in that whole villages, or the IDP camp, would suddenly wake up upon hearing the screams, women and children would huddle together in the dark, and the men would attempt to chase whatever it was away. Fear quickly spread, as the visions could be echoed by other women in the night.

These attacks were bewildering to me as the researcher in the field, in that they bore no resemblance to the relatively petty interpersonal kinds of witchcraft accusations I had seen in the country before. After years living in Sierra Leone, I had seen neighbors and even friends occasionally brought up on witchcraft charges. A fine was paid, a traditional healer called to exorcise the witch spirit, promises made to address grievances, and life moved on. *Njombo-bla* attacks were experienced fundamentally differently, and on a more dramatic scale than I (or most around me) had ever seen. Carolyn Nordstrom (1995) writes about how, during times of mass violence, social institutions and boundaries that govern life can become distorted, rent, "grotesques" of their previous forms. This was certainly the case for me and for everyone these events touched; they were partly so shocking because they bore no resemblance to the way witchcraft was normally anticipated in Sierra Leone and seemed to reflect a suddenly spiraling intensification of social tension and anxiety. Locals themselves struggled for answers, but a consensus opinion developed that was very clear about pointing the finger, at power and ethnically based jealousy. Specifically, it was assumed jealousy surrounding the rise to power of a Mende hunter-militia, known as the Kamajohs, or *kamajesia*.[3]

This chapter documents the context and implications of the event and ensuing accusations, but in my own attempts to understand and rationalize the experience, I also attempt three complementary explanatory frames.[4] I partly frame these nocturnal events within strikingly similarly described episodes of sleep paralysis, in that the assaults as narrated to me match cases described in the literature of being suddenly unable to move or speak upon either sleeping or waking and hallucinating a shape moving toward and then hovering over the body. Episodes of sleep paralysis have been shown to increase with experiences of stress and trauma (Hinton, Pich, Chhean, & Pollack, 2005; Hinton, Pich, Chhean, Pollack, & McNally, 2005; Paradis & Friedman, 2005); they have also been described through culturally informed semantics of witchcraft and nocturnal spirit attack among West African, Afro-Caribbean, and African American populations. So in some ways, this is the story of how a biological event interacts with religious belief to become a social model of discourse about wartime events. It is also the story of a collective distress idiom that evolved around social and economic tension, gender violence, and vulnerability. The fact that the *njombo-bla* only appeared to women is very significant; though it seemed theoretically possible, no one could think of a time when it had ever appeared to a man. I interpret its appearance at this time during the war as precipitated social and political tensions about displacement, gender violence, and ethnic tension, inscribing their own discourse on an expressive, collective female body, a discourse made manifest and testified through both intimate experiences and the local idioms of Mende religious culture. Thus, it may be in this context that nighttime assault was a manifestation of social, political, and economic anxieties becoming embodied in psychological experience, as a complex interaction of culture, the experience of violence, and the altered *grotesques* of wartime subjectivity.

The Conflict, the Kamajoh Movement, and the Balance of Social Power

The story of the Sierra Leone violence has by now been written many times. In March 1991, an attack on a small southern village by a group of armed Sierra Leoneans, Liberians, and Burkinabés calling themselves the Revolutionary United Front (RUF) began an eleven-year conflict in Sierra Leone. Infrastructural damage to the country has been enormous; about half of the country of 5 million became displaced at least once during the conflict. People everywhere witnessed their loved ones, homes, schools, clinics, bridges, mosques, churches, and social institutions being damaged or destroyed. Although initially supported by Charles Taylor of Liberia, the RUF quickly claimed its own populist agenda for political reform. However, their tactic of targeting civilians, and the failure of genuine political reforms to produce a lasting cease-fire, quickly fueled popular skepticism about the legitimacy of RUF's claims. Numerous attempts were made at cease-fires, amnesties, negotiated settlements, boycotts, and political power sharing, yet there were still hit-and-run guerrilla attacks, highway ambushes, burned and looted houses, destroyed or confiscated crops, rapes, maiming, and mass human rights violations. Analysts have variously attributed the violence in Sierra Leone to a mixture of personal-political grievances harbored by neighboring Liberia's former president, Charles Taylor, war-inspired exiles, disenchanted youth fighting social exclusion, failed patrimonialism, and increased criminal control over the highly profitable illicit diamond trade, which flows out of Sierra Leone into neighboring countries such as Liberia (Abdullah & Muana, 1998; Reno, 1998; Richards, 1996). It has often been pointed out that the violence in Sierra Leone could be "functional," in that it provided an ideal destabilized environment under which criminal activity like smuggling could take place (Campbell, 2002; Reno, 1997; Smillie, Gberie, & Hazleton 2000). Indeed, sometimes the forms of those waging war on either side seemed to blur; rebels would masquerade as soldiers to enter a town; soldiers masqueraded as rebels to make a living, and the word *sobel* was born.

It was in this environment of shifting identities and ambiguous loyalties that the *kamajesia* were formed. Local and national leaders had first mobilized groups of local men, many of them youths and hunters, to assist the military through their knowledge of local bush tracks and forests. Recruits initially acted as guides for the military, but as the public grew more mistrustful of soldier behavior, the guides continued to enjoy widespread admiration, and tension began to grow between the two. Tension turned to open conflict when the national political party of the president transformed the guides into a fully armed civilian militia. Known as the Kamajohs, they were fiercely loyal to the national government, yet autonomous from (and competitive with) the national army (for more detailed histories of the Kamajoh movement, see Alie, 2005; Ferme, 2001b, Muana, 1997; Zack-Williams, 1997).

But the Kamajohs were not simply a "militia"; in large part their tremendous local support and authority arose from their association with a much older "traditional" Mende society of magical and heroic hunters. Every village had a few Kamajohs before the war, but their powers were somewhat limited, to hunt or trap forest animals stealthily, for example, or to travel in the forest at night. This changed dramatically in early 1996 when a Muslim holy leader from Bo claimed to have been empowered by God with miracles to initiate men (women could not be Kamajohs) on a massive scale, and to invest them with powers hitherto unseen – abilities, for example, to divert rocket-propelled grenades, to stop automatic weapons from firing, to render the society-man impermeable to bullets, or to turn the fired bullets back upon their source. These powers last with the Kamajoh only as long as he follows very strict, specific rules – not touching dead bodies, not showing fear, not accepting anything from a woman, not stealing from the war front, or not looting. Violations render him powerless. Later that year others began to manifest this initiating ability, and initiation into the Kamajoh society began to occur on a massive scale.

What was widely perceived as a "new" power rising up from Mende land was not without regional consequence and did much to upset previously existing balances of power. Most disturbing were fears and accusations voiced by many non-Mende peoples that the Kamajohs were inherently tribalistic and were bent on setting up a Mende-dominated state. The Kamajohs were perceived as intrinsically Mende – arising from Mende areas, composed in entirety of Mende men trained in "deep" Mende lore, and believed to be gifted by God with supernatural powers expressly for the recapture of Mende homelands. Unquestionably, other ethnic groups felt threatened by this sudden power "rising up" from Mende land, which threatened to upset both local and national balances of power. Political leaders of other ethnic groups would very insistently explain to me how the Kamajohs were "an instrument" "cooked up" by people in the South and East of the country (predominantly Mende areas) "to silence" the North (areas with different ethnic groups).

The *Njombo-bla*

In the middle of this simmering ethnic tension, *njombo-bla* attacks began. They started around the town of Bo in early 1994, roughly corresponding with the rise to prominence of the Kamajohs there. They purportedly attacked fifteen women. Their appearance in Kenema in January 1997 corresponded with the arrival of Kamajohs there; there had been three attacks that spring, and by June, there were three alleged perpetrating witches all apprehended by the Kamajohs – all were from the northern, Temne ethnic group; all died (were killed) while in custody.

When I inquired at the Kamajohs' local headquarters about the incident, and asked whether I could speak with the accused men, the local spokesperson said:

> Yes! They (Temne people) are jealous! But that is not our problem; God has given *us* this power. They came into this war to deceive us ... instead of fighting, they were taking property, looting, and sharing it ... the *njombo-bla* is really just part of the jealousy ... when those (Temne) men came, it took us only twelve hours to find them, and the Kamajohs arrested three of them that were "playing that game." So we took them down (pause), and we don't know what happened to them after that. They just disappeared. So since then, we have not been hearing about any *njombo-bla* again.

The Temne people I spoke with strongly felt that these accusations were false and quietly countered their own prevailing view, that the Kamajohs were manipulating tribalistic sentiments in order to clear Temne people from southern areas, so that they could expand their own ethnically based regional operations (such as diamond mining and coffee and cocoa trading).

That I discuss the arrival of the *njombo-bla* in these sociopolitical terms does not mean that it was encountered at all levels as a social or political event. On the contrary, the *njombo-bla* appearances were profoundly frightening and deeply personal, especially to women. After many efforts, I was finally able to meet and interview Mariama, a woman in town who had suffered a *njombo-bla* attack.

The assault occurred in February 1997, while Mariama and a relief-outreach team were delivering supplies to a nearby village. I have transcribed our meeting in much detail, in an attempt to convey the profound fear that pervaded her particular encounter.[5]

I was sleeping, it was as if I was in a deep sleep, when I saw a huge man at the side of the bed – at first lying on my right hand side, and then suddenly he was standing. He came closer to me, and I said, "Who are you?" As soon as I asked this, he turned into a dog, which then jumped forward as if to have sex with me; it started fighting with me, and so I started to shout! Then my workmate Sally woke up and said, "What's happening, what's wrong?" and I shouted, "Here is this dog, trying to rape me!" As soon as I said that, the thing disappeared. I got up out of bed, and ran outside, and all the women in the other room also went out. I was afraid that no one would believe me, because I alone had seen that man....

Sally never even saw the dog. But as soon as we all went out, we heard another girl shouting, in a house close by. That girl had been sleeping with her husband, but then started shouting, "Leave me! Leave me!"

Then the men announced, "All the women should come out of their houses at once!" and we did, and sat on the verandahs with some of the boys. The men went off, some of them were Kamajohs, and started looking for the *njombo-bla....* So all of us were just sitting there, *some of us were able to get back to sleep,* but we were all afraid. Then suddenly I saw a HUGE something, high and big, and kind of a brownish red color, dark, with bulging big eyes, standing over us, and then coming towards us. So then all of us began shouting, and when we did, it bent down and took a hold of me like this.... It hit me on my leg here and here. Other women saw it, too. The men heard the shouts, came back, and the thing started away. The men pointed a flashlight at it, and it turned into a cat, and then a dog, and ran away. But it was strange – only we women saw it; the men couldn't see it, and they couldn't catch it. It was only later, after we came back the next week, that we heard that they caught a man at the place there ... the Kamajohs caught him.

As happened to the other three men in Kenema, the man arrested and accused of this attack died while in the custody of the militia.

Religious Belief in Sierra Leone

Hufford (1982, 2005) considers sleep paralysis a core event with characteristics that almost universally seem to prompt religious or spiritual explanation. Because culture provides the content and interpretations for what is seen during an episode of sleep paralysis, indigenous religious beliefs bear some elaboration.[6]

Classic anthropological texts on African religion tend to characterize witchcraft beliefs or accusations as social attempts to give structure and meaning to chaotic experiences, or as conceptions of evil that explain misfortune. More recent works have noted how new forms of religious expression can arise to allow people to engage with rapid social change and tension, that can speak to, and sometimes protest, existing structures of social power or modern uncertainties (Comaroff, 1985; Moore & Sanders, 2001). This work situates changing religious traditions within processes of fluctuating postcolonial modernity, be they market forces and structural inequality (Comaroff & Comaroff, 1993); conflict and post-conflict uncertainty (Reis, 2013); gender, generation, and fertility (Auslander, 1993); labor migration and political ambition (Geschiere, 1997); even the uneven accumulation of wealth and power remembered from the slave trade (Shaw, 2002).

These approaches have been challenged by those who suspect them of reducing religious beliefs to being merely "idioms," or misrepresentations, of reality. Ellis and Ter Haar (1998), for example, note that religious expressions are not simply metaphors for expressing social or economic relations, but rather are themselves integral parts of reality. This reality can be dark and morally ambiguous, in that people with access to the spiritual realm are often assumed to have aspirations to political power that might threaten or compete with the established order (Ter Haar & Ellis, 2009). Niehaus (1993), for instance, writing about witch outbreaks and "witch-cleansing cults" in northern South Africa, describes how a youth organization gained moral authority in part by taking it upon themselves to hunt down and attack witches – 50 were taken in a single month, 36 of them put to death. Becoming involved in communal witch hunting was deemed a social service and therefore gave the group both political and moral legitimacy. Others have written about how, during the political instability of war, religious movements can be methods to reorder power, enhancing the mobilization of people or resources (Behrend, 1999; Lan, 1985), maintaining fighting discipline or confidence, or simply intimidating the opposition (Ellis, 2007; Marwick, 1950).

Mende religious cosmology, and West African cosmology in general, allows for the accommodation of malevolent spiritual forces that can prey on people, particularly women and young children. These forces are often considered destructive, rapacious, and nocturnally predatory (Little, 1948). A "witch spirit," for instance, may commonly house itself in the body of an antisocial person but is then able to project itself outward in order to "eat away" the soul of someone else. Witches are thought to be able to drain the blood out of a person, consume flesh, destroy crops, and be able to shape-shift into dangerous animals including chimpanzees, baboons, leopards, snakes, or crocodiles (MacCormack, 1983). Jealousy and greed are the main forces thought to inspire witches to act – jealousy of accumulation, jealousy of power, or jealousy of another's fortune. Spirits can also be "bush devils," associated with a particular place (a creek, river, forest clearing, or rock) but capable of wreaking havoc on individuals or villages. Gittins, for example, speaks of the treacherous *ndohgboh jusui*, which can enter a town after making a traitorous pact with someone inside the village (Gittins, 1987). A devil might change into a dog, and then into a man, in order to gain access to a victim within a village stealthily.

Rebel behavior, in its opaqueness, destructiveness, or ferocity, was often assumed to have been obtained through pacts made with the supernatural; their actions, in fact, seemed to mimic each other. Whenever I traveled, children would admonish me to beware of the *kudwai* devil, who would hide by the side of a forest road and ambush passers-by (much as rebels did), paralyzing them with fear and then killing them. Equally terrifying were the "shape shifting" habits of rebels and of soldiers, in that one could masquerade as the other in order to gain access to a village; such characteristics became so powerfully feared in part because they resonated with these broader religious interpretations about hidden identity and shape-alteration. Any actions on the part of rebels or soldiers that might reveal or even suggest this ability would play on these local associations, compounding the public fear of the insidious and powerful nature of the transformer (Ferme, 2001a).

Spirits were seen to be active during the war. Refugees were considered more vulnerable to them. In general, malevolent spirits are associated with the night and cool nighttime breezes. So while well-built houses and villages are thought to be relatively secure, refugees and IDPs could be stuck sleeping out in the open, either in temporary dwellings in makeshift camps, or crowded outside onto verandahs and porches. Exposed in these open, cold, and damp environments, displaced people already considered themselves relatively more vulnerable to potential attack. Some were convinced that bush devils had become increasingly disturbed during the conflict, as displaced people had been forced to cut down what had been sacred areas of rainforest in order to make room for new camps. Compounding all this was the strain in obtaining sufficient food rations, especially the staples like rice and palm oil, which were considered necessary to maintain "strong blood" and good health. These vulnerabilities could result in anemia or, much worse, convulsions associated with being "eaten" by a possessing spirit.

Sleep Paralysis as an Explanatory Frame

In trying to make sense of how religious beliefs were interacting with external events surrounding the war, my first explanatory frame is sleep paralysis. In an episode of sleep paralysis, someone either falling asleep or waking up discovers that they can't move their body. Over a time period of several seconds to several minutes, the motor-inhibitory aspects of REM sleep continue, with total or partial paralysis of the skeletal muscles, while the person is in between a wake-sleep state (Hobson, 1995). If a dream state persists during this time, the person can vividly hallucinate sights, sounds, conversations, and even tactile sensations; these are hypnagogic or hypnopompic hallucinations, depending on if they occur while falling asleep or when waking up (Kryger, Roth, & Dement, 2000).

Cultural models provide the content for these experiences, in which shared beliefs can produce very vivid images that can conform to both expectations and fears, thus giving patterns of experience to members across a society (Hufford, 2005). Very often people report seeing some kind of dark, shadowy being approach. Around the world, this has been culturally explained as an "Old Hag" syndrome in Newfoundland (Hufford, 1982; Ness, 1978), alien abduction in the U.S. (McNally & Clancy, 2005), nocturnal spirit attacks ("being pushed down by a ghost") in the Cambodian population (Hinton, Pich, Chhean, & Pollack, 2005; Hinton, Pich, Chhean, Pollack, & McNally, 2005), "being ridden by a witch" among African Americans (Hall, 1993), to "being oppressed by evil spirits" among Nigerians (Ohaeri, 1997). In that visions of menacing intruders commonly incorporate sexual content and even rape, sleep paralysis provides a potential explanation for the incubus and succubus of Western cultural tradition (De Jong, 2005; McNally & Clancy, 2005; Schenk, Arnulf, & Mahowald, 2007). In a strikingly similar event, Martin Walsh (1995) describes the *popobawa* outbreaks in Zanzibar, in which an amorphous, shape-shifting demonic bat could come in the night, often accompanied by vivid sights, sounds, or smells, pressing itself on victims (primarily men), and sodomizing them. These attacks could be recognized by others nearby, who could also be attacked in turn. Many homes could be attacked simultaneously, creating general pandemonium, until the *popobawa* spirit moved on. Spanos, McNulty, Dubreuil, Piries, and Burgess (1995) note that sleep paralysis among some groups can have higher salience and "threat values," in that that which is hallucinated can generate tremendous anxiety and even post-traumatic stress. *Popobawa* assaults, for example, seemed to spread; Walsh describes how people accused of being responsible were killed by angry mobs.

Significantly for my own understanding of the njombo-bla appearance at that time during the war, researchers have found a relationship between sleep paralysis and stress, in that stress may disrupt regulatory sleep mechanisms (Fukuda, Miyasita, Inugami, & Ishihara, 1987). Hinton et al. (see Hinton, Pich, Chhean, & Pollack, 2005; Hinton, Pich, Chhean, Pollack, & McNally, 2005) note that people with traumatic histories are especially likely to have sleep paralysis, and moreover that those cultural groups that have great fear of the sleep paralysis and the entity seen during that state are likely to have high rates: an escalating spiral of anxiety may be created in which PTSD causes sleep paralysis (and associated hallucinations) and then the experience of sleep paralysis causes great fear, which in turn produces more PTSD that then causes more sleep paralysis, and so on.

It does seem plausible that sleep paralysis provides at least a partial explanation for the social epidemiology of the njombo-bla. Social stress, wartime insecurity, and the experiences of loss and suffering may predispose one to sleep paralysis; resulting anxiety over the culturally attributed cause of the nighttime terror (assaulting witches) may cause still more fear, which then spreads through a community. Once the community recognizes it as a problem, everyone becomes more anxious, which can then promote more sleep paralysis. Once sleep paralysis becomes experienced in the community, this could become a model through which the body-mind expresses distress. At least for Mariama's case (though I note above that her own report was somewhat atypical), it is not a perfect explanatory frame. It is unusual for someone to report speech during episodes of sleep paralysis (recall that Mariama reported trying to engage the njombo-bla in questioning). The episode of restraint also seems a bit different; Mariama reports struggling, whereas in classic sleep paralysis, the victim is immobilized in a swoon.[7] It is somewhat unusual that episodes of sleep paralysis would occur primarily to one gender, though women during conflict are disproportionately vulnerable to men, therefore experience higher stress and greater threat to being. Certainly within Mende religious belief, women, particularly young or pregnant women, are considered more vulnerable to nighttime attack by evil spirits. Finally, this could be a biased reporting issue, in that once sleep paralysis becomes associated with one particular gender, this association suppresses reporting by the opposite sex. Outside of the *popobawa* attacks, I do not know of other examples from the literature where the hallucinations seem to spread, in what could become a kind of community mass hysteria.[8] Sleep paralysis is complex, though, and can't be completely discounted even from Mariama's case, because there are related sleep paralysis-linked phenomenon, and unexplained nighttime terrors are more likely to occur when sleep is disrupted and threats seem to loom.

Gender Violence, Vulnerability, and Embodied Idioms of Distress

There are additional ways to frame the appearance of the njombo-bla, and people's reactions to it. As I mentioned, manifestation and response were also the products of gender violence and social vulnerability during conflict.

Even before the war, Sierra Leone ranked at the bottom of the UN Development Program's "Human Development Index." Women, with lower literacy rates, education, and income earning potential, are structurally marginalized to become particularly vulnerable during conflict. While men more often died in fighting, women I knew had been subjected to widespread sexual violence, including rape, torture, sexual slavery, and forced marriages to combatants (Henry, 2005; see also Benjamin, 2001; Coulter, 2009; Human Rights Watch, 2003). While membership in the Kamajoh society offered supernatural protection against the effects of war, that was a society for men only, and no such parallel protection existed for women.

Even while supposedly safe in the watched environment of a displaced-persons camp, women were extremely disadvantaged relative to men in terms of their income generating opportunities. In other places I've documented how young refugee men could earn a very reduced, but survivable income based on day labor, farming, trading, and smuggling (Henry 2005). This was only really enough for themselves, however; refugee women remained comparably much more vulnerable. A German-funded technical school had opened nearby to teach carpentry, masonry, and metal-working, but these were not things that women do in Sierra Leone; they were therefore unrealistic for most. A few women enrolled in masonry classes anyway with the hope that something was better than nothing, but (correctly) recognized that their futures in this area was limited at best. The largest source of income for displaced women was men.

There also exists tremendous moral tension for women displaced from conflict. From the very beginning of my fieldwork I heard stories about how single women had become much more promiscuous during the war, and how they would informally exchange "love" and sex for material and financial support. These accusations were sometimes true – displaced women were in fact compelled into taking increased numbers of short term sexual partners as an economic survival strategy. There were actually court cases where women were kicked out of IDP camps for doing this. Jita, a young woman from the IDP camp right outside the village where Mariama's attack occurred, explained it to me this way:

Before the war, you had a husband, or a close man, and the two of you could work towards a bright future. You worked together – in business, on the farm, you were together, and women didn't suffer too much. But now, during this war, they've killed a lot of men. So a woman may be left with 2, 3, 4 children, but the rebels have killed your husband. So now she has to try very hard to raise the children. Like you see women doing now in the camp – they have to get up very early in the morning, go into the forest, cut trees, and carry the firewood all the way to town to get money for food, and then come back and feed the children. So in all this, if she meets a man who wants to help her, will she sleep with him? Of course!

Given the fear of sexual slavery and wartime rape at the hands of rebels or soldiers, the economic strain of making ends meet, and the strained moral universe that women found themselves forced to navigate, it would not be unexpected for women to manifest experiences that function as "distress idioms" that allow the self to "speak" unspeakable things during times of violent unrest. In the last 25 years, medical and psychological anthropologists have detailed dozens of somatized illness experiences, each with a particular culturally informed etiology, diagnosis, meaning, style of expression, and prescribed method of healing (Csordas, 1983; Helman, 1994; Hinton, Pich, Marques, Nickerson, & Pollack, 2010; Jenkins, 1996; Kirmayer &Young, 1998; Nichter, 1981; Rubel, 1977).

Elsewhere I (Henry, 2006) document how discussions of one such illness-idiom in Sierra Leone, "*haypatɛnsi*," allowed horrific subjective experiences to become apprehended and mediated, enabling survivors to understand and express the pain of their trauma and vulnerability, and begin to move beyond it by reestablishing order and control over their lives. Though not an illness-event per se, I think it is useful to approach local beliefs and discussions surrounding the njombo-bla attacks in a similar way – where people symbolically express collective distress over violence, death, disempowerment, social tension, and moral crisis. What makes the njombo-bla attacks so different as an idiom of distress is where the culturally informed apprehension and recognition conditions a response – in this case, where outsider-men became searched for, scape-goated, and killed by militia members before they were put on trial.

Conclusions

Hollan (2004) suggests that there has been a tendency in the anthropological literature to naively interpret idioms of distress as always leading to alleviate or make suffering more manageable. As I show here, actions that surround these idioms may just as likely create new forms of suffering and/or new agents of violence; they can exacerbate existing distress, or reproduce violence in new contexts and theaters. I find it extremely significant that the *njombo-bla* seemed to only appear to women – men were initially unable to see it in its "witch form." Coupled with the violence that women experience during wartime, this means that the appearance and the attacks of the *njombo-bla*, themselves a crystallization of ethnically-based competition, takes place on the terrain of the most assailable and susceptible of society's members. In this case, women *saw what the men did not*; they gave voice to it, and testified about, what may have otherwise been left unspoken. Their active participation in the local political discourse did mobilize men, and send them off into the forest to protect themselves, their children, and their homes; it also, however, had the effect of scapegoating and killing potentially innocent people. So instead of allowing the sociopolitical tension to become diffused, the testimony in fact had the opposite effect, essentially creating more spectacular violence, making things crystallize and burst before they settled down again.[9] Das, Kleinman, Ramphele, and Reynolds (2000) and Bourgois (2001) are both instrumental here, when they point out that those who witness violence can themselves become subjects, even agents of violence, as the act of witnessing (and I would add, "testifying") becomes part of the experience of subjugation.

Clearly violent ruptures and social symptoms go far beyond visible wounds and body counts. As bodies during wartime can be expressive idioms through which personal and social suffering become manifest and potentially managed, the case of the *njombo-bla* suggests that this expression may also aggravate the extreme tensions and anxieties that underlie the grotesque forms of social and political power during war. Distress idioms are thus fundamentally ambivalent – at times able to mitigate, mediate, or heal, at times able to explosively destroy. As anthropologists, we must continue to draw together the personal and collective, psychological and political, by analyzing the messages that people convey about their anxiety, be it through the symbolic and idiomatic language of suffering, or through discussions about religious belief, social power, and witchcraft. Surely if relief is to follow experiences of mass violence, it can only follow through recognition of the multi-layered meanings through which people express distress.

NOTES

1 Before the war, it would have been unusual for a woman of Mariama's age to not yet remarry. During the war, however, with men suffering higher mortality, being away fighting, or seasonally migrating away to mine diamonds, this was less unusual, and women often complained that finding a stable man had become difficult now. Mariama herself was having an affair with a married Muslim man. She suspected the man's first wife as preventing a polygamous marriage to him, which she herself was desirous of. "No first wife is going to want a second wife who makes more money than her husband," she explained.

2 The Mende are one of the two largest ethnic groups in Sierra Leone, occupying the largest part of the south and southeast of the country. They are well studied in the literature (Ferme, 2001a; Little, 1965; MacCormack, 1983). Because the original combatants entered from the Liberia to the south and east, Mende people in these areas have been somewhat disproportionately affected by the conflict.

3 *Kamajesia* is the Mende plural form of "Kamajohs," as they became known in English (alt. spelling "Kamajor" and "Kamajo"). I use the two terms interchangeably.

4 There are dilemmas of representation here of which I am painfully aware, and which have made the writing of this difficult. How, for instance, does one portray intense personal suffering and terror without making it disappear into scholarly academic discourse, biological reductionism, or worse,

something that is itself a pornography of violence? What level of analysis allows an "engaged witness" a critical stance (Scheper-Hughes & Bourgois, 2004) that is not so solipsistic that only the ethnographer's reaction gets told? How does one reconcile writing about what were chaotic and anarchic experiences without imposing an "anesthetized," narrative order that has little relevance to the people in the throws of violence (Feldman 1995)? Like Lemelson in this volume, I myself struggle with how to frame things that resemble Western categories, but have other polyvalent cultural meanings that would make such an evaluation meaningless to the subjectivity of the people concerned. My writing here is an attempted navigation of these questions, but ultimately I write about them simply because I feel I must.

5 There are some striking differences between Mariama's personal account told to me, and the generalized account that other women (not speaking from personal experience) told each other. Most narratives, for example, told of being held down or immobilized in a swoon while sex was forced; Mariama reports fighting back. Mariama also reports talking with and trying to engage the witch spirit, which other women did not. Finding other women to speak from firsthand experience was impossible.

6 Here I find Ellis and Ter Haar's (2004) definition of religious belief useful, "a belief in the existence of an invisible world, often thought to be inhabited by spirits that are believed to affect people's lives in the material world" (p. 3). I've also benefitted from Moore and Sanders' perspective that witchcraft and the occult can be seen as a set of discourses on the contemporary human condition, "a sort of social diagnostics... that try to explain why the world is the way it is, why it is changing and moving in a particular manner at the moment" (Moore & Sanders, 2001, p. 20).

7 I am grateful to both David Hufford and Ria Reis for their feedback in this section.

8 I am also unwilling to characterize this "only" as an episode of mass hysteria, though, and instead choose to focus on what anxieties seemed to condition the experiences of what people reported and how they responded, and how those anxieties seemed to interface between the episodes of sleep paralysis and external social and political events.

9 Ria Reis (2013) similarly points out how the idiom of child witchcraft accusations can be very harmful, leading to expulsion, exorcism, or the death of a child.

REFERENCES

Abdullah, I., & Muana, P. (1998). The Revolutionary United Front of Sierra Leone: A revolt of the lumpen-proletariat. In C. Clapham (Ed.), *African guerrillas* (pp. 172–201). Oxford, UK: James Currey.

Alie, J. (2005). The Kamajor militia in Sierra Leone: Liberators or nihilists? In D. Francis (Ed.), *Civil militias: Africa's intractable security menace?* (p. 51–70). Aldershot, UK: Ashgate.

Auslander, M. (1993). Open the wombs! The symbolic politics of modern Ngoni witch finding. In J. Comaroff & J. Comaroff (Eds.), *Modernity and its malcontents* (pp. 167–92). Chicago: University of Chicago Press.

Behrend, H. (1999). *Alice Lakwena and the holy spirits: War in Northern Uganda 1985–97*. Athens: Ohio University Press.

Benjamin, J. (2001). *Women, war, and HIV/AIDS: West Africa and the Great Lakes*. Seminar for the World Bank on International Women's Day, March 8, 2001. Washington, DC: Women's Commission for Refugee Women and Children.

Bourgois, P. (2001). The power of violence in war and peace: Post-cold war lessons from El Salvador. *Ethnography*, 2, 5–34.

Campbell, G. (2002). *Blood diamonds: Tracing the deadly path of the world's most precious stones*. Boulder, CO: Westview.

Comaroff, J. (1985). *Body of power, spirit of resistance: The culture and history of a South African people*. Chicago: University of Chicago Press.

Comaroff, J., & Comaroff, J. (1993). *Modernity and its malcontents: Ritual and power in postcolonial Africa*. Chicago: University of Chicago Press.

Comaroff, J, & Comaroff, J. (1999). Response to Moore: Second thoughts. *American Ethnologist*, 26, 307–9.

Coulter, C. (2009). *Bush wives and girl soldiers: Women's lives through war and peace in Sierra Leone*. Ithaca, NY: Cornell University Press.

Csordas, T. (1983). *The rhetoric of transformation in ritual healing*. New York: Palgrave.

Das, V., Kleinman, A., Ramphele, M., & Reynolds, P. (Eds.) (2000). *Violence and subjectivity*: Berkeley: University of California Press.

De Jong, J. (2005). Cultural variation in the clinical presentation of sleep paralysis. *Transcultural Psychiatry*, 42, 78–92.

Ellis, S. (2007). *The mask of anarchy: The destruction of Liberia and the religious dimension of an African civil war*, 2nd ed. New York: New York University Press.

Ellis, S., & Ter Haar, G. (1998). Religion and politics in sub-saharan Africa. *The Journal of Modern African Studies*, 36, 175–201.

(2004). *Worlds of power: Religious thought and political practice in Africa*. London: C. Hurst.

Feldman, A. (1995). Ethnographic states of emergency. In A. Robben & C. Nordstrom (Eds.), *Fieldwork under fire* (pp. 224–53). Berkeley: University of California Press.

Ferme, M. (2001a). *The underneath of things: Violence, history, and the everyday in Sierra Leone*. Berkeley: University of California Press.

(2001b). La figure du chasseur et les chasseurs-miliciens dans le confit sierra-léonais. *Politique Africaine*, 82, 119–32.

Friedman, S., Paradis, C. M., & Hatch, M. (1994). Clinical characteristics of African American and white patients with panic disorder and agoraphobia. *Journal of Hospital and Community Psychiatry*, 45, 798–803.

Fukuda, K., Miyasita, A., Inugami, M., & Ishihara, K. (1987). High prevalence of isolated sleep paralysis: Kanashibari phenomenon in Japan. *Sleep*, 10, 279–86.

Geschiere, P. (1997). *The modernity of witchcraft: Politics and the occult in postcolonial Africa*. Charlottesville: University of Virginia Press.

Gittins, A. (1987). *Mende religion: Aspects of belief and thought in Sierra Leone*. Nettetal, Germany: Steyler Verlag – Wort und Werk.

Hall, F. (1993). Unique panic disorder presentation: "Ridden by the witch." *Clinical Psychiatry News*, 13, 25.

Helman, C. (1994). *Culture, health, and illness*, 3rd ed. Oxford, UK: Butterworth-Heinemann.

Henry, D. (2005). The legacy of the tank: The violence of peace. *Anthropological Quarterly*, 78, 443–56.

(2006). Violence and the body: Somatic expressions of trauma and vulnerability during war. *Medical Anthropology Quarterly*, 20, 379–98.

Hinton, D., Pich, V., Chhean, D., & Pollack, M. (2005). "The ghost pushes you down:" Sleep paralysis-type panic attacks in a Khmer refugee population. *Transcultural Psychiatry*, 42, 46–77.

Hinton, D. E., Pich, V., Chhean, D., Pollack, M. H., & McNally, R. J. (2005). Sleep paralysis among Cambodian refugees: Association with PTSD diagnosis and severity. *Depression and Anxiety*, 22, 47–51.

Hinton, D. E., Pich, V., Marques, L., Nickerson, A., & Pollack, M. H. (2010). Khyâl attacks: A key idiom of distress among traumatized Cambodia refugees. *Culture, Medicine and Psychiatry*, 34, 244–78.

Hobson, J. (1995). *Sleep.* New York: Scientific American Library.

Hollan, D. (2004). Self systems, cultural idioms of distress, and the psycho-bodily consequences of childhood suffering. *Transcultural Psychiatry*, 41, 62–79.

Hufford, D. (1982). *The terror that comes in the night: An experience-centered study of supernatural assault traditions.* Philadelphia: University of Pennsylvania Press.

(2005). Sleep paralysis as spiritual experience. *Transcultural Psychiatry*, 42, 11–45.

Human Rights Watch (2003). "We'll kill you if you cry:" Sexual violence in the Sierra Leone conflict. Retrieved October 10, 2006, from http://www.hrw.org/en/reports/2003/01/16/well-kill-you-if-you-cry

Jenkins, J. (1996). The impress of extremity: Women's experience of trauma and political violence. In C. Sargent & C. Brettel (Eds.) *Gender and health: An international perspective* (pp. 278–91). Upper Saddle River, NJ: Prentice Hall.

Kirmayer, L., & Young, A. (1998). Culture and somatization: Clinical, epidemiological, and ethnographic perspectives. *Psychosomatic Medicine*, 60, 420–30.

Kryger, M., Roth, T., & Dement, W. (2000). *Principles and practice of sleep medicine*, 3rd ed. Philadelphia: Saunders/Elsevier Science Press.

Lan, D. (1985). *Guns and rain: Guerrillas and spirit mediums in Zimbabwe.* London: James Currey.

Lemelson, R. (2015). "The spirits enter me to force me to be a communist": Political embodiment, idioms of distress, spirit possession and thought disorder in Bali. In D. E. and A. L. Hinton (Eds.), *Genocide and mass violence: Memory, symptom, and response.* Cambridge: Cambridge University Press.

Little, K. (1948). The function of "medicine" in Mende society. *Man*, 142, 127–30.

(1965). *The Mende of Sierra Leone: A West African people in transition.* London: Routledge Press.

MacCormack, C. (1983). Human leopards and crocodiles: Political meanings of categorical anomalies. In P. Brown and D. Tuzin (Eds.), *The ethnography of cannibalism* (pp. 51–60). Washington, DC: the Society for Psychological Anthropology.

Marwick, M. (1950). Another modern anti-witchcraft movement in east central Africa. *Africa*, 20, 100–12.

McNally, R., & Clancy, S. (2005). Sleep paralysis, sexual abuse, and space alien abduction. *Transcultural Psychiatry*, 42, 113–22.

Moore, H., & Sanders, T. (Eds.) (2001). *Magical interpretations, material realities: Modernity, witchcraft and the occult in postcolonial Africa*. London: Routledge.

Muana, P. (1997). The Kamajoi militia: Civil war, internal displacement, and the politics of counter-insurgency. *African Development*, 22, 77–100.

Ness, R. (1978). The old hag phenomenon as sleep paralysis: A biocultural interpretation. *Culture, Medicine, and Psychiatry*, 2, 15–39.

Nichter, M. (1981). Idioms of distress: Alternatives in the expression of psychosocial distress, a case study from South India. *Culture, Medicine, and Psychiatry*, 5, 379–408.

Niehaus, I. (1993). Witch-hunting and political legitimacy: Continuity and change in Green Valley, Lebowa, 1930–91. *Africa*, 63, 498–530.

Nordstrom, C. (1995). War on the front lines. In C. Nordstrom & A. Robben (Eds.), *Fieldwork under fire: Contemporary studies of violence and survival* (pp. 129–53). Berkeley: University of California Press.

Ohaeri, J. (1997). The prevalence of isolated sleep paralysis among a sample of Nigerian civil servants and undergraduates. *African Journal of Medical Science*, 26, 43–5.

Paradis, C., & Friedman, S. (2005). Sleep paralysis in African Americans with panic disorder. *Transcultural Psychiatry* 42, 123–34.

Reis, R. (2013). Children enacting idioms of witchcraft and spirit possession as a response to trauma: Therapeutically beneficial, and for whom? *Transcultural Psychiatry*, 50, 622–43.

Reno, W. (1997). African weak states and commercial alliances. *African Affairs*, 96, 65–186.

(1998). *Warlord politics and African states*. Boulder, CO: Lynne Rienner.

Richards, P. (1996). *Fighting for the rainforest: War, youth, and resources in Sierra Leone*. Oxford, UK: James Currey.

Rubel, A. (1977). The epidemiology of a folk illness: *Susto* in Hispanic America. In D. Landy (Ed.), *Culture, disease, and healing: Studies in medical anthropology* (pp. 119–28). New York: Macmillan.

Schenk, C., Arnulf, I., & Mahowald, M. (2007). Sleep and sex: What can go wrong? A review of the literature on sleep related disorders and abnormal sexual behaviors and experiences. *Sleep*, 30, 683–702.

Scheper-Hughes, N., & Bougois, P. (2004). *Violence in war and peace: An anthology*. Oxford: Blackwell.

Shaw, R. (2002). *Memories of the slave trade: Ritual and the historical imagination in Sierra Leone*. Chicago: University of Chicago Press.

Smillie, I., Gberie, L., & Hazleton, R. (2000). *The heart of the matter: Sierra Leone, diamonds, and human security*. Ottawa: Partnership Africa-Canada.

Spanos, N., McNulty, S., Dubreuil, S., Piries, M., & Burgess, M. (1995). The frequency and correlates of sleep paralysis in a university sample. *Journal of Research in Personality*, 29, 285–305.

Ter Haar, G., & Ellis, S. (2009). The occult does not exist: A response to Terrence Ranger. *Africa*, 79, 399–412.

United Nations Development Program (UNDP). (2003). Sierra Leone: human development indicators 2003. Retrieved April 2004 from http://www.hu.org/hdr2003/indicator/cty_f_SLE.html

Walsh, M. (2005). Diabolical-Delusions-and-Hysterical-Narratives-in-a-Postmodern-State. Presentation to the Senior Seminar, Department of Anthropology, University of Cambridge, February. Retrieved November 5, 2009, from http://www.scribd.com/doc/13997211/Diabolical-Delusions-and-Hysterical- Narratives-in-a-Postmodern-State

Zack-Williams, A. (1997). Kamajors, "sobel" and militariat: Civil society and the return of the military in Sierra Leonean politics. *Review of African Political Economy*, 24, 373–98.

Part III

Response and Recovery

11 The Chaplain Turns to God: Negotiating Posttraumatic Stress Disorder in the American Military

Erin Finley

In the spring of 2007, I sat down at a café in San Antonio, Texas, to talk with a recently retired army officer, whom I will call Chaplain Matthew.[1] He had spent much of the early Iraq war in Baghdad, offering spiritual guidance and counseling to American service members there. He said that many of the U.S. soldiers then fighting in Iraq were raised on after-school reruns of the 1970s show *The Brady Bunch*, with its mild portrayal of suburban family life, and that this was the kind of an ideal world they were expecting when they went to Iraq and faced the consequences of war for the first time. He reported finding that war brings about "a loss of innocence." He mused a little further about American apple pie optimism before asking, rather sharply, "But does that make 'em PTSD?"

The fact that Chaplain Matthew felt in a position to ask this question is, at base, the subject of this chapter, which briefly examines how posttraumatic stress disorder (PTSD) has been actively negotiated and contested among service members, chaplains, and mental health care providers in the U.S. military. In framing this discussion, it helps to take a step back and consider the history of PTSD itself and how it has traditionally been approached in the scholarly literature.

PTSD was formulated as a clinical diagnosis in the American Psychiatric Association's *Diagnostic and Statistical Manual of Mental Disorders, 3rd edition (DSM-III)* in 1980. The disorder has been conceptualized since that time, despite some amount of "bracket creep" across editions (McNally, 2003), as an illness characterized by symptoms of hypervigilance, avoidance, and reexperiencing, phenomena emerging in the aftermath of exposure to a traumatic event provoking "fear, helplessness, or horror in response to the threat of injury or death" (Yehuda, 2002). Within the United States, the disorder has taken on a renewed importance since September 11, 2001, for among the more than 2.4 million U.S. service members deployed to Iraq and Afghanistan, PTSD has already been diagnosed in some 274,000 individuals within the VA health care system alone (VA Office of Public Health, 2013).

Thanks in large part to important work by Allan Young (1995) on the creation of PTSD as a diagnosis in the wake of the Vietnam War, the medicalization of combat trauma in the form of PTSD has become a classic example of how experiences of suffering are interpreted and negotiated by public, political, and professional actors (Kleinman, Das, & Lock, 1997a). By the late 1980s, the diagnosis of PTSD had been internationally embraced, having morphed in the process from a "war neurosis" to an illness of the general population. The diagnosis of PTSD was increasingly assigned to survivors of noncombat traumatic experiences, including childhood abuse, rape, motor vehicle accidents, natural disasters, and so forth. In the intervening years, screening for PTSD has become a predictable feature of postconflict and postdisaster humanitarian response efforts around the world (Breslau, 2000; Summerfield, 1999), as well as a topic of considerable attention and debate within psychological anthropology (e.g., Breslau, 2004; Fassin & d'Halluin, 2007; McKinney, 2007) and transcultural psychiatry (e.g. De Jong, 2005; D. Hinton, Rasmussen, Nou, Pollack, & Good, 2009; Summerfield, 2000, 2001, 2002).

Despite the powerful example of Young's work, and his oft-quoted chastisement that PTSD as a disorder lacks "intrinsic unity" and "is glued together by the practices, technologies, and narratives with which it is diagnosed, studied, treated, and represented" (1995, p. 5), there has been little study of how PTSD is itself understood and put into practice across settings, an oversight that seems somewhat puzzling given sophisticated cultural analyses of related phenomena like trauma and suffering (as in several of the chapters in this volume). On the contrary, there has too often been a regrettable tendency to conflate discussions of *trauma*, most succinctly described as exposure to a horrific event (Weathers, 2007), with *suffering*, which represents a state of generalized individual or social distress (Kleinman, Das, & Lock, 1997b), and with PTSD, which is a biomedical category describing a cluster of symptoms so severe that they result in considerable functional impairment (Yehuda, 2002), and which occurs among only a minority of those exposed to trauma (N. Breslau et al., 1998; Perkonigg, Kessler, Storz, & Wittchen, 2000).

It may seem that the case under exploration in this chapter is different from others in this volume because the United States has not had a war on its own soil in many decades. America's recent history, rather than being one of conflict at home, has largely been one of sending warriors off to conflict elsewhere, and then welcoming them home again, if sometimes warily, when their job is done. Nonetheless, the United States is the nation whose American Psychiatric Association first formally recognized PTSD as a diagnosis in 1980, and the resulting construction of PTSD is widely used in organizing responses to trauma the world over. PTSD is the biomedical category that anthropologists and other social scientists working in conflict settings often work in opposition to, critiquing its hegemony in cultural explorations of mass trauma (e.g., Englund, 1998; Zarowsky, 2004) and using it as the authoritative global against which to compare the local.

And yet Chaplain Matthew's question points to the fact that PTSD, even in the United States and even among the combat veterans for whom the diagnosis was originally described, is far from being monolithic. Despite its cogent list of symptoms arranged in an orderly fashion on the pages of the *DSM*, a list that might lead us to believe it is an agreed-upon and bounded fact within American ethnopsychiatries (Gaines, 1992a, 1992b), PTSD remains a cultural product like any other: fluid, subject to interpretation, and often differently realized in practice than in theory. Although unquestionably important in their impact on global mental health, American understandings of combat PTSD – in terms of what PTSD is, what it represents as far as processes within the body and mind, and what actions should be taken in response to it – are far more heterogeneous and dynamic than a single (albeit oft-changing) *DSM* definition can reveal. Indeed, both lay and professional ideas of what PTSD is continue to emerge and reemerge in dialogue with shifting notions of military service, combat trauma, and what it means to be a veteran in contemporary American society. These ideas may have global impact, but they are hardly static.

During 2007–8, I spent twenty months engaging in anthropological field research in San Antonio, Texas, investigating understandings and experiences of PTSD among male veterans of Iraq and Afghanistan.[2] In the course of this work, I interviewed returning veterans who had and who did not have a diagnosis of PTSD, collecting ethnographic and epidemiologic data on their experiences of deployment, combat trauma, and the return home. In addition, I spoke with older veterans, family members, mental health clinicians, and community service providers working with veterans and active duty military personnel. When assembled, these narratives align to reveal a range of perspectives on combat PTSD, fraught and under almost constant negotiation among recent veterans and those who provide health care and other services to them.

To illustrate this tension, and the epistemic diversity that produces it, I want to take a moment to consider three events, all of which took place in the context of PTSD-related workshops held as part of a local training program for hospital-based military chaplains, and all of which emerge at the cultural intersection where military values meet the contemporary Christian chaplaincy and the nosology of professional mental health. The first was a workshop on PTSD held at Brooke Army Medical Center (BAMC), a military hospital at Ft. Sam Houston in San Antonio that is responsible for providing care to many of the Americans wounded in Iraq and Afghanistan. The second event took place at an area seminary, during the course of a day-long workshop on the spiritual aspects of trauma and healing. The third event occurred after a final workshop, again at BAMC, on the history of combat stress. The first and second workshops offer a taste of how PTSD is made sense of and made use of in different institutional settings – for example, in the military and the VA, within the Christian chaplaincy and mental health – while what happened after the third workshop offers some insight into what such negotiations may ultimately mean for military personnel and veterans struggling to manage their own suffering and distress amid the many views of PTSD available to them.

In the remainder of this chapter, I argue that in avoiding the temptation to view Western notions of PTSD as fixed and inert, and in paying particular attention to those cultural junctures where stakeholders meet and contest the meaning of trauma in a given setting, it becomes possible to elicit more nuanced comparisons of trauma and recovery across postconflict populations. I begin by outlining the cultural, historical, and structural conditions that have framed recent discussions of PTSD in the U.S. military.

Force Readiness and Self-Denial

In the charged wartime environment of the early 2000s, the U.S. Department of Defense found itself engaged in a struggle at home as well as abroad, fighting to keep the Armed Forces operating at full capacity despite an almost universal recognition that the military workforce is overstressed. Service members have been under growing strain, plagued by multiple deployments, stop-loss measures that prohibited soldiers from leaving the military when their contracts ended (Squitieri, 2004; White, 2004), and the increasing frequency with which previously nondeploying service members have been asked to deploy as support staff for combat troops.

As part of their response to the personnel crunch, U.S. military leadership at the highest levels have taken steps toward an active and aggressive response to PTSD and other forms of psychological stress among service members. These efforts have promoted better screening, greater access to health care providers, the use of more effective pharmacologic and behavioral treatments, and programs to minimize stigma around mental illness and care seeking. The new programs have built on a system of combat stress screening, prevention, diagnosis, and treatment that has been evolving since the First World War (Chermol, 1985; Shephard, 2001) and that now represents the cumulative expertise of several generations of mental health care providers.

The cultural expectations of military life, however, remain largely unchanged. Military socialization continues to reinforce the values of mental and physical toughness and showing no weakness, serving also to perpetuate the stigma associated with PTSD, which is often seen, in effect, as the inability to contribute to the well-being of the unit. Several veterans I spoke with during fieldwork described delaying care seeking despite debilitating psychological symptoms. One former marine was diagnosed with PTSD while still in Baghdad. He had survived a tour in Afghanistan with few after effects, he says, but picking up the pieces of his best friend's body after he was killed in combat drove him to the breaking point, leaving him incoherent and unable to function, breaking intermittently into sobs. Despite his diagnosis and his leadership's concern, he said, "We were so short on people that I didn't want them to pull me out. So I just sucked it up and kind of did what I needed to do to get through. And just kind of exploded when I got back."

So it is that the military's efforts to decrease stigma and improve health care access have run into direct conflict with closely guarded values of toughness and self-denial, with the result that highly divergent ideas about combat stress are regularly communicated up and down military channels. Mental health care providers may communicate very different expectations about mental health and help seeking from those conveyed by military leadership. Chaplain Matthew may have put it best when he said that he had, over the past few years, seen soldiers getting dual messages. He said that they hear "We can help!" from mental health teams, while being told, "If you're broke, we'll kick you to the curb," from the rest of the military community.

Chaplains are an often-overlooked presence in this discussion, yet they fulfill a key role within the contemporary American military; they lead religious services, offer marital and family counseling, serve as spiritual advisers, and run psycheducation and life skills classes for service members preparing to deploy or to return home from deployment. They are considered particularly vital during deployment, for while a chaplain is assigned to every army battalion (between three hundred and twelve hundred troops), mental health providers are assigned only to every brigade (twenty-five hundred to four thousand troops), leaving far more chaplains than health providers available to provide support on the ground. There is, in fact, considerable overlap between the role of the military mental health care provider and that of the chaplain. Chaplains are increasingly part of the mobile Combat Operational Stress Control (COSC) teams who have provided acute care for combat stress in Iraq and Afghanistan. Chaplains also serve as a conduit to mental health services, as service members hesitant to seek clinical treatment or without immediate access to mental health care providers may seek out a chaplain instead. Chaplains are widely touted by army clinicians as an essential part of the care network, particularly in the realm of suicide prevention; one DoD report found that, of those who committed suicide in Iraq in 2007, 36 percent had met with a chaplain in the 30 days prior to the event (MHAT, 2008).

Nonetheless, the services that chaplains are intended to provide are distinct from those of a psychiatrist, psychologist, or social worker, and chaplains are expected to refer for mental health care those whose troubles extend beyond the spiritual. One of the army chaplains I interviewed, a Methodist captain named Jose de la Garza, was attached to a combat unit during his deployment to Iraq in 2004, in a position, as he says, to "go literally and walk with a soldier on the streets of Baghdad, Afghanistan, or whatever, and be with them and be their spiritual and moral support." Soldiers who were experiencing distress could speak with him before or after weekly church services, could track him down in his office or at the medic's station, or simply walk along beside him during the course of the day's patrol. His mission for service members – whether the 550 individuals under his care in Iraq, or those wounded soldiers he serves in his more recent role as a hospital chaplain – is to do what he calls "spiritual triage," and to "find out where the soldier is at. What is the soldier's need? Is it really spiritual?" If the need is spiritual, he may provide spiritual counseling and emotional support and offer communion or other sacraments. If the need is psychological, however, he must refer.

But this very necessity raises the question of what is a "spiritual" versus a "psychological" need in this context, and indeed, the intention behind the first of the three workshops – to which I turn now – was to aid in clarifying this boundary. The workshop itself, however, reveals complex debates over the way that PTSD is talked about and defined by military personnel, debates that suggest an uncomfortable and ambiguous relationship with the very idea of PTSD. Not only do service members receive mixed messages about PTSD, but the messages themselves remain in flux.

Stress versus Disorder

The first workshop took place at Brooke Army Medical Center around the same time as my initial conversation with Chaplain Matthew. A psychologist from the VA had been invited to give a morning's seminar on PTSD for a group of the hospital chaplains, in an attempt to educate them about symptoms that should cue a referral to mental health services. The chaplain playing host to the event, held in one of the hospital's conference rooms, stood up and introduced the day's speaker, a VA psychologist named Lisa Montalvos. The presiding chaplain explained that many of those seeking mental health care at the VA go through the trauma clinic where Dr. Montalvos works and noted that PTSD was a very hot topic just then, the focus of much conversation among military leadership concerned about the extent of the problem. He noted that the audience was slightly over half army chaplains, the remainder made up of air force chaplains from nearby Lackland Air Force Base and a handful of civilians working at the local VA.

In the course of Dr. Montalvos's talk, she differentiated between Acute Stress Disorder (ASD), experienced within two days to four weeks of a trauma, and PTSD, which she said could be diagnosed only more than a month afterward. She noted that, in order to merit a diagnosis, PTSD symptoms have to last longer than one month and to cause significant social, occupational, or other impairment. She spoke at length of the treatments provided for PTSD at the Trauma Clinic, including cognitive behavioral therapy; psychoeducation in how to manage stress, anger, and sleep; and pharmacological medications. She added, "Normalizing is so important – [telling service members] that a lot of what they're going through is expected," and said that symptoms do not necessarily mean that a diagnosable disorder is present. One chaplain spoke up to say that he sees soldiers convinced that they have a full-blown disorder when they only have mild symptoms and argued that there needs to be more differentiation between posttraumatic *stress* and posttraumatic stress *disorder*. He suggested the need for a new acronym to make this distinction clearer.

Dr. Montalvos's response to this statement was interesting. She said that clinicians *do* make differentiations. She gave several examples of other possible non-PTSD diagnoses, such as Generalized Anxiety Disorder (GAD) or Personality Disorder, and pointed out that a soldier may be experiencing one of a number of different disorders. The chaplain retorted that soldiers are being told about PTSD somewhere in the system because "They don't come in thinking they have GAD." Dr. Montalvos held to her point, saying that possible PTSD cases may need to be referred for further testing, and went on to make a few additional clarifications about how a diagnosis of PTSD is made.

Watching this exchange – which the chaplain found visibly frustrating – I thought Dr. Montalvos's response largely ignored the concern he was expressing. The chaplain was worried that soldiers were being told about

PTSD and then, when they experienced distress after trauma, becoming unduly concerned that they were mentally ill. He did not think PTSD was as common an experience as would be suggested by how much he was hearing it talked about. He was expressing the desire for a more fully articulated distinction between experiencing some distress after trauma and having a full-fledged mental disorder; more than this, he wanted an acronym, an authoritative name with which to acknowledge such experiences as valid. Dr. Montalvos, operating from a clinical perspective, was thinking only about different kinds of pathologies, about the act of professional discernment involved in making an appropriate diagnosis. My impression was that the chaplain was hoping to step outside the pathology model altogether, seeking recognition that trauma may prompt reactions that are powerful without being pathological.

The presiding chaplain put in his two cents to say that trauma results in a wide spectrum of responses, not something as simple as PTSD or no PTSD. He said that a significant number of individuals deployed would admit to having some symptoms, but could not be called disordered. Clearly, he said, going through traumatic stress changes you, but the problem lies in the fact that under the current system of providing diagnosis and treatment for PTSD within both the military and the VA, you have to be either disordered or not disordered. If you are not disordered, you cannot get help. He reinforced Dr. Montalvos's emphasis on the importance of normalizing traumatic stress and reminded everyone that, in common soldier language, if you have a PTSD diagnosis, "you're crazy."

Initially, what the workshop brought out for me was the different set of concerns that the VA clinician and the military chaplains found most compelling in their interactions with soldiers' and veterans' trauma. Dr. Montalvos was focused on the professional difficulties of distinguishing between PTSD and other diagnoses, and of making sure the chaplains knew how PTSD is defined in clinical terms. Her concerns were shaped by other issues as well, not least of which is the politicization of PTSD diagnoses within the VA, a phenomenon linked with both the national discourse around rewarding veterans' service and the economics of awarding payments for service-acquired disabilities (Finley, 2011).

Meanwhile, the chaplains, drawing on their own experiences in Iraq and working as intermediaries between service members and mental health clinicians, were less concerned with the details of diagnosis and more concerned with other questions: How do we deal with post-traumatic stress in a milieu where nearly everyone has trauma exposure? How do we provide education about symptoms and care seeking without convincing everyone that he or she has PTSD? How do we get the people who need help the help they need without stigmatizing them in a military built on a standard of toughness? Their daily concerns were different, and their way of talking about PTSD symptoms as a sign of stress as opposed to disorder reflected this.

Some of this difference in perspective, as Chaplain Matthew pointed out, was disciplinary, a result of chaplains' and psychologists' having different training, goals, and epistemic orientations toward healing the wounded person. He pointed out, too, what he called the "paradox" of PTSD, which is that service members who may be terrified by the idea of a receiving a PTSD diagnosis while on active duty – at the risk of losing face, losing their security clearance, or being forced into early retirement by a medical evaluation – may take steps to seek out the diagnosis once they separate from the military and become eligible for veterans' health care and disability compensation.[3] As a result, while chaplains may find themselves in the position of needing to encourage troubled service members to seek treatment, Dr. Montalvos and other VA clinicians may at times find themselves in a different predicament, having to distinguish between those who go to the clinic seeking help and those who go seeking compensation.

I told Chaplain Matthew about the workshop later, and he jokingly summarized this conflict as the difference between "the mental health care providers, who want to provide treatment," and "the chaplains, who think all you need is Jesus."

Giving Voice to Trauma

In contrast to the hospital setting of the first workshop, the second workshop was held in a quiet classroom, surrounded by the lawns, gardens, and artful stained glass of a local theological seminary. Pastor Bill, an Evangelical pastor and "religious consultant" from the East Coast, had been invited by the chaplains' training program to hold a workshop on the spiritual aspects of trauma.[4] Many of the army and air force chaplains from the first workshop were in attendance, but on this occasion, they were joined by a larger group of civilian chaplains working at the VA or other local hospitals.

Pastor Bill, over the course of the day, spoke very little about clinical PTSD. Instead, he informed the gathered audience that the workshop was entitled "Post Traumatic Soul Disorder and Healing," seeming to propose an alternative perspective on PTSD altogether. Pastor Bill handed around an array of papers and other objects: packets of written articles and exercises, as well as a thick rubber band and two small round stones for each participant. He then told the story of the Christian saint

Ignatius, who as a young man served as a soldier until he was wounded in battle and his "dreams of military glory were shattered along with his leg." St. Ignatius's conversion to Christianity began in his sickbed, a process that Pastor Bill said he had seen many times in his work among wounded soldiers at the Walter Reed Army Hospital. Tormented by pain, struggling to reach the light of the Holy Spirit, St. Ignatius became "a soldier of Christ." Pastor Bill spoke of Ignatius's conversion as resulting from the trauma itself, his wound creating an opening for Jesus Christ to enter his heart.

Pastor Bill spent much of the morning describing trauma as a rending of the soul from itself, from the fellowship of others, and from God, drawing upon the theological writings of Thomas More, Martin Buber, and Paul Tillich. He spoke of the potential created by trauma, envisioning it as a tearing apart that can make way for transformation and growth. He warned that the danger of trauma lies in becoming stuck, immobilized, unable to heal and move forward, and was forceful in arguing that trauma demands to be spoken aloud. He used a story from the Bible (the walk to Emmaeus in the Book of Luke) to demonstrate how Jesus himself had responded to trauma, using this as a model for the role of the chaplain in healing. "In the story, Jesus walks beside them, to hear their story and let the trauma have voice. If you don't let people talk about their trauma, it stays inside and starts to fester ... unless someone walks with them through it and gives it voice." Later on, he opened the discussion to stories of grace, and a series of those present told their own stories of finding God amid great suffering and loss. This last took up a good portion of the morning.

In the afternoon, the conversation turned to the necessity for chaplains of providing good self-care, that they may be able to provide continuing ministry and support to others in need. Pastor Bill directed the group's attention to a *Newsweek* article reproduced in the packet, which told the story of a Walter Reed chaplain struggling to keep his faith amid the death and misery he saw around him. Pastor Bill asked the group how they might try to help a colleague suffering from such a crisis of faith and suggested that it can be helpful to provide visual metaphors. As an example, he explained the stones and rubber bands he had handed out earlier in the day: a rubber band to snap back from trauma, and rocks to stand on when the going gets tough.

One of the army chaplains raised his hand at this and asked, "What about when chaplains have no rubber band and no rock?" He said that, at his last posting, they had had four suicides in six weeks, an overwhelming loss for all involved, and hinted that he was experiencing a spiritual crisis of his own. The pastor responded by saying that it is necessary to listen to the soul – one's own as well as others' – and to hear when the soul is troubled. But the chaplain, who said his name was Jim, noted wryly that chaplains are not supposed to feel all this, that they are supposed to be numb and to have all the answers even when there are none.

Chaplain Jim then pointed out that counseling and mental health care are taboo for those in the military, a "career stopper." Pastor Bill made a few suggestions for accessing support beyond the traditional network, but the rest of the audience remained quiet. In contrast to the warm and open responses that had flowed after the earlier stories of finding a triune God, Chaplain Jim's story of losing him seemed to meet with a cooler reception. Later in the afternoon, toward the close of the workshop, Pastor Bill pointed out that for some burned-out and exhausted clergy the church can become part of the sickness. He noted that chaplains may at times be faced with the accusation that if their faith were stronger, the loss of it would not be an issue.

Although Pastor Bill framed the second workshop's discussion as one of trauma and the soul rather than of PTSD and its symptoms, it seems no coincidence that he called his seminar "Post Traumatic Soul Disorder." He named the concern of the day in relation to the diagnosis, perhaps seeking to challenge it, perhaps seeking to draw upon its authoritative or metaphorical power. In fact, although the language of the second workshop was very different from that of the first, there were parallels in their underlying views of trauma and its aftermath. Despite the seminary setting, the cultural frames of military life were certainly in evidence in the second workshop, with St. Ignatius presented as both a "soldier for Christ" and a bed-bound figure who must have seemed very familiar to BAMC chaplains, accustomed to ministering to those wounded in war. In both workshops, care seeking was raised as an important coping strategy, although both audiences acknowledged that military personnel have good reasons for not reaching out. But there were differences, too. Where trauma was discussed primarily as a threat in the first workshop, Pastor Bill presented it also as an opportunity, a site for transformation and growth, and focused on speaking of trauma as the primary mode of healing. And in the second workshop, a different form of posttraumatic distress was also discussed, one unnoticed in the first: the spiritual crisis.

The Space Between

A few months later, I returned to BAMC to give a presentation on the history of combat stress to another group of assembled military chaplains, many of whom had been present at the previous two workshops.

As I was standing around afterward, a man I recognized as Chaplain Jim came up and began chatting with me. He introduced himself politely and made small talk for a few minutes, and then asked casually, although watching me very closely, "So how are you doing with all this stuff?" I paused, wanting to leave room for what I suspected was coming, and answered, "Well, I had nightmares last night, if that's what you mean." Jim snorted and said, "Yeah, well." "How about you?" I asked, "How are you doing with this stuff?"

And he began to speak about how he was struggling. He said that he had been to Iraq twice, and on the very first day he had "seen stuff" and thought to himself, "Oh God, what am I in for?" He said that the other chaplains did not want to talk about it; they did not even want to hear about it. He said that there was a lot of "emotional stuffing" going on, of people trying to pretend that everything was fine. He started to say more, but his supervisor walked up just then and he stopped talking. We chatted for a little bit; the supervisor asked whether I thought there was a military culture and I said I thought so. Jim chimed in, reaching out and putting his hand on his supervisor's shoulder. He said, "Oh yeah, because we're both in the army, [he] and I are like brothers, no matter what the differences between us." His supervisor gave a short nod, damningly slight. Then, after a few minutes, he abruptly said that he and Jim had to get back to work, and the two of them shook my hand and went off together.

I ran into Jim a few minutes later as I was heading toward the hospital exit, and we walked down the long hall side by side. I noticed that he was keeping one eye out as to who was around us as we went. He said that he had found himself talking to a bunch of soldiers one night after they had a casualty in his unit, and they said, "We can always go to you, Chaplain, when we need help. But who do you go to?" He said, "I gave the chaplain's answer, which is, 'I go to God,' but ..." and he shook his head. I asked whether he had been able to find the kind of support he needs, now that he was home. He said yes, that he had had some counseling – here his voice got very quiet in the hallway – and that he had his church community, with whom he was trying to be as naked and as honest about himself as he could be. He put his hands to his chest as he said this, as though covering his heart. We realized that we were both headed back downstairs, so we took the elevator down together, not talking now that there were others around, and said our good-byes on the ground floor. As I walked out to my car, I thought back on how eager he had seemed for the chance to talk, even if only muttering in the hallway with one eye cocked to see who else might be listening.

Closing Thoughts

Of the many social fields traversed by the American men and women who have served in Iraq and Afghanistan, these workshop moments barely hint at only three: those created within professionalized VA mental health care, within the military chaplaincy, and within the realm of the U.S. Army. There are other such fields that deserve discussion: those created within families, at the level of local communities, within veterans' organizations, within the national media, and in light of the historical memory of how veterans were treated in the years after Vietnam, a legacy that comes up continually in contemporary conversations about veterans and PTSD.

And yet it is beyond the scope of this chapter to summarize understandings of trauma fully within even the military chaplaincy alone, for it remains a diverse and understudied entity. More than 60 percent of military chaplains are Evangelical Christians (as compared with 14 percent of the American population as a whole), while the rest are mostly mainline Protestant and Catholic chaplains, along with a minority representing the Jewish, Mormon, and other faiths (Brady, 2005). These denominational differences may well be reflected in diverse perspectives on trauma and healing.

What does become clear, however, is that while chaplains and mental health care providers in the military are for the most part mutually respectful and provide services that are largely complementary, contemporary discussions of PTSD remain the site of some tension. Conflicts arise over defining the boundary between PTSD and "normal" responses to trauma; between PTSD as a clinical diagnosis and PTSD as not-PTSD-at-all but a traumatic rending or a loss of innocence; between PTSD as that which is the subject of much discussion among military leadership, in workshops, and among soldiers, and PTSD that chaplains do not want to hear about from other chaplains; between posttraumatic stress *symptoms* and posttraumatic stress *disorder*.

Each of these conflicts, in turn, proved to have implications for how Chaplain Jim was attempting to manage and understand his own distress, seeking out both a church community and counseling, talking about his experience with a relative stranger (me) while feeling his story was not welcome among his colleagues (including his supervisor, whose presence silenced him). These conflicts have implications for framing interventions among active duty and former military personnel distressed by combat trauma. And their distress is great. One national study estimated that some 300,000 service members deployed to Iraq and Afghanistan have experienced PTSD and depression symptoms, only half of whom are thought to have sought treatment (Tanielian et al., 2008).

As such, we would do well to remain open and thoughtful in our analyses of how PTSD is understood and enacted both cross-culturally and across adjacent social realms within particular cultural settings. PTSD proves to be, not simply a monolithic category, but an open and idiosyncratic space for interpretation and the organization of experience. Moreover, within the constellation of the workshop moments described here, four modes of analysis stand out as particularly helpful in illuminating the relevant negotiations.

First of all, precisely because PTSD has become so profoundly medicalized, because it has become the object of professional discernment and expertise, it provides rich ground for epistemologically minded ethnography; it invites the analysis, following Young, of how its "practices, technologies, and narratives" are made use of and made sense of across a variety of clinical settings. Biomedical psychiatry is a global paradigm, but Gaines and other ethnographers have shown how its authoritative knowledge may be differently interpreted and elaborated in different cultural milieu (Gaines, 1992b). Pushing beyond the ethnomedical, I would argue that the interpretive theology of trauma offers additional territory for exploration, particularly where it intersects, as in the current example, with medical models of PTSD.

Second, the analysis of trauma and recovery also benefits from the critical and political economic analysis advocated by Kleinman, Das, and Lock (1997a) in their considerations of social suffering, and exemplified by Summerfield (1999) in his critique of trauma interventions. Without doubt, the structural requirements of retaining a large and high-functioning military force have gone a long way toward forcing the Department of Defense's hand in developing state-of-the-art screening and referral for psychological casualties.

Third, the unearthing of trauma and recovery must also remain grounded in the phenomena of human life, for it is here that the repercussions of horror and the opportunities for resilience and recovery become most clear. Epistemology can begin to seem rather thin and abstract without an appreciation for how such constructions of knowledge and perception influence the shape of life itself, played out, for example, in Chaplain Jim's soul searching and secrecy as he struggled to derive a path for his own recovery amidst the debates ongoing around him.

Finally, phenomenology itself can seem rather slim without an appreciation for how deeply trauma and recovery may be embedded in social relations.[5] Chaplain Jim's grief lay not only in the suicides he had failed to prevent, the "stuff" he had seen, and his fumbling grasp on faith, but in his unsuccessful efforts to seek out acknowledgment and consolation from his peers, a struggle that seemed inseparable from his attempt to assimilate divergent messages about PTSD. For Chaplain Jim, turning simultaneously to God and to counseling and his church community, it was not only the experience of trauma in Iraq that left him lost and liminal. It was his place, standing there in the hallways of the hospital, alone and adrift among the fields of meaning available to describe it.

NOTES

1 All names of persons have been changed.
2 Funding for this research was provided by National Science Foundation Doctoral Dissertation Improvement Grant #0650437 and a fellowship from the Emory Center for Myth and Ritual in American Life (MARIAL), a Sloan Center for Working Families. Additional support was provided by the Institute for Integration of Medicine and Science at the University of Texas Health Sciences Center, San Antonio (UTHSCSA). This research was reviewed and its conduct approved by the Institutional Review Boards of Emory University and UTHSCSA, as well as by the Research and Development Committee of the South Texas Veterans Health Care System.
3 Although the army has taken steps in recent years to revise its policy on security clearance so that individuals who report mental health concerns related to their service are not penalized (Richie, 2008), this has not always been the case and remains a widely reported concern among active duty service members.
4 It bears noting that all of the chaplains in attendance were, to my knowledge, Christian, although there is a small minority of non-Christian chaplains working in San Antonio. The local predominance of Christian chaplains, and Evangelicals in particular, reflects a growing move toward Evangelical Christianity in the U.S. military (Cooperman, 2005).
5 An observation indebted to Schutz (1970).

REFERENCES

Brady, J. (2005). Evangelical chaplains test bounds of faith in military. *All Things Considered*. Retrieved from http://www.npr.org/templates/story/story.php?storyId=4772331
Breslau, J. (2000). Globalizing disaster trauma: Psychiatry, science, and culture after the Kobe earthquake. *Ethos*, 28, 174–97.
(2004). Cultures of trauma: Anthropological views of posttraumatic stress disorder in international health. *Culture, Medicine, and Psychiatry*, 28, 113–26.
Breslau, N., Kessler, R. C., Chilcoat, H. D., Schultz, L., Davis, G. C., & Andreski, P. (1998). Trauma and posttraumatic stress disorder in the community: The 1996 Detroit areas survey of trauma. *Archives of General Psychiatry*, 55, 626–32.
Chermol, B. H. (1985). Wounds without scars: Treatment of battle fatigue in the U.S. Armed Forces in the Second World War. *Military Affairs*, 49, 9–12.

Cooperman, A. (August 30, 2005). Military wrestles with disharmony among chaplains. *The Washington Post,* August 30, 2005.

De Jong, J. (2005). Comment: Deconstructing critiques on the internationalization of PTSD. *Culture, Medicine, and Psychiatry,* 29, 361–70.

Englund, H. (1998). Death, trauma and ritual: Mozambican refugees in Malawi. *Social Science & Medicine,* 46, 1165–74.

Fassin, D., & d'Halluin, E. (2007). Critical evidence: The politics of trauma in French asylum policies. *Ethos,* 35, 300–29.

Finley, E. P. (2011). *Fields of combat: Understanding PTSD among veterans of Iraq and Afghanistan.* Ithaca, NY: Cornell University Press.

Gaines, A. D. (1992a). From *DSM-I* to *III-R;* Voices of self, mastery and the other: A cultural constructivist reading of U.S. psychiatric classification. *Social Science and Medicine,* 35, 3–24.

(Ed.). (1992b). *Ethnopsychiatry: The cultural construction of professional and folk psychiatries.* Albany: SUNY Press.

Hinton, D. E., Rasmussen, A., Nou, L., Pollack, M. H., & Good, M. J. (2009). Anger, PTSD, and the nuclear family: A study of Cambodian refugees. *Social Science & Medicine,* 69, 1387–94.

Kleinman, A., Das, V., & Lock, M. (1997a). Introduction. In A. Kleinman, V. Das, & M. Lock (Eds.), *Social suffering* (pp. ix–xxv). Berkeley: University of California Press.

(Eds.) (1997b). *Social suffering.* Berkeley: University of California Press.

McKinney, K. (2007). "Breaking the conspiracy of silence": Testimony, traumatic memory, and psychotherapy with survivors of political violence. *Ethos,* 35, 265–99.

McNally, R. J. (2003). Progress and controversy in the study of posttraumatic stress disorder. *Annual Review of Psychology,* 54, 229–52.

MHAT. (2008). *Mental Health Advisory Team (MHAT) V: Operation Iraqi Freedom 06–08: Iraq, Operation Enduring Freedom 08: Afghanistan.* Washington, DC: Office of the Surgeon, Multi-National Force – Iraq and Office of the Command Surgeon and Office of the Surgeon General, United States Army Medical Command.

Perkonigg, A., Kessler, R. C. K., Storz, S., & Wittchen, H. -U. (2000). Traumatic events and post-traumatic stress disorder in the community: Prevalence, risk factors, and comorbidity. *Acta Psychiatrica Scandinavica,* 101, 46–59.

Richie, C. E. (2008). Appearance on *Diane Rehm Show*: National Public Radio.

Schutz, A. (1970). *On phenomenology and social relations: Selected writings.* Chicago: University of Chicago Press.

Shephard, B. (2001). *A war of nerves: Soldiers and psychiatrists in the twentieth century.* Cambridge, MA: Harvard University Press.

Squitieri, T. (2004). Army expanding "stop loss" order to keep soldiers from leaving. *USA Today.* Retrieved from http://www.usatoday.com/news/nation/2004-01-05-army-troops_x.htm

Summerfield, D. (1999). A critique of seven assumptions behind psychological trauma programmes in war-affected areas. *Social Science and Medicine,* 48, 1449–62.

(2000). War and mental health: A brief overview. *British Medical Journal,* 321, 232–5.

(2001). The invention of post-traumatic stress disorder and the social useful-ness of a psychiatry category. *British Medical Journal*, 322, 95–8.

(2002). Effects of war: Moral knowledge, revenge, reconciliation, and medical-ised concepts of "recovery." *British Medical Journal*, 325, 1105–7.

Tanielian, T., Jaycox, L. H., Schell, T. L., Marshall, G. N., Burnham, M. A., & Eibner, C., et al. (2008). *Invisible wounds of war: Psychological and cognitive injuries, their consequences and services to assist recovery*. San Diego: RAND.

VA Office of Public Health. (2013). *Analysis of VA Health Care Utilization among Operation Enduring Freedom (OEF), Operation Iraqi Freedom (OIF), and Operation New Dawn Veterans. Report of the Epidemiology Program, Post-Deployment Health Group, Veterans Health Administration, Department of Veterans Affairs, released November 2013.*

Weathers, F. W. (2007). The Criterion A problem revisited: Controversies and challenges in defining psychological trauma. *Journal of Traumatic Stress*, 20, 107–21.

White, J. (2004). Soldiers facing extended tours: Critics of army policy liken it to a draft. *The Washington Post*, June 3, 2004.

Yehuda, R. (2002). Post-traumatic stress disorder. *New England Journal of Medicine*, 346, 108–14.

Young, A. (1995). *The harmony of illusions: Inventing post-traumatic stress disorder*. Princeton, NJ: Princeton University Press.

Zarowsky, C. (2004). Writing trauma: Emotion, ethnography, and the politics of suffering among Somali returnees in Ethiopia. *Culture, Medicine, and Psychiatry*, 28, 189–204.

12 Acehnese Women's Narratives of Traumatic Experience, Resilience, and Recovery

Mary-Jo DelVecchio Good

On December 26, 2004, the devastating Indian Ocean tsunami struck the coast of the Indonesian province of Aceh, killing approximately 160,000 persons. Eight months later, on August 15, 2005, representatives of the Free Aceh Movement (GAM) and the government of Indonesia signed a Memorandum of Understanding (MOU), ending an armed conflict that had ravaged civilian communities for more than two decades. In this chapter, I focus on conflict affected populations in the hills of Aceh, most of whom were beyond the reach of the tsunami's direct destruction. In particular, I address the gendered dimensions of traumatic experiences related to years of civil insecurity and armed combat. Women living in high conflict affected areas were not only exposed to combat and conflict, as were men; many were tortured physically and psychologically and humiliated. Women were also, however, protectors of their male kin, buffering their men from the military forces who hunted them. The stories women told of bravery and resilience, of defending their men, children, houses, and land during the conflict, resonate with the symbolic role of the women warriors of Aceh in times past and raise profound questions for contemporary women. What might their future hold, even as now they engage in trauma resolution, return to economically productive activities, and participate in the often-harsh gender politics of postconflict peace?

The generation-long conflict (1976–2005) between the Indonesian Military (TNI) and the Free Aceh Movement (GAM) was resolved with a remarkably effective Memorandum of Understanding, signed in Helsinki on August 15, 2005. The peace agreement between GAM and the Indonesian government granted exceptional measures of political autonomy to Aceh including the right to establish local political parties and the withdrawal of nonorganic military troops and police brigades, in exchange for the disarmament and demobilization of GAM's armed wing, the TNA (Aceh Armed Forces), thereby ending GAM's struggle for independence. Acehnese greeted the MOU initiated peace with cautiously hopeful expectations for the future, followed by a rising euphoria, a sense of freedom and excitement, as direct elections were held and local political parties were formed. The era began with demilitarization, demobilization, and reintegration of combatants. GAM combatants returned to their villages and homes. TNI soldiers were no longer on patrol in villages or at checkpoints on the byways and major highways. Interventions designed to build a lasting peace included compensation programs, economic livelihood and community development projects, projects for child development, and even psychosocial and mental health outreach programs. Funded by international donors and the World Bank, and administered by intergovernmental organizations as well as local NGOs, these projects exemplified the internationalization of peace building in Aceh. The International Organization for Migration (IOM) was charged with managing activities related to securing the peace, including an assessment of the psychosocial needs of high conflict affected rural communities. This is the project that drew my husband, Byron Good (B. Good, chapter 7, this volume), and me into Aceh – as IOM's scientific advisers on postconflict mental health projects that we designed to address "the remainders of violence" from 2005–9.[1]

The ethnographic vignettes and women's narratives I include in this chapter are drawn from my conversations, interviews, and observations carried out during our many field trips to Aceh to work on our IOM mental health projects.[2] Survey data are drawn from our IOM psychosocial needs assessment reports, studies we designed, had implemented, analyzed, and published for IOM in 2006 and 2007, and from our evaluation studies of the IOM mental health outreach interventions (B. Good & M. Good, 2010). Other data sources I draw on include Indonesian newspaper articles, glossy magazines, reports from local NGOs, political tracts, Aceh Women's League literature, and interviews with its leadership; my photos and text and e-mail correspondence with Acehnese colleagues also inform this chapter. As a participant observer engaged in mobile ethnography in Aceh's high conflict affected areas and as an ethnographer and insider of IOM's mental health endeavors in Aceh, I draw from a wide array of empirical materials I collected and analyzed from 2005 through 2010, and updated for this chapter (B. Good, M. Good, Grayman, & Lakoma, 2006; M. Good, B. Good, Grayman, & Lakoma, 2007; M. Good, B. Good, & Grayman, 2010; M. Good, 2010; M. Good & B. Good, 2013). I now turn to Acehnese women's narratives of conflict experiences and resilience.

Warrior Women

Laskar Perempuan Aceh ("Women Warriors of Aceh") headlined an article published in Banda Aceh's leading news daily in November 2008

("Si Pai Inong Laskar Perempuan Aceh," 2008). The article highlighted the legacy of women's involvement in the Acehnese Sultanate, noting that "women were not only engaged in governmental affairs but were also soldiers – a military corps of women existed since ancient times in Aceh" from the late sixteenth into the early twentieth century.[3] The article, without byline, appeared at the very moment when women combatants of GAM (Free Aceh Movement) were struggling for recognition and reintegration funds comparable to those given male GAM combatants; when village women were seeking compensation for material and personal losses and violence suffered during decades of conflict; and when "activist women" were seeking recognition as legitimate politicians, as they established local political parties and campaigned for office in the provincial assembly and district government. Word of the news story was texted to me from Aceh just prior to my initial presentation (at the American Anthropology meetings) on stories activist women told me about terrible deeds inflicted on their village communities by quite a different sort of military corps.

Women as Protectors, Not Just Victims

Women living in high conflict affected rural areas were identified as "victims" by many NGOs and governmental organizations from Aceh's new regime, but many also assumed the role of protectors of their male kin, buffering them from the military forces seeking to destroy GAM. Village women I interviewed over the course of four years spoke of the difficulties in assuming this protective role, of how they strategized to protect their children as well as other women and themselves in the face of military intrusion into daily lives. Women spoke not only about the traumas of war and the insecurity of conflict-era life, but also of their own bravery in the face of conflict horror. Their stories resonate with the popular history of Aceh's ancient and precolonial women warriors. Narrative themes included the clever management of threatening men (Indonesian military or rebel combatants); the resort to strategic creativity in the face of violence, destruction of homes, schools, mosques, fields, animals; the coping with injuries and witnessed death of spouses, children, and friends; the active search for zones and homes of safety and security. Women laced their accounts with irony and "postconflict laughter," at other times with profound sadness and deep distress (see Siapno, 2009, on postconflict humor).

Media stories such as "Aceh's Warrior Women" celebrating Acehnese historical heroines appeared frequently in the popular press during the five years of our field studies. Celebrations of contemporary women combatants also graced the pages of magazines and newspapers such as *Aceh Kita* (July 2007), and the woman GAM combatant became a media imagined romantic figure in the immediate postconflict period. These themes continue into the present (2013) as part of the public discourse in Aceh. In June 2010, enormous billboards lined Aceh's coastal highways and roundabouts in urban centers, featuring portraits of famous Acehnese women – some veiled, some not – from several historical eras. The billboards promoted the development of women's political and human rights and celebrated powerful women as historical and contemporary symbols in Acehnese political identity.[4] In July new billboards went up in the same locations featuring contemporary women politicians who were running for political office.

Gendered Violence and Early Postconflict Responses

As the first psychosocial needs assessment survey (PNA1) of thirty high conflict affected villages on Aceh's north coast drew to a close in the middle of February 2006, the field researchers requested that an IOM medical team visit a village deep in the hills of North Aceh to address extraordinarily high levels of symptoms from traumatic experience; the conflict stories were exceptionally horrific and many were "victims" of deep cruelty and loss.[5] An open clinic was scheduled at the community *meunasah* (prayer house/community center). Upon arriving at the village market, which was littered with trash and swarming with flies, we were warmly greeted by men at the coffeehouses across from the market area, with coffee and banter.

After a bit of conversation, the men began to tell stories of threats and interrogations perpetrated by the soldiers. Then the mood shifted and with levity the men told how one of their wives stepped in front of a group of Javanese soldiers threatening to shoot her husband. Throwing up her arms, she yelled at the soldiers, "I am Javanese; shoot me, not him!" The men all laughed – even a Javanese wife would bravely defend her husband. The story circulated and I heard it again later that day from women who also told it to me with laughter and then introduced me to the Javanese wife. After coffee, we walked to the community house, the *meunasah*, while the IOM vehicles followed closely according to the rules of humanitarian security control.

Several hundred people arrived over the course of the five hour "trauma clinic." As women and men spoke to the psychiatrist and doctors and nurses, they also spoke to me and my colleague from the University of Syiah Kuala. Some sat silently but many told elaborate stories of forced evacuation and ransacked houses, of women forced to watch as husbands were tortured or eviscerated, their hearts cut out. Stories of women accused of "cooking rice" for GAM and interrogated and tortured, their toenails ripped off; of women forced by the military to search for their husbands and sons in the forest; of women forced to lodge soldiers who shot up their houses in irrational fright and fear of the dark, searching for the ghosts of GAM in the rafters; of women's gardens and animals and agricultural livelihood destroyed; of forced evacuation and upon return of finding "not one plate" left intact in homes destroyed, some burned by military searching for GAM.[6]

The first two weeks of the psychosocial needs assessment survey were profoundly unsettling to us all; it was my initiation into listening to a deluge of stories hour after hour from those who had experienced militarized violence, systematic torture, irrational as well as targeted destruction, terrorizing, humiliation, and forced witnessing of the torture and killing of spouses, children, and friends. This first mobile trauma clinic led to the development of a mental health intervention, the centerpiece of which were mobile mental health outreach teams who served more than seventy-five high-conflict affected villages, treating villagers who suffered psychological and emotional disorders associated with the remainders of violence (M. Good et al., 2010).

Gender Differences in Traumatic Events

The Acehnese have a saying, "The mountain goat eats the corn; the village goat gets the beating," and it well describes the physical aggression and psychological torture ordinary villagers experienced when caught between the military and GAM during periods of intense high conflict such as those in the mountain village we visited (Aryo Danusiri's film, *The Village Goat Takes the Beating*, 1999).

The following tables illustrate in overview the gendered patterns of violence and trauma from the needs assessment surveys, which I will refer to as PNA1 (3 districts, February 2006) and PNA2 (10 districts, July, and 1 district, November 2006). Table 12.1 presents the study samples by gender for the PNA1 and PNA2 needs assessment surveys of 105 villages and 14 districts and for the evaluation study of the Direct Health and Psychosocial Assistant Program (DHPAP) that my husband and I designed, which was carried out in 20 villages, 10 in each of 2 districts (Bireuen and Aceh Utara). These evaluation interviews were conducted at three points in time, beginning at "before" treatment by the IOM mobile mental health teams, at midpoint, and after IOM treatment when patients were transferred to the local district health clinics if they continued to need treatment or when they had concluded treatment.

Table 12.1. *Gender of those assessed*

Sample by Gender of Respondent	PNA 1	PNA 2	PNA 1 and PNA 2	DHPAP T1 T 3	
Males	53%	50%	51%	30%	32%
Females	47%	50%	49%	70%	68%
Total	596	1,376	1,972	1,122	1,063

We also conducted qualitative interviews with 45 patients during the DHPAP evaluation study during the midpoint in 2008 and after treatment in 2009. In the evaluation study of the DHPAP, only 5 percent of patients were lost between Times 1 and 3 of the study.

The Cruelty of Location

Certain locales, what Jesse Grayman calls "hot spots," were infamous sites of extraordinary torture and cruelty for both men and women (M. Good et al., 2007, pp. 26–9). Within the hotspots one finds that both men and women were beaten and tortured; that villages were bombed; that schools and mosques burned and houses destroyed; and that local economies were decimated; and within such hotspots one finds that men reported suffering higher levels of beating, trauma, humiliation, and experiences of being forced to humiliate, harm, or betray others. Although sexual assault, torture, and rape of women were regarded as widespread by human rights organizations working during the conflict era, and people told our IOM research teams of seeing genital mutilations of male and female bodies tossed in ditches along the roads, few women and men reported sexual assault or torture during the PNA studies. We suspected numbers of sexual assaults and rapes were higher than reported. Our project chose not to press interviewees to revisit or reveal experiences they wished to conceal. Nonetheless, women and men reported rape or sexual assault. Physical injury was suffered by many, as was head trauma.

Tables 12.2 and 12.3 illustrate the difference in how cruelty was meted out to village men and women. The combined surveys and total mean and percentage scores presented in Tables 12.2 and 12.3 do not capture the intensity of trauma inflicted on local populations in the hot spot villages of Aceh Utara and Bireuen (PNA1 sites) and Aceh Selatan and Aceh Timor on the east and south coasts (PNA2 sites). For example, in Bireuen, 68 percent of men between the ages of 17–29 were beaten

Table 12.2. *Past traumatic events experienced by men and women (fourteen districts)*

Past Traumatic Events Experienced	Men (n = 1,006)	Women (n = 966)
Experienced combat	77%	72%
Forced to flee burning buildings	37%	33%
Forced to flee danger	47%	44%
Forced to hide	14%	9%
Beating to the body	44%	12%
Attacked with gun or knife	24%	10%
Tortured	19%	6%
Witnessed physical punishment	49%	38%
Humiliated or shamed in public	16%	8%
Rape or sexual assault	4%	5.5%
Head injuries	32%	8%
Destruction of property	43%	36%
Spouse killed	1%	5%
Child killed	4%	4%
Friend or family killed	43%	33%
Forced to give food/ shelter	21%	17%
Forced to search for GAM in forest	33%	19%

Note: On the Harvard Trauma Questionnaire with modifications, see M. Good et al., 2007.

on the head or strangled, as were 28 percent of women in the same age group. In Aceh Utara, 67 percent of men 17–29 but also 60 percent of those age 30–53 were beaten on the head or strangled, as were 29 percent of women, ages 17–29, and 27 percent of ages 30–40. More than 40 percent of men resident in East Coast and South Coast districts also suffered head trauma or strangling; women were less frequently targeted (> 10 percent) (M. Good et al., 2007).

Gender explains little of the variation in levels of psychological distress, especially at higher symptom thresholds. Rather locale and level of exposure to traumatic events are most predictive of risk of psychological distress. Odds ratios are vivid representations of the relationship between past traumatic experiences and current symptom scores on depression and PTSD measures; these models determine the risk of an individual's suffering a particular illness if exposed to certain levels of violence. Similarly, high current stressful events (such as inability to provide for one's family and other livelihood concerns) significantly increase the odds of meeting symptomatic criteria. Odds ratios calculated for the PNA1 sample found that if exposed to four or more events, an individual regardless of gender was three times more likely to meet criteria

Table 12.3. *Depression, PTSD, anxiety symptoms, and diagnoses by gender*

Formal Measures of Psychological Symptoms and Diagnoses	PNA 1 Males (n = 315)	PNA1 Females (n = 281)	PNA2 Males (n = 691)	PNA2 Females (n = 685)	PNA1 Total	PNA2 Total
Meets criteria for depressive disorder	54 %	57%	20%	26%	55%	23%
High threshold	18%	19%	6%	7%	18%	7%
Meets criteria for PTSD	37%	35%	13%	12%	36%	12%
High threshold	11%	10%	3%	3%	10%	3%
Meets criteria for anxiety disorder symptomatic	64%	75%	33%	46%	69%	39%
Anxiety high symptomatic	30%	36%	10%	8%	33%	9%

Note: See M. Good et al., 2007, p. 52.

for depression and more than six times more likely to meet criteria for PTSD than those exposed to three or fewer events. If exposed to eight to ten traumatic events, one was six times more likely to meet criteria for depression and nearly twelve times more likely to meet criteria for PTSD than if exposed to zero to three events. The findings also held for the PNA2 sample in areas with lower scores on psychiatric symptoms and severe conflict related trauma, but where forced evacuation was high. Although the odds ratios are lower, the pattern persists: Increased exposure to traumatic events is consistently associated with higher symptom scores for depression, anxiety, and PTSD, confirming the powerful relationship between traumatic events associated with conflict and continued levels of mental health disorders (see B. Good et al., 2006; M. Good et al., 2007, for additional detail).[7]

IOM launched the first mobile mental health treatment program as a pilot to 25 villages in Bireuen in January 2007. A redesigned and much larger second intervention expanded the treatment program to 50 villages in Bireuen and Aceh Utara in 2008–9. The second intervention included a longitudinal evaluation study we (M. Good and B. Good) designed using qualitative interviews and surveys to measure patient outcomes from onset through conclusion of treatment with IOM, and a six month follow-up visit. Both men and women in these patient groups exhibited higher levels of traumatic events and psychiatric symptoms than the adults surveyed in the PNA1 and PNA1, as would be expected (see B. Good & M. Good, 2010). Village women more readily sought out clinical care from the mobile mental health teams (68 percent% of patients who were interviewed at Time 3 in the longitudinal study); men and women who were treated by the IOM teams recovered at similar rates. The following ethnographic narratives illustrate traumatic experiences and complement the numbers reported in the PNA1 and PNA2 surveys.

Recovery and Reflection

The following conversations were with women who sought treatment from the IOM teams for conflict related emotional disorders and psychiatric illnesses and took place during our visits to patients currently or recently in treatment during the expanded mental health program. Village health cadre, also women, participated in these conversations as well.

Women Defenders of Children and Land: April 2008

We joined our IOM mental health outreach team on a lengthy trip deep into the Bireuen countryside. Although remote, homes along the road were strung for electricity and TV satellite dishes perched on roofs. There was no market center. The mobile clinic as usual was held in the village *meunasah,* a large, open-sided unpainted wooden structure set in an open field. As the clinic proceeded, I entered into conversation with women who were waiting to see a clinician. "Women here seem strong – who owns the houses?" There was much laughter; in chorus the women responded loudly, "Women do!" Findings from the PNA indicated how very important houses are to women; the most significant traumatic event associated with high symptoms of depression or PTSD for women was the destruction of a woman's house, even more so than the loss of a spouse to the conflict. In many locales in Aceh women are deeded their homes and even land by their parents or own their homes through customary law. There is legal variation throughout the region. (For further detail see the anthropologist James Siegel's [2003] discussion on Acehnese women's ownership of houses; see M. Good et al., 2007; M. Good et al., 2010; Siapno, 2009, on women and homes.)

The women told me how they responded to threats from the armed forces who swept into their villages. "We defended our land." "If I am to die, I will die bravely *(berani).*" "I will die with my children, and I will die defending them and defending my land." Daughters were sent to safe places, often to towns. Sons accompanied their fathers into the forest. The women stayed behind in their houses, with their small children, to guard their land and offspring. They described how soldiers aggressed them – "pulled my hair" and "crushed my toes with their boots" – in an effort to terrorize them into telling where husbands and sons were hiding. Told with fierce toughness and much animation, this was less victim talk, more solidarity talk, flecked with bravado and an admirable bemused irony. These things happened to us; we resisted. Their stance and voices conveyed a community of defiance to those of us engaged in the conversation (me, Byron, and the Acehnese women physicians). By contrast, the older men were quiet, appearing to clinicians on the team to be depressed, deeply sad, and exhausted by the conflict (M. Good, field notes and photos, April 2008).

Free Aceh Movement Women: Hasan de Tiro's GAM Women (January 2009)

My husband and I, accompanied by our IOM colleagues and district community mental health nurses, journeyed to a village near the district of Pidie to visit patients in treatment with IOM. Pidie is the birthplace of GAM in 1976 and its founder, Hasan di Tiro. We met a large woman of fifty-five who had been treated for PTSD, inability to sleep, intrusive thoughts, and bereavement over the loss of two of her sons and her husband, who were killed during conflict in combat between GAM and the TNI. She welcomed our large party into her well-furnished living room. She was a GAM leader, and her wealth and stature were material as well as political. She wore beautiful gold rings and rich silky clothing. And although Acehnese village women "dress up" at times at home as well as for trips to town, the richness of the cloth of her dress was unusually lovely. Her first comments to me were that she and her husband knew Hasan di Tiro, the founder and hero of the Aceh independence movement. They had been to his home and were friends with his family and members of his political circle. "Yes," the patient reported to the medical team's questions, she was sleeping "a lot ... maybe too much now – the pills make one very sleepy"; "yes," she no longer suffered from rumination and intrusive thoughts; "yes," she felt more herself. Once the questions about her illness experience were answered, she turned to tell me of her political life, and why and how her sons and husband had been killed. Soon her daughter joined us, and fourteen more women crowded into her living room to join us (M. Good, field notes, January 2009). Mother and daughter told stories of the world of Hasan Tiro and GAM in their village. The daughter exclaimed she too was a GAM leader.

As the younger women were becoming excited telling their conflict era stories, the patient turned to me to describe her aching knees and aching back. When I gently asked whether it might be from age, likening her aches to my own, she laughed, demonstrating how she came to have a chronic backache caused by a blow from a soldier's rifle butt. She had her arm around me, enveloping me in her silky robes, hugging me close to her, and then suddenly she swung her arm and hit me on the side of my back, on my kidney, with a good solid whack that I felt for months. Was this simply an attempt to get me to pay attention to her, now that young attractive women were telling compelling war stories to my male companions, or was it more complex? Was she demonstrating to me physically that this is what war is about (about beating, about hurt), and about how strong one has to be to bear this physical aggression. These things she let me know in one friendly but solid slap, well placed to hurt for a long time. I then listened with care to her stories of how she hid her sons and her belongings in the rafters of the house, above a false ceiling. How she strategized to prevent the soldiers from opening up the ceiling, creating distractions so her son could escape out through the gardens into the jungle; how her aches were from physical aggression at the hands of the military, not from age.

Soon after, our host let her daughter take the floor, amused too by the younger generation's stories of resistance. Her daughter and her friends animatedly told how they not only created corridors of security for the men, who had to run and hide from soldiers invading their village, but also protected each other, how the women would cordon off the soldiers who arrived to terrorize and assault. And like her mother, who had engaged in many modes of resistance, she and her friends told how the women of this village learned to deflect sexual assault from the soldiers. After one girl had been isolated and raped by a soldier, women decided to patrol the village aggressively to make certain no woman would be left alone, exposed to a soldier's assault. If a soldier appeared, women mounted a security force against any military intruder by crowding into and occupying an isolated woman's home. The image of a mass of women invading their neighbors' homes joining together against the intrusive soldiers recalls the Acehnese tales of the ancient Aceh Women Warriors – the Laskar Perempuan Aceh – and the contemporary news stories of GAM "women combatants" valorized in the newly free Acehnese press. These stories were of the same genre as those we heard in other villages of Bireuen and Aceh Utara. Women en masse would seek to protect their communities. Women formed crowds to protest against the military, going "by truckload" to military posts to shame the soldiers who took their husbands, sons, or brothers for interrogation.[8] The telling of these stories was by women recollecting compelling experiences of resistance during moments of chilling terror and conflict.

Si Pai: Armies of Evil

In July and August of 2008, we were evaluating the effectiveness of the second IOM mobile mental health outreach program and were interviewing a number of villagers who had received mental health care. It was a euphoric period in many districts of Aceh following the establishment of local political parties and direct elections of candidates. Former GAM men had been elected to office including the governor and many of the district heads. Soon local elections for provincial assembly would be held and the people of Aceh could vote for candidates from local parties rather than only from national political parties. Villagers seemed in a high mood as well, and many had Party Aceh flags plastered on their doors and windows. They praised the IOM mental health program and the teams, and even if biased given the presence of IOM project members in the village, their appreciation seemed truly genuine (Acehnese speak about themselves as being very critical and dissatisfied with many services so praise was remarkable and welcome in the view of the IOM team.) When we interviewed people treated by our mental health teams, their accounts of therapeutic benefit and recovery were remarkably impressive. Yet, what most impressed me and my colleagues were the graphic stories of chilling terror and bravery that women were still telling about life prior to the MOU, even three years after the establishment of a notable and remarkably secure peace. The interviews we conducted were also recorded and transcribed.

The following vignette illustrates the dominant theme of the conflict related stress experienced by women, not as victims, but as protectors of men against the national military soldiers (TNI). Through these villagers' stories the meanings of si *pai* in conflict era rural Aceh unfolded. As usual, our visits were very social and followed the pattern of the mobile teams' outreach program. My interview group included two young Acehnese men, a newly graduated physician trained in mental health care by IOM and a trauma specialist who was also a public mental health nurse and the IOM project field coordinator. Prior to his IOM employment, which began in 2005 after the tsunami, he worked with a famous trauma treatment center in Bireuen that cared for victims of torture during decades of conflict. We were also accompanied by a female Javanese psychologist on the IOM staff and the female village mental health cadre (all village health cadre I worked with between 2006 and

2009 were women, as they were in an earlier period when I advised faculty at University of Syiah Kuala on an Oral Rehydration Therapy for Children with Diarrhea (ORT) project, between 1988 and 1992). The mental health cadre women were trained by our IOM teams to screen their communities and identify people who had conflict related disorders and might benefit from IOM's mental health services. The mental health cadre was an exceptionally articulate thirty-two-year-old woman with a high school diploma. She introduced herself upon our meeting as an activist and took us to visit a sixty-year-old woman, who also described herself as an activist and a cultural leader of the community. For the past two months the older woman was receiving psychopharmacological treatment and brief talk therapy for depression and PTSD from the Acehnese physician and trauma specialist who accompanied me. When they asked how she was feeling, she told us that recently she awoke, suddenly able to see in a new way (Jenkins & Carpenter-Song, 2005; M. Good, 2010; Jenkins, 2010). Before taking medications, she said, everything appeared fuzzy and dark, but two months into treatment, she suddenly could see colors and people, the blue brightness of the sky, the intense green of the leaves of the plants, the veins on the leaves. She felt better physically too. She laughed as she described her improved state – amused she could have such a positive response to antidepressants and IOM care.

She also recalled how she felt before the MOU and peace, attributing her heart palpitations and hypertension to constant intense worry over her sons' being harassed by the military. She then explained the ultimate causes of her emotional distress and illness. In 2001, her teacher son was beaten at school, kicked, punched, his abdomen crushed by soldiers; he died of internal injuries two weeks later. More recently, her older son was shot by soldiers when trying to escape on his motorcycle; although he escaped, he died shortly after in the hospital. Her husband, who was hard of hearing and much older than she, "did not leave the house much" and "did not come to the son's aid even though he was shot in front of their house." She told how she and other women were emotionally and physically exhausted trying to protect their men from the soldiers. She feared for her grandchildren's future, as she had five small children to rear and educate. She attributed her heart palpitations, hypertension, headaches, fever, weight loss, and emotional distress (depression, PTSD, anxiety, bereavement) to the deaths of two of her three sons and to chronic conflict related stress and exhaustion caused by constant military harassment, aggression, interrogations, and insecurity. She feared a worse conflict might break out in the future and mused, "Where then can I run for safety?"

The village cadre was anxious to tell her story as well and she began to join in the conversation. She too worried about an outbreak of conflict in the future. Comparing the present to past terror and a feared future, she reflected:

Now at least people can go out to earn a living. In the past, it was the women who did because the men had to hide. The men could not leave the house, and if they did they could not return. In the past, danger was present every single day. When the army entered the village, we all had to hide for fear of getting shot. At night we often slept in a neighbor's house which was in better condition than mine, more solid and secure, for fear we would be accidentally shot during a fire fight. One night, I had to run and climb a fence with my two toddlers in my arms to escape to find safety when two groups of soldiers gathered in front of my house. Soldiers would often search houses at 2 or 3 AM, forcing people to go outside, to leave the house.

Both women told how they taught their own children and grandchildren, and all the village children from the time they were toddlers, to protect the whereabouts of the village men, to keep silent when the army appeared. The older woman activist explained, "We taught them," she said, "when you see the *si pai* run, hide ... if they ask you a question, say nothing.... If they show you a gun and ask if your daddy has one of these, say no; if there is a gun in the house, say no ... run, hide, do not speak to them." I was startled. "*Sipahi*?" I asked, thinking of the modern Turkish spelling, the colonial British meaning, and its recent use as *cipayo* by the rebel ETA in Basque country for the Basque police, whom rebels regarded as traitors to the Basque independence movement (Aretxaga, 2008; M. Good, 2010). The young Acehnese and Javanese were unfamiliar with the term. But both women activists, in response to my stunned interest and request for further explanation, repeatedly returned to make certain the young IOM staff as well as I understood the meaning of *si pai*, spelling it out *SI PAI* over and over again. "Yes. It is a bad word for those who do evil." "If they (the soldiers) heard us call them *si pai*, they would slit our throats." The older woman's grandson circled us waving a reedy stick, softy chanting *pa'i pa'i* as they repeated, "*Si pai* are people who do and are evil." The women repeated emphatically once again, "If they (the soldiers) heard us call them that they would slit our throats."

The women continued to elaborate. When soldiers entered the village, children ran through the village warning people, "The *si pai* are coming"; "Those who are evil (*jahat*) are coming." Soldiers threatened very young children, who became targets for interrogations. Toddlers who were two or three years old would be asked the whereabouts of their fathers, and women taught them to answer "*Hom*" (I don't know). Soldiers showed children pictures or real guns and asked even toddlers whether there were guns in their houses. When children refused to speak or tried to run away, the soldiers would point guns at them, threatening, "I'll shoot you" or would "display anger and fury."

The cadre's stories poured forth in Indonesian – a soldier pointed his gun at her forehead during a village sweep, insisting she help search for a man suspected of being GAM. When she refused, the soldier threatened, "Do you want to die?" She challenged him "NO! If you want to catch someone catch him yourself, not ask a women like me." She became furious, and took an Indonesian flag – and threw it at him – "What a damned flag. It causes people to die! Is it right that my husband and I get punished for this?" she said. She told us that women in this village displayed the national flag in front of their houses when soldiers were on patrol to deflect aggression. The soldier again pointed his gun at her, "Do you want to die?" She responded, "Yeah. Go ahead if you want to shoot a woman. But it's a shame that as a man you shoot a woman." Swearing at her, he called Acehnese men pigs and she answered: "That's right. Look; these are the children of pigs."

She then shared a story of less successful defiance. With tears of fury flowing, she recalled how a group of soldiers invaded her family house and tortured her husband. She tried to defend him and protect him from the blows of the soldiers. Her five-year-old son ran to her, and tried to hide under her skirt, and cried, "Mommy, please don't do it; if Daddy dies, let not you die too. Where am I going to go; who will care for me, if you both die?" She fell under the soldiers' boots. Her husband was tortured from 1:30 to 4:30 in the morning; their home was ransacked. It was only after the soldiers found his identity cards that they stopped. Her husband still has scars from the weapons the soldiers used to torture him. During the height of the conflict, her village was a daily battleground and men were targeted with death. If men wished to escape, to leave the village, women had to sneak them out when the roads were clear of soldiers. These actions were part of the evildoing of the contemporary *si pai* of conflict era Aceh. Both women were "activists" and involved in the politics of peace and supporters of the new Partai Aceh. Both had been protectors of their male kin, only partially successful. Victims, yes, of militarized aggression, but far more than victims. Three years after the peace agreement, post MOU, they remained anxious and cautious about the future.

Aguswandi, a scholar and a student political activist in his youth with whom I correspond, responded to my texted question about the meaning of "*si pai*" in Aceh. He texted, "It is the name for those who commit evil." The "villagers use it for the TNI" and "the term is very ancient." "It came from the elders – the old people – way back in the hills." *Si Pai* "is very strong, a potent curse, against those who do evil" (Aguswandi, text message, November 2008)" M. Nur Djuli, a GAM intellectual, member of the peace negotiating team for the MOU, and Harvard Weatherhead Fellow recently, wrote in response to my query, "The term is used by GAM for the TNI; it originally referred to Javanese slaves used by the Dutch during its war campaign in Aceh; they were very much despised by the Acehnese. A derogatory term from colonial era, it came from the word *sepoy* [British Muslim soldiers in India]. The word is not used in polite conversation much less in writing." He was surprised *Si Pai Inong* would be used as a headline in a news article extolling the Women Warriors of Ancient Aceh's Sultanates ("Si Pai Inong Laskar Perempuan Aceh," 2008).

Engaging the Peace as Recovery: Women Activists, Not Just "Victims"

By featuring Aceh's historical women warriors and sultanahs as icons to inspire contemporary women in their struggle to attain political power in the postconflict era, women's organizations are also in the process of creating a postmodern meaning to warrior women. We see an exceptionally pointed and well-funded effort to revivify the ancient image of Aceh's warrior women, rather secular, tied to Sultanate Acehnese histories. The image of powerful warrior women is perhaps more than just a local and internationally generated symbol encouraging women's empowerment and greater involvement in making a modern-day peace. It is part of a politics of recognition, acknowledging women's bravery and strengths during the long TNI-GAM conflict, when men hid and fled and destroyed, and women were interrogated, subjected to aggression, and threatened with extortion and destruction of their economic livelihood.[9] The warrior women of the political billboards, promoting justice and women's rights and urging women to become involved in contemporary democratic politics, are part of a creative reconstruction of the historical and cultural scaffolding of Aceh to produce a contemporary postconflict political subjectivity for Aceh's women (M. Good, interviews with women activists, 2009–12; LINA, 2010).[10] The Provincial Election was soon to take place after these 2008 interviews. Party flags were flying everywhere – in villages, on highways, in towns, in private as well as public spaces, in party buildings painted lipstick red if the Aceh Party, or blue if one of several others, such as SIRA. As we drove the five hours returning to Banda Aceh from our stay in Bireuen and Aceh Utara, it seemed that not all politics leads to madness and trauma. Some Acehnese experienced politics as having a healing and euphoric effect. Certainly the politics of peace appeared at the time to provide succor to at least some who have suffered "trauma" from years of conflict. Many Acehnese women would like to be players in this politics of peace, and women's empowerment groups flourish throughout the province although women politicians continue to struggle against formidable barriers of women not voting for women. In 2008 there were only five women elected to the provincial assembly and in 2010 women political activists were talking about the need for quotas. The more pessimistic view and the worries of the women activists we interviewed in our village visits seem to be in tune with the difficulty for women of winning elections. And in 2010, a district male politician and former GAM member criticized women as "unfit to lead" and a Meulaboh district head declared women were wearing pants too tight riding around on their motorcycles and must now don full length skirts, which he would provide.[11] Acehnese women activists, politicians, and scholars continue to struggle against these types of attitudes and barriers, even as they seek to open pathways for women's engagement in provincial and local politics (LINA, 2010; M. Good, interviews with women activists, 2010; Siapno, 2009).

What does being an Acehnese woman mean in this post-MOU era? The politics of peace flourished during the period I cover in this paper, and although the euphoria of earlier days following the MOU had given way to routinized security, and concerns about jobs and the economy took priority, women we interviewed remained interested in their conflict experiences, concerned about what the political future might hold for their families and children, and engaged in local politics. In this chapter, I have discussed ways Acehnese rural women who were exposed to very high levels of conflict related insecurity and traumatic events nonetheless engaged in strategic action, demonstrating "everyday resilience" as they took up the burden of defending their children, land, and community, and protecting their husbands, sons, and other male kin during the years of conflict between GAM and TNI. Jacqueline Siapno, in *Living through terror: Everyday resilience in East Timor and Aceh* (2009), argues that government rhetoric on IDPs and human rights reports "are simplistic, reducing displaced persons to easily frightened masses [or] victims.... Neither representation provides room for agency, political subjectivities, intentions, dilemmas, ambivalence, thoughts, resilience, creativity, and strategies of displaced persons" (p. 50).[12] My chapter seeks to redress this gap and to contribute to a growing literature on women, gender, and conflict in which trauma and suffering are acknowledged, but where political subjectivity, activism, creativity, and strategic experiences are highlighted, even as we document the emotional and mental health toll of remainders of violence.

Acknowledgments

Great appreciation to the Acehnese women and men who participated in these studies, the patients, cadres, and activists and politicians, as well as to our many collaborators and colleagues, including Steve Cook, Nenette Motus, and Mark Knight and Kristin Parco at IOM; Professor Sugihen Bahrein and Ibu Rosnani Sarhadin and Dr. Ibrahim Puteh at Syiah Kuala University; and the teams of doctors, nurses, and drivers who worked on the projects, particularly Hayatullah, Hafid, Nifa, Adri, and Dafi and Drs. Riska, Zubir, Fitri, Fikri, and Enny, and Pak Joe. Appreciation to the Acehnese public intellectuals and activists, including Aguswandi, Shadia Marhaban, and Nur Djuli, for their insights and reflections and critical readings, and to the Bupati of Bireuen, Tengku Nurdin Abdul Rahmann. Our University of Gadjah Mada (UGM) team, Ninik Supartini and Ibu Dewi, assisted with great competence in data preparation and analysis. A very special thank you to Jesse Grayman for more than five years of intellectual engagement on Aceh. At Harvard, appreciation to Matt Lakoma, our PNA statistician; to Sharon Abramowitz and Adia Benton for suggestions on the PNA design; and special appreciation to Devon Hinton, whose interpretation and encouragement of this chapter I greatly value.

NOTES

1 Byron Good and I are PIs on a new interuniversity partnership to improve mental health care in Indonesia, a collaboration of Harvard University with the University of Gadjah Mada in Jogjakarta and the University of Syiah Kuala in Banda Aceh, funded by USAID.

2 Our interviews were primarily conducted in Indonesian mixed with Acehnese. Anthropologically inclined Acehnese team members who accompanied us readily assisted us and translated Acehnese into Indonesian. Interviews were transcribed in Acehnese and Indonesian; Acehnese segments were translated into Indonesian by Acehnese students at UGM. I translated our interviews into English in collaboration with my Indonesian research assistants and colleagues including Acehnese Indonesians.

3 Women sultans are prominent Acehnese heroines, as are women warriors such as "Admiral Malahayati" and her "widow army" who battled the Portuguese and Dutch in the sixteenth century. Cut Nyak Dhien, a nineteenth century Acehnese heroine, is also a national icon for her "fierceness in battle" in resisting Dutch attempts to colonialize Aceh (LINA, 2010, p. 6). LINA's leaders strategically link these famous historical women with the women combatants who joined the military wing of GAM who were also known as "the widows battalion" (LINA, 2010; Shadia Marhaban, LINA [Aceh Women's League] president and cofounder, interview, 2010; M. Good, personal observations of billboard images of historically famous political and military women, June–July 2010). The Serambi news article headline consisted of two parts and led

first with a derogatory term from colonial times, *Si Pai* (military corps), and then *Inong* (women in Acehnese). I discuss this term later in the essay and its relevance to the conflict. A leading intellectual of GAM, M. Nur Djuli, was shocked to see *Si Pai* appear in a newspaper story headline. Younger people in urban Aceh are less aware of the derogatory meaning the term holds for older and rural Acehnese.

4 LINA (the Aceh Women's League) has been deeply engaged since its founding in 2006 in public education programs and conferences to teach women to take more central political roles in postconflict Aceh and represents the internationalization of the women's movement in Aceh. Shadia Marhaban, cofounder and president, was the only woman to participate in the Helsinki peace negotiations among the GAM delegation that led to the MOU ending the conflict between GAM and the government of Indonesia and its military. UNIFEM, UNFPA, UNDP, LIPI, OXFAM, GTZ (German Aid), Center for Humanitarian Dialogue based in Switzerland, Fredrich Ebert Stifung (FES), Secours Catholique Caritas, Terre des Hommes, LIPI (Indonesian Institute of Science), Olof Palme International Center, and Urban Community Mission Jakarta (PMK-HKBP) provided support for LINA activities. Billboards extolling women's rights and empowerment were funded by the EU and USAID, as well as local organizations. Clearly Western governments as well as Indonesian governmental and nongovernmental organizations invest in programs to encourage women's participation in democratic politics and community and civil society life.

5 The IOM medical team included a male Acehnese psychiatrist, a male Acehnese trauma specialist with a university public mental health degree, a female physician employed by a government district health clinic, and our Acehnese drivers, who acted as community liasons. Our research group included Byron Good, me, and Jesse Grayman.

6 See PNA1 and PNA2 reports: http://www.iom.or.id/publications/pdf/17_PNA2eng07-e.pdf and http://www.iom.or.id/publications/pdf/19_PNA-English.pdf.

7 See B. Good, M. Good, Grayman, & Lakoma, 2006, p. 28, and M. Good, B. Good, Grayman, & Lakoma, 2007, pp. 54–6.

8 In 2010, activist women in Banda Aceh were critical of how GAM used "truckloads" of women to protest on behalf of men, but male politicians did not share political positions with women. In 2013, women activists I interviewed with J. Grayman again complained about the marginalization of women in Partai Aceh politics.

9 Siapno (2009) noted that women activists she interviewed noted that "even gender roles are reversed; men and husbands use the armed conflict with TNI as an excuse not to economically support their wives, claiming it is the women, the wives who have to look for a living as it is too dangerous for men to go outside" (p. 52).

10 Once an Ottoman title for landed gentry on the empire's borderlands, and a term for the armies of the ancient Acehnese Sultanates, including the women warriors, *si pai* has been transformed in meaning during centuries of colonial rule by Dutch, British, Japanese, Javanese. During a seminar we gave at UGM, few faculty had heard the term. However, as older professors explained, *si pai*

was used for the colonial army in Java, made up of Javanese, Dutch, and those of mixed race as well as for the Indian troops of the British colonial army. The MOU agreement to demobilize and withdraw inorganic – that is, non-Acehnese – troops from the villages of Aceh and for the GAM to demobilize and give up all claims to independence suggests that at least for the moment the cursed evil embodied by the *si pai* of Jakarta has retreated, opening new political challenges and opportunities for Aceh's activist women, even as they must negotiate with their own activist men.

11 On October 8, 2010, the *Jakarta Globe* published a story by Nurdin Hasan headlined "Women Unfit to Lead Says Achenese District Council Chairman," noting, "In a move criticized as an insult to the dignity of women, an Aceh district speaker has called for the replacement of a female subdistrict head, arguing women were unfit to lead under Islamic law." Women activists we interviewed lamented the problem of getting women elected to the provincial political offices and of "dawn raids" during elections, when husbands pressured wives to vote for their male candidates.

12 Jacqueline Siapno, Philippine born, writes from the perspective of one who suffered violence and conflict, first in Aceh as the former wife of an activist later killed during the conflict by unknown forces and second as the interim first lady of the acting president of Timor Leste, whose residence was burned, forcing her to flee. She reported she was evacuated three times from her homes.

BIBLIOGRAPHY

Aretxaga, B. (2008). Madness and the politically real: Reflections on violence in postdictatorial Spain. In M. J. Good, S. Hyde, S. Pinto, & B. J. Good (Eds.), *Postcolonial disorders* (pp. 43–61). Berkeley: University of California Press.

Aspinall, E. (2006). *The Helsinki agreement: A more promising basis for peace in Aceh?* (Policy Studies 20). Washington, DC: East-West Center Washington.

Danusiri, A. (Director). (1999). *Village goat takes the beating* (Documentary). Australia: B3W Video Project, produced by D. Hanan, Monash University. Retrieved from http://www.arts.monash.edu.au/mai/films/aceh.html.

Good, B. J. (2015). Haunted by Aceh: Specters of violence in post-Suharto Indonesia. In D. E. Hinton & A. L. Hinton (Eds.), *Genocide and mass violence: Memory, symptom, and recovery*. Cambridge: Cambridge University Press.

Good, B. J., & Good, M. J. (2010). *Direct Health and Psychosocial Assistance Project (DHPAP) report*: Geneva : International Organization for Migration.

Good, M. J. (2010). Trauma in post-conflict Aceh and psychopharmaceuticals as medium of exchange. In J. H. Jenkins (Ed.), *Pharmaceutical self: The global shaping of experience in an age of psychopharmacology* (pp. 41–66). Santa Fe, NM: School for American Research Press.

Good, M. J., & Good, B. J. (2013). Perspectives on the politics of peace in Aceh, Indonesia. In F. Aulino, M. Goheen, & S. Tambiah (Eds.), *Radical egalitarianism: Local realities, global relations* (pp. 191–208). New York: Fordham University Press.

Good, M. J., Good, B. J. & Grayman, J. H. (2010). Complex engagements: Responding to violence in postconflict Aceh. In D. Fassin & M. Pandolfi

(Eds.), *Contemporary states of emergency: The politics of military and humanitarian interventions* (pp. 241–66). Cambridge, MA: MIT Press.

Good, B. J., Good, M. J., Grayman, J. H., & Lakoma, M. (2006). *Psychosocial needs assessment of communities affected by the conflict in the districts of Pidie, Bireuen, and Aceh Utara.* Geneva: International Organization for Migration.

Good, M. J., Good, B. J., Grayman, J. H., & Lakoma, M. (2007). *A psychosocial needs assessment of communities in 14 conflict-affected districts in Aceh.* Geneva: International Organization for Migration.

Good, M. J., Hyde S. T., Pinto, S., & Good, B. J. (Eds.). (2008). *Postcolonial disorders.* Berkeley: University of California Press.

Grayman, J. H., Good, M. J., & Good, B. J. (2009). Conflict nightmares and trauma in Aceh. *Culture, Medicine and Psychiatry,* 33, 290–312.

Hasan, N. (2010, October 8). "Women unfit to lead" says Acehnese district council chairman. *Jakarta Globe.* Retrieved from http://www.thejakartaglobe.com/home/women-unfit-to-lead-says-acehnese-district-council-chairman/400219.

Hyde, V. (2003). Trauma and testimony: Implications for political community. *Anthropological Theory,* 8, 293–307.

Jenkins, J. H. (Ed.) (2010). *Pharmaceutical self: The global shaping of experience in an age of psychopharmacology.* Santa Fe, NM: School for American Research Press.

Jenkins, J. H., & Carpenter-Song, E. (2005). The new paradigm of recovery from schizophrenia: Cultural conundrums of improvement without cure. *Culture, Medicine and Psychiatry,* 29, 379–413.

LINA (Liga Inong Acheh, Acheh Women's League). (2010). *Recognizing the critical role women can and must play in post-conflict society, LINA strives to empower Acehnese women to act as agents of change.*

Mangunwijaya, Y. B. (1991). *The weaverbirds.* Jakarta, Indonesia: The Lontar Foundation.

Siapno, J. A. (2009). Living through terror: Everyday resilience in East Timor and Aceh. *Social Identities: Journal for the Study of Race, Nation and Culture,* 15, 43–64.

Siegel, J. T. (2003) [1969]. *The rope of God.* Ann Arbor: The University of Michigan Press.

Si pai inong, laskar perempuan Aceh. (2008, November 23). *Serambi,* Metro Aceh section, p. 5.

Tambiah, S. J. (1996). *Leveling crowds: Ethnonationalist conflicts and collective violence in South Asia.* Berkeley: University of California Press.

13 Rwanda's *Gacaca* Trials: Toward a New Nationalism or Business as Usual?

Christopher C. Taylor

Background

By now much has been written about the Truth and Reconciliation Commissions (TRCs) in South Africa, which were designed to provide a measure of justice to those who had suffered from state-sponsored racial violence. Much of this literature has been critical (Wilson, 2001). One of the most visible apologists for the TRCs, however, was Bishop Desmond Tutu. In some of the bishop's statements, he distinguished between retributive and restorative justice, emphasizing that the true African (and superior) form of justice was restorative, while the typically Western form was retributive (Tutu, 1999)

Like South Africa, Rwanda witnessed its share of state-sponsored ethnic violence. But in contrast to South Africa, it chose to deal with its many genocide prisoners through uniquely retributive means. In the early years following the 1994 genocide, accused persons were simply thrown in jail, often on the basis of a single and unsubstantiated accusation, to be tried later by Rwanda's conventional courts. Some prisoners were tried and sentenced by these courts and a small number were executed, but Rwanda's prison population continued to grow. Rwanda's conventional justice system was overwhelmed. After considerable debate and eventual rejection of the TRC model by the Government of Rwanda (Uvin, n.d.), the trial method of *gacaca* was decided upon in 1999, a method that ideally would weld elements of restorative justice to a basically retributive core (Schabas, 2005, p. 3). In procedures similar to those of the TRCs, accused persons would receive anything from full clemency to reduced sentences in exchange for full confessions. And for those who received reduced sentences, the possibility existed to serve all or part of their remaining terms by doing communal work – *travaux d'interet general.*

The question of restorative versus retributive justice and its "Africanness" calls to mind Evans-Pritchard's (1940) work on the Nuer, one of the first anthropological works to consider a non-Western system of justice and to explain it in its own terms. In cases of homicide, the Nuer used their "leopard skin chiefs" to work toward compensating the victim's descent group with blood wealth (in the form of cattle), rather than punishing the person responsible for the homicide. They employed restorative rather than retributive means. To many students, the Nuer method raised the question of deterrence. Did a system based on restorative principles prevent future killings? Although Evans-Pritchard did not specifically address this point, it could certainly be argued that the Nuer method was likely to have had a deterrent effect. Even though killers were not deprived of life or liberty, their actions cost their agnates dearly in cattle, and these latter would be unlikely to allow their lineage mate to forget his debt to them. Any man who did not want to be indebted to his lineage mates would likely think twice before committing homicide.

There were other questions that Evans-Pritchard did not fully address. Granted, an institution existed that aimed toward compensating the victim's group rather than punishing the offender, but how often was blood wealth paid? How often did the institution of the leopard skin chief actually work? When it did, it certainly obviated the need for police, jails, and hangmen, and the question might be asked, Why does every social group not have the equivalent of the leopard skin chief institution? However, if it worked most of the time, why was it that the Nuer seemed to be so frequently embroiled in feuds? And was not feuding a structurally necessary part of Evans-Pritchard's model, part of the fission-fusion dynamics of segmentary lineage systems? There seemed to be a contradiction between two functions: one centering on homeostasis and the other on social reproduction. It was difficult to see how a single institution, one that served to resolve intragroup tensions and restore the social order to the status quo ante, could also be the one that led to the group's propagation in space and time (see Sahlins, 1968). To my mind Evans-Pritchard did not resolve this tension. He never fully answered the questions raised by his model; nor did he devote much attention to the question of vengeance. To what degree did Evans-Pritchard ignore or underreport the frequency of vengeance among the Nuer? How often, for example, did the aggrieved group simply avenge their loss of a kinsperson with another homicide, rather than await the outcome of complicated negotiations and the payment of blood wealth? Did the kinsmen of Nuer victims manifest the desire that their adversaries endure commensurate pain? And if indeed reprisal violence was carried out, at what point did the Nuer consider the score even with no further need for continued violence? Were the Nuer anything like the Cambodians whom Alex Hinton (1998) has studied, for whom the loss of honor that results when one endures an affront or an act of violence requires that reprisal violence be carried out and that it be in excess of the initial violence – the dynamics of "an eye for a tooth, a head for an eye."

These are questions that I have contemplated with regard to Rwanda ever since the 1994 genocide drove me out of that country. Until the adjudicative method of *gacaca* was instituted in 2001 (Schabas, 2005, p. 13), it seemed that many Rwandan survivors were only interested in vengeance, or, at the very least, retribution. Restorative justice was a vain hope. In previous instances of mass violence, as in 1959 when the first large-scale killings of Tutsi occurred, and until 1994, a "culture of impunity" had always prevailed. After the overthrow of the Tutsi monarchy in 1962, the victory of Hutu political parties, and independence from Belgium, many killers of Tutsi were even rewarded with government jobs. Ethnic killings continued well into the 1960s, prompting tens of thousands of Tutsi to flee to neighboring African countries. The last paroxysm of that violent phase occurred in 1973, when Defense Minister Juvenal Habyarimana, a Hutu from northern Rwanda, seized the reins of power from the country's Hutu president, Gregoire Kayibanda, ended the pogroms against Tutsi, and instituted a quota system called "regional and ethnic equilibrium."

For the next seventeen years under President Habyarimana, Rwanda was relatively free of ethnic violence, but every citizen's national ID card still bore the ethnic labels that had become obligatory during the colonial era: Tutsi, Hutu, and Twa. Between 1973 and 1990, people labeled as Tutsi were no longer being attacked in pogroms, but they found themselves doomed to second-class status. They could not serve in the military, they could not hold high government posts, and they received much less than their allotted quota (10 percent) of state jobs and secondary school and university placements. In addition, the Tutsi expatriate community in neighboring countries only grew as time went on. In the late 1980s, the Habyarimana government experimented halfheartedly with measures aimed at repatriating Rwanda's refugees, but these were ineffectual and did little to placate an increasingly well-organized, well-funded, and well-armed diaspora (Prunier, 1995). Moreover, a number of Rwandan Hutu, especially from southern Rwanda, were disgruntled after years of Habyarimana's dictatorship. Many joined with these refugee Tutsi and formed the Rwandan Patriotic Front (RPF). Most supported Yoweri Museveni's bid for power in Uganda and later became soldiers in the Ugandan army.

Facing problems in Uganda and persuaded that Habyarimana's days were numbered, soldiers from the RPF deserted the Ugandan army en masse in October 1990 and invaded Rwanda from the north (Prunier, 1995). Habyarimana's supporters and other more extreme Tutsiphobes lost no time in blaming the invasion on Tutsi in general, and once again anti-Tutsi pogroms, planned and orchestrated by people close to the central government, began anew. These culminated in the 1994 genocide, which likely took the lives of about 800,000 Tutsi and up to 100,000 Hutu opponents of the genocide.

Early Measures of Justice after the Genocide

After ending the genocide and forcing Rwandan Government Forces (RGF) into Mobutu's Zaire, the fledgling Rwandan government had to contend with instability at home and armed incursions from Zaire. The new government was shaky, consisting as it did of the RPF and several predominantly Hutu parties who had been democratic opponents of the Habyarimana regime. Not all members of the latter had been warm to the RPF in the days leading up to the genocide, as opposition to Habyarimana did not necessarily mean opposition to the principle of continued Hutu dominance. Many prominent Hutu politicians in the postgenocide government mistrusted the RPF as a majority Tutsi organization and resented the fact that real power appeared to reside with Vice President Paul Kagame, former leader of the armed wing of the RPF, the Rwandan Patriotic Army (RPA). Although some in this army were Hutu (about 20 percent), the majority of its soldiers were Tutsi. After the genocide and despite the return of thousands from the diaspora, Tutsi were now even more of a minority in the Rwandan population than they had been before. They were nervous. The Rwandan Patriotic Army's methods of retaining control over the country and preventing armed incursions were often brutal. Hutu civilians suspected of collaborating with infiltrators were killed in reprisal violence by the RPA, and soon units from it entered Zaire to attack soldiers of the former RGF and their allied Interahamwe militias. As well as armed combatants, the RPA attacked Hutu refugee camps in Zaire, killing thousands and perhaps tens of thousands in the process. Back in Rwanda measures against people accused of participation in the genocide took the form of retribution, although to them it must have seemed like simple vengeance. Tens of thousands of Hutu were thrown into crowded prisons, where hygienic conditions were substandard. At its maximum about 130,000 prisoners were so incarcerated (Human Rights Watch, 2011), and in the meantime an inadequately manned judiciary sifted through a morass of accusations at a snail's pace.

The prevailing philosophy at the time seemed to be that the "culture of impunity" could only be reversed by vengeance of sufficient magnitude, "a head for an eye." And indeed until *gacaca* was instituted in 2001, that appeared to be the modus operandi of the Rwandan Patriotic Army. In 1995 they attacked a Hutu refugee camp near the Rwandan town of Kibeho, which was sheltering thousands of people. Perhaps as many as three thousand were killed. Elsewhere in Rwanda, RPA soldiers killed thousands of Hutu in the years following their victory. This victors' justice also appeared to characterize official Rwandan state actions. In 1998 twenty-two people who had been convicted of genocide crimes were publicly executed after a trial lacking in due process (Schabas, 2005, p. 17). Until *gacaca*, it seemed that only two outcomes awaited those suspected of genocide crimes: violent death or languishing in an overcrowded Rwandan jail for the rest of one's life.

All of this imparted a tarnish to Rwanda's international image by the late 1990s. For all the stated claims of wanting to establish a nonethnic state, it seemed that Rwanda's new rulers, under strongman and later president Paul Kagame, were only doing what had been done under every other previous regime – favoring their own ethnic group, while discriminating against the disempowered one.

In this paper I wish to explore aspects of *gacaca* as these relate to the rebuilding of the Rwandan nation-state and the role of justice in this process. My thinking on this is inspired in part by B. Anderson's work regarding nationalism and its rituals (Anderson, 1991). I will also consider the degree to which *gacaca* as a state-constrained ritual has been effective in fostering a new, nonethnic form of nationalist sentiment.

Gacaca

Gacaca was resorted to when it seemed that vengeance and purely retributive methods of dealing with the genocide's aftermath would not work. Advocates for *gacaca* extolled it as a form of restorative justice (see Longman, 2009, p. 306), pointing out that sole use of retributive means undermined the proposition that the new Rwanda was intent upon becoming a state characterized by the "rule of law," and one where one's ethnicity no longer mattered. *Gacaca* is a diminutive of the noun *urucaca* meaning "grass." Translated literally, it means "little grass." The term refers to the practice of community members meeting informally outdoors on some grassy spot to adjudicate disputes among neighbors or family members. It was never a part of the formal state judicial system, but for what it was called upon to do, it usually worked fairly well. A community would convene a *gacaca* and the dispute brought before them would usually be resolved.

Today's *gacaca* is quite different. Judges, called *inyangamugayo*, are elected by local communities. They receive rudimentary judicial training but no compensation. They can impose prison sentences. *Gacaca* does not conform to the South African TRC model, although it does integrate some aspects of restorative justice. *Gacaca* is also a hybrid in that it integrates notions from Western jurisprudence and Christianity. Confession, for example, encouraged and rewarded under the new *gacaca*, never played much of a role in precolonial Rwandan ritual practice (Taylor, 1992). It only became important as a result of widespread Christian evangelization. As for Western notions of jurisprudence, not all are employed in the new *gacaca*. There is no presumption of innocence, no right to representation by a lawyer, no cross-examination of witnesses. All this imparts a certain "messiness" to *gacaca* (A. Hinton, 2010; Burnet, 2008), which undoubtedly complicates its mission.

Where the new *gacaca* departs most starkly from "tradition" is that it has become part of the state judicial system, even though under Habyarimana, local administrators sometimes resorted to ad hoc *gacaca* councils to resolve disputes among neighbors (Reyntjens, 1990). Never in the past, however, were the hopes for *gacaca* so high, and never was it called upon to heal such a profound wound in the body politic. It is hoped that the new *gacaca* will contribute to a number of goals (see Uvin, n.d.):

1. Relieve overcrowding in Rwanda's jails by remanding prisoners to the jurisdiction of local *gacaca* courts.
2. Relieve pressure on Rwanda's overly strapped conventional judicial system, which does not have sufficient numbers of qualified personnel to process all who are accused of genocidal crimes.
3. Determine what actually happened during the genocide: Who was killed, who was injured, whose property was stolen or destroyed, and who was responsible?
4. Give some measure of justice to survivors of the genocide.
5. Promote reconciliation between the ethnic groups, while reversing the "culture of impunity."
6. Strengthen the new Rwandan nation-state while enhancing the new government's legitimacy.

Doing all this is a tall order as there are tensions between some goals and others. So far *gacaca* has met with mixed success, though it is certainly to be preferred to what was occurring in the pre-*gacaca* days after the genocide. Let us take the issue of the nation-state first. Surely one of the less overtly stated goals of *gacaca* is to rebuild the Rwandan state by promoting a shared sense of Rwandan national identity. For Gellner (1997), nationalism requires the marriage of people and state. But the people half of this marriage usually implies a group that thinks of itself as a single linguistic, racial, and/or ethnic entity. Although Rwanda is linguistically unified, its three ethnic groups, Hutu, Tutsi, and Twa, have limited historical consciousness of themselves as a single people. This is true even within the most numerous group, Hutu, presently 90 percent of the population. Indeed, the ethnonym "Hutu" is relatively recent in origin, having come into use as a general term for cultivators only during the late eighteenth century (Vansina, 2000). The term derives from a military context where Tutsi warriors used support personnel, usually cultivators, whom they referred to as "Hutu" (ibid.). The term meant "social son." It was an imposed term, and not one that a group would have chosen on its own. But this was not the last indignity that cultivators would have to endure before the arrival of European colonialists. The differentiation process under way among Rwanda's peoples deepened during the nineteenth century. For example, it was at this time that corvee labor (*uburetwa*), performed for the benefit of the king and other high-ranking Tutsi, was introduced, and only cultivators, that is, Hutu, were liable to it (ibid.). This drove a political wedge between Tutsi and Hutu as the practice entailed enduring Hutu subjugation.

When the Germans established a protectorate in Rwanda at the very end of the nineteenth century, they encountered a society that was already highly stratified. But colonialism worsened conditions by introducing the ideology of biological determinism and the practice of favoring Tutsi in education and participation in the colonial state. Belgian colonialism did not substantially alter this. Finally a Tutsi-dominated system ended when the majority Hutu took control of the country at about the time of independence from Belgium (1962). This change did little to resolve ethnic and political tensions. A "Tutsicracy" simply became a "Hutucracy." Founding a state by equating Hutu ethnic identity with nationhood, as the leaders of the "Social Revolution" did after 1960, did nothing to create a nonethnic "Rwandan" identity. Tutsi came to be considered less than fully Rwandan and were termed "invaders from Ethiopia." This expression resurfaced with particular vehemence during the violence of 1990–4.

Rwanda today is not trying to invent a postnationalist state, that is, a state where notions of nationality would become irrelevant, but it is trying to instill a different form of nationalist sentiment. Ideally, this will not be dependent upon ethnic identity as the primary means of fostering solidarity. It is hoped that each citizen will identify him- or herself as a Rwandan first, rather than as a Tutsi, a Hutu, or a Twa. Regional identities such as Banyanduga (southern Rwandans) and Banyakiga (northern Rwandans) will also disappear. To that end there is no longer any mention of a person's ethnicity on official documents, for example, on one's national ID card. No longer in the new Rwanda is there a policy of ethnic and regional equilibrium. Mentioning the terms "Hutu," "Tutsi," and "Twa" has become almost taboo, and vaguely defined laws have been enacted that punish practices like "sectarianism," "divisionism," or "genocide ideology." However, the laws are often used as a foil to silence dissent (Human Rights Watch, 2011), while doing nothing to counter the impression that Rwanda has become, in the minds of many, a "thinly disguised Tutsi dictatorship" (Lemarchand, 2009, p. x).

To give one example, there is ethnic discrimination where it comes to *gacaca*. All of the *gacaca* sessions that I observed dealt with crimes that had been committed by Hutu against Tutsi. In effect, there is de facto assimilation of the terms "victim" and "genocide survivor" with Tutsi, and the term "perpetrator" with Hutu. None of the *gacaca* sessions that I observed attempted to deal with crimes committed by RPF or RPA soldiers against Hutu. I was told by *gacaca* participants that war crime accusations against RPF politicians and RPA soldiers were being handled by military and governmental authorities, but not in a public manner. As *gacaca* is quite public, this difference incites suspicions of ethnic bias among many Hutu (Longman, 2009, p. 309). In essence, the crimes of Hutu militia members are brought out in the open for all to discuss, while the crimes of RPF and RPA are dealt with less transparently. To date, only a handful of RPF and RPA members have been punished for crimes committed during the genocide or after it (Human Rights Watch, 2011). All of the latter are lower-ranking personnel; no high-ranking officers or politicians have been openly accused of war crimes and brought to justice (ibid.).

Another problem is that of who composes the *gacaca* jury. According to the design of *gacaca*, the courts are organized at the *cellule* and *secteur* levels with *inyangamugayo* elected by the local community. It would seem unlikely, then, that recent immigrants from the Tutsi diaspora would find themselves on *gacaca* juries, and yet this does occur. Moreover, some observers who have closely followed *gacaca* proceedings claim that juries presided over by Anglophone Tutsi, that is, Tutsi who in all likelihood recently immigrated to Rwanda from Uganda, are harsher than juries presided over by Hutu or Francophone Tutsi (Tutsi who resided in Rwanda prior to the genocide). Although at this point a systematic study that would elucidate this point is lacking, this is a troubling hypothesis. It is, however, one that is echoed by several expatriate Rwandans (Tutsi and Hutu) whom I have interviewed in the United States and others who continue to reside in Rwanda.

There is indeed a perception on the part of many Hutu that *gacaca* is vengeance and retribution masquerading as restoration. Furthermore, some of the *gacaca* judges have been corrupted (Burnet, 2008). This is hardly a surprising result as none receives remuneration. Rwandans report that some innocent Hutu have received long prison sentences, while others against whom the evidence was compelling have been acquitted after paying a bribe (Human Rights Watch, 2011). On the other hand, there are also cases to the contrary – innocent Hutu liberated by *gacaca* after a long period of incarceration (see later discussion). Abuses of *gacaca* may very well contribute to the fact that many Hutu witnesses brought before the tribunals are wont to dissimulate and equivocate when questions are asked of them, while truthful testimony is rare (see also Rettig, 2008, pp. 25–50). Rwanda does not have the equivalent of the U.S. Fifth Amendment, so witnesses must speak. But when they speak, they are likely either to feign ignorance or simply to lie.

Let me discuss some cases that illustrate some of *gacaca*'s shortcomings. One man who had been summoned in 2005 in Butare to give testimony before a *gacaca* court during the information gathering phase was asked what he had seen in his daily journey from his residence a fair distance away from Butare to the center of the town where he worked as a waiter in a restaurant. He responded: "It was a very troubled time. Many things were happening." When asked about the specifics, he was conveniently unable to provide any details. His answers were consistently vague. He had something with him, however, that he hoped would clarify matters and that he wanted the participants to see. It was a small sketchbook, which he referred to as the "story of my life." He leafed through the pages showing the sketches to the *gacaca* jurors present, most of whom grinned mockingly while others openly expressed exasperation. After close to an hour of this, everyone was tired of it. The witness was dismissed, no further questions.

Another witness was a woman who had been employed at the Butare hospital where many Tutsi patients had been killed. Working as a nurse during the time that people were being killed at the hospital meant that she almost certainly had either participated in the killings or been complicit in some way. When asked about this she said, "No, I was not present at the hospital at any time when killings occurred." When asked about where had she been, she replied, "I was at home." She had not seen anything; she did not know anything. And this despite the fact that other witnesses had already testified that they had seen her at the hospital during the period in question. "The witnesses are wrong," she said. "Who was your supervisor during the genocide?" a judge asked. "Sosthene Munyemana," she replied. The judge continued, "Do you know if he participated in any of the killings?" She answered, "It is possible that he did, but I had nothing to do with them."

Sosthene Munyemana is a Rwandan medical doctor with whom I have had conversations in France, and who presently resides near Bordeaux with his Tutsi wife and their five children. During much of the genocide he continued to serve as one of the chief physicians at the Butare hospital. He is suspected of having abetted or participated in the killings of hundreds of Tutsi in the hospital and near his home village of Tumbo. On several occasions, he has appeared before courts in France accused of involvement in the genocide. Though so far he has not been convicted of any genocidal crime, he continues to face legal problems. In the preceding case, the nurse's strategy seemed to be, when all else fails, deflect attention and blame onto an even bigger fish.

In another *gacaca* session in the village of Tumbo, very close to Butare, a man in his late twenties or early thirties stood before a large assembly of residents to give testimony. Several people present identified him as one of the ringleaders of an Interahamwe group who had traveled to Tumbo to seek out and kill Tutsi and Hutu moderates. "I saw you at Munyakazi's house," one witness stated. "When you and your companions left, everyone in the house had been killed."

Another witness added, "I saw you at Butera's house. Some were killed; some were left for dead, but survived; and all of their livestock and many of their belongings were stolen." This went on for quite sometime with several people offering stories of their own about the man before them. He stood before them with his hat clutched behind his back and his head slightly bowed, trying to look as unmenacing and humble as possible. "You weren't so well-behaved on the days when you came and killed people in Tumbo," someone shouted. "You are all mistaken," he said. "It must have been someone else who looked like me." "Oh, it was you all right!" someone interjected. And so it continued.

Although I was assured by some Rwandans that witnesses called before *gacaca* occasionally did something other than lie and dissimulate, I did not observe this in the sessions that I attended in 2005. I attended more than a dozen sessions and listened to many witnesses. Not one gave valuable testimony and it seemed to me, not one told the truth.

More recently during the spring of 2009, I returned to Rwanda and was able to observe a few *gacaca* tribunals, although *gacaca* is winding down and there are fewer trials. One of the tribunals took place in the Kigali suburb of Gikongo. I attended this session with a Tutsi woman named Daphrose, who had been very close to being killed during the genocide when soldiers and Interahamwe went to her home on several occasions. Managing to escape when a close Hutu friend rescued her and other family members, she returned to Rwanda after the genocide had run its course. Unlike many Tutsi survivors, she made it a point to attend as many *gacaca* sessions as she could. This was in sharp contrast to her sister, Anne-Marie, who possessed a cynical attitude toward *gacaca* and never attended any sessions. I found this attitude to be common among some Tutsi survivors. They reasoned that *gacaca* only exposes survivors to more humiliation and can even expose them to danger. If one speaks up at *gacaca*, one is identified as a potential witness who could bring about the imprisonment of a former Interahamwe member still at liberty. A friend, a family member, or the implicated Interahamwe might then try to kill the witness. I heard stories from Rwandans of witness killings of this sort, and one day while listening to a Rwandan radio station, I heard the murder of a witness announced on the news.

After I had attended a *gacaca* session with Daphrose, she began to tell me about her ordeal during and after the genocide. She had been very close to being killed and sexually assaulted during the violence. On one occasion a Rwandan government soldier ordered her to remove her clothes and then told her to lie down on her bed. Sitting at the foot of the bed, he pointed the rifle barrel directly at her vagina saying that he was going to shoot through her body. In effect, this would have resulted in the equivalent of a vagina to mouth impalement, an atrocity that some women suffered during the genocide, but by spear (see Taylor, 1999, for a discussion of the symbology of anus to mouth and vagina to mouth impalement). She pleaded with the soldier to kill her in some other fashion so as to leave her with at least a modicum of dignity. Unexpectedly, the soldier decided not to kill her, but before he left he said that others would arrive soon enough and that they would kill her. A day or so later other soldiers arrived and one of them took her to her bedroom ordering her to disrobe so that he could have sex with her. She concocted a story that she was HIV positive and that she did not wish to have his death on her soul when it came time for her to answer to God. The soldier thought about this for a moment and then did not rape her.

Because of what she had endured during the genocide, Daphrose felt that attendance at *gacaca* was necessary for the improvement of her psychological equilibrium. She also believed that it was her civic duty to help bring the perpetrators to justice. As for her mental health, she described a symptom that she referred to as *guhahamuka*. Later I would encounter this term in the stories told to me by several other Rwandan survivors. Most of them described it as a constricted feeling in the chest, a sensation that one cannot breathe properly, that the heart is out of place, and that the air one has inhaled remains trapped in the chest. Others described it as a feeling that prevents words from correctly exiting the mouth. Literally the term means "to speak while trembling," "to be unable to speak because of fear," or "to be in the grips of extreme fear."

Related to *guhahamuka* is the Rwandan folk syndrome termed *ihaha-muka*, whose chief symptom is shortness of breath. Rare before the geno-cide, *ihahamuka* has become quite common among genocide survivors (see Hagengimana & D. Hinton, 2009). *Ihahamuka* is the noun form of the verb *guhahamuka*. It names the state of being characterized by *guhahamuka*. For example, a Rwandan might say, *nahahamutse* and that would mean: "I am paralyzed by fear. I can't breathe properly. My breath and my words are caught in my chest." *Ihahamuka* is not simple fear. The term for fear in Kinyarwanda is *ubwoba*. *Ihahamuka* is an emotion that blocks your breath and your words.

Several survivors whom I interviewed told me that attending *gacaca* helped to relieve them of the feeling of *guhahamuka*. Other researchers who have worked on *gacaca* have also noted the frequent use of the word *guhahamuka* (Burnet, 2008). The term connotes obstruction and in that respect is quite close to one of the root metaphors that I hypothesize char-acterizes Rwandan traditional healing, a metaphor that opposes normal flows of bodily substances to abnormal flows (blockages, aborted flows, hemorrhagic flows) (Taylor, 1992). Undoubtedly, Western medical nos-ology would group the various symptoms termed *ihahamuka* under the rubric of posttraumatic stress disorder (PTSD), but this would obscure what is Rwandan about it. In effect, the survivors were somaticizing the experience of having endured extreme terror, but they were doing so in a culturally specific way related to their notions about the body (see Hagengimana & D. Hinton, 2009, for a discussion of how *ihahamuka* as blockage creates ontological resonances that reach from the body – as in shortness of breath, blockage of breath – into multiple other ontological domains, including trauma memory). *Gacaca*, then, despite its "messi-ness," has provided psychological relief for some survivors. This may be in part because justice is locally perceived as a means by which proper flows can be restored through the exchange of dialogue, the unearthing of truth, and the reconstitution of social order. Where crime and trans-gression disrupt the flow of social life and, concomitantly, flows of the body, justice heals.

I met Daphrose at her home and we took a taxi to a municipal office about ten minutes drive away. There a few dozen people were already waiting for the proceedings to begin. Two prison guards armed with rifles were also present guarding a prisoner dressed in a bright pink shirt with matching shorts, the standard prison uniform. The prisoner wore no restraints of any kind on his hands or feet. We waited at the municipal office for close to an hour, but it was clear that other business was being conducted in the office and that they were not about to curtail their activities to yield the building to a *gacaca* group. After a while the guards arose and, along with the prisoner, began walking away. I learned that the *gacaca* for that day would take place at a nearby school, which happened to be closed for the weekend. By the time we arrived there, a larger crowd was milling around, obviously uncomfortable about having to stand in the sunlight. Someone produced keys to the school building and soon chairs and tables were carried out. One participant began to speak, stating that it was not right that so many people had assembled and that to all appearances, the *gacaca* president and the other *inyangamugayo* had not bothered to come, nor to tell anyone that they were not coming (a not unusual occurrence, I was told, where *gacaca* was concerned). Soon, however, four *inyangamugayo* appeared, readily identifiable by the sashes worn over their shoulders. The trial could begin.

In this case the prisoner had requested the *gacaca* in order to confess his crimes and, he hoped, to receive clemency from the court. He had signed a statement while in prison. The statement was read by one of the judges. Then, people present began to advance their opinions. Many of the comments resembled this one: "We saw the prisoner and other Interahamwe at such and such a place and at such and such a time. People were killed there. Why doesn't he mention this? What about this other incident also not mentioned in his confession?" And so on.

The air of incredulity among the audience appeared to be shared by the *inyangamugayo*. One of them asked the prisoner, "Were you a member of the Interahamwe?" "No," he replied, "I had some Interahamwe friends but I never joined the organization." (This was possible in a technical sense as not all who participated in the genocidal violence were necessarily official members of the youth group associated with President Habyarimana's party, the MRND.) "Did you accompany them when they went to people's houses to rob and kill them?" a judge asked.

"Yes, I accompanied them in some instances, but I never took part in the violence," he replied. "But one witness claims to have seen you holding a rifle while you and other Interahamwe were at Kavumbi's house?" "Yes, I was holding a rifle. My companions were busying themselves with people in the other rooms in the house, but I remained by myself in the front room. I was simply acting as a guard. Someone handed me a rifle, but because I did not know how to use it, I merely held it in my hands." And so it continued. "Yes, I had Interahamwe friends and accompanied them on occasion during the genocide, but I never participated in any of the violence." "So what exactly are you confessing then?" a judge asked. This continued for some time. The accused admitted nothing save having been an accessory. The judges then withdrew to consider his plea. Finally, the session ended with a rejection of his appeal for clemency.

He was advised to resubmit a more truthful appeal in the future, one that enumerated all that he had seen and done.

This prisoner's behavior may stem from the hope that if one continues to deny them and no witness comes forward, one's crimes will be unrecognized. Or it may stem from the conviction that the promise of clemency is an empty one. Yet this is belied by the number of former genocide participants who have indeed received it. Despite this, many Hutu see *gacaca* only as victor's justice. At a *gacaca* session that I attended in the Kigali community of Biryogo during the spring of 2009, this sentiment was voiced by several who were present there. These latter had attended to observe proceedings involving a prisoner who was on trial for violence during 1994 that had not been brought to light until 2006 when he appeared before a *gacaca* court for the first time. The accused was present and dressed in the bright pink uniform of prison inmates. Two armed prison guards were also present, but they manifested little anxiety that the prisoner would try to escape or that his supporters in the audience might try to free him by force. The crime that he was being tried for that day was having participated at a barrier in the Biryogo section of Kigali and having attempted to kill a Tutsi woman there. The woman was present at the trial as a witness and would later give her testimony.

From the accusation read at the *gacaca* trial, a process that took well more than an hour, it appeared that the accused in question had been something of a political opportunist. A member of one of the democratic parties opposed to Habyarimana before the genocide, he was said to have become an Interahamwe after it started. During the genocide he was observed ferrying other Interahamwe around in a stolen car and taking them to places where people had been killed. After the genocide, it seemed that no witnesses were around to denounce him as an Interahamwe when he returned to Kigali in 1998. (Almost everyone fled Kigali at about the time the RPF took the city in 1994.) He even managed to secure a low-level functionary position in the local government. From that time on he had manifested support for the new government. In 2006, however, he was implicated at a *gacaca* session when it came to light that his past had not been unblemished. He had participated in the genocide on the side of the Interahamwe, had aided and abetted them, and had shared in the spoils looted from their victims. He was jailed at that time. But the charges of 2009 were more serious; he had been more than an accessory. He had assaulted Tutsi during the genocide and had more than likely killed some of them. Though he denied this, a Tutsi woman was present who had endured violence at his hands in 1994.

According to her she had been stopped at the barrier where the accused was serving. She endured the usual harassments. Asked for her

ID card, she claimed to have lost it. She was then accused of being an *icyitso* (traitor), the term commonly used for Tutsi. The accused took all the money and valuables on her and then began to beat her with a club, knocking her unconscious. Assuming that she was dead, he or someone else pulled her off to the side of the road and left her there with others. Miraculously, she managed to survive. When she recovered consciousness hours or days later, the barrier was no longer present, but murdered people were lying all around her. RPF soldiers were closing in on Kigali at the time and it was possible for her to make her way to the RPF lines. It was in this way that she was rescued. She had not been present at the 2006 trial of the accused because she was not living in Kigali at the time. Later she heard that her assailant was in prison and that he was attempting to gain a reprieve. No evidence had yet been presented that he had actually killed or assaulted anyone. For this reason she decided to participate in the 2009 *gacaca*.

During a break in the proceedings I chatted with three women who were in their early twenties. They approached me and between their broken French and my broken Kinyarwanda, we managed a conversation. One of the women was the daughter of the accused. Two were her neighbors and close friends. The women wondered where I was from and when I told them, they asked whether I could find a "correspondent" for them. The French term *correspondent* could be translated as pen pal, and that is at least part of what the term means when used by Rwandans. However, it also carries the hope that the pen pal will become a "sponsor" and enable the Rwandan to go to the United States to obtain an education, a well-paying job, and a better life. From there we moved on to the subject of *gacaca*. One of the women said that this *gacaca* court was a severe one and that her own father had been condemned to a heavy sentence by it several months prior to today's trial. She did not think that the accused would be shown mercy in this case and believed that the outcome was likely to be harsh. She and her companions stated that they thought *gacaca* was just a way for Tutsi to take revenge on Hutu.

After a few hours of proceedings in this case, the *inyangamugayo* – two men and two women readily distinguishable by the sashes they wore over their shoulders – withdrew to a private space. After about an hour of deliberation, they returned and pronounced the verdict: an additional seventeen years in prison. Later I saw the prisoner walking back to the Kigali prison with his two guards. He was not wearing restraints of any kind and passers-by from the neighborhood were occasionally walking up to him to chat. The guards sometimes joined in the conversation and did not seem nervous or impatient. I was surprised by their nonchalance.

As others who had attended this *gacaca* session were walking away, I talked to a few of them. Although one echoed the feelings of the young women discussed previously, three other people with whom I spoke thought that the *gacaca* in this case had done its job well. Because the accused had continued to lie about his role in the genocide and had not made a confession, he merited the additional prison time. He was getting off lightly, according to one, his life having been spared even though he himself had probably killed.

Another case, the case of Venant, is interesting because a *gacaca* tribunal liberated him from prison. Venant and other members of his family resided near Butare. At the time I met him in 2009, he was employed in Kigali. In 1994 he had been a student in Ruhengeri (a city in northern Rwanda, now renamed Musanze). When violence broke out in Kigali on April 6, 1994, his school closed. Having no reason to remain in Ruhengeri and concerned about family members in Butare, he searched for a way of getting back there. He managed to hitch a ride with an RGF officer. When he arrived in Butare, violence had not yet begun, as the prefect, who was Tutsi, had prevented it. But the calm did not last long. In late April, the prefect was assassinated and soon the genocide against Tutsi began. Though Venant himself was not Tutsi, a few members of his extended family were killed. Fearing for his own life, Venant decided to flee to Burundi. He did not stay there long. Just a few weeks after the RPF had succeeded in expelling the last Rwandan Government Forces into Zaire, Venant returned to his family's small plot of land near Butare. At first he encountered no problem from local officials. They did not believe that he had been an Interahamwe, nor that he had participated in the violence.

Some time in 1995, however, the situation changed. A neighbor decided to denounce him as an Interahamwe. Venant says that he does not understand why this neighbor acted in this way. At any rate he was arrested and put in prison. He remained there for eleven years. By 2005, however, *gacaca* was well under way in the Butare area. He decided to appeal to a *gacaca* court. His first efforts were not successful, but this was due to procedural difficulties. The appropriate witnesses had not been contacted or could not be found or some other minor problem occurred. By 2006, however, his luck changed. More thorough examination of his case revealed that there was no one who could back up the claim of the malicious neighbor. No one in the area where his family resided had seen him commit any crime during the genocide and no one had witnessed him giving aid or support of any kind to those who were committing violence. No one could say that he belonged to a group such as the Interahamwe. He was completely exonerated and released. He received no compensation for his time in prison, but at least he was free. For that reason in his discussion with me in 2009, he felt that *gacaca* was doing its job and that although it had been very slow in his case, it had ended by doing the right thing. He bore no malice toward anyone after all of this, because as he sees it, virtually all Rwandans have suffered because of the genocide and some have suffered even more than he.

Rwandans' Opinions

How Rwandans assess the efficacy of *gacaca* in rebuilding their nation varies immensely. Although further research is needed to clarify this, there are some general patterns that I observed in people's statements during the spring of 2009. Among Rwandan Tutsi who were not living in the country before or during the genocide and who recently immigrated to it – refugees from the 1960s and 1970s or their descendants (sometimes referred to as "new Rwandans") – one tends to encounter a favorable evaluation of *gacaca*. Most qualify their remarks, but say that *gacaca* has been successful on the whole. For them it has been good to see that not all Hutu joined in the killings. They are relieved that they need not have a categorical fear of Hutu.

Critical attitudes among Tutsi toward *gacaca* are more likely to be found among those who were present in Rwanda during the genocide and who managed to survive (about 20 percent or so of the pregenocide Tutsi population). Their opposition to *gacaca* spills over at times into hostility toward the "new Rwandans," whom they sometimes refer to as "conquerors." Many of them ask, If the RPF had not invaded Rwanda in 1990, would there have been a genocide in 1994? Survivors' attitudes toward *gacaca* are sometimes cynical. Although some, like Daphrose, discussed earlier, regularly attend *gacaca* meetings and will give testimony at them, it is not uncommon among survivors, like Anne-Marie, mentioned previously, to avoid *gacaca* sessions. They say that their former persecutors are able to witness their pain yet again and if they demonstrate specific knowledge about genocidal crimes, they expose themselves to violence. This is not an idle fear, as I have pointed out. Some Tutsi survivors, despite having had ample opportunity, have never attended *gacaca* at all. Attendance, supposedly obligatory, is very irregular, especially after several years of it. These latter claim that *gacaca* possesses an advantage for Hutu perpetrators, because they can receive clemency just by confessing, and that "new Rwandans" also have something to gain because then the genocide can be whitewashed, forgotten, and the "new Rwandans" can get on with the business of making money. But among these survivors there are those who speak as if there were no measure of atonement that could ever satisfy them. More recent Tutsi immigrants often express impatience with these "inconsolables." They ask questions like "How often do we need to be reminded of the genocide? When can normal life resume?"

Among Hutu, attitudes are also varied. Many who did not participate in genocidal crimes or only in crimes against property, welcomed *gacaca*, at least at first. To them, individuals were responsible for genocidal crimes and not an entire ethnic group. To these people it was necessary to identify the guilty, determine the measures of redress, and then get on with life. Other Hutu see *gacaca* as something verging on a "witch hunt" and point to instances when innocent people like Venant received lengthy prison terms. They condemn corrupt *gacaca* judges who have accepted bribes and cite occasions when *gacaca* has been used to settle personal scores unrelated to the genocide. They resent the interference of the Rwandan central government in *gacaca* and its use as a punitive tool to silence those who have openly criticized the government. Many are quick to point to the reprisal crimes committed by RPF members and RPA soldiers and the government's unwillingness to bring these people to justice.

Conclusion

Gacaca has a mixed record with some successes, but overall it has not succeeded in its most important goals. Many innocents have been liberated from Rwanda's overcrowded jails, many people guilty of genocidal crimes have been brought to justice, and *gacaca* has given psychological relief to many victims. But the trials have not contributed to the deethnicization of Rwanda's political life. If anything, *gacaca* has deepened ethnic resentments and increased the likelihood that there will be more violence in the future.

Gacaca has shown that the present government is content to accept a double standard where genocidal crimes and RPA war crimes are concerned. The former are liable to prosecution; the latter can be ignored. This does little to efface the pernicious but unstated dichotomy: Tutsi as survivors occupy the moral high ground; Hutu as perpetrators do not. During the colonial era, alleged Tutsi superiority was said to be intellectual in nature; now it is seen as moral.

In the last years of the nineteenth century before the arrival of Europeans, Rwanda was a land where the Tutsi monarchy and other high-ranking Tutsi enjoyed considerable privilege, in sharp contrast to the Hutu majority, many of whom could barely survive (Vansina, 2000). This inequality did not change appreciably during the colonial era. Instead it became bureaucratized through the indirect rule state apparatus, preferential schooling, and ethnically marked ID cards. Nevertheless, some Hutu, largely through the Rwandan Catholic Church, managed to obtain higher education. An educated Hutu elite emerged. With the aid of the Catholic Church and an abrupt change on the part of Belgian colonials, they were able to overthrow the Tutsi dominated system in the late 1950s and early 1960s. But this merely changed Rwanda into a Hutu dominated state with a Hutu autocrat at the helm. Habyarimana's coup in 1973 and his subsequent twenty-one years of rule were lighter-handed than his predecessor, Kayibanda's, but they did little to depoliticize ethnicity. Ethnic labels continued to be marked on everyone's ID card and one's ethnicity largely determined one's chances in life.

Before the RPF succeeded in stopping the genocide in 1994 and winning the war against the Hutu extremist government, high-level spokespersons in the organization had promised that their vision of a new Rwanda was one where ethnicity would no longer play an important role. This has not happened. Although there is no longer anything on one's ID card that indicates ethnicity, one's chances in life are still strongly influenced by it, just as they were under Habyarimana, Kayibanda, and before them, the Tutsi kings. *Gacaca*, had it been better planned, been better implemented, and experienced less interference from the central government, might have been able to aid in the neutralization of ethnicity in Rwanda. In that it has failed. Restorative justice has not triumphed over retribution and vengeance. It is as if Rwanda were perpetually unable to escape its perverse repetitive structures. The contradiction between the rhetoric of its present rulers and the situation on the ground has more tragic potential than that of the Nuer's homeostasis versus expansion, as it could lead to another genocide. *Gacaca* is showing that in today's Rwanda the high ideals of the RPF revolution have largely been abandoned.

BIBLIOGRAPHY

Anderson, B. (1991). *Imagined communities: Reflections on the origin and spread of nationalism*. London & New York: Verso.
Burnet, J. (2008). The (in)justice of local justice: Truth, reconciliation and revenge in Rwanda's gacaca. *Genocide Studies and Prevention*, 3, 173–93.
Evans-Pritchard, E. (1940). *The Nuer*. Oxford, UK: Clarendon Press.
Gellner, E. (1997). *Nationalism*. New York: New York University Press.
Hagengimana, A., & Hinton, D. (2009). *Ihahamuka*, a Rwandan syndrome of response to the genocide: Blocked flow, spirit assault, and shortness of breath. In D. Hinton & B. Good (Eds.), *Culture and Panic Disorder* (pp. 205–29). Stanford, CA: Stanford University Press.

Haskell, L. (2011). *Justice compromised: The legacy of Rwanda's community-based gacaca Courts.* New York: Human Rights Watch.

Hinton, A. (1998). A head for an eye: Revenge in the Cambodian genocide. *The American Ethnologist,* 25, 352–77.

Hinton, A. (2010). Introduction: Toward an anthropology of transitional justice. In A. Hinton (Ed.), *Transitional justice: Global mechanisms and local realities after genocide and mass violence* (pp. 1–22). Rutgers, NJ: Rutgers University Press.

Human Rights Watch (2011). *World Report 2011: Events of 2010.* New York: Human Rights Watch.

Lemarchand, R. (2009). *The dynamics of violence in Central Africa.* Philadelphia: University of Pennsylvania Press.

Longman, T. (2009). An assessment of Rwanda's *gacaca* courts. *Peace Review,* 21, 304–12.

Prunier, G. (1995). *The Rwanda crisis: History of a genocide.* New York: Columbia University Press.

Rettig, M. (2008). *Gacaca:* Truth, justice, and reconciliation in postconflict Rwanda? *African Studies Review,* 51, 25–50.

Reyntjens, F. (1990). Le gacaca ou la justice du gazon au Rwanda. *Politique Africaine,* 40, 31–41.

Sahlins, M. (1968). *Tribesmen.* Englewood Cliffs, NJ: Prentice Hall.

Schabas, W. (2005). Genocide trials and *gacaca* courts. *Journal of International Criminal Justice,* 3, 1–17.

Taylor, C. (1992). *Milk, honey, and money: Changing concepts of illness in Rwandan traditional medicine.* Washington, DC: Smithsonian Institution Press.

Taylor, C. (1999). *Sacrifice as terror: The Rwandan genocide of 1994.* Oxford, UK: Berg Press.

Tutu, D. (1999). *No future without forgiveness.* New York: Doubleday.

Uvin, P. (n.d.) The introduction of a modernized *gacaca* for judging suspects of participation in the genocide and the massacres of 1994 in Rwanda. Discussion paper prepared for the Belgian Secretary of State for Development and Cooperation.

Vansina, J. (2000). *Le Rwanda ancien: Le royaume nyiginya.* Paris: Karthala.

Wilson, R. (2001). *The politics of truth and reconciliation in South Africa: Legitimizing the post-apartheid state.* Cambridge and New York: Cambridge University Press.

14 Pasts Imperfect: Talking about Justice with Former Combatants in Colombia

Kimberly Theidon

"That's the most difficult thing for someone to understand about Colombia. The reason why all of us from the same country – between families, friends, neighbors – why we have to have a war. In the end, we don't know why we have it. Before we had it clear – people fought for a town, for a party, for poverty, for I don't know what all. For thousands of things. But now we don't have it clear why there's this war, and the war now just goes from revenge to revenge. That's how this war goes." – Juan, former combatant, FARC, December 2006

Introduction

A key component of peace processes and postconflict reconstruction is the disarmament, demobilization, and reintegration (DDR) of excombatants. According to the World Bank, in 2005 more than one million former combatants were participating in DDR programs in some twenty countries around the world at an estimated cost of $1.9 billion. DDR is big business, and it is serious business: Both livelihoods and lives are at stake.

Elsewhere I have argued that DDR programs imply multiple transitions: from the combatants who lay down their weapons, to the governments that seek an end to armed conflict, to the communities that receive – or reject – these demobilized fighters (Theidon, 2007, 2009). These transitions inevitably imply a complex and dynamic tension between the demands of peace and the clamor for justice. And yet, traditional approaches to DDR have focused almost exclusively on military and security objectives, a focus that in turn has caused these programs to be developed in relative isolation from the growing field of transitional justice and its concerns with historical clarification, justice, reparations, and reconciliation. Similarly, evaluations of DDR programs have tended to be technocratic exercises concerned with tallying the number of weapons collected and combatants enrolled. By reducing DDR to "dismantling the machinery of war," these programs have not considered adequately how to move beyond demobilizing combatants to facilitating social reconstruction and coexistence (Knight, Michael, & Ozerdem, 2004, p. 2).

Drawing upon ongoing research with former combatants in Colombia, I extend these arguments by considering how the stories of rank and file ex-combatants might contribute to transitioning from violence and working toward sustainable peace. A key challenge following mass violence is what to do with the thousands of low-level perpetrators whose sheer numbers may overwhelm the legal system and whose return to civilian life may generate tremendous fear and resentment. In this exploratory chapter, I discuss how these former combatants conceptualize justice, forgiveness, and reconciliation – concepts that are central concerns to the growing field of transitional justice.

From the post–World War II tribunals at Nuremberg and Tokyo to the proliferation of tribunals and truth commissions in the present, a genealogy of transitional justice illustrates how the field has both expanded and normalized (see Teitel, 2000, 2003). The burgeoning of transitional justice is often associated with the post–Cold War political climate in which a significant number of authoritarian and frequently violent nation-states began to transition toward peace and procedural democracy (for a general discussion, see Hayner, 2001). The massive scale of damage characteristic of these postconflict settings, the breakdown of legal and social institutions, and the destruction of social solidarity and civic trust indicated the need for innovations in the administration of justice. Frequently the traditional mechanisms of justice, designed to address occasional rather than chronic deviations from legal norms, failed to meet this challenge, and, with equal frequency, the legal institutions of the countries themselves had played a role in promoting or sanctioning human rights violations (see Teitel, 2000). Thus the innovative judicial and legal measures known as transitional justice sought to realign societies with norms consistent with the rule of law, respect for human rights, and liberal democracy (for further discussion, see Laplante & Theidon, 2007).

As transitional justice has expanded, so have the goals of its proponents. One area of inquiry has focused on which transitional justice mechanisms are best suited to assisting countries and their citizens in recovering from prolonged violent conflicts in which the enemy is often the government, or one's family members and neighbors (see Theidon 2004, 2012). Thus reconciliation was added to the transitional justice agenda, though remaining elusive both as a concept and as a goal.

Ethnographers of reconciliation processes have underscored the contradictory logics at work when introducing a politics of scale into one's analysis (Biggar, 2003; Borneman, 2002, 2003; Shaw 2005; Theidon 2004; Wilson 2003a, 2003b). What these studies demonstrate is the need for place-based analyses of transitional justice that permit academics and practitioners to capture locally and regionally salient definitions of justice, reparations, and reconciliation. In addition to allowing policy makers to design more relevant and effective interventions, these studies emphasize that transitions in the political realm must be accompanied by transformations at the subjective and interpersonal levels.

Among the transformations that interest me are the relationships these former combatants have to their violent pasts and to their imagined futures. How do these men and women talk about killing, about the possibility of justice, about living once again as and among civilians? Most truth-telling endeavors have focused on victims, reflecting the fact that one explicit goal of truth commissions is the writing of new national narratives that are more inclusive of groups that have been historically marginalized within the nation-state. In her influential discussion of postconflict issues, Martha Minow (1998) writes: "The most distinctive element of truth commissions, in comparison with prosecution, is the focus on victims, including forgotten victims in forgotten places" (p. 60). In contrast to legal proceedings and the aggressive questioning that characterizes them, truth commissions are considered "victim-centered" or "victim-friendly" because they include empathic listening rather than an adversarial hermeneutics of suspicion (see Hayner, 2001).

Without denying the importance of listening empathetically to victims – a group that is frequently made vulnerable as a result of structural inequalities and multiple forms of discrimination – I insist on the need to listen to the accounts of low-level perpetrators as well. Listening to both victims and perpetrators, and to those who blur the categories, is crucial to constructing "departures from violence" (see Borneman 2002, 2003). To date in Colombia the "transition" has been decidedly top-down, and the public face of the paramilitaries and the guerrilla groups are the high-level officials who have either provided "confessions" in hopes of avoiding extradition or dominated the media with their deaths. Missing from the public sphere are the stories of "ordinary combatants" who are key actors in rebuilding – or undermining – coexistence.

I begin with an overview of the Colombian political context and the challenges of implementing DDR and transitional justice measures in a "prepostconflict" setting. I then turn to my conversations with former combatants to explore how they understand justice and revenge, noting the importance of *conciencia* – conscience and consciousness – in their narratives. I follow this section with an analysis of their comments on reconciliation, including both the horizontal and vertical aspects of the term.[1] I conclude with recommendations on how and why DDR programs would benefit from considering the ways in which former combatants understand justice, forgiveness, and reconciliation in their own lives.

Colombia: A "Prepostconflict" Country

Colombia's civil war is the lengthiest armed conflict in the Western Hemisphere. What began almost five decades ago as a war waged by Marxist revolutionaries against an exclusive political system has devolved into a bloody struggle over resources: Military, paramilitary, guerrillas, domestic elites, and multinational actors vie for control of this resource-rich country.[2] In the struggle, all groups have committed serious human rights violations. Among the armed groups that are of particular interest to our discussion of demobilization processes are the Fuerzas Armadas Revolucionarias de Colombia (FARC), the Ejército de Liberación Nacional (ELN), and the Auto-Defensas Unidas de Colombia (AUC), commonly referred to as the paramilitaries.

The FARC is Colombia's oldest and largest guerrilla group, established in 1964. The FARC has its roots in the rural self-defense groups that were organized during La Violencia.[3] From its beginnings as a primarily rural based guerrilla movement, the FARC grew in both size and influence. With time, the Marxist ideology that had been a key component of its foundation ceded to a desire for territorial control and wealth. The FARC has financed itself through kidnapping, extortion, drug trafficking, and drug trade protection. In the eyes of their many critics, the FARC have become one more violent armed actor rather than a revolutionary alternative.

The second largest guerrilla movement is the ELN, which began operations in 1964. Unlike the rural FARC, the ELN was mostly an outgrowth of university unrest. The ELN's ideology, which has traditionally been considered a mixture of Cuban revolutionary theory with liberation theology, began calling for a Christian and Communist solution to the problems of poverty, political exclusion, and corruption. However, discourse and action again diverged, as the ELN lost its focus and began engaging in illegal activities to finance its actions. At present the ELN has an estimated thirty-five hundred to four thousand combatants and since July 2004 has been in sporadic peace negotiations with the Colombian government. However, as with the FARC, the ELN appears on the U.S. list of terrorist organizations. And there is another group that was placed on that same list in September 2001: the paramilitaries.

The terms "paramilitary organization" and "self-defense group" have been used to describe a variety of armed groups over the past several decades. As Winifred Tate notes, paramilitary organizations have evolved considerably since the 1960s, when U.S. military advisers first recommended the organization of "indigenous irregulars" as a fundamental component of the Colombian counterinsurgency strategy, then aimed at defeating leftist guerrilla movements (see Tate, 2007). Thus began the complicated relationship among the Colombian state, the United States government, and the alternately legal and illegal armed groups known collectively as the paramilitaries.[4] Although promoted as "self-defense committees" founded to protect local communities against the guerrillas, they came to assume greater responsibility in state-organized "search and destroy" operations seeking to eliminate the guerrillas. The use of paramilitaries as auxiliary forces assumed a central place in the government's counterinsurgency plan. Additionally, paramilitary groups would become regional elites' preferred option for protecting their interests and suppressing social protests (see García-Peña, 2009).

The 1970s and 1980s were decades in which the drug trade grew in Colombia, first with marijuana and then with cocaine. This was the fabled era of the Medellín and Cali cartels, personified by Pablo Escobar and his nouveau riche excesses (Dudley, 2003). These cartels provided a perverse but lucrative twist on the concept of family-owned businesses; within a few years, these family-based cartels controlled a billion dollar cocaine industry. It was the fusion of paramilitary organizations and drug trafficking that gave rise to the phenomenon known as *paramilitarismo* – the transformation of paramilitary groups into an economic, social, and political force that infiltrated Colombian society. Beyond the individual combatants who collectively organized into armed and lethal groups, *paramilitarismo* became a corrosive and insidious institution.

Disarmament, Demobilization, and Reintegration: Colombia's Serial Search for Peace

Throughout Colombia's lengthy internal armed conflict, each successive president has attempted some sort of military victory or, in the face of that impossibility, peace negotiations. While it is beyond the scope of this chapter to present an exhaustive review of these previous efforts, there are certain key features that warrant our attention and allow us to understand both the great challenges and the possibilities that the current demobilization process poses.

In the glossary of postconflict reconstruction and peace building, three terms are omnipresent: disarmament, demobilization, and reintegration (United Nations Department of Peacekeeping Operations [UNDPKO], 1999). As UNDPKO defines it, in the context of peace processes, disarmament consists of the collection, control, and elimination of small arms, ammunition, explosives, and light and heavy weapons from the combatants and, depending upon the circumstances, the civilian population. Demobilization is the process in which armed organizations (which may consist of government or opposition forces) decrease in size or are dismantled as one component of a broad transformation from a state of war to a state of peace. Generally demobilization involves the concentration, quartering, disarming, management, and licensing of former combatants, who may receive some form of compensation or other assistance to motivate them to lay down their weapons and reenter civilian life. Finally, reinsertion or reintegration consists of those measures directed toward ex-combatants that seek to strengthen the capacity of these individuals and their families to achieve social and economic reintegration in society. The reinsertion programs may include economic assistance or some other form of monetary compensation, as well as technical or professional training or instruction in other productive activities.

In its traditional formulation – and implementation – DDR was squarely located within a military or security framework. This focus failed to give sufficient consideration to the host communities, and to the need to consider local, cultural, or gendered conceptions of what constitutes the rehabilitation and resocialization of ex-combatants. As Colletta, Kostner, and Wiederhofer (1996) have argued in their evaluation of DDR programs in Sub-Saharan Africa, "Long-term integration is ultimately the yardstick by which the success of the DDR programme is measured," and the widespread agreement that reintegration is the weakest phase of the DDR process has prompted demands for reform. The 2006 United Nations Integrated DDR Standards (UNIDDRS) underscored the deficiency of reintegration efforts and insisted on "the need for measures to be conducted in consultation and collaboration with all members of the community and stakeholders engaged in the community, and that [DDR programs] make use of locally-appropriate development incentives."[5]

A brief overview of past DDR efforts in Colombia provides ample evidence of each of the weaknesses listed in the DDR framework. Previous efforts to demobilize the guerrillas can best be summarized by the name of one of the laws that governed the demobilization process under the Betancur administration (1982–6). Law 35 was the Law of Unconditional Amnesty in Favor of Peace, reflecting a legal environment in which blanket amnesties were offered in exchange for "peace and stability." The legal treatment of the ex-combatants was "solved" with an approach described as *olvido y perdón en pro de la paz* (forgetting and pardon in favor of peace), a broad statement that left much room for interpretation – and for manipulation. In fact, the ex-combatants enjoyed complete amnesty. In addition to this trade-off, the government failed to consider what would happen to those guerrilla combatants who demobilized. For example, Law 35 formed the basis for the La Uribe Contract of 1984 in which the FARC agreed to a cease-fire and announced the foundation of a political party, the Unión Patriótica. However, after their demobilization and reconstitution as a legitimate political party, some three thousand members of the Unión Patriótica were assassinated by the paramilitaries.[6] The government proved incapable of guaranteeing the security of the ex-combatants, and this previous experience of demobilization – and subsequent slaughter – hovers over negotiations with the guerrilla groups today.

By the presidential elections of 2002, an increasing number of Colombians demanded change. The debacle of past peace processes readied many sectors of Colombian society for someone who would take a "heavy-handed" approach to the violence. Alvaro Uribe promised to be that man. President Uribe was not inclined to attempt dialogue with the FARC, whom he considered a "terrorist threat." Rather, Uribe cautiously explored the possibility of negotiating with the paramilitaries, while promising to rein in the guerrillas. There is a certain irony to these negotiations: In part the paramilitary demobilization was an attempt to "deparamilitarize" the Colombian state. Clearly earlier government initiatives to fill its absence with civilian defense committees went beyond the state's control. Thus at some juncture the government was destined to find itself negotiating peace not only with the guerrillas but with the paramilitaries as well (García-Peña, 2005, p. 66).

Thus in August 2002, the government began negotiations with the paramilitaries. The Uribe government promoted the demobilization of individual combatants from all armed groups and began negotiations for the collective demobilization of the AUC.[7] The government named Luis Carlos Restrepo as the high commissioner for peace, and gave him the task of negotiating peace. The signing of the *Santa Fe de Ralito I* agreement on July 15, 2003, marked the beginning of formal talks between the AUC-linked paramilitary groups and the government. The terms of the agreement included the demobilization of all combatants by the end of 2005, concentrating its leadership and troops in specified locations. The negotiations also obligated the AUC to suspend its lethal activities and maintain the unilateral cease-fire, as well as aid the government in its anti-drug-trafficking efforts.

The *Sante Fe de Ralito II* agreement, signed on May, 13, 2004, set up a 368 km² "concentration zone" (*zona de ubicación*) in Tierralta, Córdoba. The concentration zone was created to facilitate and consolidate the process between the government and the AUC, to improve verification of the cease-fire, and to establish a timetable for the demobilization process. Since 2002, 30,664 AUC combatants have collectively demobilized, and almost 21,000 combatants from the FARC, ELN, and certain paramilitary blocs have individually demobilized.[8]

In addition to the preceding initiatives, on July 22, 2005, President Uribe signed Law 975, the Justice and Peace Law. The law embodies the competing tensions of peace and justice, and victim-survivors' organizations succeeded in challenging certain key aspects of the law on the grounds that it failed to provide sufficient assurance of their right to truth, justice, and reparations. Under pressure from victim-survivors' organizations and domestic and international human rights organizations, the Colombian government was forced to modify the law; although still imperfect when measured by absolute human rights standards, the Colombian Constitutional Court ruling of May 2006 did serve to strengthen the law in response to these challenges. If at one time states wielded their sovereign prerogative to issue amnesties in the name of political expediency, stability, and peace – prerogatives that characterized past demobilization efforts in Colombia – changes in international norms increasingly place limits on the granting of leniency to perpetrators, forcing governments to address transitional justice issues of truth, justice, and redress. Thus the Colombian government has been forced to implement DDR on the terrain of transitional justice, which presents both opportunities and challenges.

Methodology

Since January 2005 I have been conducting anthropological research on the individual and collective demobilization programs.[9] The first stage of the project included in-depth interviews with demobilized combatants in order to determine where to focus my case studies. The analysis of these interviews led me to select three sites with the goal of capturing regional dynamics: the shelters and *fincas* (farms) in Bogotá and on the outskirts of the city; the Reference and Opportunity Centers (CRO) in Bogotá and Medellín, and two barrios in Medellín; and the CRO in Turbo as well as three development projects in Turbo-Apartado.[10] To date my research assistant and I have interviewed 236 male and 53 female excombatants from the AUC, the FARC, and the ELN.

In addition to interviewing ex-combatants, we have interviewed representatives of state entities and NGOs as well as the military, the Catholic and Evangelical Churches, and various sectors of the host communities. Clearly the unit of analysis and intervention must extend beyond the former combatants to include their social environment. Only then can we think of how to articulate DDR with transitional justice measures. I have used an ethnographic approach in the hope of moving beyond the black and white of statistics to explore the gray zone that characterizes the complex realities of a fratricidal war.

Speaking of Justice

Justice, like beauty, is in the eye of the beholder and can be interpreted in a variety of ways. (Stover & Weinstein, 2004, p. 4., in *My Neighbor, My Enemy: Justice and Community in the Aftermath of Mass Atrocity*)

I never killed anyone. I only killed enemies in combat. (a leitmotif with former combatants from each armed group)

There are approximately fifty-six thousand demobilized combatants in Colombia, but only some 5 percent will be tried under the Peace and Justice Law and given sentences that may include incarceration (Jaramillo, Giha, & Torres, 2009, p. 36). Consequently there is a sizable group of former combatants who will receive a de facto amnesty unless creative forms of accountability are developed for low-level perpetrators. What forms of accountability – and transformation – might be possible? Perhaps understanding how these men talk about killing and justice might provide us with a place to start.[11]

During my conversations with former combatants, I have lost count of the number of times someone has insisted, "I never killed anyone. I only killed enemies in combat." At this point I strive to open a space for empathy. I assure them that I admire the efforts they are making to change their lives, and that I know how difficult it is to do so. I then ask them for help with something that is difficult for me: "When I leave here, I work with many people who consider themselves victims of this war. I remember a woman I met in Medellín who lost five sons to this violence. Five sons! And when I sit with women like her and tell her about the time I spend with all of you, I am usually asked how I can stand it. For these mothers, you embody her pain – looking at you reminds her of how much she has lost and suffered. I try to think of something to say, and it is really difficult. So what would you say to her? What would you say to a mother who has buried so many people she loved?"

The questions are invariably followed by silence. Some men then say they would explain to her that these are "things that happen during war and everyone needs to accept that." Those men are the absolute minority. Most sit back, some cry, some look as though the wind was knocked out of them. Others simply run their hands through their hair and fidget in their chairs. My aim is to create some room to acknowledge that even if they justify the killing as part of combat, those they killed were indeed people and someone grieves for them. Recognition and reckoning can begin with putting a human face to those who died regardless of the reasons given for having killed them. In the men's reactions, perhaps I am witnessing an incipient form of accountability for one's actions; this may also signal a "re-emergence of conscience."[12]

It may be more accurate, however, to speak in terms of a change in *conciencia*, a change these men associate with leaving the war behind and building "civilian" or "legal" lives. *Conciencia* (conscience or consciousness) figures prominently in our conversations, and it has various significations. It can refer to being *concientizado* by the armed group to which one belonged, with this *concientización* being a key component of the indoctrination they received. *Conciencia* also references the degree to which one was aware of his own actions and, in turn, informs the assessment of how responsible the individual is for what he or she has done. Finally, many of these former combatants differentiate between those who demobilized because of orders received versus those who have truly demobilized *por conciencia*.

Additionally, discussions of *conciencia* form part of a broader process of compartmentalization. Our conversations are replete with spatial metaphors: *en el monte* (in the mountains or the jungle); *allá* (over there); *en el otro lado* (on the other side); and the contrast made between *el monte* and *el pueblo* (town). These spatial metaphors index much more than geographical location; the men use these terms to locate both the war and their combat experiences at a distance from the person they are as they sit across from me. These spatial terms locate violent actions elsewhere, and that distance in turn marks differences in time, self, and *conciencia*. Many of these men attempt to cordon off certain actions and facets of their violent pasts by locating them in another space, time, and self. Certain moral codes pertain to certain spaces, and this compartmentalization is a powerful way of managing one's past.[13] These terms allow the former combatants to construct personal histories of discontinuity – to construct the sense of ending and of beginning that scholars associate with political transitions and processes of reconciliation. Unfortunately, the same terms that allow them to construct a new sense of self may also allow them to deny the harm they have inflicted. Given that the majority of people killed in Colombia's conflict are noncombatants, it is imperative to explore ways of closing the gap between the moral code that operated in *el monte*, and the *conciencia* necessary for these men to live once again as and among civilians.

Command Responsibility

Another facet of justice I have explored concerns the internal rules and sanctions imposed within the various armed groups.[14] For many ex-combatants from the FARC or ELN, justice is often associated with the "war councils" they participated in.[15] For instance, J. M. is a twenty-eight-year-old demobilized combatant from the ELN who spent thirteen years on a variety of fronts. He had waited for a salary that never materialized and finally "deserted" when members of the ELN assassinated his younger brother.[16] J. M. explained how the war councils operate:

Say you are in charge of handing out some *merca* (merchandise, frequently drugs), probably worth around 30,000 (pesos). But you're hungry. Well, you're not allowed to take away any of it. Say you're delivering some crackers, bread, soda – you would be punished. You can't take anything without having the commander's permission. If you screw up, you'll get a sentence, a reprimand – that is, if it's your first time. That's how the war council works. If it's your second time, you'll be killed. Because of a few crackers, you'll be killed! You'll be called in front of everybody, the war council, and you'll be shot right there, so that all your comrades, so all your compañeros can see. Of course they remain silent because otherwise they'd kill them, too. Yeah, they would call us to watch. Say you were really hungry. You didn't know. So you would eat the things. And you would be shot dead. Yeah, that's about it. That's how the war council works.

L. R.'s explanation of the way justice is understood and practiced on the battlefield did not differ much from J. M.'s. After eight years in the FARC, he explained what justice meant to him: "Justice for me is – well, you get somewhere, you get the commanders, and you call for a war council. If someone is going to be shot, if that's what you want, you'll get a war council so that you stop messing around. So, justice for me is that everyone has to pay for what he does." Importantly, the people sent to carry out the death penalty are usually rank and file members of the condemned individual's squadron.

The militarized hierarchy within each of the armed groups leads to tremendous resentment as the foot soldiers find themselves forced to carry out orders that may be at odds with what they believe is right. A number of former guerrillas spoke about "innocent compañeros" who were put to death on the basis of personal grudges or rumors. As one former combatant from the FARC explained:

"You realize that they kill your innocent compañeros (fellow soldiers). Just for rumors, because so-and-so said this or that. And you can't do a thing. You can't say anything because if you do then you get a war council too. Sometimes they (the commanders) ask for everyone's opinion, but most of the time they don't let anyone vote during a war council. You can't do anything – if you try to defend yourself or the other guy, then they shoot you too. If the commander says something and you don't agree with it, you just have to keep quiet. And if they send you to kill the guy, you also have to keep quiet. They tell you, 'if you aren't capable of killing, then tell me so I can kill you right now.' That's the phrase they use over there for anyone who isn't following order. Out there you have a war mentality. The war mentality – well, a person just doesn't think about life."

"Did you ever want to be a commander?"

"No, not really. It's really hard out there – to have that responsibility and have to respond to your superior for the lives of the men under your command. I don't like that sort of responsibility. If I were a low-level commander – say, a squadron leader – I would have to answer for everything, obey orders and everything. That's the problem. Now, it's really different if you're a high level commander because everyone under you has to obey orders. So the small commander (*comandante pequeño*) is in a constant state of contradiction. I had enough problems just being a combatant."("Alirio," Medellín, January 2007)

Our conversations are replete with references to the injustice the men experienced or witnessed at the hands of their commanders. In each of the armed groups, a double standard dictates who decides the rules and who will pay for disobeying them. Commanders may be accompanied by wives, girlfriends, and even their children; their female partners are allowed to remain and carry their pregnancies to term while low-level female combatants are routinely subjected to forced abortions; the commanders eat well while the rank and file eat whatever may be on hand; the commanders pocket illegally earned money while the foot soldiers *ponen el pecho a la guerra* – put their chest to the war, meaning they carry the load. The specific examples these former combatants cite vary across the armed group, but the resentment is shared and acute.

Additionally, justice as *lex talionis* – the proverbial eye for an eye and a tooth for a tooth – is what dominated all our conversations. I offer a quick review of the most common answers:

* "Everyone should do justice as he sees fit."
* "Justice is … well, if someone kills my father, I'll kill him."
* "Justice? The word makes no sense to me."
* "I don't think justice exists. What you gotta do is take revenge."

Even those who mentioned that justice should be administered "by God" still qualified their statements by adding that "helping him out" was not necessarily a bad thing. As J. C. told us after spending thirteen years in the AUC, "Justice? Well, supposedly God takes care of it, but God is a very busy man. You have to do it yourself – you have to help him out."

I underscore the complete absence of the state in these responses. The state as actor, an intermediary, as protagonist in the administration of justice – it simply does not appear. Moreover, for ex-combatants from the FARC and the ELN, the state was defined as intrinsically unjust and an enemy of "the people." The idea of looking to the Colombian judicial system for justice does not even enter the picture. I believe one factor that contributes to the desire for revenge that so many of these former combatants express is precisely the lack of legal alternatives for dispute resolution. However, as Minow has argued, "Finding some alternative to vengeance – such as government-managed prosecutions – is a matter, then, not only of moral and emotional significance. It is urgent for human survival" (Minow, 1998, p. 14). If one component of justice is staying the hand of vengeance, then the Colombian state must be found guilty of failing to adjudicate conflicts and punish the perpetrators.

And yet, justice consists of much more than prosecutions and adjudication. The forms of justice are diverse; understanding how these former combatants conceptualize justice and articulating their definitions with those of the victims who find themselves living with these men could assist policy makers in developing strategies "urgent for human survival." Rama Mani has written, "Justice is at once philosophical and political, public and intensely private, universal in its existence and yet highly individualized and culturally shaped in its expression" (Mani, 2002, p. 186). Exploring the multiple dimensions of justice is a crucial step in moving the methods and goals of DDR and transitional justice together. Moreover, while transitional justice is largely based on liberal legal models and concepts of justice, in practice people's justice repertoire is diverse. Justice in its retributive mode is frequently complemented by compensatory, restorative, redistributive, and divine concepts, among others. Grasping the broader dimensions of justice that animate individual and collective legal consciousness could open a path to innovative forms of assessing responsibility and settling accounts.

Living with Oneself, Living with Others

"What we're searching for is forgetting. I say let's go for it because if we don't forget we aren't doing anything. Well, it's not that we're going to forget what we learned because a person doesn't forget. But you need to get the war out of your mind. You need to leave the war behind, know that you're not stuck in this war – that you have a new life." ("Juan," former combatant, FARC, December 2006)

Reconcile: to restore to friendship, compatibility or harmony; to make consistent or congruous; *to cause to submit or to accept.* (Webster's Third New International Dictionary, 1993)

We turn now to the complex issue of reconciliation. Reconciliation is also multidimensional: the individual with him- or herself, members of a community with one another, between communities or states, between the individual and his or her god(s), and between civil society sectors and the state. I would like now to consider various aspects of the term, emphasizing the need to distinguish between vertical and horizontal reconciliation (see also Theidon, 2004).

In addition to providing the legal framework for the DDR process, the Justice and Peace Law established a National Commission on Reparation and Reconciliation (CNRR). As the name implies, part of their mandate included the elaboration of a reparations program and working toward national reconciliation. However, laws and rhetoric aside, the DDR program has been implemented in virtual isolation from the other programmatic areas of the CNRR. This isolation extends to the personnel of the various CROs, shelters, and *fincas*; they were surprised when I asked them how they address the issue of reconciliation with these former combatants. In response, I learned they do not. Indeed, one administrator in Medellín shook his head: "Reconciliation? Oh no, the topic is far too volatile."

Similarly, not one demobilized combatant with whom I have spoken is aware that his demobilization is allegedly one component of "national reconciliation" efforts. However, this is one crucial facet of that overlooked "R" in DDR. How do these men imagine life will be when they live once again among those they have harmed? Among those who consider themselves victims and may not want even to see these men's faces? I briefly cite two interviews I conducted in a *finca* outside Bogotá.

The first young man was Barney. He joined the AUC when still an adolescent because "I always loved guns. Ever since I was just a little kid, having a gun was a dream of mine." After he spoke at length about his time in the AUC, I asked whether he thought forgiveness would be possible.

"No. Forgiveness is just a word, but in the heart the resentment remains."

"So forgiving would be very difficult?"

"*Bueno*, it depends on what type of forgiveness. It might be that you can't forgive from the heart. If someone killed a family member, maybe I could forgive them with words, but in my heart the resentment would remain."

"So, where does that leave us if we want to think about reconciliation – about living together again?"

"Well, here people look at us like strange insects. But – for example in Bogotá – lots of people don't know how to look at an armed man. Lots of people don't really know how to look at an armed man, not even with the markings (*brazalete*, referring to the tattoos) of an illegal group. But the people who know, it's different. Those who have been mistreated – they're afraid, they resent you."

This young man would subsequently tell me that when he went into the nearby town, a storeowner told him he had "the face of a demobilized combatant," and told him to leave. There was no consultation with the townspeople prior to establishing the *finca*, and people wanted nothing to do with the *matones* ("killers") who "appeared overnight" in their town.

I had another lengthy conversation with Wilton, a young man from Turbo. He had been in the AUC for "four years and eight months." He missed his mother terribly but did not dare return to Turbo because he had demobilized individually "and wouldn't last for three days there because everyone knows who I was."

"Wilton, yesterday you talked a lot about God. You told me only God can forgive."

He nodded. "That's what I say. I committed a serious error. A person, a person isn't going to forgive me. The only one who can is God. In the meantime, the only one who can console me is God. Apologies yes, but forgiveness is a very big word."

"So if I commit an error, in front of the family or the person – can I say anything?"

"The family, no. The family will never forgive me. They may accept my words, but they will never forgive me."

"Even if they don't forgive you, could you live with them again – live in their town?"

"No, I couldn't. If you live there, you just don't know what might happen. We might be able to live together, but not all mixed up. God gives his touch to each human being, and to be a human being you have to work, to live through many things in your life and realize what you are doing. If not, you're not a human being. I repent for everything because I did things that weren't acceptable. Walking, doing things that aren't acceptable to God."

As Wilton and I parted that day, I asked him again whether there was anything that we could do so that he might return to Turbo. "No, I'll just have to go somewhere else. I can't show my face there."

These conversations are striking for many reasons. This was the first time in the DDR process that anyone had talked with them about what would happen when they left the shelter or *finca* – the first time "reintegration" was discussed as something other than passing by the CRO regularly for monitoring and picking up one's check. Both these former combatants as well as the surrounding communities would benefit from efforts to imagine forms of reconstructing social life, and concrete ways of implementing those ideas.

What might implementation entail? I insist first and foremost on the need to analyze local and regional specificities. The local and regional allegiances of the civilian population are crucial, and we should not lose sight of the fact that in some regions former combatants of a particular armed group may be viewed as war heroes by significant portions of the population. Consequently we must ask what sort of violence was suffered *and* practiced in various regions and by whom. Who benefited, who stood by, and who gave away a neighbor or a loved one in hopes of improving his or her own lot? Who *are* the guilty and what do people want done with those they hold responsible for their suffering? The complexity of guilt can rarely be reduced to a binary variable, and the gray zone will be vast in practice if not in narration.

Additionally, what work does the discourse of reconciliation perform in different contexts? Who "speaks it"? Which institutions authorize it and to what end? I recall a lengthy conversation I had in January 2007 with a former midlevel commander of the AUC who now directs a large nongovernmental organization dedicated to "social development." I asked whether he had given any thought to the issue of reconciliation, and he vigorously nodded. As I learned, he had organized several "reconciliation encounters" between the men who had served under him and victims who lived in the surrounding neighborhoods. I asked him how it had gone, and he smiled: "A great success. I get the *muchachos* (former combatants) and the victims together, we talk, and the victims always forgive. Always."

He then asked whether I knew what the number one problem is his city was. I shook my head, prompting the following response:

"The number one problem here is mental health. We need detraumatization (*destraumatización*) programs, for the *muchachos* (former combatants) and for the victims. We need psycho-spiritual therapy. With the victims, we need to work a great deal on spirituality. If the *muchachos* repent and apologize, the victims need spiritual therapy so they can forgive them. If the victims could get over their trauma, they would be able to forgive and forget – then they would be able to reconcile. True reconciliation is forgiving and forgetting."

This is not, to my mind, quite the way reconciliation or therapy should work. "Psychologizing" problems that have their roots in inequality, political violence, and ongoing fear does not allow policy makers to address the broader social dynamics that fuel conflict. Clearly war is not strictly a medical or psychological problem. Certainly blood is spilled; there are casualties and deaths. However, both the origins and the resolution of armed conflict go far beyond the confines of the medical model or clinical concepts of "recovery."

Additionally, I insist on moving beyond an excessively theological definition of reconciliation that too frequently locates the "failure to reconcile" in the victims, who may well demand earthly forms of justice. For example, we might consider the South African case, where the discourse of national reconciliation was largely a discourse of political and religious leaders. In his analysis of the South African TRC, Richard Wilson criticizes it for having deployed the concept of reconciliation in a top-down manner, leaving scant space to express the sentiments of retribution and revenge that operated in the local sphere (see Wilson, 2001a, 2001b). The gap between national and local processes was striking: There were no mechanisms to translate the grand vision of national reconciliation to the local level. Rather, religious and political elites appropriated the term "reconciliation" as a metanarrative to reconstruct the nation-state and their hegemony post apartheid. As Wilson (2001a, 2001b) argues, "The TRC's inability to transform the national reconciliation project into local reconciliation resulted from the lack of any mechanism for resolving conflicts locally, and for negotiating the return of former 'pariahs" to the community. In the principal areas of the conflict, the TRC was converted into a ritualized performance with little concrete organization to implement the grand vision of reconciliation" (p. 20).

For this reason, I underscore the importance of developing concrete, local mechanisms to reincorporate these demobilized combatants into the communities and barrios in which they will live. This will call for further research on locally and regionally specific definitions and practices of justice, redress, reparations, and reconciliation to ensure that third-party interventions do not, to put it colloquially, hurt more than they help.

Conclusions

Anthropologists have been accused of making the social so complex as to make it useless for any policy purposes that demand some reduction of complexity. However, in my experience it is precisely when anthropologists are able to convey the meaning of an event in terms of its location in the everyday, assuming that social action is not simply a direct materialization of cultural scripts but bears the traces of how these shared symbols are worked through, that it can be most effective. (Das, 2007, p. 217)

In this exploratory chapter I have argued for the importance of understanding how former combatants conceptualize themes that are central to the field of transitional justice and yet remain largely absent from DDR programs as they are currently designed and implemented. When considering what is involved in the concrete work of repairing the damage done to people, relationships, and societies following violence, it is clear that the moral issues of guilt, remorse, accountability, and reconciliation cannot be adequately addressed within a strict legal or security framework. These questions radiate across disciplinary and practitioner fiefdoms, as well as those that divide postconflict and peace-building interventions.

My conversations with former combatants convince me that these rank and file soldiers have much to contribute to social reconstruction, even in the "prepostconflict" context of Colombia. Combining these conversations with place-based analyses of locally and regionally salient practices of justice, punishment, and reparation could assist third parties in more effectively contributing to the work of social repair. Introducing a politics of scale into the design and implementation of both DDR and transitional justice measures could provide the synergy necessary to place these resources in the service of rebuilding both lives and livelihoods in the shadows of war.

Acknowledgments

I thank the Weatherhead Center for International Affairs, the John D. and Catherine T. Macarthur Foundation, and the International Center for Transitional Justice for the funding that made my research possible. For helpful discussions on the themes I address in this text, I thank Marcelo Fabre, Gonzalo Sanchez, Carlos Iván Degregori, Winifred Tate, Ana Patel, Eduardo Gonzalez, and Rosalind Shaw. I am grateful to Paola Andrea Betancourt for her research assistance in Colombia. Finally, my deepest gratitude goes to the many Colombians who have been generous with their time and their knowledge.

NOTES

1 See Theidon, 2004, for a discussion of horizontal and vertical reconciliation in the Peruvian context.
2 One reader questioned whether I was categorically denying the role of ideology in the conflict. I acknowledge that a number of former combatants of the FARC and, to a greater extent, the ELN cite social justice motivations for having joined the guerrilla, and I do not want to "depoliticize" the violence. However, in each instance they also refer to their sense of deception when they encountered the gap between ideology and practice, assuring me that the commanders were involved in drug production and trafficking, extortion, killing civilians, among other acts. Thus I do argue that ideology has been eclipsed by economic motivations, and by the influence of national and transnational criminal networks involved in the drug trade (see Chernick, 2007).
3 La Violencia refers to the period 1948–53, when violent confrontations between the Conservative and Liberal political parties resulted in 200,000 people dead and more than a billion dollars in property damage. For a detailed study of this period, see Germán, Fals-Borda, & Umaña-Luna, 2005.
4 The legal sponsorship for these groups was emergency Decree 3398 in 1965, subsequently transformed into Law 48 and approved by the Colombian Congress in 1968. This law allowed the government to "mobilize the population in activities and tasks to restore public order and contain the insurgent threat." In 1989, the paramilitaries were made illegal by President Barco, who suspended Decree 3398 and outlawed the use of armed civilians in army operations (see Romero, 2003).
5 United Nations Integrated Disarmament, Demobilization and Reintegration Standards, II.2.4 (2006).

6 See Steve Dudley's (2004) excellent discussion of the Unión Patriótica.
7 For a detailed analysis of the legal framework for this process and the ensuing debates, see Laplante & Theidon, 2006.
8 See the Ministry of the Interior (2011).
9 Although the individual and collective demobilization processes vary in detail, I have interviewed former combatants in both programs because I am interested in the reintegration phase and the experiences of both these demobilized combatants as well as their families and host communities.
10 The Referral and Opportunities Centers (CRO) are administered by the Ministry of the Interior and provide the demobilized with orientation, case workers, social support, and other forms of assistance.
11 For the sake of space I focus on male ex-combatants in this text. For the same reason, I present the dominant trends in my conversations. This admittedly results in a certain homogenization, but there is no way to address the full complexity of the research in this text.
12 I borrow this term from Gobodo-Madikizela (2006), who was referring to her interviews with Eugene de Kock, former head of the Valkplass unit of the South African police counterinsurgency unit. De Kock was jailed for his role in the torture and assassination of dozens of antiapartheid activists.
13 In Braithwaite's (1989) influential work on crime, shame, and integration, he states: "The point is that conscience is acquired" (p. 71). Thus I argue that these terms implying distance and change are important ways the former combatants construct new selves and lives.
14 For a fascinating discussion of the forms of justice administered by armed groups vis-à-vis the communities and regions under their dominion, see Gomez, 2001. In my conversations with former paramilitaries, they refer to the "guerra de honor" (war of honor) as the site in which justice was administered within the paramilitary organizations.
15 See Molano, 2001, for an excellent overview of guerrilla justice.
16 I never use the term "desert" when speaking with these men. Thus when the term appears it is because a former combatant used it in conversation. Words matter, and it concerns me that the former paramilitaries "demobilized" while former guerrilla members "deserted." The former does not carry the connotations of betrayal or cowardice that the latter term does. I argue for avoiding this stigmatizing term.

REFERNCES

Biggar, N. (Ed.) (2003). *Burying the past: Making peace and doing justice after civil conflict.* Washington, DC: Georgetown University Press.

Borneman, J. (2002). Reconciliation after ethnic cleansing: Listening, retribution, affiliation. *Public Culture,* 14, 281–304.

(2003). Why reconciliation? A response to critics. *Public Culture,* 15, 199–208.

Braithwaite, J. (1989). *Crime, shame and reintegration.* Cambridge: Cambridge University Press.

Castro, M. C. (1997). *Guerrilla reinserción y lazo social.* Bogotá, Colombia: Almudena Editores.

Chernick, M. (2007). FARC-EP: Las fuerzas armadas revolucionarias de Colombia-ejército del Pueblo. In M. Heiberg, B. O'Leary, & J. Tirman (Eds.), *Terror, insurgency and the state: Ending protracted conflicts* (pp. 51–82). Philadelphia: University of Pennsylvania Press.

Colletta, N., Kostner, M., & Wiederhofer, I. (1996). *The transition from war to peace in sub-Saharan Africa*. eLibary: The World Bank.

Das, V. (2007). *Life and words: Violence and the descent into the ordinary*. Berkeley: University of California Press.

Dudley, S. (2003). *Walking ghosts: Murders and guerrilla politics in Colombia*. New York: Routledge.

Falk, R. (2003). Doubting the unconditional need for retribution. *Public Culture,* 15, 91–194.

García-Peña, D. (2005). La relación del estado colombiano con el fenómeno paramillitar: Por el esclarecimiento histórico. *Analisis Politico,* 53, 58–76.

Gobodo-Madikizela, P. (2006). *A human being died that night*. New York: Portobello Books.

Gómez, G. I. (2001). La justicia comunitaria: Introduccion. In B. Sousa Santos, & M. García Vallegos, (Eds.), *El caleidoscopio de las justicias en Colombia,* Bogotá. (pp. 217–73). Columbia: Colciencias.

Gutmann, M. C. (1996). *The meanings of macho: Being a man in Mexico City*. Berkeley: University of California Press.

Guzmán, G., Orlando, F. B., & Eduardo U. L. (Eds.) (2006). *La violencia en Colombia*. Bogotá, Colombia: Ediciones de Tercer Mundo.

Hayner, P. B. (2001). *Unspeakable truths: Confronting state terror and atrocity*. New York: Routledge.

Jaramillo, S., Giha, Y., & Torres, P. (Eds.). (2009). *Disarmament, demobilization, and reinsertion amidst the conflict: The case of Colombia*. New York: International Center for Transitional Justice.

Knight, M., & Ozerdem, A. (2004). Guns, camps and cash: Disarmament, demobilization and reinsertion of former combatants in transitions from war to peace. *Journal of Peace Research,* 41, 499–515.

Laplante, L. J., & Theidon, K. (2006). Transitional justice in times of conflict: Colombia's ley de justicia y paz, *Michigan Journal of International Law,* 28, 49–108.

Mani, R. (2002). *Beyond retribution: Seeking justice in the shadows of war*. Cambridge, UK: Polity Press.

Minow, M. (1998). *Between vengeance and forgiveness: Facing history after genocide and mass violence*. Boston: Beacon Press.

Molano, A. (2001). La justicia guerrillera. In B. Sousa Santos & M. García Vallegos, (Eds.), *El caleidoscopio de las justicias en Colombia* (pp. 331–62). Bogotá, Colombia: Uniandes-Siglo del Hombre-Colciencias-CES.

Nader, L. (2003). Departures from violence: Love is not enough. *Public Culture* 15, 195–7.

Romero, M. (2003). *Paramilitares y autodefensas: 1982–2003*. Bogotá, Colombia: Editorial Planeta.

Sampson, S. (2003). From reconciliation to coexistence. *Public Culture 15,* 181–6.

Sánchez, G. & Lair, E. (Eds.). (2004). *Violencias y estrategias colectivas en la region andina*. Bogotá, Colombia: Grupo Editorial Norma.

(2004). Guerra prolongada y negociaciones inciertas en Colombia. In G. Sánchez & E. Lair, (Eds.), *Violencias y estrategias colectivas en la region andina*. Bogotá, Colombia: Grupo Editorial Norma.

Shaw, R. (2005). *Rethinking truth and reconciliation commissions: Lessons from Sierra Leone*. Washington, DC: United States Institute of Peace.

Stover, E. & Weinstein, H. M. (Eds.) (2004). *My neighbor, my enemy: Justice and community in the aftermath of mass atrocity*. Cambridge: Cambridge University Press.

Tate, W. (2007). *Counting the dead: The culture and politics of human rights activism in Colombia*. Berkeley: University of California Press.

Teitel, R. (2000). *Transitional justice*. Oxford: Oxford University Press.

(2003). Transitional justice genealogy. *Harvard Human Rights Law Journal*, 16, 69–94.

Theidon, K. (2004). *Entre prójimos: El conflicto armado interno y la política de la reconciliación en el Perú*. Lima, Peru: Instituto de Estudios Peruanos.

(2007). Transitional subjects? The disarmament, demobilization and reintegration of former combatants in Colombia. *International Journal of Transitional Justice*, 1, 66–90.

(2009). Reconstructing masculinities: The disarmament, demobilization and reintegration of former combatants in Colombia. *Human Rights Quarterly*, 31, 1–34.

(2012). *Intimate enemies: Violence and reconciliation in Peru*. Philadelphia: University of Pennsylvania Press.

United Nations Department of Peacekeeping Operations (1999). *Disarmament, demobilization and reintegration of ex-combatants in a peacekeeping environment: Principles and guidelines*. New York: Department of Peacekeeping Operations/Lessons Learned Unit.

United Nations Integrated Disarmament (2006). Demobilization and reintegration standards, II.2.4.

Webster's Third New International Dictionary (1993). Springfield, MA: Merriam-Webster.

Wilson, R. A. (2003a). Anthropological studies of national reconciliation processes. *Anthropological Theory*, 3, 367–87.

(2003b). Justice and retribution in postconflict settings. *Public Culture 15*, 187–90.

15 Atrocity and Non-Sense: The Ethnographic Study of Dehumanization

Alexandra Pillen

The second half of the twentieth century was characterized by brutal insurgency and counterinsurgency wars; civilian populations experienced extreme violence on an unprecedented scale. A challenge for anthropologists working in such war-torn societies across the globe is that of paying attention not only to rapid sociocultural change but also to processes of dehumanization and local redefinitions of what it means to be human. The non-sense and inhumanity of war thereby challenge the very definition of "anthropology," as informants claim and fear that some of those affected are no longer human. The ethnographic method is not necessarily geared toward capturing such a mood of inhumanity and lack of sense. Nonetheless, significant numbers of ethnographers are being sent to hot spots of extreme violence and asked to write narrative accounts of such zones of dehumanization. This critique of ethnography carried out in times of crisis explores the consequences of the ethnographic study of dehumanization.

In terms of research methodology and ethics, a common question relates to the ethnographer's capability to interview and work with traumatized survivors. Here, however, I move beyond this level of critique and consider the impact of the wider cultural and linguistic consequences of twentieth century waves of extreme violence on the ethnographic method. The notion of a "traumatized" population easily leads ethnographers toward understanding their findings as narratives of the traumatized, reenactments of violence, or symptoms of posttraumatic stress disorder. This approach envisages the provision of a therapeutic moral framework to a selected few within the community, while obscuring important cultural processes related to dehumanization and its reversal. In view of the moral devastation of certain communities, rehabilitation is more than a question of participation in NGO programs or traditional healing. In parallel to the reestablishment of a social order, people need to find ways to feel human again and transcend cultural meaninglessness. Such a cultural moment is not easily captured within a discourse on trauma and readily elides ethnographic representation.[1]

My argument, therefore, does not concern the cycle of violence or the trauma of survivors and their communities, articulated in psychological or sociological terms. Rather, my entry points are "culture and language" and their articulation with processes of dehumanization. A key element of this analysis concerns the simultaneous presence of contradictory moral frameworks in which wartime subjectivities are engulfed. Such contradictory moral frameworks can be exemplified in a number of ways. For example, the two conflicting realities that exist for families of the disappeared: loved ones who are at the same time both dead and alive. Indelible contradiction also emerges in the coagulation of family life and horror, revealed in the denunciation of relatives to death squads, sexual forms of torture, and more generally the intimate nature of many forms of extreme violence. For perpetrators, such contradictions are experienced as the ludic nature of killings, the festive ambience of violence, or the experience of being forced to carry out orders, including killing, against one's will. In general, I summarize such conflicting realities as the coexistence of a pre-war morality with a violent new reality in people's hearts and minds. In an affective sense, this translates as a continuous oscillation between feelings of humanity and inhumanity, normality and atrocity.

The tension between such opposing perspectives and affects, experienced simultaneously or in rapid oscillation, is not just a matter of individualized mental health but constitutes pervasive cultural realities. The simultaneity of opposed affects is here not a sign of madness or psychiatric illness, but a cultural consequence of the intimate nature of twentieth century insurgency and counterinsurgency warfare. The pervasive tension between opposing realities, forced upon people through extreme violence, has cultural and linguistic consequences. I explore the potential role of anthropology in documenting such moments of dehumanization and the fragile cultural processes of rehumanization and reconstruction of language.

Case Study: Inhumanity and Non-Sense in Southern Sri Lanka

– the sound that broke the back of words (Morrison, 1987, p. 261)

This case study of dehumanization and its ethnographic exploration is based on fifteen months of fieldwork (1996–8) in a community in southern Sri Lanka. Plagued by chronic low-intensity violence and poverty, the rural South constitutes a reservoir of violence, used by the Sri Lankan national army to recruit soldiers to fight a war against the Tamil minority (1983–2009). The condition of extreme violence was, however,

already established before the well-publicized war against Tamil sepa-
ratists and Tamil Tigers (LTTE) began. A much less well-documented
civil war or Sinhalese insurgency (by the People's Liberation Front or
JVP – Janatha Vimukthi Peramuna) led to a regime of terror and violence throughout the villages of southern Sri Lanka. This youth movement, which grew out of the Peking wing of the Ceylon Communist
Party, quickly resorted to guerrilla warfare and during the first insurgency (1971) almost managed to topple the government. After years
of severe repression, they reappeared in a more violent form, and their
struggle against state security forces and other paramilitary bodies led
to the extreme violence and dehumanization of the civil war of 1987–9.
Atrocities and massacres were committed at the hands of the Special
Task Force (the Sri Lankan state's counterinsurgency commandos) and
a staggering number of people – about forty thousand according to some
sources (Chandraprema, 1991) – disappeared or were killed extrajudi-
cially (Amnesty International, 1993). The social fabric of communities
was severely affected by a global culture of terror and counterinsurgency
warfare (see Mahmood, 2000; Sluka, 2000) as cordon and search operations led to concealed apprehension technique (CAT) commandos forcing local villagers to take part in the selection of people to be executed
or disappeared.

I conducted ethnographic fieldwork seven years after the end of the
civil war of the late eighties, known as the second JVP insurgency. A
horrendous war against the Tamil Tigers (LTTE) was still raging in the
North and East of the country. Many Sinhalese soldiers had deserted
the army and were roaming the rural countryside, armed and unemployable, perpetually hiding from security forces. Rumors circulated in the
national press that an estimated twenty thousand such deserters participated in the cycle of low-intensity violence in the midnineties; at the
same time the youth suicide rates (age fifteen to twenty-four) were the
highest in the world (LaVecchia, 1994). My research was carried out
through participant observation in the village of Udahenagama, a pseu-
donym for a conglomerate of five neighborhoods in a densely populated
rural-urban area, more accurately described as a rural slum. At the time
of the population census of 1993 this area comprised about three thousand inhabitants. People belonged to the drummers', cultivators', or jag-
gery makers' caste; a survey of each neighbourhood revealed dynamics of
revenge, as well as the number of disappeared people and victims of suicide in the research area. Strikingly, perpetrators and victims continue to
live in close proximity to each other and reconstruct their moral universe
to include neighbors responsible for the killing of loved ones. During the
civil war of the late eighties, local conflicts became the breeding ground

for extreme violence, as family members denounced each other to death squads.

The ethnographic research method was primarily based on participant observation and sociolinguistic analyses of discourses on violence. A key focus of the research was on cleansing or healing rituals (*tovil*). These thirty-hour-long rituals galvanized the community and allowed me to observe spontaneous discourses on pollution, moral malaise, dehumanization, and cultural reconstruction.

The category "youth" as I use it in this paper is polysemic. The first layer of meaning sedimented into the notion "troublesome youth," relates to the atrocities committed by local youngsters during the JVP insurgencies. Youths denounced kinsmen to death squads and engaged in brutal killings. But it was not enough to kill: Youngsters subjected corpses to mutilation – a fact that still shocks elders.

A second layer of meaning, which affects young men in southern Sri Lanka, is summarized in the expression "good for nothing" (*rastiyādu pĕte vĕtilā*). Both traditional occupations and chronic unemployment are shameful for a generation of volatile underemployed rural youths. This situation reflects the global predicament of youth: The marginalization of young people may be seen as a structural consequence of the global spread of neoliberal capitalism (Comaroff & Comaroff, 2005, p. 27). Ethnic warfare in the North and East and recruitment into the Sri Lankan national army provide a rare economic opportunity for impoverished Sinhalese youths. The predicament of rural Sinhalese youth is a cornerstone of the socioeconomic formation of chronic "ethnic" warfare (Winslow & Woost, 2004). However, a significant proportion of youths become deserters, live in fear of arrest, and are unable to search for employment. The crisis of masculinity initiated through the neoliberal transformation of an agrarian economy is deepened by militarization and desertion; all this is reflected in the term "good for nothing."

A third metaphor attached to this broader category of troublesome youth is the notion of people who behave like unsocialized wild spirits (*yakā vage minissu*). Despite the fact that most participants in the last insurgency were eliminated, chronic low-intensity violence continues to taint the image of village youth. Sinhalese soldiers who commit atrocities at the front in the North and East of the country regularly spend their holidays in their villages, and armed deserters return to theirs to hide. Rape, homicide, and suicide are part of a cycle of low-intensity violence perpetrated by unsettled youth and give rise to a potent metaphor of dehumanization. The inhumanity of violent youngsters is encapsulated in the appellation "spiritlike people."

Three key meanings thereby qualify the notion of troublesome youth: war criminals, "unemployable," and "spiritlike people." These metaphors coexist within the collective imagination even though they do not necessarily coincide within the individual lives of contemporary youths. Many men between the ages of fifteen and forty simply fit within the category of "good for nothing." Either unemployed or deserters from the army, they embody the potential for violence within the collective imagination: Their image is constructed in a mirror shattered by youth violence. As their potential violence and chronic unemployment are lumped together, meanings coalesce and a potent image emerges of spiritlike beings, lacking certain defining characteristics of humanity.

Theravada Buddhism has been the major religion on the island of Sri Lanka since the second century BC. The Sinhala Buddhist pantheon constitutes a cosmic hierarchy of Buddha, deities, humans, and spirits. Sinhalese Buddhist culture now plays a crucial role in the articulation of both nationalism and class dynamics. While the middle classes focus on the Buddha and the deities, the ritual practices of the working class and peasant Sinhalese include the lower reaches of this pantheon (Kapferer, 1983, p. 48). Traditional healers or "exorcists" (*ëduro*) engage in elaborate rituals (*tovil*) at moments when the cosmic order has been subverted by "demonic intrusion" (p. 57) and people have become possessed by evil spirits.

Traditional healers I encountered in the late nineties observed that spiritlike men are rarely afflicted by spirit possession. Unsocialized spirits or demons, "the terrors which prowl at the base of the Sinhala Buddhist cosmic hierarchy" (Kapferer, 1983, p. 51), simply do not attack such people because they are horrified by them and "shiver away" (Argenti-Pillen, 2003b, p. 113). Terrified spirits of the Sinhala Buddhist pantheon fled a human world engulfed in civil war (pp. 111–14). Such understandings reflect a pantheon in turmoil, where the relative position of humans and evil spirits is presented as potentially reversed, with some humans occupying a position below traditional monstrous beings.

I now question how such inhumanity and cosmological turmoil are reflected in linguistic and performative expressions and how this challenges an ethnographic method. This set of questions builds on the notion of inhumanity and concerns non-sense, or absence of meaning. Not only do violent people in southern Sri Lanka occupy the position of unsocialized spirits within collective representations of a postwar cosmos, but their position is consolidated by the fact that it is not threatened by beings from below. Their problematic acts sometimes extend into the arena of ritual, when they mock ritual specialists and disrupt sacrificial rites.

In the aftermath of the civil war, troublesome but innovative young men have added an element to traditional sacrifice: They themselves now offer an effigy to the spirits, despite never having been apprenticed to a ritual specialist. They thereby attempt to bring about ritual change within Sinhala Buddhist healing rituals, traditionally performed by ritual healers to cure a possessed patient. In the youths' version of the ritual, however, the effigy is cajoled like a toddler, treated like a sexual object, addressed with superior-to-inferior pronouns, and ritually abused and murdered. Bystanders attempted to placate the anthropologist and dismiss such acts as mere "nonsense" (*anang manang* or *vikāra*). Such words refer to the non-sense of people who are drunk, yet also connote the disoriented speech and confusion of the terrified who have witnessed or committed an atrocity.

Yet, as such non-sense spills into the ritual arena, and spiritlike people engage in a mockery of sacrificial acts, they as it were participate in what Malamoud (1996) called "the sacrificial definition of humanity or the ritual circumscription of violence" (pp. 98–9). I argue that by disrupting and participating in healing rituals, young men attempt to reintroduce certain aspects of their everyday world within the contours of Sinhala Buddhist civilization. In the aftermath of the ineffable violence of the civil war, innovative forms of sacrifice may represent an attempt to rebelong to society, and above all to be considered human.

Yet I would caution against ethnographic overinterpretation and optimism, as I try to discern processes of rehumanization on the basis of existing ritual and sacrificial theory (see also Argenti-Pillen, 2010). After all, my informants experienced such violent incursions into the ritual arena as yet more instances of senseless violence, and indeed non-sense. During sacrificial rituals, the young men in Sri Lanka begin by taking care of the effigy as loving fathers, but this image of intimate care is quickly replaced by an image of sexual abuse and death through murder. They thus create a tension between emotions, a rapid oscillation between the opposed meanings of family life and horror, which cannot coagulate into a single emotional state. It is this simultaneity of opposed moral frameworks and affects that the audience experiences as an instance of non-sense.

This leads to questions about the cultural definition of non-sense in the aftermath of widespread extreme violence when a culture is being threatened at its core. Such a state of not knowing – of not being able to make sense – has consequences for the ethnographic method. Informants who respond with "Don't know" or "This doesn't make sense" commonly tend to be underrepresented in the final ethnographic representation of their cultural community. Equally, a transcript's non-sense passages – the places where language breaks down – are not often selected for inclusion in a final ethnographic text. Such methodological routines might thus inadvertently turn the ethnographer away from important expressions of dehumanization and senselessness.

I propose to summarize this case material on the local definition of spiritlike people, absent spirits, non-sense, and dehumanization as an instance of "cosmological damage" in the aftermath of the extreme violence of twentieth century civil war. Cosmological damage is hereby defined as dehumanization brought about through a reattribution of monstrous and human characteristics, or a reconceptualization of the interaction between human and spirit worlds.[2]

Cosmological Damage on a Global Scale?

This case study's themes of inhuman violence, dehumanization, and cosmological damage are not unique. Theidon (2003) depicts the discursive dehumanization of Shining Path guerrillas in Peru. During the 1980s and 1990s, the refrain "living and dying like dogs" could be heard throughout the highland communities of Ayacucho, as guerrillas killed people in ways villagers would not use even to butcher their animals. The extreme violence of Shining Path guerrillas led villagers to consider them as "fallen out of humanity" and to imagine them as bodily different; literally otherworldly beings with, for example, three belly buttons, genitals in odd parts of their bodies, and green eyes all testifying to their monstrosity (pp. 11–12). Wartime cosmology thereby redefined such people as nonhuman, echoing the cosmological damage that occurred in wartorn Sri Lanka.

De Berry's (2000) work in northern Uganda allows me to take this comparison a step further. Among the Karamajong, wartime degradation and perversion of humanity are expressed as the departure of spirits. During the civil war certain categories of spirits were terrified of the noise of gunfire, ran away, and had little to do with the fighting (p. 103). De Berry points to a "disjunction" in which wartime suffering is not experienced as part of a continuum with other forms of affliction and negotiation with the realm of traditional spirits (p. 106). That even spirits should be frightened and chased out of the world testifies to a cosmology damaged by war.

A. Hinton's (2002b, 2005) work on dehumanization and Khmer Rouge genocidal ideologies reveals another example of cosmological damage, seen in the redrawing of the line between the human and animal species. In the aftermath of the carpet bombing[3] of the countryside and other atrocities committed by the Lon Nol regime, city people were robbed of their humanity, addressed as "Comrade Ox," and harmed, discarded, or disemboweled like animals by the Khmer Rouge.

I now turn to a more difficult example, which concerns the experience of the dehumanization not of others, but of oneself. Fahy's (2009) work on the North Korean famine offers a haunting glimpse at testimonies of dehumanization. With the famine came corruption, and corruption turned people into beasts; thus a "beast society" (*chimsung sawi*) emerged in North Korea (p. 236). Starving people use the metaphor "fuel" for food; living beings regard themselves as fueled (or unfueled) machines or vehicles (p. 217). Beasts, machines, vehicles – these are not comments made about a loathed other, but by themselves about their own state of dehumanization.

These examples I have commented on, from Sri Lanka, Peru, Uganda, Cambodia, and North Korea, provide a global context for the development of a definition of twentieth century cosmological damage. I propose a narrow, historically grounded definition[4] linked to the postcolonial insurgency and counterinsurgency violence of the cold war era and its immediate aftermath.[5] In other words, the notion of cosmological damage engenders questions of etiology and an imperative to investigate the cultural impact of twentieth century mass violence. Such an analysis necessarily goes beyond the historical contingencies of the dehumanization caused by colonialism or Nazism; instead it focuses on the widespread experience of extreme violence among civilian populations, and its cultural effect.

The Ethnographic Study of Dehumanization.

You forgot who you were and couldn't think it up. (Morrison, 1987, p. 251) -

Working in a community where people fear they are no longer able to make sense poses additional methodological problems. The modernist techniques of contextualization and meaning making used in anthropology – being drawn into a global system of knowledge and interests – might be at odds with the local, subtle forms of rehumanization and reconstruction of everyday life. Statements such as "I don't know," or "This doesn't make sense" should be regarded extremely seriously rather than taken as a cue for the anthropologist to search further afield for another context or a "better" informant. A cultural formation of temporary doubt needs to be carefully observed as a moment the entire community needs to go through, a cultural breathing space, which requires ethnographic respect.

Within this volume, the current chapter and chapters by Kidron and Kwon all concern spaces of relative nonintervention[6] and thereby provide a complementary image to the realities of trauma counseling, psychosocial interventions, and conflict resolution. In ethical terms, such an approach is justified, as a majority of survivors live within the interstices of the web of interventions. My analysis resonates with Kidron's chapter, which calls into question expert interventions in "silent" survivor populations that function to elicit public articulation for the purpose of therapy or national reconciliation. I suggest we add "ethnographic intervention" to Kidron's causes for concern and list ethnography as a method for the elicitation and public discussion of memories of violence.

Ethnography is an intervention in its own right, and in addition to its favoring of the most meaningful informants, ethnography has other implicit methodologies for "manufacturing sense."[7] These implicit research methods, used to "give voice" to survivors and provide meaningful observations, are of a linguistic nature and as such are determined by the ethnographer's linguistic ideology. Existing anthropological codes of ethics for ethnographers of extreme violence do not question such implicit linguistic technologies. This case study and analysis highlight the ethics of an extensive and mandatory training in linguistic anthropology as a prerequisite to the study of survivors.[8] Detailed sociolinguistic records and theoretical questions about the imposition of the semantic structure of ethnography and the linguistic ideology of European languages[9] in contexts of extreme violence become thereby the cornerstones of a revised code of ethics. Rather than selecting the most meaningful passages from observations or conversations among survivors, the ethnographer becomes a witness to the senseless nature of dehumanization[10] and the subtle reconstruction of language and humanity.

In the aftermath of the Holocaust, the poetry of Paul Celan offers a lyrical interface between non-sense and reconstructed language:

While poetry itself seems to collapse under the pressure of "this time," it also reasserts itself as the medium that recovers speaking, that moves, however tentatively, to reunite the solitary words of mad un-language to the fragile structure of poetic speech – a process during which poetry disintegrates into mad babble at the same time as it turns this mad babble back into poetry. (Weineck, 1999, 267)

What strikes Weineck is the simultaneity of opposites that emerges in the poem's advance toward madness (p. 264). The poems include quotes from one who stopped speaking (p. 265) and at times constitute a total refusal of meaning – any meaning in any ideological services (p. 266, my emphasis).

Interestingly, many ethnographers implicitly share their informants' distrust of superimposed meanings that come to the rescue at nonsensical times.[11] In Kirmayer's terms (personal communication, September 2009) this argument can be encapsulated by a question:

Can we rebuild cosmology not by asserting the grand sweep of a totalizing narrative (that may contain the seeds of a future round of mutually assured destruction), but through the more fragile, tentative, essays of lyric that invite us to a moment of trust, of intimacy and connection with another consciousness or way of being? (My emphasis)

Yet the difficulty for ethnographers is that such incipient expressions and minute processes of rehumanization are not necessarily earmarked as artistic or poetic and are therefore not easy to discern. An ethical awareness of the linguistic technologies of ethnography and an extensive training in linguistic anthropology thereby become even more essential when studying violence and dehumanization. The methodological entry point is thereby reoriented to grassroot linguistic creativity at the interface of nonsense and sense.[12] The experience is of a continuously displaced anthropology as the ethnographer moves on from one context to the next, not being able to make immediate sense of cultural and semantic insecurity. The mood becomes one of a postponed ethnography, which awaits meaning within an indefinite time frame.

The simultaneity of contradictory moral frameworks in the aftermath of extreme violence[13] cannot be fully understood within a theoretical framework guided by notions of dissociation, trauma, or psychiatric illness. I therefore opt for an anthropological discourse and theoretical analysis to summarize key aspects of this case study. Kristeva's (1980) notion of ambivalence and Deleuze's (2004) definition of displaced subjectivity both provide a set of points of comparison for further analysis. The fact that poetic or ambivalent language has considerable consequences for its subject leads Kristeva to refer to the questionable subject-in-process (p. 135). A blurred subjectivity yields to ambivalence (p. 68), or the painful tension between opposed meanings. In terms of the case material under study, I argue that the tension between humanity and experienced inhumanity or the senselessness emerging from this tension creates an ambivalence grounded in the disturbing political processes of an era of mass dehumanization.

Deleuze (2004) coins the term "displaced subjectivity," a subjectivity that is always being displaced in relation to itself (p. 261). He argues that a subterranean principle of countersense is imposed on sense, and that this is not just a momentary reversal of perspectives but a continuous motion and tension between perspectives and affects (pp. 83, 87). Deleuze's focus on the fragmented subject, lost identity, and the copresence of sense and non-sense helps to explore further the ambivalent affect and rehumanization I try to describe. The frameworks of Kristeva and Deleuze not only question the subjectivity ethnographers project upon survivors, but query the nature of ethnographic language, and the potential importance of adequately recording both ambivalence and countersense.[14]

The process of rehumanization involves a linguistic dimension, an articulation of the non-sense of one's degradation, and of the ambiguous and uncertain nature of many wartime realities (e.g. Argenti-Pillen, 2003b). A move to a more certain order of language entails the "trauma" of leaving such experiences behind, as contradictory affects are confronted with a unitary and consolidated narrative, which might not fit them.[15] It is this kind of suffering I would like to highlight: the experience of being forced in particular semantic directions without being given the space or freedom for a cultural pause in the aftermath of carnage and violence. Such a cultural pause includes an articulation of non-sense and reflections on inhumanity at the margins of recognizable forms of communication.

Such comments inevitably lead to a consideration of ethnography as a set of cultural negotiations through which ethnographers are keen to construct a swift cultural image of a postwar context. The result is an ethnographic objectification or imposition of the semantic structure of anthropology, which many might intuitively not trust in the aftermath of elite-led atrocity and violence. The easily accessible imagery of an "ethnography of suffering" thereby constitutes a type of imprisonment in understanding, an understanding that occurs all too quickly.

In such instances the cultural or political contextualization of extreme suffering through ethnography might seem rather meaningless to survivors – the ethnographic manufacture of sense experienced as infinitely less important than local microprocesses of rehumanization. Moreover, populations who still question what it means to feel human again might at times refract the image of ethnography as senseless. Following Burnside (2006), I use the term "senseless" in both a semantic and a perceptual sense. Within a philosophy of aesthetics, the notion of senselessness also connotes a numbing or anesthetic (p. 149). While I have used "non-sense" in a predominantly linguistic sense, senselessness expands the analysis to include its sensory counterpart, numbness. The risk of a senseless superimposition of meaning in the aftermath of dehumanization reverberates to ethnographers as senselessness in a sensorial sense, a much needed cultural anesthetic for haunted elites.

Yet this is not the final point in this critique of the ethnographic study of dehumanization. Ethnography can indeed be a gift for the safeguarding of a cultural pause or breathing space, but such an endeavor requires a degree of ethnographic freedom. This freedom itself requires not only detachment from the fast semantic demands of peacetime ethnographies, but also a critical consideration of the implicit linguistic methodologies deployed to construct ethnographies. A rigorous training in linguistic anthropology is thus not a mere subdisciplinary option, but a sine qua non for ethnographers of extreme violence to capture and reflect moments of precious cultural freedom[16] when addressing dehumanization and its reversal. Ethnography needs to take a step back and record cultural creativity in the aftermath of twentieth century cosmological damage. As is extensively demonstrated in Kwon's chapter in this volume, such cultural creativity extends far beyond an interaction with well-intentioned modernist interventions or paradigms. Anthropology thereby entertains the possibility that twentieth century global forms of inhumanity will lead to rehumanization and cultural reconstruction, which may well bypass the points of reference of Euro-American culture, civilization, and empire.

Acknowledgments

I am very grateful to A. Hinton and D. Hinton for inviting me to the panel "Legacies of Violence: Memory, Symptom, Intervention" at the conference of the American Anthropological Association, San Francisco (November 2008). I am especially indebted to the extensive comments and suggestions from the panel's discussant, Prof. L. Kirmayer. Research in Sri Lanka was made possible by a UCL Graduate School Fellowship, a doctoral (1996–8) and a postdoctoral (2000–1) research grant from the Harry Frank Guggenheim Foundation. I would like to extend special thanks to A. Witeska and S. Fahy, as the debates about their doctoral work have substantially influenced this paper's argument.

NOTES

1 My work is akin to the contributions by Kidron (this volume) and Kwon (this volume). Intervention or the notion of trauma is not the point of departure, but its relative absence leads to a consideration of the role of Holocaust memories in everyday life (Kidron, this volume) or the trauma endured by the dead (Kwon, this volume). I too advocate a decentralization of the discourse on trauma.

2 This case study from southern Sri Lanka can be placed on a continuum with case material by Theidon (this volume), Kohrt (this volume), and Taylor (this volume). Theidon discusses the value of an ethnographic grassroots perspective to complement integration orchestrated from above. Kohrt (this volume) and Taylor (this volume) provide a critical analysis of the potential role of

indigenous mechanisms of reconciliation. By comparison, the entry point of my analysis does not concern explicit forms of rehabilitation mediated through existing social institutions such as indigenous healing or an NGO. My case study concerns the *as yet unmediated* contributions to rehumanization initiated by people who have fallen out of humanity, or people who operate within an everyday cosmology damaged by war.

3 American warplanes were responsible for death and destruction among rural Cambodians on an unprecedented scale (A. Hinton, 2002b, pp. 267, 271). The resulting grudges and uncontrollable hatred against the urban elites were a source of motivation for unspeakable Khmer Rouge atrocities rooted in an ideology of dehumanization.

4 I therefore distinguish this cosmological damage from earlier forms of dehumanization. The prototypes of a cosmology based on dehumanization are of course colonialism and Nazism. Kuper (2002) describes the process of dehumanization of indigenous people: the common phenomenon of "equating hunting and gathering people with animals" or "hunting them down in the same way as animals" (p. 68). Likewise dehumanization (e.g.,Wolf 2002, p. 195) was an essential ingredient of a Nazi cosmology and "cosmic struggle" for domination as a master race (pp. 200, 203). Another prototypical example is the genocide in Rwanda (Taylor, 1999), framed within the context of the enduring effects of colonialism (p. 177).

5 My argument is thereby framed by the insights of Sluka's (2000) important contribution to the ethnography of violence. His work reveals striking cross-cultural similarities in the practice of state terror (p. 9), and the fact that the global rise in state terror was concentrated among Third World states in the U.S. sphere of influence (p. 8). Cycles of violence based on the phenomenon of death squads are thereby understood as a manifestation of U.S. cultural influence.

6 I am indebted to Kirmayer's suggestion (personal communication, September, 2009) to explore this approach further in relation to Sebald's (e.g., 1993) oeuvre. Sebald's prose slowly draws the reader toward a moving glimpse of absences, silences, fragmentary memories, and desolation of survivors of the Holocaust: "With every beat of the pulse, one lost more and more of one's qualities, *became less comprehensible to oneself,* increasingly abstract" (p. 56, my emphasis). Only hindsight allows Sebald to evoke the emigrants' lives in this particular manner.

7 This expression evokes A. Hinton's (2002a, 2005) anthropology of genocide. Several contributors highlight anthropology's role in the genocidal projects of modernity and its business of "manufacturing difference," a prelude to "annihilating difference."

8 Key introductory texts for ethnographers of violence are Brenneis & Macauley, 1996, and Duranti, 2009.

9 For an introduction to the notion of linguistic ideology see Woolard, 1998, or Kroskrity, 2000.

10 Nowhere did I come across a starker depiction of this predicament than in the work of the Dutch anthropologist Van de Port (1998), who set out to describe Serbian atrocities. Van de Port describes his tormenting sense of

incomprehension (p. 13) when Serbian society confronted him with a lack of concepts (p. 21), or a bewildering miscellany of opposing accounts, a cacophony of stories, a fragmented, disintegrating world (p. 22). He asks whether we really would like to read an academic text that is disturbing (p. 28). It is his informants' acquaintance with a world of inhuman experiences that leads them to highlight their ethnographer's lack of knowledge and sense of reality (p. 101). Van de Port highlights the damage war can cause to stories when a *fundamental trust in a meaningful world* has been destroyed (p. 109, my emphasis). The ethnography itself thereby becomes ironic: "The informants cannot be understood until they have been admitted to the bleak landscape of the university building, with its insipid *Ficae benjaminae* stuck in PVC plant-pots with clay grains and self-regulating moisturisers" (p. 26).

11 Fahy (2009) documents how the language that articulates suffering in North Korea is influenced by the discourse of a political elite and ideology "*which produced the suffering in the first place*" (p. 160, my emphasis). For a comparable analysis concerning Sri Lanka, see Argenti-Pillen, 2003a.

12 Fahy (2009) comments on her translation effort: "There will be the use of expressions and references which are contextually safe, and perhaps even so culturally bound as to *make little sense* outside of those settings, or they are *grammarless, fractured, without form*" (p. 233, my emphasis).

13 What I gloss here as "contradictory moral frameworks" features prominently in the chapter by Behrouzan and Fischer (this volume), as they depict "double-sided catacoustics" (hating and blaming but still loving the beauty of *nouheh*). The senselessness of a double-edged reality is best encapsulated by the phrase "this man I have nothing in common with, and who scares me; but knows how to spell my name!"

14 Lemelson's (this volume) case study of a survivor in Bali reveals this dynamic among contradictory moral frameworks, symptoms, and the ethnographic record. A familiarity with both the reality of the massacre and postmassacre social appearances is articulated as a "sense of living in two worlds," yet one of these worlds is given meaning as a spirit world. Lemelson's detailed ethnographic record reveals a typical example of the ambivalent non-sense expressions I accentuate:

> When I asked whether he believed that someone was practicing sorcery that caused his problems, however, Nyoman responded in Indonesian in a way that suggested either ambivalence or difficulty expressing himself in that language … *Definitely not, but the possibility exists.* (my emphasis)

15 This idea is raised in recent work with survivors of the Communist repressions in Poland (Witeska, 2009):

> Last year Leszek felt proud when an invitation for a presidential palace reached him. At the same time though, he feared going for the high rank official celebrations. His *doubts* made his legs cold and unable to move the night before. His dreams made him tired and nervous. His desire for resolving his *sense of guilt*, and his dream of belonging made him go. After the event, he *interpreted* his fears as a *legacy of the repressions* he went through. (p. 138, my emphasis)

The symptoms related to objectification can thereby be very similar to symptoms of trauma in the conventional sense. In other words, this linguistic or

356   *Pillen*

cultural unease and tension cause a distress, which can easily be lumped together with the distress caused by painful memories.

16 As in Fischer's (2007) analysis: "more forms of agency exist than witnessing and testifying ... witnessing and testifying are themselves *genre forms* within hierarchies of power and adjudication" (p. 437, my emphasis).

REFERENCES

Amnesty International (1993). Sri-Lanka: "Disappearance" and murder as techniques of counter-insurgency. In *Disappearances and political killings: Human rights crisis of the 1990's: A manual for action*. London: Amnesty International.

Argenti-Pillen, A. (2003a). The global flow of knowledge on war trauma: The role of the "cinnamon garden culture" in Sri Lanka. In J. Pottier, P. Sillitoe, & A. Bicker (Eds.), *Negotiating local knowledge: Identity, power and situated practice in development intervention* (pp.189–214). London: Pluto Press.

(2003b). *Masking terror: How women contain violence in Southern Sri Lanka*. Philadelphia: Pennsylvania University Press.

(2010). The fear of the sorcerer: Finding a peaceful moment for a sacrifice in Southern Sri Lanka. In A. Michaels (Ed.), *Ritual dynamics and the science of ritual*. Vol. III. *State, power and violence* (pp. 105–31). Wiesbaden, Germany: Harrassowitz-Verlag.

Behrouzan, O., & Fischer, M. J. (2015). "Behaves like a rooster and cries like a [four eyed] canine": The politics and poetics of depression and psychiatry in Iran. In D. E. Hinton & A. L. Hinton (Eds.), *Genocide and mass violence: Memory, symptom, and recovery*. Cambridge: Cambridge University Press.

Brenneis, D., & Macauley R. (1996). *The matrix of language: Contemporary linguistic anthropology*. Boulder, CO, and Oxford: Westview Press.

Burnside, S. (2006). *Senselessness in Paul Celan's Mohn und Gedächtnis. German Life and Letters*, 59, 140–50.

Casey, C. (2015). Remembering and ill health in post-invasion Kuwait: Topographies, collaborations, mediations. In D. E. Hinton & A. L. Hinton (Eds.), *Genocide and mass violence: Memory, symptom, and recovery*. Cambridge: Cambridge University Press.

Chandraprema, C. A. (1991). *Sri Lanka, the years of terror: The J. V.P. insurrection, 1987–1989*. Colombo: Lake House.

Comaroff, J., & Comaroff J. (2005). Reflections on youth: From the past to the postcolony. In A. Honwana & F. De Boeck (Eds.), *Makers and breakers: Children and youth in postcolonial Africa* (pp. 19–30). Oxford: James Currey.

De Berry, J. (2000). Life after loss: An anthropological study of post conflict recovery, Uganda. Unpublished doctoral dissertation, London School of Economics, London.

Deleuze, G. (2004). *The logic of sense*. London, New York: Continuum.

Duranti, A. (2009). *Linguistic anthropology: A reader*. Oxford: Wiley-Blackwell.

Fahy, S. (2009). Tales from the bottom of the well: Survivor testimonies from the North Korean 1990s famine. Unpublished doctoral dissertation, School of Oriental and African Studies, University of London, London.

Fischer, M. M. J. (2007). Epilogue: To live what would otherwise be unendurable: Return(s) to subjectivities. In J. Biehl (Ed.), *Subjectivity: Ethnographic investigations* (pp. 423–46). Berkeley: University of California Press.

Hinton, A. L. (2002a). The dark side of modernity: Toward an anthropology of genocide. In A. L. Hinton (Ed.), *Annihilating difference: The anthropology of genocide* (pp. 1–40). Berkeley: University of California Press.

(2002b). A head for an eye: Revenge in the Cambodian genocide. In A. L. Hinton (Ed.), *Genocide: An anthropological reader* (pp. 254–85). Oxford & Malden: Blackwell.

(2005). *Why did they kill? Cambodia in the shadow of genocide.* Berkeley: California University Press.

Kapferer, B. (1983). *A celebration of demons: Exorcism and the aesthetics of healing in Sri Lanka.* Oxford and Washington, DC: Berg, Smithsonian Institution Press.

Kidron, C. A. (2015). Embodying the distant past: Holocaust descendant narratives of the lived presence of the genocidal past. In D. E. Hinton & A. L. Hinton (Eds.), *Genocide and mass violence: Memory, symptom, and recovery.* Cambridge: Cambridge University Press.

Kohrt, B. A. (2015). The role of traditional rituals for reintegration and psychosocial wellbeing of child soldiers in Nepal. In D. E. Hinton & A. L. Hinton (Eds.), *Genocide and mass violence: Memory, symptom, and recovery.* Cambridge: Cambridge University Press.

Kristeva, J. (1980). *Desire in language: A semiotic approach to literature and art.* New York: Columbia University Press.

Kroskrity, P. V. (2000). Regimenting languages: Language ideological perspectives. In P. V. Kroskrity (Ed.), *Regimes of language: Ideologies, polities and identities* (pp. 1–34). Oxford: James Currey.

Kuper, L. (2002). Genocide: Its political use in the 20th century. In A. L. Hinton (Ed.), *Genocide: An anthropological reader* (pp. 48–73). Oxford and Malden, MA: Blackwell.

Kwon, H. (2015). The Vietnam War traumas. In D. E. Hinton & A. L. Hinton (Eds.), *Genocide and mass violence: Memory, symptom, and recovery.* Cambridge: Cambridge University Press.

Lavecchia, C., Lucchini F., & Levi, F. (1994). Worldwide trends in suicide mortality 1955–1989. *Acta Psychiatrica Scandinavica*, 90, 53–64.

Lemelson, R. (2015). "The spirits enter me to force me to be a communist": Political embodiment, idioms of distress, spirit possession, and thought disorder in Bali. In D. E. Hinton & A. L. Hinton (Eds.), *Genocide and mass violence: Memory, symptom, and recovery.* Cambridge: Cambridge University Press.

Mahmood, C. K. (2000). Trials by fire: Dynamics of terror in Punjab and Kashmir. In J. A. Sluka (Ed.), *Death squad: The anthropology of state terror* (pp. 70–90). Philadelphia: University of Pennsylvania Press.

Malamoud, C. (1996). *Cooking the world: Ritual and thought in ancient India.* New York: Oxford University Press.

Morrison, T. (1987). *Beloved.* London: Vintage.

Sebald, W. G. (1993). *The emigrants.* London: The Harvill Press.

Sluka, J. A. (2000). Introduction: State terror and anthropology. In J. A. Sluka (Ed.), *Death squad: The anthropology of state terror* (pp. 1–45). Philadelphia: Pennsylvania University Press.

Summerfield, D. (2002). Effects of war: Moral knowledge, revenge, reconciliation, and medicalised concepts of "recovery." *British Medical Journal*, 325, 1105–7.

Taylor, C. (1999). *Sacrifice as terror: The Rwandan genocide of 1994*. Oxford and New York: Berg.

Taylor, C. C. (2015). Rwanda's *gacaca* trials: Towards a new nationalism or business as usual? In D. E. Hinton & A. L. Hinton (Eds.), *Genocide and mass violence: Memory, symptom, and recovery*. Cambridge: Cambridge University Press.

Theidon, K. (2003). Justice in transition: The micropolitics of reconciliation in postwar Peru. *Journal of Conflict Resolution*, 50, 1–25.

——— (2015). Pasts imperfect: Talking about justice with former combatants in Colombia. In D. E. Hinton & A. L. Hinton (Eds.), *Genocide and mass violence: Memory, symptom, and recovery*. Cambridge: Cambridge University Press.

Van De Port, M. (1998). *Gypsies, wars, and other instances of the wild: Civilization and its discontents in a Serbian town*. Amsterdam: Amsterdam University Press.

Weineck, S. M. (1999) Logos and *pallaksch*: The loss of madness and the survival of poetry in Paul Celan's "Tübingen, Jänner." *Orbis Litterarum*, 54, 262–75.

Winslow, D., & Woost, M. D. (2004). *Economy, culture, and civil war in Sri Lanka*. Bloomington and Indianapolis: Indiana University Press.

Witeska, A. (2009). The landscapes of Polish memory: Conflicting ways of dealing with the communist past in a Polish town. Unpublished doctoral dissertation, University College London, UK.

Wolf, E. R. (2002). National socialist Germany. In A. L. Hinton (Ed.), *Genocide: An anthropological reader* (pp. 192–207). Oxford and Malden, MA: Blackwell.

Woolard, K. A. (1998). Introduction: Language ideology as a field of enquiry. In B. Schieffelin, K. Woolard, & P. Kroskrity (Eds.), *Language ideologies: Practice and theory* (pp. 3–47). New York: Oxford University Press.

16 Growing Up on the Front Line: Coming to Terms with War-Related Loss in Gonagala, Sri Lanka

Kenneth E. Miller and Sulani Perera

On the night of September 18, 1999, a platoon of the Liberation Tigers of Tamil Eelam (also known as the LTTE or Tamil Tigers), armed with scythes and machetes, quietly crossed the rice paddies that separate the largely Tamil district of Batticaloa from the ethnically diverse district of Ampara, in eastern Sri Lanka. Moving through the paddies toward the Sinhalese farming village of Gonagala, the Tigers split into two groups, one composed solely of men, the other of both male and female cadres. As the two groups approached the houses closest to the edge of the rice fields, the villagers slept, unaware of the massacre that was about to unfold.

By morning, fifty-four people had been murdered, including twelve children. According to survivors, the group of male Tigers only killed men, while female Tigers were actively involved in the killing of women and children. In one house, twenty people had been participating in a religious ritual to mark the death of another villager three months earlier; all but one person in the house were killed during the attack, including nine members of a single family.

After the massacre, many families, particularly those living closest to the border, began leaving their homes at night, afraid of another attack. They sought shelter in the homes of family, friends, or neighbors farther from the front line; in some cases, when no other shelter could be found, they simply cleared a spot in the jungle where they could spend the night. Just before sunrise, they would return to their homes, so that children could attend school and parents could work in the rice paddies or in their homes. This nightly migration continued on and off for nearly eight years, stopping during a temporary cease-fire, restarting when the cease-fire collapsed, and then stopping again when the Tigers lost their military base in Batticaloa in 2007.

The massacre in Gonagala occurred three days after the Sri Lankan air force bombed the marketplace in the Tamil community of Puthukkudiruppu, killing twenty-two civilians including two children.

Although it has been suggested that the attack on Gonagala was a retaliation for the air force bombing, the actual motivation for the massacre remains a matter of speculation. Gonagala was by no means the worst of the numerous massacres committed by the Tigers; the list of their mass attacks against civilians is long and victims numbered more than one hundred in some instances. These massacres must be viewed against a backdrop of prolonged civil war over LTTE demands for a separate homeland, a demand that arose after peaceful attempts at social change by Tamils were met by increasingly intense state-sponsored violence. The civil war in Sri Lanka was prolonged and bloody, marked by rampant violations of human rights on both sides, by the militarization of Sri Lankan society, by recurrent suicide attacks engaged in by so-called Black Tigers (an elite unit of the LTTE), and by the disappearance, torture, and killing of suspected LTTE militants and sympathizers by government forces. By the time of the LTTE's military defeat in 2009, more than seventy thousand people were estimated to have died in the war (BBC, 2009).

The documentary film *Unholy Ground* (www.unholygroundfilm.com)[1] explores the impact of the Gonagala massacre on six survivors, all of whom lost family members during the attack. The film crew was primarily Sri Lankan, including two residents of Gonagala, who worked as an interviewer and a photographer. Another key partner was the staff of a local organization, the Centre for Psychosocial Care (CPC). CPC has provided psychosocial assistance to Gonagala and other war- and disaster-affected communities in Ampara District. The participation of these local actors with strong ties to the village was critical to our ability to make the film, given the villagers' understandable wariness toward outsiders asking questions about a terrifying and deeply painful event and the impact it has had on their lives.

In addition to examining the ways in which villagers' lives were changed by the massacre, *Unholy Ground* explores the diverse pathways that the survivors have followed in coming to terms with their experiences of loss, in a context of ongoing vulnerability and continual disruption. We also examine the pivotal and at times complex role of Buddhism in helping to shape the community's understanding of, and response to, the deaths of their loved ones.

The six survivors featured in the film include a woman who lost three of her four children; a man who lost his wife and three children; a man who lost his wife, son, daughter-in-law, and infant grandson; another man who lost nine family members who were attending the community ritual mentioned earlier; and two girls who both lost their fathers. In the remainder of this chapter, we focus on the two girls, Sharmali and Samanthi. Our aim is to illustrate briefly three points:

1. Despite exposure to a similarly terrifying and painful event (the murder of their fathers), the two girls have followed very different paths and reached quite different places in the healing process. This underscores the important point that knowing about a potentially traumatic event does not, by itself, permit us to predict a particular mental health or psychosocial outcome for any individual.

2. Key factors in their social environments have either fostered or impeded the healing process for the two girls. Any understanding of the mental health effects of organized violence must take into account the social ecology of survivors, and in particular the ways in which aspects of that ecology may promote or impede the healing process and foster or undermine people's resilience.

3. Although the focus in much of the literature on mental health in conflict settings is on PTSD, the salient and enduring mental health difficulty in Gonagala, eight years after the massacre, is persistent grief, and in some cases, clinical depression. As a growing number of writers have begun to argue, the fascination with PTSD may at times reflect the interest of Western researchers and clinicians more than it does the priorities of particular war-affected populations (Barenbaum, Ruchkin, & Schwab-Stone, 2004; Miller, Kulkarni, & Kushner, 2006; Summerfield, 1999). This is not to suggest that PTSD symptoms were not widespread immediately after the massacre; by all accounts they were; however, trauma symptoms have largely abated with the passing of time for most villagers, while intense sadness – and for some people, other symptoms of depression – persist.

Struggling with Grief

Sharmali is a sweet, shy, and soft-spoken seventeen-year-old, who was ten years old the night her father was killed. She has vivid memories of the event:

That day it was only my dad, mom, me, and my younger brother at home. Around 2:00 AM we heard a sound and when we tried to go outside we saw someone flashing a light. Then all four of us went into one room and because we could not go outside we closed the door to that room really well. We didn't know who was coming. First they broke down the back door and came inside the house and then kicked the front door and broke it. Then we closed the door and placed the bed in front of it, and Mom and Dad leaned against the door. Then someone came to the door and we heard speaking in Tamil. They tried to open the door but they could not. They started to cut the door. Then they saw my mom and asked us to come out. Then once we came out they asked us to give them money and they put the mattress from the other room in the middle of the room we were in. Then two people held onto Dad's hands. Mom screamed, saying, "Please don't do anything!" Then they held a gun to Mom's chest and said, "If you scream we'll kill you." Then my younger brother and I hung onto Dad's hands. They said they would send him home in the morning, and told us to go to sleep. We could hear sounds from the outside. Two people took him by his hand and left. Then we saw him only in the morning [crying]. We even heard gunshots from houses in the upper part of the village. In the morning the police had come, somehow the police came and they went over to the paddy fields and fired shots. Then several people came and that is when we saw him there, by the jackfruit tree.

After the massacre, Sharmali's family left their home each night for about four years, until a local armed militia, called the Homeguard, was formed to protect the village. The presence of the Homeguard provided a greater feeling of safety to the village, and many families, including Sharmali's, began staying in their houses at night. Unable to work the paddy fields without her father's help, Sharmali's mother rented out the fields to generate income. Their small house is dark and sparsely furnished, and there is a heaviness that pervades it. Sharmali said her grief has not abated much since the incident, and she thinks about her father constantly, especially when she is at home. Her paternal grandmother recently died but was alive, though in poor health, when we made the film and lived with the family. When we interviewed the grandmother, she could not speak about her deceased son without weeping to the point where she was almost unable to talk.

Sharmali described her relationship with her mother as quite conflictual, and her mother readily acknowledged hitting Sharmali when she becomes angry with her. Sharmali is quite sure that her father would not be so harsh with her:

He didn't drink, he never yelled at us, and he took us to school in the morning. When Mom yells at me, I think of my father. I think if Dad were here he wouldn't yell like that.

Sharmali has friends with whom she speaks freely, but since she recently dropped out of school after scoring poorly on her O-Level exams, she now spends most of the day in the house. She would like to attend a vocational school; however, her mother does not allow her to leave the village as she considers it too dangerous, because young men might flirt with her and thereby damage her reputation. Sharmali was unable to articulate any plans or hopes she might have for the future.

Sharmali's mother, now forty-three, was also interviewed for the film. Throughout the interview, she smiled at unexpected times, laughing as she stated that "sadness is for weak people," and "there is no point in being sad." When asked why she thought her mother-in-law and daughter were still so grief-stricken eight years after the massacre, she shook her head, reiterated her belief that sadness was for weak people, and said simply that Sharmali is still so sad because she thinks about her father so much of the time. As Sharmali sat nearby listening to the interview and crying, her mother explained her reaction to the death of her husband within a Buddhist framework:

I don't have any sadness about anyone. The Tigers attacked. We exist and then we don't. We too will die someday. There is no point in being sad. For some people it is because they have attachments that they feel sad. After the Tigers attacked, even children were mutilated. It happened because they had *karma*. Because we didn't have *karma* it didn't happen to us. The Tigers had held a gun to my chest and told us not to scream. If I had died it would have been over then. It is because I didn't have *karma*. It is because of *karma* that it happened and I feel no sadness about anybody. There is no point in crying.

Other people interviewed for the film also suggested that sadness, according to their Buddhist faith, should not be enduring, because attachments are transient and experiences of change and loss are inherent in life. Yet most of the people we interviewed also recognized that strong attachments do develop within families, and that deep sadness is a natural reaction to the loss of loved ones, especially in such a premature and violent way. One man, who lost four family members (including an eighteen-month-old grandson) in the attack, described his struggle between his understanding of Buddhism and the reality of his distress in this way:

When you think about the Buddhist faith, it is not something that we should be really upset about. There is not a lot of sadness that we should experience. They had committed some sin and somehow received its negative consequences. When I think about the other side though, my heart hurts. They were brutally killed. It was not like they had grown old. The sadness is still there. I live like a human being. I eat and dress and live. But when I remember it, when I come home from the fields, my heart stings.

In framing her negative view on sadness within a Buddhist framework, Sharmali's mother revealed a religious understanding that is quite selective, for Buddhism also prioritizes compassion and a gentle acknowledgment of one's experience. Indeed, one of the village monks, interviewed for the film, described how he comforted villagers after the attack by sharing with them a popular story about the Buddha, meant to illustrate the Buddhist belief that grief is a common human experience (and not a sign of weakness, as Sharmali's mother asserted). According to the story, the Buddha sought to comfort a grieving mother by encouraging her to go through her village and find a family in which nobody had died. The woman returned to the Buddha comforted by the realization that loss, though painful, was also a shared experience and that she was not alone with her experience of grief. The story resonated with many villagers, who stated that they found comfort in the realization that they were not alone with their grief in the wake of the massacre. Unfortunately, in Sharmali's home there is still very little space for grief. Paradoxically, this may have had the effect of keeping her grief (and that of her grandmother) alive and salient in her ongoing experience. In refusing to empathize with Sharmali's sadness, and indeed criticizing it as a sign of weakness, her mother may be unintentionally helping to maintain in her daughter the very emotional experience she so dislikes.

Transcending Tragedy

Samanthi was also ten years old when her father was killed in the attack on Gonagala. A bright, playful, and outgoing adolescent of seventeen, she, like Sharmali, has vivid memories of the night of the massacre and the murder of her father:

That day the Tigers came and they broke the door down and came inside our house. They took our father and asked for money; they took him away, saying they would return him in the morning. But they didn't return him in the morning and they took the money as well. So that day, Father was there in the porch, all cut up.

Although she becomes visibly sad when speaking of her father, Samanthi said that she is normally happy, an observation confirmed by her mother. Samanthi said that she becomes sad when she remembers her father, and that in those moments the sadness feels as strong as it did eight years ago. When that happens, she talks with her mother, a warm and compassionate woman who cried quietly when talking about the death of her husband and the challenges of raising the three children by herself: "Since her father is not there, everything that is done by a father and by a mother, I do for my children." Samanthi is quite close to her mother and finds comfort in talking with her, whether about sadness related to losing her father or any other problems she might have.

At first, we were extremely sad; we had an unbearable kind of sadness. After a little time had passed, it's not that we forgot, but nonetheless, with the strength I got from my mother, I was able to mend my heart a little, and did my schoolwork and lived. My mother – now when such things happen, when I have a personal problem, I take it to my mother; my mother tells me how to solve it, in this way.

Samanthi said that talking with her mother, and sharing her sadness in this way, is quite helpful, and allows her to move through the sadness and shift back into pleasurable activities and a happier mood. She loves to dance, which she does at school, and dreams of one day being a dance teacher. She also delights in helping her younger sister with her school-work and is an avid reader.

Now when I recall the incident when my father died I get very sad, but at other times when I'm spending time with my mother, my older brother, and younger sister, I live happily. When I get to school I get together with my friends, and when I'm exercising, when I'm dancing, I'm happy.

Like many families who lost members in the attack, Samanthi and her family found comfort in the religious ritual of *dane*, an alms-giving ceremony in which the family prepares a meal for the village monks, who in turn offer guidance and support in what is generally a two day communal gathering. *Dane* is meant to earn merit or good *karma* for the deceased, so that they will never again suffer such a terrible fate in a future life as they did during the massacre. *Dane* is a source of great comfort to those families who can afford it.

To this day, since my father's death, every year we give alms; even if we can't do so at home, we give alms to the temple – at least a meal – in a way that we can afford. For about three years we did it at home, then considering my mother's economic condition, we did it in a way that we can afford. I think that by giving alms like that my father will receive at least a little bit of merit. According to our religious beliefs we think so. So because we love our father a lot, we give alms and in that way we mend our hearts a little.

Samanthi lives with her mother, brother, and younger sister, who was born soon after the attack. Their simply decorated house has a warm and inviting feel, enhanced by the frequent laughter of Samanthi's nine-year-old sister. Although they are poor and had to sell some of their land to raise money, they still have enough land to grow rice and other food for their own consumption; Samanthi made a point of noting that the family is able to live within its means. Her mother does not conceal her sadness and is comfortable supporting her children when they become sad. Although this does not seem to lessen the intensity of the feelings of grief when they arise, it does create a space in which Samanthi's grief can be experienced, arising and diminishing, so that it is neither pervasive nor constant. Having experienced the brutal murder of her father as a child, Samanthi has a delight in much of her life and hopefulness for the future that reflect a genuine process of healing, fostered by her mother's consistent support, her family's capacity to engage in *dane*, and her own internal resources.

Summary

The different developmental pathways followed by Sharmali and Samanthi following the massacre likely reflect a constellation of factors at different ecological levels. Individually, each has allotted her own coping strategies, strengths, and vulnerabilities to the monumental task of grieving the murder of her father and moving on with life. Sharmali and Samanthi are friends, and Samanthi wondered aloud whether perhaps Sharmali has had a more difficult time because she is shy and does not talk readily with others about problems she is having. In contrast to Samanthi, who is outgoing and clearly at ease in social situations, Sharmali is quite introverted, a characteristic that may have made it difficult for her to reach out for emotional and practical support over the years.

Both young women have found comfort in the religious ritual of *dane* and the belief that by giving alms, they are earning merit for the deceased fathers (on the centrality of bereavement among Cambodian refugees who survived the genocide, and the importance of rituals for the deceased in trauma recovery, see D. Hinton, Peou, Joshi, Nickerson, & Simon, 2013). The village temple is nearby, and clearly it has played an important role in the healing process of all of the survivors of the Gonagala massacre. However, Sharmali and Samanthi have experienced quite different environments within their families. Samanthi's mother has sought to support her daughter's (and her own) grieving process, while encouraging her academic achievements and her growth as a dancer. In contrast, Sharmali's mother has had a more difficult time managing her daughter's sadness and supporting her efforts within and outside school. Both women (mothers) are practicing Buddhists, yet their understandings of Buddhism have shaped their reactions to the experience of loss in very different ways. For Samanthi's mother, the Buddhist emphasis on *compassion* was clearly a central element of her faith and her approach to life; for Sharmali's mother, the concept of *nonattachment* was particularly salient and was instrumental in helping her minimize the emotional impact of her husband's death (on the use of Buddhist doctrine and practice to recover from trauma among Cambodian refugees, see Nickerson & D. Hinton, 2011). It is interesting to consider that Buddhism also speaks of the danger of *aversion*, the avoidance of unpleasant feelings and experiences. Aversion may lead to an inability to experience one's own difficult emotions or to tolerate the painful feelings of other people; this in turn may impede healing from experiences of loss or emotional injury (Kornfield, 1993).

In making the film *Unholy Ground*, we were struck by the remarkable strength of many of the people we met. Many of the villagers we interviewed had put their lives back together and found new sources of meaning and hope following a profound tragedy that initially left everyone we met in a state of despair. At the same time, we were also struck by the enduring nature of people's grief, and the vulnerability that some individuals, such as Sharmali, continued to experience eight years after the massacre. The persistence of such grief and vulnerability may suggest the limits of the extent to which people can fully heal in the wake of mass tragedy. However, we also believe that effective interventions can foster the healing process significantly, by supporting survivors and their families economically, psychosocially, and spiritually. For example, livelihood support to lessen economic distress within Sharmali's family, coupled with spiritual guidance and emotional support to help her mother tolerate feelings of sadness with greater compassion, might have lessened Sharmali's grief and enabled her to reengage more fully with life.

The various pathways followed by the survivors of the Gonagala massacre illustrate the complexity of predicting mental health and psychosocial well-being solely on the basis of knowledge of prior exposure to potentially traumatic life experiences. Although the correlation between war exposure and level of distress is consistently positive, exposure by itself is a highly imperfect predictor, rarely accounting for more than 25 percent of the variance in levels of distress or symptomatology (Miller & Rasmussen, 2010). Numerous factors influence the ways in which people react to, and are affected by, exposure to organized violence, including extreme acts of violence such as the massacre described in this paper. Although signs of extreme distress (i.e., symptoms of trauma, depression, and anxiety) are ubiquitous in the immediate aftermath of such experiences, there is growing evidence that for the majority of people such distress diminishes with the passing of time and a supportive environment; that is, healing – a "mending of the heart" as the Gonagala survivors described it – seems to be the rule rather than the exception. It may be an imperfect healing, with moments of pain and vulnerability resurfacing as reminders evoke distressing memories. And because experiences of loss change the social and material environments of survivors, emotional pain may relate as much to ongoing experiences of social isolation or poverty (when a breadwinner is killed) as they do to the original experience of loss. In any case, our experience making the film *Unholy Ground* underscored for us the importance of honoring the capacity to heal from the most devastating events, while also recognizing that holistic, culturally grounded assistance may also facilitate the healing process.

It is also important to consider the variability that exists within any cultural context when examining the influence of culture on experiences of loss and healing. Theravadan Buddhism as practiced in Sri Lanka was clearly a critical force in shaping the reactions of Sharmali and Samanthi, as well as their mothers, to their experiences of war-related loss. Yet a variety of individual factors in turn shaped the ways in which Buddhism was understood and utilized in responding to those losses. Certainly, an understanding of Buddhism is critical to comprehending the impact of the Gonagala massacre; however, it is also essential to explore variations of Buddhist belief and experience among the villagers, as well as a host of other individual and familial factors (e.g., temperament, prior trauma history, family support, financial circumstances) that invariably influence the process of healing from trauma and loss.

NOTES

1 The film was directed by Ken Miller and coproduced by Ken Miller, S. Manohaari Habaragamua, M. A. J. Ranawake, and Gaithri Fernando.

REFERENCES

Barenbaum, J., Ruchkin, V., & Schwab-Stone, M. (2004). The psychosocial aspects of children exposed to war: Practice and policy initiatives. *Journal of Child Psychology and Psychiatry*, 45, 41–62.
BBC. (2009). Quick guide: Sri Lanka. Retrieved March 12, 2009, from http:// news.bbc.co.uk/2/hi/ south_asia/6065646.stm
Hinton, D. E., Peou, S., Joshi, S., Nickerson, A., & Simon, N. (2013). Normal grief and complicated bereavement among traumatized Cambodian refugees: Cultural context and the central role of dreams of the deceased. *Culture, Medicine, and Psychiatry*, 37, 427–64.
Kornfield, J. (1993). *A path with heart.* New York: Bantam.
Miller, K. E., Kulkarni, M., & Kushner, H. (2006). Beyond trauma-focused psychiatric epidemiology: Bridging research and practice with war-affected populations. *American Journal of Orthopsychiatry*, 76, 409–22.
Miller, K. E., & Rasmussen, A. (2010). War experiences, daily stressors, and mental health in conflict and post-conflict settings: Bridging the divide between trauma-focused and psychosocial frameworks. *Social Science and Medicine*, 70, 7–16.
Nickerson, A., & Hinton, D. E. (2011). Anger regulation in traumatized Cambodian refugees: The perspectives of Buddhist monks. *Culture, Medicine, and Psychiatry*, 35, 396–416.
Summerfield, D. (1999). A critique of seven assumptions behind psychological trauma programmes in war-affected countries. *Social Science and Medicine*, 48, 1449–62.

17 The Role of Traditional Rituals for Reintegration and Psychosocial Well-Being of Child Soldiers in Nepal

Brandon A. Kohrt

Raj became a soldier in the Maoist People's Liberation Army when he was fourteen years old. He joined after Maoist youth threatened to kill his father. Raj deserted his battalion after two years in the Maoist army. Maoists and the Nepal government signed peace accords ending the decade-long People's War shortly after Raj's return home. The end of war and return home did not abate Raj's suffering. Memories of his friends' deaths in combat plagued him. Prior to joining the Maoists, he had been a shamanic healer. However, the actions he committed as a Maoist soldier such as touching dead bodies and eating with other castes disturbed his ancestral deity. Without the protection of this deity, Raj lost his healing abilities, and his family became vulnerable to physical and spiritual afflictions. To free Raj from his war memories and restore his healing abilities, Raj's family summoned a traditional healer. The healer performed a ritual of *man baadhne* – binding the heart-mind. The ritual temporarily abated his distress and partially restored his healing abilities. When members of a nongovernmental organization (NGO) aiding child soldiers asked Raj what assistance he required, he requested funds to participate in additional rituals to appease the family's ancestral deity, enabling his full recovery and assuring his family's well-being.

Maya joined the Maoists voluntarily when she was fourteen years old. She returned home after a year of service. Maya was concerned that she had abandoned her parents. She did not participate in any rituals upon returning home; she had no desire to participate in them. She was particularly reluctant to consider the *Swasthani* ritual. This ritual, performed only by women, is a month-long fast to atone for one's sins and assure the well-being of male relatives. Adult women advised that girl soldiers participate in the Swasthani to prevent negative consequences of their sins committed as Maoist soldiers such as traveling with men, interacting with other castes, and being physically active during menstruation. If girl soldiers did not perform this ritual, they endangered their future husbands and sons, according to elder women. Maya dismissed their concerns. She focused on opening a small store in her village. It would

369

be the first store in her village operated by a woman of her ethnic group. Maya asked NGO workers for a loan to help start the business.

Introduction

Using traditional rituals to support children affected by mass violence is a burgeoning trend in humanitarian psychosocial interventions. The goal of this chapter is to discuss how such rituals can be beneficial for reintegration of child soldiers as well as the limitations of using such rituals. The psychosocial community's interest in rituals grows out of their focus on "the close connection between psychological aspects of our experience (our thoughts, emotions and behavior) and our wider social experience (our relationships, traditions, and culture)" (Psychosocial Working Group, 2003). Psychosocial practitioners, as well as anthropologists and other social scientists, have questioned the appropriateness of Western psychiatric therapies for survivors of mass violence, especially for children (Bracken & Petty, 1998; Psychosocial Working Group, 2003; Summerfield, 1998). They argue that psychiatric approaches have the potential of doing more harm than good.

Presenting them as an alternative to psychiatric care, psychosocial practitioners implement interventions such as vocational training, working with water and sanitation programs, education, school-based social activities, sports groups, self-help discussions, and play activities for children (Psychosocial Working Group, 2003). Psychosocial interventions categorized as targeting "culture and values" provide opportunities for normal religious practice and work with traditional, religious healing sources. Similarly, international psychosocial guidelines advise interventionists to "learn about and, where appropriate, collaborate with local, indigenous and traditional healing systems" (IASC, 2007, p. 136).

Donor and implementing humanitarian agencies have promoted traditional rituals for reintegration of child soldiers. Reintegration is the third part of the DDR (disarmament, demobilization, and reintegration) framework in postconflict settings (see Theidon, this volume). Reintegration returns ex-combatants to civilian life. In Sierra Leone, communities and families employed "rituals of welcome" to incorporate returned girl soldiers into acceptable social positions (McKay & Mazurana, 2004). Honwana (2006) describes traditional healers in Angola conducting communal cleansing rituals for child soldiers to purify them of their exposure to killing. In Mozambique, traditional healers facilitated reintegrating ex-combatants by "taking the war out of the people" (Nordstrom, 1997, p.146). Rituals have tremendous potential to aid children and communities in a manner that is culturally congruent

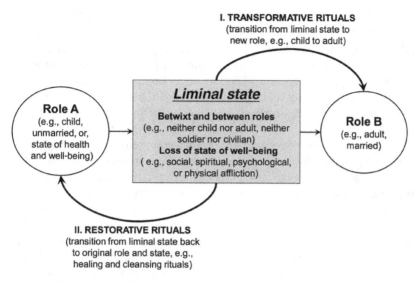

I. TRANSFORMATIVE RITUALS
(transition from liminal state to
new role, e.g., child to adult)

Role A
(e.g., child,
unmarried, or,
state of health
and well-being)

Liminal state

Betwixt and between roles
(e.g., neither child nor adult, neither
soldier nor civilian)
Loss of state of well-being
(e.g., social, spiritual, psychological,
or physical affliction)

Role B
(e.g., adult,
married)

II. RESTORATIVE RITUALS
(transition from liminal state back
to original role and state, e.g.,
healing and cleansing rituals)

Figure 17.1. Classification of rituals.

with locally available resources and practitioners. However, rituals have potential negative consequences.

Anthropological approaches to rituals are helpful to understand the positive and negative implications of these practices. A key component of rituals is *liminality*. Turner (1967) discusses liminality as ambiguity at the borders between spaces, times, and roles; it is "betwixt and between." Rituals can be dichotomized, albeit rather crudely, as *transformative* versus *restorative*. Both types involve movement through liminal states. Rites of passage exemplify transformative rituals such as social role changes from child to adult, from bachelor to married person, or from community member to leader. In contrast, healing ceremonies exemplify restorative rituals wherein persons regain a position of health from a liminal state of sickness, whether it is a spiritual, psychological, or physical ailment (see Figure 17.1). Restorative rituals include the regaining of a lost social role: A woman considered religiously impure or polluted may undergo a ritual to regain her ability to marry.

Former child soldiers find themselves in a liminal state. They are not active combatants; nor are they civilians. Families react with fear and suspicion to child soldiers and do not treat them as they do other children in the community (Betancourt, Agnew-Blais, Gilman, Williams, & Ellis, 2010; Boyden, 2003). Many adults see child soldiers as threatening and morally corrupted (Boyden, 2003). Many of the approaches to rituals, especially those for child soldiers, have focused on restorative ceremonies to regain putative innocence and be nonthreatening to adults. The rituals may restore health by removing spiritual and other afflictions acquired through participation in war. Afflictions may affect whole families and communities. Through ritual, child soldiers have the possibility of regaining social status wherein adults do not perceive them as threatening, morally corrupt, and harbingers of spiritual and physical violence.

While the benefit of restorative rituals is apparent from a social cohesion perspective, there are potential threats to well-being in those rituals. Rituals of resocialization may entail a cost to participants. For example, child soldiers are threatening to adults because they do not fall into socially expected roles of submission to adult authority. Rituals may restore the expected socially submissive role of children, but this may represent a lost opportunity for children to gain a greater voice in social processes. The issue of girl soldiers exemplifies this challenge. Traditional rituals often reinforce gender discrimination by promoting the status of "(older) males" and "threaten the human security and well-being of women and girls" (Denov, 2007). Furthermore, Denov adds, "when assessing whether 'culture is always right,' one cannot discount … the reality and implications of gendered exclusionary practices." Girl soldiers are particularly threatening for patriarchal societies. Therefore, adults use ritual to disempower girls and restore them to socially acceptable subjugated roles. This raises the question of whether restorative rituals are the best practice for reintegration of child soldiers, particularly for girl soldiers.

Psychosocial interventionists thus find themselves at the intersection of competing ideologies. On the one hand, psychosocial programs operate from a desire to follow rights-based frameworks that advocate gender equity and inclusion of children in communal and social processes. On the other hand, psychosocial practitioners advocate following community-initiated approaches and traditional practices, which may be rooted in processes of exclusion such as patriarchy and ethnic discrimination. Therefore, a critical eye is required to examine the need for promoting rituals and who will benefit most so that children receive optimal support rather than potential harm from such practices.

Methods

Nepal is a landlocked country north of India and south of the Tibetan autonomous region of China, with a population of 28 million. Nepal's population comprises more than sixty ethnic and caste groups. There is a history of hegemonic dominance by Hindu high castes (Bahun and Chhetri) over those deemed low caste (Dalit) and minority ethnic groups (Janajati), who are predominantly Buddhist and shamanist. In 1996, the Communist Party of Nepal (Maoists) declared war on the government of Nepal, which at the time was a Hindu monarchy. After a decade of war with more than sixteen thousand deaths, the parties signed peace accords in 2006.

During the war, the Maoist army and government security forces conscripted individuals less than eighteen years of age. These child soldiers assumed myriad roles including as soldiers, spies, porters, cooks, propaganda workers, and cultural program dancers. After the war, child soldiers experienced reintegration difficulties such as lack of support by the community, rejection by the family, and denial of education and employment (Kohrt et al., 2010a). When girl soldiers returned home, families often neglected and abused them. The community viewed the girls as no longer pure or respectable because they operated outside appropriate social norms during their time with Maoists (Kohrt, Tol, Pettigrew, & Karki, 2010b). Therefore, understanding the role of rituals in reducing stigma and facilitating healthier and more successful reintegration is crucial.

The findings are drawn from a mixed-methods study of the mental health and psychosocial consequences of children's participation in armed groups and subsequent reintegration (Kohrt et al., 2008). The study was conducted from 2007 through 2008 with a Nepali NGO, Transcultural Psychosocial Organization (TPO) Nepal. The qualitative component of the larger study included participatory approaches (Karki, Kohrt, & Jordans, 2009), narrative focus group discussions (N = 25 groups) with children and community members, key informant interviews (N = 152) with children and community members, and case studies (N = 24) of child soldiers. Pseudonyms are used for case studies. The quantitative results are from a sample of 142 child soldiers.

Findings

Types of Rituals

Participants identified rituals either currently being employed or potentially employable for returned child soldiers. Figure 17.2 illustrates social domains such as rituals practiced with the family (e.g., *kul devta puja*, *bhaakal*) versus within school (e.g., Saraswati puja). Some rituals crosscut domains and include multiple components such as *kul devta puja* (worship of ancestral deities). *Dhaami-jhankri* (shamanic healers) lead many rituals.

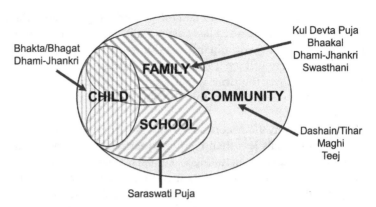

Figure 17.2. Rituals identified by community members for returned children.

1. *Bhaakal* – The *bhaakal* ritual was the most commonly described ritual and most frequently practiced ritual for returning child soldiers. Turner (1931, p. 473) defines *bhaakal* as

a pledge, consisting of [money] and some rice put on one side when a man wishing for some boon (such as health) promises to perform a sacrifice to one of the greater gods (the similar pledge made to a *kul-deutā* [ancestral spirit] is called *bādhā*).

Parents performed *bhaakal* to assure safe return of child soldiers. They did this through *kul devta puja*, the worship of a family's ancestors thanking them for the safe return of children.

UPPER CASTE WOMAN: Families or communities do rituals for the children when they return. *Bhaakal* is practiced for different reasons. When children become sick, we do *bhaakal* so that they become well again. Parents also do this with the hopes that a child will pass his school exams. They may put lights around the temple when doing *bhaakal*.

A man from a Janajati ethnic group in northeastern Nepal stated, "Families and community members do rituals for the children. Families do *bhaakal*. It is different in every region based on the traditions there. Here people fast and set pigeons free to offer a *bhaakal*." A man in midwestern Nepal described the reasoning behind performing *bhaakal*: "Parents think Maoists took their children because their *kul devta* (ancestral deity) was angry with them, so they do *bhaakal* for the return of their family members." A woman in northeastern Nepal explained that *bhaakal* benefited children: "After the *dhaami* (shaman) did *bhaakal*, the children felt better."

Bhaakal represents a restorative ritual that can reintegrate a child into the family network. The ceremony helps children move from the liminal state between Maoist soldier identity and identity as a family member. Children often reported a reluctance to return home because of concern that their family would not accept them. Child soldiers also reported that parents did not treat them as well as their siblings. The *bhaakal* ritual symbolized parental acceptance. The practice of *bhaakal* made the children feel welcome when they returned. A child from midwestern hills explained, "When I came back, my family took me to the *dhaami* (traditional healer), and two roosters were sacrificed as *bhaakal*."

2. *Man baadhne* – *Man baadhne* is ritual binding of the heart-mind. The *man* (heart-mind) is the organ of emotion, memory, and desire. Distress in the heart-mind manifests as sadness, bad memories, nightmares, worries, and uncontrolled desires (Kohrt & Harper, 2008). The *man* influences the *dimaag*, the brain-mind, which controls social behavior. When the heart-mind fills with strong and overwhelming emotions or desires, the brain-mind is not able to regulate behavior. Brain-mind damage manifests as acting *paagal* (mad or psychotic) including actions such as aggressive behavior, violence toward others, distraction, being lost in thought, wandering aimlessly, and acting inappropriately for one's social position, which is based on gender and caste.

Child soldiers and adults in the community reported that problems in the heart-mind and brain-mind were common among returnees (Kohrt & Maharjan, 2009). They described flashbacks, intrusive memories, and ruminations about traumatic events – all evidence of heart-mind disruption. Other problems included impulsivity, inability to concentrate, and aggression – symptoms of brain-mind dysfunction resulting from overactive heart-minds. Families summoned traditional healers, who conducted *man baadhne* to reduce distressing memories and prevent heart-mind activity from overwhelming the brain-mind. In the ritual, a shaman transfers overwhelming emotions from the child to a transitional object such as an egg, which he places at crossroads to feed spirits, or a chicken, which he sacrifices and consumes. A second use for the *man baadhne* ritual was to prevent ex-combatants from returning to the Maoists. Parents called upon shamans to bind the heart-mind of child soldiers to prevent the desire to return from becoming too strong to ignore.

The *man baadhne* ritual, therefore, is also restorative because it moves children from a liminal state of distress and restores them to a condition of well-being and putative psychological normalcy. Child soldiers who underwent this said it helped them with traumatic memories and psychological problems. Families reported that after children had their heart-minds bound by shamans, behavior improved. Moreover, the binding of potential desires to rejoin the Maoists made families feel more secure in their children's position as civilians, not soldiers. *Man baadhne* appeared to be successful and effective for improving interpersonal relationships within the family and for children to address their own worries, fears, and anger.

3. *Swasthani* – Parents and other adult community members feared that girl soldiers had lost their purity by being Maoist soldiers. Adults occasionally referred to this explicitly as fears that girls lost their virginity. However, more often, adults described this as loss of Hindu *ritual* purity such as tainting of one's caste purity. The loss of a daughter's purity has ramifications for the extended family network. Many adult women did not interact with girl soldiers because they were impure and would contaminate others. Adults in the community, particularly older women, suggested taking part in the Swasthani ritual to increase social acceptance, improve marriage prospects, and allow girls to participate in other religious activities and festivals.

The *Swasthani* is a ritual text originating in Nepal. The *Swasthani* comprises multiple narratives about Hindu women who have sinned in their current or prior lifetimes. These sins influence the lives of husbands and sons. The narratives suggest that anger and negative emotions displayed toward men result in deformity, misfortune, and despair in the next life (Bennett, 1983). The early death of a husband is his wife's fault. Women are responsible for maintaining their husbands' long lives. "Some sin in a previous life causes a woman to become a widow in this one" (Bennett, 1983, p. 219). The *Swasthani* includes tales of women's redemption. Women atone for their sins through prolonged fasts and subjugation to men in their lives. Throughout January, women, mostly upper-caste Hindu women, read the *Swasthani* and fast, mimicking the actions of the narratives' heroines. This prevents their sins from having a negative effect on the men in their lives.

The Swasthani ritual is as a restorative ritual that repositions girl soldiers within preconceived culturally acceptable roles. The Swasthani ritual was the closest model to a cleansing ritual for girl soldiers in Nepal. While it provided an opportunity for social acceptance, it threatened the autonomy and striving for gender equality that motivated girls to join the Maoists.

Case Studies

Raj: Maoists and Traditional Healing

The following account of Raj illustrates motivations for engaging in ritual, the specific use of the *man baadhne* ritual, and some of the reasons why many families did not employ rituals. This account from Raj explains how he became a child soldier and the experiences that distressed him.

RAJ: My father was plowing his field. Two Maoist boys, two girls, and the commander of the group came and started beating my father so badly that he almost died. My father was innocent but the Maoist soldiers accused him of speaking against them. I felt so helpless watching them accuse my father. I could not do anything for him because I was so scared that the Maoists would kill me. My father lost consciousness from the torture.... A few days later, the Maoists came to my house and threatened to kill my father if I did not go with them. I pleaded with them. I told them that I wanted to stay and finish my schooling, but they did not listen to me. They forced me to go with them. I was fourteen years old at that time.

Many of my friends and I were injured. Many people died in one battle. On that day, I did not think I would survive. I thought that day was my last.... Many friends were dying. One friend asked me for water as he was dying. I could not do anything for him because the battle was very dangerous. I still get scared and start sweating when I think of that day. I especially remember that friend asking me for water as I ran away from him. I cannot do any work if I think of that day. I get very disturbed and want to be by myself in a quiet place. I need to stay busy. That helps me to forget about that day. This kind of experience creates a bad impact in our society for a long time.

In addition to being a child soldier, Raj was a traditional healer.

RAJ: My grandfather was a shaman. Two years after my grandfather passed away, I started becoming possessed. Then I took my grandfather's drum and went to the cremation grounds at night. One day, when I was possessed, the deity started speaking through me. He said, "After your grandfather died, I have appeared to you. You should go to the river, take a bath, and purify yourself. Worship me to become a shaman."

The Maoists reject traditional shamanistic healing. The Maoists have advocated the use of "scientific" medicine and the end of reliance upon "superstitious" traditional healing. They have banned shamanic rituals throughout the country. "The Maoists are seeking to replace traditional shamanic community ceremonies with their own community building rituals. They want to supplant the shamanic/superstitious community rituals" (De Sales, 2006). During their association with Maoists, child soldiers beat shamans, burned ritual sites, and urinated on ritual artifacts.

RAJ: The Maoists did not believe in such superstition. They said it was worthless. They don't believe in God. I have seen Maoists beating shamans. And they rip up the shamans' books or throw them away. While I was with the Maoists, I could not do anything that my deity told me to do. I did not have any problems with my deity while in the Maoist army at the beginning, but later I had to carry dead bodies. Then I started having a possession sickness.

Handling corpses is one of the most polluting activities in Hinduism, similar to eating beef or touching a woman during her menstrual period. Polluted individuals cannot communicate effectively with their gods. In Raj's case, touching corpses had polluted him and offended his shamanic deity. The offended deity then began to possess him in the form of sickness rather than endow him with healing powers.

RAJ'S MOTHER: The shaman god became angry at Raj because he had to carry dead bodies and eat anything that he found. He couldn't follow the rules of the shaman god so he started shivering [he began having convulsions]. He dreamed only about war. He has nightmares. Raj was a very jolly person but since he came back from the Maoists, he sits only by himself and does not want to go near to the people and talk with them. He worries all the time. He is very sad because he had to quit his studies. His heart-mind is full of sadness. He speaks very little these days. He is not happy at all.

To address Raj's distress, his family chose to summon a shamanic healer. The healer selected the *man baadhne* ritual because it would reduce the intrusive recollections of Raj's war experiences. The family sacrificed one of their few chickens for the ritual. The shaman moved Raj's distressing emotions to the sacrificial chicken. The ritual helped reduce some of his anger and irritation with others. Intrusive memories abated partially but still distressed him occasionally. His family also saw some improvement in Raj, with the qualification that he does remain withdrawn and shows happiness only rarely.

Raj was concerned that the ritual did not fully restore his purity and consequently his shamanic deity would not return all his healing powers. The polluting experiences with the Maoists required a larger ceremony, a ceremony he and his family could not afford. The ceremony would appease the deity and cleanse him of the polluting effects of having carried dead bodies.

RAJ: We do not have the money to follow what my deity told us to do. I still have not done the *puja* (ceremony) that the deity told me to do. I think my parents and my brother also have become sick because of this. We are hoping to do the *puja* soon.

Raj's case illustrates the benefit of a restorative ritual to reduce distress. Raj hoped to find an NGO to support additional ritual activity to regain healing abilities and reduce the threat of sickness and misfortune for other family members.

Maya: Gender, Ethnicity, and Rituals for Girl Soldiers

Maya's account demonstrates the limitations of traditional healing to facilitate reintegration. Unlike Raj, Maya joined the Maoists voluntarily.

MAYA: I thought that if I joined the Maoists, I could beat people. I thought the Maoists would back me up. I threatened people who gambled and played cards by burning all their cards. I spent a year with the Maoists.

Maya is from the Chepang ethnic group of Mongolian descent, who were traditionally hunter-gatherers living in the forests and low hills. The Chepang are an ethnic group historically not subscribing to the caste system; nevertheless, they are at the mercy of caste hierarchy. Maya explained that her main experience with people not from her ethnic group was in school.

MAYA: While I was studying in the school, the Chhetri, Bahun, and Tibetans would dominate us. They tried to harass us and we would quarrel on the school bench. We sometimes fought. I was foolish. I didn't tolerate it if anyone looked down on me or said anything rude to me. I would beat them and sometimes I got hurt too while trying to hurt others....

We were the lowest level of society. Everyone despised us and made fun of us. Nowadays our tribe is still very weak. We eat if we can find some food, otherwise we starve. Other tribes have education and employment so they have good food to eat. We don't have anything so what would we eat? People treat our tribe like animals. We are hated, exploited, and trapped because we collect roots and yams to feed ourselves.

Maya went on to describe a changing ethnic and political landscape. These changes were set in motion before the People's War and a major part of the Maoist rhetoric during the People's War:

MAYA: Anyone can do anything now. We are no less than anyone else. We spread the awareness that we can do many things. Society and times are changing.... I try to encourage others and create awareness among my neighbors and among my tribe that they should learn skills, get employment, and educate our children. Whenever I hear someone use derogatory words to refer to our tribe, I immediately scold them. They don't dare to use slang in front of me. People in our tribe are becoming aware of their rights with the help of many organizations. Radio and television programs now also present positive stories about Chepang people.... I feel confident that I can and will do something to improve the lives of the Chepang.

Girls saw the Maoists as an opportunity to join strong women and escape from patriarchy and gender-based violence.

COMMUNITY HEALTH WORKER: Maya told me patrolling RNA [Royal Nepal Army] soldiers and armed police raped two or three Chepang women from this village when the women were collecting grass and wood. Maya had known that RNA soldiers and police behave this way toward Chepang and Dalit [low-caste] women. When Maya heard of this event in her own community, she was so enraged that she decided to join the Maoist party to take revenge on those rapists. Then she met the commander of a Maoist party traveling with a friend and asked them if she could join the party.

The Maoists were successful in recruiting women because of the history of gender discrimination and legacy of violence against women perpetrated by government security forces.

When girl soldiers returned to their villages, they encountered discrimination manifested as concerns about ritual purity. Girl soldiers in areas that were predominantly Hindu reported that when they returned to their communities, adults excluded them from many activities. The girl soldiers had become polluted because they were outside the watchful eye of a male relative. Villagers assumed girl soldiers were sexually active or impure by violating caste regulations. A male high-caste health worker in eastern Nepal said, "Young people just join the Maoists because of 'free sex,'" with the term "free sex" emphasized in English. In public, people would insult the girls, calling them *"nakachari, kumari keti chhaina, keta-haruko sutne ochhyaan"* (girl of poor character, "loose bird," not a virgin like the Kumari, a bed for boys to sleep upon). Maya described her perception of sexual relations among the Maoists:

MAYA: It might be partially true, and that's why people talk about it. We were accustomed to caring for senior and junior commanders. But I didn't see any bad things, and I didn't hear any bad things either while I was there. I don't think they do such things there. While I was with the Maoists, I didn't hear about any unpleasant things. Many people in the villages talk about it. I think ignorant people say it happens with the Maoists, but I still think that such bad things don't happen there. Both men and women have so many things to do there, how would we have time for these things? We have to be ready to run away at any moment. I think these ideas just come from people outside of the party.

One girl from the central hills of Nepal who did not join the Maoists explained the public perception:

SIXTEEN-YEAR-OLD DALIT GIRL: Everyone treats girls badly who leave the village. As soon as she leaves, everyone assumes she took off with some boy and is now impure. I also thought of going to join the Maoists. I want to escape all the hardship of life here. So, I thought I must go and join up. Instead of suffering here, it would be better to deal with the Maoists. But, then I would stop and think and my senses would return. Girls' heart-minds at this age constantly go back and forth. At 15 or 16 years old, it is difficult to grasp the importance of your decisions. I realize that in an instant a girl's life could be ruined forever. But, so many of my friends have joined and left.

The Swasthani ritual was a potential restorative ritual for girls to regain purity in the eyes of the adult public. However, girl soldiers almost unanimously rejected the Swasthani ritual. Girls explained that they joined the Maoists in order to escape patriarchal societal norms. Performance of the Swasthani would be a reversion of this. The restorative ritual would reposition them in the disempowered state they originally fled. This restorative ritual illustrates a one-sided trade-off; it may lead to greater acceptance among adult upper-caste women in the community, but it involves the girls' symbolically rejecting their ideals of gender equality. The Swasthani thus is an example of a ritual that Denov (2007) would highlight as reinforcing the threat to women's safety and security rather than promoting it.

When asked about participating in rituals, Maya said that it was superstitious and backward. Instead, she focused on the rights of women and her ethnic group. Rather than asking an NGO for assistance with a ritual, she asked for funds to start a small business.

MAYA: The NGO helped me open a grocery shop. I have a business with total transactions of 700 to 800 *rupiya* daily [$11–13]. Now I feel my status improving and I feel that I can do something. The grocery shop that I started with an investment of 8000 *rupiya* [$130] has a net worth of 35,000 *rupiya* [$580]....

I wish to expand this grocery into the "Chepang Wholesale Shop" and do some remarkable work for the Chepang tribe. I would do even better if the NGO invested more money for me. I would like to show that even an insulted outcast girl can do work like this.

For Maya, the transformation to a successful businesswoman was a greater priority than participation in restorative rituals to meet expectations for essentialized gender norms of purity.

Ritual Use among Child Soldiers

To place these two case studies in the broader context of child soldier experiences, this section presents the quantitative results of ritual use among 142 child soldiers (see Table 17.1). Twenty percent of girl soldiers participated in rituals after reintegration compared with 13 percent of boys; however, there was no statistical difference by gender in ritual participation (OR = 1.61, 95 percent CI 0.65–3.97). Eighteen percent of Hindu child soldiers versus 7 percent of non-Hindus participated in rituals; this was also nonsignificant (OR = 2.84, 95 percent CI 0.35–22.87). Among girls, there was a difference by ethnicity, with significantly less participation by Dalit girls compared with Janajati and high-caste girls (χ^2 = 10.34, p = .006) (see Table 17.2).

Table 17.1. *Demographics and ritual participation*

Characteristics	No. (%)
Gender	
Girls	75 (53%)
Boys	67 (47%)
Religion	
Hindu	128 (90%)
Other	14 (10%)
Ethnicity	
High-caste	45 (32%)
Dalit	46 (32%)
Janajati	51 (36%)
Current belief in ritual	
No belief	46 (32.4%)
A little belief	37 (26.1%)
Moderate belief	36 (25.4%)
Strong belief	23 (16.2%)
Participated in ritual before association	
Yes	56 (47%)
No	64 (53%)
Participated in ritual during association	
Yes	2 (1%)
No	140 (99%)
Participated in ritual after association	
Yes	24 (17%)
No	118 (83%)
Ever participated in rituals	
Yes	71 (50%)
No	71 (50%)
Interest in future participation in rituals	
Yes	69 (62%)
No	42 (38%)

The most common types of rituals were either *puja* (worship/prayer), which encompassed a broad range of individual, family, and collective worship, or *phakphuk*, which are *dhaami-jhankri* (shamanic) healings (see Table 17.3). *Puja* often involved *bhaakal* assuring and celebrating safe return. Child soldiers said *puja* demonstrated family membership and reestablished ritual practice. *Man baadhne* (heart-mind binding), within the *phakphuk* category, alleviated spiritual afflictions and prevented children from rejoining the Maoists. The amount of belief in traditional rituals endorsed by children or adults showed no association with rates of ritual performance.

Table 17.2. *Ritual participation by gender and caste/ethnicity*

	High-Caste (n = 45)	Dalit (n = 46)	Janajati (n = 51)	Group Difference (chi-square)
Girls	8 (36%)	1 (3%)	6 (29%)	P = .006
Boys	3 (13%)	3 (21%)	3 (10%)	P > .05
Total	11 (24%)	4 (9%)	9 (18%)	P > .05

Discussion

Traditional rituals have the potential to promote psychosocial well-being during reintegration of child soldiers. Rituals such as *bhaakal* and *man baadhne* have restorative potential to return children to their prior position in the family and recover health. NGOs could choose to support these rituals through economic support to fund rituals, which may represent significant cost to poor families. However, this presents a challenge to NGOs with regard to spending money on costly rituals versus supporting children enrolling in school or vocational training. For Raj, would there be greater benefit in funding the ritual he requests to restore his healing deity or in funding vocational training to increase his opportunities for employment, which would then allow him to pay for rituals? One should find the answer by considering cost-effectiveness, local opportunities for income generation, the ability to collaborate with traditional healers in different communities, and the psychosocial status of particular children. For example, a healing ritual may be necessary for Raj before he feels he can successfully participate in job training.

The infrequent use of rituals – endorsed by one in six children – raises the question of whether ritual promotion should be a priority versus education, vocational training, or specialized mental health services. Advocating cleansing rituals for girls in Nepal is problematic because of the conflict in this instance between human rights promotion emphasizing gender equity and a local tradition emphasizing female subservience. Cleansing rituals such as the Swasthani may lead to increased community acceptance of girl soldiers. However, from a gender rights perspective and from the perspective of most girl soldiers, this ritual participation represents patriarchal subjugation. For girl soldiers, restorative rituals to achieve religious purity entail too great a cost of personal models of agency. It is poignant that the one girl soldier who did participate in the Swasthani ritual was from the Magar minority ethnic group; she

Table 17.3. *Rituals by type, reason, and participants*

Reason for Ritual	Gender		Ethnicity			Ritual Type			Total
	Girls	Boys	High-Caste	Dalit	*Janajati*	*Puja*	*Phakphuk*	Other	
Treat spiritual/supernatural affliction	4	2	1	3	2	0	6	0	6 (25%)
Demonstrate family membership	5	1	3	0	3	6	0	0	6 (25%)
Reestablish ritual practice	2	2	3	0	1	4	0	0	4 (17%)
Assure and celebrate safe return	1	2	1	0	2	2	0	1	3 (13%)
Prevent return to Maoists	1	1	1	0	1	1	1	0	2 (8%)
Evoke support from others	0	1	1	0	0	1	0	0	1 (4%)
Physical illness (fever)	0	1	0	1	0	0	1	0	1 (4%)
Mental suffering (fear/fright)	1	0	1	0	0	0	1	0	1 (4%)
Total	15	9	11	4	9	14	9	1	24 (100%)

was not a high-caste Hindu girl. This girl explained her Swasthani participation as "if other women can do this, I am going to do it as well." For her this was a subversive act of participation asserting her agency rather than viewing it as a cleansing ritual for her sins. Ultimately, rituals are not risk-free simply because they are not Western psychological interventions. Traditional rituals may be rooted in exclusionary symbolism that marginalizes women, when viewed from a Western perspective on gender relations.

What is the potential role for *transformative* rather than *restorative* rituals for the reintegration of child soldiers? Are there activities that would help children reintegrate and be socially accepted while being consistent with the ideology of children, especially girls? If one views culture as a static and monolithic entity, finding such rituals is problematic. However, cultures are in constant flux with changing models and practices. The cultures of Nepal represent not only hegemony of Hinduism as practiced by elites, but also cultures of modernity, cultures of human development and foreign aid, cultures of global capitalism, media cultures, cultures of information technology, and cultures of Maoism and other political ideologies. It is important for anthropologists and other social scientists to consider how rituals from these other cultural frameworks could be transformative. For example, Maya described her appreciation for the inclusion of ethnic minorities in media and her personal interest in business culture. How could rituals in this domain be transformative to foster successful reintegration?

The complexity and dynamic nature of rituals present challenges for NGOs and donor agencies who wish to encourage or implement rituals to facilitate psychosocial recovery of violence-affected populations. Wholesale advocacy of traditional rituals without careful evaluation can present risks of harm no less potent than wholesale importation of Western-based approaches. The awareness that cultures are not static and monolithic combined with a framework for evaluation is necessary to understand rituals before inclusion in psychosocial programming. Through careful consideration of the goals of rituals, beneficiaries, practitioners, and potential harm, researchers and NGO workers will be able to foster environments of well-being for child soldiers and other populations affected by mass violence.

Acknowledgments

Thanks to Ian Harper, Andrew Rasmussen, Devon Hinton, Alex Hinton, and Theresa Betancourt for their comments on this chapter. Thanks to the staff of TPO Nepal and study collaborators: Mark Jordans, Wietse

Tol, Rohit Karki, Manju Adhikari, Renu Shrestha, Reena Thapa, Ramesh Karki, Suraj Koirala, Sujen Maharjan, and Robert Koenig.

REFERENCES

Bennett, L. (1983). *Dangerous Wives and Sacred Sisters: Social and Symbolic Roles of High-Caste Women in Nepal.* New York: Columbia University Press.

Betancourt, T. S., Agnew-Blais, J., Gilman, S. E., Williams, D. R., & Ellis, B. H. (2010). Past horrors, present struggles: The role of stigma in the association between war experiences and psychosocial adjustment among former child soldiers in Sierra Leone. *Social Science & Medicine*, 70, 17–26.

Boyden, J. (2003). The moral development of child soldiers: What do adults have to fear? *Peace and Conflict: Journal of Peace Psychology*, 9, 343–62.

Bracken, P., & Petty, C. (1998). *Rethinking the trauma of war.* New York: Free Association Books.

De Sales, A. (2006). The Maoists and the shamans: A tale of bullets, hail, and prejudices. Paper presented at the Social Science Baha: Lecture Series XVII, Patan, Nepal.

Denov, M. (2007). Is culture always right? The dangers of reproducing gender stereotypes and inequalities in psychosocial interventions for war-affected children. In L. Dowdney (Ed.), *Psychosocial Web Page*. London: Coalition to Stop the Use of Child Soldiers.

Honwana, A. (2006). *Child Soldiers in Africa*. Philadelphia: University of Pennsylvania Press.

IASC. (2007). *Guidelines on mental health and psychosocial support in emergency settings.* Geneva: Inter-Agency Standing Committee.

Karki, R., Kohrt, B. A., & Jordans, M. J. D. (2009). Child led indicators: Pilot testing a child participation tool for psychosocial support programmes for former child soldiers in Nepal. *Intervention: International Journal of Mental Health, Psychosocial Work & Counselling in Areas of Armed Conflict*, 7, 92–109.

Kohrt, B. A., & Harper, I. (2008). Navigating diagnoses: Understanding mind-body relations, mental health, and stigma in Nepal. *Culture, Medicine & Psychiatry*, 32, 462–91.

Kohrt, B. A., Jordans, M. J. D., Tol, W. A., Perera, E., Karki, R., Koirala, S., & Upadhaya, N. (2010a). Social ecology of child soldiers: Child, family, and community determinants of mental health, psychosocial well-being, and reintegration in Nepal. *Transcultural Psychiatry*, 47, 727–53.

Kohrt, B. A., Jordans, M. J. D., Tol, W. A., Speckman, R. A., Maharjan, S. M., Worthman, C. M., & Komproe, I. H. (2008). Comparison of mental health between former child soldiers and children never conscripted by armed groups in Nepal. *Journal of the American Medical Association (JAMA)*, 300, 691–702.

Kohrt, B. A., & Maharjan, S. M. (2009). When a child is no longer a child: Nepali ethnopsychology of child development and violence. *Studies in Nepali History and Society*, 14, 107–42.

Kohrt, B. A., Tol, W. A., Pettigrew, J., & Karki, R. (2010b). Children and revolution: The mental health and psychosocial wellbeing of child soldiers in Nepal's Maoist Army. In M. Singer & G. D. Hodge (Eds.), *The War Machine and Global Health* (pp. 89–116). Lanham, MD: Altamira Press/Rowan & Littlefield.

McKay, S., & Mazurana, D. (2004). *Where are the girls? Girls in fighting forces in northern Uganda, Sierra Leone, and Mozambique.* Montreal: Rights and Democracy.

Nordstrom, C. (1997). *A Different Kind of War Story.* Philadelphia: University of Pennsylvania Press.

Psychosocial Working Group. (2003). Psychosocial intervention in complex emergencies: A framework for practice. In T. P. W. Group (Ed.), *Working Paper* (p. 2). Edinburgh: Queen Margaret University College.

Summerfield, D. (1998). Protecting children from armed conflict: Children affected by war must not be stigmatised as permanently damaged. *British Medical Journal, 317*(7167), 1249.

Theidon, K. (2015). Pasts imperfect: Talking about justice with former combatants in Colombia. In D. E. Hinton & A. L. Hinton (Eds.), *Genocide and mass violence: Memory, symptom, and recovery.* Cambridge: Cambridge University Press.

Turner, R. L. (1931). *A comparative and etymological dictionary of the Nepali language.* London: K. Paul, Trench, Trubner.

Turner, V. W. (1967). *The Forest of Symbols: Aspects of Ndembu Ritual.* Ithaca, NY: Cornell University Press.

Commentary

Wrestling with the Angels of History: Memory, Symptom, and Intervention

Laurence J. Kirmayer

[...] The colonel returned with a sack used to bring groceries home. He spilled many human ears on the table. They were like dried peach halves. There is no other way to say this. He took one of them in his hands, shook it in our faces, dropped it into a water glass. It came alive there. I am tired of fooling around he said. As for the rights of anyone, tell your people they can go fuck themselves. He swept the ears to the floor with his arm and held the last of his wine in the air. Something for your poetry, no? he said. Some of the ears on the floor caught this scrap of his voice. Some of the ears on the floor were pressed to the ground.

May 1978 (Forché, 1981, p. 15)

Introduction

The opening quote from Carolyn Forché's documentary poem *The Colonel*, drawn from her experiences in El Salvador in the late 1970s, confronts us with the terror and absurdity of mass atrocities. Living in the aftermath of war, with perpetrators still in power and only a fragile order restored, how can memory contain the horror and the loss? Must survivors turn away from the past in order to survive? And if silence is required for survival, what becomes of the history needed to provide a moral compass and guide efforts to rebuild a just society? Ears pressed to the ground, can the dead and dismembered hear stories the living are compelled to forget?

The violence described in the essays in this volume is massive not just in its scale or scope – with large numbers of people or whole populations facing terror, injury, loss, and death – but also in its effects, tearing down social structures and rending the fabric of communities, peoples, or nations. As such, the remainders of violence can be seen at the levels of body, self, and society. The responses at each level have their own dynamics, involving physiological, psychological, and social processes that range from the intimate sphere of family systems to the wider arenas of neighborhood, community, nation, and the international networks of global society.

These systems are deeply interconnected and we need interdisciplinary perspectives to trace the effects up and down these levels.

In recent years, social science and psychiatric approaches to violence have been dominated by the metaphor of trauma. In their Introduction, the editors raise basic questions about the nature of "trauma experience," the recollection of traumatic memories, and the cultural and biosocial shaping of individual and collective forms of suffering and healing. All of these questions treat trauma as a given, a starting point that does not require further specification or clarification. But *trauma*, in our present context, has at least four different meanings: (1) wounding violence, which may be an expectable (if not ordinary) aspect of the human condition; (2) violence that has lasting effects on physical and mental health, the prototype of which has become posttraumatic stress disorder (PTSD); (3) states of extremity that break out of all bounds of reason, containment, and control, to violently disrupt and destroy the social order; and (4) an open-ended set of diverse and shifting sorts of events that are linked metaphorically to one of the first three meanings.

The contributors speak to all of these senses of trauma. They recognize massive violence as a *tremendum* that can not only destroy lives but subvert cosmologies – but they also trace the impact of subtler or more insidious forms of structural violence embedded in routines of the ordinary. Trauma is part of local forms of life, and the phenomenology of trauma is deeply embedded in social relations. One crucial element common to all of these papers is the concern to situate trauma in the contexts of everyday life at local, regional, and international levels. This need for contextualization should be obvious, but, outside the discourse of anthropology, trauma often is treated as self-evidently basic and as determining its own outcome or else as something that utterly defies description, the disaster that transcends any human capacity to articulate. In contrast, as the contributions to this volume make abundantly clear, the experience of and response to mass violence evokes intense interpretive activity that reflects culture and politics as much as human biology.

The contributors to this volume examine the legacy of genocide and mass violence on multiple levels, exploring the interconnections of personal and social memory, symptom and social rupture, and intervention. This concluding commentary will follow the organization of the book in terms of three intersecting areas: narrative and memory, symptom and social rupture, and posttrauma response and intervention. Although the chapters are grouped into these three themes, they are necessarily crosscutting. Memory, symptom, and intervention form interactive systems: The narratives and embodied processes of learning and memory shape symptom experience and expression. Interventions that work with memories to effect change inevitably act to support and stabilize some narratives while undermining, discounting, and displacing others. This suggests one way that integration of the personal, social, and political can occur in theory and practice, namely, by tracing the systemic loops that link memory, symptoms, and responses.

Trauma Memory as Narrative, Embodiment, and Enactment

Memory defines trauma, linking current suffering to past events through recollection (Young, 2004). But there are many varieties of memory, some of which can be narrated as stories, others that are embodied dispositions to respond in ways that reveal a history of violence. Narratives of trauma include personal and collective, informal or improvised, and formal, official versions. These narratives are enacted by individuals as autobiographical stories, identities, symptoms, and rhetorical claims to power and moral authority. They also are part of collective enactments through the commemorations or memorialization of shared history that serve the myths and ideologies that define group identities. Both the individual self and the institutions of society are based on discursive practices. Remembering and retelling can therefore serve to reconstruct identity at both individual and communal levels.

In his chapter for this volume, Heonik Kwon describes how the state-instituted "heroic memory" of war in postwar Vietnamese society changed domestic space. Political campaigns substituted the commemoration of heroic war dead for the traditional cult of ancestors. Against this official version, villagers have improvised other ways to acknowledge the moral complexity of local history. Everyday acts of commemoration – kowtowing and offering incense to the ancestors of the household – have been transformed by adding a second gesture, "turning the body to the opposite side to repeat the action towards the street-wandering ghosts." This act recognizes persisting wounds associated with the ghosts of those who suffered unjust deaths and whose apparitions remind villagers of their own enduring pain and loss.

In Vietnamese thought, there is a moral economy to death. A violent, unjust death and the memory of its terror can trap the soul in a negative afterlife. In this terrible state, the soul must relive the violent event again and again. The My Lai villagers with whom Kwon worked mentioned the names of certain older villagers as the most grievous victims of the 1968 massacre, and these names belonged to families whose genealogy was decimated by the violence. The decimated family genealogy provoked the strongest sense of injustice and moral indignation in other communities affected by civilian massacres. A grievous death in this context is not only the destruction of innocent lives but also a crisis in the social foundation of commemoration. The dead have an inalienable right to be liberated from their violent history, and the protection of this right depends on the secular institutions of commemoration. Commemoration then is a process that supports the moral structures of society and works therapeutically at both individual and collective levels.

Kwon describes the ontology that brings to life the suffering of the dead as a parallel to the psychodynamics of traumatic memory in the survivor, so that we might say, without irony, that the dead *embody* the disavowed, unspeakable, and unresolved experiences of the living. The experience of the dead constitutes a realm of moral imagination, both for individuals and communities, through the cultural ontology of forms of death and the social regulation of commemorative action. This, in turn, opens up the possibility of a new form of political action, in which the dead speak back to the living, challenging collective silence, seeking acknowledgment, restitution, and repair; from their position beyond the mundane world, the dead can challenge the oppression of everyday life and the political arrangements that try to suppress or rewrite history.

Trauma memory faces other social and political forces of silencing and suppression in the work of Erin Finley, who describes how the diagnosis of PTSD figures in the psychological, moral, and spiritual dilemmas faced by military chaplains and counselors working with veterans of recent conflicts. The meanings of PTSD and modes of expression of trauma-related suffering are "fraught and under almost constant [re]negotiation." This renegotiation is possible because of the "epistemic diversity" that arises from competing ways of knowing, forms of truth, and authority. Far from the fixed entity defined by psychiatric diagnostic criteria, Finley argues that semiotics of PTSD are fluid, negotiable, and under constant challenge. The epistemic frames at play reflect competing political, religious, and sociomoral systems of meaning.

Despite acknowledging the emotional impact of war on veterans, the military values toughness and self-control. To maintain solidarity with their unit, soldiers must not show signs of emotional vulnerability or weakness. Efforts to recognize and help veterans with trauma-related disorders directly conflict with these core values. Psychiatric illness is prima facie evidence of weakness. Indeed, in the common parlance of soldiers, if you have PTSD you are crazy. Finley describes episodes with two soldiers she calls "the Marine" and "the Chaplain" who must hide their suffering and find ways to suppress their feelings because they do not want to appear weak and incompetent or even "crazy." Far from protecting the sufferer from stigma or moral opprobrium, the diagnosis of PTSD constitutes a social stigma that many struggle to avoid.[1]

Despite the stigma, the construct of PTSD provides a way to articulate certain kinds of distress and resist the silencing and suppression of suffering that are part of the emotional regulation of institutions like the military. Finley's examination of the pragmatics of the use of the PTSD diagnosis shows how it functions as "an open and idiosyncratic space for interpretation and the organization of experience." But in the social system of the military it is difficult to find space for any counternarrative. Chaplain Jim is reduced to catching a few private words with Finley in the corridor after a meeting about his personal struggles, apparently valuing this space "in between" where he can voice his doubts without immediate pressure to contain his feelings and conform to an official story.

For the Chaplain, though, suffering may also have a spiritual meaning. He performs "spiritual triage" to decide whom to refer for psychological intervention and who has a problem that is better understood and addressed through spiritual counseling, prayer, and ritual. Finley also describes the work of the Evangelical Pastor Bill who gives workshops on "Post Traumatic Soul Disorder." Finley suggests the interpretive theology of trauma has important intersections with medical models of PTSD and offers much territory for exploration. At the same time, the military setting makes it easy to see some of the social economic constraints on discourse that have shaped PTSD and trauma talk from its inception (Young, 1995). These larger social structural forces impact on the process of working through trauma on an individual level where people must use the cultural or institutional narratives on offer or actively resist them to devise their own heterodox versions of the meanings and consequences of mass violence.

The interaction of trauma narratives and norms of expression is also evident in the chapter by Conerly Casey on the experience of those who, as children, witnessed the 1990 Iraqi invasion of Kuwait. For Kuwaitis, psychological distress is highly stigmatized with consequences for family reputation, marriage, and community relations. Somatic distress due to physical illnesses, however, is more socially accepted, especially when the illness is attributed to exposure to war contaminants or other "outside assaults." Indeed, seen as the result of attacks from outside, somatic symptoms become vectors of a specific type of memory with clear moral implications. Many young adults do not believe government reports that attribute prevalent somatic symptoms to stress rather than the effects of environmental contaminants spread during the war. Psychological explanations for their suffering are not reassuring or empowering and may be viewed as evidence of official denial and betrayal. Persistent somatic symptoms speak back forcefully to this betrayal.

For the young adults who experienced the 1990 Iraqi invasion of Kuwait, the 2003 U.S. war in Iraq was a trigger, elicitor, or amplifier of symptoms rooted in past trauma. The amplification of trauma reflected the convergence of past and present memories evoked by the sensorial qualities of experiences and the emotional resonances of specific events and moral predicaments. The wars were associated with strong feelings of betrayal and abandonment. These sentiments have their own power as organizers of memory. Familial, social, and national stories; commemorative events and topographical reminders, such as bombed out buildings; have all functioned as what Casey terms "emotive institutions," anchoring and eliciting affect. These institutions are both evocative symbols and contexts or arenas for ritual and commemorative performance. Those who witnessed the Iraqi invasion as children vividly recalled the dangers of Iraqi checkpoints, and the destruction of community centers, religious sites, public parks, schoolyards, and marketplaces. Many of the damaged sites have never been repaired, but have been marked with plaques describing particular incidents of violence, ensuring they retain a place in collective memory. The "post" of "posttrauma" then is an altered landscape, one that may not only be scarred but, in some ways, unstable. In Kuwait, the violence has left great feelings of uncertainty, and many young people have an escape plan, with a passport or visa that will let them leave quickly if necessary.

War changed the physical landscape, giving it new affective contours, charged with meaning and populated with memories of dangerous figures. There are many topographical referents to the invasion that inscribe trauma into "Kuwaiti cityscapes." These topographies vary according to individuals' experiences, constituting a sort of urban memory theater. The environmental damage visited on the landscape during the war also has a moral meaning, and, together, memory and morality shape bodily experience.[2] The health consequences of violence then stem not just from the immediate impact of events, but from the ways in which they situate the self in a landscape of memory and identity.

Landscapes of a different sort figure in the chapter by Orkideh Behrouzan and Michael Fischer on echoes of the revolution and violent conflicts in Iran. The persistence of traumatic memory is intrinsic to its psychobiology and social dynamics, but in the case of the Iranian diasporic community, it has been intensified by the regime change and transformation of society in ways that have turned fantasies of return into nightmares. Behrouzan and Fischer describe a sonic landscape of echoes of the past that includes spaces for expression that have been found on the Internet, in dreams, and in popular media, after political repression has shut down the agora.

They note the difficulties of communication across the generations of the Iranian revolution. Persian cultural and religious traditions of mourning and melancholia valorize grief and the commemoration of loss, but within Iran these have been appropriated and subverted by the state. Persian cinema has been an important arena of expression and offers a kind of dreamwork. Films can tell family stories against a backdrop of larger political stories that may be harder and more dangerous to tell.

The weaving of satellite television and the Internet into the fabric of Iranian diasporic culture provides new media for the culture of metaphors. Internet blogs form communities in which the tokens of identity and exchange are dreams. The dreams and nightmares recounted are remixes: cutting, layering, and blending disparate images and themes drawn from contemporary Persian culture. The Internet and popular psychology also go hand in hand. The "rise of the psychiatric self" among Iranians is reflected in psychiatric, psychological, and self-help talk shows that attract calls from all strata of society, rural as well as urban. Along with this is a shift from the indirection and allusion of poetry to explicitly psychological language. Pop psychological language creates a space to name and acknowledge certain personal and collective realities. Work on the self is a political project and the "traumatic dream work of the present" is both an undercurrent to contemporary community and a site of protopolitical discourse that can cut across the generations.

The intergenerational transmission of memory and identity is central to Carol Kidron's work on embodiments of memory in the developmental experiences of children of Holocaust survivors. For many of this second generation, the histories of their parents' suffering was shrouded in "oppressive silence," but Kidron shows how silence itself maintains traces of the past and can constitute a powerful mode of communication and remembrance within the family. She also points to the value of silence as an alternative to the insistent efforts of psychotherapies to promote disclosure, confession, and testimony. Personal memories need not enter the social sphere to have meaning and value; they can remain within the inner world of the individual or the family as private knowledge.

Kidron approaches memory in terms of embodiment, as prereflexive and prerational. For example, she describes one mother's Proustian moment at the kitchen sink, smelling potato peelings and being catapulted back to a mode of existence in which potato peels were the only sustenance. The Holocaust survivor, like Billy Pilgrim in Vonnegut's (1969) *Slaughterhouse-five*, has become unstuck in time. This temporal dislocation is part of the depersonalization and derealization that often follow severe traumatic experience. The sufferer is on a chronotopic forced march under leaded skies down slopes of affect-laden memory. Kidron speaks of the dark cloud of mood conveying the memory of the Shoah.

As the reference to Proust suggests, however, such temporal, sensory, and affective processes are central to the organization and experience of ordinary memories as well as traumatic events. Indeed, through metaphor, sensory memory provides the ground for the scaffolding or more abstract reflection and rationality. At the same time, our metaphoric constructions, sustained by dominant narratives, reshape our sensory and temporal experience. Hence, there is a circular causality in the sensory construction and embodiment of memory and experience.

When memories circulate in local worlds they can be taken up by others in ways not intended by their original bearer. Kidron's own work with psychotherapy groups in Israel illustrates how transgenerational processes of remembering can be put to political ends (Kidron, 2004). Through direct and indirect means, the state appropriates and regulates personal memory to serve collective identity and stake moral claims.[3] What makes trauma memory special then is not just the biology of fear conditioning, but the way the politics of memory *as* identity determine the narrative templates and metaphors that organize remembering.

This political structuring and appropriation of memory is an undercurrent in the discussion by Vincent Crapanzano of the predicament of the children of the Harkis, Algerians who served the French army. The Harkis faced torture and ostracism in Algeria and incarceration in detention camps in France, suffering "the pathologies of abjection." They now face painful historical memories and a collective "wound" that, as Crapanzano notes, "we all too readily describe as trauma and embed in our psychological understanding."

Like Kidron, Crapanzano is concerned with the transmission of memory across the generations, here shaped by French and Algerian politics. The experiences of betrayal and abandonment "serve to bind the Harkis in a single, dispersed community of memory, the particular contents of which they seem incapable telling their children." Betrayal and abandonment engender thoughts and feelings particularly liable to be the motive for and focus of obsessive ruminations. For the children, who have never heard the details of their fathers' experiences, a shifting, fragmentary, and generic story must take the place of specific memories. This incompleteness is a cause of both rumination and, ultimately, dissatisfaction, in that it makes it impossible to take the full measure of their parents' suffering or achieve some closure. The lack of content leads to a vague, generic account of Harki history. The part of experience that is clear, unequivocal, and directly available to the second generation is the community's continued lack of recognition. Consequently, many of the younger generation have become involved in political activism, lobbying for recognition and compensation for the sacrifices their parents made for France.

The Harkis have come to see their predicament as a "fated destiny," and Crapanzano sets his reflections in the larger frame of notions of contingency (as destiny, fate, fortune, or luck). Various ontologies, ethnopsychologies, and systems of religious belief connect contingency to a sociomoral order with assumptions about freedom, risk, responsibility, and blame. Causal explanation assigns moral significance and points toward what must be done in terms of apology and restitution. In accounting for events, how and why narratives may be quite separate: the how providing mechanistic explanation, the why, moralistic evaluation. And the failure to provide a coherent why itself stands as a sign of the enormity of events: "There are stories whose aim is to call attention to the impossibility of ever answering the ultimate why. They turn impossibility into a rhetorical figure, playing on mystery, the harrowing acknowledgement of the unexplainable." This is the genre of the story of Job and its modern echoes. Indeed, we can build theologies on this experience of the inexplicable (Mosès, 2009).

Unexplained, hard, refractory contingency is both troubling and fascinating – and demands explanatory work on both counts. Literary genres provide ways of narrative ordering, smoothing, and containment; they specify appropriate whys and wherefores for the apparently contingent or, by giving an explicit place to the contingent, create a metaorder that contains disorder (e.g., an all powerful God whose actions are beyond human understanding). Individuals may shift among alternative accounts because any narrative is limited in its ability to contain the chaos and contradiction produced by massive violence.

In the case of the Harkis, the collective story overshadows any individual's account, which remains unclear in its details and potentially damning if revealed. Hence, the collective obligation to remember hides the individual impossibility of recollection. The collective story surpasses the individual both because this individual story has been elided or suppressed and because it is this collective story that constitutes the individuals as Harki and that valorizes an otherwise marginal and troublesome identity. The narrative becomes what Crapanzano calls a "frozen story" – a fixed and formulaic account that cannot grow and evolve because it must serve as a historical anchor of collective identity.

Symptom, Communication, and Social Repertoire

Trauma is associated with a wide variety of symptoms some of which have been portrayed as specific to violence but most of which occur in many contexts. Symptoms may arise from physiological perturbations and become stabilized as persistent disorders through several mechanisms: the ongoing effect of unrelenting external stressors, physiological final common pathways involving altered neural regulatory systems, and vicious circles in which the symptom is amplified by feedback, through psychophysiological loops within the person and social-interactional loops involving interpersonal processes (Kirmayer & Bhugra, 2009). The psychological responses to violence include not only the fears, anxieties, and avoidance behaviors characteristic of PTSD but also panic, anger, grief, and demoralization (Afana, Pedersen, Rønsbo, & Kirmayer, 2010; D. Hinton, Rasmussen, Nou, Pollack, & M. Good, 2009; D. Hinton, Peou, Joshi, Nickerson, & Simon, 2013; Silove et al., 2009). When violence is perpetrated by those we have previously trusted and depended on, the result is an added trauma of betrayal at different levels including family, institutional authority, community, and nation.

Among the symptoms and experiences viewed as distinctive to trauma and its aftermath are feelings of horror and the uncanny. In his chapter for this volume, Byron Good considers his own experiences of the uncanny in Aceh, Indonesia, where he co-led an IOM program to identify and treat trauma after the tsunami. The tsunami that took so many lives also swept aside the long-standing military conflict, ushering in a postconflict era. However, the apparent calm is haunted by ghosts of the past.

Living with ghosts and specters is more than a metaphor for the anxieties associated with both public and private space in a regime where so much of historical memory has been suppressed. The "eerie moments when the ghosts of violence refuse to be quiet" that Good describes point to the survivors' experiences not simply of intrusive thoughts but of entities or beings. The notion of spirits and specters references and depends on a cultural ontology, but the ease with which we can be led to an ontology of ghosts and spirits – which need not be uncanny (they can be friendly and familiar) – reflects our cognitive capacities to attribute agency and to personify other agents as human like us.

For Freud, the uncanny (*unheimliche*) is something that is secretly familiar, but has been repressed and then restored to consciousness only in some shadowy form (Freud et al., 1976). It is not some intrinsic strangeness of events, then, but their active repression that makes them return as phantoms and apparitions. In a sense, the uncanny is what should have remained hidden but has come to light. But where does this demand for invisibility originate?

From a neurophenomenological point of view, the ghosts of mass violence reflect the horror and incongruity of the original events, and their echoes in feelings of dislocation, depersonalization, and derealization. Ethologists and comparative psychologists might argue that it is some essential strangeness, incongruity, and indeterminacy, defined against evolutionary ecological norms, that makes certain events horrible and haunting. For example, D. O. Hebb (1946) described the terror of chimpanzees when they saw the plaster death mask of another chimpanzee.

Intense experiences of the uncanny can be evoked by images of damaged or distorted bodily integrity. But this sense of strangeness also can be evoked by images that do not represent injury or death.[4] The violent and grotesque are only two of many routes to the uncanny. As Kafka's fictions showed, events can be horribly mundane and yet create quite the same dread and chill of the uncanny because they violate our basic expectations for safety, coherence, and agency in everyday life. In the settings Byron Good describes, perhaps the most direct source of feelings of the uncanny is the history of political repression that produced categories of the unspeakable and the transgressive that continue to configure social spaces in ways that create intimations of great danger. The eerie or uncanny then can arise from the circumstances of impossible social performances like meeting one's former torturer in a café or living daily life beside a neighbor who killed one's father.

Ordinarily, the uncanny is a fleeting feeling that subsides over time with familiarity. Images of horror and incongruity can lose their emotional shock value with exposure. But there is much in the nature of mass violence that prevents this process of refamiliarization. In particular, mass violence can disrupt the moral and symbolic order that creates and protects the spaces in which exposure can occur safely. Citing Derrida, Good suggests that when ontologies are ruptured, they give rise to "hauntologies." Apparitions continue to hover at the margins of awareness, in the frightening imagery of ghosts and nightmares, and can be self-perpetuating as they prompt fears that circulate through gossip and mass media, maintaining high levels of anxiety within a community.

In these situations, activities like art and psychotherapy can work to reestablish a sense of safety. The dramatic performance by Butet Kartaredjasa, recounted by Byron Good, shows how theater can provide a transitional space where the audience can watch the actor play with the ghosts of violence – exerting some control over their comings and goings by regulating aesthetic distance. The ghosts can be invoked and invited onstage, because this is a play, and in a playful, comic, or elegiac mode, the ghosts' threat – to remember their sundered lives; naming names, places, events – is aestheticized, muted, and controlled.

Good describes the suffering associated with the conventional symptoms of PTSD and the value of psychiatric treatment with medication and psychosocial support and counseling. It seems a bitter irony, though, that it was only by eliding details about the perpetrators of political violence that government support and funding could be secured to treat some of the aftermath of the violence. The tsunami provided a politically neutral form of violence on which to focus attention. And the individual treatment interventions many received did not provide a place for basic processes of recognition, restitution, and reconciliation. The ghosts of the past then must follow the scripts given them by the powers that be. They can express their resistance in symptoms, intrusive memories, and performances in designated places that are clearly "just play."

In his essay for this volume, Robert Lemelson also traces the legacy of violence in Indonesia to the world of ghosts. He presents the case of "Nyoman," a Balinese man who lives with the repeated intrusions of apparitions that he calls "shadows" (in Indonesian, *bayangan*). Nyoman describes himself as living in two worlds: that of his community and the realm of the spirits. Nyoman traces his illness back to 1965, when he witnessed the massacre of fellow villagers during the mass violence. His problems with anxiety and social withdrawal began after this terrifying experience, which weakened his "life force" (Balinese, *bayu*), with persistent symptoms of feeling his heart beating rapidly, and a sensation of "inner pressure" weighing down his body. He had other symptoms typical of PTSD including being jumpy and easily startled and frequent nightmares with images of people being butchered. He avoided social gatherings and public places and stopped participating in community work projects.

Another layer was added to his suffering with the death of a newborn child some years later. In addition to ordinary expressions of grief, he experienced an intensification of his social anxiety and avoidance and began to have more unusual experiences with auditory and visual hallucinations. He began seeing small black figures, which he believed to be spirits known as the *wong samar*, which are widely recognized in Bali as potential causes of illness or emotional problems. In Balinese cosmology, many different sorts of spirits and ghosts are believed to inhabit rivers, graveyards, ravines, and trees. When offended, these spirits can cause illness and emotional or interpersonal problems.

Although the spirits occupy a different realm, their ability to cause illness depends on conditions in the mundane social world. When political changes occurred in Indonesia in 2002 and it became more possible to speak of the conflicts of the past, the spirits returned and began asking Nyoman to join the Communist Party. To protect himself from these subversive spirits, Nyoman took to wearing a military camouflage jacket and helmet, which he believed constituted an effective barrier to spirits trying to enter his body. Antipsychotic medication also helped to reduce his hallucinations and other symptoms.

Lemelson's detailed account of Nyoman's symptoms illustrates how culture shapes the phenomenology of psychopathology. Symptomatology is cognitively mediated through interpretive processes, but it is also shaped by social practices that reference specific levels or domains of experience and that constitute various sorts of spirit beings as real and important for social order and well-being. The spirit realm parallels the mundane world but may afford greater fluidity and possibilities for transformation. Nyoman has effected a truce with the *wong samar* by symbolically renouncing his former political affiliations.

Although much of the focus in psychiatry has been on symptoms directly attributed to exposure to violence, the subsequent life contexts of survivors are key determinants of their illness experience. Nadia El-Shaarawi explores the predicament of Iraqi refugees in Egypt. Their health and well-being are linked not so much to experiences in Iraq as to the subsequent difficulties of life in Egypt and, especially, to uncertainties and anxieties about their future. The symptom of tiredness (*ta'abana*) emerged in many of her interviews and was described as a deep and overwhelming sense of physical exhaustion that was attributed to stressful life circumstances. Other common symptoms included a mix of anxiety and depression, which were traced to experiences of torture and other violence endured before fleeing Iraq but also to their ongoing predicament as exiles in Egypt. They called this complex condition *hala nufsia*, a "psychological situation," reflecting the centrality of loss, fear, and demoralization in their lives.

The aftermath of mass violence may be internal displacement or forced migration, and the ability to find safe haven and embark on future-oriented projects is essential for the well-being of survivors (Beiser, 2009). Different stances taken toward migration affect subsequent mental health; these stances are determined as much by the reception in the host society as they are by any characteristics of the individual (Porter, 2007). For those actively seeking asylum, uncertainty and delays in the refugee determination process are major causes of distress (Silove, Steel, & Watters, 2000). If asylum is granted, they may come to see themselves as immigrants building a new life, as part of growing diasporic communities, or else as exiles, perennial strangers in a strange land. Those who have no possibility of permanent residence or citizenship may have feelings of not belonging that reinforce their sense of exile. If the place of exile is not adopted as a new home but viewed only as a temporary way station, then life is lived in a provisional way. This liminal state of waiting may be a major contributor to distress because it suspends life projects that would otherwise be absorbing and provide some answer to the ruptures and losses resulting from past violence.

A central interest of cultural psychiatry has been in culture-specific symptoms and syndromes, and many of the papers in this volume describe symptoms related to trauma that are shaped by ethnophysiological ideas linked to larger ontologies. In their chapter, Devon Hinton and colleagues examine the relevance of culture-specific symptomatology in assessing trauma-related distress. As part of a needs assessment survey in rural Cambodia among villagers who had suffered under the Khmer Rouge regime, they developed the Cambodian Symptom and Syndrome Inventory (C-SSI), which consists of 12 somatic symptoms (including dizziness, blurry vision, tinnitus, headache, neck soreness, shortness of breath, cold hands and feet) and five cultural syndromes (weak heart, *khyâl* attack, *khyâl* hitting up from the stomach, fear of *khyâl* overload, and fear of neck vessel rupture). They suggest these symptoms and syndromes result from four sets of interacting processes: the biology of trauma, which leads to increased arousal and reactivity; ethnophysiological notions, which amplify specific sensations through attention, attribution, and interpretation; metaphoric resonances and elaborations that relate the symptoms to cultural idioms of distress; and specific, personal, and idiosyncratic associations of the symptom with past trauma events or responses.

They compared the relationship of past trauma events to a measure of PTSD symptom severity and to the C-SSI to assess which scale was a more sensitive indicator of trauma-related symptomatology. Exposure to traumatic events was more strongly correlated with the culture-specific measure. Some of the effects of trauma were seen in culture-specific syndromes or fears, which themselves may give rise to vicious circles of symptom amplification through processes of biolooping that link psychophysiological processes and sociosomatic idioms of distress.

Clearly, the conventional symptoms of PTSD listed in diagnostic criteria are "just the tip of the iceberg." The same situations that lead to PTSD also result in multiple other somatic symptoms and syndromes that often cooccur. The severity of particular types of symptoms may reflect differences in physiopathology or in culturally mediated salience through mechanisms of attention and attribution. The development of culture-specific measures to explore salient symptoms in other contexts may reveal new aspects of psychobiological processes, as well as social-semiotic processes that contribute to vicious circles that cause persistent symptoms and dysfunction. As D. Hinton and colleagues have shown in other work, these culture-specific symptoms can be the target of tailored interventions built on the principles of cognitive behavior therapy. Understanding the cultural shaping of distress and designing effective interventions will require a multidimensional approach that integrates psychophysiological, semiotic, and interactional models.

The challenge of integrating alternative explanatory frameworks for symptoms is evident in the chapter by Doug Henry, who describes episodes of nocturnal rape attacks of Mende women living in IDP camps in Sierra Leone. These *njomb-bla* attacks involved an apparition in the night like a dark mist that put a woman into an immobilized state, undressed her, and then forced sex. In addition to the possibility of actual sexual violence, Henry considers three complementary explanatory frames for these reports of nocturnal attacks: episodes of sleep paralysis, expressions of vulnerability to gender violence, and reflections of larger social tensions related to war and displacement.

The experience of spirit attacks fits within a larger Mende religious system and cosmology. The action of the spirits reflects an intelligible moral order in which "jealousy and greed are the main forces thought to inspire witch attacks." Spirits are associated with the night and were thought to be more active during the war; refugees were particularly vulnerable. Hence, the explanation of the attack was culturally plausible. However, the *njomb-bla* attacks bore little resemblance to witch attacks that might have occurred sporadically before the war.

Sleep paralysis (also discussed by D. Hinton and colleagues in relation to Cambodian villagers) has a universal physiological core that gives rise to a specific phenomenology, which is culturally shaped and interpreted (Kirmayer, 2009). Stress and trauma can increase the frequency of episodes of sleep paralysis. News that someone experienced a witch attack served to make others apprehensive about suffering the same kind of violence. By increasing arousal and interfering with sleep, this might have increased the incidence of sleep paralysis.

The complaint of nocturnal rape by a spirit was a culturally salient way to express distress and articulate anxieties related to the precarious situation faced by women in the IDP camps. The *njomb-bla* attacks allowed them to express distress over violence, loss, and moral crises. However, Henry notes, this expression did not appear to function in an adaptive way to reduce tension or root out violence but actually exacerbated feelings of anxiety and led to the death of possibly innocent men accused of these attacks. The rape attacks then became part of the circulation of terror in ways that were unregulated and that served to exacerbate cycles of violence rather than dampen them.

Alexandra Pillen describes the ways in which violence that is extreme in its savagery, scale, and scope can attack not only individuals' sense of coherence but the collective forms of order embedded in and expressed through cultural and religious cosmologies. In Sri Lanka, "images of displaced spirits and a cosmology damaged by war go hand in hand with representations of dehumanization and inhuman people." The spirits of the Sinhala Buddhist pantheon fled in terror from the chaotic violence of the civil war. For some Sinhalese, youth who have committed atrocities and senseless violence that transgress all social mores have become "spiritlike people," lacking in full human personhood, and frightening both to humans and to spirits.[5] Even the unsocialized spirits or demons that cause illness among people are horrified by these other-than humans and "shiver away" from them. The violence of war then transcends the ordinary forms of evil that are understood and managed through relationships with the spirit world. Pillen notes other examples of such fracturing of cosmologies in the violence in Peru, Uganda, and Cambodia and the famine in North Korea.

There are plenty of frightening images of demons, death, and aggression in Sinhalese mythology but they usually follow familiar scripts (Kapferer & Papigny, 2005). The damage to the cosmology results from the deliberately transgressive nature of the political violence. Pillen suggests that the subsequent acts of mockery and disruptions of healing rituals by youth may reflect efforts by these youth to reenter the social order, finding a place for the "limit experiences" they have endured as perpetrators and witnesses to extreme violence, and so to become human again.

Pillen discusses the role of the artist in reconstructing a shattered cosmology, reassembling its elements, beginning with the most personal reflections, giving them form and materiality and drawing them into the social sphere, even into confrontation with the forces that would seek to fracture and abscond with the world or remake it in their own violent image. Art provides unique modalities to order and contain the chaotic and inexpressible through silence, non-sense, and new forms of representation.[6]

Ethnographic interviewing itself is also a kind of intervention, in which empathy, active listening, and bearing witness create opportunities to recollect, make meaning of senseless violence, and articulate a coherent narrative. However, in searching for coherence, thick description, and articulate informants, ethnographers downplay the shallow, empty, and incoherent or simply inchoate. In her chapter, Pillen speaks for the importance of fractured narratives both as expressions of injury and as early attempts at the reconstruction of meaning that must follow disaster. "A cultural formation of temporary non-sense needs to be carefully observed as a cultural moment the entire community goes through" (p. 10).[7] She suggests that rather than emphasizing empathic connection as a direct route to emotional meaning, sensitivity to language can open up new possibilities to apprehend the struggle to make sense of a fractured reality. Rhetoric and poetics, in particular, offer tools for exploring the pragmatics of meaning making at the precipice of madness (Kirmayer, 2007).

Postconflict Response and Intervention

Following Fassin and Rechtman (2009), the editors recognize the irony of interventions that dehistoricize collective violence by medicalizing it and interpreting it through the contemporary moral economy of victimhood. A focus on individual psychopathology deflects attention from the projects of collective identity, ethnicity, and nationalism that give rise to mass violence and that continue to shape postconflict efforts at reconciliation. Interventions designed to rebuild communities after mass violence, including trials, truth and reconciliation commissions, and other forms of restorative justice, all depend on addressing historical traditions that have framed the relationships among groups and that provide the moral imagination with possibilities for peaceful coexistence with those perceived as 'other'.

We have endogenous healing mechanisms at the level of neurobiological responses to trauma as well as cognitive-emotional processes of meaning making that undergird social processes of contrition, expiation, and forgiveness, reparation, restitution, healing, and recovery. These are guided by collective narratives rooted in notions of morality and personhood. At the same time, mental health professionals and other stakeholders actively intervene to shape personal representations of trauma to fit specific notions of health and well-being. These refigured narratives influence historical memory and the political uses of trauma as a symbol of collective injury and injustice.

Of course, the postconflict situation is not simply one of rebuilding meaning out of ashes and nonsense but a rhetorical arena that is always heavily constrained by ongoing politics that make some narratives tolerable and safe and others provocative, dangerous, or simply unthinkable. People living in the aftermath of large-scale violence rarely have the freedom to explore their experience without facing threats both internally (in their own psychic economy) and externally in the politics of postconflict reconstruction.

Drawing from her work in Aceh, Indonesia, Mary-Jo DelVecchio Good explores some gendered aspects of trauma experience. She contrasts the experiences of men and women during and after the conflict. At the height of the conflict, woman were often in the position of having to protect the men as well as their children, and they appealed to cultural-historical forms of female heroism to evade or resist their attackers and to valorize their struggles in later retelling.

In a related epidemiological study, the most significant event associated with symptoms of depression or PTSD for women in Aceh was the destruction of their home, and this effect was stronger than that of losing a spouse. This speaks to the woman's central role of maintaining the household, and the extent to which it constitutes her social capital and ability to sustain and protect herself. For women in the postconflict setting, stories told with laughter and irony served to affirm their resilience and communal solidarity in the face of memories of violence and violation. The image of the powerful warrior woman, which invokes a local Acehnese history distinct from the images of women in Indonesian or global Islam, is part of a politics of recognition that honors their own communal identity.

Mary-Jo DelVecchio Good is particularly interested in the nature of postconflict subjectivity, explored through careful attention to narratives as well as empathic connections with the people she seeks to understand. For the most part, this method seems to offer ready access to experience, but she describes one startling interaction with a woman, with whom she felt she had good rapport, who suddenly gave her a sharp jab in the back as if to unsettle her. Her surprise was a reminder of the limits of empathy even as her lingering discomfort yielded new insight into the damage to trust and safety that remains for many in the wake of mass violence.

The dilemmas of confronting traumatic memory may be particularly severe for perpetrators, who have much to gain by forgetting. Reflecting on her ethnographic work with former combatants in Colombia's long civil war, Kimberly Theidon discusses the dynamics of disarmament, demobilization, and reintegration (DDR) programs on the ground. DDR programs tend to focus on military and security issues, collecting weapons and reassigning people to civilian settings, but the tasks of reconstructing lives are far broader and more challenging. The transition from conflict to peace requires reconfiguring identities and communities in ways that test the limits of human imagination and compassion.

Theidon focuses on how former combatants think about justice, forgiveness, and reconciliation. She insists on the importance of understanding the lives of the perpetrators of violence and not reducing their predicament to a simple calculus of good and evil. She confronts these men with the perspective of their victims by asking them what she should say when she interviews a mother who lost her sons in the violence. The men respond with varying degrees of empathy; many try to compartmentalize their consciousness, locating the violence at a distant place and time. This allows the former combatant to construct his current self as discontinuous with and distinct from the perpetrator who carried out violent acts. The process of social reintegration involves the management of some emerging level of consciousness and conscience (*concienca*) of the implications of their actions and their location in larger systems of power and oppression. This begins for some with recognition of the human implications of their actions that preclude their rejoining the communities, villages, families to which they once belonged.

Theidon's work shows how reconciliation remains elusive. True reconciliation depends not on simply burying the past in an unmarked grave, but recognizing the guilty and considering what can be done to ameliorate the suffering they have caused. In any real event, victims, perpetrators, and bystanders do not occupy hermetically contained or isolated social positions; they are connected in complex ways that follow the lines of transgression of the violence they have engendered or endured.

Religious systems offer moral exemplars and logics of contingency that can help survivors of mass violence find ways to continue. Kenneth Miller and Sulani Perera discuss the experience of survivors of the massacre in Gonagala, Sri Lanka, in which Tamil Tigers slaughtered whole families, including children. They focus on two cases drawn from their documentary film *Unholy Ground*, which presents the stories of survivors grappling with loss. Consistent with other studies, it is not the symptoms of PTSD but persistent grief and depression that are most challenging for many of the survivors.

The two people they describe follow divergent trajectories in their postconflict adaptation. To some extent this reflects differences in personality, with one being shy or reserved and the other more outgoing and socially at ease. In addition, differences in preexisting family relationships shape the meaning and impact of their losses and coping strategies. More broadly, the social ecology of each person appears to be a crucial determinant of outcome. This ecology includes ongoing networks of relationships within the family, the village, and the larger society. An ecosystemic view points to the importance of psychosocial interventions to promote social integration and engagement in activities that can support the person emotionally, but also economically and spiritually.

Buddhism plays an important role in adaptation for many Sinhalese. The notion that loss is inevitable and must be accepted because all attachments are transient helps some to frame the violence they have experienced as part of a larger, universal human predicament. This Buddhist perspective is a source of comfort and acceptance for some, while others feel compelled to show a façade of equanimity that is difficult to sustain and that silences expressions of grief within the family. Ritual alms giving to the village monks serves to reaffirm and actively support a coherent moral order and aids the gradual process of mending the hearts of those with grievous losses.

Christopher C. Taylor discusses the dilemmas surrounding the use of village-level courts or *gacaca* in postgenocide Rwanda. The *gacaca*, originally used to adjudicate minor disputes, were pressed into service to deal with larger ruptures following the genocide. Many felt that the only way the culture of impunity could be combated would be through reprisals of sufficient magnitude to balance the past aggression. The *gacaca* were invoked to try to prevent such retributive escalation.

Taylor notes that some traditional forms of justice in Africa have adhered to what has been called restorative justice as a way to manage the desire for vengeance by focusing on compensating the wronged party rather than punishing the guilty. Restorative justice is an alternative to retributive justice that works to maintain reciprocity and social homeostasis. In the aftermath of violent ruptures, it can work to repair the political structures and relationships that weave the fabric of communal life. The *gacaca* involved a hybrid of retributive and restorative justice. It could sentence people convicted of serious crimes, but those who made full and open confessions of less serious transgressions could be required to compensate their victims, symbolically or otherwise.

In all of the *gacaca* sessions that Taylor observed in 2005, the accused and other witnesses obviously lied. It is no surprise that people deal with this volatile and dangerous situation by evasion and dissimulation. Yet, in his later observations of *gacaca* in 2009, Taylor found victims who stated that attending these hearings had helped them manage troubling symptoms of *guhahamuka*, feelings of tightness in the chest and shortness of breath associated with intense fear. In effect, the *gacaca* provided a site for in vivo exposure therapy for some survivors. Other survivors chose not to attend *gacaca* for precisely the same reason – to avoid reexperiencing unbearable memories. The *gacaca* also prompted migration to cities and emigration by those eager to avoid village justice. A community survey of twelve hundred Rwandans in 2006 found high levels of distress among *gacaca* witnesses and no evidence that levels of depression or PTSD were lower in communities where *gacaca* had operated for somewhat longer periods, casting doubt on the mental health benefits of trauma testimony in this setting (Brounéus, 2010). At the same time, though opinions differ on the ethnic and political biases inherent in the process, to the extent that it can and does elicit confessions and apologies, demand restitution, and mete out severe punishments, the *gacaca* has served to reassert a moral order. Taylor concludes that it remains to be seen to what extent the *gacaca* will contribute to viable reconstruction of communities and the nation-state. At the very least, conjoining restorative and retributive justice may be advancing a process of moral education: Vengeance killing has diminished or stopped, the death penalty has been abolished, and a sense of belonging to a nonethnic nation may have been strengthened in some communities.

Although the international NGO response in the aftermath of mass violence has emphasized psychosocial support rooted in Western notions of counseling and psychotherapy,[8] every society has indigenous systems of helping and healing that can be mobilized to foster recovery and reintegration. Brandon Kohrt describes three different types of ritual among Hindus in Nepal that have been used to address different aspects of the symbolic damage done by participation in the violence.

In some cases, parents understand that their children were taken by the Maoists because ancestral deities were angry with the family. Hence, rituals to thank the ancestors for returning the children are appropriate and can help those children feel accepted and support their reintegration into the family and community. In other cases, feelings of sadness, troubling memories, nightmares, worries, and uncontrolled desires are viewed as signs of trouble with the heart-mind that require ritual healing. As well, children who exhibit aggressive or violent actions, mental distraction, or other behaviors judged socially inappropriate for their gender and caste may be considered *paagal* (mad or psychotic) because they have suffered damage to the *dimaag*, or brain-mind. In such cases, traditional healers can conduct specific rituals to bind the heart-mind and provide relief from these symptoms.

A third type of ritual has been used to address the predicament of girls or young women whose experiences as soldiers have rendered them ritually impure. A specific ritual can be performed to cleanse and restore purity and reposition the girl within culturally appropriate roles. However, Kohrt found that most girls rejected this ritual because it signaled a return to the gender discrimination and subordination maintained by patriarchal society. Many girls were drawn to the Maoist movement in the first place because of the history of gender discrimination and violence against women by government forces, and they were loath to give up the gains in status won during their time as soldiers.

The Inter-Agency Standing Committee Guidelines (2007) for intervention recommend collaboration with indigenous healers, but this practice raises complex ethical and pragmatic issues. Kohrt shows how the meaning of traditional practices varies by gender, caste, and class as well as with family structure and process. As a result, traditional healing can be helpful or harmful in specific cases. Rituals that reassert conventional gender roles may undermine the gains in equality achieved by participation in the Maoist army. On the other hand, for youth who are committed to a religious path, rituals can serve as powerful vehicles for reintegration.

Sites of Rupture, Resistance, and Repair

The ethnographic studies in this volume describe geographically distant and culturally diverse settings where people have experienced markedly different forms of mass violence. Despite these differences, there are many crosscutting themes. Massive violence breaks down the bonds of communal solidarity and undermines the sense of moral order. Survivors of mass violence use the available social and cultural resources to work through the suffering left by trauma and loss and rebuild viable communities. In many settings, there are specific ritual practices and institutions that have been put to new purposes: containing anxious and intrusive images and nightmares and helping individuals work through traumatic memories; restoring purity and social status to promote social integration; and meting out justice in the form of punishment and restitution. Religion provides a structure for these rituals and makes them part of larger systems of meaning.

Trauma counselors and other mental health practitioners, as well as popular media, promote psychological idioms as a way to express distress and point to strategies for healing. However, in most postconflict situations, talk about past violence remains fraught for many reasons. The psychological impact of recollection can be severe, and others may be unwilling or unable to bear witness and help carry the story. The history may be threatening to a fragile political order that fears opening old wounds. The recollection of violence may be dangerous for the spirit world, as well. In all these cases, people find zones of mediation that lie outside the official, collective, and controlled spaces of narration. These may be special types of gathering like the Rwandan *gacaca* described by Taylor or the artistic performance discussed by Byron Good, moments in the interstices of institutional spaces and routines like the corridor when Finley had her conversation with a military chaplain, the liminal spaces of religious rituals studied by Kohrt and his colleagues, or the virtual meeting spaces of global communities woven together by the Internet discussed by Behrouzan and Fischer.

Trauma creates ruptures in memory and experience that make people strangers to themselves and others. Working through the self-estrangement and social ruptures requires spaces that allow the flexibility to reconfigure identity and renegotiate roles. But trauma also calls for ways of challenging and resisting the oppressive structures that cause, maintain, and, inevitably, follow mass violence.

Table C.1 summarizes some of the sites of rupture and repair discussed in the contributions to this volume. These spaces, realms, or registers provide some elbow room or slippage, where survivors of mass violence

Table C.1. *Sites of rupture, resistance, and repair in mass violence*

Realms of Experience	Descriptive Languages	Injuries or Ruptures	Idioms of Distress	Sites of Resistance and Repair
Body	Physiological	Incurable wounds and scars	Symptoms and syndromes	Medical care, healing *temenos*
Self/person	Psychological	Fragmented self, emptiness, madness	Personal memory, internal conflict	Psychotherapy, dreams, fantasy
Interpersonal relationships	Moral	Capricious evil, inhumanity, loss of trust	Wrongdoing, revenge, redress	Family, communal activities, Internet
Communal/ political	Justice/human rights	Unjust social order, absence of safety	Collective memory, history, speaking truth to power	Court, *gacaca*, TRC
Spirit world	Religious	Damaged cosmology	Grievously injured spirits, witchcraft	Shrine, cemetery, ritual space

can challenge cultural forms or dominant narratives and push back against constraints. They allow this resistance partly because they partially escape surveillance and control by powerful interests that would enforce a single ideological account of history; by allowing circulation of these warded-off ideas and experiences, they also help keep memory alive.

There are several points to be made about these multiple levels or realms of experience and explanation:

1. The realms of experience reflect ontologies, that is, notions of what the world is made up of, including bodies, persons, relationships, families, clans, communities, nations, peoples, and spirits. In their Introduction, the editors suggest that the integration of biology and culture needed in trauma theory can be approached by considering the "ontological spaces" that shape subjectivity and provide the institutional and conceptual resources that people use to make sense of massive violence and rebuild their lives and communities. However,

these ontologies need not involve elaborate or explicit metaphysical systems, theories, or beliefs. They may be known and lived as a mixture of tacit knowledge or intuitions and situated social practices or institutional routines.

2. Each of these entities or kinds of being has its own languages of description and notions of order and disorder as well as its own dynamics that can give rise to violent ruptures and injuries or damage to individuals and to the social fabric. Each level provides settings for action and sites of production of narratives, memories, and discourses, as well as symptoms and afflictions, and corresponding interventions.

3. There are individuals and institutions warranted to speak the appropriate languages, diagnose the conditions of order or disorder, and intervene at each level. At the same time, each person makes use of available cultural idioms to articulate his or her own suffering. The observed cultural idioms of distress are the result of interactions of biology, individual agency, and interpretive and discursive forms that are socially mediated and constrained.

4. There are socially created and prescribed sites for engaging and talking about these levels or aspects of experience. One can take part in these conversations, rituals, or negotiations without actually knowing or subscribing to an ontology or any specific expectation. All that is essential is a commitment to follow the social forms and subject oneself (or be subjected) to these ways of acting. New experiences can emerge through our imaginative capacities and individual agency, the performative functions of language that conjures things into being by saying, and the responses of others who agree to follow a complementary script.

5. The levels or domains are linked through both material and discursive processes. Although the effects of violence may be seen or felt in distinctive ways at each level, mass violence affects all of these sites, disrupting the order of each level as well as the coordination or coherence across levels.

These realms of experience are embedded in local and global social ecosystems.

The importance of these ecosystems is evident, for example, in ethnographic studies of reconciliation processes like Theidon's, which show the "contradictory logics" at work. The grand narratives of reconciliation taken from religious myths and exemplars meet the vagaries of human frailty on the ground. This can be understood in terms of the complexities of human motivation, the lasting traces of violence in memory and emotion, and, as Theidon suggests, the situated, place-based dynamics of social identity and positioning.

Beyond the local social ecology, the postconflict predicaments of survivors of mass violence reflect not just their preconflict positions and trajectories or the brute effects of violence, but also structural inequalities and injustices that have global origins (Farmer, 2004). The consequences of mass violence then must be understood in the context of the enduring forms of economic inequity and the influence of powerful agencies and institutions that seek not only to survive but to capitalize on catastrophe through mobile capital and strategic maneuvering (Klein, 2007).

Conclusion

A Klee painting named *"Angelus Novus"* shows an angel looking as though he is about to move away from something he is fixedly contemplating. His eyes are staring, his mouth is open, his wings are spread. This is how one pictures the angel of history. His face is turned toward the past. Where we perceive a chain of events, he sees one single catastrophe which keeps piling wreckage and hurls it in front of his feet. The angel would like to stay, awaken the dead, and make whole what has been smashed. But a storm is blowing in from paradise; it has got caught in his wings with such a violence that the angel can no longer close them. The storm irresistibly propels him into the future to which his back is turned, while the pile of debris before him grows skyward. This storm is what we call progress. (Benjamin, 1968, p. 257)

The last century has produced a terrible burden of catastrophes so that we can say, with Blanchot, that we are all living after the disaster. What captures the backward gaze of Benjamin's angel of history is not nostalgia for a past Eden, or a romantic rebellion against the progress of modernity, but absolute horror at the growing pile of human debris left behind. The angel is an otherworldly being, a messenger from beyond, but also an embodiment of our longing for redemption. While the storm from paradise pushes us forward, compassion would have us turn back, standing against the wind, to retrieve, remember, and restore what has been lost.

Witnessing, remembering, and recounting the history and experience of mass violence depend on the dynamics of memory itself, which includes embodied, psychological, and social processes. Indeed, there are many kinds of memory reflecting the diverse systems in brain, body, and society that are marked, changed, transformed, or even created by events and that can be said to hold records. Despite this rich and varied archive, memory is often fragmentary, unstable, and incomplete. Narrative accounts are always reconstructions and undergo smoothing and restructuring to fit narrative templates. Traumatic memories do persist, and some of this is due to the indelibility of fear conditioning – ensuring that once burned twice shy – but there are other mechanisms that work to keep trauma memories alive (McNally, 2003). The obdurate, persistent parts of traumatic memory have multiple roots: physical scars that inscribe history on the body in ways that are at once indexical, metonymic, and metaphorical; classical conditioning that results in automatic or reflexive responses; autobiographical narratives that sustain identity and self-presentation; social norms and institutions that govern collective acts of remembering; moral commitments that we struggle to honor and uphold; myths and ideologies that set the boundaries of what we defend as sacred and inviolable.

Remembering, therefore, involves not only the neurobiology of memory but also family dynamics, individual and collective constructions of identity, the geography of memorial landscapes, and the political uses of events. Collective memory is a function not just of the witness and the storyteller but of the audiences that participate in the memory's performance and transmission. These audiences (real or imagined, present in the flesh or virtual) are central to the moral significance of remembering. Forgiving and forgetting are regulated by and sustain specific moral regimes where they may be the object of struggle and contestation. An example from my own local context can serve to illustrate this moral struggle in closing.

From to 1869 to the 1980s, the Canadian government mandated a system of residential schools for Aboriginal children, run by the churches, with the express purpose of forced assimilation (Milloy, 1999). About 150,000 children went through these schools, where, in addition to harsh suppression of their language, cultural and spiritual traditions, and painful separations from their families, many experienced physical and sexual abuse. On June 11, 2008, the prime minister of Canada stood in the House of Commons to make a formal statement of apology to former students of the Indian Residential Schools. He faced the leaders of Aboriginal nations and others who stood in the gallery and there were crowds gathered on Parliament Hill for this event. The media carried stories of Residential School experiences. With the apology was the announcement of further efforts at restorative justice: compensation payments for residential school survivors and a Truth and Reconciliation Commission (Castellano, Archibald, & DeGagné, 2008).

A cynical observer might see all of this as the government's attempt to contain the threat represented by the many lawsuits pending over the harm caused by the residential schools. Clearly, the government would like to have a final resolution and "turn the page." However, at a societal level, the act of apology provided basic recognition that opens onto a new relationship, with continued dialogue at many levels. The testimony collected through the TRC will find its way into history books, museums, and other places where the work of collective memory and commemoration can continue. Even the initial recognition had immediate effects that transcended political rhetoric. At a meeting in Montreal soon after the official apology, an Aboriginal scholar told the story of returning to her rural community to have nuns from a nearby institution, who had previously evaded or denied the history of the Indian residential schools, approach her in tears with personal apologies, ready for a new kind of conversation.

Yet newspapers that day also carried a photograph of residential school survivor Geronimo Henry's clenched fist, tattooed with "M R.S. #48 survivor," and quoted his comment that this was "just a bunch of words" – too little and too late to help the many whose lives were destroyed.[9] Those who insist on remembering the violence or who cannot escape it play a crucial role in our moral economy. They bear the burden of historical memory that can spur others to continue to strive for justice. The labor of memory is essential to building a just society. Remembering works against the "institutionalized forgetfulness" or collective amnesia welcomed, or deliberately engineered, by those in power. Acts of commemoration are essential to recognize and learn from the suffering of the other. The challenge is how to do this without rewounding and igniting a cycle of violence driven by the desire for retribution.

TRCs can be ritualized performances that record suffering and assert lofty values without engaging the lived experience of suffering and the dilemmas of postconflict coexistence (Avruch, 2010). To understand paths to reconciliation, we need to look more locally at how people actually manage the day-to-day encounters, the upwellings of grief and anger, the paroxysms of mistrust and paranoid fear that are part of the legacy of mass violence. Apology is a step toward a new sort of relationship and, when it concerns collective violence, toward a new relationship between communities. Forms of expiation and restitution must follow. Forgiveness may be yet another step in this process, but it does not turn the page. It is simply another turn in an unfolding story in which each participant reshapes the other's narrative.

For indigenous peoples in the Americas, the notions of historical trauma, loss, and grief have become popular ways to understand the origins of contemporary forms of social suffering. Historical trauma is a way of configuring cultural memory, linking the story of each individual to the collective wounds of a people. The narrative of historical trauma situates individual and collective suffering in social and historical context. It serves to reduce individual blame and directs attention to sources of injustice in social and political events. In so doing, it organizes and motivates action to redress past wrongs. However, by framing individuals as victims it may reinforce a sense of being damaged and create feelings of entitlement. Linking the consequences of this historical violence to current psychiatric illness (e.g., residential school syndrome) is a way to valorize the sufferer but risks stigmatizing the survivor and whole communities.

For trauma stories to function as personal and collective history, there must be public places for them to be told, acknowledged, and retold. The political recognition of collective identity and history can help create this place for individuals to tell their stories. Individuals' stories, in turn, can serve as testimony to ground collective history and call for further moral and political response. Countervailing political forces can make certain stories hard to imagine and to tell to others. Nevertheless, as the accounts in this volume make clear, despite the difficulty of understanding and articulating the experience of mass violence, survivors continue to wrestle with the angels of history. In joining with them, we hope to regain some essential human truth and sustainable community.

NOTES

1 Recent efforts to establish diagnoses of Mild Traumatic Brain Injury for veterans from Iraq or Afghanistan also aim to sidestep the negative view of mental disorders, substituting a grave neurological diagnosis that commands respect. An information sheet from the U.S. Department of Veteran Affairs Mental Illness Research, Education and Clinical Center states: "Brain injuries are the 'signature wounds' of our Global War on Terrorism. Returning combat veterans may not know they have suffered such a wound. That is why VA doctors want these 'new warriors' and their families to have this information" (http://www.mirecc.va.gov/docs/visn6/TBI-pocketcards-vet-family. pdf, accessed June 4, 2011). For the many soldiers who do have troubling symptoms, the passage from medically unexplained symptom to neurological disorder may then be swift and decisive.

2 This inscription of history into landscape is especially powerful for indigenous peoples who define their sense of self and personhood in explicit relation to the physical environment. Whitbeck and colleagues (2004) have shown how specific memories and symptoms associated with historical trauma may be felt at particular places. In our own work on resilience among indigenous peoples, the Mohawk of Kahnewake speak of the painful memories associated with the creation of the St. Lawrence Seaway (Kirmayer, Dandeneau, Marshall, Phillips, & Williamson, 2011). Long after the historical events of colonization, symbols of collective trauma are present in the landscape as vivid expressions of structural violence and ongoing discrimination.

3 For example, Yad Vashem, the Israeli Holocaust museum, in its most recent revision, acknowledges a wider range of experiences of the Holocaust than it did in the past, including North African Jews and others. But all of the

recorded testimonies on display present Hebrew speakers. Along with other choices of exhibit as well as the architecture and siting of the museum, this serves to convey an implicit narrative arc from oppression to liberation culminating in arrival in Israel and, hence, links redemption with the creation and survival of the Jewish state (Goldberg, 2012).

4   Artificial intelligence researchers who construct humanoid robots describe the "uncanny valley," the place along the continuum of similitude where plastic faces are creepy because they are close but not-quite human (Seyama & Nagayama, 2007). Something is being violated in these simulacra, some essential aspect of the human cleaved off, distorted, or reversed.

5   People invoke different metaphors of dehumanization depending on cultural contexts, for example, as animals (subhuman) or as machines (nonhuman) (Haslam, Loughnana, Reynolds, & Wilson, 2007), but as the Sinhalese examples suggest, this list is not exhaustive and the metaphors can be blended and extended in novel ways.

6   Indeed, for Lyotard (1992), the unique function of modern art is precisely to bear expressive witness to the inexpressible and this requires new expressive forms. In visual art, one thinks immediately of the work of Anselm Kiefer (Lauterwein, 2007); in poetry, Paul Celan (Felstiner, 2001); in narrative art, see, for example, W. G. Sebald's (1996, 2001) limning of the ineffable of the Shoah in his novels of lost memory or Nathan Englander's (2007) burlesque of the craziness of Argentina's dirty war.

7   We can recognize different cultural forms of emptiness and senselessness – distinguishing gibberish, craziness, wildness, ineffability, speechlessness, and nothingness. For example, Paul Celan's poem *Tübingen, Jänner*, a meditation on Holderlein's madness, ends with the nonsense words "Pallaksch, pallaksch" (Celan & Hamburger, 2002). Celan's poem moves from hermetic imagery toward stuttering, stammering, and babble. Since the time of Plato, madness has been a privileged point of entry into understanding the uniqueness of poetry compared to other modes of speaking, but the breakdown in language with Holderlein's madness also speaks to the larger breakdown of language in the wake of the Holocaust (Weineck, 1999, p. 263). The barbarians are those who babble – and in the wake of the barbarians, babble is all that is left to us. Madness is a kind of visitation of the divine that leads the poet to speak in tongues, a kind of fluent babble. Words have immediate sensual qualities, which Celan keeps negating, dissolving, or surpassing (Burnside, 2006). In this way, he speaks to (and instantiates) the predicament of poesis through language that has lost its communal ground or had it undermined and disfigured, rendered uncanny by the violence of the other who admits no Other. Emptiness can be deadness like Agamben's (1999) description of the *Muselmann* of the death camps, located beyond empathy with that racialized epithet, the emptiness of the blank canvas, or the alchemists' *nigredo*, calling forth creativity out of darkness, or even the emptiness of the clear mind of the meditator realizing the co-constructed nature of experience. Mass violence and genocide have been recognized as catastrophes that transcend our powers of expression (Blanchot, 1986). Yet narratives can provide the framework and emplotment we need to understand something of the radical alterity

inherent in the experience of disaster. The evocative power of lyric can present still more of the unreconstructed, raw, inchoate aspect of memory and experience. Can we rebuild cosmology then not by asserting the grand sweep of a totalizing narrative – that may contain the seeds of a future round of mutually assured destruction – but through the more fragile, tentative essays of lyric that invite us to a moment of trust, of intimacy and connection with another consciousness or way of being?

8 Humanitarian organizations train and employ large numbers of trauma workers, who, once the work of the NGO is complete, move into the larger society with a new set of skills and perspectives. These mental health workers may incorporate new psychological and moral language into their self-narratives and deploy these ways of thinking in their work. In this way, they convey a set of moral ideas and practices with the potential to reconfigure the self, gender roles, and relationships in family and communal life. The training these trauma workers receive has substantial similarities across diverse programs and usually includes notions about the therapeutic value of listening, respecting cultural difference, and sharing painful experiences. In some settings, much of the training is experiential, and the workers themselves experience the effects of listening and confiding their own life stories and trauma narratives. In so doing, they come to value these modes of relating not just as technical means to a therapeutic end, but as part of a set of moral values and commitments that can provide comfort, safety, and a renewed capacity for trust in the wake of violence and uncertainty. Some counselors may experience an improvement in their own well-being as a result of the training, and this would tend to deepen their commitment to the values of the profession and the intervention program. Indeed, trauma counselor training and the employment opportunities it opens up provide a way to transform a personal history of trauma into social capital. At the same time, the idiom of trauma and the ways of interacting as a counselor are consistent with bureaucratic and technocratic norms of order and rationality that may conflict with other local cultural values. The personal and political are fused in the persona of the psychosocial counselor – although the political is given a distinctly psychological slant. In effect, trauma workers become proponents of new forms of social life, the purveyors of new narratives of the self and modes of interaction, with a measure of moral authority and social position that enable them to spread the good word. In some ways, the moral work of trauma counselors parallels the impact of psychotherapy in Western countries, where it has enormously influenced popular culture with ideas about child rearing, intimate relationships, and the project of self-realization. The moral language of psychodynamic psychotherapy owes much, in turn, to Judeo-Christian tradition. Beyond symptom management, social support, and reintegration, counseling may include notions of acceptance and forgiveness with their roots in a Christian soteriology. The experience of training as a counselor, therefore, may be an awakening to both psychological and political issues along with the acquisition of tools to begin to work for change.

9 *The Globe and Mail* (Toronto), Thursday, June 12, 2008, p. A1.

REFERENCES

Afana, A., Pedersen, D., Rønsbo, H., & Kirmayer, L. J. (2010). "Endurance is to be shown at the first blow": Social representations and reactions to traumatic experiences in the Gaza Strip. *Traumatology*, 16, 73–84.

Agamben, G. (1999). *Remnants of Auschwitz: The witness and the archive.* Cambridge, MA: MIT Press.

Avruch, K. (2010). Truth and reconciliation commissions: Problems in transitional justice and the reconstruction of identity. *Transcultural Psychiatry*, 47, 33–49.

Beiser, M. (2009). Resettling refugees and safeguarding their mental health: Lessons learned from the Canadian Refugee Resettlement Project. *Transcultural Psychiatry*, 46, 539–83.

Benjamin, W. (1968). Theses on the philosophy of history. In *Illuminations: Essays and Reflections*. New York: Schocken Books.

Blanchot, M. (1986). *The writing of the disaster [L'ecriture du désastre].* Lincoln: University of Nebraska Press.

Brounéus, K. (2010). The trauma of truth telling: Effects of witnessing in the Rwandan *gacaca* courts on psychological health. *Journal of Conflict Resolution*, 54, 408–37.

Burnside, S. (2006). Senselessness in Paul Celan's *Mohn und Gedächtns*. *German Life and Letters*, 59, 140–50.

Castellano, B. M., Archibald, L., & DeGagné, M. (Eds.) (2008). *From truth to reconciliation: Transforming the legacy of residential schools.* Ottawa, Canada: Aboriginal Healing Foundation.

Celan, P., & Hamburger, M. (2002). *Poems of Paul Celan.* New York: Persea Books.

Englander, N. (2007). *The ministry of special cases.* New York: Alfred A. Knopf.

Farmer, P. (2004). An anthropology of structural violence. *Current Anthropology*, 45, 305–25.

Fassin, D., & Rechtman, R. (2009). *The empire of trauma: An inquiry into the condition of victimhood.* Princeton, NJ: Princeton University Press.

Felstiner, J. (2001). *Selected poems and prose of Paul Celan.* New York: W. W. Norton.

Forché, C. (1981). *The country between us.* Port Townsend, WA: Copper Canyon Press.

Freud, S., Strachey, J., Cixous, H., & Dennomé, R. (1976). Fiction and its Phantoms: A Reading of Freud's Das Unheimliche (The "Uncanny"). *New Literary History*, 525–645.

Goldberg, A. (2012). The 'Jewish narative' in the Yad Vashem global Holocaust museum. *Journal of Genocide Research*, 14(2): 187–213.

Good, B. J. (2015). Haunted by Aceh: Specters of violence in post-Suharto Indonesia. In D. E. Hinton & A. L. Hinton (Eds.), *Genocide and mass violence: Memory, symptom, and recovery.* Cambridge: Cambridge University Press.

Haslam, N., Loughnana, S., Reynolds, C., & Wilson, S. (2007). Dehumanization: A new perspective. *Social and Personality Psychology Compass*, 1, 409–22.

Hebb, D. O. (1946). On the nature of fear. *Psychological Review*, 53, 259–76.

Hinton, D. E., & Hinton, A. L., Eng, K. T. (2015). Key idioms of distress and PTSD among rural Cambodians: The results of a needs assessment survey.

In D. E. Hinton & A. L. Hinton (Eds.), *Genocide and mass violence: Memory, symptom, and recovery*. Cambridge: Cambridge University Press.

Hinton, D. E., Peou, S., Joshi, S., Nickerson, A., & Simon, N. (2013). Normal grief and complicated bereavement among traumatized Cambodian refugees: Cultural context and the central role of dreams of the deceased. *Culture, Medicine, and Psychiatry*, 37, 427–64.

Hinton, D. E., Rasmussen, A., Nou, L., Pollack, M. H., & Good, M. J. (2009). Anger, PTSD, and the nuclear family: A study of Cambodian refugees. *Social Science and Medicine*, 69, 1387–94.

Inter-Agency Standing Committee. (2007). *IASC guidelines on mental health and psychosocial support in emergency settings*. Geneva: Inter-Agency Standing Committee.

Kapferer, B., & Papigny, G. (2005). *Tovil: Exorcism & healing rites*. Negombo: Viator.

Kidron, C. A. (2004). Surviving a distant past: A case study of the cultural construction of trauma descendant identity. *Ethos*, 31, 513–44.

Kirmayer, L. J. (2007). Celan's poetics of alterity: Lyric and the understanding of illness experience in medical ethics. *Monash Bioethics Review*, 26, 21–35.

(2009). Nightmares, neurophenomenology and the cultural logic of trauma. *Culture, Medicine and Psychiatry*, 33, 323–31.

Kirmayer, L. J., & Bhugra, D. (2009). Culture and mental illness: Social context and explanatory models. In I. M. Salloum & J. E. Mezzich (Eds.), *Psychiatric diagnosis: Patterns and prospects* (pp. 29–37). New York: John Wiley & Sons.

Kirmayer, L. J., Dandeneau, S., Marshall, E., Phillips, M. L., & Williamson, K. J. (2011). Rethinking resilience from indigenous perspectives. *Canadian Journal of Psychiatry*, 56, 84–91.

Klein, N. (2007). *The shock doctrine: The rise of disaster capitalism*. New York: Metropolitan Books/Henry Holt.

Kwon, H. (2015). The Vietnam War traumas. In D. E. Hinton & A. L. Hinton (Eds.), *Genocide and mass violence: Memory, symptom, and recovery*. Cambridge: Cambridge University Press.

Lauterwein, A. (2007). *Anselm Kiefer/Paul Celan: Myth, mourning and memory*. London: Thames & Hudson.

Lemelson, R. (2015). "The spirits enter me to force me to be a communist": Political embodiment, idioms of distress, spirit possession, and thought disorder in Bali. In D. E. Hinton & A. L. Hinton (Eds.), *Genocide and mass violence: Memory, symptom, and recovery*. Cambridge: Cambridge University Press.

Lyotard J-F. (1992). *The inhuman: Reflections on time*. Chicago: University of Chicago Press.

McNally, R. J. (2003). *Remembering trauma*. Cambridge, MA: Belknap Press of Harvard University Press.

Milloy, J. S. (1999). *A national crime: The Canadian government and the residential school system, 1879 to 1986*. Winnipeg, Canada: University of Manitoba Press.

Mosès, S. (2009). *The angel of history: Rosenzweig, Benjamin, Scholem*. Stanford, CA.: Stanford University Press.

Porter, M. (2007). Global evidence for a biopsychosocial understanding of refugee adaptation. *Transcultural Psychiatry*, 44, 418–39.

Sebald, W. G. (1996). *The emigrants*. New York: New Directions.

(2001). *Austerlitz*. New York: Random House.

Seyama, J., & Nagayama, R. S. (2007). The uncanny valley: Effect of realism on the impression of artificial human faces. *Presence*, 16, 337–51.

Silove, D., Brooks, R., Bateman Steel, C. R., Steel, Z., Hewage, K., Rodger, J., & Soosay, I. (2009). Explosive anger as a response to human rights violations in post-conflict Timor-Leste. *Social Science and Medicine*, 69, 670–7.

Silove, D., Steel, Z., & Watters, C. (2000). Policies of deterrence and the mental health of asylum seekers. *Journal of the American Medical Association*, 284, 604–11.

Vonnegut, K. (1969). *Slaughterhouse-five; or, The children's crusade, a duty-dance with death*. New York: Delacorte Press.

Weineck, S. -M. (1999). Logos and Pallaksch. The loss of madness and the survival of poetry in Paul Celan's "Tübingen, Jänner." *Orbis Litterarum*, 54, 262–75.

Whitbeck, L. B., Adams, G. W., Hoyt, D. R., & Chen, X. (2004). Conceptualizing and measuring historical trauma among American Indian people. *American Journal of Community Psychology*, 33, 119–30.

Young, A. (1995). *The harmony of illusions: Inventing posttraumatic stress disorder*. Princeton, NJ: Princeton University Press.

(2004). When traumatic memory was a problem: On the historical antecedents of PTSD. In G. M. Rosen (Ed.), *Posttraumatic stress disorder: Issues and controversies* (pp. 127–46). New York: John Wiley & Sons.

Index